Please remember th;
and that it belongs ~
p~~~~~~~~~~
not write in this,

D0912061

# Philosophical Ethics

## An Introduction to Moral Philosophy

168762
VC M.Ed.

# Philosophical Ethics

## An Introduction to Moral Philosophy

### THIRD EDITION

Tom L. Beauchamp

*Georgetown University*

Boston   Burr Ridge, IL   Dubuque, IA   Madison, WI
New York   San Francisco   St. Louis
Bangkok   Bogotá   Caracas   Lisbon   London   Madrid   Mexico City
Milan   New Delhi   Seoul   Singapore   Sydney   Taipei   Toronto
2001

# McGraw-Hill Higher Education

*A Division of The McGraw-Hill Companies*

PHILOSOPHICAL ETHICS: AN INTRODUCTION TO MORAL PHILOSOPHY

Copyright © 2001, 1991, 1982 by The McGraw-Hill Companies, Inc. All rights reserved. Printed in the United States of America. Except as permitted under the United States Copyright Act of 1976, no part of this publication may be reproduced or distributed in any form or by any means, or stored in a database or retrieval system, without the prior written permission of the publisher.

This book is printed on acid-free paper.

2 3 4 5 6 7 8 9 0 FGR/FGR 0 9 8 7 6 5 4 3 2 1

ISBN 0-07-229721-2

Editorial director: *Jane Vaicunas*
Sponsoring editor: *Monica Eckman*
Developmental editor: *Jennie Katsaros*
Senior marketing manager: *Daniel M. Loch*
Project manager: *Kelly L. Delso*
Production supervisor: *Kari Geltemeyer*
Freelance design coordinator: *Craig E. Jordan*
Cover illustration: *Laura Stutzman*
Compositor: *GAC/Indianapolis*
Typeface: *10/12 Times Roman*
Printer: *Quebecor Printing Book Group/Fairfield*

**Library of Congress Cataloging-in-Publication Data**

Beauchamp, Tom L.
    Philosophical ethics : an introduction to moral philosophy / Tom L. Beauchamp.—3rd ed.
        p.     cm.
    Includes bibliographical references and index.
    ISBN 0-07-229721-2 (softcover : alk. paper)
    1. Ethics. I. Title.
    BJ1012 .B4 2001
    170—dc21

                                                          99-047187

http://www.mhhe.com

*For Karine, Zachary, and Ruthie,*
*who make life come alive*

# Contents

# Preface to the Third Edition

The objective of this book is to provide a thorough grounding in the main types of moral philosophy. Short readings from classical and contemporary writers are included to facilitate this goal. A secondary but important design of the book is to help students become aware of situations that require moral reflection, judgment, and decision, at the same time revealing the complexities that surround moral choices and the framing of public policies. My aim has been to develop a pedagogically sound book with substantive arguments, readable materials, and practical significance.

The moral philosophies of Aristotle, Hume, Kant, and Mill are at the core of the book's structure, but their philosophical commitments are placed in the context of today's moral problems and philosophical controversies, especially those that have been prominent in moral philosophy in the last thirty years. I have emphasized philosophical argument in these four philosophers, attending to historical background and textual exegesis only as necessary to help the student understand their writings. In short, historical figures are examined both for their theories and for the way they continue to inform contemporary moral thinking.

History is reordered in Chapters 4 through 7 for pedagogical reasons. Utilitarianism is the least intricate of the theories and in many respects the easiest to learn. Kantian theories are most easily learned and appreciated as a reaction to certain alleged deficiencies in utilitarianism. Aristotelian theories, understood here as a type of virtue ethics, are best presented as an alternative to the obligation-based utilitarian and Kantian accounts. Finally, Humean theories are eclectic and have a foot in various types of ethical theory.

There are innumerable changes in this third edition. Every chapter has been rewritten to bring it up to date and to satisfy suggestions made by instructors who have used the text. Approximately one-third of the selections are new. Chapter 1 has been substantially reduced in size so that students are not unduly delayed with preliminary materials. Chapter 7, on Hume and Humean theories, has been heavily reshaped, with some of the material from that chapter moved to Chapter 8, which has an entirely new set of selections.

**xi**

Many friendly critics helped improve this volume in the first and second editions, and I again acknowledge their efforts. In the first edition, R. Jay Wallace critiqued virtually every paragraph; and in the first two editions, Ruth Faden and Hugh LaFollette made very significant suggestions for improvement. For some comments on earlier materials that led to Chapters 2, 7, 8, and 9, I am indebted to Richard Wasserstrom, Alasdair MacIntyre, Robert L. Simon, Joel Feinberg, James Childress, Burton Leiser, Norman Daniels, Norman Bowie, and Louis Katzner. I have received many helpful suggestions for improvements in this edition from students and faculty who have used the text in the classroom. I am especially grateful to Kevin Gibson and William J. Talbot. Special thanks must be given in this third edition to Gregory Pence and Sven Sherman-Peterson—as to David DeGrazia and Jeff Kahn in the second edition. They worked through the entire set of revisions and conducted research on new source material. They also helped in teaching the new material to students and evaluating its strengths and weaknesses. Moheba Hanif took the manuscript through innumerable drafts and stylistic changes. I am very grateful for all this assistance.

Tom L. Beauchamp

# PART ONE

# *Fundamental Questions*

# Morality and Moral Philosophy

In this book we encounter some perplexing moral problems that help us understand the moral philosophy at the core of the book. Each chapter begins with a case study that poses a moral problem. Various aspects of the case are then analyzed in the chapter. The case study that introduces this first chapter may seem to present only a moral *wrong*, not a moral *problem*. On closer inspection, however, this case helps us understand not only moral problems but why we regard such matters as moral at all.

## THE WATERGATE COVERUP

In March 1973, a convicted burglar named James McCord wrote to a judge named John Sirica that the White House was covering up the fact that five men had been hired by high White House officials to burglarize Democratic headquarters in the Watergate apartment-hotel complex. A month later, on April 30, 1973, White House counsel John Dean was fired by President Richard Nixon after Dean refused to is-sue a fictitious report that denied a coverup in the Watergate scandal.

Two months after his firing, Dean gave public testimony before Congress re-garding the Watergate scandal that ultimately led to Nixon's resignation. Dean tes-tified in remarkable detail about how the highest-ranking White House officials, including President Nixon, had approved the burglary and then obstructed justice in attempting a coverup of potentially damaging information about their activities. According to Dean, when the men who burglarized Democratic headquarters were arrested, those responsible at the White House intentionally effected the massive coverup. There was never any question of making the full story public; it was as-sumed in this tight circle that the facts must be concealed. There were, however, dif-ferent reasons for the coverup: Some White House officials feared prosecution, some feared impeachment, and some feared the overthrow of the country by radi-cals. Nevertheless, the imperative to cover up was, according to Dean, accepted spontaneously, unanimously, and without serious question.

Millions of people who followed this testimony, including Dean himself, thought that this burglary and the subsequent coverup were *morally wrong*, whether or not they turned out to be *illegal*. They considered such actions to be moral offenses, even if they were not punishable by law. It was eventually established that the break-in was illegal, and Dean himself was imprisoned for his role, but there was never any official judgment or pronouncement about the immorality of the break-in. Indeed, one of the early witnesses in congressional hearings on the Watergate scandal, Bernard Barker, defended the burglary as both patriotic and morally proper, no matter its legality.

## MORALITY

As we reflect on Dean's testimony and the events surrounding Watergate, several philosophical questions emerge about the morality of these activities. What made this burglary wrong? Is it the mere fact of its being a burglary? If so, how can a fact constitute a wrong? Is morality comprised of facts? Do we need a philosophical theory to determine the rightness or wrongness of the burglary—or, rather, does a philosophical theory merely draw on social morality, thus *assuming* rightness or wrongness?

These questions are philosophical, and we will meet such questions many times in this book. As an initial response, it seems clear that the words "ethics" and "morality" cannot be confined to *philosophical* contexts. The terms "ethical theory" and "moral philosophy" refer exclusively to philosophical reflection on morality. The purpose of ethical theory is to introduce clarity, substance, and precision of argument into the domain of morality. Comprehensive ethical theories attempt to provide a normative framework for understanding and responding to problems in living a moral life. Usually such a framework takes the form of a theory of right action, but it may also take the form of a theory of good character.

The term "morality," by contrast to "ethical theory" and "moral philosophy," is used to refer to conventions in society about right and wrong human conduct. These beliefs are expressed through terms such as "good," "bad," "virtuous," "praiseworthy," "right," "wrong," "ought," and "blameworthy." However, several areas of conduct other than ethics also use action-directing words such as "good" and "bad" to evaluate human endeavors. Religion, law, etiquette, and politics are examples. We may ask, then, "What is distinctive about morality?" or, more generally, "How is morality distinct from other areas of human endeavor in which normative judgments occur?"

### Morality as a Social Institution

Morality is a social institution, composed of a set of standards pervasively acknowledged by the members of a culture. It is comprised of practices that—together with other kinds of customs, rules, and mores—are transmitted from generation to generation. Morality thus has an enduring social status as a body of guidelines for conduct. Similar to political constitutions and natural languages, morality exists prior to the acceptance (or rejection) of its standards by particular individuals. Individuals do not create morality by making their own rules, and morality cannot be purely a personal policy or code.

   We learn these social requirements and their appropriate applications as we grow up, along with other important social rules, and this is one reason why it is sometimes difficult to distinguish moral rules from other rules. For example, we are constantly bombarded in our early years with rules such as "Don't swim near the rocks," "Don't cross the street without looking both ways," and "See your dentist for an annual checkup." Most of these rules are instructions in our own interest, teaching us about various kinds of *prudent behavior.*

   We also learn rules of several different kinds. We are told by parents, teachers, and peers that certain things ought or ought not to be done because they affect the interests of other people: "Don't color your sister's photographs," "Don't lie to your father and mother," "It is better to give than to receive," and "Respect the rights of others." These are elementary instructions in morality because they express what society expects of us in terms of taking the interests of other people into account. We thus learn about *moral* behavior. But we learn rules of other types as well.

## Morality and Law

One group of rules that we learn early in life are the rules of law, and these rules are often confused with moral rules. This confusion is understandable. Morality and law are both social institutions, and they share concerns over matters of great social importance. They also share in common certain basic principles, obligations, and criteria of evidence. Law can even serve as the public's agency for translating morality into explicit social guidelines and practices and for stipulating punishments for offenses.

   A surprising number of people tend to think "If it's legal, it's moral." Many thousands of people who followed the events in the Watergate scandal took just this view: If nothing legally wrong had been done, then there was no moral fault or blame either. Moral evaluation, however, needs to be carefully distinguished from legal evaluation. The law is not the repository of a society's moral standards and values, even when the law is directly concerned with moral problems. A law-abiding person is not necessarily morally sensitive or virtuous, and the fact that something is legally acceptable does not imply that it is morally acceptable. For example, a person who has a joint bank account with another person is legally authorized to withdraw all the money from the account, but it hardly follows that the person is morally authorized to do so. What legally is a withdrawal may morally be a theft.

   In the Watergate affair, it seems clear in retrospect that the planned burglary was morally wrong even if no court had ever been persuaded that a legal wrong had occurred (as at one time seemed a possible outcome of the case). The actions that took place in the White House constituted moral offenses whether punishable by law or even governed by law. For example, the coverup led to several legally punishable cases of perjury by high officials, including Dean and Attorney General John Mitchell. Their acts would have been condemnable lies from a moral point of view even if these figures had been found innocent of the perjury charges. There also were charges of "political espionage" by White House officials—a legally suspect category in this case, but a most important matter in judging the moral character of those so charged. President Nixon himself was never legally punished, though he was widely considered to have committed the most egregious moral lapse of all by fostering an environment of immoral conduct in the White House that permitted the scandal to occur. It has often been observed that the Watergate affair provoked widespread lack of confidence in the United States in the moral integrity of politicians and high officials. This is a matter of the highest moral importance in a culture, though it has no direct legal significance.

Finally, it deserves note that we commonly use moral principles to formulate and to criticize the law. In his famous "Letter from the Birmingham City Jail," Martin Luther King, Jr. argued that racial segregation was immoral, even though it was legal in many parts of the United States at the time. King wrote that "any law that degrades human personality is unjust. It gives the segregator a false sense of superiority, and the segregated a false sense of inferiority. . . . [It relegates] persons to the status of things. So segregation is not only politically, economically, and sociologically unsound, but it is morally wrong and sinful."[1]

## The Universality in Morality

The most abstract and sweeping principles of morality—such as, "Do not kill"—are, in effect, found in all cultures. These shared principles are sometimes referred to as the "common morality." Common morality is not a (specific) morality or a theory; it is simply shared morality. In recent years, the favored category to express shared universal moral content has been human rights (see the Feinberg, Okin, and Waldron selections in Chapter 8), but obligations can also be expressed in universal form. Typical of the principles that persons in all cultures seem to affirm are "Tell the truth," "Obtain consent before invading another person's body," "Do not cause pain," "Do not deprive of liberty," and "Do not steal or otherwise deprive of goods." Several of these fundamental moral values were violated by White House officials in the Watergate affair.

These norms constituting shared morality certainly do not comprise all of morality; the morality we share is only a small slice of the entire moral life. Morality more broadly understood includes divergent moral norms and positions that spring from particular cultural, philosophical, and religious roots. Many people, including many philosophers, are skeptical that the common morality has very much content at all. That is, they think that virtually nothing in the way of substantive moral content is shared across cultures. This issue will be considered in depth in Chapters 2, 3, and 8 in this text.

But before we get to those chapters, one widely held belief about morals deserves attention: When we judge an act morally right or wrong (e.g., "The deception at the White House was a moral outrage") or make a judgment about moral character (e.g., "Nixon was absolutely not to be trusted"), we do not believe our declaration is like a judgment of mere taste or preference (e.g., "This banana is delicious"). Mere preferences vary from individual to individual, but sound ethical judgments that derive from the common morality seem to transcend such individual

[1]Martin Luther King, Jr., "Letter from Birmingham City Jail," in James Melvin Washington, ed., *A Testament of Hope: The Essential Writings and Speeches of Martin Luther King, Jr.* (San Francisco: Harper, 1991).

preferences, holding interpersonally despite the fact that it is an individual who makes the judgment. For example, the rule that misleading deception in politics is morally unacceptable seems to be a universalizable moral rule, not merely a custom preferred in a few countries or by a few persons.

Although this argument makes good sense of our beliefs about fundamental moral principles, such as not harming others, it makes far less sense of many particular moral judgments (e.g., "John Dean's testimony was morally courageous") and of codes of ethics intended for specific areas of conduct, such as professional ethics. On the one hand, universality seems to be a way in which morality protects against bias, prejudice, and idiosyncratic preference. On the other hand, a *claim* of universality may itself be no more than an individual or parochial prejudice. How to sort out this problem is one of the central questions in Chapter 2.

## THE NATURE OF A MORAL POSITION

This text contains selections by philosophers who take a *moral position* on issues. We now have an understanding of the nature of morality, but virtually nothing has been said about the distinction between taking a moral position and taking some other kind of position. In the Watergate scandal, it was clear from the start that many citizens, politicians, prosecutors, and the like, were taking moral positions about theft, deception, secret wiretapping of private citizens, the moral integrity of the officials involved, and many other moral matters. Less clear is what makes such positions moral, if they are moral. Ronald Dworkin attempts in the following essay to explain the necessary ingredients that distinguish a moral position from a preference, prejudice, or a mere parroting of social platitudes. He also exposes the flaw in thinking that the norms operative in a society constitute a *moral* position.

# *The Concept of a Moral Position**

### Ronald Dworkin

We might start with the fact that terms like "moral position" and "moral conviction" function in our conventional morality as terms of justification and criticism, as well as of description. It

*Reprinted by permission of the publisher from: *Taking Rights Seriously* by Ronald Dworkin, Cambridge, Mass.: Harvard University Press. Copyright © 1970 by NYRV, Inc. and 1977 by Ronald Dworkin.

is true that we sometimes speak of a group's "morals," or "morality," or "moral beliefs," or "moral positions" or "moral convictions," in what might be called an anthropological sense, meaning to refer to whatever attitudes the group displays about the propriety of human conduct, qualities, or goals. We say, in this sense, that the morality of Nazi Germany was based on prejudice, or was irrational. But we also use some of these terms, particularly "moral position" and "moral conviction," in a discriminatory sense, to contrast the positions they describe with prejudices, rationalizations, matters of personal aversion or taste, arbitrary stands, and the like. One use—perhaps the most characteristic use—of this discriminatory sense is to offer a limited but important sort of justification for an act, when the moral issues surrounding that act are unclear or in dispute.

Suppose I tell you that I propose to vote against a man running for a public office of trust because I know him to be a homosexual and because I believe that homosexuality is profoundly immoral. If you disagree that homosexuality is immoral, you may accuse me of being about to cast my vote unfairly, acting on prejudice or out of a personal repugnance which is irrelevant to the moral issue. I might then try to convert you to my position on homosexuality, but if I fail in this I shall still want to convince you of what you and I will both take to be a separate point—that my vote was based upon a moral position, in the discriminatory sense, even though one which differs from yours. I shall want to persuade you of this, because if I do I am entitled to expect that you will alter your opinion of me and of what I am about to do. Your judgment of my character will be different—you might still think me eccentric (or puritanical or unsophisticated) but these are types of character and not faults of character. Your judgment of my act will also be different, in this respect. You will admit that so long as I hold my moral position, I have a moral right to vote against the homosexual, because I have a right (indeed a duty) to vote my own convictions. You would not admit such a right (or duty) if you were still persuaded that

I was acting out of a prejudice or a personal taste.

I am entitled to expect that your opinion will change in these ways, because these distinctions are a part of the conventional morality you and I share, and which forms the background for our discussion. They enforce the difference between positions we must respect, although we think them wrong, and positions we need not respect because they offend some ground rule of moral reasoning. A great deal of debate about moral issues (in real life, although not in philosophy texts) consists of arguments that some position falls on one or the other side of this crucial line.

It is this feature of conventional morality that animates Lord Devlin's argument that society has the right to follow its own lights. We must therefore examine that discriminatory concept of a moral position more closely, and we can do so by pursuing our imaginary conversation. What must I do to convince you that my position is a moral position?

(*a*) I must produce some reasons for it. This is not to say that I have to articulate a moral principle I am following or a general moral theory to which I subscribe. Very few people can do either, and the ability to hold a moral position is not limited to those who can. My reason need not be a principle or theory at all. It must only point out some aspect or feature of homosexuality which moves me to regard it as immoral: the fact that the Bible forbids it, for example, or that one who practices homosexuality becomes unfit for marriage and parenthood. Of course, any such reason would presuppose my acceptance of some general principle or theory, but I need not be able to state what it is, or realize that I am relying upon it.

Not every reason I might give will do, however. Some will be excluded by general criteria stipulating sorts of reasons which do not count. We might take note of four of the most important such criteria:

(*i*) If I tell you that homosexuals are morally inferior because they do not have heterosexual desires, and so are not "real men," you would reject that reason as showing one type of prejudice. Prejudices, in general, are postures of judgment that take into account considerations our conventions exclude. In a structured context, like a trial or a contest, the ground rules exclude all but certain considerations, and a prejudice is a basis of judgment which violates these rules. Our conventions stipulate some ground rules of moral judgment which obtain even apart from such special contexts, the most important of which is that a man must not be held morally inferior on the basis of some physical, racial or other characteristic he cannot help having. Thus a man whose moral judgments about Jews, or Negroes, or Southerners, or women, or effeminate men are based on his belief that any member of these classes automatically deserves less respect, without regard to anything he himself has done, is said to be prejudiced against that group.

(*ii*) If I base my view about homosexuals on a personal emotional reaction ("they make me sick"), you would reject that reason as well. We distinguish moral positions from emotional reactions, not because moral positions are supposed to be unemotional or dispassionate—quite the reverse is true—but because the moral position is supposed to justify the emotional reaction, and not vice versa. If a man is unable to produce such reasons, we do not deny the fact of his emotional involvement, which may

have important social or political consequences, but we do not take this involvement as demonstrating his moral conviction. Indeed, it is just this sort of position—a severe emotional reaction to a practice or a situation for which one cannot account—that we tend to describe, in lay terms, as a phobia or an obsession.

(*iii*) If I base my position on a proposition of fact ("homosexual acts are physically debilitating") which is not only false, but is so implausible that it challenges the minimal standards of evidence and argument I generally accept and impose upon others, then you would regard my belief, even though sincere, as a form of rationalization, and disqualify my reason on that ground. (Rationalization is a complex concept, and also includes, as we shall see, the production of reasons which suggest general theories I do not accept.)

(*iv*) If I can argue for my own position only by citing the beliefs of others ("everyone knows homosexuality is a sin"), you will conclude that I am parroting and not relying on a moral conviction of my own. With the possible (though complex) exception of a deity, there is no moral authority to which I can appeal and so automatically make my position a moral one. I must have my own reasons, though of course I may have been taught these reasons by others.

No doubt many readers will disagree with these thumbnail sketches of prejudice, mere emotional reaction, rationalization and parroting. Some may have their own theories of what these are. I want to emphasize now only that these are distinct concepts, whatever the details of the differences might be, and that they have a role in deciding whether to treat another's position as a moral conviction. They are not merely epithets to be pasted on positions we strongly dislike.

(*b*) Suppose I do produce a reason which is not disqualified on one of these (or on similar) grounds. That reason will presuppose some general moral principle or theory, even though I may not be able to state that principle or theory, and do not have it in mind when I speak. If I offer, as my reason, the fact that the Bible forbids homosexual acts, or that homosexual acts make it less likely that the actor will marry and raise children, I suggest that I accept the theory my reason presupposes, and you will not be satisfied that my position is a moral one if you believe that I do not. . . .

(*c*) But do I really have to have a reason to make my position a matter of moral conviction? Most men think that acts which cause unnecessary suffering, or break a serious promise with no excuse, are immoral, and yet they could give no reason for these beliefs. They feel that no reason is necessary, because they take it as axiomatic or self-evident that these are immoral acts. It seems contrary to common sense to deny that a position held in this way can be a moral position.

Yet there is an important difference between believing that one's position is self-evident and just not having a reason for one's position. The former presupposes a positive belief that no further reason is necessary, that the immorality of the act in question does not depend upon its social effects, or its effects on the character of the actor, or its proscription by a deity, or anything else, but follows from the nature of the act itself. The claim that a particular position is axiomatic, in other words, does supply a reason of a special sort, namely that the act is immoral in and of itself, and this

special reason, like the others we considered, may be inconsistent with more general theories I hold.

The moral arguments we make presuppose not only moral principles, but also more abstract positions about moral reasoning. In particular, they presuppose positions about what kinds of acts can be immoral in and of themselves. When I criticize your moral opinions, or attempt to justify my own disregard of traditional moral rules I think are silly, I will likely proceed by denying that the act in question has any of the several features that can make an act immoral—that it involves no breach of an undertaking or duty, for example, harms no one including the actor, is not proscribed by any organized religion, and is not illegal. I proceed in this way because I assume that the ultimate grounds of immorality are limited to some such small set of very general standards. I may assert this assumption directly or it may emerge from the pattern of my argument. In either event, I will enforce it by calling positions which can claim no support from any of these ultimate standards *arbitrary,* as I should certainly do if you said that photography was immoral, for instance, or swimming. Even if I cannot articulate this underlying assumption, I shall still apply it, and since the ultimate criteria I recognize are among the most abstract of my moral standards, they will not vary much from those my neighbors recognize and apply. Although many who despise homosexuals are unable to say why, few would claim affirmatively that one needs no reason, for this would make their position, on their own standards, an arbitrary one.

(*d*) This anatomy of our argument could be continued, but it is already long enough to justify some conclusions. If the issue between us is whether my views on homosexuality amount to a moral position, and hence whether I am entitled to vote against a homosexual on that ground, I cannot settle the issue simply by reporting my feelings. You will want to consider the reasons I can produce to support my belief, and whether my other views and behavior are consistent with the theories these reasons presuppose. You will have, of course, to apply your own understanding, which may differ in detail from mine, of what a prejudice or a rationalization is, for example, and of when one view is inconsistent with another. You and I may end in disagreement over whether my position is a moral one, partly because of such differences in understanding, and partly because one is less likely to recognize these illegitimate grounds in himself than in others.

Dworkin's thoughtful analysis raises a number of questions. Reasons for a belief can be defended sincerely and dispassionately, yet have little or nothing to do with morality. Such reasons may even be supported by what Dworkin refers to as "general" (normative) theories, yet the theories too may have little or nothing to do with morality or moral philosophy. Dworkin might say that these general theories must be *moral* theories, but then he would risk begging the question of what a moral position is.

Dworkin seems to think that only a restricted class of general ethical theories counts as providing "very general standards" and "ultimate grounds" for our more particular moral judgments. He notes that moral reasons "presuppose some general moral principle or theory," by which he presumably means a well-defended *moral theory*. Chapters 4 through 7 in this book explore the issue of what counts as an acceptable moral theory, and we can postpone further discussion of these matters until we come to those chapters.

## THE OBJECT OF MORALITY

Another important question is, "What is the object, point, or goal of morality?" We often try to understand why we have institutions in terms of their goals, functions, or objects. For example, the object of medicine is to improve health and combat disease, the object of business is to provide a service and produce a profit, and the object of social research is to develop knowledge about social life. It seems reasonable, then, to try to understand why we have the institution of morality in terms of its object, goal, or function. This assumes, of course, that there is some specifiable object of morality. This assumption may turn out to be mistaken, but it is no more implausible than the assumption that the object of medicine, social research, or business can be made explicit.

G. J. Warnock has presented a widely discussed thesis about the object of morality. He holds that morality functions to ameliorate or counteract the tendency for things to "go badly" in human relationships. Conditions naturally and inevitably deteriorate in human affairs, in his estimation, as a result of our limited resources, limited sympathy, and limited information. For example, we have institutions that house prisoners because they are persons who do not have enough of what they want in life, fail in their responsibilities to others, and make things "go badly" in society. Of course, one need not go to the extreme of prison life to observe deteriorating human relationships. Child abuse, battered women, litigation, broken contracts, contested divorces, political refugees, and dissolving partnerships are everyday examples.

In the following selection, Warnock argues that the object of morality is to contribute to the betterment of the human condition by countering the limited sympathies that persons have for one another, which can lead to unfortunate or even tragic situations.

# The Object of Morality*

## G. J. Warnock

It seems to me that to understand some species of evaluation (as contrasted perhaps with mastering it as a mere drill) is essentially a matter of grasping what its object is, what it is done *for;* and indeed if—*only* if—one understands this, can one be in any position to assess the appropriateness, or even relevance, of the standards and criteria employed.

Consider, for instance, the "grading" of candidates in a school-leaving examination. Clearly, in considering how this is or should be done, it is essential to be clear as to what it is being done for. Is it the object, for instance, to determine and indicate how well candidates are judged to *have* done certain work at school? Or is it, differently, to indicate how well they are judged *likely* to do certain things in [the] future, for instance in employment or at universities? Conceivably one might hold that these come to the same, on the ground that what a candidate has done is the only

sound, or only assessable, indicator of what he may be expected to do; but if that is not so, clearly the two objects would make appropriate and relevant the employment of different criteria. Then again, it might be the object, or part of the object, to reward or reprove, encourage or stimulate, the examinees themselves; and this too would make "grading" a different sort of exercise.

Now it is not impossible to raise the question: what is *moral* evaluation for? What is its point? Why do we distinguish between, say, actions as morally right or wrong, between people or qualities of character as good or bad? Why do we teach children to do this, by precept or example? Why do we think it worth doing? What are we trying to achieve, or bring about, by doing it? Well, it is by and large—with qualifications already noted—evaluation *of* the actions of rational beings. It does not seem plausible that in doing this we are simply, so to speak, disinterestedly awarding marks, for no particular reason or purpose, to ourselves or others. There is, it seems obvious here, some general

*From G. J. Warnock, *The Object of Morality* (London: Methuen & Co., 1971), pp. 15–18, 21–23, 26.

practical end in view; and if so, it may seem manifest that the general object must be to bring it about, in some way or other, that rational beings act, in some respects or other, *better* than they would otherwise be liable to do. Put more pompously, the general object of moral evaluation must be to contribute in some respects, by way of the actions of rational beings, to the amelioration of the human predicament—that is, of the conditions in which *these* rational beings, humans, actually find themselves. Accordingly, I take it to be necessary to understanding in this case to consider, first, what it is in the human predicament that calls for amelioration, and second, what might reasonably be suggested (to put it guardedly) as the specific contribution of "morality" to such amelioration. How are things liable to go wrong? And how exactly—or, perhaps, plausibly—can morality be understood as a contribution to their going better? . . .

It seems reasonable, and in the present context is highly relevant, to say, without necessarily going quite so far as Hobbes did,[1] that the human predicament is inherently such that things are liable to go badly. This seems to be inherently so, but not completely hopelessly so; that is, there are circumstances, not in the least likely to change significantly or to be changed by our own efforts, which cannot but tend to make things go badly, but also something at least can be done, many different things in fact, to make them go at least somewhat better than they would do, if no such things were done at all. . . .

Now some human needs, wants, and interests are, special and exceptional circumstances apart, just naturally satisfied by the human environment and situation, and others frustrated. For instance, there is naturally available in the atmosphere of the planet, without any intervention of ours, enough air for everybody to breathe (not always clean air, but that is another matter); and there are doubtless some things that people want to do, or perhaps would like to do, or wish that they could do, which are simply physically impossible—either completely so, for everybody, or impossible in certain conditions, or for certain people. But, uncontroversially, over an enormous range of needs, wants, and interests, these are neither just naturally satisfied, nor naturally, ineluctably frustrated. In an enormous range of cases, something both needs to be done, and also at least in principle could be done. And of course this is where practical problems arise. . . .

What we need now to bring in might be called limited rationality, and limited sympathies. In the first place it may be said—certainly with extreme vagueness, but still with pretty evident truth—that human beings in general are not just naturally disposed always to do what it would be best that they should do, even if they see, or are perfectly in a position to see, what that is. Even if they are not positively neurotic or otherwise maladjusted, people are naturally somewhat prone to be moved by short-run rather than long-run considerations, and often by the pursuit of more blatant, intense, and obtrusive satisfactions rather than of those cooler ones that on balance would really be better. . . .

Next, limited sympathies. This may even be too mild a term for some of the things that I have in mind. One may say

[1] *Leviathan*, I, c. 13.

for a start, mildly, that most human beings have some natural tendency to be more concerned about the satisfaction of their own wants, etc., than those of others. A man who does not like being hungry, and who is naturally inclined to take such steps as he can to satisfy his hunger, may very well care less, even not at all, about the hunger of others, and may not care at all whether anything is done to satisfy them. Even if he does care to some extent about others, it is quite likely to be only about *some* others—family, friends, class, tribe, country, or "race." There is also, besides complete or comparative indifference, such a thing as active malevolence, perhaps even purely disinterested malevolence; a man will sometimes be not only unconcerned about, but actively malevolent towards, others whom he may see as somehow in competition with himself, and sometimes perhaps even towards some whose frustrations or sufferings are not even supposed to be for the advancement of any interest of his own. There are two obvious ways in which, consequentially, things in the human predicament are liable to go badly. For people are not simply confronted, whether as individuals or groups, with the problems of getting along satisfactorily in material conditions that may, in varying degrees, be ungenial or hostile. They are also highly vulnerable to other people; and they often need the help of other people. But, given "limited sympathies," it cannot be assumed that needed help will naturally be forthcoming; and it cannot even be assumed that active malevolence will *not* be forthcoming. And perhaps above all, there may be the impossibility of trust. Whether, in pursuit of some end of my own, I need your help, or merely your non-interference, I may well be unable

to trust you either to co-operate or to keep out of it, if I think that you are not only much less concerned about my ends and interests than your own, but possibly even actively hostile to my attainment of my ends. If so, then it may be impossible for either of us to do, either separately or together, things that would be advantageous to us both, and which perhaps we both clearly see would be advantageous to us both; and it may be necessary for us individually to do things, for instance in self-protection, the doing of which may be exceedingly laborious, wasteful, and disagreeable. It will be obvious that all this applies as fully to relations between groups as between individuals; and indeed that distrust and active hostility between groups has been, in the human predicament, as frequent and constant as between individuals, and vastly more damaging.

So far we have not, I think, said anything seriously disputable, or at all unfamiliar. It is obvious that human beings have, in general, an *interest* in the course of events in which they are involved: for, though they may indeed want some things which they would not be at all the better for having, they do have many entirely harmless and proper and reasonable wants; and they also have interests and actual needs, satisfaction of which may be absolutely necessary for their well-being. But the course of events is not at all likely, without their intervention, to go in a way at all satisfactory to them; and even with intervention, there is still so much that may go wrong. Resources are limited; knowledge, skills, information, and intelligence are limited; people are often not rational, either in the management of their own affairs or in the adjustment of their own affairs in relation to others.

Then, finally, they are vulnerable to others, and dependent on others, and yet inevitably often in competition with others; and, human sympathies being limited, they may often neither get nor give help that is needed, may not manage to cooperate for common ends, and may be constantly liable to frustration or positive injury from directly hostile interference by other persons. Thus it comes about that—as Hobbes of course most memorably insisted—there is in what may be called the human predicament a certain "natural" tendency for things to go very badly; meaning thereby not, of course, in this connection, *morally* badly, but badly merely in the sense that, given the above-mentioned wholly indisputable facts about people and the circumstances in which they exist, there is the very evident possibility of very great difficulty in securing, for all or possibly even any of them, much that they want, much that it would be in their interest to have, even much that they need. And the facts that make this so are facts about the *human* predicament; there is probably no great interest in speculating about possible circumstances of other conceivable species of rational beings, but still it is worth bearing in mind that the facts we have so summarily surveyed are *contingent* facts. It is easy enough to see in general terms how very different the

situation would be if the beings concerned were less vulnerable, less aggressive, less egotistical, less irrational, more intelligent, more self-sufficient, and more favoured by material circumstances. . . .

Now, the general suggestion that (guardedly) I wish to put up for consideration is this: that the "general object" of morality, appreciation of which may enable us to *understand* the basis of moral evaluation, is to contribute to betterment—or non-deterioration—of the human predicament, primarily and essentially by seeking to countervail "limited sympathies" and their potentially most damaging effects. It is the proper business of morality, and the general object of moral evaluation, not of course to add to our available resources, nor—directly anyway—to our knowledge of how to make advantageous use of them, nor—again, not directly—to make us more rational in the judicious pursuit of our interests and ends; its proper business is to expand our sympathies, or, better, to reduce the liability to damage inherent in their natural tendency to be narrowly restricted. We may note at once that, if this is, as I think, in a sense the most important of the built-in tendencies of things to go wrong, the present suggestion fits well with the common idea that there is something peculiarly *important* about morality.

If Warnock is correct about the object of morality, his analysis helps explain pervasive features of the moral life. We are all aware that many persons are disposed to attend to the concerns of some favored persons in their lives to the exclusion or detriment of others. We are also familiar with the human tendency not to intercede to prevent harm from occurring to other persons, especially when those persons are strangers or live in distant lands. It is noncontroversial that we must avoid *causing* harm to others, even when they are complete strangers. Much more controversial is

the claim that morality actually requires us to *contribute* to and *promote* the betterment of the human condition by giving our time and resources to improve the lives
of others—for example, by preventing harmful conditions or eliminating starvation
or aggression in wars that occur in foreign nations.

In Chapter 4, we will examine a theory that takes the very strong view that we
must *maximize* the welfare of others—the primary object of morality in this theory.
We will evaluate the correctness of this strong thesis in several subsequent chapters.

## APPROACHES TO THE STUDY OF MORALITY

Four ways of studying moral beliefs and moral philosophy have dominated the
literature of ethics. Two of these approaches describe and analyze morality without
taking moral positions. These approaches are therefore called "nonnormative." Two
other approaches do involve taking moral positions, and are therefore called
"normative." This division of approaches to the study of morality can be outlined as
follows:

A  Nonnormative approaches
   1  Descriptive ethics
   2  Metaethics
B  Normative approaches
   3  General normative ethics
   4  Practical normative ethics

It would be a mistake to regard these categories as expressing approaches that cannot be used together. They are often undertaken jointly by a single author in a single article or book. Nonetheless, these distinctions are important and serviceable
when understood as broad polar contrasts exemplifying models of inquiry.

### Nonnormative Approaches

First among the two nonnormative fields of inquiry into morality is *descriptive
ethics,* or the factual description and explanation of moral behavior and beliefs.
Anthropologists, sociologists, and historians who study moral behavior employ this
approach when they explore whether and in what ways moral attitudes, codes, and
beliefs differ from person to person and from society to society.

Descriptive ethics investigates a wide variety of moral beliefs and behavior, including methods of brutality, the treatment of the aged, kinship systems, morality in
professional organizations, and abortion practices. Although philosophers do not
generally concentrate on descriptive ethics in their work, some have combined descriptive ethics with philosophical ethics by analyzing, for example, the ethical
practices of Native American tribes. These philosophers, like social scientists, have
raised questions about the apparent relativity of moral judgments and rules (issues
addressed in Chapter 2 of this text).

*Metaethics* (literally meaning "above ethics") is the second nonnormative approach to morality. It involves analysis of the meanings of central terms in ethics

such as "right," "obligation," "good," "virtue," and "responsibility." The proper analysis of the term "morality" is an example we have already discussed. Attention will be paid to the meanings of moral terms throughout this text. In addition, the structure or logic of moral reasoning is examined in metaethics, including the nature of moral justification and inference. Such problems are explored in Chapter 3.

## Normative Approaches

We can now consider the third and fourth ways of studying morality. *General normative ethics* is the philosophical attempt to formulate and defend basic moral principles and standards of virtue. In contrast to the term "morality," as analyzed above, the terms "ethical theory" and "moral philosophy" refer to reflection on the nature and justification of right actions. Many people go through life with an understanding of morality largely dictated by their culture. Other persons are not satisfied simply to conform to the morality of society. They want difficult questions answered: Is what our society forbids wrong? Are social values the best values? What is the purpose of morality? Does religion determine morality? Do the moral rules of society fit together in a unified whole? If there are conflicts and inconsistencies in our practices and beliefs, how should they be resolved? What should people do when facing a moral problem for which society has, as yet, provided no instruction?

Moral philosophers seek to answer such questions and to put moral beliefs and social practices of morality into a more unified and defensible package of guidelines and concepts. Sometimes this task involves challenging traditional moral beliefs by assessing the quality of moral arguments and suggesting modifications in existing beliefs. Morality, we might say, consists of what persons ought to do in order to conform to society's norms of behavior, whereas ethical theory concerns the philosophical reasons for or against the morality that is stipulated by society or by some social group.

Ideally, any ethical theory will provide reasons for adopting a system of moral principles or standards of virtue and will defend claims about the range of their applicability. Some philosophers have argued that there is one and only one fundamental principle determining right action. It is, roughly, the following: An action is morally right if, and only if, it produces at least as great a balance of value over disvalue as any available alternative action. This is known as the principle of utility, and philosophers who subscribe to it are referred to as "utilitarians." One member of the team of burglars in the Watergate scandal offered a half-hearted utilitarian defense of his actions by contending that a favorable balance of good over harm resulted from the burglary.

Nonutilitarians claim that one or more fundamental principles of ethics differ from the principle of utility. These are usually principles of strict obligation, such as "Never treat another person merely as a means to your own goals." This principle means that it is immoral, for example, to deceive, coerce, or fail to consult with others merely in order to promote your goals. Many philosophers who accept a nonutilitarian account of the principles of moral obligation are referred to as "deontologists." These problems in ethical theory are examined in Chapters 4 through 7 in this text.

The principles, virtues, and forms of reasoning found in general normative ethics are sometimes used to reflect on moral problems such as abortion, widespread hunger, fairness in journalism, and truthfulness in law and business. The use of moral action-guides in these contexts is commonly referred to as "practical ethics" or "applied ethics" ("practical normative ethics" in the outline above). These terms came into vogue in the 1970s when philosophical ethics began to address issues in professional ethics as well as social problems such as capital punishment, abortion, environmental responsibility, and affirmative action. Several of these problems are attended to in Chapters 8 to 10 of this text.

In recent years the teaching of practical ethics in professional schools has been conducted largely by analysis of case studies, where the hope is to teach students how to identify moral principles relevant to cases, as well as forms of reasoning that might be employed. The present text follows the model of using cases, but without engaging in extensive case analysis. Each chapter begins with a brief case relevant to the more abstract matters of theory discussed in the chapter—like the Watergate case explored in this chapter—and the case is then invoked throughout the chapter to illustrate specific issues and principles.

It is important to appreciate when reflecting on these cases that there are sharp limits to what may be expected of moral philosophy in the way of applying principles and resolving moral problems. The fundamental business of moral philosophy has always been to provide a theory or justification of moral rules, not a specification or application of the rules directly to problems of social morality. Moral philosophy helps us think clearly about these problems, but it is no panacea for resolving them.

## THE REMAINDER OF THIS TEXT

Now that we have some idea of morality and its object, as well as some idea of how it can be studied and perhaps augmented or applied, the remaining nine chapters can be outlined.

Chapter 2 continues the considerations begun in Chapter 1 by examining relativism, moral disagreements, plural and conflicting values, and egoism. In Chapter 3, attention shifts to the topic of justification in ethics, including problems of how to justify ultimate moral principles, theories of justification, the distinction between facts and values, and the justification of morality. It is useful to have studied these topics before considering the major theories of normative ethics: utilitarian theories, deontological and Kantian theories, virtue theories, and Humean theories. Presentations of these theories in Chapters 4 through 7 are woven together with a detailed analysis of the works of the writers often regarded as their primary historical spokesperson: the English philosopher John Stuart Mill, the German philosopher Immanuel Kant, the ancient Greek philosopher Aristotle, and the Scottish philosopher David Hume.

Chapters 8 through 10 then proceed to topics that have been the focus of sustained inquiry in recent years: rights, justice, and liberty. These chapters are not developed in conjunction with the study of historical figures of major influence, but several recent philosophical works that have made a major impact in philosophy are examined. These include works by figures we will have already encountered in Chapters 2 through 7, including John Rawls, Robert Nozick, Joel Feinberg, John Mackie, Alasdair MacIntyre, and John Stuart Mill.

## SUGGESTED SUPPLEMENTARY READINGS

Abelson, Raziel, and Kai Nielsen: "History of Ethics," in Paul Edwards, ed., *The Encyclopedia of Philosophy* (New York: Macmillan Company, 1967), vol. 3, pp. 81–117.

Copp, David: *Morality, Normativity, and Society* (New York: Oxford University Press, 1995).

Donagan, Alan: *The Theory of Morality* (Chicago: University of Chicago Press, 1977), chaps. 1–2.

Frankena, William K.: *Ethics,* 2d ed. (Englewood Cliffs, NJ: Prentice-Hall, 1973).

Gert, Bernard: *Morality: A New Justification of the Moral Rules* (New York: Oxford University Press, 1988), chaps. 1–5.

Gewirth, Alan: *Reason and Morality* (Chicago: University of Chicago Press, 1978), chap. 1.

Gowans, Christopher W., ed.: *Moral Dilemmas* (New York: Oxford University Press, 1987).

MacIntyre, Alasdair: *A Short History of Ethics* (New York: Macmillan Company, 1966).

Mackie, John L.: *Ethics: Inventing Right and Wrong* (Harmondsworth, England: Penguin Books, 1977).

May, Larry, and Stacey Hoffman, eds.: *Collective Responsibility: Five Decades of Debate in Theoretical and Applied Ethics* (Lanham, MD: Rowman & Littlefield, 1991).

Nielsen, Kai: "Problems of Ethics," in Paul Edwards, ed., *The Encyclopedia of Philosophy* (New York: Macmillan Company, 1967), vol. 3, pp. 117–34.

Rachels, James: *The Elements of Moral Philosophy* (New York: Random House, 1986).

Regan, Tom, ed.: *Matters of Life and Death,* 3d ed. (New York: Random House, 1992).

Reich, Warren, ed.: *Encyclopedia of Bioethics,* 2d ed. (New York: Macmillan, 1995).

Richardson, Henry: "Specifying Norms as a Way to Resolve Concrete Ethical Problems," *Philosophy & Public Affairs,* 19 (1990): 279–310.

*Routledge Encyclopedia of Philosophy* (London, England: Routledge, 1998). On-line edition available.

Scheffler, Samuel: *Human Morality* (New York: Oxford University Press, 1993).

Singer, Peter, ed.: *A Companion to Ethics* (Cambridge, England: Blackwell, 1991).

———: *Practical Ethics,* 2d ed. (New York: Cambridge University Press, 1993).

Warnock, Geoffrey J.: *The Object of Morality* (London: Methuen and Company, 1971).

Williams, Bernard: *Ethics and the Limits of Philosophy* (Cambridge, MA: Harvard University Press, 1985).

Winkler, Earl R., and Jerrold R. Coombs, eds.: *Applied Ethics: A Reader* (Cambridge, England: Blackwell, 1993).

# CHAPTER 2

# *Relativity, Pluralism, and Individuality in Morals*

## MERCY KILLING IN CANADA

When the first European explorers sailed into the region of Hudson Bay (now in northern Canada), they were in search of a northwest passage across the American continent. They chanced upon a few extraordinary customs among tribal nations. Members of some tribes in the region had a custom of killing their parents when they became old and incapable of supporting themselves by their labor. Elderly parents were strangled by their children, who, natives believed, had an obligation to perform this ritual act. It was considered an act of benevolence, not an act of cruelty. First, a grave was dug for the parent. The parent then descended into the grave, had a drink or two with his or her children, and perhaps smoked a pipe. When the parent signified a readiness to proceed, two of his or her offspring placed a thong around the parent's neck and pulled violently until the parent was strangled. Should a tribe member suffer the misfortune of having no children to perform this duty, the custom was to request the service from friends. However, friends were not under the same obligation as children, and in some cases the request was refused. A refusal was viewed as a humiliation for the person making the request; dying for the sake of the group was a point of honor in these tribes.

These seventeenth-century practices may today seem little more than remote facts of history, but assisted death that involves killing another human being remains a very live issue in Canada. A celebrated 1993 Canadian Supreme Court decision narrowly upheld (by a 5 to 4 vote) a legal ban on physician-assisted suicide. But then, in the years 1996–98, there emerged the following controversial case: A man named Paul Mills was a patient in the Queen Elizabeth II Health Sciences Center in Halifax, Nova Scotia. Mills had undergone ten unsuccessful operations for throat cancer. He was dying, and a life-support system had been withdrawn at the request of his family. It was thought that he would die a natural death within a few hours.

However, the heavy sedation he had been given was not having its intended effect. Mills was suffering from infection and experiencing "tremendous discomfort" and "excruciating pain," as hospital officials put it. Mills's physician was Nancy

Morrison; it was her decision how to alleviate his pain and discomfort. On November 10, 1996, she administered to Mills a dose of potassium chloride, an agent that is generally not used in pain control and that, in sufficient quantity, stops the heart. (Potassium chloride is used in some states in the United States as an agent to execute prisoners.) Mills died shortly thereafter. His family was unaware of the injection.

After an internal review at the hospital led to a suspension of Dr. Morrison for three months, the specifics of her action were reported to legal authorities by a person familiar with the case. On May 6, 1997, Dr. Morrison was indicted for first-degree murder; police searched the hospital and seized records. The charge was that she had intentionally hastened death. Canadian law prohibits intentional acts of hastening death, but it recognizes that doctors sometimes inject agents, using substances such as morphine, that unintentionally cause death when the intention is to alleviate pain and discomfort. This "hastening" of death is legal. Prosecutor Craig Botterill argued that the fact that Morrison's act was a "mercy killing" made no difference: Mercy killing is not a recognized excuse or category in Canadian law. However, Botterill also said that *if* there were a statute in Canadian law called "compassionate homicide," he would have charged Morrison with that crime.

Morrison pleaded not guilty. After more than one failed attempt to prosecute her, charges were thrown out on February 27, 1998. A judge determined that there was a lack of legal evidence sufficient to sustain the charge of first-degree murder. The judge and everyone involved in this case was aware that there is vast disagreement in Canada among doctors, lawyers, ethicists, and other citizens about the moral justifiability of what Morrison had done. She had unintentionally provoked a national debate about whether it is best to die a slow but painful death, or best to die quickly with a physician's assistance. At one point, Prime Minister Jean Chretien promised to bring this matter to a vote in Canada, but neither the prime minister nor the parliament has yet brought the issue to a vote.

The Nova Scotia College of Physicians and Surgeons—a licensing authority—subsequently acted on a formal complaint against Morrison that could cause suspension of her license to practice medicine. Meanwhile, she continued to practice and teach medicine (at Dalhousie University), but not in the intensive care unit where this case arose.[1]

## RELATIVISM IN MORALS

We are so accustomed to disagreements over moral problems, such as those in these two cases of "mercy killing," that we often despair of reaching agreement on the issues. Doubts that we can reach agreement are fed by popular aphorisms that morality is more properly a matter of taste than reason, that beliefs are ultimately

---

[1]The example from Hudson Bay is adapted from Karl Duncker, "Ethical Relativity," *Mind,* 48 (1939): 39–56. Duncker extracts it from Sir Henry Ellis's *Voyage for the Discovery of a North-West Passage.* The case of Nancy Morrison is written from numerous articles (1996–99) in Canadian newspapers and medical journals. Some parts of the case rely upon reports by Canadian physicians.

arbitrary, and that there is no neutral standpoint from which to evaluate disagreements. On the one hand, we may be inclined to think that moral views are based simply on how one feels or on how a culture accommodates the desires of its people, not on objectively justifiable principles. On the other hand, we tend to view morality as more than a matter of individual taste or self-interest, and we find ourselves judging many actions and beliefs with a certainty that we are right. Most of us have had the experience of being firmly convinced that another person, group, or nation is acting unjustly and ought to be punished, and we do not regard our convictions in these circumstances as mere matters of feeling or taste.

Among the most common conceptions of morality is that all moral beliefs and principles are relative to the convictions of individual cultures or persons. One person's or one culture's values, relativists maintain, do not legitimately govern the conduct of others. Even if tribal customs at Hudson Bay required the death of superannuated parents, no person reared in a different culture would feel constrained by these customs. Similarly, the thousands of physicians who today are willing to actively assist their patients in dying are counterbalanced by thousands of physicians who are utterly opposed to such assistance. Many people have therefore concluded that moral rightness and wrongness vary from place to place or person to person, without any absolute or universal moral standards that could be applied to all persons at all times.

Moral relativism is no newcomer to the scene of moral philosophy. Ancient thinkers were as perplexed by cultural and individual differences as modern thinkers. Nevertheless, it was easier in former times to ignore cultural differences than it is today, because there was once greater uniformity within cultures and less commerce between them. Any contemporary pluralistic culture is saturated with diversity of belief and lifestyle. Nonetheless, we reject the idea that this diversity compels us to tolerate racism, social-caste systems, sexism, genocide, and a wide variety of other inequities that we believe to be morally wrong.

In order to be as clear as possible about the different types of relativism, its two main forms—cultural and normative—will be discussed separately in the following pages.

## Cultural Relativism

Cultural relativists appeal to anthropological data indicating that moral rightness and wrongness vary from place to place and that there are no absolute or universal moral standards that could apply to all persons at all times. They maintain that rightness is contingent on cultural beliefs and that the concepts of rightness and wrongness are meaningless apart from the specific contexts in which they arise. The claim is that patterns of culture can only be understood as unique wholes and that moral beliefs about normal behavior are closely connected in a culture. From this perspective, a moral standard is simply a cultural product.

Psychological and historical versions of this thesis hold that the moral beliefs of individuals vary on the bases of historical, environmental, and familial differences. The weight of this anthropological, psychological, and historical evidence suggests to many observers that moral beliefs are relative to groups or individuals and that there are no transcendent universal norms. One anthropologist, Ruth Benedict, even argues that the term "morality" *means* "socially approved habits," and the expression "It is morally good" is *synonymous* with "It is habitual."[2]

Both moral philosophy and ordinary moral belief are challenged by cultural relativism. In the following article, J. L. Mackie explains why. He tries to turn our normal assumptions upside down by maintaining that relativism is defensible and that ordinary moral beliefs in opposition to relativism are indefensible.

# Relativism and the Claim to Objectivity*

## J. L. Mackie

. . . [T]he main tradition of European moral philosophy includes the . . . claim . . . that there are objective values. . . .

. . . [T]his objectivism about values is not only a feature of the philosophical tradition. It has also a firm basis in ordinary thought, and even in the meanings of moral terms. . . . The ordinary user of moral language means to say something about whatever it is that he characterizes morally, for example a possible action, as it is in itself, or would be if it were realized, and not about, or even simply expressive of, his, or anyone else's, attitude or relation to it. But the something he wants to say is not purely descriptive, certainly not inert, but something that involves a call for action or for the refraining from action, and one that is absolute, not contingent upon any desire or preference or policy or choice, his own or anyone else's. . . .

. . . [O]rdinary moral judgments include a claim to objectivity, an assumption that there are objective values in just the sense in which I am concerned to deny this. And I do not think it is going too far to say that this assumption has been incorporated in the basic, conventional, meanings of moral terms. . . . The traditional moral concepts of the ordinary man as well as of the main line of western philosophers are concepts of objective value. But it is precisely for this reason that linguistic and conceptual analysis is not enough. The claim to objectivity, however ingrained in our language and thought, is not self-validating. It can and should be questioned. But the denial of objective values will have to be put forward not as the result of an analytic approach, but as an "error theory," a theory that although most people in making moral judgements implicitly claim, among other things, to be pointing to something objectively prescriptive, these claims are all false. It is this that makes the name "moral scepticism" appropriate.

But since this is an error theory, since it goes against assumptions ingrained in our thought and built into some of the ways in which language is used, since it

*From *Ethics: Inventing Right and Wrong* by J. L. Mackie (Penguin Books, 1977), pp. 33, 35, 38. Copyright © J. L. Mackie, 1977. Reproduced by permission of Penguin Books Ltd.

[2]Ruth Benedict, "Relativism and Patterns of Culture," in Richard B. Brandt, ed., *Value and Obligation* (New York: Harcourt Brace and World, 1961), p. 457.

conflicts with what is sometimes called common sense, it needs very solid support. It is not something we can accept lightly or casually and then quietly pass on. If we are to adopt this view, we must argue explicitly for it. . . .

The argument from relativity has as its premiss the well-known variation in moral codes from one society to another and from one period to another, and also the differences in moral beliefs between different groups and classes within a complex community. Such variation is in itself merely a truth of descriptive morality, a fact of anthropology which entails neither first order nor second order ethical views. Yet it may indirectly support second order subjectivism: radical differences between first order moral judgements make it difficult to treat those judgements as apprehensions of objective truths. But it is not the mere occurrence of disagreements that tells against the objectivity of values. Disagreement on questions in history or biology or cosmology does not show that there are no objective issues in these fields for investigators to disagree about. But such scientific disagreement results from speculative inferences or explanatory hypotheses based on inadequate evidence, and it is hardly plausible to interpret moral disagreement in the same way. Disagreement about moral codes seems to reflect people's adherence to and participation in different ways of life. The causal connection seems to be mainly that way round: it is that people approve of monogamy because they participate in a monogamous way of life rather than that they participate in a monogamous way of life because they approve of monogamy. Of course, the standards may be an idealization of the way of life from which they arise: the monogamy in which

people participate may be less complete, less rigid, than that of which it leads them to approve. This is not to say that moral judgements are purely conventional. Of course there have been and are moral heretics and moral reformers, people who have turned against the established rules and practices of their own communities for moral reasons, and often for moral reasons that we would endorse. But this can usually be understood as the extension, in ways which, though new and unconventional, seemed to them to be required for consistency, of rules to which they already adhered as arising out of an existing way of life. In short, the argument from relativity has some force simply because the actual variations in the moral codes are more readily explained by the hypothesis that they reflect ways of life than by the hypothesis that they express perceptions, most of them seriously inadequate and badly distorted, of objective values.

But there is a well-known counter to this argument from relativity, namely to say that the items for which objective validity is in the first place to be claimed are not specific moral rules or codes but very general basic principles which are recognized at least implicitly to some extent in all society—such principles as provide the foundations of what Sidgwick has called different methods of ethics: the principle of universalizability, perhaps, or the rule that one ought to conform to the specific rules of any way of life in which one takes part, from which one profits, and on which one relies, or some utilitarian principle of doing what tends, or seems likely, to promote the general happiness. It is easy to show that such general principles, married with differing concrete circumstances, different existing social patterns or different preferences, will beget different specific moral rules; and there is some plausibility in the claim that the specific rules thus generated will vary from community to community or from group to group in close agreement with the actual variations in accepted codes. . . .

[P]eople judge that some things are good or right, and others are bad or wrong, not because—or at any rate not only because—they exemplify some general principle for which widespread implicit acceptance could be claimed, but because something about those things arouses certain responses immediately in them, though they would arouse radically and irresolvably different responses in others. "Moral sense" or "intuition" is an initially more plausible description of what supplies many of our basic moral judgements than "reason." With regard to all these starting points of moral thinking the argument from relativity remains in full force.

Philosophical counterarguments have been advanced in criticism of the kind of cultural relativism presented by Mackie. Among the best-known criticisms is the argument that there is a universal structure of human nature, or at least a universal set of human needs, that leads to the adoption of similar moral principles in all cultures. This empirical issue cannot be resolved here, but we can point to a matter that presents a problem for Mackie. He and other relativists seem to hold that significant differences in moral belief and judgment show that the standards that underlie those beliefs and judgments are different. This is a highly controversial inference.

Although cultural practices and individual beliefs vary, it does not follow that people *fundamentally* disagree about ultimate moral standards. Two cultures may agree about an ultimate principle of morality, yet disagree about how to apply the principle in a particular situation or policy. For example, individuals might differ over an appropriate set of actions to protect the environment not because they have a different set of standards in their environmental ethics, but because they hold different factual views about how certain discharges of chemicals and airborne particles will or will not harm the environment. They might invoke identical normative standards in supporting policies to protect the environment, and yet wind up making different recommendations because of their different beliefs about *facts*.

In the case that introduced this chapter we saw that some seventeenth-century tribes in northern Canada considered it a moral duty to kill elderly parents. Although the practice of killing one's parents horrified the first European explorers to the region and would horrify most of us today, this does not necessarily imply that we would disagree with the tribes on their underlying standards of morality. Their actions could well have been based upon standards we would accept, such as that one ought to treat one's parents with benevolence, love, and respect. Because of the different circumstances the tribes lived in, and the different factual beliefs they held, the same standards appear to have led to different particular moral judgments.

This possibility suggests that a basic or fundamental conflict between cultural values is present only if cultural disagreements about proper principles or rules occur at the level of *ultimate* moral principles. Otherwise, the apparent disagreements can be understood in terms of, and perhaps be arbitrated by, appeal to deeper shared values. If a moral conflict were truly fundamental, then the conflict could not be removed even if there were perfect agreement about the facts of a case, about the concepts involved, and about background beliefs.

We need, for this reason, to distinguish relativism of judgments from relativism of standards: When people differ about whether one policy for keeping hospital information confidential is more acceptable than another, they clearly differ in their judgments, but they need not have different moral standards of confidentiality or different goals of protecting confidentiality. Even if relativism of judgments is true, there may not be a relativism of standards.

This possibility is important for two reasons. First, many arguments intended to prove cultural relativism appeal to facts about a relativism of judgment; these facts are *claimed* to support a relativism of standards. Yet, as we have seen, the latter does not follow from the former. Second, many people reject the idea that rigid moral rules allow no flexibility in individual judgment, and it seems to them that relativism is therefore preferable to a nonrelativistic perspective. A relativism of judgment that allows for flexibility in judgments is consistent with a denial of the relativism of moral standards. You and I might agree that, generally speaking, we should keep our promises (we both accept the rule of promise keeping), and yet disagree about whether we should keep our promises in a particular kind of circumstance (say, when the person to whom we made a promise turns out to be untrustworthy).

However, these observations do not determine whether a relativism of standards is true, and this has generally been the major problem about relativism. Several controversial questions about this form of relativism are addressed in the following essay by Richard Brandt. Brandt argues that although cultural relativism is subject to strong objections, *ultimate disagreements* in morals may be inevitable, including ultimate disagreements over standards themselves.

# *Relativism and Ultimate Disagreements about Ethical Principles**

## Richard B. Brandt

Suppose that Eskimos, through their experience with the hardships of living, think of parricide as being normally the

*From Richard B. Brandt, *Ethical Theory* (Englewood Cliffs, N.J.: Prentice-Hall, Inc., 1959), pp. 100–3, 285–6, 287–8. Reprinted by permission of the author and the publisher, Prentice-Hall, Inc.

merciful cutting short of a miserable, worthless, painful old age. And suppose the Romans think of parricide as being normally the getting rid of a burden, or a getting one's hands on the parent's money—an ungraceful, selfishly motivated aggression against one whose care and sacrifices years ago have made the child's life a rich experience. The Eskimos are more-or-less unconsciously taking for granted that putting a parent to death is euthanasia under extreme circumstances; the Romans are more-or-less unconsciously taking for granted that putting a parent to death is murder for gain. In this case, although the Romans and the Eskimos may use the very same words to describe a certain sort of act—and then may express conflicting ethical appraisal of it—actually in some sense they have in mind quite different things. The Eskimos, perhaps, are accepting something of the kind *ABCD;* the Romans are condemning something of the kind *ABFG.* In this situation, we do not want to say there is necessarily any ultimate disagreement of principle between them.

When, then, do we want to say there is ultimate disagreement about ethical principles? . . .

It is not easy to answer the question whether there is ultimate disagreement on ethical principles between different groups. Most of the comparative material assembled, for instance by Westermarck, is of little value for this purpose, for in large part what it tells us is simply whether various peoples approve or condemn lying, suicide, industry, cleanliness, adultery, homosexuality, cannibalism, and so on. But this is not enough. We need, for our purpose, to know how various peoples *conceive* of these things. Do they eat human flesh because they like its taste, and do they kill slaves merely for the sake of a feast? Or do they eat flesh because they think this is necessary for tribal fertility, or because they think they will then participate in the manliness of the person eaten? Perhaps those who condemn cannibalism would not do so if they thought that eating the flesh of an enemy is nec-

essary for the survival of the group. If we are to estimate whether there is ultimate disagreement of ethical principle, we must have information about this, about the beliefs, more or less conscious, of various peoples about what they do. However, the comparative surveys seldom give us this.

In view of the total evidence, then, is it more plausible to say that there is ultimate disagreement of ethical principle, or not? Or don't we really have good grounds for making a judgment on this crucial issue?

First of all, we must report that no anthropologists, as far as the writer knows, today deny that there is ultimate disagreement—although doubtless many of them have not posed the question in exactly the above form. (*Almost* no philosophers deny it either.) This seems a matter of importance, because, even if they have not explicitly argued the matter out, their intuitive impression based on long familiarity with some non-Western society should carry considerable weight. However, we must concede that no anthropologist has offered what we should regard as really an adequate account of a single case, clearly showing there is ultimate disagreement in ethical principle. Of course, we must remember that this lack of information is just as serious for any claim that there is worldwide *agreement* on some principle.

Nevertheless, the writer inclines to think there is ultimate ethical disagreement, and that it is well established. Maybe it is not very important, or very pervasive; but there is some. Let us look at the matter of causing suffering to animals. It is notorious that many peoples seem quite indifferent to the suffering of animals. We are informed that very often, in Latin America, a chicken is *plucked alive,* with the thought it will be more succulent on the table. The reader is invited to ask himself whether he would consider it justified to pluck a chicken alive, for this purpose. Or again, take the "game" played by Indians of the Southwest (but learned from the Spaniards, apparently), called the "chicken pull." In this "game," a chicken is buried in the sand, up to its neck. The contestants ride by on horseback, trying to grab the chicken by the neck and yank it from the sand. When someone succeeds in this, the idea is then for the other contestants to take away from him as much of the chicken as they can. The "winner" is the one who ends up with the most chicken. The reader is invited to ask himself whether he approves of this sport. The writer had the decided impression that the Hopi disapproval of causing pain to animals is much milder than he would suppose typical in suburban Philadelphia—certainly much milder than he would feel himself. For instance, children often catch birds and make "pets" of them. A string is tied to their legs, and they are then "played" with. The birds seldom survive this "play" for long: their legs are broken, their wings pulled off, and so on. One informant put it: "Sometimes they get tired and die. Nobody objects to this." Another informant said: "My boy sometimes brings in birds, but there is nothing to feed them, and they die."[1] Would the reader approve of this, or permit his children to do this sort of thing?

Of course, these people might believe that animals are unconscious automata, or that they are destined to be rewarded many times in the afterlife if they suffer

[1]See the writer's *Hopi Ethics: A Theoretical Analysis* (Chicago: University of Chicago Press, 1954), pp. 213–5, 245–6, 373.

martyrdom on this earth. Then we should feel that our ethical principles were, after all, in agreement with those of these individuals. But they believe no such thing. The writer took all means he could think of to discover some such belief in the Hopi subconscious, but he found none. So probably—we must admit the case is not definitively closed—there is at least one ultimate difference of ethical principle. How many more there are, or how important, we do not say at present.

Possibly we need not go as far afield as Latin America or the Hopi to establish the point. The reader *may* have argued some ethical point with a friend until he found that, as far as he could tell, there were just some matters of principle on which they disagreed, which themselves could not be debated on the basis of any further common ground. In this case, the conclusion is the same. Note, however, that we say only "may have argued." Some people say they cannot remember ever having had such an experience; and perhaps the reader has not. In this case, we do not need to go afield.

It is obvious that if there is *ultimate* disagreement of ethical opinion between two persons or groups, there is also disagreement in *basic* principles—if we mean by "basic ethical principle" . . . the principles we should have to take as a person's ethical premises, if we represented his ethical views as a deductive system. We have so defined "ultimate disagreement" that a difference in the ethical theorems of two persons or groups does not count as being "ultimate" if it can be explained as a consequence of identical ethical premises but different factual assumptions of the two parties. Since ultimate ethical disagreements, then, cannot be a consequence of the factual assumptions of the parties, it must be a consequence of their ethical premises. Hence, there is also disagreement in "basic" principles. Our conclusion from our total evidence, then, is that different persons or groups sometimes have, in fact, conflicting basic ethical principles. . . .

There are some more detailed questions, then, that we may well ask ourselves. For instance, we may ask: Is relativism true for *all* topics of moral assessment, for perhaps 50 percent, or perhaps for only 1 percent? Or again, is relativism true for all topics except perhaps for those about which we have no strong feelings anyway, or is it true also for some topics (for example, slavery) of strong concern to us? Or, and this is obviously the most important issue, on *exactly which topics* are conflicting ethical views supportable, and on which topics must we say that all valid views are in agreement? . . .

On this matter there has been a marked change of opinion among social scientists in the past twenty years. There was a time when anthropologists like Ruth Benedict proclaimed the equal validity of the most diverse modes of living and ideals for humanity. The megalomania of the Kwakiutl, the repressed sobriety of the Pueblo, and the paranoia of the Dobuan culture were different value systems; but it would be ethnocentric, she thought, to make judgments about the relative merits of the systems. Since that time, however, anthropologists have turned attention to the similarities between societies, and to the functioning of social systems, to the analysis of institutions in terms of their capacity to minister to essential human wants and the maintenance of the social group as a continuing entity. These new interests have led to the following results.

First, it has come to be agreed that certain features of a culture system are essential for the maintenance of life, and that a system of values that permits and sanctions these forms is inevitable in society.[2] For instance, every society must provide for mating and for the rearing of offspring. Again, it must provide for the education of the offspring in the performance of those tasks that are necessary for survival. Moreover, in a complex society there must be differentiation of jobs, assignment of individuals to these jobs and the means for training them for adequate performance, and provision of motivation to do the jobs. Sufficient security must be provided to prevent serious disruption of activities, for example, security against violent attack. And so on.

It must be no surprise, therefore, to find that certain institutional forms are present in all societies: such as the family with its responsibilities for training children and caring for the aged, division of labor between the *sexes* (and occupational differences in more complex societies), games or art or dance, and so on.[3]

Second, anthropologists have come to find much more common ground in the value systems of different groups

---

[2]See D. F. Aberle et al., "The Functional Prerequisites for a Society," *Ethics,* 49 (1949), 100–11.

[3]See G. P. Murdock, "The Common Denominator of Cultures," in R. Linton, ed., *The Science of Man in the World Crisis* (New York: Columbia University Press, 1945); and C. Kluckhohn, "Universal Categories of Culture," in A. L. Kroeber, ed., *Anthropology Today* (Chicago: University of Chicago Press, 1953).

than they formerly did. As Professor Kluckhohn recently put it:

> Every culture has a concept of murder, distinguishing this from execution, killing in war, and other "justifiable homicides." The notions of incest and other regulations upon sexual behavior, of prohibitions upon untruth under defined circumstances, of restitution and reciprocity, of mutual obligations between parents and children—these and many other moral concepts are altogether universal.[4]

There are other universals we could mention: disapproval of rape, the ideal for marriage of a lifelong union between spouses, the demand for loyalty to one's own social group, recognition that the interests of the individual are in the end subordinate to those of the group. . . .

What is proved by these observations of anthropologists? First, that there is much agreement about values, especially important values, which provides

[4]C. Kluckhohn, "Ethical Relativity: Sic et Non," *Journal of Philosophy,* **52** (1955), pp. 663–77.

some basis for the resolution of disputes, even if we set aside completely considerations of validity, and assume there is no such thing as a "valid" value. Second, some values, or some institutions with their supporting values, are so inevitable, given human nature and the human situation in society as they are, that we can hardly anticipate serious questioning of them by anybody— much less any conflicting "qualified attitudes," that is, conflicting attitudes that are informed (and so on).

Thus, ethical relativism may be true, in the sense that there are *some* cases of conflicting ethical judgments that are equally valid; but it would be a mistake to take it as a truth with pervasive scope. Relativism as an emphasis is misleading, because it draws our attention away from the central identities, from widespread agreements on the items we care most about. Furthermore, the actual agreement on the central things suggests the possibility that, with better understanding of the facts, the scope of agreement would be much wider.

Those opposed to relativism need not be dismayed by Brandt's conclusions. Suppose that certain persons or cultures *do not* agree on ultimate principles, so that their ultimate moral standards are in fact culturally relative. It does not follow from this disagreement that there is no ultimate standard or set of standards that everyone ought to accept. Consider, as an analogy, the phenomenon of religious diversity. That there exist many apparently incompatible, fundamental religious beliefs does not mean that there is no single *correct* set of religious or atheistic propositions. Given current anthropological data, one might be skeptical that there could be a compelling argument in favor of one system of religion or morality. But nothing more than a cautious approach to inquiry seems justified by the facts adduced by anthropology; and nothing more than cautious inquiry would be justified if fundamental conflicts of belief were discovered.

These considerations do not definitively refute all forms of relativism. They show only why philosophers have generally been disenchanted with cultural relativism. We need now to consider a second form of relativism.

## Normative Relativism

Cultural relativists might reasonably be said to hold that "what is right at one place or time may be wrong at another." But this statement is ambiguous and may just as well be used to express a second form of relativism. Some relativists interpret the statement to mean that what is right in one context is wrong in another: What was right at Hudson Bay three centuries ago may be wrong now in Halifax, and may have been wrong then in London. What is wrong for physicians to do in Halifax now may be right for them to do in Amsterdam. This thesis is normative, because it makes a value judgment about what is right or wrong; it delineates which standards or norms legitimately determine right and wrong behavior.

There are two forms of normative relativism: a *group* form and an *individual* form. A group or society determines right and wrong in the group form. An individual person decides the right and the wrong in the individual form.

Normative relativism has sometimes been crudely translated as "anything is right or wrong whenever some individual or some group sincerely thinks it is right or wrong." For example, a national registry for a military draft would be right for those who sincerely believe it is right and wrong for those who sincerely believe it is wrong. However, less crude formulations of the position can be given, and more plausible examples can be adduced. One can hold the view, for example, that in order to be right something must be *conscientiously,* and not merely customarily, believed. In the case of group relativism, one might maintain that a belief is right if it is part of a reflectively developed, traditional moral code of rules—for example, a conscientiously adopted code of ethics accepted by an international professional organization. Formulated in this way, it seems plausible to say that a person ought to act on whatever he or she believes; or, in the case of a group, one ought to obey the group's rules.

It is not an attractive prospect to try to mix these two forms of normative relativism by accepting them both. Individual beliefs too often conflict with group beliefs. In the examples given above, it is easy to imagine a conscientious objector strongly opposing a particular group's principles, even though the individual is a member of the group.

Support might be claimed for normative relativism in the widespread belief that it is inappropriate and ultimately indefensible to criticize one culture from the partialities of another. It might be argued that we should not criticize the inhabitants of Hudson Bay or a physician like Nancy Morrison for their acts of mercy killing, and that others should likewise not criticize prohibitions on euthanasia in another culture. On the basis of such convictions, normative relativism has sometimes been formulated to assert that it is morally illegitimate to apply any standard whatever to another culture (or, alternatively, to another individual). The idea is that the validity of standards is limited in scope and the standards themselves are binding only in a specific domain, just as principles of etiquette and custom are binding only in certain locations.

The evident inconsistency of this form of relativism with many cherished and central moral beliefs is a strong reason to question it. No general theory of normative relativism is likely to convince us that *all* beliefs and acts of others—even conscientiously held beliefs—are correct, although that is exactly the general commitment of this theory. The idea that practices such as sexual exploitation, terrorism, slavery, and genocide cannot be evaluated across cultures by some common standards seems patently unacceptable. It is one thing to suggest that these practices might be excused, still another to suggest that they are correct or right, as this theory does.

There are some related puzzles about normative relativism that have never been satisfactorily answered by its defenders. One set of problems turns on changes of belief and the status of abandoned beliefs. If a conscientious objector believed strongly that he or she must resist all wars, but changed this belief after the beginning of World War II to cover only *some* wars (as happened with a large number of conscientious objectors), can one assume that one view was correct for this person at one time and another view correct at another time? If a person is forever changing beliefs, is it always a morally right belief only for the duration that it is held? When a former terrorist shudders in horror at the thought of what he or she believed last year, is it correct to say that what the terrorist did last year was right at the time, but wrong now?

In the case of the group form of normative relativism, what are we to think when a person simultaneously belongs to several groups or societies, some of whose moral standards conflict with the standards of others? Here normative relativism seems to require that individuals hold inconsistent beliefs. Suppose I am dying, and I belong to a death counseling group that accepts assisted suicide, but assisted suicide is strictly prohibited by my religion and by a professional association to which I belong. What am I bound to do if I am a normative relativist? Or, if I am a Quaker of deep religious convictions that conflict with my country's generally accepted rules of obligation to serve one's country in war, wherein do my obligations lie?

One problem in unraveling these puzzles is that the concept of a social group is difficult to interpret. Americans, for example, differ in beliefs as often as they agree, and members of seemingly more homogeneous groups, such as Roman Catholics, often are in open conflict over matters of belief. Significant moral disagreement can emerge within all such groups. These matters need to be clarified before normative relativism will appear a plausible ethical theory.

Finally, as noted above, it has often been said that one of the virtues of both cultural and normative relativism is that they are committed to promoting tolerance of diversity and dissent. But if "promote" here means that they defend a *standard* of tolerance, these forms of relativism are caught in theoretical inconsistency. The universal normative principle that we should tolerate the views of others, or that it is right not to interfere with others, is precluded by the strictures of both forms of relativism, because this proposition entails a nonrelative account of what one should do. There is nothing internal to cultural or individual relativism that suggests an individual should accept any standard other than what the individual or his or her culture believes to be correct. Both forms of relativism are in principle committed to a denial of even the existence of a normative rule of tolerance that transcends what cultures or individuals happen to believe. If there can be relativity of belief for every moral proposition, as relativists insist, then there can be relativity of belief regarding whether the practices of another society or person are to be tolerated. Indeed, if one's group accepts principles of intolerance, then one is bound to practice intolerance by the commitments of normative relativism.

The relativist cannot hold that a principle of tolerance is demanded by morality itself, because this appeal is nonrelativistic and opens the door to other nonrelative standards. A moral commitment to tolerance of other practices and beliefs thus leads inexorably to the abandonment of relativism.

It may be possible to defend some still-to-be-considered form of relativism against these criticisms. But, of the forms studied here, no compelling version has emerged. It would probably not repay the effort at this stage of our inquiry to concoct ingenious qualifications of these relativist views. As we shall now see, concern about relativism probably mislocates the deepest moral problems. More bothersome are issues of moral pluralism, multiculturalism, and moral disagreement, to which we now turn.

## MORAL DISAGREEMENT

### Diverse and Conflicting Values

Even if moral beliefs are not relative to persons or groups, we still encounter plenty of moral disagreement. Even universal principles must allow for diversity in the ways in which the universal principles are specified. Universal principles must be specified to suit the needs of particular contexts and to overcome their intrinsic lack of specific action-guiding content. This perspective on universal norms allows one to accept moral pluralism, including the version now often called multiculturalism, while rejecting a relativism of *fundamental* principles. The claim is that in different cultures, groups, and individuals, specification yields different norms; and many differences are acceptable—that is, several alternative specifications of general, nonrelative, obligations are coherent with the fundamental principles that form the core of morality itself.

This theory allows one to criticize morally unacceptable conduct that violates universal standards while remaining sensitive to legitimate cultural and individual differences. That is, it allows one to hold that there is a moral order in which certain types of conduct and cultural practices are nonnegotiable violations of human rights, but that many cultural variations violate no universal principle at all. (This thesis as applied to universal rights is treated in Chapter 8.)

Nonetheless, there is a disturbing intractability about some moral conflicts and disagreements, and we cannot always reasonably expect to agree about the morality of premarital sex, abortion, bluffing in business deals, providing national health insurance to all citizens, committing the mentally disturbed to institutions without their consent, civil disobedience, and so forth. The idea that there is an irreducible moral pluralism involving incomparable values presently receives support from a number of moral philosophers, one of whom will now be considered. Alasdair MacIntyre reaches largely skeptical conclusions in the following article. He believes that moral pluralism renders at least some moral disagreements systematically unresolvable, because the rival premises used by disputing parties cannot be made compatible. He also believes that there is no rational way to assess the claims of one argument against another. MacIntyre's theory about ultimate disagreement could be used to support individual relativism, but he argues instead for the conclusion that neither the common morality nor the moral theory developed by philosophers is powerful enough to overcome the radical forms of moral disagreement that we encounter both in daily life and in philosophy.

# *Moral Disagreements**

## Alasdair MacIntyre

I do not want to attend to the details of [moral] disagreements, so much as to the fact of disagreement. For I take it that the inability of professional moral philosophers to resolve disagreement about the concept of morality and the meaning of such words as "moral" and "ethical" through argument is related to the inability of ordinary moral agents to resolve their disagreements about which moral principles are the correct ones. Consider two important contemporary moral debates.

*1. A:* A just war is one in which the good to be achieved outweighs the evils involved in waging the war and in which a clear distinction can be made between combatants—whose lives are at stake—and innocent noncombatants. But in modern war, calculation of future escalation is never reliable and no practically applicable distinction between combatants and noncombatants can be made. Therefore no modern war can be a just war and we all *now* ought to be pacifists.

*B.* If you wish for peace, prepare for war. The only way to achieve peace

is to deter potential aggressors. Therefore you must build up your armaments and make it clear that going to war on any scale is not ruled out by your policies. A necessary part of making this clear is being prepared both to fight limited wars and to go not only to, but beyond the nuclear brink on certain types of occasion. Otherwise you will not avoid war *and* you will lose.

*C:* Wars between the Great Powers are purely destructive and all of them ought to be opposed by revolutionaries; but wars waged to liberate oppressed groups and peoples, especially in the Third World, are a necessary and therefore justified means for destroying exploitation and domination.

*2. A:* Everybody has certain rights over their own person, including their own body. It follows from the nature of these rights that at the stage when the embryo is essentially part of the mother's body, the mother has a right to make her own uncoerced decision on whether she will have an abortion or not. Therefore each pregnant woman ought to decide and ought to be allowed to decide for herself what she will do in the light of her own moral views.

*B:* I cannot, if I will to be alive, consistently will that my mother should have had an abortion when she was

*From The Belmont Report: Ethical Principles and Guidelines for the Protection of Human Subjects of Research,* Appendix I, DHEW Publication (OS) 78-0013 (Washington, D.C.: Government Printing Office, 1978).

pregnant with me, except if it had been certain that the embryo was dead or gravely damaged. But if I cannot consistently will this in my own case, how can I consistently deny to others the right to life that I claim for myself? I would break the so-called Golden Rule unless I denied that a mother has in general a right on abortion. I am not of course thereby committed to the view that abortion ought to be legally prohibited.

*C:* Murder is wrong, prohibited by natural and divine law. Murder is the taking of innocent life. An embryo is an identifiable individual, differing from a new-born infant only in being at an earlier stage on the long road to adult capacities. If infanticide is murder, as it is, then abortion is murder. So abortion is not only morally wrong, but ought to be legally prohibited.

About these two arguments I want to make four major points. The first concerns the systematically unsettleable and interminable character of such arguments. Each of the protagonists reaches his conclusion by a valid form of inference from his premises. But there is no agreement as to which premises from which to start; and there exists in our culture no recognized procedure for weighing the merits of rival premises. Indeed it is difficult to see how there could be such a procedure since the rival premises are—to borrow a term from contemporary philosophy of science— incommensurable. That is to say, they employ and involve concepts of such radically different kinds that we have no way to weigh the claims of one alternative set of premises over against another. In the first debate an appeal to an Aristotelian concept of justice is matched against an appeal to a Machiavellian concept of interest and both are attacked from the standpoint of a Fichtean con-

ception of liberation. We have no scales, no set of standards, by which to assess the weight to be given to justice thus conceived over against interest thus conceived or liberation thus conceived. Similarly, in the second debate an understanding of rights which owes something to Locke and something to Jefferson is counterposed to a universalizability argument whose debt is first to Kant and then to the gospels and both to an appeal to the moral law as conceived by Hooker, More, and Aquinas.

Secondly, in this unsettleable character, in this use of incommensurable premises, these debates are clearly typical of moral argument in our society. If the debates had been about euthanasia instead of abortion or social justice instead of war, the characteristics of the arguments would have been substantially the same. Perhaps not all moral disagreement in our society is of this kind, but much is and the more important the disagreement the more likely it is to have this character.

Thirdly—and this is the point of my excursion into the characteristics of moral disagreement—there are crucial links between this kind of disagreement among ordinary moral agents over which moral principles we are to adopt and the current disagreements between moral philosophers about how morality is to be defined. Indeed, one not uncommon type of argument used by contemporary moral philosophers has been of the form: if $X$'s account of morality is accepted, then such-and-such moral principles would be acceptable; but those moral principles are precisely unacceptable, and therefore $X$'s account of morality must be rejected. . . .

This conceptual connection between the content of moral principles and the definition of morality will perhaps be best elucidated by considering its historical explanation. When I characterized the rival moral premises of contemporary debates as Aristotelian, Machiavellian, Fichtean, and so on, I suggested something of the wide range of historical sources on which contemporary moral argument draws, but I did so by using the names of philosophers as a kind of allusive shorthand. Three points need to be made in a more extended way. The first is that the origins of contemporary moral debates are not to be found only or even mainly in the writings of philosophers, but in the forms of argument which informed whole cultures and which the writings of philosophers articulate for us in exceptionally clear and accessible ways: Aristotle is being treated here as a spokesman for at least a central strand in the culture of fourth-century Athens, Fichte as related in a similar way to [the] nineteenth century.

Secondly, the premises of contemporary moral debate have not merely been inherited; they have also been torn from the social and intellectual contexts in which they were originally at home, from which they derived such force and validity as they possess. What we have

inherited are *only* fragments and one reason why we do not know how to weigh one set of premises against another is that we do not know what force or validity to grant to each of them in isolation.

Thirdly, as the conceptual connection between the content of morality and its definition would lead us to expect, this fragmented inheritance is embodied in our rival definitions of morality as well as in our rival sets of moral principles. . . .

Fourthly, . . . the peculiar function of evaluative expressions in our discourse is to refer us to impersonal standards of value, to give reasons whose force is independent of who utters them. The implication is that in this part of our discourse we ought to be able to arrive at rational agreements on central, if not always on peripheral, issues. Yet the state of moral argument in our culture shows this not to be so. We therefore seem to be in a dilemma: *either* we have to reject the presuppositions of the dominant culture of our own society *or* we have to reject the possibility of rationality in moral argument. But the roots of this dilemma are, so I have suggested, historical.

Many philosophers have a more optimistic outlook on the problem of moral pluralism than does MacIntyre. Even when faced with an intractable pluralism, they think we can generally make constructive judgments that balance competing and conflicting values. They believe that reason and judgment can be invoked to reflect on troublesome moral problems even in the absence of a unified moral theory. It clearly does not follow from the fact of plural and conflicting values that there is no way to make comparisons between reasoned judgments. Indeed, it is especially important to resist the conclusion that a plurality of values by itself stifles sound deliberation, justification, and decision-making.

Consider an analogy to situations in which we must make choices between plural and conflicting values in our personal lives. Often these choices are moral ones and are based on sources of value such as specific obligations to one's nation or family, the rights of other individuals, or one's own personal projects; but such personal choices also reach far beyond moral choices. For example, our budget may require that we make a choice between buying textbooks for a college course or buying a train ticket home for a vacation period. Not having the textbooks will be an inconvenience, because library books will have to be used on reserve. Not visiting home will make parents unhappy and cause us distress over not being able to visit old friends. The choice may not be easy, but we think through the alternatives, deliberate, and reach a conclusion. We do not believe that we cannot make comparisons between the values that are in conflict; nor do we think that a plurality of values squelches sound deliberation and decision-making.

Here deliberation involves weighing and assessing several considerations such as obligations to parents and friends, responsibilities when taking a course, convenience, and the like. Plural values are clearly involved: happiness, money, family obligations, and convenience, to name a few. Our problem is ultimately to rate one set of values as preferable to the other set, a problem we usually surmount without suffering a crippling defeat because of the conflict that confronts us. In making our decisions, we may decide that several outcomes are both reasonable and acceptable. Even so, we must decide which is the best option. When we make poor judgments, we can still reflect on, and deliberate about, why our choices were less than sound or acceptable.

Plural and conflicting values occur not only in these cases of everyday morality and personal choice, but also in philosophical ethical theory. As Chapters 4 through 7 of this book amply illustrate, philosophical ethics presents a body of sharply conflicting and rival theories. Compelling arguments have been offered for these theories, and many philosophers have, as a result, concluded that several sources and forms of value must be accepted in philosophical ethics. A pluralist in ethical theory is one who accepts the view that there are several compelling forms of moral theory. If we pool the insights of these theories rather than choosing sides and squabbling about the one correct general theory, then we might hope to get somewhere not only in easing controversy but also in attempting to develop a philosophical ethic.

Whether moral theory should employ this model is one among many questions to be discussed in later chapters. But even if a pluralistic model of this form is acceptable, there remains the problem of how to manage disagreement in circumstances of conflict and controversy, the topic to which we now turn.

### The Resolution of Moral Disagreements

Can we hope to resolve moral controversies and disagreements? If so, on what principles or procedures can we be expected to rely? In ethics, law, and public policy, agreement between parties with widely divergent value commitments often occurs, and strategies of action to resolve moral problems can therefore be formed even in the presence of underlying disagreements. Agreement may sometimes be achieved on a code or policy without underlying justification for the positions taken. For example, it is common for members of ethics committees in business and in politics to agree about the unacceptability of certain actions, despite underlying disagreements over the justification and status of a particular principle or theory of ethics. Deep *theoretical* disagreements thus need not lead to disagreements in *practical* decision-making.

Undoubtedly no single set of considerations will ever prove consistently reliable as a means of ending moral disagreement and controversy. Resolutions of cross-cultural conflicts such as those presented in the Hudson Bay case will continue to be elusive. This fact points to the incomplete character of moral principles, reasoning, and theory. Such incompleteness may reflect the complex and sometimes dilemmatic character of the moral life rather than inherent defects in philosophical theories or the common morality. However, we know that several methods for dealing constructively with moral disagreements have been employed in the past, and each deserves recognition as a method of constructively contending with disagreement.

**Obtaining Objective Information**   Many moral disagreements can be eased by obtaining factual information. It has often been assumed that moral disputes are produced solely by differences over moral principles or their interpretation and application, rather than by a lack of information. However, as we saw when considering cultural relativism, differences in factual belief about the nature of an afterlife or the harm that will be produced by some contemplated action may be at the heart of apparent moral disagreements. For example, debates about capital punishment have foundered for decades on the factual issue of whether the threat of capital punishment effectively deters crime. Massive factual evidence has been marshaled inconclusively on both sides of the issue. This problem is factual; it is not a dispute over a moral principle or its proper application (though this is not to say that all disputes about capital punishment are factual ones).

New scientific information about possible dangers to the public involved in certain kinds of research has sometimes turned surging moral controversies in unanticipated directions. Controversies about toxic substances in the workplace, nuclear plants, research on human intelligence, cloning, and fluoridation, among others, are laced with issues over both values and facts. Current controversies over whether there should be compulsory screening for AIDS often turn on factual claims about how the human immunodeficiency virus (HIV) is transmitted, how much can be learned by screening, how many persons are threatened, whether health education campaigns can successfully teach safe sex practices, and the like.

**Providing Definitional Clarity**   Second, controversies have been calmed by reaching conceptual or definitional agreement over the language used by disputing parties. For example, controversies over the morality of euthanasia are often needlessly entangled because disputing parties use different senses of the term "euthanasia" and have invested heavily in their particular definitions. It may be that one party equates euthanasia with mercy killing and another party equates it with voluntarily elected natural death. Some even hold that euthanasia is by definition nonvoluntary mercy killing. Any resulting moral controversy over "euthanasia" is ensnared in terminological problems, rendering it doubtful that the parties are even discussing the same problem.

The Hudson Bay and Nancy Morrison cases present similar problems, because it is doubtful that what many think of as "killing" would be so described by the Hudson Bay tribes or by Dr. Morrison. It is still unclear today exactly what "killing" means in English, including the extent to which it carries moral censure. There may be no agreed-upon point of contention in some controversial cases, because the parties will be addressing entirely separate issues through their conceptual assumptions. Conceptual clarity and agreement provides no guarantee that a dispute will be settled, but it can help advance discussion of the issues.

**Adopting a Code**    Third, resolution of moral problems can be facilitated if disputing parties can come to agreement on a common set of moral guidelines, such as a professional code of ethics. If this method requires a complete shift from one starkly different moral point of view to another, disputes will virtually never be eased; differences that divide persons at the level of their most cherished principles are deep divisions, and conversions are infrequent. Nonetheless, various forms of discussion and negotiation can lead to the adoption of a new or changed moral framework that can serve as a common basis for discussion and judgment.

An example is found in a United States national commission that was at one time appointed to study ethical issues in research involving human subjects. It began its deliberations by unanimously adopting a common framework of moral principles that provided the general background for deliberations. Commissioners developed a framework of three moral principles: respect for persons, beneficence, and justice. These principles were analyzed in detail in the light of contemporary philosophical ethics and then applied to a range of moral problems that confronted the commission.[3] This common framework of moral principles facilitated discussion of the controversies the commissioners addressed and led to many agreements that might otherwise have been impossible.

Virtually every professional association has a code of ethics, and the reason these codes exist is to give guidance in a circumstance of uncertainty or dispute. This body of rules includes codes of medical, nursing, and research ethics, which apply respectively to all persons in the relevant professional roles.

**Using Examples and Counterexamples**    Fourth, resolution of moral controversies can be aided by use of example and counterexample. This form of debate occurred, for example, when the aforementioned national commission considered the level of risk that can justifiably be permitted in scientific research involving children as subjects, when no therapeutic benefit is offered to the child. On the basis of principles of acceptable risk used in their previous deliberations, the commissioners were at first inclined to accept the view that only procedures involving

---

[3]These principles were published in National Commission for the Protection of Human Subjects of Biomedical and Behavioral Research, *The Belmont Report: Ethical Principles and Guidelines for the Protection of Human Subjects of Research,* Publication No. (OS)78-0012 (Washington, DC: Government Printing Office, 1978).

low or minimal risk could be justified in the case of children (where "minimal risk" refers analogically to the level of risk present in standard medical examinations of patients). However, examples were also cited indicating that significant diagnostic, therapeutic, and preventive advances in medicine might not have occurred if procedures that posed a higher level of risk had not been employed. Counterexamples of overzealous researchers who placed children at too much risk were then presented and the debate continued for several months.

Eventually, the majority of commissioners abandoned their original view that nontherapeutic research presenting more than minimal risk was unjustified. Instead, they accepted the position that a higher level of risk can be justified by the benefits provided to other children (e.g., when terminally ill children are used as research subjects in the hope that something will be learned about their disease that will eventually help other children). Once a consensus on this particular issue crystallized, resolution was quickly achieved on the larger moral controversy about the involvement of children as research subjects.

**Analyzing Arguments**   Finally, one of the most common methods of philosophical inquiry is exposing the inadequacies, gaps, fallacies, and unexpected consequences of an argument. If an argument rests on accepting two incoherent points of view, say, then pointing out the incoherence will require a change in the argument. Exposing the unexpected consequences of a person's position functions similarly. For example, writers often express opinions about the nature of human life when treating issues such as abortion and fetal rights. Some writers on these topics have not appreciated that their arguments about life—used, for example, in discussing fetuses and individuals who are irreversibly comatose—are so broad that they may carry unintended implications for the lives of infants, nonhuman animals, or other groups. Their arguments implicitly provide reasons they had not noticed for denying rights to infants (rights that adults have), or for granting (or denying) the same rights to fetuses that infants have, and in some cases for granting (or denying) the same rights to animals that infants have.

It may be correct to hold that infants have fewer rights than adults, or that fetuses and animals should be granted the same rights as infants. The point is that if a moral argument leads to conclusions that a proponent is not prepared to defend and did not previously anticipate, the argument will have to be changed, and this process may reduce the distance between the parties who were initially in disagreement. This style of argument may be supplemented by one or more of the other four ways of reducing moral disagreement.

Some moral disagreements may not be resolvable through any of the five means discussed here, as MacIntyre strongly hints in his essay. No contention has been made in this section that moral disagreements can always be resolved, or even that every rational person must accept the same method for approaching such problems. There is always a possibility of ultimate disagreement in both theory and practice. However, *if* something is to be done about these problems of justification in contexts of controversy, a resolution is likely to be facilitated by using the methods outlined in this section.

# EGOISM

Relativism, pluralism, and moral conflict threaten the objectivity of morals and raise questions about the place of personal judgment in the moral life. The problem of egoism also challenges objectivity, especially the notion that morality requires impartial judgments, and it raises profound questions about the role of the individual. Rather than emphasizing *diversity*, egoism accentuates the role that *self-interest* plays, or ought to play, in our lives.

The problem of egoism has familiar origins. We have all been confronted with a need to decide about spending money on ourselves or on some worthy charitable enterprise. For example, we give self-interest priority over the interests of others when we elect to purchase new clothes for ourselves rather than contribute to a university scholarship fund for poor students. Egoism generalizes beyond these familiar occasions to all human choices. The egoist contends that choices invariably involve, or perhaps should involve, self-promotion as their sole objective: One's only proper goal and perhaps only moral duty is self-promotion. The following list, which derives from C. D. Broad, illustrates the motives that egoists have in mind when they speak of desires for self-promotion:

> Desire for self-preservation
> Desire for happiness
> Desire for self-respect
> Desire to get and keep property
> Desire for self-assertion
> Desire for affection[4]

Egoism has received favorable treatment from many academic psychologists and political theorists, but the theory has never fared well among moral philosophers, who have variously judged it to be unprovable, false, inconsistent, or irrelevant to morality. Objections to egoism will be considered later, after we have examined the nature of egoism, its two types, and the arguments advanced in defense of these types.

## Two Types of Egoism

Everyone has heard the advice that one should try to maximize one's personal good in any given circumstance. This counsel is generally put in looser terms, such as "You're a fool if you don't always look out for yourself first." This advice seems unacceptable in light of common moral requirements. Morality requires that we return a lost puppy to its owner even if we become enamored of it, and that we correct bank statements containing errors in our favor. Yet, why should we look out for the interests of others on such occasions? This question has troubled many reflective persons, some of whom have concluded that acting against one's interest is contrary

---

[4]C. D. Broad, *Ethics and the History of Philosophy* (London: Routledge and Kegan Paul, 1952; fac. ed. Westport, CT: Hyperion Press, 1979), pp. 218–31. Broad also notes that some special relationships prompt egoistic desires. They include the relation of ownership, the relation of blood-kinship, love and friendship, and membership in institutions.

to reason. These thinkers have viewed conventional morality as tinged with irrational sentiment and indefensible constraints on the individual. These are the supporters of "ethical egoism," which may be roughly defined as the theory that the only valid moral standard is the overriding *obligation* to promote one's personal well-being.

This form of egoism must be distinguished from a second type, "psychological egoism," which is a psychological rather than an ethical theory. This theory concerns human motivation and offers an explanation, as contrasted with a justification, of human conduct. It says that people always do what pleases them or what is in their interest. Sometimes it is put in the stronger form that we not only *do* always maximize our good, but that we psychologically *cannot* act voluntarily against what we believe to be in our best interest. For example, it could be maintained that the people of Hudson Bay who requested to be executed could not have acted otherwise, given their beliefs about how much they might suffer in the future and how they would fare in an afterlife. Regardless of whether the theory is formulated as "We do act egoistically" or "We must act egoistically," typical ways of expressing this viewpoint are these: "People are at heart selfish, even if they appear to be unselfish"; "People always look out for Number One first"; and "In the long run, everybody always does what he or she wants to do."

Psychological egoism presents a serious challenge to moral philosophy. If correct, there could be no purely altruistic or moral motivation (as we commonly use the term "moral"). Normative ethics presupposes that one *ought* to behave in accordance with moral principles, whether or not such behavior promotes one's interests. If people are so constituted that they always act in their interests, it would be absurd to demand that they act contrary to this self-interest. We need, then, to examine psychological egoism in some detail.

## Psychological Egoism

Those who promote psychological egoism do so because they are convinced through observation of themselves and others that people are thoroughly self-centered. Conversely, those who reject the theory are impressed with examples of altruistic behavior in the lives of saints, heroes, and public servants, and with many compelling studies of unselfish behavior in contemporary psychology. To them it seems undeniable that there are at least some outstanding examples of preeminently unselfish actions. Those who take this view often cite practices such as taking personal risk in hastening the death of patients, as in the Morrison case. Such actions can be viewed as paradigmatically *unselfish*. Opponents of egoism consider even the acts performed at Hudson Bay by the elders as sacrificial, performed for the sake of society's younger and more productive members, who otherwise would be short of food and housing.

Defenders of psychological egoism are not impressed by these examples. They do not contend that people always behave in an outwardly selfish manner. These egoists maintain that, no matter how self-sacrificing a person's behavior may seem at times, the desire behind the action is always selfish: In the long or the short run, one is ultimately out for oneself. In their view, an egoistic action is perfectly compatible with behavior that we standardly refer to as altruistic. The clever person who is self-interested can appear to be the most unselfish person around; whether a person is acting egoistically depends on the motivation behind the behavior. An apparently altruistic person may simply believe that an unselfish appearance best promotes his or her long-range interests. The fact that some "sacrifices" may be necessary in the short run thus fails to count against egoism (see the selection by Gauthier below).

A politician, for example, may work tirelessly for his or her constituents in order to promote the appearance of sacrifice and unselfishness. If the politician does so solely in order to be reelected (presumably the best way to promote his or her objectives), then that person has adopted an egoistic policy. Any clever egoist would act in this way, because an unselfish demeanor is almost universally praised and a selfish one likewise almost universally condemned. The psychological egoist maintains that all persons who expend effort to help others, and promote the general welfare, even risking their lives for the welfare of others, are, on close inspection, acting to promote themselves or protect themselves psychologically from criticism, guilt, and the like.

Perhaps the best way to investigate the claims made in theories of psychological egoism is to reflect on two examples, one apparently in support of psychological egoism, the other in apparent conflict. The first example is fictional, but it has long inspired philosophers attracted to psychological egoism. It has its philosophical origins in a famous passage from Book 2 of Plato's *Republic*. A figure named Glaucon relates a story about Gyges, a young man who was able to get rid of all the normal conventions and cultural constraints that operate in society, and so was left to his basic human instincts. Gyges, a shepherd, was tending his flock when suddenly an earthquake split the ground before him into a deep chasm. After the earthquake passed, Gyges, astonished by the sight, entered the chasm, where he found a tomb in the form of a hollow brazen horse. Inside the tomb was a naked boy, save for a gold ring on one finger. Gyges took the ring, and later, while attending a gathering of shepherds, innocently turned the top part of the ring to the inside of his hand. At once he became invisible, and his companions commented that he must have slipped out of the room. Gyges found he could appear and disappear at will by manipulating the ring. After this discovery, this previously innocent and honest shepherd contrived to become a courier who took messages from small villages to the court of the king. Once inside the court, he seduced the queen, and with her help murdered the king and seized the throne.

Now, says Glaucon, suppose that there were two such rings and that one was given to the most just of all persons. How would that person behave? No one, suggests Glaucon, would have such iron strength of mind as to stand fast in doing right or to keep hands off another's property when that person could do anything and have anything he or she wanted with a maximum of ease. Such a person would have a god's powers and would behave no better than the most unjust person. Glaucon concludes that we do what is morally right only under social compulsion. For our purposes, his point is that all persons perform morally obligatory actions only because they are culturally conditioned to do so or because they seek personal gain through their performance.

The second example is not hypothetical. It is an actual story reported in the *Washington Post*:

### Doorman Bequeaths $100,000

When you make $60 a week and you spend 42 years opening Mayflower Hotel doors for those much richer, you learn—by osmosis and advice—how to make a little money become a lot of money.

Until his death three weeks ago, William H. (Mike) Mann applied his lessons. When his will was submitted for probate there this week, it was Washington-area children and invalids who reaped the benefits.

Mann's will leaves $100,000 in stocks and savings to 10 area charities, in equal parts. The money has been building and multiplying—and has never been touched—since Mann joined the Mayflower as a busboy at the hotel's opening in 1925. He was doorman at the time of his death. . . .

Concentrating on blue-chip stocks and occasionally on the surefire dividends of savings accounts, Mann always handled his transactions himself. . . .

As a bachelor living in an $85-a-month apartment near the Mayflower, Mann had few expenses. "He never looked like he had a dollar or a friend," [Milton] Kronheim recalled. . . .

[The benefactors] are Children's Hospital, the Hebrew Home for the Aged, the Little Sisters of the Poor, St. Ann's Infant Asylum, the Men of St. John's, the Jewish Social Service Agency, the Ner Israel Rabbinical College in Baltimore, the Florence Crittenden Home, the Linwood Children's Center in Ellicott City, and the Columbia Lighthouse for the Blind.[5]

The egoist will attempt to explain away Mike Mann's alleged altruism. The egoist will argue that even if Mann deceived himself into thinking that he was acting from a sense of charity or duty, beneath the surface he was acting for a reward, because he knew his action would be publicly acclaimed, and stories recounting it would appear in newspapers. He would receive fame and glamour as a memorial, and for him this was psychologically satisfying, and for that reason a goal worthy of pursuit. Mann did not act primarily for the sake of the unfortunate, but, rather, so that people would remember him when he died and for the pleasure their expected acclaim brought him while he lived. The egoist might even hypothesize that Mann acted as he did for the sake of rewards in heaven or to boost his pride and avoid shame. Most plausibly of all, it might be argued, Mike Mann's greatest satisfactions were found in small daily kindnesses to others, such as opening doors for famous people, who responded with like kindnesses. The underlying principle is that everyone always acts for his or her greatest personal satisfaction, which is sometimes found not in power, riches, and fame, but in doing for other people what makes them happy.

Those who object to psychological egoism will reply that Mike Mann was always a retiring individual who shied away from public recognition and who did not believe either in the existence of God or in the possibility of an afterlife. They will note that to support altruism is not to assert that we are *always* altruistic. As David Hume maintained (in a passage to be examined in Chapter 7), the altruist insists

---

[5]Reprinted with permission from the *Washington Post* (November 11, 1970), p. A28.

only that "it is sufficient for our present purposes, if it be allowed . . . that there is some benevolence, however small, infused into our bosom; . . . some particle of the dove kneaded into our frame, along with the elements of the wolf and the serpent."[6] Hume adds immediately that egoism rests on an impoverished model of moral psychology. A devoted mother is among his favorite examples:

> Tenderness to their offspring, in all sensible beings, is commonly able alone to counterbalance the strongest motives of self-love, and has no manner of dependence on that affection. What interest can a fond mother have in view, who loses her health by assiduous attendance on her sick child, and afterwards languishes and dies of grief, when freed, by its death, from the slavery of that attendance? . . .
>
> These and a thousand other instances are marks of a general benevolence in human nature, where no *real* interest binds us to the object. And how an *imaginary* interest, known and avowed for such, can be the origin of any passion or emotion, seems difficult to explain.[7]

Hume thinks that natural benevolence, sympathy, fellow-feeling, concern for others, and the like, are ingredients in human nature.

Those who, like Hume, are opposed to egoism argue that to say a person derives satisfaction from doing something is markedly different from saying that something is done for the *sake* of the satisfaction. As they see it, Mike Mann did not act for the sake of satisfaction, even if he derived satisfaction from his actions. These critics of egoism will also insist that the egoistic argument confuses *self-motivation* with *selfish motivation*. Every voluntary act is self-motivated and stands to be self-gratifying; the act, after all, involves doing something in order to achieve one's goals, to satisfy one's desires, and to fulfill one's interests. Those who requested to be killed at Hudson Bay had definite goals in mind, and they may have been gratified by their children's or friends' responses. However, it does not follow from either self-motivation or the satisfaction of desire that an act is selfishly motivated or performed for the sake of satisfaction.

Whereas desire for personal gain is often the motivating factor in human actions, there are many forms of desire, some directed toward the interests of others. For example, if I see a clerk cheating a blind man at a railroad station, I may be motivated by a desire to see justice done or at least to see the facts set straight, just as in studying philosophy I am motivated by the desire to know something about ethical values. But the fact that I am motivated by these desires does not prove that I am motivated by the *satisfaction* that follows the success of the venture. As Bishop Joseph Butler pointed out,[8] the satisfaction of any desire is necessarily one's personal satisfaction, whether the desire be for self-gratification, a child's welfare, revenge, pity, or malice. But it is not true that all impulses have for their objects "states of the self." For example, sympathy and malice are not directed at

---

[6]David Hume, in Tom L. Beauchamp, ed., *An Enquiry concerning the Principles of Morals* (Oxford, England: Oxford University Press, 1998), sect. 9, par. 4.

[7]Ibid., appendix 2, pars. 9 and 11.

[8]Joseph Butler, *Fifteen Sermons Preached at the Rolls Chapel* (1726), in vol. 2 of W. E. Gladstone, ed., *The Works of Joseph Butler;* reissued and edited by Raymond Frey, 3 vols. (Bristol, England: Thoemmes Press, 1995), especially preface and sermons 1–3, 11–12.

producing personal happiness, although both come from within and may produce happiness.

If the arguments thus far are correct, psychological egoism is a difficult theory to defend. However, it is also difficult to produce a definitive refutation of it, owing to unresolved questions about human motivation. Every time a case of benevolent behavior is presented, the egoist responds that the person acted for *underlying* egoistic reasons. In Mike Mann's case, we saw how the egoist theory alleges that he saved and then gave away his money in order to be well regarded by others. When the nonegoist provides evidence that Mann did not care about reputation, the egoist responds that he did it for rewards in heaven. When it is shown that he did not believe in God or immortality, the egoist says that he did what he did out of guilt. If a psychiatrist then shows that he is remarkably free of guilt, the egoist may retrench and say (reminiscent of Glaucon), "Look, he passed up an opportunity to enjoy almost everything this world has to offer. Doesn't this prove that he must have done it for some kind of personal gain or perhaps for avoidance of some kind of displeasure? Surely there must be some unconscious desires or wishes that are operative."

Unargued assumptions at work in the egoist's strategy here become apparent. No longer armed with relevant evidence, and in the face of counterevidence, the egoist asserts an a priori thesis about an empirical question. The egoist winds up with an ad hoc, a priori, and unempirical defense.

### Ethical Egoism

Many problems about psychological egoism stem from its status as an empirical theory of motivation. This problem does not attend ethical egoism, however, because it is a normative ethical theory independent of psychological assumptions. Because self-promotion is the sole valid standard of behavior recognized in ethical egoism, an ethical egoist says that in any given circumstance one should assess the available options and then perform whatever action promises to be maximally self-promoting. However, egoistic calculation of this sort is compatible with several different formulations of the basic egoistic position.

One form of egoism is *individualistic*: "I ought to promote myself above others at all times." This assertion is more akin to a personal creed than an ethical theory, because it does not apply beyond oneself. It would be a self-defeating theory if one were to advocate it publicly, because to instruct others in its wisdom could lead them to accept it for themselves, and this acceptance would in turn undermine the promotion of one's interests above theirs. A second form of egoism is not individualistic but has similar problems: "Everyone ought to promote my interests above the interests of all others." This view is patently implausible both psychologically and as a moral theory. The most plausible form of ethical egoism is a third version: "Everyone ought to promote himself or herself above all others at all times." Hereafter, this *universal* form of egoism will be the only one discussed.

Perhaps the most plausible foundation for ethical egoism is in the writings of Thomas Hobbes, a well-known seventeenth-century British philosopher. According to one interpretation he is not an egoist at all, because, in his theory, once one has consented to the rules of civilized society (which it is to one's advantage to do), there will be times at which one ought to act altruistically, as altruism has previously been described. However, it is also reasonable to attribute a strong foundation for ethical egoism to Hobbes, and this interpretation will alone be considered here.

For Hobbes, good and evil are closely connected with pleasure and pain for the individual person. The word "good" is associated with whatever is the object of a person's appetite or desire, and evil is the object of aversion. "Good and evil," he says, "are names that satisfy our appetites." The good is what we promote for ourselves, the evil what we wish to avoid. Considered independently of the social constraints in civilized society, our personal appetites alone "measure" good and evil, right and wrong, justice and injustice: "It is natural, and so reasonable, for each individual to aim solely at his own preservation or pleasure."[9]

Hobbes's argument can be recast in the following form: Any clever person will realize that he or she has no moral obligations to others besides those that are voluntarily assumed. One should accept moral rules and assume specific obligations only when doing so promotes one's own self-interest. One may take the offensive and bring some benefit or liberty to oneself, or one may adopt a more defensive strategy by avoiding the enmity and limited sympathies of others; but any intelligent person will see that it is personally advantageous to make all such decisions in the light of self-interest. Moreover, one should obey moral rules and laws only in order to protect oneself and to bring about a situation that is personally advantageous. One should renege on an "obligation" whenever it becomes clear that it is to one's long-range disadvantage to fulfill the obligation. Thus, when confronted by the questionable trustworthiness of a colleague or an incompetent administration at one's place of employment, one is under no obligation to obey the law, tell the truth, or fulfill one's contracts. These obligations exist only because one assumes them, and one ought to assume them only as long as doing so promotes one's interest.

What now can be said by way of criticism of this Hobbesian universal ethical egoism? One objection is that the theory gives incompatible directives in circumstances of moral conflict. According to universal egoism, both parties in a circumstance of conflict *ought* to pursue their individual interests exclusively. Suppose, for example, that it is in the interest of an antiwar demonstrator to stop railroad shipments of dangerous chemicals used in the construction of bombs and that it is in the railroad's interest to prevent the antiwar demonstrator from stopping the shipments. Egoism counsels both parties to pursue their interests exclusively; indeed, universal egoism holds both pursuits to be morally required.

This situation's oddity can be highlighted by assuming that the antiwar demonstrator is an egoist. In order to be a consistent egoist, the demonstrator must maintain that the railroad ought to pursue its interest, which would involve thwarting the demonstrator's own antiwar objectives. In thus striving for theoretical consistency, the egoist supports a theory that works against self-interest, and so seems to fall into practical inconsistency in the attempt. Another way of looking at this example is to see the egoist as having incompatible objectives. The egoist says that everyone

[9]See Thomas Hobbes, in Edwin Curley, ed., *Leviathan* (1651) (Indianapolis: Hackett, 1994), chaps. 14–15; and Ferdinand Tönnies, ed., *The Elements of Law*, 2d ed., with a new Introduction by M. M. Goldsmith (New York: Barnes & Noble, 1969), chap. 1.

ought to seek maximal personal satisfaction, yet the universalist character of the theory makes maximization of the egoist's own satisfaction implausible. (An *individual* rather than universal egoism can escape this criticism, but at a price that has been previously noted.)

The most plausible egoistic reply is that the objection springs from a misunderstanding of the rules and policies an ethical egoist would actually accept. If everyone were to act on more or less fixed rules such as those found in common moral and legal systems, this arrangement would produce the most desirable state of affairs from an egoistic point of view. The reason is that these rules arbitrate conflicts and make social life more agreeable for everyone. These rules would include, for example, familiar moral and legal principles of justice that are intended to make everyone's life and property more secure and stable. Only an unduly narrow conception of *genuine* (long-term) self-interest, the egoist might argue, leads critics to think that the egoist would not willingly observe such rules of justice, because it is clearly in one's self-interest to do so. If society can be structured to resolve personal conflicts through courts and other peaceful means, the egoist will see it as in his or her interest to accept those binding social arrangements, just as the egoist will see it as prudent to treat other individuals well in his or her personal contacts with them.

The egoist is saying not that his or her best interests are served by promoting the good of others, but rather that *personal* interests are served by observing impartial rules irrespective of the outcome for others who live in society. The egoist does not care about the welfare of others except insofar as it affects her or his welfare. The egoist might extend this argument as follows: Egoism gives the best answer to the question, "Why be moral?" (which is addressed in Chapter 3): One ought to be moral because being moral is in one's long-range interest. Just as egoism supplies the final justification for doing anything, so it provides the final justification for adopting a moral way of life.

In the following selection David Gauthier develops such a line of thought. Gauthier argues that an egoist will in fact best maximize his or her self-interest by adopting the standards of morality. *Only* by adopting moral standards and agreeing to constrain the pursuit of self-interest will the egoist be able to cooperate with other members of society to mutual advantage. This argument turns on the distinction between long-term and short-term self-interest. His claim is that it is in the egoist's long-term self-interest to become a cooperating moral person, even though this may conflict with his or her short-term self-interest. Such conflicts are a common part of life, and we frequently counsel our friends and family members to pursue their long-term, or enlightened, self-interest over tempting short-term rewards. As an example, suppose someone chooses to take more than his or her fair share of the profits generated by a joint business venture with a partner. In the short term, the person gains more money than he or she would have gotten from a fair division of the profits. However, if the partner discovers the cheat and refuses to participate in any future business ventures, then all the future benefits the person could have reaped from further cooperation will be lost. In the long run it would have been better off to divide the profits fairly even from the egoistic perspective.

The benefits that a person may expect from a course of action, such as reaping money by cheating a business partner, are referred to by Gauthier as the "payoff."

The planned course of action itself is termed the "strategy." When the egoist considers whether to steal from his or her partner, he or she wants to know which strategy yields the highest payoff. Gauthier argues that egoists often face what he calls strategy-payoff conflicts, like that faced by the egoist businessperson. In the face of this problem, Gauthier contends that it is in the egoist's enlightened self-interest to cooperate with other people by acting morally. In this way, the happy outcome is a recommendation by the egoist of exactly what is recommended by morality.[10]

# The Incompleat Egoist*

## David Gauthier

"Egoism . . . is the doctrine which holds that we ought each of us to pursue our own greatest happiness as our ultimate end."[1] Thus G. E. Moore, who proceeded to charge this doctrine with "flagrant contradiction."[2] "The egoistic principle," Brian Medlin asserted, "is inconsistent." [3] In levelling these accusations, Moore and Medlin have been representative of a host of philosophers who have found egoism wanting in rationality. But why accuse the egoist? Left to himself, surely he seeks only to do as well for himself as possible, and this intent, if not wholly attractive, seems to fall squarely within the confines of the economist's utility-maximizing conception of practical rationality—hardly, then, what we should expect to find contradictory or inconsistent. Philosophers are blessed with both talent for and desire of finding paradox where other mortals suspect none, yet what, *rationally,* could be at fault with the attempt to do as well for oneself as possible?

As a philosopher, I have up my sleeve what, if not truly paradoxical, should seem unexpectedly puzzling. But the questions I shall raise about egoism come, not from the traditional philosophical repertoire, but rather from the theory of rational choice. . . .

The claim that egoism is self-defeating may be illustrated by an example long familiar among game theorists and now widely known to philosophers—the Prisoners' Dilemma. Jack and Zack are prisoners charged with a serious crime; each must choose between a confession that implicates the other and non-confession. If only one confesses, he is rewarded for turning state's evidence with a light sentence, while the other receives the maximum. If both confess, each receives a heavy sentence,

*From David Gauthier, "What Can an Egoist Do?" in Sterling M. McMurrin, ed., *The Tanner Lectures on Human Values* (Salt Lake City: University of Utah Press, 1984), vol. 5.

[1]G. E. Moore, *Principia Ethica* (Cambridge: At the University Press, 1903), p. 96.

[2]Ibid., p. 102.

[3]Brian Medlin, "Ultimate Principles and Ethical Egoism," *Australasian Journal of Philosophy* 35 (1957), p. 118.

[10]See also the collection of relevant materials in David P. Gauthier and Robert Sugden, eds., *Rationality, Justice and the Social Contract: Themes from Morals by Agreement* (Ann Arbor: University of Michigan Press, 1993).

but short of the maximum. If neither confesses, each will be convicted on a lesser charge and receive a sentence slightly heavier than that which would reward turning state's evidence. Jack reasons that, if Zack confesses, then he avoids the maximum sentence by confessing himself, whereas if Zack does not confess, then he gains the lightest sentence by confessing. Whatever Zack does, Jack does better to confess. Zack of course reasons in a parallel way. Given that neither is able to affect the other's choice by his own, each does better to confess, whatever the other may choose to do. Jack and Zack each maximizes his value by confessing. Each receives a heavy sentence. If neither had confessed, each would have received a lighter sentence. Jack and Zack have both satisfied the requirements of egoism and have reached a mutually costly outcome. The requirements, then, should not always be satisfied. Egoism is self-defeating. . . .

To show that egoism is self-defeating is no simple matter. As we shall see, it is not enough to show that egoists, in maximizing actor-relative value, fail to do as well for themselves *collectively* as they might. . . . We must rather show that each person's following self-interest is harmful to himself, that each fails to do as well for himself *individually* as he might. Only an argument addressed to the individual egoist can hope to show that *his* ways are self-defeating. But we may begin from the perspective of everyone, from the failure of egoists to do as well for themselves as possible, and then show how this perspective may be linked to that of the individual. And so we may begin with the Prisoners' Dilemma. . . . Let us review exactly what the Dilemma shows. Each prisoner—Jack and Zack as I called them in the preceding part—has a strategy that

is a best response to whatever strategy the other chooses. This strategy is confession. But the outcome if each chooses his best response is disadvantageous to both. Both would do better if both chose the alternative strategy—non-confession or silence. Each does best to confess whatever the other does, but each does better if neither confesses than if both confess. . . .

What the Dilemma reveals is that in some situations, his [the egoist's] choice does not give effective expression to his concern. Selecting among strategies, the egoist may be unable to maximize his payoff given the payoffs of others, and so may be unable to obtain some benefit that he could enjoy at no cost to others. Let us then say that the egoist faces *strategy–payoff conflict*. This is the general problem that the Dilemma reveals. . . .

Egoists are defeated by the existence of strategy–payoff conflict. But no individual egoist is defeated. No individual can improve his own lot. The remedy is not for individuals to choose differently, in a non-egoistic way, but rather for them to prevent strategy–payoff conflicts from arising. Those who would otherwise expect to find themselves paying the costs of such conflicts may have good reason to provide for sanctions, through binding agreements or external enforcement, that alter the payoffs. . . . These are the classic devices, proposed by Thomas Hobbes long before the theory of games revealed the precise structure giving rise to conflict. Covenants—but not covenants without the sword . . . —and the sovereign who enforces covenants and structures social institutions to prevent free-riding bring order to the egoists' world. These precautionary devices themselves involve costs that egoists would prefer to avoid, and Hobbes may be accused of failing to give sufficient consideration to these costs, but the world is under no obligation to accommodate itself to all of our preferences. There is nothing self-defeating in the need to cope with structures of interaction that in themselves impede persons seeking the greatest possible realization of their actor-relative values. . . .

Two cooperators will each do better than two non-cooperators. The problem, as we have seen, is that a non-cooperator paired with a cooperator will do better still, and at the cooperator's expense.

Suppose then that an actor is *conditionally* disposed to cooperate in Prisoners' Dilemma situations, and more generally in all situations involving strategy–payoff conflict. She does not unthinkingly opt for a cooperative strategy. Instead, she forms an expectation about the strategy choices of her partners (or opponents) and conforms her own choice to that expectation. She chooses cooperation as a response to expected cooperation, and non-cooperation as a response to expected non-cooperation. . . .

The egoist seeks to maximize actor-relative value given his expectations about the strategies others will choose. But their choices, and so his expectations, may be affected by his egoistic, maximizing policy; others, anticipating his choice, respond in a maximizing manner. The cooperator refrains from seeking to maximize value given her expectations about the strategies others will choose. And their choices, and so her expectations, may be affected by her cooperative policy; other cooperators, anticipating her choice, respond in a cooperative manner. . . . The conditional cooperator refrains from making the most of her opportunities, yet she finds herself with opportunities

that the egoist lacks, and so may expect payoffs superior to those that he can attain. . . .

I claim, then, that given the capacity to choose between egoism and conditional cooperation, and given also sufficient ability to identify the dispositions of others and to make oneself identifiable in turn, a rational person will choose to dispose herself to conditional cooperation. This choice is itself an egoistic one; she maximizes her expected actor-relative value in so choosing among possible dispositions to choose. But its effect is to convert her from an egoist to a cooperator, to a person who, in appropriate circumstances, does not choose egoistically. . . .

Egoism does indeed contain the resources for its own reform. The egoist is able to recognize the self-defeating character of his disposition to choose, and so has reason to select an alternative disposition. But the reform that the egoist carries out is not one internal to his original egoistic position. Choosing conditional cooperation is the egoist's last act as an egoist, and in that act the self-defeating character of egoism is affirmed. . . .

Cooperation requires a real measure of constraint. If we relate morality to the disposition to cooperate, then moral theory will be, or at least will include, that part of the theory of rational choice that is concerned with the formulation of principles for cooperative interaction. These principles perform the traditional constraining role of morality in such a way that their rationality must be recognized by all those who, sharing the egoist's view of value and reason, realize the self-defeating character of his choices.

In the Prisoners' Dilemma the selection of cooperative strategies is unproblematic. But this is not generally true in strategy–payoff conflict. In the Dilemma there is but one plausible way of cooperating. . . . But in most strategy–payoff conflicts there are many ways of cooperating—many outcomes that are both optimal and superior for each person to what she could expect were each to seek directly to maximize value. Moral principles must enable us to select among these possibilities. If they are to be used effectively as an alternative to general egoism, then they must be reasonably simple and clearly established in accepted social practices and institutions. Cooperation depends on the ability of each cooperator to anticipate the choices of her fellows, and this is possible in general only if those choices reflect widely shared principles.

We should expect moral principles for mutually beneficial cooperation to require such traditional virtues as truth-telling and promise-keeping, as honesty, gratitude, and reciprocal benevolence. But we should not expect all of traditional morality to pass the scrutiny imposed by the cooperative standpoint. In relating morality to ratio-

nal choice we seek to derive principles independent of any appeal to established practice. We are not concerned with reflective equilibrium. Although it would be surprising, did no commonly recognized moral constraints relate to mutually beneficial cooperation, yet traditional morality as such may be no more than a ragbag of views lacking any single, coherent rationale. My account of morality does not attempt to refine our ordinary views, but rather to provide constraint with a firm foundation in rational choice. . . .

Each person prefers to cooperate with others on terms as advantageous to herself as possible. But each must recognize that everyone has this preference. And so no one can expect others, insofar as they are rational, to accept terms of cooperation less advantageous than the least advantageous terms she herself will accept. The recognition of mutual rationality leads to the requirement that moral principles be mutually acceptable. . . .

So what should an egoist do? Why, he should become a cooperator and consent to morality.

A response to a sophisticated egoist of the sort Gauthier envisions was once considered by Hume in an extension of his argument considered previously (and to be examined further in Chapter 7). Hume recognized that circumstances sometimes arise in which persons will hurt their own interests by acting in accordance with moral rules, such as rules of justice. In a famous passage,[11] he considers the acts of a "sensible knave" who *occasionally* acts unjustly while concealing his immoral acts through deception. Hume maintains that the knave's true interests are subject to competing interpretations. On the one hand, as Gauthier's analysis emphasizes, the knave is constantly in danger of exposing his deception and cunning to others, with the ruinous consequence of a loss of reputation and future trust." On the other hand, the knave might be willing to assume this risk and sacrifice his peace of mind and

[11]*An Enquiry concerning the Principles of Morals,* sect. 9, pars. 22–25.

sense of integrity for a shot at increasing his worldly benefits. The knave will have his own perspective on how to balance the benefits, risks, and losses of his activities, and his balance could easily differ from another person's evaluation.

Hume, like Gauthier,[12] believes that acting morally returns benefits to the actor, because it produces favorable responses in other persons. Hume too appeals to the knave's instinctive self-interest as a reason for acting in accordance with moral rules of justice. The problem, however, is that acting unjustly does *sometimes* seem to be personally beneficial. Truly clever knaves seem to be able to selectively screen out those aspects of morality that do not serve their self-interest. The knave can agree that Hume and Gauthier correctly present the advantages of rules of justice for all members of society and still ask why these rules should be followed on *every* occasion. Hume's purpose in presenting and then dismissing his knave may not be to respond to this question with definitive answers as much as to reassure readers who already possess a sense of justice and a well-formed character that these possessions are worthy and ultimately rewarding in themselves—something the knave fails to appreciate.

Neither Gauthier nor Hume may have penetrated to the main moral objection to egoism. Many people believe that egoism is an evil doctrine—indeed, not a *moral* doctrine at all. This is because it advocates the overriding pursuit of selfish goals even when such pursuits lead to deception, fraud, and suffering. For example, egoism in principle supports extreme cruelty to animals whenever someone finds pleasure in inflicting pain on them (and can conceal their acts from other humans). Ethical egoism seems to advise us to ignore the welfare of others, to not pay uncollectible debts, to plagiarize where our theft cannot be detected, and to ignore commitments or avoid work through convenient excuses.[13]

Whether the sophisticated version of egoism presented by Gauthier and Hume leads to such forms of immoral behavior is far from clear, and not a matter that can be pursued further at this point. However, it should be noted that in each ethical theory that we encounter in Chapters 4 through 7, egoistic theories and motives are treated as morally improper. In these four chapters, we will study the theoretical framework used to support the claim of their wrongness.

## SUGGESTED SUPPLEMENTARY READINGS

### Relativism

Benedict, Ruth: *Patterns of Culture* (New York: Pelican Books, 1946), especially chap. 7.
Brandt, Richard B.: *Ethical Theory* (Englewood Cliffs, NJ: Prentice-Hall, 1959), especially chap. 11, "Ethical Relativism."

[12]On the comparison of Hume's view and Gauthier's, see Gauthier's treatment of the sensible knave problem in the context of self-interested motives for accepting the rules of justice, with a reply by Annette Baier: Gauthier, "Artificial Virtues and the Sensible Knave," *Hume Studies,* 18 (1992): 401–27; Baier, "Artificial Virtues and the Equally Sensible Non-Knaves: A Response to Gauthier," *Hume Studies,* 18 (1992): 429–39.

[13]See R. B. Brandt, *A Theory of the Good and the Right* (Oxford, England: Clarendon Press, 1979), p. 270 (and see rev. ed., Amherst, NY: Prometheus Books, 1998), for a list of egoistic commitments and for an objection to egoism of the sort discussed in this paragraph.

Copp, David: *Morality, Normativity, and Society* (New York: Oxford University Press, 1995).

Dascal, Marcelo, ed.: *Cultural Relativism and Philosophy* (Leiden, Netherlands: Brill, 1991).

Harman, Gilbert, and Judith Jarvis Thomson: *Moral Relativism and Moral Objectivity* (Cambridge, MA: Blackwell, 1996).

Krausz, Michael, ed.: *Relativism: Interpretation and Confrontation* (Notre Dame, IN: University of Notre Dame Press, 1989).

Krausz, Michael, and Jack W. Meiland, eds.: *Relativism: Cognitive and Moral* (Notre Dame, University of Notre Dame Press, 1982).

Ladd, John, ed.: *Ethical Relativism* (Belmont, CA: Wadsworth Publishing Company, 1973).

Moser, Paul K.: *Philosophy After Objectivity: Making Sense in Perspective* (New York: Oxford University Press, 1993).

Okin, Susan Moller, et al., eds.: *Is Multiculturalism Bad for Women?* (Princeton, NJ: Princeton University Press, 1999).

Pittman, John, ed.: *African-American Perspectives and Philosophical Traditions* (New York: Routledge, 1997).

Rorty, Richard: *Objectivity, Relativism, and Truth: Philosophical Papers I* (Cambridge, England: Cambridge University Press, 1991).

Taylor, Charles, and Amy Gutmann, eds.: *Multiculturalism: Examining the Politics of Recognition* (Princeton, NJ: Princeton University Press, 1994).

Wong, David: "Relativism," in Peter Singer, ed., *A Companion to Ethics* (Cambridge, England: Blackwell, 1991).

Wong, David B.: *Moral Relativity* (Berkeley: University of California Press, 1984).

## Disagreement and Pluralism

Beauchamp, Tom L.: "Ethical Theory and the Problem of Closure," in Arthur Caplan, H. T. Engelhardt, Jr., and Daniel Callahan, eds., *Closure of Scientific Disputes* (New York: Cambridge University Press, 1984), pp. 27–48.

Hampshire, Stuart: *Morality and Conflict* (Cambridge, MA: Harvard University Press, 1983).

Honderich, Ted, ed.: *Morality and Objectivity* (London: Routledge and Kegan Paul, 1985).

Misak, Cheryl J.: *Truth, Politics, Morality: Pragmatism and Deliberation* (New York: Routledge, 1999).

Nagel, Thomas: "The Fragmentation of Value," in *Mortal Questions* (Cambridge, England: Cambridge University Press, 1979).

Phillips, D. Z., and H. O. Mounce: *Moral Practices* (New York: Schocken Books, 1970), especially chap. 9, "Moral Disagreement."

Sinnot-Armstrong, Walter: *Moral Dilemmas* (Oxford, England: Basil Blackwell, 1988).

Stocker, Michael: *Plural and Conflicting Values* (Oxford, England: Clarendon Press, 1990).

Wallace, James D.: *Moral Relevance and Moral Conflict* (Ithaca, NY: Cornell University Press, 1988).

Williams, Bernard: "Conflicts of Values," in *Moral Luck* (Cambridge, England: Cambridge University Press, 1981).

## Egoism

Baier, Kurt: *The Moral Point of View* (Ithaca, NY: Cornell University Press, 1958), chap. 8.

————: "Egoism," in Peter Singer, ed., *A Companion to Ethics* (Cambridge, England: Blackwell, 1991).

Blum, Lawrence A.: *Friendship, Altruism, and Morality* (London: Routledge and Kegan Paul, 1980).

Brandt, Richard B.: *Ethical Theory* (Englewood Cliffs, NJ: Prentice-Hall, 1959), chap. 14.

Butler, Joseph: *Fifteen Sermons Preached at the Rolls Chapel*, in D. D. Raphael, ed., *British Moralists, 1650–1800* (Oxford, England: Clarendon Press, 1969), vol. 1, pp. 323–77.

Gauthier, David P., ed.: *Morality and Rational Self-Interest* (Englewood Cliffs, NJ: Prentice-Hall, 1970).

————: *Morals by Agreement* (New York: Oxford University Press, 1986).

————, and Robert Sugden, eds.: *Rationality, Justice and the Social Contract: Themes from Morals by Agreement* (Ann Arbor: University of Michigan Press, 1993).

Kalin, Jesse: "On Ethical Egoism," *American Philosophical Quarterly, Monograph Series No. 1: Studies in Moral Philosophy* (1968), pp. 26–41.

MacIntyre, Alasdair: "Egoism and Altruism," in Paul Edwards, ed., *The Encyclopedia of Philosophy* (New York: Macmillan Company, 1967), vol. 2, pp. 462–66.

Mansbridge, Jane J., ed.: *Beyond Self-Interest* (Chicago: University of Chicago Press, 1990).

Milo, Ronald D., ed.: *Egoism and Altruism* (Belmont, CA: Wadsworth Publishing Company, 1973).

Morillo, Carolyn R.: "The Reward Event and Motivation," *Journal of Philosophy,* 87 (April 1990): 169–86.

Nagel, Thomas: *The Possibility of Altruism* (Oxford, England: Clarendon Press, 1970).

Nielsen, Kai: "Egoism in Ethics," *Philosophy and Phenomenological Research,* 19 (1959).

Nozick, Robert: "On the Randian Argument," *The Personalist,* 52 (1971): 282–304.

Rachels, James: "Two Arguments against Ethical Egoism," *Philosophia,* 4 (1974): 297–314.

Schmidtz, David: "Self-Interest: What's in It for Me?" *Social Philosophy and Policy,* 14 (1997): 107–21.

Sober, Elliot: "What Is Psychological Egoism?" *Behaviorism,* 17 (1989): 89–102.

## CHAPTER 3

# Justification and Truth

## ORGAN PROCUREMENT POLICIES

Hall-of-fame baseball great Mickey Mantle was suffering from three liver diseases and needed a liver transplant in mid-1995. Unlike many people who need transplants, Mr. Mantle almost immediately received the liver he needed. His case brought widespread attention to the system used to procure and distribute organs, and also publicized the plight of thousands of persons on waiting lists to receive tissues and organs. It was said that Mr. Mantle received his liver so quickly because he met the criterion of urgent need. This criterion applies only to patients in a hospital intensive care unit where their doctors anticipate that they have less than a week to live without a transplant. Mantle was at the time the only patient in Dallas, Texas, in the category of urgent need (so-called Status 1) and was in a particular area of the United States in which livers were fairly readily available. The liver was authorized by a nonprofit, independent organ procurement organization.

However, the integrity and justifiability of the system of distributing organs came under deep suspicion as a result of what the public perceived as the privilege of a celebrity to jump to the top of the waiting list, which is ranked by medical and scientific criteria as well as length of time on the list. Just before Mantle, Pennsylvania Governor Robert Casey had received both a liver and a heart on only one day's notice. Questions were also raised due to the fact that Mantle had also seriously damaged his liver by a forty-two-year history of heavy drinking of alcohol. There was strong feeling in the public that the liver award was not justified and should have gone to someone who had no history of persistent drinking. Media in various parts of the country received angry phone calls from citizens expressing their outrage and threatening to destroy their donor cards.

The justice and the justifiability of the present system for distributing organs is an important and much debated moral question. However, many commentators have suggested that issues of distributing organs are less important than the need for a system of *procuring* organs that will eliminate the shortage of organs and therefore eliminate problems of their fair distribution. From this perspective, it is less important whether Mr. Mantle justifiably received an organ so quickly and more important whether the system we use to procure organs is itself justified.

The advent of immunosuppressive therapies (those that suppress rejection mechanisms and facilitate transplantation) in the early 1980s dramatically increased the urgent need for tissues and organs. Medical successes have led to long waiting lists, which increase in size each year. Many patients die as a result, and others live in a severely compromised state prior to receiving a transplant. To many observers this seems a moral failure, utterly without justification, especially since we know that organs are retrieved in most nations from only 15 to 20 percent of those whose organs are of value and could be procured at the time of death.

The scarcity of organs and tissues has prompted a number of proposals for reform of the current system of procurement by finding a more efficient policy that is also morally justified. The system used in many countries is to make decisions about donation through a donor card. In practice, however, few individuals sign donor cards, the cards are rarely available at the time of death, the cards are sometimes improperly executed, and procurement teams virtually always ask for family consent even if the decedent left a valid donor card that required no additional consent. This system has not worked efficiently.

As a result, various public policies have been considered, and some adopted, that aim to procure organs more efficiently. Some people have maintained that we can obtain many more organs if we circumvent the requirement of patient or family consent. One way to do so is by *presuming* consent to a dead person's tissues or organs. Laws have been passed in some states in the United States and in Europe that rely heavily on this notion of "presumed consent," which has been used as a justification for methodical retrieval of organs or tissues when no objection to retrieval has been publicly registered. The policy is straightforward: All legally competent persons are provided with the opportunity to refuse to donate. Each person is presumed to have consented to donation unless a refusal to donate has been registered. However, many people find this policy unjustifiable because it does not require direct patient or family *consent*—the only kind of meaningful consent, they think.

Several alternative policies of procurement have been suggested to increase organ availability. One approach that has generally been viewed as extreme is to create a public market in tissues and organs, including policies that would provide financial incentives to the family of the deceased to authorize organ retrieval. This option has been declared illegal in most nations because of concerns about exploitation of persons desperate for funds. There is also concern that this policy would seriously damage public altruism in the giving of tissues and organs.

Another alternative is known both as *required response* and as *mandated choice*. The proposal is that all competent adults be required by law to express their preferences about tissue and organ donation—for example, when applying for or renewing a driver's license. Individuals could either accept or reject the status of "donor." The moral justification of this proposal is its unattenuated fidelity to individual autonomy (see Chapters 5 and 10). However, this policy also excludes the rights of families to control the process, which is a powerful reason in the minds of many for thinking that this policy is unjustifiable.

Some commentators recommend still more sweeping changes that would make organ procurement a community project of routinely collecting organs unless objections are registered, rather than a matter of individual or family decisions. The routine retrieval of tissues and organs from all dead persons is claimed by proponents to be justified on grounds that members of a community have an obligation to provide other persons with objects of lifesaving value when no cost to themselves is required. These policies suggest community ownership of (or at least rights of control over) body parts. This approach gives more authority and control to the state and to medical institutions than do most policies governing medical interventions. For this reason, some view routine collection as conflicting deeply with individual and family rights.[1]

## MORAL ARGUMENTS AND MORAL JUSTIFICATION

Almost everyone interested in moral problems at some point asks whether certain views about what is morally good and right can be justified. As we saw in Chapter 2, we resist the thesis that something is right or justified merely because it is *believed* to be right. But what is meant by "justification," and how do we know when a belief or action is justified?

"Justification" has more than one meaning in English, and has independent histories of use in theology, law, philosophy, and other disciplines. In its most general sense, justification means to show to be right, to vindicate, to furnish adequate grounds for, to warrant, and the like. The underlying idea is proving one's case by presenting sufficient grounds for believing, acting, asserting, preferring, and the like. Here there is a need to distinguish between an *attempted* justification and a *successful* justification.

Problems of justification involve problems of soundness in argument, including problems of method (how premises are produced) and logic (how conclusions are produced). Logic is that branch of philosophy concerned with the relationship between premises and their conclusions, especially with how conclusions are correctly derived in arguments. An argument is a group of statements standing in relation to one another; one statement in the group, the conclusion, is claimed either to be the consequence of, or to be justified by, the other statements.

In a newspaper interview several years ago, the millionaire oilman H. L. Hunt was asked to justify his statement that "I would starve if I earned less than a million dollars a week." He offered the following reason: "Our family spends 13 times that

---

[1]See Jeremiah G. Turcotte, "Transplantation: A Frontier for Bioethics and Bioscience," in Michael G. Phillips, ed., *Organ Procurement, Preservation and Distribution in Transplantation*, 2d ed. (Richmond, VA: UNOS, 1996), pp. 13–22; Patricia A. Marshall, David C. Thomasma, Abdallah S. Daar, "Marketing Human Organs: The Autonomy Paradox," *Theoretical Medicine*, **17** (1996): 1–18; U.S. General Accounting Office, *Organ Transplants: Increased Effort Needed to Boost Supply and Ensure Equitable Distribution of Organs. Report* (Washington, DC: GAO, 1993); United Network for Organ Sharing (UNOS), Histocompatibility Committee, "The National Kidney Distribution System: Striving for Equitable Use of a Scarce Resource," *UNOS Update*, **11** (August 1995): 31–32; Laurie Goodstein, "Crying Foul over Mantle: Liver Transplant Sparks Ethics, Alcoholism Debate," *Washington Post*, June 10, 1995, p. B1; Oscar Bronsther et al., "Prioritization and Organ Distribution for Liver Transplantation," *Journal of the American Medical Association,* **271** (January 12, 1994): 140–43; B. J. Katz, "Increasing the Supply of Human Organs for Transplantation: A Proposal for a System of Mandated Choice," *Beverly Hills Bar Journal*, **18** (1985): 152.

sum—$13 million—in keeping our food, oil, ranching, real estate, and other activities as going concerns." Hunt gave a good reason for needing $1 million a week: He had to pay his debts. But did he give a good reason for fearing starvation and ruin? Did he justify his claim? Many will say that, given the same premises, conclusions utterly at odds with Hunt's can be drawn, for example, that he could live in the lap of luxury for the remainder of his life if he simply sold off his assets.

In general, every argument, no matter how complex, can be put into the following form:

$X$ is correct; therefore, $Y$ is correct.

or

Because $X$ is correct, $Y$ is correct.

Unfortunately, arguments are rarely presented in this simplified form. More often, we find them submerged in complex and intricate patterns of discourse, disguised by rhetoric, irrelevancies, redundancies, and subtle connections with other arguments. A premise may be compounded with an exhortation, or a description, or an aside having no bearing on the point. People also rarely argue by using premises arranged in a logical order, all leading rigorously to some clear conclusion. Sometimes, the conclusion is the first statement uttered; sometimes, the conclusion is so obvious in the context that it goes unstated. The same is true of premises; they may be left at the level of suggestion or only elliptically expressed. These complexities heighten the difficulty of finding or formulating an argument and seeing whether a claim is justified.

## INTERNAL AND EXTERNAL JUSTIFICATIONS

A condition that some philosophers place on justification is the following:

> Justification occurs if and only if there is successful appeal to an independent standard that validates as correct what is claimed to be correct.

Unless a standard is independent of what needs to be justified, we seem to beg the question by *presupposing* the judgments or standards we are presumably defending. If, for example, I am attempting to justify the right to free speech, I beg the question if I invoke nothing but premises that presuppose the right to free speech. I need some form of justification external to this right; for example, I need to appeal to the disastrous social consequences that would occur if we fail to recognize the right.

Nevertheless, despite its apparent plausibility, this condition of independence creates problems for justification and method in ethics, and in philosophy generally. First, is it possible to justify *ultimate* or *final* moral premises under this requirement of an independent standard? Suppose we ask for a justification of the whole corpus of our moral beliefs. What could count as a justificatory standard that is independent of the system of moral beliefs? Is there any truly external condition that is plausibly a justifying condition?

## The Internal-External Distinction

Internal justifications occur within an established institution or system of thought. For example, principles and forms of justification appropriate to the fields of law, theology, history, accounting, and science are accepted by persons who work in those fields. Problems of justification are treated by reference to accepted rules and reigning standards of evidence, reasoning, and argument. All internal problems of justification of particular moral judgments and principles assume the legitimacy of "higher," more general standards, which are the necessary conditions of their correctness. The higher standards have still more general conditions of their correctness in the form of more fundamental principles or reasons. This process of justification cannot go on forever. At some point, the highest or most fundamental level must be reached, the level of ultimate principles required for the correctness of all other principles. At least the model of internal justification points to this conclusion.

External justification, by contrast to internal, attempts to address the problem of justifying principles at the ultimate level (rather than assuming these principles). External justification seeks to justify an entire institution of beliefs and reasoning, the relevant set of internal principles. To challenge an entire structure of beliefs is tantamount to challenging the defensibility of the basic standards of a theory, field, or institution. Thus, a challenge to scientific reasoning, theological reasoning, or legal reasoning that calls into question the complete structure of justifying principles in one of these disciplines can be answered only by showing that the ultimate principles defining the field can *themselves* be justified. In the case of morality, we are interested in whether an external justification of the basic standards of the moral way of life—the institution of morality, as it was called in Chapter 1—can be given.

## The Regress of Justification

Many philosophers believe that external justification creates an absurd demand that cannot be fulfilled and involves a misconception of the basis and nature of justification. If every standard used to justify another standard is unjustified, then there cannot in principle be an adequate foundation for moral judgments or for the institution of morality (or for anything else). The "Independence Condition," critics claim, introduces a crippling regress bound to eventuate in skepticism. More than one way of dealing with such skepticism has been proposed, as we will see later in this chapter, but this section will be confined to two theories that have specifically addressed the issue of external justification. The first is based on the growth of moral convictions in a moral tradition and the second on what is generally called pragmatic justification.

**Moral-Tradition Justifications**   Many contemporary philosophers reject the demands of external justification and the attendant conception of levels. They hold that such "foundationalism" in ethical theory needlessly promotes skepticism and a philosophical deadlock over justification. They maintain that it is a false conception to suppose that everything is open to the need for further justification. As we widen the scope of our reasons, at some point we will find not a new level of justification, but rather a final level of *description* that expresses our most general commitments. This level *is* the final level of justification.

Explanation in science is frequently used in this context as an analogue to morality: In scientific explanation we cannot go on forever justifying beliefs in terms of more general premises; at some point, we reach a final level comprised of our most general laws, forms of evidence, and other general commitments in science. In morals, logic, science, and elsewhere when we reach the ultimate level of our framework principles, we can provide nothing more than an *internal* justification in which basic beliefs have been located and described.

From this perspective, human society is governed by a set of moral commitments that constitute the terms of social cooperation, and these provide the framework within which a moral philosopher thinks. Moral beliefs and the institution of morality cannot be separated from the moral matrix of beliefs that has grown up and been tested over time; the package of beliefs cannot be justified in bits and pieces or by an historical look at the logic of moral discourse. Morality is an internal component of a tradition; justification is internal to traditions, and internal only.

**Pragmatic Justifications**   A second response to the demand for external justification is a pragmatic theory initially spearheaded by Herbert Feigl and Wesley Salmon.[2] They distinguish *validation*, or internal justification, from *vindication*, or external justification. To validate is to appeal correctly to principles already accepted within an institution or system of thought. Validating principles serve as the framework for internal justification, and they warrant individual inferences. If one asks for an external justification of these internal validating principles, vindication is requested. Vindication is pragmatic. Once an operative purpose or objective of an institution or system of thought has been identified, a set of standards is considered most suitable, and therefore is vindicated, if it can be shown to be better for reaching these objectives than any alternative set of standards. The set of principles that best achieves a stated goal should be adopted.

To understand the pragmatic character of this strategy of justification, consider the "best" strategy for playing football. Which "theory of football" ought to be adopted by coaches? Many kinds of plays and rules are taught to players, and behind these rules are more complex principles and strikingly different "theories" of the game. As long as one presupposes a system or theory of the game, the rules and judgments taught to players are internally justified by the principles and theories. However, if a justification of coach $X$'s theory of the game is requested, then only an external justification would be adequate, because the request in effect says, "Why this theory of football rather than that one?" According to the pragmatic

---

[2]Herbert Feigl, "De Principiis Non Disputandum . . . ?" in Max Black, ed., *Philosophical Analysis* (Ithaca, NY: Cornell University Press, 1950), pp. 119–56; Wesley Salmon, *The Foundations of Scientific Inference* (Pittsburgh: University of Pittsburgh Press, 1966); and "Symposium on Inductive Evidence," *American Philosophical Quarterly,* 2 (1965): 265ff.

theory of vindication, that set of principles or theory is best which is most suitable for fulfilling one's objectives in playing football. If the objective of football games is winning, say, then a theory is pragmatically justified if it is most effective in deploying (similarly talented) players so that the team wins more often than it would by following any other theory of the game. Obviously, things would change if the objective were teaching good sportsmanship, say, rather than *winning*.

The same approach presumably will externally justify a *moral* framework of rules or guides to action. The justification rests on the framework's suitability for fulfilling the objectives the institution of morality is intended to serve. If a set of standards is most suitable for this objective, that set and no other is justified. The assumption is that there is a goal or purpose of morality; and, as we saw in Chapter 1, this assumption is plausible. There G. J. Warnock argued that morality's fundamental objective is to ameliorate or counteract the tendency for things to go badly in human affairs as a result of the limited resources, sympathy, information, and intellectual abilities of our fellow human beings. In theory, the object of morality is to better the human condition by countervailing limited sympathies that lead to social conflicts. If this statement of the *goal* of morality is correct, then the pragmatic approach holds that a system of moral guides is justified if, and only if, it is the most suitable means for achieving this goal.

The pragmatic account obviously presupposes that one can identify both the meaning and the purpose of "morality," but it should be acknowledged that these are formidable tasks (see Chapter 1). If morality is a complex enterprise with numerous goals, a framework of principles best suited to achieve a single goal (such as Warnock's) may be unsuited to achieve other goals. Additionally, if no set of standards can reliably be predicted to achieve the goals of morality, then our choice of standards seems arbitrary. Yet, it is of the highest importance in the pragmatic theory that the goal or objective of morality not be a matter of personal choice, because then any goal whatever could be stated as the right goal, and, consequently, any "moral theory" whatever could be justified merely by specifying the goal of morality so that the desired theory was the best means to that goal.

However, it has not been the purpose of this section to deal exclusively or primarily with the place of the pragmatic theory of justification. The point has been to show the difference between an internal and an external justification, and to emphasize that it is appropriate to ask for an internal or an external justification of any moral belief, principle, code, or theory. We can use this background to address what some philosophers have judged to be one of the most important questions about moral justification: "Why be moral?"

## The Justification of Morality

Can we justify the belief that we ought to be persons of good moral character or ought to live a moral life? The "ought" in this statement cannot be a *moral* ought if the problem of begging the question is to be surmounted. The question presupposes that we know what morality requires and asks for a justification of living by moral standards. The question is, "Even if one can determine by reference to morality what one morally ought to do, why ought one to do what morality requires?" For example, suppose you knew that the morally right act is to serve as an organ or tissue donor. Why should you live up to that obligation?

Some have maintained that this question is senseless, because it asks for a good reason for doing something when a reason has already been provided. From this perspective, if a reason is a good *moral* reason, then it is a good reason period, because moral reasons are by their nature good reasons, and it makes no sense to ask questions if good answers are already known. To ask such senseless questions would be tantamount to asking what one ought to do when one already knows. P. H. Nowell-Smith once stated the point very succinctly: "The question 'Why should I do what I see to be [morally] right?' is not just an immoral question, but an absurd one. . . . In conceding that it is the right thing to do, he has already conceded that [a person] ought to do it."[3]

We need to ask whether this claim of absurdity harbors a confusion—perhaps a confusion between internal and external justification. The question is not, "Why, from a moral (internal) point of view, should one be moral?" Rather, it is, "Why, from a nonmoral (external) point of view, should one be moral?" Although this seems an odd question from the moral point of view, it is not odd if we consider the conflicts that occur between a moral way of life and other ways of life, or even between moral decisions and decisions made on nonmoral bases. Many of us have been tempted to override moral reasons by appeal to attractive nonmoral reasons, including religious reasons, political reasons, and self-interested reasons. A relative of a person needing a kidney transplant might know that the morally right thing to do is to donate his or her kidney, yet have reasons of self-interest to incline him or her against donation. Self-interest might be served by refusing to help. Why should such a person, or anyone else, act on moral reasons in such circumstances rather than on reasons of self-interest? Why should he or she not act immorally or as they please?

The question "Why be moral?" has seldom been treated as focusing on why a *group* should accept morality. The question has generally been interpreted as focusing on why an *individual* should adopt and give supremacy to a moral way of life. One might again adopt a Hobbesian approach by arguing that a moral way of life pragmatically overcomes many disadvantages that one would encounter if one did not live by moral standards. A moral way of life seems clearly preferable to a life of punishment, rejection, and isolation.

Here Hobbes's answer seems less than compelling, however, because a justification of morality in terms of self-interest is subject to the following objection (which recalls our discussion of both Hobbes and Hume's sensible knave in Chapter 2): It is true that I would be advantaged if everyone else acted morally and that I should attempt to escape the sanctions that would be imposed on me for my immoral acts, but these premises provide no compelling reason why I should act morally or be moral instead of merely pretending to act morally. If one could succeed in making one's self-interest paramount while inducing others to make the demands of morality paramount, would this not seem, from the pragmatic point of view, the best

---

[3]P. H. Nowell-Smith, *Ethics* (Baltimore: Penguin Books, 1954), pp. 41ff.

possible world for oneself? But this response is tantamount to rejecting a moral way of life rather than accepting it.

It is always possible that in some sense of a "better life," some persons will have a better life if they do not live up to morality's demands. This might be a better life from, say, a religious or political standpoint. One would have to supply the crucial sense of a better life and argue for the point of view that it is better than morality. This problem must now be confronted directly.

## ULTIMATE JUSTIFICATION
## AND INDIVIDUAL CHOICE

If, as earlier suggested, the regress of moral justification is unstoppable in the pursuit of an external justification, we cannot reasonably expect to reach an ultimate level that answers the question, "Why should I be moral?" Is it, then, a matter of elective choice, made by each individual, to live either a moral way of life, a nonmoral way of life, or a partially moral way of life? This would be a choice for which no external justification of the choice is available. The most likely appeals would be to morality itself, to self-interest, or to some source of directive norms such as a religious tradition.

A long philosophical tradition holds that acceptance of morality is not a matter of either reason or justification; rather, it is a matter of commitment, feeling, sentiment, or choice of the most abiding and significant sort. Many theologians have offered this appraisal of religious faith, which they construe as a commitment for which there is no justification by reason (only a justification by the quality of faith itself). Perhaps morality is similar: Ultimate choices and commitments must be made by each individual, and justification is a matter of the quality of the commitment made.

This approach has been criticized as irrational and arbitrary, like a game of chance. However, this analogy to chance seems inaccurate. A person can choose in light of a wealth of information about what it would be like to live *different* ways of life that involve the acceptance of different principles. The person could debate the options with others and could choose in light of both the available information and the perspectives on that information provided by others. This is a form of deliberative choice, if not justification, much like choosing between a vacation on the coast or a vacation in the mountains: In the end, one chooses the vacation (or the way of life) that one finds most attractive in the light of the assembled information about both.

On this hypothesis, no ultimate reason can be given—only a *choice* that is up to each individual. On the one hand, the choice of a moral way of life has seemed to some writers no more justifiable than the choice of some alternative way of life. On the other hand, some writers have argued that the analogy to religious commitment considered earlier is indeed appropriate: In the end, a religious way of life and a moral way of life both rest on faith.

In the following article, William Frankena argues that a *philosophical* defense of morality as a way of life rests in important respects on faith. He postulates that one would choose to be moral if one knew clearly what one wanted and what the facts of one's situation were. He admits that his postulation rests on an "article of faith," though he also holds that "this faith is rational" because a process of justification can be given that underwrites the choice.

# Why Be Moral?*

## William K. Frankena

[Suppose one] asks what is the rational thing to choose, all things considered; prudence, morality, and whatnot. Then one is asking what one *would* choose, as far as one can see, *if* one were completely clear-headed and fully knowledgeable about oneself and everything involved. What could be more rational than such a decision? If I am right, then something is rational for one to choose if one would choose it under those conditions. *Rational* thus means "would be chosen under such conditions." And then it is an open question, not only whether being moral is rational, but also whether being prudent or self-interested is. . . .

I [wish to dispute] the assumption that a course of action or a way of life, to be rational for me to adopt, must be such as to give me the best or highest score in the long run, or for the time I can reasonably expect to have, in terms of something like pleasure, satisfaction, fulfillment, happiness, flourishing, or achievement of excellence—in short, that it is never rational to pursue a course that involves any sacrifice on one's part or results or may be expected to result in anything less than such a highest score for oneself. . . .

What worries me is the assumption that one can show being moral to be rational only if one can show that it gives one the best score for one's life, all things considered. It would, after all, be paradoxical if the only way to justify a nonegoistic enterprise like morality were by use of an egoistic argument. Besides, I do not believe that being moral will always give one the best score even if one considers the contribution that being moral makes to one's good or happiness, though I agree that this contribution is a great one. I believe, rather, that morality sometimes requires genuine sacrifice, and may even require self-sacrifice. . . .

If, in order for an individual to be rational, being moral must yield him or her the best score in some longrun way, then the rationality of genuine sacrifice, supreme or not supreme, cannot be proved, even if one has strong, deeply-rooted interests in one's fellows. For genuine sacrifice means taking a course of action that makes one's total score in life less than it would be otherwise. It can therefore be rational for a person only if it represents a course that person would choose "on the whole if all the consequences of all the different lines of conduct open to him were accurately foreseen and adequately realized in imagination at the present point of

*From. William K. Frankena, "Lecture Three: Why Be Moral?" *Thinking about Morality* (Ann Arbor: University of Michigan Press, 1980), pp. 85–94.

time," to borrow words Sidgwick used in defining the notion of "a man's future good on the whole."[1]

It may be thought that I am making a distinction without a difference. Not so. There is a difference between the life that gives one the best score and the life one would prefer given complete knowledge and a perfect realization of what is involved. One might, all things considered, prefer a life that does not yield one the best score, precisely on the ground that it has morality on its side. To give me my best score, a life must include my being around to collect the results, but a life involving self-sacrifice may not allow me to do this. Nevertheless, I might prefer it if I knew all about myself and the world. . . . We cannot know for certain that being moral is rational either for anyone or for everyone. We are, however, still ahead *if* we can say more in favor of believing *this* than we can in favor of believing that being moral is for the good of everyone in the sense of always giving him or her the better score. I am convinced that we can. In the first place, we can, of course, say for it everything that can be said for the coincidence of being moral with self-interest, which is a great deal. Here I would stress both of the lines of argument mentioned earlier, i.e., the one that points out how much happiness there is in relating well to others, and the one that centers on the thought that virtue is its own reward. The good life for anyone consists primarily of enjoyments of various kinds and of the achievement of such excellence as one is capable of; the first argument emphasizes the former component, the second

the latter. To make the second clearer, I may observe that being moral entails achieving a certain kind of excellence, namely excellence as judged from the moral point of view; that this is a kind of excellence which requires no special ability or gift, as artistic and athletic excellence do (even a person of ordinary talents can become a very good person); and that it is a peculiarly important sort of excellence just because it is excellence in one's relations to other persons and sentient beings as well as to oneself. The facts about mental illness show how significant for human life such relations and performing well in them are. . . .

I think one can also claim, judging by the case of Socrates and many others, that those who have been moral would choose to be so again if they could look back over their actions from the vantage point of perfect hindsight.

Finally, there is the matter of self-respect. Moral philosophers have been making much of its importance lately, but they were anticipated by Aldo Leopold who wrote, "Voluntary adherence to an ethical code elevates the self-respect of the sportsman, but . . . voluntary disregard of the code degenerates and depraves him."[2] His point is that self-respect presupposes that one sees oneself as moral. What is self-respect? I suggest that it is a conviction that one's character and life will be approved by any rational being who contemplates it from the moral point of view. One can claim that having this belief about oneself is a primary human good, as John Rawls does in his widely read and much discussed book, *A Theory of Justice,* but it is not just a good that is to be added in, along with

---

[1] Henry Sidgwick, *Methods of Ethics,* 7th ed. (London: Macmillan & Co., Ltd., 1907), pp. 111–2.

[2] Aldo Leopold, *A Sand County Almanac* (New York: Ballantine Books, Inc., 1970), p. 232.

other goods or evils, in determining one's score. Rather, I believe, it is a judgment about oneself that one cannot make if one sees oneself as always looking for the best score for oneself, as never willing to make a genuine sacrifice, however small. The importance of self-respect is not so much that it improves one's score as that it may lead one to prefer a life in which it is present to one from which it would be absent but which would yield a better score. Why can it do this? I believe it is because we are so constituted that we cannot clear-headedly respect ourselves unless we perceive ourselves as respecting others. At any rate, our need for self-respect and its dependence on our being moral are important evidence that we may prefer being moral to having the highest score. . . .

We can safely assert, although we cannot know, that at least some people are so built that they would choose to be moral if they were clear-headed and logical and knew all about themselves and the alternative lives open to them. For them, being moral is rational, even if it involves sacrifice. This is an important result. We can then infer that for certain kinds of persons it is rational to be

moral. But, of course, this leaves open the possibility that for others it is not. Are we left with the conclusion that whether one should be moral or not depends on what kind of a person one is, as some, including myself, have suggested? That is all we can be sure of, and it is important, because no one of us can know with certainty what kind of a person he or she is at any point in time (or only in a Day of Judgment, if there will be one, when it will be too late). However, in view of what has been said, it seems to me reasonable to *postulate* that everyone is so constituted by nature, antecedently to any conditioning he or she may receive, that he or she would choose to live a moral life if the stated conditions were fulfilled. This cannot be proved, and so must remain a postulate, but it also cannot be disproved, and one who would be moral must affirm it. Why then should one be moral? Why is it rational to be moral? Because one would choose to be moral if one clearly knew what one was about. This is an article of moral faith. Being moral is rational if this faith is rational, i.e., if one would espouse it if one knew what everything is about—a possibility that at least cannot be ruled out.

At least two problems threaten this strategy of justifying morality by sheer choice and faith. The first is that the most obvious reasons for choosing a moral way of life would seem to be *moral*. This risks begging the question by providing a moral justification of morality; but in light of theories such as the pragmatic justification mentioned above, it may be best to acknowledge that the only justification of morality is fulfilling the social purpose that the institution serves. The second issue is whether these matters can be decided by reason or rationality. Must the final appeal be to rationality or to faith? Some hold that it is rational to be moral because the rational person would choose to be moral on the basis of comprehensive knowledge and deliberation (see Kant's theory in Chapter 5). However, an alternative is that our commitment to a way of life may be based on whether we have a sufficiently strong *desire* to live the moral life, a stronger desire than we have to live some alternative form of life (see Hume's theory in Chapter 7). If so, perhaps desire rather than choice is the key category for understanding ultimate moral commitment.

The distinction between being motivated by a desire and being motivated by (and justified by) reason will be addressed in detail in Chapters 5 and 7. But we need first to examine the difference between cognitivist theories of morality, in which some appeal to reason or knowledge is central, and noncognitivist theories, in which some appeal to desire, attitude, or commitment is central.

## COGNITIVISM

Issues about whether a choice for or against morality is based on knowledge or rather on desire invite consideration of the following two broad questions about morality:

1. Is there moral knowledge? (And do moral statements make knowledge claims?)
2. Is there moral truth? (And do moral judgments make truth claims?)

These questions should be situated in the context of the justification of claims to knowledge, which is properly the domain of epistemology. These questions are ones of *moral epistemology.*

Ordinary moral discourse suggests that we possess moral knowledge (see the selection by Mackie below), as when we say, "He's a cruel man who deserves to be punished." Some philosophers have tried to reinforce this view by basing ethics on ethical properties, which they think can be known either by intuition, by reason, or by an examination of the facts. Others have doubted these philosophical claims, and two opposed schools of thought, known as cognitivism and noncognitivism, have been locked in a sustained debate over how to answer questions 1 and 2 above.

Controversy between these approaches often turns on an understanding of different functions served by the language of morals. Each theory might be said to develop an account of the meaning of moral language and to rely on an underlying general theory of the meaning of words. Noncognitivists (1) deny that moral language reports something to be the case, (2) deny that moral assertions are either true or false, and (3) deny that there is moral knowledge. Cognitivists, by contrast, believe that moral language reports something to be the case, that moral propositions are either true or false, and that we have moral knowledge. Note that a cognitivist need not claim that moral propositions are true, only that these propositions make truth claims and that they are *either* true *or* false.

Cognitivism was probably the dominant metaethical theory until the middle of the twentieth century. Its two primary forms are naturalism and intuitionism, although we will see in Chapters 4 through 7 that there are a large number of ways to defend cognitivism.

## Naturalism and the Naturalistic Fallacy

The naturalists believe that value judgments can be justified through a method that parallels procedures in disciplines such as history, psychology, and the sciences. Here values are viewed as a species of fact. In value judgments, as in scientific judgments, a property is attributed to some subject. In "Mantle was courageous," for example, the value predicate "courageous" is applied to, or conjoined with, the subject "Mantle." The naturalist holds that all value predicates can be defined in terms of, or translated into, factual predicates. For example, a naturalist might hold that "the President acted properly" can be translated as "the President acted in accordance with the ideals of behavior adopted by his culture"—a factual and, in principle, confirmable statement.

Different naturalistic theories provide different definitions or translations of value predicates, but they are united in believing that value words can, without loss, be understood in terms of factual predicates. The principle is that if we can understand what value words mean or refer to, we can determine how to justify them. For example, if the word "good" *means* "that which is desired by the majority in a culture," we can show that something *is* good by showing what is in fact desired by the majority.

Naturalism has the attractive feature of modeling moral justification on factual justification, which presumably we already understand. However, naturalistic theories have tended to stumble over two problems. The first problem has been dubbed by G. E. Moore, the "naturalistic fallacy." In all naturalistic theories, it is possible to derive an "ought" statement, or a value statement, about what is good from an "is" or factual statement, because "ought" (and any other value term such as "good") can be defined in terms of what "is." For example, if "One ought to do $X$" means "One is required by the legal and moral code of one's society to do $X$," then "One ought to stop one's car at red lights" can be deduced from "One is required by the legal and moral code of one's society to stop one's car at red lights."

If "good" simply meant a factual property such as "required by the prevailing moral code," Moore argues, we could never meaningfully raise the question, "Is the prevailing code good?" This query would be like asking, "Is that which is the prevailing code the prevailing code?" (because "good" and "prevailing code" have the same meaning). Moore's contention is that in naturalism, for anything whatever with a value property, we can always ask meaningfully, "But is it good?" or "But is it right?" If this open question holds for all natural properties, Moore argues, then naturalism must be based on the false assumption that "good" is synonymous with some term that refers to a natural property.

Moore's thesis that "good" in ordinary language cannot be equated with any naturalistic term (or terms) seems flawless, but naturalists would probably not disagree. Naturalists regard ethical terms such as "good," "right," and "duty" as vague in ordinary language. They hold that these words need a clarifying definition. One naturalist, R. B. Perry, explicitly maintains that his purpose is to refine value terms on the basis of a theoretical analysis of their meanings. Perry dismisses Moore's argument in these words: "Theory of value is in search of a *preferred meaning*. The problem is to define, that is, *give a meaning* to the term, either by selecting from existing meanings, or by *creating a new meaning*."[4]

Moore's argument may nonetheless be right in spirit. Many philosophers have thought that Moore should have aimed his argument directly at the problem of how value judgments can be derived from factual judgments: How can an ethical argument move from purely factual premises, so-called *is statements,* to purely evaluative conclusions, so-called *ought statements?* According to this line of thought, when presenting a moral argument, one must include "ought" statements somewhere in one's premises, independent of factual statements, if one is to include an "ought" in one's conclusion.

The following argument schema can be used to illustrate this fact-value problem:

*M* cannot survive without *S*'s bone marrow.

Therefore, *S* ought to donate his bone marrow.

Here, an "ought" statement is allegedly derived from an "is" statement, but is the derivation fallacious? As far as logic is concerned, the conclusion does not follow. The sheer fact that *M* cannot survive is not logically powerful enough to entail anything about what *S* ought to do. A further value premise is needed to make the argument valid:

*M* cannot survive without *S*'s bone marrow.

Everyone ought to help others survive through bone marrow transplant donations.

Therefore, *S* ought to donate his bone marrow.

The new value premise bridges the logical gap between a factual premise and a value conclusion. But prior to adding a value premise, it was possible to assert the first premise while denying the conclusion, and no use of logic alone could convince us otherwise.

This argument seems to refute any naturalism holding that value judgments cannot be a species of factual judgments. But is this argument correct? Perhaps, as Perry's strategy suggests, we need to revise the meaning of value terms in ethical theory, showing their direct connection to factual terms. If "right action," for example, were defined by a naturalist as "any action supported by a moral rule accepted in the culture," then we would have a *naturalistic* definition that properly linked facts and values. Of course, naturalistic theories still must show that there are plausible factual properties to make the link. We will return to this problem after a look at intuitionistic theories.

---

[4]Ralph Barton Perry, *Realms of Value* (Cambridge, MA: Harvard University Press, 1954), pp. 2ff.; italics added.

## Intuitionism

A second form of cognitivism is "intuitionism," which views value properties as *unlike* the factual properties to which naturalists appeal. Intuitionists believe that terms such as "good," "right," and "courage" do not refer to something that can be known through sense experience or through empirical methods of research. For example, if I say, "Pumpkin pie is orange," I have cited the natural property orange, but statements such as "Pumpkin pie is good" possess no parallel natural property in intuitionist theory.

Critics of intuitionism ask, "How can it be *known* whether a value judgment is either true or false?" Intuitionists answer, "By intuition." We directly apprehend the presence of a value property without the aid of any form of direct sensory experience or empirical testing. At times during the history of modern philosophy, this view has been extremely popular. Major eighteenth-century philosophers, including Francis Hutcheson, maintained that we possess a mental faculty of moral intuition ("the moral sense"), and that through this faculty we come to have moral knowledge. Leading nineteenth- and twentieth-century philosophers, among them G. E. Moore and W. D. Ross (see Chapter 5), also believed in moral knowledge of moral facts founded in self-evident truths. They accepted what has been called a "foundationalist" conception of justification and truth, and Moore added a metaphysical account of value properties that was independent of natural facts and properties.

Moore argued that a proposition of the form "*X* is good" refers to a unique property (goodness), and whenever we speak of something as "good," we are ascribing this property to it. We cannot define "good" through other terms; "good" refers to goodness, which is an ultimate, unobservable, and unanalyzable property. Value judgments can be true or false in this theory, because subjects referred to as good, virtuous, and so forth, either do or do not have the value property attributed to them.

In this tradition, analogies have often been made to maturity of thought and to mathematical thinking, in which basic truths are intuitively known and obvious to those with sufficient mathematical background. Ross, who will be studied closely in Chapter 5, held that the basic principles of ethics are known only after a person has achieved an appropriate stage of moral development or maturity. Just as a scientist can "see" or "interpret" many things that baffle a nonscientist, so a person of moral experience can "see" the rightness, wrongness, or virtuousness of basic moral principles. Like problems in mathematics, self-evident propositions require reflection and insight. Even the greatest mathematicians have to be instructed in basic mathematics by others, and there is no reason, according to Ross, why we should trust less in reason when it comes to morality than we trust a mathematical axiom when it comes to mathematics. In both domains, we accept propositions that cannot be proved and that need no proof.

Persons not attracted to intuitionism have been puzzled why anyone would believe in a theory in which it seems that anything at all can be justified, including prejudices and rationalizations. This theory seems so opposed to the forms of moral reasoning and justification that were discussed earlier in this chapter that many have regarded it as an abandonment of critical thinking—a way of treating mere opinion as if it were justified and true. The intuitionist appeal makes the theory seem

burdened with a view of morality and language according to which moral judgments ascribe properties that are queer or mysterious; and the faculty of intuition involved seems no less shrouded in mystery. Moreover, the language of morals has
numerous functions, such as prescribing, that do not appear to ascribe any properties to things.

Because of these problems, intuitionism and other cognitive theories have been
under sustained attack from noncognitivists, who find the epistemological and
metaphysical commitments of cognitivism recondite and unconvincing.

## NONCOGNITIVISM

The noncognitivist typically begins with the function of moral (and of all value)
discourse. Sometimes, value language is used to express feelings, as when we say
"Ah, how sweet it is!" after a victory or "More, more!" after hearing a stirring violin
performance. Sometimes, we use moral language for exhorting, pleading, or expressing our feelings; on other occasions, we are attempting to persuade; on still
other occasions, we issue commands. In carrying out these objectives, say noncognitivists, we are not uttering true or false statements, not reporting something
to be the case, and not referring to value properties. These themes of *not* knowing and *not* making truth claims give this theory its somewhat awkward title,
"noncognitivism."[5]

The general label "noncognitivism" covers a wide variety of theories, some with
little in common. The leading forms of noncognitivism will therefore be treated
separately.

### The Emotive Theory and the Attitude Theory

Perhaps the starkest form of the noncognitivist theory is *emotivism*. Bertrand
Russell elegantly affirmed the essence of this theory in his essay "Science and
Ethics" by proposing that ethics consists of a set of desires rather than a set of true
or false statements. Expressions of desire, he maintained, are akin to matters of taste
verbalized in sentences such as "Oysters are bad." Ethics and politics are attempts
to enlist allies by showing them that their desires harmonize.

This theory was brought to prominence by Alfred Ayer, who maintained that
moral utterances are like ejaculations of, or displays of, emotion. "Abortion, no!"

---

[5]The noncognitivist believes that although the normative judgments made in *morality* are noncognitive, *moral philosophy* is a cognitive enterprise. This leads the noncognitivist to what was once an immensely influential thesis in philosophy: Normative ethics, being noncognitive, is not the proper province of philosophy; philos-ophy, being cognitive, must confine its attention to conceptual and logical questions about ethics. This thesis presumes a sharp distinction between normative ethics and metaethics, and philosophers at one time routinely invoked this distinction as justification for an exclusive preoccupation with metaethics. However, the claimed distinction between these two approaches has come under attack in recent years. Many philosophers now en-gage in both metaethics and normative ethics in the same piece of work. See the history, distinctions, and ar-ticles in Stephen Darwall, Allan Gibbard, and Peter Railton, eds., *Moral Discourse and Practice: Some Philosophical Approaches* (New York: Oxford University Press, 1997).

and "Women's rights, yeah!" function in this theory as models of moral disapproval and approval, and hence as models of claims of moral wrongness and moral rightness. The sentence "The donor of the liver for Mickey Mantle did what he ought to have done" expresses our feelings of approval or disapproval toward the man who donated his organs, but such feelings are neither true nor false. They also cannot rationally be defended, are neither objective nor cognitive, and contain no appeal to reason.

To say, however, that there is no role for *reason* is not to affirm that there is no role for rational *argument*. Emotivists recognize that we are forever trying to resolve disputes by persuading other persons to accept our point of view. In moral arguments, say emotivists, we are operating on the assumption that the persons with whom we are disputing a point already share some of our fundamental evaluative commitments. Hence, we hope to point out certain facts, anecdotes, motives, or beliefs that we think the person may not know or may have overlooked in order to change the person's emotive reaction.

A related but less extreme theory than emotivism may be called the attitude theory. It was developed by C. L. Stevenson, who held that moral judgments express speakers' attitudes and are generally uttered with the intention of evoking similar attitudes in others. His technique was to show dual, interconnected uses for value terms, which he called the *emotive* and the *descriptive* meanings of value terms.

Emotive meaning is the power or tendency a word has acquired, through historical association, to express attitudes or to evoke effective responses. Examples are "death sentence," "genocide," "socialized medicine," and "democracy," all of which can evoke powerful negative or positive responses. Descriptive meaning is the tendency of a word to affect cognition (after a process of conditioning in the proper use of the word), that is, to describe or characterize something. "Cousin" and "cranial hemorrhage" are nonvalue terms with a descriptive function, although they can also have an attached emotive meaning, depending on how they are used.

Stevenson argues that value terms need never be completely emotive, in the way the words "alas" and "hurrah" are. Consider, for example, the value predicate "good." He contends that sometimes "This is good" has the descriptive meaning of "This has qualities or relations *X, Y,* and *Z*." For example, a "good" college president may be one who (*X*) is an industrious executive and fund-raiser, (*Y*) is honest and tactful with university personnel, and (*Z*) commands wide respect for his or her intellectual abilities and charitable activities. This usage might be thought to be purely descriptive, but Stevenson rejects this interpretation. His claim is that the descriptive part of the pattern (that is, the possession of properties *X, Y,* and *Z*) is always accompanied, either explicitly or implicitly, by a "laudatory emotive meaning which permits it to express the speaker's approval, and tends to evoke the approval of the hearer."[6]

In general, Stevenson argues that there is a continuum in our usage of value terms, from pure emotive expressiveness to nearly pure descriptive reference. Despite his belief that value judgments are neither true nor false, Stevenson provides some role for reasoned argument in ethics. Because attitudes depend on

---

[6]C. L. Stevenson, *Ethics and Language* (New Haven, CT: Yale University Press, 1944), pp. 9, 33, 207ff.

beliefs, the whole point of moral argument may be to change attitudes by citing beliefs that tend to have a psychological impact on attitudes. For example, if I disfavor legislation requiring all persons to wear seat belts in automobiles, I could be influenced to change my mind by others who tell me that thousands of lives and millions of dollars in public funds have been saved by such legislation. Moral language appears objective and factually justified, according to Stevenson, because facts often do causally affect attitudes. Stevenson concludes that our *fundamental* moral beliefs rest on attitudes that themselves do not have the support of facts, in which case there is no way that we can either be persuaded rationally to abandon our moral beliefs or provide an ultimate justification of them.

## Prescriptivism

During the second half of the twentieth century, emotivism and the attitude theory received sustained criticism. One theory proposed as a replacement was prescriptivism, which is generally considered a form of noncognitivism. It is associated largely with one name, that of R. M. Hare. Value judgments are seen by Hare as having a prescriptive or action-guiding function absent in purely factual judgments. Evaluative language in general is viewed as functioning to commend or condemn particular courses of action or belief, not to make truth claims. The foundations of normative ethics, as well as all value judgments, are *prescriptive*. Factual discourse, by contrast, is not action-guiding, but deals instead with descriptions and causal explanations of human or natural phenomena. There is an unbridgeable logical gap between the statements in these two domains, according to prescriptivism.

In Hare's view, moral language functions differently from language expressing an emotion or an attitude; a person who commends or condemns something uses specifiable *criteria* for value words, and can support value judgments by appeal to reasons for making the judgments. Consider, for example, Hare's analysis of the statement "That's a good strawberry." This assertion is not identical in meaning to "That's a strawberry, and it is sweet, juicy, firm, red, and large." These are factual properties that the strawberry possesses, and they often are the criteria we invoke in defending our judgment that a strawberry is good. Nonetheless, terms describing these factual properties do not mean what "good" means, and "good" cannot be reduced to a list of such properties. If a lengthy list were prepared of all the factual properties of strawberries—redness, sweetness, firmness, juiciness, and so forth—then the strawberry would merely be described but not evaluated. A term having commending power, such as "good," must be employed to serve the value function.

Hare maintains that the word "good" has a common meaning in all its uses, functioning as "the most general adjective of commendation." But while the *meaning* of "good" is always the same, the *criteria* of goodness shift from context to context and from type to type: The criteria for something's being a good cactus are different from those of a good sunset or a good surgical procedure. Learning the criteria of goodness applicable to a new class of items may always be a new lesson, but we are able to use "good" for entirely new classes of objects, and a different lesson in meaning is never involved once we understand the word's commending function.

The criteria for the application of "good" clearly vary in relation to the class of objects being evaluated, but they also differ from person to person, as when we disagree over the properties of (criteria for) good strawberries and good automobiles. Items we evaluate factually either do or do not have the properties we rely on their having when we say they are good; but our *choice* of properties (the criteria) is not a factual matter. "The judge gave a good legal argument in the case" is a value judgment that can be justified by pointing to the features of legal justification that make arguments good under some assumed set of criteria—for example, precedents in the law are followed, the judge does not let personal views interfere with the responsibilities of being a judge, and the opinion is tightly formulated using strict definitions. However, the initial selection of criteria of good legal decisions depends on a value judgment.

How does a prescriptivist suggest that we *justify* our acceptance of moral principles? In a discussion of "decisions of principle," Hare considers how we learn action-guides. He points out that the "learning of principles" is learning to do acts of a certain kind in a certain kind of situation. In any but the most elementary kind of instruction, an opportunity must be provided for the learner to make decisions for himself or herself and, in so doing, to examine and sometimes to modify the principles being taught. The factor of personal decision, Hare argues, is no less crucial to the morally good person than to the driver of an automobile. That is, one's principles may require judgment when putting them into practice and may also require modification by the user.

As we mature and encounter unanticipated circumstances, we begin to question our old principles and sometimes are forced to make decisions of principle. Ordinarily, says Hare, we justify our decisions by appeal to an action's probable effects and to the principles governing the action. But if we are asked for a full and complete justification, we will deliberate about both effects and principles, as well as about the effects that accompany the *use* of certain principles. A complete justification of a decision would consist in a complete account of the decision's effects, the principles employed, and the effects of using those principles in relevantly similar circumstances.

Suppose that after such a complete attempt at justification, a person is still not satisfied and asks, "Why should I live like that?" This question is similar to the "why-be-moral" question discussed earlier in this chapter. Here, claims Hare, there is no further answer to give, because we have already said everything we could by way of justification. We can only ask the person to make up his or her mind about which way one ought to live. In the end, everything pertaining to the choice of retaining one's old principles or finding new ones rests upon a decision of principle; individuals must decide for themselves whether to accept a course of conduct such as the moral life.

Hare's account of justification has been criticized as too lenient and as inconsistent with the limits morality places on justified actions. One critic, Philippa Foot, asks the following rhetorical question: "Is it open to us to *choose* what the criteria for determining moral goodness shall be?" Put another way, are we free to choose what counts as evidence for moral goodness, or is what counts as evidence restricted by the institution of morality itself? As Foot sees it, Hare's philosophy leads to the implausible position that anything at all can be counted as a "good reason" for a value judgment (moral or nonmoral) if we *choose* to make it a good reason:

> [According to prescriptivism] one man may say that a thing is good because of some fact about it, and another may refuse to take that fact as any evidence at all. . . . It follows that a moral eccentric could argue that a man was a good man because he clasped and unclasped his hands, and never turned NNE after turning SSW. He could also reject someone else's evaluation simply by denying that his evidence was evidence at all.[7]

Foot proposes instead that "criteria for the goodness of each and every kind of thing . . . are always determined, and not a matter for decision." In support of her contention, she points out that we cannot in general choose criteria for the goodness of something; for example, we cannot choose criteria for a good knife, a good farmer, or a good reader. In these evaluations, and no less in moral evaluations, the point of the activity and the function of the objects involved impose a limit upon what the criteria of goodness can be. If someone does not adhere to these standards in commending relevant items, Foot believes, we cannot understand that person as speaking from a *moral* point of view.

G. J. Warnock argues for this same thesis with a direct reference to the meaning of the term "morality" (here assuming the analysis of the goal of morality that he provided in Chapter 1 of this text):

> Not just anything can function as a criterion of *moral* evaluation. . . . That there *are* such limits seems to me perfectly evident. . . . The limits are set somewhere within the general area of concern with the welfare of human beings. . . . The *relevance* of considerations as to the welfare of human beings *cannot*, in the context of moral debate, be denied. (Again, of course, we do not *choose* that this should be so; it *is* so, simply because of what "moral" means.)[8]

Hare's prescriptivism has been discussed for five decades, and many criticisms have been leveled against it. It has been maintained, for example, that we not only prescribe with ethical language, but also advise, admire, exhort, reward, report, implore, deplore, and confess. These sometimes tedious criticisms are important for ethical theory, but they may here be set aside in order to consider some other features of noncognitivism. Many philosophers have argued against noncognitivism, but some of the fiercest critics are actually sympathetic with the noncognitivist thesis that there are no moral truths. This brings us to the subject of moral realism.

## MORAL REALISM AND ANTIREALISM

In contemporary philosophy the cognitivism-noncognitivism debate is sometimes presented as a debate about realism versus antirealism. A moral realist is a cognitivist who holds that some moral statements report a state of affairs and are true. An antirealist is either a noncognitivist, or one who believes that all moral claims that report a state of affairs are false. This debate is entangled with related controversies

---

[7]Philippa Foot, "Moral Beliefs," *Proceedings of the Aristotelian Society,* 59 (1958–1959): 83ff.
[8]G. J. Warnock, *Contemporary Moral Philosophy* (New York: St. Martin's Press, 1967), pp. 67ff.

about realism in other areas of philosophy (in particular, epistemology, metaphysics, philosophy of science, and philosophy of mind). We will get a thorough sense of the philosophical debate in the essays below by David McNaughton and John Mackie.

## Moral Realism

Moral realists believe that there are moral facts to which we can appeal in defense of moral judgments. They see the proper goal of moral theory as the discovery and description of these facts. These philosophers accept a *truth* theory that appeals to some procedure for identifying moral truths.

However, moral realists do not always agree about which arguments succeed or how to determine truth. The nature and acceptability of the truth conditions for moral statements is the premiere issue, but the term "moral realism" should be understood as a general label that is neutral as to which truth conditions count. The truth conditions can be (1) psychological (subjective), if they are found in human subjective responses; (2) sociological (intersubjective), if they are found in conventions or in practices of human groups; or (3) ontological (nonsubjective, or objective), if they are found in objective conditions that are independent of human contributions. A theory based on any of these three foundations will count as moral realism if it renders at least some moral statements literally true, in accordance with a truth theory and not an error theory such as Mackie's (which allows "truth" only relative to prior choice, as we saw in Chapter 2 and will experience in the next section as well).

Diverse philosophers provide accounts that fit one of these three descriptions of moral realism. For example, R. B. Perry (see pp. 70–71) appeals to truth-conditions of type (1): He defines "value" in terms of human interests, arguing that moral truth is traceable to interests. In particular, he defines goodness in terms of a person's positive interest in things, and badness in terms of negative interests. He then defines *moral* goodness as "harmonious happiness."[9] In his early and best known work, John Rawls (see pp.91–94) defends truth-conditions of type (2): He argues that moral truth rests on what rational agents ideally would agree to when forging a social contract.[10] G. E. Moore (see pp. 70–72) defends truth-conditions of type (3): He argues that certain valuable items (for example, beautiful objects) have their value independent of human beliefs and that moral truth rests on objective, nonnatural properties. The term "good" names the simple property "goodness," which is shared by all things that are good. Value judgments can be true or false in his theory, because subjects referred to as good, virtuous, and the like, either do or do not have the property attributed to them.[11]

---

[9]R. B. Perry, *Realms of Value: A Critique of Human Civilization* (Cambridge, MA: Harvard University Press, 1954), esp. pp. 2–3, 90–91, 101–9, 119, 134. For a more comprehensive and updated account of naturalism and truth conditions in moral realism, see David O. Brink, *Moral Realism and the Foundations of Ethics* (New York: Cambridge University Press, 1989). Brink discusses the differences between naturalism and non-naturalism on pp. 156–66.

[10]John Rawls, *A Theory of Justice* (Cambridge, MA: Harvard University Press, 1971), pp. 17–21.

[11]G. E. Moore, *Principia Ethica* (Cambridge, England: Cambridge University Press, 1903), pp. 6–8, 84.

The antirealist's primary concern has historically been to refute (3). Antirealists ridicule fanciful ideas such as those about "nonnatural properties." However, W. D. Ross, a defender of (3), rightly pointed out that "it is surely a strange reversal of the natural order of thought to say that our admiring an action either is, or is what necessitates, its being good. We think of its goodness as what we admire in it, and as something it would have even if no one admired it, something that it has in itself."[12] An honest person does seem to *be* honest, whether or not someone recognizes the person's property of honesty; and the property of honesty does not seem to disappear if the person lives in a culture that does not recognize or value honesty.

Although the dominant view in philosophy in the last fifty years has probably been that (3) is not defensible, some of the most celebrated philosophers in this century have defended it. They use the language of morals to report what they believe to be moral facts independent of the beliefs of any user of the language; and they believe this to be the only way to understand what we are asserting when we use the language of morals. They believe that we do not mean to refer to subjective states, relative standards, and the like, but rather to what is right and wrong, good and bad.

These philosophers find a view such as Mackie's unacceptable because he makes truth strictly relative to standards created and then perpetuated in traditions. They point to a familiar problem: We criticize morally bad actions and judgments by using standards *external to* those in any tradition, and thus our evaluations transcend beliefs internal to those systems. Realists object to the idea that the sociohistorical origin of beliefs about what is true or justified can itself determine what *is* true or justified. How *X* came to be regarded expresses a context of origin, whereas appropriate reasons for accepting *X* express the context of truth and justification. Of what possible interest, then, could historical traditions or subjective criteria be to justification in ethics?

In the following essay, David McNaughton supplies a statement of the arguments needed to defend moral realism.

# Morality—Invention or Discovery?*

## David McNaughton

There are two contrasting feelings about our moral life that all of us share to some extent. On the one side, we often feel that morality is an area of personal decision; a realm in which each of us has the right to make up his or her own mind about what to do. While other people may offer advice on what we should do and what moral principles we should adopt they have no authority to tell us how to live our lives. . . .

This view of moral choice sits unhappily with the second feeling that we all share, namely that it is often difficult,

*From David McNaughton, *Moral Vision: An Introduction to Ethics* (Oxford, England: Basil Blackwell, 1988).

[12]W. D. Ross, *The Right and the Good* (Indianapolis: Hackett Publishing Co., 1990), p. 89.

when faced with some pressing and perplexing moral problem, to discover which answer is the right one. If I am puzzled as to what I ought to do then I am likely to feel that what matters is not that the answer I arrive at should be mine, one for which I am prepared to assume ultimate responsibility, but that it be the correct answer. I do not think of my choice as determining the right answer; on the contrary, I wish my choice to be determined by the right answer. . . .

The feeling that we have to discover which moral values are correct, rather than invent them, leads naturally to the view that there are moral truths. Moral truth is thought of as independent of whatever moral decisions we may happen to reach. What we aspire to in our moral thinking, on that view, is to get to that moral truth. On the other side, the feeling that values are a product of our choices leads equally naturally to the contrary view that there is no moral truth; there is nothing independent of our choices that could possibly determine which consistent system of moral values is the correct one.

In developing the view that the answers to moral questions are independent of us and need to be discovered, it was natural to draw on the interrelated concepts of truth, belief and reality. The notion of truth is intimately connected with that of belief. Beliefs aim at truth; they are true if they hit their mark, false if they miss it. If we discover that two of our beliefs are inconsistent then we must abandon at least one of them because two inconsistent beliefs cannot both be true. That our beliefs are consistent is a necessary condition for their being true, but is not, as we have just seen, sufficient for truth. Consistency within our system of beliefs is thus no guarantee that they are true. Whether or not our

beliefs are true depends on something independent of them, namely reality: the way things are, the way the world is. It follows that our moral beliefs will be true if things are, morally, as we suppose they are.

This view, which springs from the second feeling about ethics, might best be called *moral realism,* for it insists that there is a moral reality which is independent of our moral beliefs and which determines whether or not they are true or false. It holds that moral properties are genuine properties of things or actions; they are, as it is sometimes picturesquely put, part of the furniture of the world. We may or may not be sensitive to a particular moral property, but whether or not that property is present does not depend on what *we* think about the matter. . . .

The moral realist thinks of moral views as being purely cognitive; they are simply beliefs about the way the world is, morally speaking. His irrealist opponent claims that what is distinctive about moral views is that they contain a non-cognitive element, an element from the feeling or emotional side of our natures. We may, therefore, call such a position *moral non-cognitivism.* . . .

The non-cognitivist sees evaluative thought in general, and moral experience in particular, as possessing two quite distinct aspects. We can illustrate this by referring to [the] example of . . . children throwing stones at [a] dog. First, we have some beliefs about what we take the facts to be; we might acquire these by actually seeing the children behaving this way or by being told about it. If our beliefs about the facts are inaccurate or incomplete then this may invalidate the moral judgement we form on the basis of those beliefs. Our beliefs need to be sensitive to the facts, to the way the world is. Second, we are so constituted, whether by nature or upbringing, that we react to this behaviour with revulsion. This reaction is the work of our feelings and it reveals something about *us,* but nothing about the world. Since people differ in their emotional make-up, it is possible for two people to agree about all the facts and yet differ in the values they assign to those facts. We might express this by, saying that people can agree in belief but disagree in moral attitude. . . .

The moral realist denies the existence of that sharp and significant division between fact and value which is the hallmark of his opponent's position. In the realist's view, moral opinions are beliefs which, like other beliefs, are determined true or false by the way things are in the world. It follows that moral questions are as much questions of fact as any other. In rejecting the divide between facts and values the realist rejects the other distinctions which stem from that basic contrast, such as that between beliefs and attitudes, or between descriptive and evaluative meaning. Where the non-cognitivist sees division, the realist finds unity.

The realist maintains that the structure of our ordinary moral thought supports his case. Moral utterances appear to be perfectly ordinary statements which are capable of being true or false in just the way that other statements are. We believe that some moral views are correct and others incorrect and that in morality, as in other areas of life, we can be mistaken about which is which. Moreover, our experience of the world seems to include experience of value; we can see the beauty of a summer landscape or the goodness in someone's face. The main realist charge against non-cognitivism is that it gives a seriously distorted account of the nature of morality; if non-cognitivism were correct then many of our present moral practices and our beliefs about the structure of moral thought would have to be revised or abandoned. . . .

The realist is committed, as I expressed it at the beginning of the chapter, to the claim that "moral opinions are beliefs which, like other beliefs, are determined true or false by the way things are in the world." This way of putting it, true so far as it goes, serves to distinguish moral realism from non-cognitivism, but it does not adequately capture what is distinctive about the realist position. To understand what more needs to be added we must examine the debate between realists and irrealists, since non-cognitivism is not the only form of moral irrealism.

Debates between realists and irrealists are by no means confined to ethics but occur in virtually all areas of philosophy. The realist affirms that some particular kind of thing or property exists; the irrealist denies it. As so often in philosophy, we can become clearer about just what the realist is affirming by finding out what it would be to deny it; that is, by looking more closely at irrealism in general.

Debates about whether some entity or property exists are common in the history of human thought, and they are sometimes settled on the side of irrealism. There is a large range of things in whose existence we have ceased to believe: fairies, witches, phlogiston, the ether, the four humours of the body. In denying the existence of such entities we have typically rejected all talk of such things as false. We have looked at the world and found that it contains no fairies. If there are no fairies at the bottom of anybody's garden then there can be no facts about them and no true stories in which they figure. Any tendency to talk as if there really were such beings must be rejected as the product of delusion or fancy.

Philosophers are notoriously given to claiming that certain sorts of thing or property do not exist. From within some particular philosophical perspective certain kinds of fact can appear utterly mysterious; it may seem that the world could not contain any such things. Indeed, there is almost nothing whose existence has not been denied by some philosopher—physical objects, conscious states, numbers and, of course, values. As with the refusal to allow fairies into one's scheme of things, it is possible for a philosopher who denies the existence of something to hold that all claims about such things are simply false. Or, even more drastically, he can declare all statements about the offending entities to be unintelligible or meaningless.

Such a stark rejection of some large area of human thought and discourse would, however, raise serious questions about what we have all been doing when we talked or thought in the rejected manner. The realization, as I grow up, that there are no fairies and no Santa Claus only requires a small adjustment to my view of the world, one which I can easily accommodate. But how could it be that all of us were quite mistaken in supposing there to be physical objects, such as tables, chairs and other people; or what sense can we make of the thought that, in using moral language, we have all been in error, or even speaking nonsense? . . .

To deny that there are moral truths runs counter to our normal thought and speech. The non-cognitivist sought to avoid that conclusion by reminding us that describing someone else's remark as true or false is a way of endorsing or rejecting the opinion he expressed. Since we can endorse and reject attitudes as well as beliefs, moral utterances can appropriately be thought of as true or false. To the realist, the non-cognitivist's reinstatement of the conception of moral truth appears merely cosmetic. Such a thin account of moral truth, precisely because it does not carry any metaphysical implications of the sort that the non-cognitivist would disown, is unlikely to lay to rest the kinds of worry that were raised by the original suggestion that there was no room in moral thought for the notion of truth. We are still left, for example, with the possibility . . . that there might be an indefinite number of internally consistent but incompatible moral systems.

The realist can push home this attack by pointing out that the non-cognitivist's attenuated concept of moral truth leaves us without the resources to express, or even think, quite commonplace thoughts. To see this, we need to look at our normal conception of truth which, the realist maintains, is far richer and more substantial than that provided by the thin account. In particular, we think of truth as something independent of the views of any individual. On this richer conception there can be a mismatch between my beliefs and the truth of the matter. All of us, unless we are unusually arrogant, will admit that we are fallible, that some of our opinions may be, indeed no doubt are, in error.

The non-cognitivist account leaves no room, however, for the thought that I am morally fallible, that some of my moral convictions may be mistaken. I cannot express this thought by supposing that some of them might be false, for that would imply a standard of truth and falsity which was independent of my individual opinion. Nor, obviously, can I suppose that my attitudes may not fit the moral facts, for there are no moral facts for them to fit. The only way that I might express the thought that I am fallible about moral questions is to admit that I may come, at some later stage, to have some different attitudes from the ones that I now have. But this is not what we were looking for. The thought that I might now be in error is not equivalent to the thought that I might come to have some different views later. To admit that my views might change over time is not in itself to express any opinion about whether or not my current views may be mistaken.

Nor can we make sense of the notion of moral perplexity. If there is no truth of the matter, what are we puzzled about? Not about choosing the correct attitude but, presumably, about choosing an attitude which we are prepared to act on. Once again, this is not what we were looking for. To worry about which of two courses of action is the right one is not the same as to worry about which of two choices I can live with.

The realist charge is that non-cognitivism seriously distorts our conception of morality and denies that we can make sense of thoughts that appear perfectly intelligible. By adopting the thin account of truth the non-cognitivist may have disguised the degree to which his understanding of moral thought differs from the normal one but, as the arguments of the last two paragraphs show, differences will still emerge. Even if we allow to the non-cognitivist that there is a sense in which moral attitudes can be said to have a truth-value it is not the same sense as that in which factual beliefs can be true or false. And that is the realist complaint. . . .

It is a striking feature of our moral experience . . . that situations in which we find ourselves make moral demands on us; we recognize that we are morally required to act in a certain way. . . . Claims that morality makes on us appear to be quite independent of our desires—they may even conflict with what we want. . . .

Non-cognitivism, in maintaining that value is the product of the agent's desire, reverses the relation between desirability and desire which we find in moral experience. We take it that we desire certain things because we see them to be desirable; non-cognitivism insists that they are only desirable because we desire them. If an agent has no desire to act in a certain way then he will not hold that course of action to be the right one, for to take up a moral attitude is to be disposed to act in the appropriate way. . . .

The non-cognitivist makes great play with the supposed gap between facts and values; no set of factual statements, it is claimed, can entail an evaluative conclusion. The realist can agree that, generally speaking, no set of non-moral statements can entail a moral conclusion, but he rejects the non-cognitivist's explanation of why this is so and denies that the gap has the importance the non-cognitivist ascribes to it.

The non-cognitivist believes that the existence of such a gap is to be explained by reference to the distinction between descriptive and evaluative meaning. The realist has a more mundane explanation which does not require the construction of an elaborately bifurcated theory of meaning. . . .

The realist thinks of the non-moral properties of an action as fixing or determining its moral properties. It is in virtue of various non-moral facts about what happens if someone induces heroin addiction in his children that such a deed would be abhorrent. We all appeal to such non-moral facts as reasons in support of the conclusion that such behaviour would be wrong. . . .

From the fact that all the objects in the world are physical objects it does not follow that all the properties of these objects are physical properties, if by that we mean the sorts of properties that figure in physics. Only if it is held that science gives an exhaustive account of all the properties that exist is there a threat to realism about properties, such as evaluative properties, which do not figure in the scientific story. But there are reasons for resisting a thorough-going physicalism, one that allows no room for non-physical properties, states or processes.

The existence of states of consciousness provides a well-known difficulty for extreme physicalism. To feel a pain, to hear a sound, to smell an odour, are quite distinctive conscious experiences which would surely have to figure in any complete account of what it is to be a human being. Yet they seem to be excluded from the extreme physicalist picture of the world. What is going on physically when I am in pain is, presumably, such things as certain receptors in my skin being excited and electrical signals being sent along nerve fibres to my brain. But if the physical story exhausts all that is really happening in the world then there is no room, in a complete account of reality, for what it is like to be in pain, for the way I experience these events on the inside.

A more modest physicalism would allow the existence of what are often called *emergent* non-physical properties. Thus, for example, when the brain and central nervous system of an organism reach a sufficient complexity there emerge conscious states of awareness, such as feeling pain. A full description of the organism and its properties would have to include the fact that it was in pain. Being in pain is not a physical property, nor is it reducible to a physical property. Talk about consciousness is ineliminable; no purely physical description of the organism, remarks about what brain fibres are firing and so on, would convey the same information as the inside story of what it was like to have those experiences. A purely physical account would always leave something out. . . .

Modest physicalism can encompass moral realism. Moral properties would then be seen as non-physical properties which emerged from complex inter-relationships between flesh and blood physical objects, namely human beings. It certainly seems plausible . . . to suppose that the moral properties of an agent or action are fixed by its non-moral properties. For example, it is in virtue of the non-moral facts about heroin addiction and my relation to my children that it would be wrong for me to introduce them to the drug. There may well be a hierarchy of emergent properties; the non-moral ones, from which the moral ones emerge, may themselves emerge from more basic properties. The modest physicalist will insist that there is some point in the chain of emergence below which we only find physical properties.

Modest physicalism does not sell science short. It admits that we live in a physical world and that science is the method by which we explore its physical nature. But it resists any pretension that science might have to give a complete and exhaustive account of every aspect of the world and of the way we experience it. It leaves room for the existence of properties that are not quantifiable and measurable but which are none the less real. Within such a framework, the moral realist may reasonably argue that moral properties should be allowed their proper place in the world.

McNaughton's arguments center on a comparison between ethics and other fields, such as the natural and social sciences, in which we presumably accept objectivity, truth, and the reality of the subject matter. Few doubt that the sciences examine real objects and events that exist independently of the minds that examine them. Nor do we doubt that these fields produce some form of knowledge. It is reasonable therefore to ask whether ethics compares favorably or unfavorably with the sciences. Philosophers such as Bertrand Russell and A. J. Ayer have taken this question seriously and concluded that ethics suffers by comparison, because it is not objective and cannot be confirmed in the way the sciences are. Other philosophers, notably the intuitionists, maintain that ethics compares favorably to the sciences.

These questions resemble other traditional questions in philosophy about the status of claims to knowledge. Physical theory is an attempt to describe the physical world, and physical realism is the claim that some form of fact allows us to succeed in describing the world. Scientific discourse, in this theory, refers to properties of the world that are real, and the sciences progressively yield knowledge about the world. Similarly, moral realism is the claim that some form of fact or reality allows us to succeed in describing the moral world, and that moral theory progressively yields knowledge about the moral universe. In this conception, moral discourse refers to properties of persons, actions, and institutions that are real and about which we are able to achieve real knowledge.

McNaughton leaves us with the conclusion that moral realism does not in any way challenge the scientific world view. Moral properties are caused by very complex states of the world, but they should not be identified with those states, just as consciousness should not be identified with the brains from which it emerges. Physical science can help explain how and why moral phenomena exist, but it does not explain away such phenomena. Moral realism coheres with both our scientific understanding and with our moral experience; there is no need to choose between scientific objectivity and moral objectivity.

## Antirealism

Moral realism is a cognitivist theory, but cognitivism is *not* confined to the theory that we know truths of morality. The position is broader: A cognitivist believes (1) that moral statements purport to report moral facts, and (2) that these reports are either true or false. This position is compatible with asserting that all moral statements purporting to report an objective state of affairs turn out to be *false*. The latter cognitivist theory is one form of antirealism, and an important one.

We have already had an introduction to this theory in Chapter 2, where we studied John Mackie's "error theory." We saw that Mackie attempts to discredit the common belief that moral statements are objectively true by arguing that they rest on a subjective basis, and that claims to objectivity, truth, realism, and the like, are erroneous. Mackie maintains that his inquiry is about what in fact exists, not a thesis about the meanings of words or the nature of concepts. It is a theory about goodness, not about what the word "good" means.

Mackie believes that both "the main tradition of European moral philosophy" and "ordinary moral judgment" stand opposed to his claim that moral statements are in error. In Mackie's view, we are almost all inclined to believe, prior to the study of moral philosophy, that ethics "is more a matter of knowledge and less a matter of decision." It is this claim to objective knowledge that prompts Mackie to develop his "error theory." In the following essay, which builds on the article in Chapter 2, Mackie clarifies this error theory (as a form of antirealism).

# Subjectivism, Objectivism, and the Error Theory*

## J. L. Mackie

. . . What is often called moral subjectivism is the doctrine that, for example, "This action is right" *means* I approve of this action; or more generally that moral judgements are equivalent to reports of the speaker's own feelings or attitudes. But the view I am now discussing is to be distinguished in two vital respects from any such doctrine as this. First, what I have called moral scepticism is a negative doctrine, not a positive one: it says what there isn't, not what there is. It says that there do not exist entities or relations of a certain kind, objective values or requirements,

which many people have believed to exist. Of course, the moral sceptic cannot leave it at that. If his position is to be at all plausible, he must give some account of how other people have fallen into what he regards as an error, and this account will have to include some positive suggestions about how values fail to be objective, about what has been mistaken for, or has led to false beliefs about, objective values. But this will be a development of his theory, not its core: its core is the negation. Secondly, what I have called moral scepticism is an ontological thesis, not a linguistic or conceptual one. It is not, like the other doctrine often called moral subjectivism, a view about the meanings of moral statements. Again, no doubt, if it is to be at all plausible, it will have to give some account of their meanings. . . .

From *Ethics: Inventing Right and Wrong* by J. L. Mackie (Penguin Books, 1977), pages 17–18, 25, 27, 38, 29, 48, 49. Copyright © J. L. Mackie, 1977. Reproduced by permission of Penguin Books.

. . . The denial that there are objective values does not commit one to any particular view about what moral statements mean, and certainly not to the view that they are equivalent to subjective reports. No doubt if moral values are not objective they are in some very broad sense subjective, and for this reason I would accept "moral subjectivism" as an alternative name to "moral scepticism." But subjectivism in this broad sense must be distinguished from the specific doctrine about meaning referred to above. Neither name is altogether satisfactory: we simply have to guard against the (different) misinterpretations which each may suggest. . . .

## Standards of Evaluation

One way of stating the thesis that there are no objective values is to say that value statements cannot be either true or false. But this formulation, too, lends itself to misinterpretation. For there are certain kinds of value statements which undoubtedly can be true or false, even if, in the sense I intend, there are no objective values. Evaluations of many sorts are commonly made in relation to agreed and assumed standards. The classing of wool, the grading of apples, the awarding of prizes at sheepdog trials, flower shows, skating and diving championships, and even the marking of examination papers are carried out in relation to standards of quality or merit which are peculiar to each particular subject-matter or type of contest, which may be explicitly laid down but which, even if they are nowhere explicitly stated, are fairly well understood and agreed by those who are recognized as

judges or experts in each particular field. Given any sufficiently determinate standards, it will be an objective issue, a matter of truth and falsehood, how well any particular specimen measures up to those standards. Comparative judgements in particular will be capable of truth and falsehood: it will be a factual question whether this sheepdog has performed better than that one.

The subjectivist about values, then, is not denying that there can be objective evaluations relative to standards, and these are as possible in the aesthetic and moral fields as in any of those just mentioned. More than this, there is an objective distinction which applies in many such fields, and yet would itself be regarded as a peculiarly moral one: the distinction between justice and injustice. In one important sense of the word it is a paradigm case of injustice if a court declares someone to be guilty of an offence of which it knows him to be innocent. More generally, a finding is unjust if it is at variance with what the relevant law and the facts together require, and particularly if it is known by the court to be so. More generally still, any award of marks, prizes, or the like is unjust if it is at variance with the agreed standards for the contest in question: if one diver's performance in fact measures up better to the accepted standards for diving than another's, it will be unjust if the latter is awarded higher marks or the prize. In this way the justice or injustice of decisions relative to standards can be a thoroughly objective matter, though there may still be a subjective element in the interpretation or application of standards. But the statement that a certain decision is thus just or unjust will not be objectively prescriptive: in so far as it can be simply true it leaves open the question whether there is any objective requirement to do what is just and to refrain from what is unjust, and equally leaves open the practical decision to act in either way.

Recognizing the objectivity of justice in relation to standards, and of evaluative judgements relative to standards, then, merely shifts the question of the objectivity of values back to the standards themselves. The subjectivist may try to make his point by insisting that there is no objective validity about the choice of standards. Yet he would clearly be wrong if he said that the choice of even the most basic standards in any field was completely arbitrary. The standards used in sheepdog trials clearly bear some relation to the work that sheepdogs are kept to do, the standards for grading apples bear some relation to what people generally want in or like about apples, and so on. On the other hand, standards are not as a rule strictly validated by such purposes. The appropriateness of standards is neither fully determinate nor totally indeterminate in relation to independently specifiable aims or desires. But however determinate it is, the objective appropriateness of standards in relation to aims or desires is no more of a threat to the denial of objective values than is the objectivity of evaluation relative to standards. In fact it is logically no different from the objectivity of goodness relative to desires. Something may be called good simply in so far as it satisfies or is such as to satisfy a certain desire; but the objectivity of such relations of satisfaction does not constitute in our sense an objective value. . . .

# The Argument from Queerness

Even more important . . . and certainly more generally applicable, is the argument from queerness. This has two parts, one metaphysical, the other epistemological. If there were objective values, then they would be entities or qualities or relations of a very strange sort, utterly different from anything else in the universe. Correspondingly, if we were aware of them, it would have to be by some special faculty of moral perception or intuition, utterly different from our ordinary ways of knowing everything else. These points were recognized by Moore when he spoke of nonnatural qualities, and by the intuitionists in their talk about a "faculty of moral intuition." Intuitionism has long been out of favour, and it is indeed easy to point out its implausibilities. What is not so often stressed, but is more important, is that the central thesis of intuitionism is one to which any objectivist view of values is in the end committed: intuitionism merely makes unpalatably plain what other forms of objectivism wrap up. Of course the suggestion that moral judgements are made or moral problems solved by just sitting down and having an ethical intuition is a travesty of actual moral thinking. But, however complex the real process, it will require (if it is to yield authoritatively prescriptive conclusions) some input of this distinctive sort, either premisses or forms of argument or both. When we ask the awkward question, how we can be aware of this authoritative prescriptivity, of the truth of these distinctively ethical premises or of the cogency of this distinctively ethical pattern of reasoning, none of our ordinary accounts of sensory perception or introspection or the framing and confirming of explanatory hypotheses or inference or logical construction or conceptual analysis, or any combination of these, will provide a satisfactory answer; "a special sort of intuition" is a lame answer, but it is the one to which the clearheaded objectivist is compelled to resort. . . .

## Conclusion

I have maintained that there is a real issue about the status of values, including moral values. Moral scepticism, the denial of objective moral values, is not to be confused with any one of several first order normative views, or with any linguistic or conceptual analysis. Indeed, ordinary moral judgements involve a claim to objectivity which both non-cognitive and naturalist analyses fail to capture. Moral scepticism must, therefore, take the form of an error theory, admitting that a belief in objective values is built into ordinary moral thought and language, but holding that this ingrained belief is false. As such, it needs arguments to support it against "common sense." But solid arguments can be found. The considerations that favour moral scepticism are: first, the relativity or variability of some important starting points of moral thinking and their apparent dependence on actual ways of life; secondly, the metaphysical peculiarity of the supposed objective values, in that they would have to be intrinsically action-guiding and motivating. . . .

Mackie is not satisfied to end his analysis of morality with the claim that moral statements are false. As an antirealist, he need not abandon support of morality or the possibility of internally justifying moral claims; it is only realism that must be abandoned. This rejection of realism leaves open whether we should *accept or reject* moral judgments and practices, and, if so, which ones. Mackie also recognizes that he needs to explain why common sense and much of moral philosophy have been led into error through an assumption of realism.

Mackie is a skeptic about the objectivity of values—their reality—but he is not a skeptic about morality, which he accepts as a viable and vital social institution. He believes that we create moral rules as a social unit. He believes there can be justification in ethics by appeal to intersubjective standards, meaning that social agreements provide our basic values. For example, we would morally justify a policy or system of procuring human organs by appeal to standards of collecting organs that we had agreed to, and not in any other way. Mackie insists that "intersubjectivity is not objectivity." As long as belief in objective truth in morals is not assumed, Mackie is even willing to say that moral statements have truth values. For example, it is true that we should not steal from others, but this truth is entirely dependent upon prior agreements about property and theft.

Mackie insists that accepting truth and objectivity as entirely relative to inter-subjectively accepted standards forces us to give up belief in the objectivity of those standards. Somewhere in the foundations of all moral beliefs there must be some standard that cannot be objectively validated and is "constituted by our choosing or deciding to think in a certain way." (Thus, there is no form of "external justification" of the sort discussed earlier in this chapter.) The two main arguments Mackie relies upon to support these positions are (1) "the argument from relativity," as presented in Chapter 2, and (2) "the argument from queerness," found in the selection above.

From the perspective of the two arguments, Mackie has a ready reply to McNaughton. Mackie is aware that common moral belief assumes objective moral truth, and in this regard he need not disagree with McNaughton. However, Mackie would presumably disagree with McNaughton's claim that moral realism in any significant sense of the term is compatible with the world view of physical science. He argues that moral properties are very different from physical properties, and that while claims about physical properties are either true or false, claims about moral properties are only true or false relative to a set of invented standards.

Consider McNaughton's claim that in virtue of heroin's addictive properties, it would be wrong for a man to introduce his children to it. McNaughton holds that this wrongness is an objective moral fact, whether or not any human beings know that it is. Mackie would surely agree with McNaughton that introducing children to heroin would be wrong, but he would argue that it would be wrong because of a set of moral standards that hold in the society he and McNaughton happen to belong to. Mackie would argue that absent a set of moral standards, there is no fact indicating that it is wrong to introduce one's children to heroin. He would not disagree with McNaughton's moral judgment; rather, he would disagree with any moral realist's claim that this shared judgment has the objective status of a moral fact. Similarly, it would be wrong not to give Mickey Mantle a liver if he best satisfied the public criteria of distribution, but Mackie would insist that there are multiple sets of criteria to which we could agree. At some point a social choice has to be made, and it could go one of several ways.

However, the moral realist is not without a rejoinder. In an influential reply to Mackie, David Brink argues that Mackie's theory rests upon the claim that moral properties, unlike other properties, are queer or mysterious. Brink claims that this is simply not true; moral properties and other types of properties are simply not constituted by *material (physical)* properties[13]—just as biology is not reducible to physics. Even if biological facts emerge from facts in physics and chemistry, biological facts are very different from facts in the latter two fields. Mackie's arguments about the queerness of moral facts could just as easily apply to biological facts; moral facts are therefore not any more mysterious than other facts that we all take to be objective. If there is nothing especially queer or mysterious about moral facts, Brink argues, we ought to accept the theory most in accord with our moral beliefs, and this is moral realism, by Mackie's own admission.

---

[13]David O. Brink, *Moral Realism and the Foundations of Ethics*, pp. 171–4.

In the end, Mackie understands morality as a persisting set of social practices pertaining to what is demanded, enforced, and condemned in a social setting. The moral realist sees a lot more than this in morality. We will return to some of these issues in the next four chapters, especially in Chapter 7, where we explore how Mackie builds on and departs from David Hume's theory of ethics.

## REFLECTIVE EQUILIBRIUM

Many philosophers have tried to circumvent problems of cognitivism and non-cognitivism by appeal to a model known as the "reflective equilibrium" or the "coherence" model of justification. Reflective equilibrium is a method formulated by John Rawls that views justification in ethics as a reflective testing of our moral beliefs, moral principles, theoretical postulates, and other relevant moral beliefs in order to make them as coherent as possible.

In developing and refining a system of ethics, Rawls argues, it is appropriate to start with the broadest possible set of considered judgments about a subject and to erect a provisional set of principles that reflects them. *Considered judgments* is a technical term referring to "judgments in which our moral capacities are most likely to be displayed without distortion." Examples are judgments about the wrongness of racial discrimination, religious intolerance, and political conflict of interest. By contrast, judgments in which one's confidence level is low or in which one is influenced by the possibility of personal gain are excluded. Starting with paradigms of what is morally right or wrong, one searches for principles that are consistent with these paradigms as well as one another. Such principles and considered judgments are taken, as Rawls puts it, as "provisionally as fixed points," but also as "liable to revision." The goal is to match and prune considered judgments and principles in an attempt to make them coherent.[14]

This model looks for the best approximation to full coherence under the assumption of a never-ending search for consistency in the face of unanticipated situations. As we confront new experiences, the theory will be further modified. It is unreasonable to suppose that we will at some point be able to terminate this process of abandoning and modifying beliefs through reflective equilibrium. A moral theory should be viewed more as a process than as a finished product; and moral problems like the best system for organ procurement and distribution should be viewed as social projects in constant need of adjustment by reflective equilibrium.

From this perspective, moral thinking is similar to forms of theorizing well beyond ethics: Hypotheses must be tested, buried, or modified through experimental thinking. Justification is not merely invoking general action-guides nor an appeal to past and present experience. Many different considerations provide reciprocal support in the attempt to fit moral beliefs into a coherent unit. As Rawls suggests in

---

[14]John Rawls, *A Theory of Justice* (Cambridge, MA: Harvard University Press, 1971), pp. 20ff, 46–48. See also Rawls's references to reflective equilibrium in his later book, *Political Liberalism* (New York: Columbia University Press, 1996), esp. pp. 8, 381, 384, and 399.

the following selection, we can expect to modify or supplement our principles and judgments in a way that does the least damage to the system of beliefs.

# Some Remarks about Moral Theory*

## John Rawls

It seems desirable at this point, in order to prevent misunderstanding, to discuss briefly the nature of moral theory. I shall do this by explaining in more detail the concept of a considered judgment in reflective equilibrium and the reasons for introducing it.

Let us assume that each person beyond a certain age and possessed of the requisite intellectual capacity develops a sense of justice under normal social circumstances. We acquire a skill in judging things to be just and unjust, and in supporting these judgments by reasons. Moreover, we ordinarily have some desire to act in accord with these pronouncements and expect a similar desire on the part of others. Clearly this moral capacity is extraordinarily complex. To see this it suffices to note the, potentially infinite number and variety of judgments that we are prepared to make. The fact that we often do not know what to say, and sometimes find our minds unsettled, does not detract from the complexity of the capacity we have.

Now one may think of moral philosophy at first (and I stress the provisional nature of this view) as the attempt to describe our moral capacity. . . . This enterprise is very difficult. For by such a description is not meant simply a list

*From John Rawls, *A Theory of Justice* (Cambridge, MA: The Belknap Press of Harvard University Press, 1971).

of the judgments on institutions and actions that we are prepared to render, accompanied with supporting reasons when these are offered. Rather, what is required is a formulation of a set of principles which, when conjoined to our beliefs and knowledge of the circumstances, would lead us to make these judgments with their supporting reasons were we to apply these principles conscientiously and intelligently. A conception of justice characterizes our moral sensibility when the everyday judgments we do make are in accordance with its principles. These principles can serve as part of the premises of an argument which arrives at the matching judgments. We do not understand our sense of justice until we know in some systematic way covering a wide range of cases what these principles are. Only a deceptive familiarity with our everyday judgments and our natural readiness to make them could conceal the fact that characterizing our moral capacities is an intricate task. The principles which describe them must be presumed to have a complex structure, and the concepts involved will require serious study. . . .

We can note whether applying these principles would lead us to make the same judgments about the basic structure of society which we now make intuitively and in which we have the greatest confidence; or whether, in cases where our present judgments are in doubt and given with hesitation, these principles offer a resolution which we can affirm on reflection. There are questions which we feel sure must be answered in a certain way. For example, we are confident that religious intolerance and racial discrimination are unjust. We think that we have examined these things with care and have reached what we believe is an impartial judgment not likely to be distorted by an excessive attention to our own interests. These convictions are provisional fixed points which we presume any conception of justice must fit. But we have much less assurance as to what is the correct distribution of wealth and authority. Here we may be looking for a way to remove our doubts. . . .

A useful comparison here is with the problem of describing the sense of grammaticalness that we have for the sentences of our native language. In this case the aim is to characterize the ability to recognize well-formed sentences by formulating clearly expressed principles which make the same discriminations as the native speaker. This is a difficult undertaking which, although still unfinished, is known to require theoretical constructions that far outrun the ad hoc precepts of our explicit grammatical knowledge. A similar situation presumably holds in moral philosophy. There is no reason to assume that our sense of justice can be adequately characterized by familiar common sense precepts, or derived from the more obvious learning principles. A correct account of moral capacities will certainly involve principles and theoretical constructions which go much beyond the norms and standards cited in everyday life. . . .

So far, though, I have not said anything about considered judgments. Now, as already suggested, they enter as those judgments in which our moral capacities are most likely to be displayed without distortion. Thus in deciding which of our judgments to take into account we may reasonably select some and exclude others. For example, we can discard those judgments made with hesitation, which we have little confidence. Similarly, those given when we are upset or frightened, or when we stand to gain one way or the other can be left aside. All these judgments are likely to be erroneous or to be influenced by an excessive attention to our own interests. Considered judgments are simply those rendered under conditions favorable to the exercise of the sense of justice, and therefore in circumstances where the more common excuses and explanations for making a mistake do not obtain. The person making the judgment is presumed, then, to have the ability, the opportunity, and the desire to reach a correct decision (or at least, not the desire not to). Moreover, the criteria that identify these judgments are not arbitrary. They are, in fact, similar to those that single out considered judgments of any kind. And once we regard the sense of justice as a mental capacity, as involving the exercise of thought, the relevant judgments are those given under conditions favorable for deliberation and judgment in general.

I now turn to the notion of reflective equilibrium. . . . In describing our sense of justice an allowance must be made for the likelihood that considered judgments are no doubt subject to certain irregularities and distortions despite the fact that they are rendered under favorable circumstances. When a person is presented with an intuitively appealing account of his sense of justice (one, say, which embodies various reasonable and natural presumptions), he may well revise his judgments to conform to its principles even though the theory does not fit his existing judgments exactly. He is especially likely to do this if he can find an explanation for the deviations which undermines his confidence in his original judgments and if the conception presented yields a judgment which he finds he can now accept. From the standpoint of moral philosophy, the best account of a person's sense of justice is not the one which fits his judgments prior to his examining any conception of justice, but rather the one which matches his judgments in reflective equilibrium. As we have seen, this state is one reached after a person has weighed various proposed conceptions and he has either revised his judgments to accord with one of them or held fast to his initial convictions (and the corresponding conception).

The notion of reflective equilibrium introduces some complications that call for comment. For one thing, it is a notion characteristic of the study of principles which govern actions shaped by self-examination. Moral philosophy is Socratic: we may want to change our present considered judgments once their regulative principles are brought to light. And we may want to do this even though these principles are a perfect fit. A knowledge of these principles may suggest further reflections that lead us to revise our judgments. This feature is not peculiar though to moral philosophy, or to the study of other philosophical principles such as those of induction and scientific method. For example, while we may not expect a substantial revision of our sense of correct grammar in view of a linguistic theory the principles of

which seem especially natural to us, such a change is not inconceivable, and no doubt our sense of grammaticalness may be affected to some degree anyway by this knowledge. But there is a contrast, say, with physics. To take an extreme case, if we have an accurate account of the motions of the heavenly bodies that we do not find appealing, we cannot alter these motions to conform to a more attractive theory. It is simply good fortune that the principles of celestial mechanics have their intellectual beauty.

There are, however, several interpretations of reflective equilibrium. For the notion varies depending upon whether one is to be presented with only those descriptions which more or less match one's existing judgments except for minor discrepancies, or whether one is to be presented with all possible descriptions to which one might plausibly conform one's judgments together with all relevant philosophical arguments for them. In the first case we would be describing a person's sense of justice more or less as it is although allowing for the smoothing out of certain irregularities; in the second case a person's sense of justice may or may not undergo a radical shift. Clearly it is the second kind of reflective equilibrium that one is concerned with in moral philosophy. To be sure, it is doubtful whether one can ever reach this state. For even if the idea of all possible descriptions and of all philosophically relevant arguments is well-defined (which is questionable), we cannot examine each of them. The most we can do is to study the conceptions of justice known to us through the tradition of moral philosophy and any further ones that occur to us, and then to consider these.

Unfortunately, an inherent vagueness in the idea of reflective equilibrium has left it open to more than one interpretation. For example, at what task is the theory directed? Under this method we might be reflecting on communal policies, on a moral philosophy, or on an individual's moral beliefs. The focus might be on judgments, on policies, on cases, or on finding moral truth. Moreover, it is not very clear how we should and should not achieve coherence, or how to know when we have done so.

For example, to take a relatively uncomplicated example in the ethics of organ transplantation, imagine that we are attracted to each of the following two moral considerations: (1) Distribute organs by expected number of years of survival (in order to maximize the organ's utility), and (2) distribute organs by time on the waiting list (in order to give every candidate an equal opportunity). The second is much more favorable to transplant candidates like Mickey Mantle, but why should we choose this rule rather than the other rule? As they stand, these two distributive principles are not coherent, because use of either will undercut or eliminate the other. We can retain both (1) and (2) in a defensible theory of fair distribution, but to do so we will have to introduce limits on these principles that specify when they do and do not apply. These limits and accounts will, in turn, have to be made coherent with other principles and rules, such as norms regarding discrimination against the elderly, the allocation of scarce medical resources, and the role of ability to pay in paying for medical procedures.

This analysis suggests that all moral systems present some level of indeterminateness and incoherence. All lack power to eliminate various conflicts among principles and rules. So understood, coherence and reflective equilibrium are not achieved merely by an absence of inconsistencies in the stated norms in a system. Coherence is a matter of the further development and mutual support of norms.

Several philosophers have endeavored to characterize reasoning within the model of reflective equilibrium in a nontrivial manner, but currently available accounts all need further work. As is widely appreciated in philosophy, the theory is promising, but underdeveloped.

## CONCLUSION

In this chapter we have canvassed several theories of justification and truth. Throughout Part One (Chapters 1 through 3), we have primarily dwelled on what are called second-order or metaethical issues—that is, those concerned with metaphysical, epistemological, conceptual, and psychological issues about morality and moral judgments. These are questions about whether morality is objective or subjective, prescriptive or descriptive, relative or nonrelative, rational or emotive, and the like. First-order issues of ethics, by contrast, are normative; they concern what is basic in our systems of moral belief and determinative of right and wrong as well as virtue and vice. In the next four chapters, we will examine four classics of ethical theory, each of which presents a theory about the foundations of ethics.

## SUGGESTED SUPPLEMENTARY READINGS

### Moral Justification and the Justification of Morality

Baier, Kurt: *The Moral Point of View: A Rational Basis of Ethics* (Ithaca, NY: Cornell University Press, 1958), especially chaps. 8, 11, 12.

Becker, Lawrence C.: *On Justifying Moral Judgments* (New York: Humanities Press, 1973).

Copp, David: "Explanation and Justification in Ethics," *Ethics,* 100 (1990): 237–58.

Dancy, Jonathan: *Moral Reasons* (Cambridge, MA: Blackwell, 1993).

DeBruin, Debra A.: "Can One Justify Morality to Fooles?" *Canadian Journal of Philosophy,* 25 (1995): 1–32.

Gauthier, David: *Practical Reasoning: The Structure and Foundations of Prudential and Moral Arguments and Their Exemplification in Discourse* (Oxford, England: Clarendon Press, 1963), especially chaps. 6–8.

Gert, Bernard: *Morality: A New Justification of the Moral Rules* (New York: Oxford University Press, 1988), especially chaps. 2, 5–7, 11.

Goldman, Alan H.: *Moral Knowledge* (New York: Routledge, 1988).

Honderich, Ted, ed.: *Morality and Objectivity* (London: Routledge & Kegan Paul, 1985).

"Justification": (Special Issue), *The Monist,* 71 (July 1988).

Nielsen, Kai: "Is 'Why Should I Be Moral?' an Absurdity?" *Australasian Journal of Philosophy,* 36 (1958): 25–32.

Ruse, Michael: *Taking Darwin Seriously: A Naturalistic Approach to Philosophy* (Amherst, NY: Prometheus Books, 1998).

Sinnot-Armstrong, Walter, and Mark Timmons, eds.: *Moral Knowledge?: New Readings in Moral Epistemology* (Oxford, England: Oxford University Press, 1996).

Williams, Bernard: *Ethics and the Limits of Philosophy* (Cambridge, MA: Harvard University Press, 1985).

### Cognitivism, Noncognitivism, and Moral Realism

Audi, Robert: *Moral Knowledge and Ethical Character* (New York: Oxford University Press, 1997).

Ayer, Alfred J.: *Language, Truth and Logic,* 2d ed. (New York: Dover Publications, Inc., 1936), especially chap. 6.

Bennett, Jonathan: "The Necessity of Moral Judgments," *Ethics,* 103 (1993): 458–72.

Blachowicz, James: "Reciprocal Justification in Science and Moral Theory," *Synthese,* 110 (1997): 447–68.

Blackburn, Simon: *Essays in Quasi-Realism* (New York: Oxford University Press, 1993).

Boyd, Richard N.: "How to Be a Moral Realist," in Geoffrey Sayre-McCord, ed., *Essays on Moral Realism* (Ithaca, NY: Cornell University Press, 1988), pp. 181–228.

Brink, David O.: *Moral Realism and the Foundations of Ethics* (New York: Cambridge University Press, 1989).

————: "Moral Conflict and Its Structure," *Philosophical Review,* 103 (1994): 215–47.

Copp, David: *Morality, Normativity, and Society* (New York: Oxford University Press, 1995).

Copp, David, and D. Zimmerman, eds.: *Morality, Reason, and Truth* (Totowa, NJ: Rowman and Littlefield, 1984).

Dancy, Jonathan: "Ethical Particularism and Morally Relevant Properties," *Mind,* 90 (1981): 367–85.

————: *Moral Reasons* (Cambridge, England: Blackwell, 1993).

Darwall, Stephen, Allan Gibbard, and Peter Railton, eds.: *Moral Discourse and Practice: Some Philosophical Approaches* (New York: Oxford University Press, 1997).

Ewing, Alfred C.: *The Definition of Good* (New York: Macmillan Company, 1947).

Fearn, Joe: "Seeing Aspects, Seeing Value," *Sorites* (April 1998): 32–46.

Foot, Philippa: *Virtues and Vices* (Oxford, England: Basil Blackwell, 1978).

————: "Moral Realism and Moral Dilemma," *The Journal of Philosophy,* 80 (1983): 379–98.

French, Peter A., Theodore E. Uehling, Jr., and Howard K. Wettstein, eds.: *Realism and Antirealism* (Minneapolis: University of Minnesota Press, 1988).

Fuller, Michael B.: *Truth, Value, and Justification* (Brookfield, VT: Avebury, 1991).

Haldane, John, and Crispin Wright, eds.: *Reality, Representation, and Projection* (New York: Oxford University Press, 1993).

Hare, Richard M.: *The Language of Morals* (Oxford: Oxford University Press, 1952).

————: *Moral Thinking* (New York: Oxford University Press, 1981).

Horgan, Terence, and Mark Timmons: "From Moral Realism to Moral Relativism in One Easy Step," *Critica,* 28 (1996): 3–39.

Hursthouse, Rosalind, Gavin Lawrence, and Warren Quinn, eds.: *Virtues and Reasons: Philippa Foot and Moral Theory* (New York: Clarendon/Oxford Press, 1995).

Lemos, Noah M.: *Intrinsic Value: Concept and Warrant* (New York: Cambridge University Press, 1994).

Lieberman, Marcel S.: *Commitment, Value, and Moral Realism* (New York: Cambridge University Press, 1998).

Loeb, Don: "Moral Realism and the Argument from Disagreement," *Philosophical Studies,* 90 (June 1998): 281–303.

Mele, Alfred R.: "Internalist Moral Cognitivism and Listlessness," *Ethics,* 106 (1996): 727–53.

Mizzoni, John: "Moral Realism, Objective Values, and J. L. Mackie," *Auslegung,* 20 (Winter 1995): 11–24.

Moore, George Edward: *Principia Ethica* (Cambridge, England: Cambridge University Press, 1903).

Paul, Ellen Frankel, Fred D. Miller, Jr., and Jeffrey Paul, eds.: *Cultural Pluralism and Moral Knowledge* (New York: Cambridge University Press, 1994).

Perry, Ralph Barton: *General Theory of Value: Its Meaning and Basic Principles Construed in Terms of Interest* (Cambridge, MA: Harvard University Press, 1950).

Quinn, Warren: "Truth and Explanation in Ethics," *Ethics,* 96 (1986): 524–44.

Railton, Peter: "Moral Realism," *Philosophical Review,* 95 (1986): 163–207.

———: "Moral Realism: Prospects and Problems," in Walter Sinnott-Armstrong and Mark Timmons, eds., *Moral Knowledge?*(above).

Rorty, Richard: *Truth and Progress: Philosophical Papers III* (Cambridge, England: Cambridge University Press, 1998).

Ross, William David: *The Right and the Good* (Oxford, England: Oxford University Press, 1930).

———: *Foundations of Ethics* (Oxford: Clarendon Press, 1939).

Sayre-McCord, Geoffrey, ed.: *Essays on Moral Realism* (Ithaca, NY: Cornell University Press, 1988).

———: "The Metaethical Problem," *Ethics,* 108 (October 1997): 55–83.

Smith, Michael: "Realism," in Peter Singer, ed., *A Companion to Ethics* (Cambridge, England: Blackwell, 1991).

Stevenson, Charles L.: *Ethics and Language* (New Haven, CT: Yale University Press, 1944).

———: *Facts and Values: Studies in Ethical Analysis* (New Haven: Yale University Press, 1963).

Tännsjö, Torbjörm: *Moral Realism* (Savage, MD: Rowman & Littlefield Publishers, 1990).

Urmson, J. O.: *The Emotive Theory of Ethics* (New York: Oxford University Press, 1969).

## Reflective Equilibrium

Brandt, R. B.: "The Science of Man and Wide Reflective Equilibrium," *Ethics,* 100 (1990): 259–78.

D'Agostino, Fred: "Relativism and Reflective Equilibrium," *Monist,* 71 (1988): 420–36.

Daniels, Norman: "Wide Reflective Equilibrium and Theory Acceptance in Ethics," *Journal of Philosophy,* 76 (1979): 256–82.

———: *Justice and Justification: Reflective Equilibrium in Theory and Practice* (New York: Cambridge University Press, 1996).

———: "Wide Reflective Equilibrium in Practice," in L. W. Sumner and J. Boyle, eds., *Philosophical Perspectives on Bioethics* (Toronto: University of Toronto Press 1996), pp. 96–114.

DePaul, Michael R.: *Balance and Refinement: Beyond Coherence Models of Moral Inquiry* (London: Routledge, 1993).

Holmgren, M.: "The Wide and Narrow of Reflective Equilibrium," *Canadian Journal of Philosophy,* 19 (1989): 43–60.

Nielsen, Kai: "Relativism and Wide Reflective Equilibrium," *Monist,* 76 (1993): 316–32.

# PART TWO

# Classical Ethical Theories

## CHAPTER 4

# Mill and Utilitarian Theories

## HEALTH POLICY FOR HYPERTENSION

In the mid-1970s two professors at Harvard, Milton Weinstein and William B. Stason, did a study on high blood pressure in American society.[1] These two researchers concluded that 17 percent of the adult American population, or 24 million persons, had problems with high blood pressure. They found that even minimally adequate treatment for these persons would cost over $5 billion annually, that close to 50 percent of the affected population were not aware that they already had problems, and that only about one-sixth of that group was currently receiving proper medical treatment and control.

Weinstein and Stason wanted to determine the most cost-effective way to handle the problem of hypertension. Data from screening programs that identified people who did not know they had high blood pressure revealed that it was not cost-effective to try to inform these persons of their problem unless they were already under a physician's care. This was because, in general, people who were informed of their condition through massive screening and education programs were not likely to report to a physician for treatment, and those who did subsequently see a physician usually did not properly adhere to the recommended therapy.

As their research developed, Weinstein and Stason discovered (somewhat surprisingly) that it was more cost-effective to target three specific groups in an attempt to reduce this general public health problem, rather than to launch a community-wide campaign. These groups were (1) younger men, (2) older women, and (3) known patients with very high blood pressure. When the researchers combined these findings with their previous findings that large-scale public screening and informational programs were not medically effective, they were led to conclude that:

> A community with limited resources would probably do better to concentrate its efforts on improving adherence of known hypertensives, even at a sacrifice in terms of the numbers screened. This conclusion holds even if such proadherence interventions are rather expensive and only moderately effective, and even if screening is very inexpensive. . . .

[1]See *Hypertension* (Cambridge, MA: Harvard University Press, 1976); *New England Journal of Medicine,* 296 (1977): 716–21; *Hastings Center Report,* 7 (October 1977).

Finally, screening in the regular practices [of physicians] is more cost-effective than public screening.

Weinstein and Stason were bothered by their recommendation because implicitly it meant that, if the government followed it, the country's poorest sector, which is in greatest need of medical attention, would not be provided with any benefits of high blood pressure education and management. Full public screening would be sacrificed in order to achieve greater success for the community as a whole; only persons known to have high blood pressure, and who were already in contact with a physician about their problem, would be recontacted. These investigators were concerned because a public health endeavor aimed expressly at the economically better-off sector of society seemed unjust to the poor and minorities. Yet the statistics were compelling: No matter how carefully planned the efforts, nothing worked efficiently except programs directed at those already in touch with physicians. Moreover, Weinstein and Stason knew that it was unrealistic, and perhaps unwarranted in light of other health needs, to expect new allocations of public health money to control high blood pressure. They also knew that it would take massive new allocations to begin to help the poorer sections of society.

Medical research since the Weinstein and Stason study has continued to support their findings. Nonadherence to treatment programs for hypertension is one of the most important antecedent conditions leading to serious hypertension-related medical problems. In poor sections of inner cities, such nonadherence is much higher among patients who are screened and treated for hypertension in the emergency room than for those treated by their own primary care physicians. This problem is significant because many poor people do not have primary care physicians.

Research also indicates that the prevalence of hypertension is 50 percent higher among African-American populations than among whites. Low economic status is also correlated with fewer visits per year to physicians' offices. Thus, the problems identified by Weinstein and Stason remain largely unchanged: A greater net improvement in overall public health is likely to be achieved by targeting patients who have and who visit primary care physicians, yet such a strategy is likely to result in underserving poor and minority populations who already suffer disproportionately from health problems.[2]

Weinstein and Stason recommended what they explicitly referred to as a "utilitarian" set of criteria for allocation. As we will see in this chapter, their study is useful for illustrating the utilitarian approach to morals as well as for noting disagreements that have emerged among utilitarians. Their recommendations must not be taken, however, as perfectly representative of all forms of utilitarian thinking, for reasons now to be considered.

---

[2]Jane Morley et al., "Hypertension Control and Access to Medical Care in the Inner City," *American Journal of Public Health,* 88 (November 1998): 1696–99; Steven Shea et al., "Correlates of Nonadherence to Hypertension Treatment in an Inner-City Minority Population," *American Journal of Public Health,* 82 (December 1992): 1607–12.

## THE OBJECTIVES OF NORMATIVE THEORIES

It has often been said that ethical theory arises because we need to *defend* our moral judgments. To demonstrate through an ethical theory that one is justified in holding a moral view requires making one's principles explicit and defending those principles systematically. This chapter concentrates on one such theory, utilitarianism, but at the outset some discussion is needed to explain the objectives of ethical theories.

Many circumstances of moral conflict puzzle us deeply. Dilemmas occur whenever good reasons for mutually exclusive alternatives can be cited. These reasons are usually rooted in conflicting principles that seem to obligate a person to perform two mutually exclusive actions in circumstances in which only one can be performed. For example, consider the following two principles:

$P_1$:   You ought to tell the truth. (For example, physicians should tell the truth to patients.)

$P_2$:   You ought to avoid causing harm to innocent persons. (For example, physicians should avoid causing harm to innocent patients.)

Both principles $P_1$ and $P_2$ seem acceptable and defensible, at least intuitively. Yet on some occasions we determine that we can protect the innocent only by not telling the truth. For example, a physician decides that telling the truth to a patient about the risks of an unavoidable procedure will make that patient extremely nervous and fearful immediately before a dangerous operation that the patient needs to meet with courage and equanimity in order to have a chance of survival. When such intuitively satisfying principles come into conflict, as they often do in the moral life, we hope to be able to appeal to a higher principle to resolve the problem.

An instinctive intellectual desire suggests to us the need for a principle that can tell us how to handle this and other circumstances of conflict. Utilitarianism and other ethical theories have been fashioned to serve this role. Utilitarians agree on the following principle:

$P_u$:   An act is right if, and only if, it can be reasonably expected to produce the greatest balance of good or the least balance of harm.

Presumably this principle tells us exactly how to proceed when we have a conflict of principles.

However, as we will see in this chapter, many believe that there are fatal counterexamples to this utilitarian principle. Some objections to utilitarianism are based on individual rights, some on competing principles, and some on an appeal to virtues. As a consequence, alternative ethical theories have emerged. One important species is deontological theories. The view behind many (although not all) of these theories is that:

$P_d$:   An action is right if and only if the action satisfies some nonutilitarian conditions $C_1, C_2, C_3, \ldots C_n$.

A major problem in ethical theory has been how to formulate $C_1$ through $C_n$. A comprehensive ethical theory attempts to solve this problem, as we will see in the present chapter and in Chapters 5 through 7. However, the lack of agreement about $C_1$ through $C_n$ renders ethical theory highly controversial. Utilitarianism is perhaps the most controversial ethical theory of all.


## THE UTILITARIAN CONCEPTION OF MORALITY

Many prominent writers in ethical theory, including utilitarians, have held that there is one and only one supreme principle of morality, which justifies all obligations and standards. Utilitarianism is one of several consequentialist ethical theories. Consequentialism asserts that actions are right or wrong according to their consequences, rather than because of any intrinsic features they may have, such as truthfulness or fidelity. What makes an action morally right or wrong is the total good or evil it produces. This contention distinguishes utilitarianism from theories maintaining that the act itself has moral value apart from the good or evil produced.

To understand utilitarianism, consider the hypertension example that begins this chapter: If one kind of health program benefits more persons than an alternative program would, then there are moral grounds for choosing it because of the greater benefit (unless other moral reasons based on utilitarian considerations prevent that choice). The utilitarian maintains that one must choose the action that would produce the best consequences for all persons affected by that action. This advice springs from two connected theses of critical importance to utilitarianism: (1) that an action or practice is right (when compared with any alternative action or practice) if it leads to the greatest possible balance of good consequences or to the least possible balance of bad consequences in the world as a whole, and (2) that the concepts of duty, obligation, and right are subordinated to, and determined by, that which maximizes the good.

Utilitarian views of roughly this description have been embraced during many periods in the history of ethical theory, but the earliest significant utilitarian philosophical writings were those of Jeremy Bentham (1748–1832) and John Stuart Mill (1806–1873). (David Hume's substantially different appeals to utility are examined in Chapter 7.) Bentham was trained in law and regarded utilitarianism as a practical system for legislators, not merely an abstract ethical theory. Just as investigators Weinstein and Stason were interested in a morally appropriate public health policy, Bentham was interested in a moral perspective that would underwrite legal reforms.

Bentham's ideas developed in part from a disenchantment with the British legal system. He argued that the purpose of law is to promote the welfare of citizens, not to enforce divine commands, impose severe punishments, or protect so-called natural rights. He thought the British system for classifying crimes, for example, was deficient because it based its determination of the gravity of offenses on outdated, brutal, and costly views about punishment. As an alternative, Bentham suggested that crimes be classified according to the offense's level of seriousness, and that the levels of seriousness should be determined by the unhappiness and misery a crime visits on its victims and society. Accordingly, his revisions in the classification of crimes were intended to bring about revisions in the severity of criminal punishments. Bentham's rule was that the punishment for a crime should only be stringent enough to cancel the advantage gained by committing the crime, and should not be any greater than needed to deter the offender and others. This led Bentham to oppose the death penalty. Moreover, Bentham believed that an act should be classified as criminal only if it causes harmful consequences to others. He thus opposed criminal sanctions against "crimes" between consenting adults, such as gambling, because they produce no harmful consequences to the parties involved. His thinking is typical of many utilitarian writers.

Bentham was among the earliest and most influential utilitarians, but the major exponent of utilitarianism is generally regarded to be John Stuart Mill, author of *Utilitarianism* and *On Liberty.* Mill was a member of Parliament for a short period of time and was, like Bentham, involved in a number of legal reform movements. He introduced a bill to extend the suffrage to women in 1867, though it was unsuccessful. Mill's involvement in legal reform is apparent throughout his philosophy, which was influenced by his legislative goals.

*Utilitarianism* was not an early work in Mill's career. It was not published in final form until 1863, when Mill, at age fifty-seven, had corrected what he considered to be flaws in, and incomplete aspects of, Bentham's moral philosophy. In *Utilitarianism,* Mill begins by arguing that moral philosophers have left a train of unconvincing and incompatible theories throughout the history of philosophy. We seem, he says, to be no closer to solving the problem of a criterion of right and wrong than we were in the days of Socrates, who, Mill thinks, asserted the theory of utilitarianism against the popular morality of the sophists.

He proposes a single standard for morals and legislation to determine which ends are worthy—a standard that allows us to decide objectively what is right and wrong. Mill argued for two different foundations of utilitarianism: (1) a *normative* foundation in the principle of utility, and (2) a *psychological* foundation in a theory of human nature. The principle of utility, or the "greatest happiness" principle, he declared to be the basic foundation of morals: "Actions are right in proportion as they tend to promote happiness, wrong as they tend to produce the reverse of happiness, i.e., pleasure or absence of pain." Pleasure and freedom from pain are the only things desirable as ends, and all desirable things (which are numerous) are desirable either for the pleasure inherent in them, or as means to promote pleasure and prevent pain. Mill's second foundation of utilitarianism derives from his belief that all persons have a basic desire for unity and harmony with their fellow human beings. Just as we feel horror at crimes, he says, so we have a basic moral sensitiveness to the needs of others. His idea seems to be that we have a natural but limited sympathy toward our fellows. The purpose of morality is at once to promote our natural sympathies and to combat their limitations; the principle of utility is regarded by Mill as the best means to these ends.

In the following excerpt, Mill explicates utilitarianism and expresses its connection to a theory of justice.

# Utilitarianism*

## John Stuart Mill

## Chapter 1

### General Remarks

There are few circumstances among those which make up the present condition of human knowledge, more unlike what might have been expected, or more significant of the backward state in which speculation on the most important subject still lingers, than the little progress which has been made in the decision of the controversy respecting the criterion of right and wrong. . . .

On the present occasion, I shall, without further discussion of the other theories, attempt to contribute something towards the understanding and appreciation of the Utilitarian or Happiness theory, and towards such proof as it is susceptible of. It is evident that this cannot be proof in the ordinary and popular meaning of the term. Questions of ultimate ends are not amenable to direct proof. Whatever can be proved to be good, must be so by being shown to be a means to something admitted to be good without proof. The medical art is proved to be good, by its conducing to health; but how is it possible to prove that health is good? The art of music is good, for the reason, among others, that it produces pleasure; but what proof is it possible to give that pleasure is good? If, then, it is asserted that there is a comprehensive formula, including all things which are in themselves good, and that whatever else is good, is not so as an end, but as a mean, the formula may be

*From John Stuart Mill, *Utilitarianism* (1863), chaps. 1, 2, 5.

accepted or rejected, but it is not a subject of what is commonly understood by proof. We are not, however, to infer that its acceptance or rejection must depend on blind impulse, or arbitrary choice. There is a larger meaning of the word proof, in which this question is as amenable to it as any other of the disputed questions of philosophy. The subject is within the cognizance of the rational faculty; and neither does that faculty deal with it solely in the way of intuition. Considerations may be presented capable of determining the intellect either to give or withhold its assent to the doctrine; and this is equivalent to proof. . . .

## Chapter 2

### What Utilitarianism Is

The creed which accepts as the foundation of morals, Utility, or the Greatest Happiness Principle, holds that actions are right in proportion as they tend to promote happiness, wrong as they tend to produce the reverse of happiness. By happiness is intended pleasure, and the absence of pain; by unhappiness, pain, and the privation of pleasure. To give a clear view of the moral standard set up by the theory, much more requires to be said; in particular, what things it includes in the ideas of pain and pleasure; and to what extent this is left an open question. But these supplementary explanations do not affect the theory of life on which this theory of morality is grounded—namely, that pleasure, and freedom from pain, are the only things desirable as ends; and that all desirable things (which are as numerous in the utilitarian as in any other scheme) are desirable either for the pleasure inherent in themselves, or as means to the promotion of pleasure and the prevention of pain.

Now, such a theory of life excites in many minds, and among them in some of the most estimable in feeling and purpose, inveterate dislike. To suppose that life has (as they express it) no higher end than pleasure—no better and nobler object of desire and pursuit—they designate as utterly mean and grovelling; as a doctrine worthy only of swine, to whom the followers of Epicurus were, at a very early period, contemptuously likened; and modern holders of the doctrine are occasionally made the subject of equally polite comparisons by its German, French, and English assailants.

When thus attacked, the Epicureans have always answered, that it is not they, but their accusers, who represent human nature in a degrading light; since the accusation supposes human beings to be capable of no pleasures except those of which swine are capable. If this supposition were true, the charge could not be gainsaid, but would then be no longer an imputation; for if the sources of pleasure were precisely the same to human beings and to swine, the rule of life which is good enough for the one would be good enough for the other. The comparison of the Epicurean life to that of beasts is felt as degrading, precisely because a beast's pleasures do not satisfy a human being's conceptions of happiness. Human beings have faculties more elevated than the animal appetites, and when once made conscious of them, do not regard anything as happiness which does not include their gratification. I do not, indeed, consider the Epicureans to have been by any means

faultless in drawing out their scheme of consequences from the utilitarian principle. To do this in any sufficient manner, many Stoic, as well as Christian elements require to be included. But there is no known Epicurean theory of life which does not assign to the pleasures of the intellect, of the feelings and imagination, and of the moral sentiments, a much higher value as pleasures than to those of mere sensation. It must be admitted, however, that utilitarian writers in general have placed the superiority of mental over bodily pleasures chiefly in the greater permanency, safety, uncostliness, &c., of the former—that is, in their circumstantial advantages rather than in their intrinsic nature. And on all these points utilitarians have fully proved their case; but they might have taken the other, and, as it may be called, higher ground, with entire consistency. It is quite compatible with the principle of utility to recognize the fact that some *kinds* of pleasure are more desirable and more valuable than others. It would be absurd that while, in estimating all other things, quality is considered as well as quantity, the estimation of pleasures should be supposed to depend on quantity alone.

If I am asked what I mean by difference of quality in pleasures, or what makes one pleasure more valuable than another, merely as a pleasure, except its being greater in amount, there is but one possible answer. Of two pleasures, if there be one to which all or almost all who have experience of both give a decided preference, irrespective of any feeling of moral obligation to prefer it, that is the more desirable pleasure. If one of the two is, by those who are competently acquainted with both, placed so far above the other that they prefer it, even though knowing it to be attended with a greater amount of discontent, and would not resign it for any quantity of the other pleasure which their nature is capable of, we are justified in ascribing to the preferred enjoyment a superiority in quality, so far outweighing quantity as to render it, in comparison, of small account.

Now it is an unquestionable fact that those who are equally acquainted with, and equally capable of appreciating and enjoying, both, do give a most marked preference to the manner of existence which employs their higher faculties. Few human creatures would consent to be changed into any of the lower animals, for a promise of the fullest allowance of a beast's pleasures; no intelligent human being would consent to be a fool, no instructed person would be an ignoramus, no person of feeling and conscience would be selfish and base, even though they should be persuaded that the fool, the dunce, or the rascal is better satisfied with his lot than they are with theirs. . . . Whoever supposes that this preference takes place at a sacrifice of happiness—that the superior being, in anything like the equal circumstances, is not happier than the inferior—confounds the two very different ideas, of happiness, and content. It is indisputable that the being whose capacities of enjoyment are low, has the greatest chance of having them fully satisfied; and a highly-endowed being will always feel that any happiness which he can look for, as the world is constituted, is imperfect. But he can learn to bear its imperfections, if they are at all bearable; and they will not make him envy the being who is indeed unconscious of the imperfections, but only because he feels not at all the good which those imperfections qualify. It is better to be a human being dissatisfied than a pig satisfied; better to be Socrates dissatisfied than a fool satisfied. And if the fool, or the pig, is of a different opinion, it is because they only know their own side of the question. The other party to the comparison knows both sides. . . .

I must again repeat, what the assailants of utilitarianism seldom have the justice to acknowledge, that the happiness which forms the utilitarian standard of what is right in conduct, is not the agent's own happiness, but that of all concerned. As between his own happiness and that of others, utilitarianism requires him to be as strictly impartial as a disinterested and benevolent spectator. In the golden rule of Jesus of Nazareth, we read the complete spirit of the ethics of utility. To do as one would be done by, and to love one's neighbour as oneself, constitute the ideal perfection of utilitarian morality. As the means of making the nearest approach to this ideal, utility would enjoin, first, that laws and social arrangements should place the happiness, or (as speaking practically it may be called) the interest, of every individual, as nearly as possible in harmony with the interest of the whole; and secondly, that education and opinion, which have so vast a power over human character, should so use that power as to establish in the mind of every individual an indissoluble association between his own happiness and the good of the whole; especially between his own happiness and the practice of such modes of conduct, negative and positive, as regard for the universal happiness prescribes: so that not only he may be unable to conceive the possibility of happiness to himself, consistently with conduct opposed to the general good, but also that a direct impulse to promote the general good may be in every individual one of the habitual motives of action, and the sentiments connected therewith may fill a large and prominent place in every human being's sentient existence. . . .

## Chapter 5

## On the Connexion between Justice and Utility

In all ages of speculation, one of the strongest obstacles to the reception of the doctrine that Utility or Happiness is the criterion of right and wrong, has been drawn from the idea of Justice. . . .

Each person maintains that equality is the dictate of justice, except where he thinks that expediency requires inequality. The justice of giving equal protection to the rights of all, is maintained by those who support the most outrageous inequality in the rights themselves. Even in slave countries it is theoretically admitted that the rights of the slave, such as they are, ought to be as sacred as those of the master; and that a tribunal which fails to enforce them with equal strictness is wanting in justice; while, at the same time, institutions which leave to the slave scarcely any rights to enforce, are not deemed unjust, because they are not deemed inexpedient. Those who think that utility requires distinctions of rank, do not consider it unjust that riches and social privileges should be unequally dispensed; but those who think this inequality inexpedient, think it unjust also. Whoever thinks that government is necessary, sees no injustice in as much inequality as is constituted by giving to the magistrate powers not granted to other people. Even among those who hold levelling doctrines, there are as many questions of justice as there are differences of opinion about expediency. . . .

Justice implies something which it is not only right to do, and wrong not to do, but which some individual person can claim from us as his moral right. No one has a moral right to our generosity or beneficence, because we are not morally bound to practise those virtues toward any given individual. And it will be found with respect to this as with respect to every correct definition, that the instances which seem to conflict with it are those which most confirm it. For if a moralist attempts, as some have done, to make out that mankind generally, though not any given individual, have a right to all the good we can do them, he at once, by that thesis, includes generosity and beneficence within the category of justice. He is obliged to say, that our utmost exertions are *due* to our fellow creatures, thus assimilating them to a debt; or that nothing less can be a sufficient *return* for what society does for us, thus classing the case as one of gratitude; both of which are acknowledged cases of justice. Wherever there is a right, the case is one of justice, and not of the virtue of beneficence, and whoever does not place the distinction between justice and morality in general where we have now placed it, will be found to make no distinction between them at all, but to merge all morality in justice. . . .

It is no objection against this doctrine to say, that when we feel our sentiment of justice outraged, we are not thinking of society at large, or of any collective interest, but only of the individual case. It is common enough certainly, though the reverse of commendable, to feel resentment merely because we have suffered pain; but a person whose resentment is really a moral feeling, that is, who considers whether an act is blamable before he allows himself to resent it—such a person, though he may not say expressly to himself that he is standing up for the interest of society, certainly does feel that he is asserting a rule which is for the benefit of others as well as for his own. If he is not feeling this—if he is regarding the act solely as it affects him individually—he is not consciously just; he is not concerning himself about the justice of his actions. This is admitted even by anti-utilitarian moralists. . . .

When we call anything a person's right, we mean that he has a valid claim on society to protect him in the possession of it, either by the force of law, or by that of education and opinion. If he has what we consider a sufficient claim, on whatever account, to have something guaranteed to him by society, we say that he has a right to it. If we desire to prove that anything does not belong to him by right, we think this done as soon as it is admitted that society ought not to take measures for securing it to him, but should leave it to chance, or to his own exertions. . . .

To have a right, then, is, I conceive, to have something which society ought to defend me in the possession of. If the objector goes on to ask why it ought, I can give him no other reason than general utility. If that expression does not seem to convey a sufficient feeling of the strength of the obligation, nor to account for the peculiar energy of the feeling, it is because there goes to the composition of the sentiment, not a rational only but also an animal element, the thirst for retaliation; and this thirst derives its intensity, as well as its moral justification, from the extraordinarily important and impressive kind of utility which is concerned. The interest involved is that of security, to every one's feelings the most vital of all interests. Nearly all other earthly benefits are needed by one person, not needed by another; and many of them can, if necessary, be cheerfully foregone, or replaced by something else; but security no human being can possibly do without. . . .

The principle, therefore, of giving to each what they deserve, that is, good for good as well as evil for evil, is not only included within the idea of Justice as we have defined it, but is a proper object of that intensity of sentiment, which places the Just, in human estimation, above the simply Expedient.

Most of the maxims of justice current in the world, and commonly appealed to in its transactions, are simply instrumental to carrying into effect the principles of justice which we have now spoken of. That a person is only responsible for what he has done voluntarily, or could voluntarily have avoided; that it is unjust to condemn any person unheard; that the punishment ought to be proportioned to the offence, and the like, are maxims intended to prevent the just principle of evil for evil from being perverted to the infliction of evil without justification. The greater part of these common maxims have come into use from the practice of courts of justice, which have been naturally led to a more complete recognition and elaboration than was likely to suggest itself to others, of the rules necessary to enable them to fulfill their double function, of inflicting punishment when due, and of awarding to each person his right.

That first of judicial virtues, impartiality, is an obligation of justice, partly for the reason last mentioned; as being a necessary condition of the fulfilment of the other obligations of justice. But this is not the only source of the exalted rank, among human obligations, of those maxims of equality and impartiality, which, both in popular estimation and in that of the most enlightened, are included among the precepts of justice. In one point of view, they may be considered as corollaries from the principles already laid down. If it is a duty to do to each according to his deserts, returning good for good as well as repressing evil by evil, it necessarily follows that we should treat all equally well (when no higher duty forbids) who have deserved equally well of us, and that society should treat all equally well who have deserved equally well of it, that is, who have deserved equally well absolutely. This is the highest abstract standard of social and distributive justice; towards which all institutions, and the efforts of all virtuous citizens, should be made in the utmost possible degree to converge. But this great moral duty rests upon a still deeper foundation, being a direct emanation from the first principle of morals, and not a mere logical corollary from secondary or derivative doctrines. It is involved in the very meaning of Utility, or the Greatest-Happiness Principle. That principle is a mere form of words without rational signification, un-less one person's happiness, supposed equal in degree (with the proper allowance made for kind), is counted for exactly as much as another's. Those conditions being supplied, Bentham's dictum, "everybody to count for one, nobody for more than one," might be written under the principle of utility as an explanatory commentary. The equal claim of everybody to happiness in the estimation of the moralist and the legislator, involves an equal claim to all the means of happiness, except in so far as the inevitable conditions of human life, and the general interest, in which that of every individual is included, set limits to the maxim; and those limits ought to be strictly construed. As every other maxim of justice, so this, is by no means applied or held applicable universally; on the contrary, as I have already remarked, it bends to every person's ideas of social expediency. But in whatever case it is deemed applicable at all, it is held to be the dictate of justice. All persons are deemed to have a *right* to equality of treatment, except when some recognised social expediency requires the reverse. And hence all social inequalities which have ceased to be considered expedient, assume the character not of simple inexpediency, but of injustice.

For utilitarians the principle of utility does not compete with other principles, because only utilitarian considerations are relevant to moral decision-making. The principle of utility is the principle from which all other principles are derived or validated; it is an absolute rule that serves, in Mill's words, as a "common umpire" in all instances of conflicting obligations. Although utilitarianism is an *absolutism of principle,* no moral action and no rule other than the principle of utility is absolutely wrong in itself, and consequently, no *rule* in the system of utilitarian rules is unrevisable. Even rules against killing or rules protecting liberty may be revised or substantially overturned.

## THE CONCEPT OF UTILITY

Utilitarianism is commonly recognized as having a strong intuitive appeal: The view that agents should perform actions that will produce more good for people than any other action seems both attractive and innocent. Nonetheless, important objections have been raised against utilitarianism. Both sides of this dispute will be presented and assessed here.

All utilitarians share the conviction that human actions are to be morally assessed in terms of their production of maximal value or goodness. But how are we to determine what things are valuable and to be achieved in any given circumstance? What does the notion of "utility" involve? Major disputes have erupted among utilitarians on this point.

Many, although not all, utilitarians agree that ultimately we ought to act to bring about circumstances that are *intrinsically,* rather than *extrinsically,* valuable. This distinction deserves elaboration. An intrinsic value is one that we wish to possess and enjoy for its own sake and not for something to which it leads. These values are "agent-neutral," meaning they do not vary from person to person; they are good in themselves and not merely good as a means to something else. An extrinsic value, by contrast, is one that we wish to possess as a means to another end. Wealth is an example. The possession of wealth is usually valued not for the sake of having stacks of money but, rather, because the money can be used to purchase important goods and services in life. Money, we might say, is good only as a means to other things. But some things that money will buy—for example, the pleasures of eating artfully and tastefully prepared meals—seem good in themselves. They are intrinsically valuable apart from the consequences they produce. Utilitarians have traditionally believed that we ought to seek and promote experiences and conditions that are good in themselves, and that all extrinsic goods or instrumentally valuable things are ultimately to be produced for the sake of obtaining intrinsic goods.

Because intrinsic values such as the pleasure of eating delicious food have no moral significance, what is *morally* good must be distinguished from what is *intrinsically* good. Utilitarians hold that the moral quality of actions is to be determined by our efforts to maximize the production of such nonmoral intrinsic values as pleasure and health (nonmoral because they are the general goal of many human activities, such as art, athletics, and learning, and thus not distinctly moral values comparable to fulfilling a moral obligation). Consider again the research study of hypertension discussed at the beginning of this chapter. The pursuit of health is not in itself a moral endeavor, and a normal blood pressure is not a moral good in the way virtuous conduct is. However, when public health officials act to promote or improve public health through policies, the moral worth of their actions is determined by their efforts to maximally promote the health of others, while minimizing risks.

For Bentham and Mill, ethical theory is grounded in a theory of the general goal of life, which they claim is the pursuit of pleasure and the avoidance of pain. The production of pleasure and pain assumes moral and not merely personal significance for them when the consequences of actions importantly affect pleasurable or painful states of existence for others. Moral rules and moral and legal institutions such as criminal punishment, as they see it, are grounded in such a general theory of the goals and values of life. Morally good actions are determined by reference to these final values. Utilitarians have not always agreed on these goals and values, but one main task for many utilitarians has been to provide an acceptable theory that explains why certain things are intrinsically good and that also includes lists and categories of such goods.

A distinction between *hedonistic* and *pluralistic* utilitarianism has been drawn within utilitarian theories committed to intrinsic value. Bentham and Mill are hedonistic utilitarians because they conceive of utility entirely in terms of happiness or pleasure. In effect, they argue that the good is equivalent to happiness, which is equivalent to pleasure (although they do not argue that the word "good" *means* happiness or pleasure in ordinary language). All other things are valuable only as means to the production of pleasure or the avoidance of pain. Bentham, for example, viewed utility as that aspect of any action or practice that tends to produce different pleasures in the form of benefit, advantage, good, the prevention of pain, and so forth:

> Nature has placed mankind under the governance of two sovereign masters, *pain* and *pleasure*. It is for them alone to point out what we ought to do, as well as to determine what we shall do. On the one hand the standard of right and wrong, on the other the chain of causes and effects, are fastened to their throne. They govern us in all we do, in all we say, in all we think. . . . The *principle of utility* recognises this subjection, and assumes it for the foundation of that system, the object of which is to rear the fabric of felicity by the hands of reason and of law. Systems which attempt to question it, deal in sounds instead of sense, in caprice instead of reason, in darkness instead of light. . . .
>
> By utility is meant that property in any object, whereby it tends to produce benefit, advantage, pleasure, good, or happiness, (all this in the present case comes to the same thing) or (what comes again to the same thing) to prevent the happening of mischief, pain, evil, or unhappiness to the party whose interest is considered: if that party be the community in general, then the happiness of the community: if a particular individual, then the happiness of that individual. . . .
>
> To take an exact account then of the general tendency of any act, by which the interests of a community are affected, proceed as follows. Begin with any one person of those whose interests seem most immediately to be affected by it. . . . Sum up all the values of all the *pleasures* on the one side, and those of all the pains on the other. The balance, if it be on the side of pleasure, will give the *good* tendency of the act upon the whole, with respect to the interest of that *individual* person; if on the side of pain, the *bad* tendency of it upon the whole.
>
> Take an account of the *number* of persons whose interests appear to be concerned; and repeat the above process with respect to each. *Sum up* the numbers expressive of the degrees of *good* tendency, which the act has, with respect to each individual, in regard to whom the tendency of it is *good* upon the whole: do this again with respect to each individual, in regard to whom the tendency of it is *bad* upon the whole. Take the *balance;* which, if on the side of *pleasure,* will give the general *good tendency* of the act, with respect to the total number or community of individuals concerned; if on the side of pain, the general *evil tendency,* with respect to the same community.[3]

---

[3]From Jeremy Bentham, in J. H. Burns and H. L. A. Hart, eds., *An Introduction to the Principles of Morals and Legislation,* with an Introduction by F. Rosen (New York: Clarendon Press, 1996).

For philosophers like Bentham and Mill, the principle of utility demands that we perform actions that produce the maximum possible happiness. Mill went to considerable lengths to clarify his broad use of the term "happiness." He insisted that happiness does not refer merely to "pleasurable excitement," but rather encompasses a realistic appraisal of the pleasurable moments afforded in life, whether they take the form of tranquility or passion. Because Bentham believed both that pleasure and freedom from pain are the only desirable ends and that pleasures and pains could be measured and compared, he was led to argue (as in the passage just quoted) that pleasure and pain can be measured by a hedonic calculus. To determine an action's moral value, the actor is exhorted to add up the total happiness to be produced, subtract the pains involved, and then determine the balance, which expresses the moral value of the act. Thus, one is enjoined literally to *calculate* what ought morally to be done.

One objection to this form of utilitarianism is that the quantification of intrinsic value is either impossible or impractical. Whatever the merit of this objection, which is considered further in the final section of this chapter, even Mill and Bentham realized that it is impractical in daily affairs to pause and rationally calculate on every occasion which choices must be made. They did not expect individuals to engage in formal calculations of the type involved in Weinstein and Stason's study of hypertension. They maintained that we must rely heavily on our common sense, our habits, and our past experience. For example, we know that driving recklessly at high speeds is risky and that utility is maximized by careful driving. Mill and Bentham were agreed that we can ask for only reasonable predictability and choice, not perfect predictability.

Mill and Bentham were also aware that many human actions do not appear to be performed merely for the sake of happiness. For example, highly motivated professionals can work to the point of exhaustion for the sake of knowledge they hope to gain, although they might have chosen different and more pleasurable pursuits. Mill's explanation of this phenomenon is that these persons are initially motivated by thoughts of success or money, both of which promise pleasure or happiness, much in the way some students are attracted to college by the prospect that higher education will lead to a more prosperous life. Along the way, the activity—here, pursuit of knowledge—can become directly productive of happiness; or money or prestige may remain associated with an ultimate goal of pleasure, despite their not actually deriving much, if any, pleasure from the activity.

Some utilitarian philosophers have not looked favorably on the pleasure-centered conception of intrinsic value championed by Bentham and Mill. Pluralistic utilitarian philosophers, unlike hedonists, argue that there is no single goal or state constituting *the* good and that many values besides happiness possess intrinsic worth—for example, friendship, knowledge, love, courage, health, beauty, and perhaps moral qualities such as fairness. According to one defender of this view, G. E. Moore, even certain states of consciousness involving intellectual activity and aesthetic appreciation possess intrinsic value apart from their pleasantness. These pluralistic utilitarians argue that if pleasure or happiness were the sole good, then goods such as knowledge, love, friendship, and beauty would be good only because they produced pleasure or happiness. Yet, they believe these goods are good independent of any pleasure they may produce.

Imagine a world in which there is, say, sexual pleasure and no other good. In this world goods such as knowledge and beauty are absent, yet sexual pleasure produces more total happiness than exists in another world in which these goods are abundantly present. If the world involving only sexual pleasure offers more total happiness than the other world, a pure, quantitative hedonist must say it is a better or more desirable world. To many, this assumption seems a serious flaw in hedonistic utilitarianism, because they do not regard a world of abundant pleasure as being as *valuable* as a world having other forms of intrinsic value. Those who subscribe to a pluralist approach prefer to interpret the principle of utility as demanding that rightness or wrongness be assessed in terms of the greatest aggregate good, which is determined by multiple intrinsic goods.

Both the hedonistic and the pluralistic approaches have seemed to some recent philosophers relatively useless for purposes of objectively aggregating widely different interests in order to determine where maximal value, and, therefore, right action, lies. It is difficult and perhaps impossible to determine objectively what is intrinsically good on any given occasion, and this problem leads many utilitarians to interpret the good as that which is subjectively desired or wanted: the *satisfaction* of desires or wants is regarded as the goal of our moral actions. This third approach is based on individual *preferences,* and utility is analyzed in terms of an individual's actual preferences, rather than in terms of intrinsically valuable experiences. To maximize an individual's utility is to maximize the satisfaction derived from what he or she has chosen or would choose from the available alternatives. To maximize the utility of all persons affected by an action or a policy is to maximize the utility of the aggregate group.

This maximization is exactly what Weinstein and Stason attempted to achieve through their recommendation about public programs to treat hypertension, although here, as elsewhere in the formulation of policies, it is difficult to know what individuals actually prefer (e.g., whether they wish to be let alone or to be notified about their health problems). Nonetheless, those who adopt the preference model believe it is far easier to determine aggregate needs based on preferences than to calculate maximal value in terms of some ad hoc or dubious general conception of pleasurable or objectively good states of affairs. This approach is indifferent to hedonistic and pluralistic views of intrinsic value. What is "intrinsically" valuable is what each individual prefers to obtain, and utility is translated into the satisfaction of those needs and desires that individuals themselves choose to satisfy.

This utilitarian approach to value based on preferences is seen by many as superior to its predecessors for two reasons. First, recent disputes about hedonism and pluralism have proved difficult to resolve. One's choice of a range of these values in constructing a general theory of utility seems decisively affected by personal experience. This problem is avoided by using the preference approach, because there is no general theory of value or utility that ranges across individuals. Second, in order to make utilitarian calculations and interpersonal comparisons, it is necessary to measure values. According to Bentham and Mill, we must be able to measure happy and unhappy states and then compare one person's level of happiness with another's in order to decide which is quantitatively greatest. Later in this chapter, we will encounter a criticism of utilitarianism to the effect that we cannot objectively measure and compare the level of happiness of different individuals. Whatever the merits of this criticism, it does make sense to measure preferences more or less objectively by devising a utility scale that measures relative strengths of individual and group preferences. This procedure or its rough equivalent is used whenever municipalities vote on increased spending proposals and whenever polls are taken to ascertain which candidate among a range of alternative choices for public office is preferred.

The preference-utility approach may enjoy these advantages, but it is not trouble-free. A problem arises if individuals have morally unacceptable preferences (according to, say, conventional moral norms). For example, a person's strong sexual preference may be to rape young children, but this preference is morally intolerable. We discount this preference because it leads to immoral acts. Utilitarianism based purely on subjective preferences is satisfactory, then, only if a range of "acceptable" values can be formulated, where acceptability is agent-neutral and thus not a matter of preferences. This latter formulation has proved difficult in theory, and it may be inconsistent with a pure preference approach, because that approach logically ties human values to preferences, which by their nature are not agent-neutral.

Nonetheless, replies to this objection are open to utilitarians. First, because people are generally not perverse and have morally acceptable values, utilitarians believe they are justified in proceeding under the assumption that the preference approach is not fatally marred by a speculative problem. As Mill noted, any ethical theory whatever may lead to unsatisfactory outcomes if one assumes a certain degree of idiocy. Second, utilitarians sometimes argue that acceptable values are restricted to the objects of a *rational* desire, that is, to objects that any individual might rationally desire. Privacy, for example, is rationally desirable, but chopping off a neighbor's head in private is not. Third, because perverse desires undercut the objectives of utilitarianism by creating conditions productive of unhappiness, the desires could be disallowed. As Mill argued in the preceding selection, the cultivation of certain kinds of desires is built into the formulation of the "ideal" of utilitarianism, whereas others are excluded. For example, we might refuse to acknowledge someone's preference to taunt and jeer at mentally handicapped persons, not only because these preferences obstruct the preferences of the retarded but because, more generally, such preferences destroy or undermine respect for the preferences of all persons. Thus on utilitarian grounds some preferences deserve to be ignored in a calculus of goods. In this account, the principle of utility allows us to exclude some preferences on more general utilitarian grounds, once an experiential basis has been established.

However, even if people are not generally perverse and the ideals of utilitarianism are well entrenched in society, some rational agents may have preferences that are immoral or unjust by common standards. The utilitarian may therefore need a criterion of value to supplement preference. The attempt to exclude certain preferences in a *preference-based* theory of value does not seem consistent with the axioms of the theory. Moreover, agent-neutral values (intrinsic values) rather than subjective values seem essential in order to exclude some preferences in favor of others.

## ACT UTILITARIANISM

A significant controversy has arisen within utilitarianism over whether the principle of utility is to be applied to particular *actions* in particular circumstances or to *rules* of conduct that determine whether acts are right or wrong. For the rule utilitarian, actions are justified by appeal to rules such as "Don't deprive persons of freedom of opportunity." These rules are justified by appeal to the principle of utility. An act utilitarian justifies actions by direct appeal to the principle of utility without the buffer of rules.

David Hume perceptively noticed several differences between act and rule utilitarians, although he did not employ this terminology. First, he noticed that we are at times *motivated* to observe a moral rule because of the rule's position in a system of social rules. If there were no general scheme of rules of justice, for example, we might not be motivated to perform such morally praiseworthy actions as hiring new employees without respect to race, sex, or religion. Second, he noticed that there was a distinction between the claim that moral rules, such as that of truth-telling, generally have social utility and the claim that every single act of truth-telling has social utility. Moral rules condemn lying, according to this view, but occasionally lying to someone can have overriding utility in particular circumstances. Hume observed that rules that are justified by their general utilitarian consequences may, in particular circumstances, require us to perform actions that do not maximize utility in those circumstances. Fulfilling a contract to spray a farmer's tract of land with a pesticide, for example, falls under a rule that one should abide by one's promises. This is a commendable social rule, justified by utility. Nonetheless, fulfilling one's obligations under this rule could endanger the public interest on some occasions.

Let us now explore this elementary formulation of the differences between act and rule utilitarians with a closer look at each of the two schools. Act utilitarianism is often characterized as a "direct" or "extreme" theory, because the act utilitarian asks only, "What good and evil consequences will result directly from this action in this circumstance?" and not, "What good and evil consequences will result generally from this *sort* of action?" An action is morally right if, and only if, it produces at least as great a balance of value over disvalue as any other action open to the person; or, in short, the right act is that which has the greatest utility *in the circumstances*. This posture seems appropriate for utilitarians, because the theory aims fundamentally at maximizing value, and the direct way of achieving this goal would seem to be that of maximizing value on every single occasion.

This position does not demand, however, that every single time we act, we must determine what should be done without reference to general guidelines. We learn from past experience, and the act utilitarian does permit summary rules of thumb. The act utilitarian regards generalizations such as "You ought to tell the truth" as useful but not unmodifiable prescriptions. However, the act utilitarian insists that the main question is always, "What should I do now?" and not, "What has proved generally valuable in the past?" Act utilitarians think observances of a general rule (of truth-telling in this case) do not always promote the general good. An investigative reporter seeking facts for a newspaper, for example, might have to lie and break laws of privacy and confidentiality; yet the act utilitarian might judge these acts justifiable in contexts in which information critical for the public good could not otherwise be obtained. Because human situations are infinitely variable, rules of thumb devised from previous cases may not suffice in a new circumstance. An act utilitarian thus would not hesitate to break any rule if its violation would lead to the greatest good for the greatest number.

Consider the following case, which actually occurred in the state of Kansas. An old woman lay ill and dying. Her suffering was now too much both for her and for her faithful husband of fifty-four years to stand, and she requested that he kill her. Stricken with grief but unable to bring himself to perform this act, the husband hired another man to kill her. Soon after, the agreement was consummated. An act utilitarian might reason that in this case, hiring another to kill a loved one was justified although in general such a practice cannot be condoned. After all, only the woman and her husband were directly affected, and relief of her pain was the main issue. It would be unfortunate, the act utilitarian might reason, if the "rules" against killing failed to allow for selective killings of this sort, because it is difficult to generalize from case to case. In a criminal trial, however, a jury convicted the husband of murder in this case and sentenced him to twenty-five years in prison. An act utilitarian might maintain that such a legalistic application of rules of criminal justice inevitably leads to injustices, and that rule utilitarianism cannot escape this consequence of a rule-based position.

This example indicates why act utilitarians regard rule utilitarians as unfaithful to the fundamental demand of the principle of utility. As Hume points out, there are many cases in which abiding by a generally beneficial rule will not prove maximally beneficial to the group of persons affected in the circumstances. Why, then, ought the rule to be obeyed if obedience does not maximize value? The contemporary act utilitarian J. J. C. Smart has argued that the rule utilitarian has no adequate reply to this criticism. In this passage, Smart further defends the act utilitarian use of rules of thumb and habitual actions in light of this criticism.

# An Outline of a System
# of Utilitarian Ethics*

## J. J. C. Smart

We may choose to habituate ourselves to behave in accordance with certain rules, such as to keep promises, in the belief that behaving in accordance with these

*From J. J. C. Smart, "An Outline of a System of Utilitarian Ethics," in J. J. C. Smart and Bernard Williams, *Utilitarianism: For and Against* (Cambridge, England: Cambridge University Press, 1973). Reprinted with permission of Cambridge University Press.

rules is generally optimific, and in the knowledge that we most often just do not have time to work out individual pros and cons. When we act in such an habitual fashion we do not of course deliberate or make a choice. The act-utilitarian will, however, regard these rules as mere rules of thumb, and will use them only as rough guides. Normally he will act in accordance with them when he has no time for considering probable consequences or when the advantages of such a consideration of consequences are likely to be outweighed by the disadvantage of the waste of time involved. He acts in accordance with rules, in short, when there is no time to think, and since he does not think, the actions which he does habitually are not the outcome of moral thinking. When he has to think what to do, then there is a question of deliberation or choice, and it is precisely for such situations that the criterion is intended.

It is, moreover, important to realize that there is no inconsistency whatever in an act-utilitarian's schooling himself to act, in normal circumstances, habitually and in accordance with stereotyped rules. He knows that a man about to save a drowning person has no time to consider various possibilities, such as that the drowning person is a dangerous criminal who will cause death and destruction, or that he is suffering from a painful and incapacitating disease from which death would be a merciful release, or that various timid people, watching from the bank, will suffer a heart attack if they see anyone else in the water. No, he knows that it is almost always right to save a drowning man, and in he goes. Again, he knows that we would go mad if we went in detail into the probable consequences of keeping or not keeping every trivial promise: we will do most good and reserve our mental energies for more important matters if we simply habituate ourselves to keep promises in all normal situations. Moreover, he may suspect that on some occasions personal bias may prevent him from reasoning in a correct utilitarian fashion. Suppose he is trying to decide between two jobs, one of which is more

highly paid than the other, though he has given an informal promise that he will take the lesser paid one. He may well deceive himself by underestimating the effects of breaking the promise (in causing loss of confidence) and by overestimating the good he can do in the highly paid job. He may well feel that if he trusts to the accepted rules he is more likely to act in the way that an unbiased act-utilitarian would recommend than he would be if he tried to evaluate the consequences of his possible actions himself. . . .

On these occasions when we do not act as a result of deliberation and choice, that is, when we act spontaneously, no method of decision, whether utilitarian or non-utilitarian, comes into the matter. What does arise for the utilitarian is the question of whether or not he should consciously encourage in himself the tendency to certain types of spontaneous feeling. There are in fact very good utilitarian reasons why we should by all means cultivate in ourselves the tendency to certain types of warm and spontaneous feeling.

Though even the act-utilitarian may on occasion act habitually and in accordance with particular rules, his criterion is, as we have said, *applied* in cases in which he does not act habitually but in which he deliberates and chooses what to do. Now the right action for an agent in given circumstances is, we have said, that action which produces better results than any alternative action. If two or more actions produce equally good results, and if these results are better than the results of any other action open to the agent, then there is no such thing as *the* right action: there are two or more actions which are *a* right action. However, this is a very exceptional state of affairs, which may well never in fact occur, and so usually I will speak loosely of the action which is *the* right one. . . .

It is true that the general concept of action is wider than that of deliberate choice. Many actions are performed habitually and without deliberation. But the actions for whose rightness we as agents want a criterion are, in the nature of the case, those done thinkingly and deliberately. An action is at any rate that sort of human performance which it is appropriate to praise, blame, punish or reward, and since it is often appropriate to praise, blame, punish, or reward habitual performances, the concept of action cannot be identified with that of the outcome of deliberation and choice. With habitual actions the only question that arises for an agent is that of whether or not he should strengthen the habit or break himself of it.

Smart's defense of act utilitarianism may rest, in the final analysis, on the belief that we will improve rather than harm the moral life if we practice *selective obedience* to rules, because such behavior will not erode either moral rules, our general respect for morality, or our habituated tendencies toward the common good. Rules, then, introduce stability in the moral life, but are not binding guides inasmuch as they should be modeled on dispensable rules of thumb.

Act utilitarianism of the sort Smart defends has been subjected to sharp criticism by both rule utilitarians and antiutilitarians. A major reason for its rejection is the claim that utilitarianism sometimes sanctions injustice and violations of rights. The argument is not that act utilitarianism always sanctions unjust actions, but that under certain hypothetical conditions immoral acts would be "morally demanded" if utility considerations alone prevail. Bearing in mind that act utilitarians consider *all* consequences of individual actions, reflect on the following classic counterexample that has been offered against act utilitarianism: A small town is disorganized and in economic distress. Unemployment is high and leadership is chaotic. The citizenry is depressed and unhappy. All the major social problems could be resolved by enslaving a small portion of this citizenry. The general level of happiness in the society would be increased by having a slave system, and the slaves would be no worse off in material terms than they were previously. Yet, it seems blatantly immoral to enslave a few in the service of the majority. The majority, we believe, has no right to treat the minority in this way. The principle of utility seems immoral if it could *under any circumstances* permit such a practice.

Another standard counterexample to act utilitarianism springs from wrong but undetectable actions. This objection is captured in the following hypothetical sequence of events. Suppose that you have made a promise to a close and faithful friend, a person whom you admire and respect, and from whom you have received many favors. Your friend, who will soon die of cancer, has asked you to deliver money after his death to an uncle who has helped him in the past, and you have promised to do so; but you know that this uncle is rich and will squander the money. Suppose now that the valuable consequences of not fulfilling the promise are greater than valuable consequences of keeping it. No act-utilitarian reason requires you to keep your promise, but, in fact, there does seem to be a good (nonutilitarian or rule-utilitarian) reason for keeping it—namely, that you promised.

These counterexamples show that act utilitarianism may be inconsistent with the common moral consciousness. That many have thought these criticisms sufficient to refute act utilitarians is, of course, no proof that the counterexamples are adequate. The act utilitarian might reply that although, ordinarily, promises should be kept and rights carefully guarded in order to maintain a climate of trust and security, such considerations fail to apply in cases in which more good would be produced by breaking promises and setting rights aside. The act utilitarian appreciates that such views may be inconsistent with ordinary moral convictions in some cases, but will add that we need to revise our ordinary convictions, not repudiate act utilitarianism. There is no reason to suppose that the common moral consciousness is reliable in all circumstances, and there is some reason to suppose that ordinary morality is tainted by various prejudices and outdated beliefs. Smart has argued that sometimes theory should take precedence over common morality, rather than assuming the priority is always the other way around. He also points out that *all* the consequences involved in having slave-owning societies and breaking promises would have to be taken into account when considering what should be done in single cases, including whether ordinary morality needs augmentation.

Act utilitarians also might maintain that making exceptions to standard rules is *consistent* with the common moral consciousness, because we all sometimes make exceptions to moral rules without any sense of committing a moral wrong. Using a different approach, the act utilitarian might point out that our common judgments are not settled in many cases. In effect, the act utilitarian is doing what philosophers have done and have been expected to do at least since Socrates: submitting the great moral issues of the day to philosophical scrutiny and eliciting reflection in the form of both theoretical and practical judgment. In the hypertension example, rule utilitarians might hold that treating all groups equally produces more long-term happiness because it produces social trust and respect among different classes. If the utilitarian's conclusions turn out to be radically different from the common morality, this too may not be so different from the conclusions reached by many other philosophers.

Weinstein and Stason's study of hypertension, described at the beginning of this chapter, provides a useful example of these act-utilitarian counterreplies. Ordinarily, one would strongly resist (for moral reasons) excluding the poor and minority groups from receiving public health benefits. Yet, the recommendations proffered by Weinstein and Stason give us pause to reconsider our "ordinary moral convictions" precisely *because* we have been given utilitarian reasons for reconsideration.

## RULE UTILITARIANISM

The counterexamples and objections considered in the preceding section are directed exclusively at act utilitarianism. They work less well as objections to rule utilitarianism, which maintains that rules have a central position in morality and cannot be compromised by the utilitarian demands of a particular situation. Such compromise would threaten the integrity and existence of moral rules, each of which was originally adopted because its general observance would maximize social utility better than any alternative rule (or lack of rule). It is, for example, morally wrong to cheat on examinations, income tax returns, and specifications for building houses, because the consequences of permitting or neglecting such actions would be disastrous. Rules are justified when they are the rules that maximize utility upon general acceptance of, and conformity to, them. An act's conformity to a socially valuable rule makes the action right—whereas, for the act utilitarian, the beneficial consequences of the act alone make it right or wrong.

The rule utilitarian believes this position is not vulnerable to objections to act utilitarianism encountered previously, because rules are not subject to the peculiar demands of individual circumstances. Rules are firm and protective of all classes of individuals, just as human rights are rigidly protective of all individuals independent of social circumstances. If the basic moral rules composing morality as we know it are sanctioned by utility, then it is hard to see how we can be led by these rules to immoral actions in particular circumstances.

Some rule utilitarians emphasize the utility of whole *codes* or *systems* of rules, rather than independent rules. Among the defenders of this position is the contemporary American philosopher Richard Brandt. He believes that the rightness or wrongness of individual acts is determined exclusively by reference to moral rules in an optimal code or system of rules. The system is assessed as a whole in terms of its utilitarian consequences. An optimal code is not to be understood as the body of rules that would, if everyone always conformed to the rules, maximize utility. This ideal is hopeless as a practical matter, because a code must take account of human desires and weaknesses, as well as social costs such as those of teaching and enforcing rules. The optimal code is the overall system of rules that realistically would have the effect of maximizing utility. This criterion roughly parallels the notion that a political constitution is to be judged by whether it maximizes social utility through all the articles and amendments it contains as a whole, inasmuch as the constitution's utility cannot be proved by considering each article or amendment in isolation from the others.

This moral-code approach allegedly has unique advantages. First, it gives us a solid basis on which to distinguish between what is obligatory and what is not: a rule states a true prima facie obligation if and only if (and to the degree that) the ideal or optimal code would need the rule in order to minimize harms and promote benefits. Second, persons are more likely to act to maximize utility throughout a society by the public advocacy of a whole system of rules, rather than by merely testing and attempting to gain adherence to single rules, each in isolation from others. Most of us are motivated to the acceptance of a whole way of life that is moral, and we think of morality as a system of integrated principles and rules. This thesis and others are explored in the following essay by Brandt.[4]

---

[4]Although this piece was published in 1967, Brandt continued to hold the views expressed in it until his death. For some later statements of his views, see his "Problems of Contemporary Utilitarianism: Real and Alleged," in Norman E. Bowie, ed., *Ethical Theory* (Indianapolis: Hackett Publishing Co., 1983); *Morality, Utilitarianism, and Rights* (New York: Cambridge University Press, 1992).

# Some Merits of One Form
# of Rule Utilitarianism*

## Richard B. Brandt

For convenience I shall refer to [my] theory as the "ideal moral code" theory. The essence of it is as follows: Let us first say that a moral code is "ideal" if its currency in a particular society would produce at least as much good per person (the total divided by the number of persons) as the currency of any other moral code. (Two different codes might meet this condition, but, in order to avoid complicated formulations, the following discussion will ignore this possibility.) Given this stipulation for the meaning of "ideal," the Ideal Moral Code theory consists in the assertion of the following thesis: *An act is right if and only if it would not be prohibited by the moral code ideal for the society; and an agent is morally blameworthy (praiseworthy) for an act if, and to the degree that, the moral code ideal in that society would condemn (praise) him for it.* . . .

For a moral code to have currency in a society, two things must be true. First, a high proportion of the adults in the society must subscribe to the moral principles, or have the moral opinions, constitutive of the code. Exactly how high the proportion should be, we can hardly decide on the basis of the ordinary meaning of "the moral code"; but probably it would not be wrong to re-

quire at least 90 percent agreement. . . . Second, we want to say that certain principles *A, B,* etc., belong to the moral code of a society only if they are recognized as such. That is, it must be that a large proportion of the adults of the society would respond correctly if asked, with respect to *A* and *B,* whether most members of the society subscribed to them. . . .

We must now give more attention to the conception of an ideal moral code, and how it may be decided when a given moral code will produce as much good per person as any other. We may, however, reasonably bypass the familiar problems of judgments of comparative utilities, especially when different persons are involved, since these problems are faced by all moral theories that have any plausibility. We shall simply assume that rough judgments of this sort are made and can be justified.

(*a*) We should first notice that, as "currency" has been explained above, a moral code could not be current in a society if it were too complex to be learned or applied. We may therefore confine our consideration to codes simple enough to be absorbed by human beings, roughly in the way in which people learn actual moral codes. . . .

(*b*) In deciding how much good the currency of a specific moral system would do, we consider the institutional setting as it is, as part of the situation. We are asking which moral code would produce the most good in the long run in this setting. One good to be reckoned, of course, might be that the currency of a

*From Richard B. Brandt, "Some Merits of One Form of Rule-Utilitarianism," a paper presented at a conference on moral philosophy, the University of Colorado, October 1965, revised and published in *University of Colorado Studies,* 1967, pp. 39–65. Reprinted by permission of the author and the University of Colorado Press.

given moral code would tend to change the institutional system.

(*c*) In deciding which moral code will produce the most per person good, we must take into account the probability that certain types of situation will arise in the society. For instance, we must take for granted that people will make promises and subsequently want to break them, that people will sometimes assault other persons in order to achieve their own ends, that people will be in distress and need the assistance of others, and so on. . . .

(*d*) It would be a great oversimplification if, in assessing the comparative utility of various codes, we confined ourselves merely to counting the benefits of people doing (refraining from doing) certain things, as a result of subscribing to a certain code. To consider only this would be as absurd as estimating the utility of some feature of a legal system by attending only to the utility of people behaving in the way the law aims to make them behave—and overlooking the fact that the law only reduces and does not eliminate misbehavior, as well as the disutility of punishment to the convicted, and the cost of the administration of criminal law. In the case of morals, we must weigh the benefit of the improvement in behavior as a result of the restriction built into conscience, against the cost of the restriction—the burden of guilt feelings, the effects of the training process, etc. . . .

It has been thought that the implications of rule-utilitarianisms for two types of situation are especially significant: (*a*) for situations in which persons are generally violating the recognized moral code, or some feature of it: and (*b*) for situations in which, because the moral code is generally respected, max-

imum utility would be produced by violation of the code by the agent. An example of the former situation (sometimes called a "state of nature" situation) would be widespread perjury in making out income tax declarations. An example of the latter situation would be widespread conformity to the rule forbidding walking on the grass in a park.

What are the implications of the suggested form of rule-utilitarianism for these types of situation? Will it prescribe conduct which is not utility maximizing in these situations? If it does, it will clearly have implications discrepant with those of act-utilitarianism—but perhaps unpalatable to some people.

It is easy to see how to go about determining what is right or wrong in such situations, on the above described form of rule-utilitarianism—it is a question of what an "ideal" moral code would prescribe. But it is by no means easy to see where a reasonable person would come out, after going through such an investigation. . . .

Far from "collapsing" into act-utilitarianism, the Ideal Moral Code theory appears to avoid the serious objections which have been leveled at direct [act] utilitarianism. One objection to the latter view is that it implies that various immoral actions (murdering one's elderly father, breaking solemn promises) are right or even obligatory if only they can be kept secret. The Ideal Moral Code theory has no such implication. For it obviously would not maximize utility to have a moral code which condoned secret murders or breaches of promise. W. D. Ross criticized act-utilitarianism on the ground that it ignored the personal relations important in ordinary morality, and he listed a half-dozen types of moral rule which he thought captured the main themes of thoughtful morality: obligations of fidelity, obligations of gratitude, obligations to make restitution for injuries, obligations to help other persons, to avoid injuring them, to improve one's self, and to bring about a just distribution of good things in life. An ideal moral code, however, would presumably contain substantially such rules in any society, doubtless not precisely as Ross stated them. So the rule-utilitarian need not fail to recognize the personal character of morality. . . .

The Ideal Moral Code theory has the advantage of implying that the moral rules recognized in a given society are not necessarily morally binding. They are binding only in so far as they maximize welfare, as contrasted with other possible moral rules. Thus if, in a given society, it is thought wrong to work on the Sabbath, to perform socially desirable abortions, or to commit suicide, it does not follow, on the Ideal Moral Code theory, that these things are necessarily wrong. The question is whether a code containing such prohibitions would maximize welfare. Similarly, according to this theory, a person may act wrongly in doing certain things which are condoned by his society. . . .

Let us examine the implications of the Ideal Moral Code theory by considering a typical example. Among the Hopi Indians, a child is not expected to care for his father (he is always in a different clan), whereas he is expected to care for his mother, maternal aunt, and maternal uncle, and so on up the female line (all in the same clan). It would be agreed by observers that this system does not work very well. The trouble with it is that the lines of institutional obligation and the lines of natural affection do not coincide, and, as a result, an elderly male is apt not to be cared for by anyone.

Can we show that an "ideal moral code" would call on a young person to take care of his maternal uncle, in a system of this sort? (It might also imply he should try to change the system, but that is another point.) One important feature of the situation of the young man considering whether he should care for his maternal uncle is that, the situation including the expectations of others being what it is, if he does nothing to relieve the distress of his maternal uncle, it is probable that it will not be relieved. His situation is very like that of the sole observer of an automobile accident; he is a mere innocent bystander, but the fact is that if he does nothing, the injured persons will die. So the question for us is whether an ideal moral code will contain a rule that, if someone is in a position where he can relieve serious distress, and where it is known that in all probability it will not be relieved if he does not do so, he should relieve the distress. The answer seems to be that it will contain such a rule: we might call it an "obligation of humanity." But there is a second, and more important point. Failure of the young person to provide for his maternal uncle would be a case of unfairness or free riding. For the family system operates like a system of insurance; it provides one with various sorts of privileges or protections, in return for which one is expected to make certain payments, or accept the risk of making certain payments. Our young man has already benefited by the system, and stands to benefit further; he has received care and education as a child, and later on his own problems of illness and old age will be provided for. On the other hand, the old man, who has (we assume) paid such premiums as the system calls on him to pay in life, is now properly expecting, in accordance with the system, certain services from a particular person whom the system designates as the one to take care of him. Will the ideal moral code require such a person to pay the premium in such a system? I suggest that it will, and we can call the rule in question an "obligation of fairness." So, we may infer that our young man will have a moral obligation to care for his maternal uncle, on grounds both of humanity and fairness.

Despite Brandt's attempt to put distance between rule and act forms of utilitarianism, an unresolved question remains: Can rule-utilitarian theories escape the very criticism they advance against act utilitarianism? Moral rules themselves often come into conflict in the moral life. On some occasions, for example, one must steal in order to preserve a life, or lie in order to preserve a secret one vowed to keep, or break a rule of confidentiality in order to protect a person endangered by its maintenance. In these cases, it must be decided which rule has priority. Are there rules that determine, at some second level, the relevance of other moral rules? Or must rule utilitarians admit that some moral decisions do not turn on rules? Even if everyone agreed on the same rules and on their interpretation, in one situation it might be better to break a confidence in order to protect someone, while in another circumstance it might be better to keep the information confidential.

Mill briefly considered this problem of conflict and argued that the principle of utility should itself decide in any given circumstance which rule is to take priority over another rule. However, if this solution is accepted by rule utilitarians, then their theory seems to rely directly on the principle that one must decide *in particular situations* which action is preferable to alternative actions in the absence of a governing rule. This problem has led some to say that whenever rule utilitarianism is applied to concrete problems and dilemmas in the moral life, it cannot be distinguished from act utilitarianism. If this assertion is correct, then all the same criticisms and counterexamples that rule utilitarians bring against act utilitarians may fit rule utilitarianism itself.

The rule utilitarian, however, need not capitulate to this reduction of rule theory to act theory. The rule utilitarian can reply that a sense of relative weight and importance should be built into the rules themselves, in so far as is possible. The weight and importance attached to a rule are based on the relative social utility produced by having the rule—a judgment that must be made in advance of particular circumstances. For example, the rule utilitarian might argue that rules prohibiting punishment of the innocent are of such vital social significance (i.e., have such paramount social utility) that they can never be overridden by appeal to rules protecting the public against criminal activities, even if grave problems of public safety are at stake.

This rule-utilitarian strategy of relative (a priori) weighting should be adequate to handle some problems of conflict, but even the rule utilitarian must acknowledge that weights cannot be so definitely built into principles that irresolvable conflicts among rules will never arise. What the rule utilitarian will *not* acknowledge is that this problem is unique to rule utilitarianism. Every ethical theory seems to have practical limitations in cases of conflict. This problem is with the moral life itself, and is not unique to rule theory.

Act utilitarianism, too, seems faced with this problem, because circumstances will arise in which the principle of utility directs us to two equally attractive alternatives, only one of which can be pursued. The principle of utility itself cannot resolve this problem of conflict. In such cases, Smart argues, the act utilitarian will say, "There is no such thing as *the* right action: there are two or more actions which are *a* right action." Notice, however, that this same strategy is open to the rule utilitarian: In case of an irresolvable conflict between equally weighted rules, there is no such thing as *the* right action; there are two or more right actions.


## CRITICISMS AND DEFENSES OF UTILITARIANISM

We have seen that utilitarians, especially act utilitarians, have been criticized for allowing the majority interests to override the rights or legitimate interests of a minority. In this section, we pursue criticisms of utilitarianism further. Most, but not all, of these criticisms raise the question of whether consequences for human welfare are all that matter in morality. We will also consider replies that utilitarians might offer to these criticisms. This dialectical exchange of criticism and defense is extremely important, inasmuch as these arguments have played a central role in recent moral philosophy.


### Problems in Measuring Goodness and Comparing Utilities

One criticism of utilitarians centers on their apparent commitment to the measurement and comparison of goodness. Hedonistic and pluralistic utilitarians suggest that goods can be measured and the utilities of different persons compared, and yet they have not shown how to do so. They have also disagreed among themselves about the role of qualitative judgments. Mill argued that according to Bentham's account of utility, it would be better to be a satisfied pig than a dissatisfied Socrates. Mill believed that human experience reveals that some pleasures are qualitatively better than others—for example, that Socratic pleasures of the mind are qualitatively better than purely bodily pleasures. Mill thus had to grapple with additional problems about how to weigh qualitative considerations.

Because utility is to be maximized, a utilitarian choice involves comparing the different possible utilities of an action and making interpersonal utility calculations. But can individual goods or units of goodness be quantified and compared to determine whether one is better than another? Is there any nonarbitrary way of establishing a common unit and baseline for comparison? How does one compare the value of a good college education with the value of regular medical checkups, or public health education with publicly funded clinics for checkups? In the hypertension study, could one determine the public interest by quantifying and comparing the goods of affected parties?

It is difficult to rank personal preferences, and still more difficult, perhaps methodologically impossible, to compare one person's preferences with those of others. Although we can imagine creating utility scales for particular individuals by testing the strength of their preferences, we have no basis for comparing these scales to one another. Yet some comparison is required if one is to *maximize* the utility of everyone affected by one's actions.

Sometimes tacked onto this methodological problem is an informational difficulty: Even if we could create utility scales and methods of comparing them, the volume of information that would be necessary to carry out the utilitarian objective would be unacquirable. For example, in deciding whether to add a new county hospital, county officials would have to calculate all the utilities and disutilities of each possible hospital and its location for all county citizens. This calculation would have to include their preferences on taxes and county services, and should include the interests of future generations of citizens no less than the present generation.

A utilitarian reply to these criticisms is that every day we make crude, rough-and-ready comparisons of values, including pleasure and pain. For example, we decide to go to the theater rather than a baseball game, because we think it will be more pleasurable or will satisfy more members of a group than the game. At work, we devise systems of office management to reduce friction. In public policy more funds are allocated for cancer research than for the treatment of hypertension, and so forth. It is easy to overestimate the demands of utilitarianism, as well as the precision with which it may be employed.

## Does Utilitarianism Demand Too Much?:
## The Problem of Requiring Supererogatory Acts

A second criticism is that utilitarianism demands too much in the moral life, because the principle of utility is a *maximizing* principle. The argument is that utilitarians cannot maintain a crucial distinction between (1) *morally obligatory actions* (those required by a moral obligation) and (2) *supererogatory actions* (those above the call of moral obligation and done from personal ideals). This objection has been registered by Alan Donagan, who proposes situations in which, although it is our firm moral conviction that an action would be supererogatory rather than obligatory, utilitarians are still committed by their theory to regard the action as obligatory.[5] Rule utilitarians too must accept the commitment, Donagan says, because "there would be more good and less evil in society as a whole if the rule were adopted." For example, Donagan imagines a society with utilitarian rules dictating occasions on which "one person should die for the people."

Donagan would presumably regard suicide for those among the elderly and the disabled who are no longer of use to society and drain its resources as illustrations of an act that might be considered supererogatory but could never be rightly

[5]Alan Donagan, "Is There a Credible Form of Utilitarianism?" in Michael D. Bayles, ed., *Contemporary Utilitarianism* (Garden City, NY: Doubleday and Company, 1968). For an important and related criticism of utilitarianism, see Bernard Williams, *Ethics and the Limits of Philosophy* (Cambridge, MA: Harvard University Press, 1985), p. 77.

considered obligatory. A less extreme example would be a requirement that large amounts of personal income be given to charity whenever utilitarian goals would be served. One can think of many examples of Donagan's rule, including heroic sacrifice of bodily parts such as kidneys and hearts. If utilitarianism makes all such actions obligatory, then it does seem a defective theory. Donagan argues that *all* utilitarians face these problems, because none can rule out the ever-present possibility that what is now considered supererogatory will, through a changing social situation, become obligatory by utilitarian standards. As Donagan puts it, utilitarians cannot account for the distinction between obligatory and supererogatory acts, because their theory tends to be intolerant of the distinction or to eliminate it entirely.

A rule utilitarian must allow for the possibility that any type of action might become obligatory, because the acceptance or rejection of an action in utilitarianism depends upon existing social conditions. To this extent, Donagan is entirely correct. Nonetheless, under almost all social conditions, utility would not be served by having rules such as a rule requiring suicide, although one might in extreme cases be obligated to perform what would ordinarily be considered a supererogatory act. If this is correct, then utilitarianism may not deviate radically from conventional views about what is and is not obligatory.

Consider the following example of extreme "social" conditions: In Nazi Germany, some prisoners at the Treblinka concentration camp were ordered to exterminate their fellow prisoners by opening gas valves. Many committed suicide rather than carry out the order. Presumably their reasons for suicide were that they were obligated not to kill innocent persons and that suicide at their own hands was the only acceptable alternative. These prisoners felt obligated to commit suicide in order to preserve their moral integrity. However, the reason for the *obligation* (let us suppose that here suicide was the only morally satisfactory alternative) in this case is the requirement *to protect* (themselves and others) *from harm,* not some rule that specifically requires suicide. Even in this extreme case, a rule utilitarian would not propose a new rule requiring suicide. The rule utilitarian would hold that virtually all circumstances of obligation in extreme cases can be handled in this way.

The rule utilitarian also holds that in any moral code there is a point of diminishing returns concerning the number of rules that are publicly promulgated. There ought not to be so many rules that people cannot acquaint themselves with all of them, or rules that apply only infrequently, or rules that are so heavily qualified with exceptions that their interpretation is difficult. Because moral rules restrict choice, the social value derived from having a rule must be greater than the value that would be gained by not having one. Moreover, it is doubtful that any rule directly requiring recognizably supererogatory actions could achieve any positive end that the basic and stable rules of morality could not. The kinds of examples envisaged by Donagan—such as "one person should die for the people"—would likely lead to considerable disutility because of the confusion, insecurity, and distrust they would unleash on society.

Nevertheless, a rule utilitarian must leave open *in principle* the question of whether, under some social conditions, a rule requiring extraordinary acts such as suicide might validly be made a matter of social obligation rather than personal choice. A rule utilitarian must, for example, applaud the Hudson Bay tribes' rule that required mercy killing of the elderly. Survival at a decent level of human existence depended in that community upon the institutionalization of this rule in their moral code, and it was fairly applied. One can also think of dire social circumstances that might involve a similar rationing of life. For example, imagine that a large plane has been forced down in a remote, snowy region where it is invisible from the air. Outsiders do not know where the plane has crashed, and rescue efforts are precluded until the weather warms and the snow melts. Imagine a moral code devised in such a minisociety: A contract is agreed to by all that cannibalism is necessary in order for some to survive until the spring thaw. Those who will be devoured will be chosen at random, and ones so selected must commit suicide (so that no one can be prosecuted later). The normal rules against murder will prevail.

Rule utilitarians would hold that under these and other extreme circumstances, a rule requiring suicide should impartially control everyone's conduct and ought to be given a prominent place in the moral code of the society. Under these circumstances, not committing suicide would encourage and perhaps produce a general breakdown in the orderly system, so that none could live. A utilitarian who adopted this argument might escape Donagan's censure, because what in conventional cases is either supererogatory or excusably wrong (beyond a normal obligation) becomes obligatory for theoretically sound reasons. The rule utilitarian believes that unpalatable rules are not dictated except in unpalatable circumstances beyond the normal range of morality, and thus that Donagan's objection fails to overturn the utilitarian philosophy.

### Does Utilitarianism Permit Too Much?: The Problem of Unjust Distributions

A third criticism is that utilitarianism permits too much—in particular, that it permits the interests of the majority to overrun the rights of minorities and in various ways leads to injustice, especially to unjust social distributions. This criticism envisions situations in which demands of justice conflict with demands of utility, a clear tip that utility alone is not the whole of morality and that, in making utility the whole, utilitarianism overvalues communities or aggregate groups while undervaluing individuals. We already encountered one form of this criticism when discussing the slave society and punishment of the innocent. Many philosophers believe this general objection can, with but slight reformulation, be extended to cover all forms of utilitarianism.

Consider again the slave society. If a slave society produced the greatest happiness for the greatest number, it would seem that a rule utilitarian would have to say that the *practice* of slavery in that society was morally obligatory. This suggests that the principle of utility is not broad enough to capture our sense of distributive justice. If this criticism can be sustained, the principle of utility will have to be supplemented by nonutilitarian principles of justice.

Mill resists this conclusion. Book V, his final book in *Utilitarianism*, is devoted to the subject of justice. Mill knew there were tensions between the idea of firm principles of justice and utilitarian balancing, and he knew that many people resist accepting utilitarianism because they think justice rather than utility is the criterion of some judgments of right and wrong. People generally think the superior binding force of justice means that it has a noncontingent status and is not a matter of efficient distribution to the greatest number. To overcome this problem, Mill proposed that all persons have moral rights in justice. Justice is simply the name for the strongest set of obligations generated by the principle of utility; these obligations entail a correlative right in a person or persons. As such, principles of justice are dependent upon, rather than independent of, utility.

But Mill's critics have wondered how utilitarianism supports these protections of the individual. How, they ask, can utilitarians support documents such as the Bill of Rights to the U.S. Constitution, which rigidly protects citizens from unreasonable interventions in the name of the public good. Utilitarian reasoning, as critics see it, is closely connected to cost-benefit analysis, which requires that an evaluation of all the benefits and costs of a potential program or action be made in order to determine which among alternative programs or actions is to be recommended. Cost-benefit analyses may reveal that a particular government program or a new technology will prove highly beneficial, and yet provision of this benefit might function prejudicially in a free-market economy by denying basic medical or welfare services to disadvantaged members of society. Planning efforts employing cost-benefit analysis are thus morally mistaken, say these critics, because they fail to account for our sense of distributive justice. Weinstein and Stason's study of hypertension is a perfect example.

Mill and other utilitarians might reply to these objections by agreeing that it is not always permissible to follow the dictates of one-time or short-range calculations of costs and benefits. For example, suppose that crop dusting were done with a new pesticide that significantly increased the profits of an agribusiness over the profits that would be realized using a less toxic but less effective pesticide. But suppose the more profitable pesticide kills, on the average, 2 of every 295 farm workers who are exposed to the spraying for more than a year. A rule utilitarian would agree that it would be immoral to use the pesticide, even if statistical calculations indicate a highly favorable overall cost-benefit equation. The argument might be similar for Weinstein and Stason's recommendation about hypertension, which is squarely based on cost-benefit considerations: If deserving individuals would be harmed or unjustifiably neglected by government health programs, the programs must be modified. The rule utilitarian bases this reply on a framework of moral rules that recognizes cost efficiency as constituting only *one* of a series of factors that must be considered in determining health policy. Findings about how to maximize health (per public dollar invested) for individuals must be considered along with moral rules governing just distribution and fair opportunity.

Thus, from a utilitarian perspective, rights can legitimately constrain direct appeals to utility maximization as long as the justification of the rights is itself based in a system of rules that maximizes utility. The only additional qualification that must be introduced into this account is that when rights come into conflict, that conflict can be adjudicated only by direct appeal to the principle of utility.

The above criticisms of utilitarianism can be further clarified by drawing a distinction between *classic* utilitarianism and *average* utilitarianism. Classic utilitarianism understands utility in terms of maximizing the overall sum of net utility produced for aggregate groups, whereas average utilitarianism understands utility in terms of maximizing the average of the utility produced for each member of the group, which is aggregate utility divided by the total number of affected individuals. Average utilitarianism can be formulated with a built-in egalitarian requirement that utility be distributed equally to individuals in the group, and this distributional idea may help defeat some of the above objections. This assumes, of course, that average utilitarianism is consistent with the very maximizing rule that governs utilitarian thinking.

## Is Utilitarianism Inconsistent with the Value of Autonomy?

The concerns about whether an unconstrained utilitarianism adequately protects rights can be extended to questions about whether utilitarianism can adequately support respect for autonomy (and corresponding rights to liberty; see Chapter 10). In utilitarianism, autonomy is to be protected *because* its protection promotes well-being for autonomous individuals. Autonomy and individuality therefore are valuable only derivatively; they are extrinsic values leading to the intrinsic value of welfare. Yet there is a strong conviction in some philosophers that this approach undervalues autonomy, personal integrity, and personhood.

Utilitarianism looks at persons (at least for purposes of ethical theory) as sites at which desires and their fulfillment or nonfulfillment occur. Moral obligations then turn on producing utility at these sites. But are persons merely repositories for a set of utilities? Or has the utilitarian accepted a ridiculously narrow view of the nature of a person? What are we to say of nonutility considerations, such as personal integrity, friendship, and familial ties? Is there a general indifference in utilitarianism to the separateness, uniqueness, and identity of individuals?

Philosopher Bernard Williams has argued that utilitarianism abrades personal integrity because it requires one to be as morally responsible for the consequences one fails to prevent as for those one directly causes—even when the former is not of one's own doing. An example is found in utilitarian Peter Singer, who defends an "obligation to assist" such that "if it is in our power to prevent something bad from happening, without thereby sacrificing anything of comparable moral importance, we ought, morally, to do it."[6] This principle requires us to alleviate a harmful condition even if we had no causal role in bringing it about, and Singer insists that the principle applies not only to saving a drowning child from a pond, but to assisting persons who live in poverty. Singer thus requires that we give money to alleviate earthquake disasters, homelessness, and malnutrition in children until we reach a level at which, by giving more, we will cause as much suffering to ourselves as we relieve through our gifts.

Williams objects to such theories. He points out that in order to achieve this goal one would constantly be giving up the projects and commitments in life that one cares deeply about. He states his objection as follows:

[6]Peter Singer, "Famine, Affluence, and Morality," in William Aiken and Hugh LaFollette, eds., *World Hunger and Morality*, 2d ed. (Upper Saddle River, NJ: Prentice Hall, 1996), p. 28.

How can a man, as a utilitarian agent, come to regard as one satisfaction among others, and a dispensable one, a project or attitude round which he has built his life, just because someone else's projects have so structured the causal scheme that that is how the utilitarian sum comes out?" . . . [This demand] is to alienate him in a real sense from his actions and the source of his action in his own convictions. . . . This is to neglect the extent to which *his* actions and *his* decisions have to be seen as the actions and decisions which flow from the projects and attitudes with which he is most closely identified. It is thus, in the most literal sense, an attack on his integrity.[7]

Williams's criticism is closely connected to the earlier criticism that utilitarians require too much (in the form of supererogation) in the moral life. If each agent must make the happiness of all persons a matter of personal responsibility, this demand is burdensome. John Mackie has said that this utilitarian "test of right actions" will fail both because it is too onerous and because it is so thoroughly removed from our experience as to be "the ethics of fantasy." Mackie agrees with Williams that universal utilitarian expectations demand that people strip themselves of the things we value most in life—close affections, private pursuits, and many kinds of competition.[8]

These criticisms by Williams and Mackie are closely related to some criticisms advanced by Robert Nozick in *Anarchy, State, and Utopia*. Nozick argues that utilitarianism wrongly understands persons and allows some people to be used as "tools" for the good of others. In so doing utilitarianism ignores the separateness of persons and illegitimately treats society as if it were one social entity whose good we ought to maximize. Nozick argues that there is no such social entity; there are only individuals, each with his or her own goals. To treat someone as a means in order to bring about good consequences for others is to fail to respect that person as an individual.

# *Moral Constraints and Moral Goals**

### Robert Nozick

This question assumes that a moral concern can function only as a moral *goal,* as an end state for some activities to achieve as their result. It may, indeed, seem to be a necessary truth that "right,"

*From Robert Nozick, *Anarchy, State, and Utopia* (New York: Basic Books, 1974).

"ought," "should," and so on, are to be explained in terms of what is, or is intended to be, productive of the greatest good. . . . It is often thought that what is wrong with utilitarianism (which *is* of this form) is its too narrow conception of good. Utilitarianism doesn't, it is said, properly take rights and their non-violation into account; it instead leaves

[7]See "A Critique of Utilitarianism," in J. J. C. Smart and Bernard Williams, *Utilitarianism: For and Against* (Cambridge, England: Cambridge University Press, 1973), pp. 116–7.

[8]J. L. Mackie, *Ethics: Inventing Right and Wrong* (New York: Penguin Books, 1977), pp. 129, 133.

them a derivative status. Many of the counterexample cases to utilitarianism fit under this objection, for example, punishing an innocent man to save a neighborhood from a vengeful rampage. But a theory may include in a primary way the nonviolation of rights, yet include it in the wrong place and the wrong manner. For suppose some condition about minimizing the total (weighted) amount of violations of rights is built into the desirable end state to be achieved. We then would have something like a "utilitarianism of rights"; violations of rights (to be *minimized*) merely would replace the total happiness as the relevant end state in the utilitarian structure. (Note that we do not hold the nonviolation of our rights as our sole greatest good or even rank it first lexicographically to exclude trade-offs, if there is some desirable society we would choose to inhabit even though in it some rights of ours sometimes are violated, rather than move to a desert island where we could survive alone.) This still would require us to violate someone's rights when doing so minimizes the total (weighted) amount of the violation of rights in the society. For example, violating someone's rights might deflect others from *their* intended action of gravely violating rights, or might remove their motive for doing so, or might divert their attention, and so on. A mob rampaging through a part of town killing and burning *will* violate the rights of those living there. Therefore, someone might try to justify his punishing another *he* knows to be innocent of a crime that enraged a mob, on the grounds that punishing this innocent person would help to avoid even greater violations of rights by others, and so would lead to a minimum weighted score for rights violations in the society.

In contrast to incorporating rights into the end state to be achieved, one might place them as side constraints upon the actions to be done: don't violate constraints $C$ such as the right of each individual to dispose of his or her property as he or she sees fit. The rights of others determine the constraints upon your actions. (A *goal-directed* view with constraints added would be: among those acts available to you that don't violate constraints $C$, act so as to maximize goal $G$. Here, the rights of others would constrain your goal-directed behavior. I do not mean to imply that the correct moral view includes mandatory goals that must be pursued, even within the constraints.) This view differs from one that tries to build the side constraints $C$ *into* the goal $G$. The side-constraint view forbids you to violate these moral constraints in the pursuit of your goals; whereas the view whose objective is to minimize the violation of these rights allows you to violate the rights (the constraints) in order to lessen their total violation in the society.

The claim that the proponent of the ultraminimal state is inconsistent, we now can see, assumes that he is a "utilitarian of rights." It assumes that his goal is, for example, to minimize the weighted amount of the violation of rights in the society, and that he should pursue this goal even through means that themselves violate people's rights. Instead, he may place the nonviolation of rights as a constraint upon action, rather than (or in addition to) building it into the end state to be realized. The position held by this proponent of the ultraminimal state will be a consistent one if his conception of rights holds that your being *forced* to contribute to another's welfare violates your rights, whereas someone else's not providing you with things you need greatly, including things essential to the protection of your rights, does not *itself* violate your rights, even though it avoids making it more difficult for someone else to violate them. (That conception will be consistent provided it does not construe the monopoly element of the ultraminimal state as itself a violation of rights.) That it is a consistent position does not, of course, show that it is an acceptable one.

Isn't it *irrational* to accept a side constraint *C*, rather than a view that directs minimizing the violations of *C*? (The latter view treats *C* as a condition rather than a constraint.) If nonviolation of *C* is so important, shouldn't that be the goal? How can a concern for the nonviolation of *C* lead to the refusal to violate *C* even when this would prevent other more extensive violations of *C*? What is the rationale for placing the nonviolation of rights as a side constraint upon action instead of including it solely as a goal of one's actions?

Side constraints upon action reflect the underlying Kantian principle that individuals are ends and not merely means; they may not be sacrificed or used for the achieving of other ends without their consent. Individuals are inviolable. More should be said to illuminate this talk of ends and means. Consider a prime example of a means, a tool. There is no side constraint on how we may use a tool, other than the moral constraints on how we may use it upon others. There are procedures to be followed to preserve it for future use ("don't leave it out in the rain"), and there are more and less efficient ways of using it. But there is no limit on what we may do to it to best achieve our goals. Now imagine that there was an overrideable constraint *C* on some tool's use.

For example, the tool might have been lent to you only on the condition that *C* not be violated unless the gain from doing so was above a certain specified amount, or unless it was necessary to achieve a certain specified goal. Here the object is not *completely* your tool, for use according to your wish or whim. But it is a tool nevertheless, even with regard to the overrideable constraint. If we add constraints on its use that may not be overridden, then the object may not be used as a tool *in those ways. In those respects,* it is not a tool at all. . . .

A specific side constraint upon action toward others expresses the fact that others may not be used in the specific ways the side constraint excludes. Side constraints express the inviolability of others, in the ways they specify. These modes of inviolability are expressed by the following injunction: "Don't use people in specified ways." An end-state view, on the other hand, would express the view that people are ends and not merely means (if it chooses to express this view at all), by a different injunction: "Minimize the use in specified ways of persons as means." Following this precept itself may involve using someone as a means in one of the ways specified. Had Kant held this view, he would have given the second formula of the categorical imperative as, "So act as to minimize the use of humanity simply as a means," rather than the one he actually used: "Act in such a way that you always treat humanity, whether in your own person or in the person of any other, never simply as a means, but always at the same time as an end."[1]

---

[1]*Groundwork of the Metaphysic of Morals.* Translated by H. J. Paton, *The Moral Law* (London: Hutchinson, 1956), p. 96.

Side constraints express the inviolability of other persons. But why may not
one violate persons for the greater social
good? Individually, we each sometimes
choose to undergo some pain or sacrifice for a greater benefit or to avoid a
greater harm: we go to the dentist to
avoid worse suffering later; we do some
unpleasant work for its results; some
persons diet to improve their health or
looks; some save money to support
themselves when they are older. In each
case, some cost is borne for the sake of
the greater overall good. Why not, *similarly,* hold that some persons have to
bear some costs that benefit other persons more, for the sake of the overall social good? But there is no *social entity*
with a good that undergoes some sacrifice for its own good. There are only
individual people, different individual
people, with their own individual lives.
Using one of these people for the benefit of others, uses him and benefits the
others. Nothing more. What happens is
that something is done to him for the
sake of others. Talk of an overall social
good covers this up. (Intentionally?) To

use a person in this way does not sufficiently respect and take account of the
fact that he is a separate person,[2] that his
is the only life he has. *He* does not get
some overbalancing good from his sacrifice, and no one is entitled to force this
upon him—least of all a state or government that claims his allegiance (as other
individuals do not) and that therefore
scrupulously must be *neutral* between
its citizens.

The moral side constraints upon what
we may do, I claim, reflect the fact of
our separate existences. They reflect the
fact that no moral balancing act can
take place among us; there is no moral
outweighing of one of our lives by
others so as to lead to a greater overall
*social* good. There is no justified sacrifice of some of us for others. This
root idea, namely, that there are different individuals with separate lives
and so no one may be sacrificed for
others, underlies the existence of moral
side constraints. . . .

[2]See John Rawls, *A Theory of Justice,* sects. 5, 6, 30.

### Does Utilitarianism Overplay "Impartiality"?

Consider now a criticism of utilitarianism advanced by one of Bentham's contemporaries who was himself an ardent and uncompromising utilitarian: William Godwin (1756–1836). Godwin repudiated as utterly immoral any claim to have an
obligation unless the obligation rested on "the general welfare." Suppose there is a
fire, said Godwin, and you can either save an archbishop or his chambermaid, who
happens to be your mother. The matter is clear to Godwin; morally, you must save
the archbishop because of his potential for good works. The special relationship between you and your mother is irrelevant—unless, Godwin acknowledged later in his
writings, the cultivation of domestic affections could themselves be construed as
contributing to the general happiness. This example raises the problem of whether a
utilitarian adduces an unacceptable premise of impartial, universalistic obligation.

There is an additional problem about what Godwin, Mill, and others call "the
general welfare" and "all those affected by an action." Whose welfare is at stake?

The members of a community? The members of the human species? All sentient animals? Here we have a debate over whose interests are to count, and how heavily they are to count. If this matter cannot be decided within utilitarianism, it seems that the utilitarian must appeal to a set of values independent of the utilitarian framework. The adoption of any such value is tantamount to a denial of the adequacy of utilitarianism as a moral system.

## CONCLUSION

We have seen that utilitarianism offers the broad outlines of a theory of moral justification and moral reform. Utilitarians invite us to consider the whole point or function of morality as a social institution, where the term "morality" comprises all common rules of justice and the moral life. The point of morality, they insist, is to promote human welfare by minimizing harms and maximizing benefits. There would be no reason to have moral codes and understandings unless they served this purpose. Many utilitarians regard the principle of utility as the sole correct means of protecting individual rights and maintaining broad social objectives. How else, the utilitarian might ask, could one justify the requirements of the moral point of view if not by appeal to the goal of promoting human welfare or preventing evil?

## SUGGESTED SUPPLEMENTARY READINGS

### Classics of Utilitarianism

Bentham, Jeremy: *Introduction to the Principles of Morals and Legislation* (1789), in W. Harrison, ed., *A Fragment on Government* (Oxford, England: Hafner Press, 1948).

Mill, John Stuart: *On Liberty* (London: J. W. Parker, 1859). Many editions.

———: *Utilitarianism* (London: Longmans, Green, and Company, 1863). Many editions.

Moore, George E.: *Principia Ethica* (Cambridge, England: Cambridge University Press, 1903).

———: *Ethics* (New York: Oxford University Press, 1965), especially chaps. 1, 2, and 5.

Sidgwick, Henry: *The Methods of Ethics,* 7th ed. (London: Macmillan and Company, 1963), especially I.9, II.1, III.11–13, and IV.1–5.

### Commentaries on Mill

Brink, David O.: "Mill's Deliberative Utilitarianism," *Philosophy and Public Affairs,* 21 (Winter 1992): 67–103.

Crisp, Roger: *Routledge Philosophy Guidebook to Mill on Utilitarianism* (New York: Routledge, 1997).

Donner, Wendy: *The Liberal Self: John Stuart Mill's Moral and Political Philosophy* (Ithaca, NY: Cornell University Press, 1991).

Dryer, Douglas P.: "Mill's Utilitarianism," in John M. Robson, ed., *Collected Works of John Stuart Mill* (Toronto: University of Toronto Press, 1969), vol. 10.

Gorovitz, Samuel, ed.: *Mill: Utilitarianism, with Critical Essays* (New York: Bobbs-Merrill Company, 1971).

Gray, J. N.: *John Stuart Mill's Doctrine of Liberty: A Defence* (London: Routledge and Kegan Paul, 1983).

Habibi, Don: "J. S. Mill's Revisionist Utilitarianism," *British Journal for the History of Philosophy,* 6 (1998): 89–114.

Lyons, David, ed.: *Mill's Utilitarianism: Critical Essays* (Lanham, MD: Rowman & Littlefield, 1997).

Skorupski, John, ed.: *The Cambridge Companion to Mill* (New York: Cambridge University Press, 1998).

Smith, James M., and Ernest Sosa, eds.: *Mill's Utilitarianism: Text and Criticism* (Belmont, CA: Wadsworth Publishing Company, 1969).

## Contemporary Utilitarianism

Adams, R. M.: "Motive Utilitarianism," *Journal of Philosophy,* 73 (1976): 467–81.

Bailey, James Wood: *Utilitarianism, Institutions, and Justice* (New York: Oxford University Press, 1997).

Bayles, Michael D., ed.: *Contemporary Utilitarianism* (Garden City, NY: Doubleday and Company, 1968).

Brandt, Richard B.: *A Theory of the Good and the Right* (Oxford, England: Clarendon Press, 1979).

————: "Problems of Contemporary Utilitarianism: Real and Alleged," in Norman E. Bowie, ed., *Ethical Theory* (Indianapolis: Hackett Publishing Co., 1983).

————: *Morality, Utilitarianism, and Rights* (New York: Cambridge University Press, 1992).

————: "Conscience (Rule) Utilitarianism and the Criminal Law," *Law and Philosophy,* 14 (1995): 65–89.

Braybrooke, D.: "The Choice between Utilitarianisms," *American Philosophical Quarterly,* 4 (1967): 28–38.

Diggs, B. J.: "Rules and Utilitarianism," *American Philosophical Quarterly,* 1 (1964): 32–44.

Feinberg, Joel: "The Forms and Limits of Utilitarianism," *Philosophical Review,* 76 (1967): 368–81.

Feldman, Fred: *Utilitarianism, Hedonism, and Desert* (Cambridge, England: Cambridge University Press, 1997).

Frey, R. G., ed.: *Utility and Rights* (Minneapolis: University of Minnesota Press, 1984).

Griffin, James: *Well-Being: Its Meaning, Measurement, and Importance* (Oxford, England: Clarendon Press, 1986).

Hare, Richard M.: *Moral Thinking: Its Levels, Method and Point* (Oxford: Clarendon Press, 1981).

————: *Essays in Ethical Theory* (Oxford: Oxford University Press, 1989).

Hart, H. L. A.: "Between Utility and Rights," in *Essays in Jurisprudence and Philosophy* (Oxford: Oxford University Press, 1983).

Hodgson, Dennis H.: *Consequences of Utilitarianism* (Oxford: Clarendon Press, 1967).

Hooker, Brad: *Rationality, Rules, and Utility: New Essays on the Moral Philosophy of Richard B. Brandt* (Boulder, CO: Westview, 1994).

Kagan, Shelly: *The Limits of Morality* (Oxford: Clarendon Press, 1989).

Levy, Sanford S.: "Utilitarian Alternatives to Act Utilitarianism,"
*Pacific Philosophical Quarterly,* 78 (March 1997): 93–112.

Lyons, David: *Forms and Limits of Utilitarianism* (Oxford: Clarendon Press, 1965).

————: "Utility and Rights," *Nomos,* 24 (1982): 107–38.

Narveson, Jan: *Morality and Utility* (Baltimore: Johns Hopkins University Press, 1967).

Powers, Madison: "Repugnant Desires and the Two-Tier Conception of Utility," *Utilitas,* 6 (November 1994): 171–6.

Quinton, Anthony: *Utilitarian Ethics* (LaSalle, IL: Open Court, 1988).

Sartorius, Rolf E.: "Utilitarianism and Obligation," *Journal of Philosophy,* 66 (1969): 67–81.

Scarre, Geoffrey: *Utilitarianism* (New York: Routledge, 1996).

Scheffler, Samuel, ed.: *The Rejection of Consequentialism* (Oxford, England: Clarendon Press, 1982).

————: *Consequentialism and its Critics* (Oxford: Oxford University Press, 1988).

Schneewind, Jerome B.: *Sidgwick's Ethics and Victorian Moral Philosophy* (Oxford: Clarendon Press, 1977).

Sen, Amartya, and Bernard Williams, eds.: *Utilitarianism and Beyond* (Cambridge, England: Cambridge University Press, 1982).

Sikora, Richard I.: "Utilitarianism: The Classical Principle and the Average Principle," *Canadian Journal of Philosophy,* 5 (1975): 409–19.

Singer, Peter: *Animal Liberation* (New York: Avon Books, 1990).

Smart, J. J. C.: "Extreme and Restricted Utilitarianism," *Philosophical Quarterly,* 6 (1956): 344–54.

————, and Bernard Williams: *Utilitarianism: For and Against* (Cambridge, England: Cambridge University Press, 1973).

Thomson, Judith Jarvis: "Goodness and Utilitarianism," *Proceedings of the American Philosophical Association,* 67 (October 1993): 145–59.

# Kant and Deontological Theories

## PLUTONIUM SECRETS

In August 1944, a young chemist named Don Mastick was examining a radioactive metal at a secret laboratory in Los Alamos, New Mexico. A year later, this metal—plutonium—would power the bombs dropped on Japan, but at this point Mastick was toiling to build up the supply of plutonium at Los Alamos. Unbeknownst to him, a chemical reaction was occurring inside the vessel that contained his plutonium; it exploded, throwing plutonium into Mastick's face and mouth, causing him to ingest bits of the metal.

Mastick's stomach was pumped immediately, but the health director at Los Alamos realized that there was no way to determine how much plutonium had been retained or what its effects might be. The laboratory's director, eminent nuclear physicist J. Robert Oppenheimer, immediately authorized studies to ascertain how to detect the presence of plutonium and its effects in the body. Mastick's accident was framed by health officials in terms of what was known about previous workers with radium. They too had ingested radioactive material, and some had suffered from a frightful bone disease of the jaw and other bone cancers. The question now hanging over Los Alamos was whether plutonium could cause a similar tragedy in workers.

In truth, little was known about this occupational health question, yet the question potentially affected hundreds of workers. Extrapolation from radium was helpful, but ultimately not reliable. The available animal data suggested that plutonium would deposit in a part of the bone associated with bone growth, but little was known about its effects. Oppenheimer therefore authorized new research involving animal and human subjects. For unknown reasons, he wrote: "I feel that it is desirable if these [experiments] can in any way be handled elsewhere not to undertake them here."

From April 1945 to July 1947, a program of human subjects research was initiated to try to learn how to protect personnel from plutonium exposure. Seventeen patients were intentionally injected with plutonium at three university hospitals in the United States: the University of California at San Francisco (UCSF), the University of Chicago, and the University of Rochester (and one additional patient at Oak Ridge Hospital, Tennessee). The purpose of this research was to determine the excretion rate of plutonium in humans. These plutonium experiments were not regarded by investigators at the time as highly risky. On the basis of the experiences with radium, it was not expected that there would be any immediate (i.e., short-term) side effects or illness. However, virtually nothing was known about long-term risk.

The injections of plutonium that took place at UCSF have been particularly carefully studied. Work began with some studies on rats and cancer conducted by Dr. Joseph Hamilton. In January 1945, Hamilton decided "to undertake, on a limited scale, a series of metabolic studies with [plutonium] using human subjects." The purpose "was to evaluate the possible hazards . . . to humans who might be exposed to them."

Three patients—known as CAL-1, CAL-2, and CAL-3—were injected at UCSF. Fifty-eight-year-old Albert Stevens was CAL-1. He was chosen because he was thought to have advanced stomach cancer and was not expected to live very long. However, soon after the injection, it was discovered that he had only a benign gastric ulcer, not cancer. The researchers collected materials from his body for almost a year, studying them for plutonium. Stevens lived for many years thereafter, but was never told about the experimentation.

CAL-2 was a four-year-old Australian boy suffering from osteogenic sarcoma. He was selected in April 1946. Simeon Shaw had bone cancer and had been flown from Australia for what had been anticipated by his Australian doctors to be advanced medical treatment. He was given some treatment, injected with plutonium, and his samples studied. Approximately one month after being injected, Shaw returned to Australia. No follow-up study was conducted, and he died in January 1947.

CAL-3 was a railroad porter named Elmer Allen, who was believed to have bone cancer. He was injected in July 1947. Allen lived until 1991, apparently a long-term cancer survivor.

There was never any expectation on the part of the experimenters that the injections for these three patients would be of therapeutic value or have any form of medical benefit. It appears that no form of consent was obtained or was expected to be obtained by the physicians involved in the first two cases. Some consent for experimentation was obtained from CAL-3, but it was not consent to *nontherapeutic* experimentation.

Although performed largely in secret, some of this work was known publicly as early as 1951. It was discussed in the 1970s and 1980s, but did not generate a substantial controversy until 1993, following the work of a persistent investigative reporter in Albuquerque, New Mexico. On January 7, 1994, UCSF Chancellor Joseph Martin appointed an ad hoc committee to investigate allegations of abuse by studying the history of UCSF involvement. After a year of investigating documents and debating the issues, this committee filed its report in February 1995. The ad hoc committee confirmed that the "injections of plutonium were not expected to be, nor were they, therapeutic or of medical benefit to the patients."

The ad hoc committee found that written consent was rare, disclosure narrow, and the permission of patients not typically obtained even for nontherapeutic research during this period. They found that it is not known exactly what these research subjects were told or what they understood. They also found that the word "plutonium" was classified at the time; it is therefore certain that it was not used in any explanations that might have been made to patient-subjects. The committee noted that in a recorded oral interview in 1979, one of the three original UCSF investigators, Kenneth Scott, said that he never told the first subject what had been injected into him. Scott added that the experiments were "incautious" and "morally wrong."

Nonetheless, the ad hoc committee wrote, "At the time of the plutonium experiments, [today's issues about proof of consent] were not discussed. . . . [O]verall, the Committee believes that practices of consent of the era were inadequate by today's standards, and even by standards existing at the time." However, it also found that the experiments themselves were "consistent with accepted medical research practices at the time."

In an appendix to the ad hoc committee's report, a lawyer and committee member, Elizabeth Zitrin, concluded that even if the experiments were consistent with accepted medical practices at the time, "it does not make them ethical. And they were not consistent with the highest standards of the time articulated by the government, the profession, or the public." The chairman of the ad hoc committee, Roy Filly, responded that this comment by the lawyer held investigators to an unrealistically high standard of research ethics.[1]

## THE DEONTOLOGICAL CONCEPTION OF MORALITY

In Chapter 4 we saw that a fundamental distinction has been adopted in modern ethical theory between consequentialist theories and nonconsequentialist theories. We also saw that the dominant form of consequentialist theory, utilitarianism, has been subjected to stern criticism. Many have concluded that this theory must be abandoned entirely. The theories to be studied in the present chapter hold that some actions must be right or wrong for reasons other than their good consequences. These theories are often called "deontological"—a term derived from the Greek *deon* for "duty" or "obligation." Keeping a personal promise, not abandoning a friend,

---

[1]This case was developed from the following sources: Advisory Committee on Human Radiation Experiments, *Final Report of the Advisory Committee on Human Radiation Experiments* (New York: Oxford University Press, 1996); Keay Davidson, "Questions Linger on 1940s UCSF Plutonium Shots," *The San Francisco Examiner* (February 23, 1995), p. A6; University of California at San Francisco (UCSF), *Report of the UCSF Ad Hoc Fact Finding Committee on World War II Human Radiation Experiments* (February 1995, unpublished but released to the public); Elizabeth A. Zitrin and Roy A. Filly, UCSF, "Report of the UCSF Ad Hoc Fact Finding Committee," Letters, Appendices; J. Newell Stannard, *Radioactivity and Health: A History* (Oak Ridge, TN: Office of Scientific and Technical Information, 1988); Don Mastick, telephone interview with Steve Klaidman, 23 July 1995; Kenneth Scott, interviewed by Sally Hughes (University of California Oral History Project), transcript of audio recording, 17 December 1979, pp. 49–50.

repaying a debt, and not shattering a contractual obligation are *obligatory,* according to these theories, whether or not utility is maximized. This conclusion is not meant to suggest that utilitarians denigrate or downgrade such relationships. They do not. The point is that deontologists do not believe that the moral principles governing these relationships are *justified* on consequentialist grounds.

Deontologists argue that moral standards exist independently of utilitarian ends and that the moral life is wrongly conceived in terms of means and ends. An act or rule is right, they maintain, insofar as it satisfies the demands of some overriding (nonutilitarian) principle or principles of obligation. For example, suppose someone defames another's character and thereby damages that person's reputation and career. The action is defamation, and the damage is a consequence of the defamation. The consequence is separable from the action. Deontologists believe that defamation can be wrong even if it turns out that social utility is *maximized* by the action of defamation.

A deontologist could similarly analyze the deception involved in the plutonium experiments by distinguishing the act of deceiving subjects from the harm to subjects that might have resulted from the act. One could offer a utilitarian justification for the research in terms of the contribution made by the research to protecting those who worked with plutonium (through knowledge of the effects of radiation on the body), as well as advancing the cold war effort to build an adequate military defense. Researchers could argue that they minimized serious risks by this research, while imposing only minimal risks on subjects. A deontologist, however, might argue in response that such deception is a wrong-making characteristic of any action and that, in the case of the plutonium studies, it was unjustifiable unless subjects were at least informed that they were being placed at risk and that some disclosures about the research were made to them. In general, deontologists urge us to consider that such actions are morally wrong not because of their consequences, but because the action itself constitutes a moral violation.

Deontological theory has been explicated in contrast to consequentialist theory in several different ways. One leading theory is based on the idea of "deontological constraints"; this approach will be examined later in this chapter (see the selection by Nagel). But first, we will examine John Rawls's account of the relation between the good and the right, which has been one of the most popular explications of the difference between deontological and consequentialist theories in recent years. A consequentialist theory (as we saw in Chapter 4) understands the good as independent of the right, and the right is then analyzed or defined in terms of that which maximizes good. As Rawls defines them, the reverse is the case: Deontological theories either do not construe the good as independent of the right or do not view the right as that which maximizes good. In Rawls's own deontological theory the right restricts what may count as the good and the right does not maximize the good.

The following selection is from Rawls's contractarian theory in *A Theory of Justice.* He explains why deontologists believe that utilitarianism must be replaced by a theory that more adequately captures our moral values. Since Rawls's particular interest is in the theory of justice, his point here is that our considered judgments about social justice require a deontological, not a utilitarian, theory.

# Utilitarianism and Deontology*

## John Rawls

My aim is to present a conception of justice which generalizes and carries to a higher level of abstraction the familiar theory of the social contract as found, say, in Locke, Rousseau, and Kant. In order to do this we are not to think of the original contract as one to enter a particular society or to set up a particular form of government. Rather, the guiding idea is that the principles of justice for the basic structure of society are the object of the original agreement. They are the principles that free and rational persons concerned to further their own interests would accept in an initial position of equality as defining the fundamental terms of their association. These principles are to regulate all further agreements; they specify the kinds of social cooperation that can be entered into and the forms of government that can be established. This way of regarding the principles of justice I shall call justice as fairness.

Thus we are to imagine that those who engage in social cooperation choose together, in one joint act, the principles which are to assign basic rights and duties and to determine the division of social benefits. Men are to decide in advance how they are to regulate their claims against one another and what is to be the foundation charter of their society. Just as each person must decide by rational reflection what constitutes his good, that is, the system of ends which it is rational for him to pursue, so a group of persons must decide

once and for all what is to count among them as just and unjust. The choice which rational men would make in this hypothetical situation of equal liberty, assuming for the present that this choice problem has a solution, determines the principles of justice.

In justice as fairness the original position of equality corresponds to the state of nature in the traditional theory of the social contract. This original position is not, of course, thought of as an actual historical state of affairs, much less as a primitive condition of culture. It is understood as a purely hypothetical situation characterized so as to lead to a certain conception of justice. Among the essential features of this situation is that no one knows his place in society, his class position or social status, nor does any one know his fortune in the distribution of natural assets and abilities, his intelligence, strength, and the like. I shall even assume that the parties do not know their conceptions of the good or their special psychological propensities. The principles of justice are chosen behind a veil of ignorance. This ensures that no one is advantaged or disadvantaged in the choice of principles by the outcome of natural chance or the contingency of social circumstances. Since all are similarly situated and no one is able to design principles to favor his particular condition, the principles of justice are the result of a fair agreement or bargain. For given the circumstances of the original position, the symmetry of everyone's relations to each other, this initial situation is fair between individuals as moral persons, that is, as rational beings with their own ends and capable,

*From John Rawls, *A Theory of Justice* (Cambridge, MA: Harvard University Press, 1971).

I shall assume, of a sense of justice. The original position is, one might say, the appropriate initial status quo, and thus the fundamental agreements reached in it are fair. This explains the propriety of the name "justice as fairness": it conveys the idea that the principles of justice are agreed to in an initial situation that is fair. . . .

Our social situation is just if it is such that by this sequence of hypothetical agreements we would have contracted into the general system of rules which defines it. Moreover, assuming that the original position does determine a set of principles (that is, that a particular conception of justice would be chosen), it will then be true that whenever social institutions satisfy these principles those engaged in them can say to one another that they are cooperating on terms to which they would agree if they were free and equal persons whose relations with respect to one another were fair. They could all view their arrangements as meeting the stipulations which they would acknowledge in an initial situation that embodies widely accepted and reasonable constraints on the choice of principles. The general recognition of this fact would provide the basis for a public acceptance of the corresponding principles of justice. No society can, of course, be a scheme of cooperation which men enter voluntarily in a literal sense; each person finds himself placed at birth in some particular position in some particular society, and the nature of this position materially affects his life prospects. Yet a society satisfying the principles of justice as fairness comes as close as a society can to being a voluntary scheme, for it meets the principles which free and equal persons would assent to under circumstances that are fair. In this sense its members are au-

tonomous and the obligations they recognize self-imposed. . . .

The striking feature of the utilitarian view of justice is that it does not matter, except indirectly, how this sum of satisfactions is distributed among individuals any more than it matters, except indirectly, how one man distributes his satisfactions over time. The correct distribution in either case is that which yields the maximum fulfillment. Society must allocate its means of satisfaction whatever these are, rights and duties, opportunities and privileges, and various forms of wealth, so as to achieve this maximum if it can. But in itself no distribution of satisfaction is better than another except that the more equal distribution is to be preferred to break ties. It is true that certain common sense precepts of justice, particularly those which concern the protection of liberties and rights, or which express the claims of desert, seem to contradict this contention. But from a utilitarian standpoint the explanation of these precepts and of their seemingly stringent character is that they are those precepts which experience shows should be strictly respected and departed from only under exceptional circumstances if the sum of advantages is to be maximized. Yet, as with all other precepts, those of justice are derivative from the one end of attaining the greatest balance of satisfaction. Thus there is no reason in principle why the greater gains of some should not compensate for the lesser losses of others; or more importantly, why the violation of the liberty of a few might not be made right by the greater good shared by many. It simply happens that under most conditions, at least in a reasonably advanced stage of civilization, the greatest sum of advantages is not attained in this way. No doubt the strictness of common sense precepts of justice has a certain usefulness in limiting men's propensities to injustice and to socially injurious actions, but the utilitarian believes that to affirm this strictness as a first principle of morals is a mistake. For just as it is rational for one man to maximize the fulfillment of his system of desires, it is right for a society to maximize the net balance of satisfaction taken over all of its members. . . .

On this conception of society separate individuals are thought of as so many different lines along which rights and duties are to be assigned and scarce means of satisfaction allocated in accordance with rules so as to give the greatest fulfillment of wants. The nature of the decision made by the ideal legislator is not, therefore, materially different from that of an entrepreneur deciding how to maximize his profit by producing this or that commodity, or that of a consumer deciding how to maximize his satisfaction by the purchase of this or that collection of goods. In each case there is a single person whose system of desires determines the best allocation of limited means. The correct decision is essentially a question of efficient administration. This view of social cooperation is the consequence of extending to society the principle of choice for one man, and then, to make this extension work, conflating all persons into one through the imaginative acts of the impartial sympathetic spectator. Utilitarianism does not take seriously the distinction between persons. . . .

Utilitarianism is a teleological theory whereas justice as fairness is not. By definition, then, the latter is a deontological theory, one that either does not specify the good independently from the right, or does not interpret the right as

maximizing the good. (It should be noted that deontological theories are defined as non-teleological ones, not as views that characterize the rightness of institutions and acts independently from their consequences. All ethical doctrines worth our attention take consequences into account in judging rightness. One which did not would simply be irrational, crazy.) Justice as fairness is a deontological theory in the second way. For if it is assumed that the persons in the original position would choose a principle of equal liberty and restrict economic and social inequalities to those in everyone's interests, there is no reason to think that just institutions will maximize the good. (Here I suppose with utilitarianism that the good is defined as the satisfaction of rational desire.) Of course, it is not impossible that the most good is produced but it would be a coincidence. The question of attaining the greatest net balance of satisfaction never arises in justice as fairness; this maximum principle is not used at all. . . .

The principles of right, and so of justice, put limits on which satisfactions have value; they impose restrictions on what are reasonable conceptions of one's good. In drawing up plans and in deciding on aspirations men are to take these constraints into account. Hence in justice as fairness one does not take men's propensities and inclinations as given, whatever they are, and then seek the best way to fulfill them. Rather, their desires and aspirations are restricted from the outset by the principles of justice which specify the boundaries that men's systems of ends must respect. We can express this by saying that in justice as fairness the concept of right is prior to that of the good.

The category "deontology" accommodates a broader set of theories than does utilitarianism, which is restricted to those theories that accept the principle of utility as primary. Rawls's theory is only one of many deontological theories. There is no parallel substantive principle or systematic deontological account shared by all deontological theories, but to be deontological, the theory must contain some conditions under which some moral obligations are not defeated by consequential claims. Some grounds of obligation independent of the production of good consequences are at least sometimes sufficient to defeat appeals to consequences, *no matter what the consequences.*

Deontologists may envisage only one supreme principle, a *monistic* theory; or they may accept more than one fundamental principle, a *pluralistic* theory. The most influential monistic theory is that of Immanuel Kant, an eighteenth-century German philosopher who profoundly influenced Rawls. The most widely examined pluralistic theory is W. D. Ross's, whose views we will examine after treating Kant's theory.

## KANT'S ETHICS

It is almost universally agreed that Kant is the greatest philosopher to emerge in German philosophy. Kant developed a highly original philosophical framework in order to account for the validity of moral rules. He tried to show that the validity of rules is grounded in pure reason, not in intuition, conscience, or the production of utility. Morality, as he saw it, provides a rational framework of principles and rules that guides and places obligations on everyone. The roots of morality are in principles of reason that all rational agents possess in common. Kant thought, as have many philosophers since Plato, that reason can be in conflict with desire. When this occurs, reason can resist and then subject desire to its control, which conclusively shows that individuals are not simply at the mercy of a clash of desires. Kant saw us as creatures with the power to resist desire, with the freedom to do so, and with the capacity to determine our lives solely by rational considerations. Kant calls this capacity to act from reason "practical reason."

Kant's views are remote (in the extreme) from the utilitarian conviction that pleasure or some other intrinsic good is the object of morality. He believed that an action is right if, and only if, it conforms to a moral rule that a rational agent (person) would necessarily follow if the agent were acting in accordance with reason. Kant thought that we should put aside all considerations of utility and self-interest in our moral lives, because the moral worth of an agent's action depends exclusively on the moral acceptability of the principle of duty from which that agent is acting (the principle of duty that determines the agent's *will*). An action therefore has moral worth only when a universally valid norm is the action's sole motive.

Kant emphasizes performing one's duty (obligation) for the sake of duty alone. All persons, he insists, must act not only *in accordance with* but *for the sake of* obligation. That is, a person's motive for acting must rest in a recognition that what he or she intends is demanded by an obligation. For example, if an employer discloses a health hazard in a plant to an employee only because the employer fears a lawsuit, and not out of a belief in the importance of truth-telling or a concern about the employee's health, then the employer has done the right thing but deserves no moral credit for the action. It is not good enough, in Kant's view, that one discharge one's obligations by performing the morally correct action, because one could perform one's obligation for self-interested reasons having nothing to do with morality. If one does what is morally right simply because one is scared, because one derives pleasure from doing that kind of act, because one is selfish, or because the action is in one's interest, there is nothing morally praiseworthy about the action.

## Three Principles

Kant provides three principles, or propositions, in the first section of his work *Foundations of the Metaphysics of Morals,* from which the selection that follows is extracted. Each proposition explicates his theory of moral worth. The "First Proposition" (Principle, Remark) is formally stated as follows: "An act must be done from obligation in order to have moral worth." An action has moral worth, that is, only if a morally valid rule of obligation determines that action. No action has moral worth exclusively from the effects brought about by the action.

The "Second Proposition" in the *Foundations* is, "An action's moral value is due to the maxim from which it is performed, rather than to its success in realizing some desired end or purpose." A maxim is a practical principle or proposition that prescribes some action. The question for Kant is not whether a maxim is generally good, but whether it is unconditionally good, and so a universally valid principle of obligation. Even a motive of benevolence will be morally unworthy unless there is an accompanying motive of obligation. Acts of benevolence are not necessarily morally good. For example, consider a judge who lets a criminal go free out of benevolence or a man who neglects his wife because he is treating his friends benevolently.

The "Third Proposition," which Kant says follows from the first two, is formally stated as follows: "Obligation is the *necessity* of an action performed from *respect* for law." Kant seems to mean that one has an obligation to do something if and only if one would necessarily do it out of respect for law. Necessity only comes from laws, not from mere subjective maxims. We must, then, will an action on the basis of an objective principle that all rational agents would accept. Kant believes that human beings are naturally constituted to feel respect for this law.

## Autonomy and Heteronomy

When a person behaves according to binding, universal moral rules, Kant considers that person to have an *autonomous* will. Kant contrasts autonomy with what he calls "heteronomy," the will's determination by persons or conditions other than oneself. Under heteronomy, Kant includes any source of determining influence or control over the will, internal or external, except a determination of the will by moral principles.

If reason is enslaved to passion or to a will that is directed by desire, a person is heteronomous or under the control of affective or sensuous impulses that are not of his or her choosing. This heteronomy is not mere persuasive influence for Kant. It is causal necessitation. Any principle not based on autonomy of the will cannot form the will's law, and thus acting from desire, fear, impulse, or habit is no less heteronomous than actions manipulated or coerced by others. Kant sees suicide, for example, as an action involving subservience to a source of legislation not one's own.

To say that an agent must "accept" a moral principle in order to be autonomous does not mean either that the principle is subjective or that each individual must create (author or originate) his or her moral principles. Kant requires only that each individual *will the acceptance* of the moral principles to be acted upon in the moral life. A person's autonomy consists in the ability to govern through moral principles that rationality determines to be authoritative. Were the obligations not willingly assumed by the individual, reason would still demand their assumption.

Interpreters of Kant have sometimes distorted this thesis by presenting Kant as a defender of the libertarian principle that every individual has the right to legislate rules and make personal decisions, and hence to be his or her "own" person through individualistic self-rule. In this conception, "autonomy" is the capacity of persons to reflect on and take responsibility for the kind of persons they want to be. What makes a life *that* person's life is that it is shaped by his or her choices. This conception of autonomy, however, is emphatically *not* Kant's. The vernacular of autonomy in contemporary moral theory has generally been erected on individualistic foundations (see pp. 161-64 below), but Kant's theory of autonomy is confined to moral self-legislation: If a person freely determines the principles under whose direction he or she will act, the person is a law-giver unto himself or herself, and thus is autonomous.

For Kant what morality requires is determined by what we would do "if reason completely determined the will."[2] A self-imposed rule morally subjects the person to obligation; but Kant insists that this subjection is consistent with *moral* autonomy. Because the person accepts and wills the principle determining the action, the person is complying with his or her own rule, not with a foreign influence or source of obligation.[3]

In a notable rebuttal to Kant, Henry Sidgwick objected that the principles of the scoundrel and the principles of the saint could both be selected autonomously. This objection, however, springs from a misunderstanding of Kant. As John Rawls puts it, a free self *could* choose as a scoundrel would, but free and equal rational beings expressing their nature would not make the choices of a scoundrel. It is not only the *liberty* to choose that characterizes autonomous choice; such choice must conform to what free and rational beings would select as expressing "their autonomous nature as rational."[4]

---

[2]Kant, *The Critique of Practical Reason*, Lewis White Beck, trans. (Indianapolis: Bobbs-Merrill, 1956), p. 18.
[3]Kant, *Foundations of the Metaphysics of Morals*, p. 58.
[4]Rawls, *A Theory of Justice*, pp. 252, 256. See also, "A Kantian Conception of Equality," *Cambridge Review* (February 1975): 97ff.

Any philosophy in which the right to individual choice can legitimately outweigh the dictates of objective moral principles of obligation is very alien to Kant's moral theory. The freedom of personal moral opinions is an absurdity as such, and any action from personal freedom that violates morality on grounds of the conscientious judgment of the free person stands to be condemned.

Kant often speaks in rather opaque language, at least by contemporary standards, but his moral philosophy has been and continues to be enormously influential. The following selection provides further details and arguments on the themes discussed thus far.

# The Good Will and the Categorical Imperative*

## Immanuel Kant

Nothing in the world—indeed nothing even beyond the world—can possibly be conceived which could be called good without qualification except a *good will*. Intelligence, wit, judgment, and the other talents of the mind, however they may be named, or courage, resoluteness, and perseverance as qualities of temperament, are doubtless in many respects good and desirable. But they can become extremely bad and harmful if the will, which is to make use of these gifts of nature and which in its special constitution is called character, is not good. It is the same with the gifts of fortune. Power, riches, honor, even health, general well-being, and the contentment with one's condition which is called happiness, make for pride and even arrogance if there is not a good will to correct their influence on the mind and on its principles of action so as to make it universally conformable to its end. . . .

Some qualities seem to be conducive to this good will and can facilitate its action, but, in spite of that, they have no intrinsic unconditional worth. They rather presuppose a good will, which limits the high esteem which one otherwise rightly has for them and prevents their being held to be absolutely good. Moderation in emotions and passions, self-control, and calm deliberation not only are good in many respects but even seem to constitute a part of the inner worth of the person. But however unconditionally they were esteemed by the ancients, they are far from being good without qualification. For without the principle of a good will they can become extremely bad, and the coolness of a villain makes him not only far more dangerous but also more directly abominable in our eyes than he would have seemed without it.

The good will is not good because of what it effects or accomplishes or because of its adequacy to achieve some proposed end; it is good only because of its willing, i.e., it is good of itself. And, regarded for itself, it is to be esteemed

*From Immanuel Kant, *Foundations of the Metaphysics of Morals,* Lewis White Beck, trans. (Indianapolis: Bobbs-Merrill Company, Inc., 1959), pp. 9–10, 16–19, 24–25, 28.

incomparably higher than anything which could be brought about by it in favor of any inclination or even of the sum total of all inclinations. Even if it should happen that, by a particularly unfortunate fate or by the niggardly provision of a stepmotherly nature, this will should be wholly lacking in power to accomplish its purpose, and if even the greatest effort should not avail it to achieve anything of its end, and if there remained only the good will (not as a mere wish but as the summoning of all the means in our power), it would sparkle like a jewel in its own right, as something that had its full worth in itself. Usefulness or fruitlessness can neither diminish nor augment this worth. . . .

An action performed from duty does not have its moral worth in the purpose which is to be achieved through it but in the maxim by which it is determined. Its moral value, therefore, does not depend on the realization of the object of the action but merely on the principle of volition by which the action is done, without any regard to the objects of the faculty of desire. . . . It is clear that the purposes we may have for our actions and their effects as ends and incentives of the will cannot give the actions any unconditional and moral worth. Wherein, then, can this worth lie, if it is not in the will in relation to its hoped-for effect? It can lie nowhere else than in the principle of the will, irrespective of the ends which can be realized by such action. . . .

Now, as an act from duty wholly excludes the influence of inclination and therewith every object of the will, nothing remains which can determine the will objectively except the law, and nothing subjectively except pure respect for this practical law. This subjective element is the maxim that I ought to follow such a law even if it thwarts all my inclinations.

Thus the moral worth of an action does not lie in the effect which is expected from it or in any principle of action which has to borrow its motive from this expected effect. For all these effects (agreeableness of my own condition, indeed even the promotion of the happiness of others) could be brought about through other causes and would not require the will of a rational being, while the highest and unconditional good can be found only in such a will. Therefore, the pre-eminent good can consist only in the conception of the law in itself (which can be present only in a rational being). . . .

But what kind of a law can that be, the conception of which must determine the will without reference to the expected result? Under this condition alone the will can be called absolutely good without qualification. Since I have robbed the will of all impulses which could come to it from obedience to any law, nothing remains to serve as a principle of the will except universal conformity of its action to law as such. That is, I should never act in such a way that I could not also will that my maxim should be a universal law. Mere conformity to law as such (without assuming any particular law applicable to certain actions) serves as the principle of the will, and it must serve as such a principle if duty is not to be a vain delusion and chimerical concept. The common reason of mankind in its practical judgments is in perfect agreement with this and has this principle constantly in view.

Let the question, for example, be: May I, when in distress, make a promise with the intention not to keep it? I easily distinguish the two meanings which the question can have, viz., whether it is prudent to make a false promise, or whether it conforms to my duty. Undoubtedly the former can often be the case, though I do see clearly that it is not sufficient merely to escape from the present difficulty by this expedient, but that I must consider whether inconveniences much greater than the present one may not later spring from this lie. Even with all my supposed cunning, the consequences cannot be so easily foreseen. Loss of credit might be far more disadvantageous than the misfortune I now seek to avoid, and it is hard to tell whether it might not be more prudent to act according to a universal maxim and to make it a habit not to promise anything without intending to fulfill it. But it is soon clear to me that such a maxim is based only on an apprehensive concern with consequences.

To be truthful from duty, however, is an entirely different thing from being truthful out of fear of disadvantageous consequences, for in the former case the concept of the action itself contains a law for me, while in the latter I must first look about to see what results for me may be connected with it. For to deviate from the principle of duty is certainly bad, but to be unfaithful to my maxim of prudence can sometimes be very advantageous to me, though it is certainly safer to abide by it. The shortest but most infallible way to find the answer to the question as to whether deceitful promise is consistent with duty is to ask myself: Would I be content that my maxim (of extricating myself from difficulty by a false promise) should hold as a universal law for myself as well as for others? And could I say to myself that everyone may make a false promise when he is in a difficulty from which he otherwise cannot escape? I immediately see that I could will the lie but

not a universal law to lie. For with such a law there would be no promises at all, inasmuch as it would be futile to make a pretense of my intention in regard to future actions to those who would not believe this pretense or—if they over-hastily did so—who would pay me back in my own coin. Thus my maxim would necessarily destroy itself as soon as it was made a universal law.

I do not, therefore, need any penetrating acuteness in order to discern what I have to do in order that my volition may be morally good. Inexperienced in the course of the world, incapable of being prepared for all its contingencies, I ask myself only: Can I will that my maxim become a universal law? If not, it must be rejected. . . .

Our concern is with actions of which perhaps the world has never had an example, with actions whose feasibility might be seriously doubted by those who base everything on experience, and yet with actions inexorably commanded by reason. For example, pure sincerity in friendship can be demanded of every man, and this demand is not in the least diminished if a sincere friend has never existed, because this duty, as duty in general, prior to all experience, lies in the idea of a reason which determines the will by a priori grounds.

It is clear that no experience can give occasion for inferring the possibility of such apodictic laws. . . .

Nor could one give poorer counsel to morality than to attempt to derive it from examples. For each example of morality which is exhibited to me must itself have been previously judged according to principles of morality to see whether it is worthy to serve as an original example, i.e., as a model. By no means could it authoritatively furnish the concept of morality. Even the Holy

One of the Gospel must be compared with our ideal of moral perfection before He is recognized as such. . . .

From what has been said it is clear that all moral concepts have their seat and origin entirely a priori in reason. This is just as much the case in the most ordinary reason as in reason which is speculative to the highest degree. It is obvious that they cannot be abstracted from any empirical and hence merely contingent cognitions. In the purity of their origin lies their worthiness to serve us as supreme practical principles, and to the extent that something empirical is added to them just this much is subtracted from their genuine influence and from the unqualified worth of actions. Furthermore, it is evident that it is not only of the greatest necessity in a theoretical point of view when it is a question of speculation but also of the utmost practical importance to derive the concepts and laws of morals from pure reason and to present them pure and unmixed, and to determine the scope of this entire practical but pure rational knowledge (the entire faculty of pure practical reason) without making the principles depend upon the particular nature of human reason as speculative philosophy may permit and even sometimes find necessary. But since moral laws should hold for every rational being as such, the principles must be derived from the universal concept of a rational being generally.

### The Idea of a Categorical Imperative

Kant's supreme principle or moral law is a *categorical imperative* that every moral agent recognizes (consciously or unconsciously) in accepting an action as morally obligatory. To understand why Kant's categorical imperative is "imperative," consider his fanciful example of a "holy will." A holy will is a perfectly rational will that always acts (by its nature) on moral maxims and is never inclined otherwise. This holy being does not say, "I must do $X$," but only "I will do $X$." There is no need to impose rules on a divine will because such a will is not subject to inclination, desire, and the like. But we human beings are imperfect rational creatures subject to desires, and hence need rules imposed on us. These rules are imperatives or prescriptions enjoining us to do or not to do something. Hence we receive them as compelling or necessitating our action.

The categorical imperative is to be contrasted with what Kant calls a *hypothetical imperative,* which has the form, "If I want to obtain end *e,* then I *must* obtain means *m.*" Suppose I say, "If I am to buy a house, then I must work hard to make enough money for a down payment." This prescription tells me what I must do, provided that I already have certain desires or interests; but the "must" is not a moral "must." You can make the same point using the word "ought," thus making the statement appear like a statement of obligation. An example would be, "If you want to get an A on the next test in ethics, you ought to study Kant diligently." Much of human conduct is governed by these hypothetical imperatives.

However, moral imperatives, in Kant's view, tell us what must be done irrespective of our desires. He thinks we must not commit suicide, for example, even should we wish to do so. A categorical imperative does not counsel, but tells you what you must do whether or not you want or desire to do it. It requires unconditional conformity by all rational beings, regardless of the circumstances. Kant expresses his views on imperatives as follows:

> If the action is good only as a means to something else, the imperative is hypothetical; but if it is thought of as good in itself, and hence as necessary in a will which of itself conforms to reasons as the principle of this will, the imperative is categorical. . . . The former present the practical necessity of a possible action as a means to achieving something else which one desires (or which one may possibly desire). The categorical imperative would be one which presented an action as of itself objectively necessary, without regard to any other end. . . .
>
> All sciences have some practical part which consists of problems of some end which is possible for us and of imperatives as to how it can be reached. These can therefore generally be called imperatives of skill. Whether the end is reasonable and good is not in question at all, for the question is only of what must be done in order to attain it. The precepts to be followed by a physician in order to cure his patient and by a poisoner in order to bring about certain death are of equal value in so far as each does that which will perfectly accomplish his purpose. . . .
>
> Skill in the choice of means to one's own highest welfare can be called prudence in the narrowest sense. Thus the imperative which refers to the choice of means to one's own happiness, i.e., the precept of prudence, is still only hypothetical; the action is not absolutely commanded but commanded only as a means to another end.[5]

Kant's categorical imperative asserts that "I ought never to act except in such a way that I can also will that *my maxim become a universal law*." Kant says that all imperatives of obligation (all "ought" statements that morally obligate) can be supported from this one principle. The categorical imperative, he maintains, is a canon of the acceptability of all moral rules, that is, a criterion for judging the adequacy or acceptability of those maxims that direct actions. The categorical imperative adds nothing to a maxim's *content;* it only decrees which maxims are objective or valid by sorting out those which are universalizable. Because it mentions nothing about the content of moral rules, it is often said to be a purely formal principle. It does not, for instance, dictate a statement similar to "An action is right if, and only if, it produces the greatest good." The categorical imperative offers the form that any rule must have in order to be an acceptable rule of morality.

To be universalizable, according to Kant, a maxim must be capable of being conceived and willed without contradiction. Kant gives several examples of moral maxims that are supported by, and made imperative by, this principle: "Help others in distress," "Do not commit suicide," and "Work to develop your abilities." His chief example of deceitful promising (see the preceding selection) perhaps best illustrates his categorical imperative, and in reflecting on this example, one might consider whether he would categorically denounce the deception involved in the plutonium experiments.

When we examine the maxim of Kant's man who deceitfully promises ("Whenever I need money, I will borrow it and promise to pay it back, knowing that I cannot do so"), we discover, according to Kant, that the man's maxim is incapable of

[5]Kant, *Foundations of the Metaphysics of Morals,* pp. 30–33.

being conceived and willed without contradiction. It is contradictory and inconsistent with what it presupposes: The maxim would make the purpose of promising itself impossible, because no one would believe the promise. Other examples function similarly. For instance, rules of lying are inconsistent with the practices of truth-telling they presuppose, and rules permitting cheating on tests are inconsistent with the practices of honesty on exams they presuppose. If everyone were permitted to cheat, neither exams nor cheating would have any meaning.

The idea of a formal principle of consistency is somewhat obscure in Kant's philosophy, but it can be simplified to make a very worthy point. One of the clearest cases of an immoral action is when a person attempts (in an inconsistent manner) to make an exception for himself or herself, or when a group seeks a special exemption for itself. For example, a person may sell a car at a high price by lying about its condition, although that person would denounce this same act of lying when buying a car from someone else. For Kant, such "excepting" actions are necessarily immoral, irrespective of circumstances; they cannot be made universal.

However, Kant's philosophy and his examples have troubled many readers. Numerous immoral actions do not seem very easily pronounced "contradictory." For example, Kant's formula does not work as well for the kind of deceit present in the plutonium experiments, in which there is no direct parallel to a promise. Few philosophers would hold, as Kant appears to, that universalizability is both necessary and sufficient for determining the moral acceptability of rules, although many concur that universalizability is a necessary condition of ethical judgments, rules, and principles.

This problem is partially alleviated when Kant goes on to state his categorical imperative in a different formulation. This second form of the categorical imperative is probably more widely quoted and endorsed in contemporary philosophy than the first form; for example, it has been repeatedly quoted by critics of research that is conducted without obtaining informed consent. Kant's second formulation stipulates that "one must act to treat every person as an end and never as a means only." This imperative insists that one must treat other persons as having their autonomously established goals, and that one must never treat others purely as the means to one's own self-determined goals.

Critics of the plutonium experiments have argued that this form of inattentiveness and exploitation occurred throughout the research. They maintain that the patients involved in these experiments were seriously wronged by the failure to obtain consent, having been treated purely as a means to the ends of science and government. Critics also argue that the patients were *wronged* even if they were not actually physically or mentally *harmed* by the plutonium injections. Although the UCSF investigating committee was unwilling to reach such strong conclusions about either wrongdoing or harm, Kantian critics maintain that there is ample evidence in these cases to show both clear wrongdoing and moral culpability for what was done.

It has often been said that Kant asserted categorically that we should never treat another as a means to our ends. This interpretation, however, misrepresents his views. He argues only that we must not treat another *exclusively* as a means to our ends. When secretaries are asked to type manuscripts, or human research subjects are asked to volunteer to test new drugs, they are treated as a means to someone else's ends, but they are not used exclusively for others' purposes, because they do not become mere servants or objects. Kant does not prohibit this use of persons. His imperative demands only that we treat such persons with all the respect and moral dignity to which all persons are entitled at all times, including those times when they are used as means to the ends of others. To treat persons *purely* as means, according to Kant, is to disregard their personhood by exploiting or otherwise using them without regard to their thoughts, interests, and needs.

We shall return to this topic in the later section in this chapter on respect for persons and their autonomy.

## PRIMA FACIE OBLIGATIONS

Moral philosophers have with increasing frequency come to regard all obligations and rights not as absolute standards but as strong moral demands that may be validly overridden when they compete with other principles. *Pluralistic* deontologists affirm more than one basic rule or principle. The most widely discussed pluralistic theory is that of W. D. Ross, who begins with what he judges to be flaws in Kant's system. In particular, Ross objects to Kant's absolutism, that is, the idea that moral rules are categorical imperatives admitting of no exceptions. Morality is constituted by categorical rules for Kant. It follows from his theory that we should never infringe on them, even if we have what seems to be a good moral reason to act otherwise—as when we need to lie to protect someone in danger.

A problem with Kant's theory is how to handle conflicting obligations that give incompatible directives, both of which cannot be fulfilled. For example, I have promised to take my children on a long-anticipated trip, but now find that if I do so, as promised, I cannot assist my sick mother in the hospital, who desperately needs me to help her make decisions with her doctor. Sometimes, the conflict arises from a single moral rule rather than from two different rules in conflict, as, in this example, when one has made two now conflicting promises. Suppose I long ago promised my children that I would take them on the trip, but also long ago promised my mother that I would always assist her in making crucial decisions with her doctor. To what form of judgment, overarching rule, or part of a theory can I appeal to resolve these conflicts?

Ross thinks that Kant gives no real answer to this question because he makes *all* the rules absolute. I cannot both take my children on a trip and help my mother in the hospital at the same time; yet Kant seems to require me to do both. Ross proposes to resolve this problem through a theory that defends several basic and irreducible moral principles that express "prima facie obligations." Our promises create obligations of fidelity, wrongful actions create obligations of reparation, and the generous gifts of our friends create obligations of gratitude. Ross defends several additional obligations as well, including obligations of self-improvement, nonmaleficence, beneficence, and justice. These obligations do not derive from either the principle of utility or Kant's categorical imperative. Ross's list of duties is not based on any overarching principle. He defends it simply as a reflection of our ordinary moral beliefs and judgments.

According to Ross, we intuit these general obligations; but we do not intuit what is right in a particular situation, because reasoning is required. He argues that we must find the "greatest obligation" in any circumstance by finding the "greatest balance" of right over wrong in that circumstance. In the case of a conflict of obligations, we must determine which action or actions would bring about the greatest balance. Here Ross introduces a distinction between *prima facie* obligations and *actual* obligations. He uses the phrase "prima facie duty" to indicate an obligation that presumes fulfillment unless it conflicts on a particular occasion with an equal or stronger obligation. A prima facie duty is always right and binding, all other things being equal. "Prima facie duty" in this sense means "conditional on not being overridden or outweighed by competing moral obligations." One's "actual obligation" is determined by an examination of the respective weights of the competing prima facie obligations.

Prima facie obligations are not absolute, but they have greater moral significance than mere rules of thumb. For example, to call promise-breaking prima facie wrong means that whenever an act involving promise-breaking occurs, the act is wrong unless some more weighty moral consideration is overriding in the circumstances. Breaking a moral rule is not like breaking a rule of thumb, which is a matter of elective choice. For Ross, moral rules have objective standing, just as they do for Kant, even though the standing is not absolute.

As Ross admits, neither he nor any other deontologist has been able to present a system of moral rules free of conflicts and exceptions. Nonetheless, Ross and other Kantians have argued that making moral rules into prima facie rules rather than the absolute rules demanded by Kant is a step in the right direction. A Kantian can in principle reconcile virtually everything in Ross's model of prima facie rules with Kant's account of morals by maintaining that we *justify the system of prima facie rules* on the basis of the categorical imperative, without having to maintain that *each rule* is a categorical imperative. This is all we can expect Kant's system to provide, from Ross's perspective. He expresses his general views both on prima facie obligations and on the correctness of a rule-deontological theory in the following selection.

# *What Makes Right Acts Right?*\*

## W. D. Ross

When a plain man fulfills a promise because he thinks he ought to do so, it seems clear that he does so with no thought of its total consequences, still

\*From W. D. Ross, *The Right and the Good* (Oxford, England: Clarendon Press, 1930). Reprinted by permission of Oxford University Press.

less with any opinion that these are likely to be the best possible. He thinks, in fact, much more of the past than of the future. What makes him think it right to act in a certain way is the fact that he has promised to do so—that and, usually, nothing more. That his act will produce the best possible consequences is not his reason for calling it right. What lends colour to [utilitarianism] . . . is not the actions (which form probably a great majority of our actions) in which some such reflection as "I have promised" is the only reason we give ourselves for thinking a certain action right, but the exceptional cases in which the consequences of fulfilling a promise (for instance) would be so disastrous to others that we judge it right not to do so. It must of course be admitted that such cases exist. If I have promised to meet a friend at a particular time for some trivial purpose, I should certainly think myself justified in breaking my engagement if by doing so I could prevent a serious accident or bring relief to the victims of one. And the supporters of the view we are examining hold that my thinking so is due to my thinking that I shall bring more good into existence by the one action than by the other. A different account may, however, be given of the matter, an account which will, I believe, show itself to be the true one. It may be said that besides the duty of fulfilling promises I have and recognize a duty of relieving distress, and that when I think it right to do the latter at the cost of not doing the former, it is not because I think I shall produce more good thereby but because I think it the duty which is in the circumstances more of a duty. This account surely corresponds much more closely with what we really think in such a situation. If, so far as I can see, I could bring equal amounts of good into being by fulfilling my promise and by helping someone to whom I had made no promise, I should not hesitate to regard the former as my duty. Yet on the view that what is right is right because it is productive of the most good, I should not so regard it. . . .

I suggest "*prima facie* duty" or "conditional duty" as a brief way of referring to the characteristic (quite distinct from that of being a duty proper) which an act has, in virtue of being of a certain kind (e.g., the keeping of a promise), of being an act which would be a duty proper if it were not at the same time of another kind which is morally significant. Whether an act is a duty proper or actual duty depends on *all* the morally significant kinds it is an instance of. . . .

There is nothing arbitrary about these *prima facie* duties. Each rests on a definite circumstance which cannot seriously be held to be without moral significance. Of *prima facie* duties I suggest, without claiming completeness or finality for it, the following division.

(1) Some duties rest on previous acts of my own. These duties seem to include two kinds, (*a*) those resting on a promise or what may fairly be called an implicit promise, such as the implicit undertaking not to tell lies which seems to be implied in the act of entering into conversation (at any rate by civilized men), or of writing books that purport to be history and not fiction. These may be called the duties of fidelity. (*b*) Those resting on a previous wrongful act. These may be called the duties of reparation. (2) Some rest on previous acts of other men, i.e., services done by them to me. These may be loosely described as the duties of gratitude. (3) Some rest on the fact or possibility of a distribution of pleasure or happiness (or of the means thereto) which is not in accordance with the merit of the persons concerned; in such cases there arises a duty to upset or prevent such a distribution. These are the duties of justice. (4) Some rest on the mere fact that there are other beings in the world whose condition we can make better in respect of virtue, or of

intelligence, or of pleasure. These are the duties of beneficence. (5) Some rest on the fact that we can improve our own condition in respect of virtue or of intelligence. These are the duties of self-improvement. (6) I think that we should distinguish from (4) the duties that may be summed up under the title of "not injuring others." No doubt to injure others is incidentally to fail to do them good; but it seems to me clear that non-maleficence is apprehended as a duty distinct from that of beneficence, and as a duty of a more stringent character. It will be noticed that this alone among the types of duty has been stated in a negative way. An attempt might no doubt be made to state this duty, like the others, in a positive way. It might be said that it is really the duty to prevent ourselves from acting either from an inclination to harm others or from an inclination to seek our own pleasure, in doing which we should incidentally harm them. But on reflection it seems clear that the primary duty here is the duty not to harm others, this being a duty whether or not we have an inclination that, if followed, would lead to our harming them; and that when we have such an inclination, the primary duty not to harm others gives rise to a consequential duty to resist the inclination. The recognition of this duty of non-maleficence is the first step on the way to the recognition of the duty of beneficence; and that accounts for the prominence of the commands "thou shalt not kill," "thou shalt not commit adultery," "thou shalt not steal," "thou shalt not bear false witness," in so early a code as the Decalogue. . . .

If the objection be made that this catalogue of the main types of duty is an unsystematic one resting on no logical principle, it may be replied, first, that it makes no claim to being ultimate. It is a *prima facie* classification of the duties which reflection on our moral convictions seems actually to reveal. And if these convictions are, as I would claim that they are, of the nature of knowledge, and if I have not misstated them, the list will be a list of authentic conditional duties, correct as far as it goes though not necessarily complete. The list of *goods* put forward by the rival theory is reached by exactly the same method—the only sound one in the circumstances—viz. that of direct reflection on what we really think. Loyalty to the facts is worth more than a symmetrical architectonic or a hastily reached simplicity. If further reflection discovers a perfect logical basis for this or for a better classification, so much the better.

It may, again, be objected that our theory that there are these various and often conflicting types of *prima facie* duty leaves us with no principle upon which to discern what is our actual duty in particular circumstances. But this objection is not one which the rival theory is in a position to bring forward. For when we have to choose between the production of two heterogeneous goods, say knowledge and pleasure, the "ideal utilitarian" theory can only fall back on an opinion, for which no logical basis can be offered, that one of the goods is the greater; and this is no better than a similar opinion that one of two duties is the more urgent. . . .

It is necessary to say something by way of clearing up the relation between *prima facie* duties and the actual or absolute duty to do one particular act in particular circumstances. If, as almost all moralists except Kant are agreed, and as most plain men think, it is sometimes right to tell a lie or to break a promise, it must be maintained that there is a difference between *prima facie* duty and actual or absolute duty. When we think ourselves justified in breaking, and indeed morally obliged to break, a promise in order to relieve some one's distress, we do not for a moment cease to recognize a *prima facie* duty to keep our promise and this leads us to feel, not indeed shame or repentance, but certainly compunction, for behaving as we do; we recognize further, that it is our duty to make up somehow to the promisee for the breaking of the promise. We have to distinguish from the characteristic of being our duty that of tending to be our duty. Any act that we do contains various elements in virtue of which it falls under various categories. In virtue of being the breaking of a promise, for instance, it tends to be wrong; in virtue of being an instance of relieving distress it tends to be right. Tendency to be one's duty may be called a parti-resultant attribute, i.e., one which belongs to an act in virtue of some one component in its nature. *Being* one's duty is a toti-resultant attribute, one which belongs to an act in virtue of its whole nature and of nothing less than this. . . .

Our judgments about our actual duty in concrete situations have none of the certainty that attaches to our recognition of the general principles of duty. A statement is certain, i.e., is an expression of knowledge, only in one or other of two cases: when it is either self-evident, or a valid conclusion from self-evident premises. And our judgments about our particular duties have neither of these characters. . . .

The general principles of duty are obviously not self-evident from the beginning of our lives. How do they come to be so? The answer is, that they come to be self-evident to us just as mathematical axioms do. We find by experience that this couple of matches and that couple make four matches, that this couple of balls on a wire and that couple make four balls; and by reflection on these and similar discoveries we come to see that it is of the nature of two and two to make four. In a precisely similar way, we see the *prima facie* rightness of an act which would be the fulfillment of a particular promise, and of another which would be the fulfillment of another promise, and when we have reached sufficient maturity to think in general terms, we apprehend *prima facie* rightness to belong to the nature of any fulfillment of promise. What comes first in time is the apprehension of the self-evident *prima facie* rightness of an individual act of a particular type. From this we come by reflection to apprehend the self-evident general principle of *prima facie* duty. From this, too, perhaps along with the apprehension of the self-evident *prima facie* rightness of the same act in virtue of its having another characteristic as well, and perhaps in spite of the apprehension of its *prima facie* wrongness in virtue of its having some third characteristic, we come to believe something not self-evident at all, but an object of probable opinion, viz. that this particular act is (not *prima facie* but) actually right.

There can be little doubt that Ross's distinction between types of duty makes a great deal of sense. But it does not solve the difficulty, as Ross recognized, of how to reason and what to do when prima facie rules conflict. A pluralist like Ross may have to admit that a moral system gives us little guidance about which rules or principles take priority in situations of conflict. Ross holds, possibly without good reason, that the principle of nonmaleficence (noninfliction of harm) takes precedence over the principle of beneficence (production of benefit) when the two come into conflict, but he gives no defense of this thesis and no account of the priorities among the other principles, except to say that several obligations (such as keeping promises) have "a great deal of stringency." Ultimately, Ross quotes Aristotle: "The decision rests with perception," but this appeal seems no real solution. Ross thus seems to have solved Kant's problem about conflict only to have generated another problem of parallel difficulty.

## RESPECT FOR PERSONS
## AND RESPECT FOR AUTONOMY

Several times in this chapter the categories of "person," "autonomy," and "human dignity" have been mentioned. They played a role in our discussion of Kant's second formulation of the categorical imperative, in the case of the plutonium investigators who failed to treat their subjects with respect for their autonomy, and in Kant's linking of personal dignity with autonomous legislation. These pivotal moral concepts, centering on the nature of persons and our responsibilities to them, occupy a special place in Kant's theory and in deontological ethics more generally.

Although respect for persons is a principle as deep-seated as any in morality, little agreement exists about the nature and strength of the obligations owed to persons, and still less agreement about what is to be respected, why it is to be respected, and under which conditions respect is not required. In this section we look more closely at these moral notions.

### Are Persons Special?

We can start with the question, "Why is the category of persons special?" Kant and many other deontologists have maintained that persons are special because they alone perform actions out of moral autonomy. Animals may perform ably in a laboratory experiment, and their performances might lead us to say that they act on reasons, but their reasons are not *moral* reasons; apparently a practical moral will is lacking in nonhuman animals. Because humans act morally and have autonomous wills, they possess value independent of any circumstance, role, or contribution that might confer value on them, such as their service to the community or their generosity toward an adoring child. Persons and only persons, say many Kantians, have this unconditional value, which endows them with dignity. Kantians argue that it is therefore inappropriate to treat persons as if they had the value possessed by animals and natural objects, which is a value strictly conditional on circumstances and instrumental only.

The theory of moral personhood underlying this theory is controversial, but it seems safe to assume that a creature (which in theory could be other than human) is a moral person if (1) it is capable of making moral judgments about the rightness and wrongness of actions, and (2) it has motives that can be judged morally. These are moral-capacity criteria, not conditions of morally correct action or character. An individual could be immoral and still qualify for moral personhood.

In some Kantian theories, any entity qualifying for moral personhood is a member of the moral community and qualifies for its benefits, burdens, protections, and punishments; any entity lacking moral personhood fails to qualify. It is central to the institution of morality that moral persons deserve respect and are to be judged as moral agents. Moral persons know that we can condemn their motives and actions, blame them for irresponsible actions, and punish them for immoral behavior.

The moral protections afforded by this community may be *extended* to weak and vulnerable human beings who are not or not yet persons—for example, fetuses, severely brain-damaged patients, and various dementia patients. We might also extend protections to nonhuman animals. But moral standing for all these individuals must rest on some basis other than personhood. For example, they might enjoy moral standing because they possess the capacity for pain, suffering, and emotional deprivation: properties that will not make them moral persons but will qualify them for moral protections.

As noted in the plutonium cases, it was not uncommon in the 1940s and 1950s for physicians to use patients as subjects in experiments without their knowledge or consent. This seems a clear affront to persons who are capable of giving an informed consent to involvement in the research—as CAL-1 and CAL-3 could have done. But potentially hazardous nontherapeutic experimentation is no less questionable with classes of individuals who are not (or are not *yet*) persons. CAL-2 was a very sick four-year-old boy. He likely did not have the form of moral autonomy envisioned by Kant, and on some criteria he may not even have been a person. Yet this fact seems in no way to give him a reduced moral status.

## Moral Autonomy and Individual Autonomy

We have seen that Kantian theory is based on *moral*, rather than *individual* personhood and autonomy. This distinction is of major importance. Moral autonomy is self-governance by giving oneself moral rules (moral guides to behavior), whereas individual autonomy is self-governance by acceptance of any kind of rules or guides to behavior (such as legal requirements, reasons of prudence, or professional objectives). A morally autonomous action involves willing moral principles and acting in accordance with them, whereas an individually autonomous action requires no such moral condition. Because individual autonomy can be moral, immoral, or amoral, moral autonomy is one kind of individual autonomy. The account of autonomy presented by Kant is exclusively an account of moral autonomy (to act individually without the warrant of morality is to act nonautonomously in their accounts), while the accounts by Mill and Hume, for example, presuppose individual autonomy and are only secondarily concerned with moral autonomy.

**Moral Autonomy and Kantian Respect for Persons.**   It may seem odd that Kant understands the term "autonomy" exclusively in terms of moral governance, thereby excluding nonmoral personal choice from the realm of the autonomous. However, "autonomy" serves for him as a technical term in moral theory with a systematic deemphasis on individual choice as something that deserves respect for moral reasons. Only a general, anonymous, and universal perspective is appropriate in Kantian morality.

Kantian theories of moral autonomy often recognize the moral and social importance of individual freedom, rights, and social liberties, but they distinguish these categories of liberty from those of autonomy. Autonomy is for them a morally weighted notion; liberty is not. They further insist that a person's *belief* that an action is morally obligatory is not sufficient to render the action morally autonomous. The obligation must *be* a moral obligation, and the person's motive must be a moral motive, for an action to be autonomous. Following the lines of the categorical imperative, the Kantian principle of respect for persons is that we must always treat persons (autonomous agents) as ends in themselves, and never merely as a means to the ends of others.

Whether in the end this Kantian thesis about respect applies only to autonomous persons and not to nonautonomous individuals (infants, the severely retarded, the mentally ill, and the like) is a difficult matter in Kantian moral theory, but one on which little turns for our purposes. More important is the contrast between Kantians and those who defend respect for individual autonomy.

**The Principle of Respect for Individual Autonomy.**   A moral principle of respect for individual autonomy specifies a duty to respect the autonomous actions of others, whether or not these actions conform to moral obligations. At first sight, this thesis seems to suggest that we must tolerate immoral actions by others. Closer inspection shows that the principle of respect for individual autonomy derives from commonsense views about the moral importance of being left free to make choices. The principle requires that we enable persons to act autonomously, generally by not interfering with them as they carry out their goals in life. For example, informed hospital patients have the right to refuse self-regarding, life-sustaining medical intervention and die as a result. The principle of respect for (individual) autonomy suggests that the morally appropriate response is to leave the choice up to the individual, even if we believe the choice is wrong.

The supporter of individual autonomy takes the view that we have a fundamental moral obligation to respect autonomous agents by duly recognizing their considered value judgments and outlook, including their right to their beliefs and their right to take actions based on those beliefs, even if we consider them to be foolish, deviant, or perilous for the individual. We respect the rights of those who wish to drive race cars, enter Golden Gloves competitions, or hang-glide, for example, whether or not we think the risks excessive and the enterprises foolish. In evaluating the self-regarding actions of others, this principle requires that we respect them as individuals with the same right to their judgments as we possess; they, in turn, are obligated to treat us in the same way. (See, further, the discussion of John Stuart Mill on "individuality" in Chapter 4 and the accounts of liberty in Chapter 10.)

However, this principle of respect does not entail that we must respect immoral actions by others. If persons violate rules of justice or break the law, we are not required to respect their actions. John Rawls has argued that it is morally misguided to permit violations of basic moral principles on grounds that the action is autonomous. Even courageous and conscientious actions need not merit respect. Without establishing moral boundaries of accountability, Rawls argues, "autonomy is likely to lead to a mere collision of self-righteous wills."

> [I]t is not true that the conscientious judgments of each person ought absolutely to be respected; nor is it true that individuals are completely free to form their moral convictions. These contentions are mistaken if they mean that, having arrived at our moral opinions conscientiously (as we believe), we always have a claim to be allowed to act on them.[6]

The principle of respect for autonomy is therefore merely a prima facie principle, to use Ross's language, and can be overridden by competing considerations. We will encounter some premier problems about when the principle of respect for autonomy is validly overridden by another moral principle when we come to the topics of legal moralism, offensiveness, and paternalism in Chapter 10.

## The Concept of Respect and the Object of Respect

The concept of respect at work in both respect for persons and respect for autonomy has not been carefully treated thus far. We now turn to this problem.

Respect has been variously defined as a disposition to consider the desires and actions of other persons, an attitude of sympathy toward other persons, taking the other person's perspective, and an acknowledgment of the dignity of other persons. There is something correct about each of these explications, but also problems with each. Respect for persons, or for their autonomy, necessarily involves a favorable attitude of evaluation and does not encompass the kind of attitude involved in respect for enemies or respect for the dangerous acts of a crazy person. The relevant general meaning of the word "respect" is esteeming, valuing, or prizing so as to treat with consideration, deference, or noninterference. Nonetheless, as we saw previously, morality does not require us to respect actions that are opposed to morality. It would be misguided to respect courageous actions that violate moral principles. Autonomy must be respected only if an autonomous action is a morally acceptable action. This means that it is appropriate in some cases *not* to respect certain autonomous actions, either by ignoring, disallowing, refusing to accept, or otherwise showing active disrespect.

This conclusion raises questions about the basis of respect. Kant said that respect is the acknowledgment of another's dignity, which is of priceless worth:

> [Each person] possesses a dignity (an absolute inner worth) whereby he exacts the respect of all other rational beings . . . and can esteem himself on a footing of equality with them.
>
> The humanity in one's person is the object of the respect which he can require of every other human being. . . . He should always pursue his end with an awareness of the sublimity of his moral nature. . . .
>
> From the fact that one is capable of such internal legislation and that the (physical) man feels himself compelled to venerate the (moral) man in his own person, there must also follow exaltation and the highest self-esteem. This is the feeling of one's inner worth

---

[6]Rawls, *A Theory of Justice*, § 78. See Chapter 9 in the present book for an explication of Rawls's theory of justice.

(*valor*), according to which he is above all price (*pretium*) and possesses an inalienable dignity.[7]

This analysis seems to switch from respect to dignity, and runs a risk of circularity. In Kant's philosophy perhaps the best definition of "dignity" treats it in terms of free rational agents who are ends in themselves. However, this analysis fails to acknowledge the dignity of these who lack the capacity for autonomy; it is circular as an explication of autonomy, because autonomy is defined in terms of dignity. If the Kantian holds that the *value* of persons is found in their autonomy, that is, in their rational capacity to prescribe laws for themselves, and this value is explicated in terms of dignity, then autonomy and dignity are interchangeable notions. Both provide the grounds of the obligation to respect persons.

Supplying a more adequate account of dignity and respect has proved troublesome for Kantians. It is also unclear whether we respect persons because they are persons rather than for some more limited characteristics they possess, such as honesty, integrity, and professionalism. Joel Feinberg explains why these terms have proved particularly difficult to analyze.

> Various terms from the metaphysical vocabulary "explain" human worth only by renaming that which is to be explained. Thus, without further explanation, the fact that all human beings are "persons, not things" or the claim that "men are ends in themselves" do not clearly account for the equality of human worth. Similarly, that men are "sacred" or of "infinite value" are other (and perhaps better) ways of putting the claim of equal worth, but not descriptions of the grounds of that worth. If "sacred" (like "precious") is best defined as being the proper object of a certain kind of attitude, then the fact of a man's sacredness cannot be invoked in justification of that attitude without a kind of trivializing circularity.[8]

The Kantian theory seems in the end to presuppose that the attitude of respect for autonomy is *fundamental* in ethics, and as such not to be defensible or explicable in terms of any other notion.

## DEONTOLOGICAL CONSTRAINTS

We have seen throughout this chapter that one of the central claims of deontological ethics is that certain actions may not be performed, come what may. In the plutonium case, the researchers thought that by experimenting on a few individuals they could help achieve several worthy social goals such as protecting workers in the nuclear industry and developing an adequate defense for western nations in the face of possible Soviet aggression. Even if achieving these goals would have good consequences for millions of people, deontologists maintain that the way the researchers treated their subjects was unethical because they violated fundamental constraints on how we can permissibly treat persons.

---

[7]Kant, *The Metaphysical Principles of Virtue*, pt. I, James W. Ellington, trans., in Kant, *Ethical Philosophy* (Indianapolis: Hackett Publishing Co., 1983), pp. 97–98.
[8]Joel Feinberg, *Social Philosophy* (Englewood Cliffs, NJ: Prentice-Hall, 1973), pp. 92–93.

These constraints are commonly referred to as "deontological constraints." Robert Nozick and Bernard Williams (see Chapter 4 on both) and other writers we have met in this text argue that these deontological constraints operate on our actions even when we can bring about a good state of affairs. In a much discussed example, should I kill an innocent person in order to save two innocent persons from being killed by someone else? To kill the innocent person is a violation of his right to life. A believer in deontological constraints holds that this person's right or a (correlative) duty not to take the person's life morally prohibits my killing the person.

Deontological constraints are essentially negative duties—that is, they specify what we cannot justifiably do to others even in the pursuit of worthy individual or social goals; however, they do not specify any actions that we should perform for the sake of others. For example, it would be a violation of a deontological constraint to steal a sibling's share of the family inheritance, but deontological constraints do not tell us how to divide wealth among siblings.

The concept of deontological constraints highlights an obvious difference between deontologists and utilitarians. The latter require us to determine the best possible objective state of affairs, irrespective of the position of particular agents who act in those states of affairs. Utilitarians demand an external, impartial view of the situation so that each person's interests are weighed equally. From this perspective, one's own position, role, and sense of integrity have no independent force; they are only important insofar as they are factors in the calculus of utilities. Whereas rule utilitarians might argue that the best possible state of affairs would be produced by a rule banning physician-assisted suicide, they would argue for such a rule from an external, objective standpoint. Only the likely consequences of banning or allowing such actions would be considered, and they would consider the fact that it would be the doctor herself who killed the patient to be irrelevant. For the utilitarian, it doesn't really matter who brings the best possible state of affairs about; all that matters is that good outcomes are in fact produced.[9]

Many deontologists, however, maintain that factors such as one's role or sense of integrity have independent moral weight. Imagine that a terminally ill patient in extreme pain asks his physician to kill him. The man's family agrees with this decision, and the doctor realizes that everyone will be better off if the man dies. Nonetheless, our deontologist doctor believes that her role as a physician, as well as her own sense of moral integrity, prevents her from taking this man's life. Similarly in the plutonium case, a physician might feel constrained from engaging in nontherapeutic human experimentation irrespective of the good consequences that would follow from the experimental work. Here deontological constraints are *agent-relative,* as they make reference to the values and judgments of particular persons such as physicians and scientists. Deontologists argue that the agent's perspective is important in moral deliberation, and that who performs an action and how a good state of affairs is to be brought about matter irrespective of consequences. As moral agents we should not be the direct cause of certain harms befalling others, even if we cannot actually prevent those harms from occurring. In the case of the

---

[9]For an example of such a utilitarian approach to moral rules, see Richard B. Brandt, *Morality, Utilitarianism, and Rights* (New York: Cambridge University Press, 1992).

doctor with the terminally ill patient, the doctor should not kill the patient even though she cannot prevent him from dying because she believes that doctors should never take human lives.

The idea that these constraints are agent-relative has been very important in recent moral philosophy, but there are puzzling aspects to this position. To return to our original example, if killing an innocent person is bad, then why can I not act to minimize the number of killings that will occur; but if I do so act, then I will do precisely what I cannot do (namely, kill the innocent person)—the so-called paradox of deontology. In the following selection, Thomas Nagel tries to make sense of deontological constraints, agent-relativity, and two different perspectives that might be taken on the morality of the situation. He maintains that deontological constraints are an important part of our morality and that they have powerful subjective force.

# The Limits of Objectivity*

## Thomas Nagel

Deontological constraints . . . depend not on the aims or projects of the agent but on the claims of others. Unlike autonomous reasons, they cannot be given up at will. If they exist, they restrict what we may do in the service of either agent-relative or agent-neutral goals.

Whatever their explanation, they are conspicuous among the moral appearances. Here is an example to focus your intuitions.

You have an auto accident one winter night on a lonely road. The other passengers are badly injured, the car is out of commission, and the road is deserted, so you run along it till you find an isolated house. The house turns out to be occupied by an old woman who is looking after her small grandchild. There is no phone, but there is a car in the garage, and you ask desperately to borrow it and explain the situation. She

doesn't believe you. Terrified by your desperation, she runs upstairs and locks herself in the bathroom, leaving you alone with the child. You pound ineffectively on the door and search without success for the car keys. Then it occurs to you that she might be persuaded to tell you where they are if you were to twist the child's arm outside the bathroom door. Should you do it?

It is difficult not to see this as a serious dilemma, even though the child's getting his arm twisted is a minor evil compared with your friends' not getting to a hospital. The dilemma must be due to a special reason against *doing* such a thing. Otherwise it would be *obvious* that you should choose the lesser evil, and twist the child's arm.

Common moral intuition recognizes several types of deontological reasons—limits on what one may do to people or how one may treat them. There are the special obligations created by promises and agreements; the restrictions against lying; the prohibitions against violating various individual rights, rights not to be

*From Thomas Nagel, "The Limits of Objectivity," in Sterling M. McMurrin, ed., *The Tanner Lectures on Human Values* (Salt Lake City: University of Utah Press, 1980), vol. 1.

killed, injured, imprisoned, threatened, tortured, coerced, robbed; the restrictions against imposing certain sacrifices on someone simply as means to an end; and perhaps the special claim of immediacy, which makes distress at a distance so different from distress in the same room. There may also be a deontological requirement of fairness, of evenhandedness or equality in one's *treatment* of people. . . .

In all these cases it appears that the special reasons, if they exist, cannot be explained simply in terms of *agent-neutral* values, because the particular relation of the agent to the outcome is essential. Deontological constraints may be *overridden* by agent-neutral reasons of sufficient strength, but they are not themselves to be understood as the expression of agent-neutral values of any kind. It is clear from the way such reasons work that they cannot be explained by the hypothesis that the violation of a deontological constraint has high negative agent-neutral value. Deontological reasons have their full force against *your doing* something—not just against its *happening.*

For example, if there really are such constraints, the following things seem to be true. It seems that *you* shouldn't break a promise or tell a lie for the sake of some benefit, even though you would not be required to forego a comparable benefit in order to prevent someone else from breaking a promise or telling a lie. And it seems that you shouldn't twist the arm of a small child to get its grandmother to do something, even if the thing is quite important—important enough so that it would not be reasonable to forego a comparable benefit in order to prevent someone else from twisting a child's arm. And it may be that you shouldn't *engage in* certain

kinds of unfair discriminatory treatment (in an official role, for example) even to produce a good result which it would be unreasonable to forego in order to prevent similar unfairness by *others*. . . .

Deontological restrictions, if they exist, apply to everyone: they are mandatory and may not be given up like personal ambitions or commitments.

There is no doubt that ideas of this kind form an important part of common moral phenomenology. Yet it is tempting to think that the whole thing is a kind of moral illusion resulting either from innate psychological dispositions or from crude but useful moral indoctrination. But this hypothesis faces problems in explaining what the illusion *is*. It may be a good thing if people have a deep inhibition against torturing children even for very strong reasons, and the same might be said of other deontological constraints. But that does not explain why we cannot come to *regard* it as a mere inhibition which it is good to have. An illusion involves a judgment or a disposition to judge, and not a mere motivational impulse. The phenomenological fact that has to be accounted for is that we seem to apprehend in each individual case an extremely powerful agent-relative *reason* not to torture a child. This presents itself as the apprehension of a *truth,* not just as a psychological inhibition. And the claim that such an inhibition is in general very useful does nothing to justify or explain the conviction of a strong reason in every individual case. That conviction is what has to be analyzed and accounted for, and accepted or rejected according to whether the account gives it an adequate justification.

I believe that the traditional principle of double effect. . . . provides a rough guide to the extension and character of deontological constraints. . . . The principle says that to violate deontological constraints one must maltreat someone else *intentionally*. The maltreatment must be something that one does or chooses, either as an end or as a means, rather than something one's actions merely cause or fail to prevent, but that one doesn't aim at.

It is also possible to *foresee* that one's actions will cause or fail to prevent a harm that one does not *intend* to bring about or permit. In that case it is not, in the relevant sense, something one *does,* and does not come under a deontological constraint, though it may still be objectionable for impersonal reasons. (One point worth stressing: the constraints apply to intentionally *permitting* as well as to intentionally *doing* harm. Thus in our example, there would be the same kind of objection if *with the same end in view* you permitted someone else to twist the child's arm. You would have let it happen *intentionally,* and that would be different from a failure to prevent such an occurrence because you were too engaged in doing something *else* which was more important.)

So far this is just moral phenomenology: it does not remove the paradox. *Why* should we consider ourselves far more responsible for what we do (or permit) intentionally than for consequences of action that we foresee and decide to accept but that do not form part of our aims (intermediate or final)? How can the connection of ends and means conduct responsibility so much more effectively than the connection of foresight and avoidability?

It is as if each action produced a special perspective on the world, determined by intention. When I twist the child's arm intentionally I incorporate that evil into what I do: it is my creation

and the reasons stemming from it are magnified from my point of view so that they tower over reasons stemming from greater evils that are more "distant" because they do not fall within the range of intention.

That is the picture, but how can it be correct?

I believe that this is one of those cases in which the removal of paradox is not a philosophical advance. Deontological reasons are essentially problematic, and the problem is an instance of the collision between subjective and objective points of view. The issue is whether the special, personal perspective of agency has fundamental significance in determining what people have reason to do. The question is whether, because of this perspective, I can have sufficient reason not to do something which, considered from an external standpoint, it would be better if I did. That is, *things* would be better, what *happened* would be better, if I twisted the child's arm than if I did not. But I would have *done* something worse. If considerations of what I may do, and the correlative claims of my victim, can outweigh the substantial impersonal value of what will happen, that can only be because the perspective of the agent has an importance in practical reasoning that resists domination by a conception of the world as a place where good and bad things happen, and have their value without perspective. . . .

Let me try to say where the strength of the deontological view lies. We may begin by considering a curious feature of deontological reasons on which I have not yet remarked. Intention appears to magnify the importance of *evil* aims by comparison with *evil* side effects in a way that it does not magnify the importance of *good* aims by comparison with *good* side effects. We are supposed to avoid using evil means to produce a good end, even though it would be permissible to produce that good end by neutral means with comparably evil side effects.

On the other hand, given two routes to a legitimate end, one of which involves *good* means and *neutral* side effects, and the other of which involves *neutral* means and slightly *better* side effects, there is no reason to choose the first route. Deontological reasons tell us only *not* to aim at *evil;* they don't tell us *to* aim at *good,* as a means. Why should this be? What is the relation between evil and *intention,* or *aiming,* that makes them clash in a special and intense way?

The answer emerges if we ask ourselves what is the essence of *aiming,* what differentiates it from merely producing a result knowingly?

The difference is that action intentionally aimed at a goal is *guided* by that goal. Whether the goal is an end in itself or only a means, action aimed at it must follow it and be prepared to adjust its pursuit if deflected by altered circumstances. Whereas an act that merely *produces* an effect does not *follow* it, is not *guided* by it, even if the effect is foreseen.

What does this mean? It means that to aim at evil, *even as a means,* is to have one's action *guided* by evil. One must be prepared to adjust it to insure the production of evil: a falling off in the level of the desired evil must be grounds for altering what one does so that the evil is restored and maintained. But the *essence* of evil is that it should *repel* us. If something is evil, our actions should be guided, if they are guided by it at all, toward its elimination rather than toward its maintenance. That is what evil *means.* So when we aim at evil we are

swimming head-on against the normative current. Our action is guided by the goal at every point in the direction diametrically opposite to that in which the value of that goal points. To put it another way, if we aim at evil we make what we do in the first instance a positive rather than a negative function of evil. At every point, the intentional function is simply the normative function reversed, and from the point of view of the agent, this produces the acute sense of doing something awful.

If you twist the child's arm, in our example, your aim is to produce pain. So when the child cries, "Stop, it hurts!" his objection corresponds in perfect diametrical opposition to your intention. What he is pleading as your reason to stop is precisely your reason to go on. If it didn't hurt, you would twist harder, or try the other arm. You are pushing directly and essentially against the normative force intrinsic to your goal, for it is the production of pain that guides you. It seems to me that this is the essence of deontological constraints. What feels peculiarly wrong about doing evil intentionally even that good may come of it is the headlong striving against value that is internal to one's aim. . . .

But all this still leaves unsettled the question of justification. For it will be objected that if one aims at evil as a means only, then one's action is not really being guided by evil but by overall good, which includes a *balance* of goods and evils. So when you twist the child's arm, you are guided by the aim of rescuing your injured friends, and the good of that aim dominates the evil of the child's pain. The immediacy of the fact that you must try to produce evil as a subsidiary aim is phenomenologically important, but why should it be morally important?

Here I think we have come down to a fundamental clash between perspectives. The question is whether to disregard the resistance encountered by my immediate pursuit of evil, in favor of the overall value of the results of what I do. When I view my act from outside, and think of it as resulting from a choice of the impersonally considered state of the world in which it occurs, this seems rational. In thinking of the matter this way, I abstract my will and its choices from my person, as it were, and even from my actions, and decide directly among states of the world, as if I were taking a multiple-choice test. If the choice is determined by what on balance is impersonally best, then I am guided by good and not by evil.

But the self that is so guided is the objective self which regards the world impersonally, as a place containing TN [Thomas Nagel] and his actions, among other things. It is detached from the perspective of TN, for it views the world from nowhere within it. It chooses, and then TN, its instrument, or perhaps one could say its agent, carries out the instructions as best he can. *He* may have to aim at evil, for the impersonally best alternative may involve the production of good ends by evil means. But he is merely following orders.

To see the matter in this light is to see both why the appeal of agent-neutral, consequentialist ethics is so great and why the contrary force of agent-relative, deontological ethics is so powerful. The detached, objective view takes in everything and provides a standpoint of choice from which all choosers can agree about what should happen. But each of us is not only an objective self but a particular person with a particular perspective; we act in the world with that perspective, and not only from the point of view of a detached will, selecting and rejecting world-states. So our choices are not merely choices of states of the world, but of *actions.* From this point of view, the pursuit of evil in twisting the child's arm looms large. The production of pain is the immediate aim, and the fact that from an external perspective you are choosing a balance of good over evil does not cover up the fact that this is the kind of action you are undertaking.

This account of the force of deontological reasons applies with special clarity to the constraint against doing harm as a means to your ends. A fuller deontological theory would have to explain the different types of normative grain against which one acts in breaking promises, lying, discriminating unfairly, and denying immediate emergency aid. It would also have to deal with problems about what exactly is being aimed at in cases of action that can be described in several different ways. But I believe that the key to understanding any of these moral intuitions is the distinction between the internal viewpoint of the agent in acting and an external, objective viewpoint which the agent can also adopt. Reasons for action look different from the first point of view than from the second.

Nagel's claim is that when we take the internal perspective, we see that it would be wrong to do certain things, such as twisting the little boy's arm. However, Nagel does not claim that a person can never legitimately violate deontological constraints or never take an external, impartial perspective. While Nagel thinks we will likely feel guilt, regret, or a sense of moral violation if we violate a deontological constraint, critics wonder why this should be so, especially if we have acted, from an external perspective, to produce the best state of affairs. This problem takes us to some of the criticisms that can be offered of deontological theories generally, and Kantian theories in particular.

## CRITICISMS AND DEFENSES OF DEONTOLOGICAL THEORIES

We can now investigate some criticisms of Kantian and other deontological theories that have been expressed in contemporary philosophy, together with some responses that deontologists might offer to these criticisms.

### The Problem of Covert Consequential Appeals

Kant asserts that actions are determined to be right or wrong independently of particular consequences, whereas Ross admits that consequences are relevant to moral thinking, although not the only consideration. A utilitarian response is that Ross is more insightful than Kant, but that, in the end, all deontologists always do covertly appeal to consequences in order to demonstrate the rightness of actions. For example, John Stuart Mill argues that in Kant's theory the categorical imperative demands that an action be morally prohibited if "the *consequences* of [its] universal adoption would be such as no one would choose to incur." Kant fails "almost grotesquely," as Mill puts it, to show that any form of contradiction appears when we universalize immoral rules of conduct. Instead, Kant's theory relies on a covert appeal to the utilitarian principle that if the consequences of the universal performance of a certain type of action can be shown to be undesirable overall, then that sort of action is wrong.

One defense of Kant against these charges is that he does not demand that we disregard consequences altogether, as if an action could be determined to be morally right (or wrong) without regard to its consequences. Kant holds only that the features of an action making it right are not dependent upon any particular outcome. An action's consequences often cannot be separated from the nature of the action itself, so consequences too must be considered when an agent universalizes the action in order to determine whether it is permissible. Kant may occasionally overstate his views by too strongly condemning consequential reasoning, but many of his writings indicate that he was more than willing to consider consequences as an integral part of the universalization process. Kant does not say, then, that an action can be universalized without universalizing its consequences, and few Kant scholars think otherwise.[10]

---

[10]David Cummiskey argues that consequences were important to Kant, and that considerations of consequences are not inconsistent with his moral theory. See Cummiskey, *Kantian Consequentialism* (New York: Oxford University Press, 1996).

Another deontological reply can be drawn from the style of argument that we have seen Thomas Nagel pressing against utilitarians, namely, that consequentialist reasoning can never fully account for the importance of character and personal integrity. Consider a well-known example from Bernard Williams: George, who has a wife and two children, is out of work when a friend offers him a job that would involve studying ways to conduct chemical and biological warfare. George believes that he cannot accept this particular job because of his moral scruples about such research. Yet he needs the money to restore family stability and to meet his children's needs. Furthermore, George knows that the other candidate for the position would pursue the research overzealously and uncritically if he were hired.

George has an opportunity to help his family and perhaps to prevent a destructive fanatic from obtaining a potentially dangerous job. Moreover, it appears that the public would benefit from George's accepting the position, because he will be more responsible in evaluating the research and will have a voice in seeing that it is not abused. Nevertheless, his conscience stands in the way. George's conscience might, on the one hand, direct him to refuse the position because it involves immoral research, but on the other hand, direct him to accept the position because it will prevent the research from being pursued by fanatics and will also benefit his family. According to Williams, George faces a moral tragedy and cannot preserve his integrity if he follows strictly consequential reasoning.

## The Problem of Nonsystematization

A second, but related, criticism has been brought against *pluralistic* deontological theories by, among others, *monistic* deontological thinkers. The contention is that pluralistic theories lack unity, coherence, and systematic organization. These critics suggest that, whereas the principle of utility tells us what makes right actions right on all occasions, thinkers such as Ross provide nothing beyond a disconnected list of diverse right-making considerations. If one takes the basic tasks of philosophical ethics to be that of providing ultimate reasons for our moral judgments, then pluralistic deontological theories (and Kantian theories that offer a plurality of categorically imperative principles) fail.

In Chapter 2, we saw Thomas Nagel defending the view that an unconnected heap of obligations must be accepted as an ineradicable feature of morality, and thus that there can be no unifying moral principle. Nagel's position could be taken as one form of reply to these critics of pluralistic deontology. Ross himself was well aware of at least some parts of this criticism, and he acknowledged that his catalog of obligations is unsystematic and probably incomplete. His response follows the lines drawn in one of his criticisms of Kant's appeal to a single categorical imperative. He finds that critics are forcing an "architectonic" of "hastily reached simplicity" on ethics. This reply is an attempt to turn the tables on his critics. Whereas they maintain that his views lack systematic unity, he sees that disunity as an integral feature of the very moral life that he is examining. Untidiness and complexity may be unfortunate features of morality, but if they nonetheless are true characterizations, then Ross's theory of morality can hardly be faulted for incorporating them. Indeed, it is the obligation of a moral philosopher to point out a lack of systematic unity if it is inescapable.

Ross might additionally have argued (although he does not) that deontological theories are no worse off than utilitarian theories in this regard. Rule utilitarianism contains an extremely abstract principle of obligation based on certain views about goodness, from which a number of rules of obligation are supported. These rules are not given systematic unity in utilitarian theories (beyond their derivation from the principle of utility itself). Ross could point out that the general demand to act on the most pressing prima facie obligation is a rule that provides all the cohesion and unity that can be expected.

## Limitations of the Models of Contract and Law

Kantian theories concentrate on *lawful* obligations, and recent Kantian theories such as Rawls's feature the idea of *contractual* obligations. These theories emphasize autonomous choice among free and equal agents, but critics question whether freedom, choice, equality, contract, law, and the staples of the Kantian theory deserve to be elevated to a central position in moral theory (even if they are central in legal or political theories). These categories are valued so highly that central goals of morality become the protection of freedom, equal consideration of persons, and impartial reflection and treatment. Morality mediates interpersonal conflict and protects us against harms. Conformity to general rules becomes the mechanism through which these goals are to be accomplished. But, some critics now ask, is this any way to understand the most prominent and meaningful dimensions of the moral life, as we experience and live it?

The terms of social cooperation are often, these critics say, unchosen, intimate, and between unequals. A Kantian deontological model fails to appreciate that parents, for example, do not see their responsibilities to their children in terms of contracts but rather in terms of care, needs, sustenance, and loving attachment. Only if all forms of moral relationship—our moral sentiments, motivations, and virtues— could be reduced to a law-governed exchange would such forms of caring be reducible to contract. But this is where we see how inappropriate the models are and how much our moral vision would change if we substituted models such as intimate relationships in the family, benevolent dispositions, and cooperation and interdependence in institutions where unequals meet as both friends and strangers (a hospital, for example, governed as it is by a network of medical and nursing ethics focused on care, compassion, and treatment). Here, autonomous choice takes a back seat to moral community and to basic responses to another's needs (see, further, Chapter 8 on communitarianism).

From the perspective of these critics, contract and law are suitable metaphors for expressing the way traders, entrepreneurs, and capitalists see markets, but not suitable as a way of capturing much that is central to the moral point of view. Kantian models may not rest on a moral mistake, but the charge is that they do rest on too narrow a conception of morality. And historically, the effect of this narrowness has been momentous, critics say, because utilitarian and deontological theories of law, contract, and obligation have so dominated moral philosophy as to drown out anyone who speaks in a different voice. These critics also argue that theorists of the *ideal* society, such as Rawls, give us no guidance in the everyday, practical world of moral conduct, which is the dimension that moral traditions do attempt to address.

Critics who take this line need not argue that we should drop categories of obligation altogether, only that we find room in our moral theories for care, love, trust, gentleness, and the like, as fundamental moral categories. They are arguing that the rights-and-obligations approach that has dominated moral philosophy fails to capture the meaning and content of what we will call in Chapter 7 "virtue ethics." For example, if we look at virtues such as "gentleness," it is unlikely that their moral importance can be fully appreciated in terms of moral rules, especially if the rules are the categorical rules Kant makes essential to morality.

This is a portentous criticism, but we are not yet ready to assess it properly. We need first to obtain a background in virtue theory (from which some of the preceding criticism emanates) and then a background in Chapter 7 on Hume's ethics (from which much of the rest of the criticism emanates).

## CONCLUSION

Deontological theories bring together a wide variety of moral considerations. Much is attractive in these theories, and many moral beliefs may rest on the foundations they describe. For all of his opacity, Kant's philosophy of treating persons as autonomous ends is a matter of fundamental importance, and Ross's account of prima facie obligation is almost universally recognized for its contribution to ethical theory. However, many philosophers are concerned that the problems that plague deontological theories cannot be resolved in deontological categories, and they have chosen to defend some alternative approach. Two popular replacements for, or perhaps supplements to, deontological and utilitarian theories are virtue theories and theories that rely on sentiments and convention in morals. These are the topics of the next two chapters.

## SUGGESTED SUPPLEMENTARY READINGS

### Kant's Works

Kant, Immanuel: *Critique of Practical Reason*, Lewis White Beck, trans. (Indianapolis: Bobbs-Merrill Company, 1956).

————: *Lectures on Ethics*, Louis Infield, trans. (New York: Harper Torchbooks, 1963).

————: *The Metaphysical Elements of Justice*, John Ladd, trans. (Indianapolis: Bobbs-Merrill Company, 1965).

————: *Ethical Philosophy*, J. W. Ellington, trans. (Indianapolis: Hackett Publishing Co., 1983).

————: *Groundwork for the Metaphysics of Morals*, Thomas E. Hill and Arnulf Zweig, eds. (Oxford, England: Oxford University Press, forthcoming).

## Kantian Ethics and Commentaries on Kant

Aune, Bruce: *Kant's Theory of Morals* (Princeton, NJ: Princeton University Press, 1979).

Baron, Marcia: "Kantian Ethics and Supererogation," *Journal of Philosophy,* 84 (1987): 237–62.

————: *Kantian Ethics Almost Without Apology* (Ithaca, NY: Cornell University Press, 1995).

Broad, C. D.: *Five Types of Ethical Theory* (London: Routledge and Kegan Paul, 1930), chap. 5.

Cummiskey, David: *Kantian Consequentialism* (New York: Oxford University Press, 1996).

Gowans, Christopher W.: "Intimacy, Freedom, and Unique Value: A 'Kantian' Account of the Irreplaceable and Incomparable Value of Persons," *American Philosophical Quarterly,* 33 (January 1996): 75–89.

Guyer, Paul, ed.: *The Cambridge Companion to Kant* (New York: Cambridge University Press, 1992).

————: "The Possibility of the Categorical Imperative," *Philosophical Review,* 104 (July 1995): 353–85.

————: "The Value of Agency," *Ethics,* 106 (1996): 404–23.

Harrison, Jonathan: "Kant's Examples of the First Formulation of the Categorical Imperative," *Philosophical Quarterly,* 7 (1957): 50–62.

Herman, Barbara: *The Practice of Moral Judgment* (Cambridge, MA: Harvard University Press, 1993).

Hill, Thomas E., Jr.: "Kantian Constructivism in Ethics," *Ethics,* 99 (1989).

————: *Dignity and Practical Reason in Kant's Moral Theory* (Ithaca, NY: Cornell University Press, 1992).

————: "Moral Dilemmas, Gaps, and Residues: A Kantian Perspective," in H. E. Mason, ed., *Moral Dilemmas and Moral Theory* (New York: Oxford University Press, 1996).

Korsgaard, Christine M.: "Kant's Formula of Universal Law," *Pacific Philosophical Quarterly,* 66 (1985): 24–47.

————: "The Right to Lie: Kant on Dealing with Evil," *Philosophy and Public Affairs,* 15 (1986): 325–49.

————: *Creating the Kingdom of Ends* (Cambridge, England: Cambridge University Press, 1996).

Louden, Robert: *Kant's Impure Ethics: From Rational Beings to Human Beings* (New York: Oxford University Press, 1999).

McCarty, Richard: "Moral Conflicts in Kantian Ethics," *History of Philosophy Quarterly* (January 1991): 65–79.

Mulholland, Leslie A.: *Kant's System of Rights* (New York: Columbia University Press, 1990).

Nell (O'Neill), Onora: *Acting on Principle: An Essay on Kantian Ethics* (New York: Columbia University Press, 1975).

————: *Constructions of Reason: Explorations of Kant's Practical Philosophy* (Cambridge, England: Cambridge University Press, 1989).

————: "Kantian Ethics," in Peter Singer, ed., *A Companion to Ethics* (Cambridge, England: Blackwell, 1991).

Paton, Herbert J.: *The Categorical Imperative* (Chicago: University of Chicago Press, 1948).

Ross, W. D.: *Kant's Ethical Theory* (Oxford, England: Clarendon Press, 1954).

Schneewind, J. B.: "Kant and Natural Law Ethics," *Ethics,* 104 (1993): 53–74.

Sherman, Nancy: "Concrete Kantian Respect," *Social Philosophy and Policy,* 15 (Winter 1998): 119–48.

Sullivan, Roger J.: *Immanuel Kant's Moral Theory* (Cambridge, England: Cambridge University Press, 1989).

Wolff, Robert P., ed.: *Kant: Foundations of the Metaphysics of Morals; Text and Critical Essays* (Indianapolis: Bobbs Merrill, 1969).

————: *The Autonomy of Reason: A Commentary on Kant's "Groundwork of the Metaphysics of Morals"* (New York: Harper and Row, 1973).

## Contemporary Deontological Writings and Critiques

Baier, Annette: "The Need for More than Justice," *Canadian Journal of Philosophy,* supplementary vol. 13 (1987): 41–56.

Baier, Kurt: *The Moral Point of View: A Rational Basis of Ethics* (Ithaca, NY: Cornell University Press, 1958).

Dancy, Jonathan: "An Ethic of Prima Facie Duties," in *A Companion to Ethics* (Cambridge, England: Blackwell, 1991).

Donagan, Alan: *The Theory of Morality* (Chicago: University of Chicago Press, 1977).

Ellis, Anthony: "Deontology, Incommensurability and the Arbitrary," *Philosophy and Phenomenological Research,* 52 (December 1992): 855–75.

Foot, Philippa: "Morality as a System of Hypothetical Imperatives," *Philosophical Review,* 81 (1972): 305–16.

Freeman, Samuel: "Utilitarianism, Deontology, and the Priority of Right," *Philosophy and Public Affairs,* 23 (Fall 1994): 313–49.

Gert, Bernard: *Morality: A New Justification of the Moral Rules* (New York: Oxford University Press, 1988).

Hooker, Brad: "Ross-Style Pluralism versus Rule-Consequentialism," *Mind,* 105 (October 1996): 531–52.

Howard-Snyder, Frances: "Rule Consequentialism Is a Rubber Duck," *American Philosophical Quarterly,* 30 (July 1993): 271–7.

Hurley, Paul: "Scheffler's Argument for Deontology," *Pacific Philosophical Quarterly,* 74 (June 1993): 118–34.

Korsgaard, Christine M.: *The Sources of Normativity* (New York: Cambridge University Press, 1996).

McMahon, Christopher: "The Paradox of Deontology," *Philosophy and Public Affairs* (1991): 350–77.

McNaughton, David: "An Unconnected Heap of Duties?" *Philosophical Quarterly,* 46 (1996): 433–47.

McNaughton, David, and Piers Rawling: "Deontology and Agency," *Monist,* 76 (January 1993): 81–100.

————: "On Defending Deontology," *Ratio,* 11 (April 1998): 37–54.

Pietroski, Paul: "Prima Facie Obligations: Ceteris Paribus Laws in Moral Theory," *Ethics,* 103 (April 1993): 489–515.

Rawls, John: *A Theory of Justice* (Cambridge, MA: Harvard University Press, 1971).

————: "The Priority of Right and Ideas of the Good," *Philosophy and Public Affairs,* 17 (1988): 251–76.

————: *Political Liberalism* (New York: Columbia University Press, 1996).

Ross, W. D.: *Foundations of Ethics* (Oxford, England: Clarendon Press, 1939).

————: *The Right and the Good* (Indianapolis: Hackett Publishing Co., 1988).

Scanlon, T. M.: *What We Owe to Each Other* (Cambridge, MA: Belknap Press of Harvard University Press, 1998).

Walen, Alec: "Doing, Allowing, and Disabling: Some Principles Governing Deontological Restrictions," *Philosophical Studies,* 80 (1995): 183–215.

Warnock, Geoffrey J.: *The Object of Morality* (London: Methuen and Company, 1971).

## Respect for Persons and Respect for Autonomy

Beauchamp, Tom L., and James F. Childress: "The Principle of Respect for Autonomy," in *Principles of Biomedical Ethics,* 4th ed. (New York: Oxford University Press, 1994), chap. 3.

Benn, Stanley I.: *A Theory of Freedom* (Cambridge, England: Cambridge University Press, 1988).

Christman, John, ed.: *The Inner Citadel: Essays on Individual Autonomy* (New York: Oxford University Press, 1989).

Cranor, Carl: "Toward a Theory of Respect for Persons," *American Philosophical Quarterly,* 12 (October 1975).

Darwall, Stephen: "Two Kinds of Respect," *Ethics,* 88 (1977): 36–49.

————: "Agent Centered Restrictions from the Inside Out," *Philosophical Studies,* 50 (1986): 291–319.

DeGrazia, David: "Great Apes, Dolphins, and the Concept of Personhood," *Southern Journal of Philosophy,* 35 (1997): 301–20.

Dennett, Daniel: "Conditions of Personhood," in Amelie O. Rorty, ed., *The Identities of Persons* (Berkeley: University of California Press, 1976): 175–96.

Downie, R. S., and Elizabeth Telfer: *Respect for Persons* (London: George Allen and Unwin, 1969).

Dworkin, Gerald: *The Theory and Practice of Autonomy* (Cambridge, England: Cambridge University Press, 1988).

Hill, Thomas E., Jr.: *Autonomy and Self-Respect* (Cambridge: Cambridge University Press, 1991).

Lomasky, Loren: *Persons, Rights, and the Moral Community* (Oxford, England: Oxford University Press, 1987).

Patterson, Francine, and Wendy Gordon: "The Case for the Personhood of Gorillas," in Paola Cavalieri and Peter Singer, eds., *The Great Ape Project* (New York: St. Martin's Press, 1993): 58–77

Young, Robert: *Personal Autonomy: Beyond Negative and Positive Liberty* (New York: St. Martin's Press, 1986).

## CHAPTER 6

# Aristotle and Virtue Theories

## THE VIRTUES OF JANE ADDAMS

The case with which this chapter begins, unlike cases in other chapters, describes the life of a single individual, Jane Addams. This remarkable person was born in Cedarville, Illinois, in 1860. When only three years old, she lost her mother, and by her own account her father was the "supreme affection" of her youth and easily the dominant influence on her life. He was a diligent, successful, and generous man— a mill owner, banker, and member of the state senate. Nominally a Quaker, he despaired of what he called "theological doctrine." He preferred to rely exclusively on integrity, self-respect, and conscience. He was widely regarded as a virtuous man— a person of kindly spirit and a pillar of tolerance. He imparted his moral beliefs to his daughter, insisting on integrity and honesty above everything else.

Jane's stepmother held out other goals for her. In accordance with the family's prominent social position, she hoped that Jane would cultivate the traditional refinements and social graces expected of upper-class women during the nineteenth century; but Jane Addams's social conscience resisted this course. She worried that in "being educated," she had "lost that simple and almost automatic response" of sympathy in "the mere presence of suffering or of helplessness." During Jane's postcollege years, her stepmother moved to Baltimore and introduced Jane to "the Johns Hopkins University society," complete with its wealth, traditionalism, lavish homes, and dresses from Paris. Jane found, however, that the people she met in Baltimore were often wasteful and misdirected, and her exposure to them was on the whole a disillusioning experience. She came to feel "maladjusted," "nervous," and "useless." In 1887, when she had been out of college for several years and had done nothing she considered of importance, she journeyed to Europe. There she made the important and life-altering decision that, despite her upbringing and the ambitions others held out for her, she could never lead a life of ease. She decided that she was "absolutely at sea so far as any moral purpose was concerned," and her trips to London in particular made her aware of "hideous human need."

In the midst of her crisis of conscience, she sat one day in a German cathedral whose stained-glass windows, as she recalled, pictured "Greek philosophers as well as Hebrew Prophets, and . . . saints." One window, showing Martin Luther affixing his decrees, particularly affected her. "The saints," she decided, "embodied fine action." That evening she formulated an idea that had been germinating for some time: the idea of a settlement house to serve immigrants and the poor. When she returned to the United States, she bought an old mansion on Chicago's West Side. Owned by an affluent real estate dealer named Hull, the mansion, which had once been a grand estate, was now an isolated remnant of the past in a slum-ridden section of the city. It wa there that, in 1889, Jane Addams established what was to become the world-famous Hull House, and in the process fixed the course of her life over the next forty years.

During these forty years, Jane developed her settlement house on Chicago's West Side into a great institution of social work—though she always considered it primarily a social experiment. In its initial year alone, over 50,000 needy persons visited Hull House for some form of attention, and in the second year the number exceeded 100,000. Her institution cared for hundreds of people every day. Its stated purposes were to provide a center for social and cultural life and to improve living conditions in the industrial districts of Chicago. Classes were provided from kindergarten through adult education, cooperative boarding houses were established, and attempts were made to find employment for the unemployed. Although cautioned by police about the dangers of the neighborhood, Jane went everywhere, usually unaccompanied, and often late at night.

At first, her neighbors were suspicious of Jane's efforts, but, as one of them later recalled, she won them over by her "uniform kindness and courtesy." They came to regard her as a good neighbor in every sense of the term. This was not so much because of her administrative talent or her contributions to the community, but rather because of her conscientiousness, concern, and compassion for others. Jane was considerate of everyone, sensitive to their needs and concerns as individuals, and genuinely cared that they do well. She also cared about their collective labors and was willing to make personal sacrifices to help them succeed. In short, she was a benevolent person—like her father, a model of virtue.

As her operation expanded, Jane began to give public lectures aimed at helping the rich and the middle class understand "how the other half lives." She had debated the famous orator William Jennings Bryan (the Democratic presidential nominee) in her college days and was known for her quiet oratory. She desired, above all, to cultivate in the people she addressed, especially the women, what she regarded as a natural sympathy and tendency toward virtue. She also found time to lecture about, and campaign widely for, the abolition of child labor, improved factory laws, court reform, and women's suffrage. She showed a consistent loyalty to every one of these projects, and sometimes exhausted herself in their pursuit. Eventually, Jane Addams and her Hull House acquired national renown. She became politically active, seconding the nomination of Theodore Roosevelt for President, involving herself in a major train strike, and promoting peace movements. She opposed the United States' entry into World War I, and her stand on the issue tested some of her most important friendships, straining even her close association with the philosopher John Dewey.

Not everyone was convinced of her complete dedication to social ideals and to the poor. In the summer of 1896, Jane met Russian writer Leo Tolstoy, who had renounced a life of wealth in favor of a peasant existence. The sleeves of Jane

Addams's dress, said Tolstoy critically, had enough material in them to make an entire frock for a young girl. He also accused her of being an absentee landlord, because she had kept her family's property in order to support her work. After reflecting on the encounter with Tolstoy, she determined that he was "more logical than life warrants." Nevertheless, she resolved to move among working people more than ever before.

Jane Addams wrote several books, some scholarly works. She was known as a first-rate theoretician, especially on matters pertaining to the fledgling fields of sociology and social work. One of her books, *Democracy and Social Ethics,* influenced American pragmatists as much as they had influenced her. By 1931, when she received the Nobel Peace Prize, she was internationally famous. Characteristically, she refused to embrace the comfortable and well-to-do part of American society that finally welcomed her. Usually a gentle person, in 1932, at more than seventy years of age, she gave a strongly worded address at Swarthmore College entitled "Our National Self-Righteousness." She denounced what she saw as a deep mood of "impatience with differing opinions." These criticisms seemed only to enhance her image in certain academic and political circles. Bryn Mawr College awarded her its highest prize, and her friend John Dewey traveled to the ceremony to see her receive it. In March 1934, the University of California celebrated its fiftieth anniversary by conferring honorary degrees on three persons: U.S. President Herbert Hoover, Jane Addams, and a former Hull House resident named Frances Perkins, who had risen to become Secretary of Labor. Hoover and Perkins refused to be photographed together, but both were delighted to be photographed with Jane Addams.

Jane Addams has often been described as a saint. In an article in the journal *Daedalus,* she was praised as one of America's few true heroines, and the American philosopher William James once wrote to her in admiration, "I do not know why you should always be right, but you always are. You inhabit reality." In 1935, at age seventy-five, she received the American Education Award for teaching "by precept and example." Later that same year, Jane died of cancer. In England, John Burns eulogized her as a saint of the modern era, and in the United States, journalist Walter Lippmann said that under her direction, Hull House had been a "cathedral of compassion." A Greek newspaper in Chicago asserted simply, "We of foreign birth have lost our best friend and the only one who understood us."[1]

## THE CONCEPT OF VIRTUE

In Chapters 4 and 5 two types of principle-based or obligation-based theories of right and wrong actions, rules, and policies were examined. These theories do not typically emphasize the agents or actors who perform actions, have motives, and

---

[1]Sources for this case include Henry Steele Commager, Foreword to Jane Addams, *Twenty Years at Hull House* (New York: New American Library of World Literature, 1961), pp. vii–xvi; Jill Conway, "Jane Addams: An American Heroine," *Daedalus,* 93 (Spring 1964): 761–80; Christopher Lasch, ed., *The Social Thought of Jane Addams* (Indianapolis: Bobbs-Merrill Company, 1965); James Weber Linn, *Jane Addams* (New York: Greenwood Press, 1968).

follow principles. Instead, they focus on *acts* or *rules* abstracted from individuals. Yet we commonly make judgments about good and evil persons, their traits of character, and their willingness to perform actions. Jane Addams has been praised as much for her saintly character as for her actions, and we make many comparable judgments about the virtues and vices of persons we encounter. We say they are saintly or despicable, hateful or lovable, noble or ignoble, and so forth. We thus judge the virtues and moral worth of persons as agents, and not merely their fulfillment of obligation or their production of good consequences.

"Virtue ethics," as it will be called here, presents a challenge to deontological and utilitarian theories. For all their differences, utilitarians and deontologists conceive of moral philosophy and the demands of morality similarly: Ethics provides general guides to action and begins with the question, "What morally ought we to do?" By contrast, in the classical Greek philosophy represented by Plato and Aristotle, the cultivation of virtuous traits of character is viewed as one of morality's primary functions. The aim of classical philosophers was not unlike Jane Addams's desire that people cultivate a tendency to virtuous conduct.

An ethics of virtue turns on an assessment of moral traits that establish a person's moral character. In the theater, for example, certain traits of actors and actresses may mark them as having a distinct character on stage (i.e., a distinct quality in acting). On some occasions, their performance will be better than others, but this fluctuation will not change their "virtue" or character as performers and will not alter the traits that mark their performances. Most of us have a moral character that similarly varies over time in its strength and predictability (e.g., from occasional moral weakness), but we also tend to exhibit typical moral behaviors. A person may also be of virtuous character in *some* respects (e.g., possess conscientiousness and trustworthiness), but suffer from deficiencies in other respects (e.g., lack of patience and tolerance).

In recent years, a number of philosophers have proposed that ethics should abandon its preoccupation with principles of obligation, directive rules, and judgments of right and wrong and return to Aristotle's emphasis on human flourishing, which underlies his conception of the moral value of persons. In some measure we have already encountered judgments of virtue in Chapters 4 and 5, although not Aristotelian judgments. Kant emphasized the motives of the person of good will, and Mill mentioned the difference between judgments of action and judgments of character. Mill noted explicitly that "utilitarian moralists have gone beyond almost all others in affirming that the motive has nothing to do with the *morality* of the action, though much with the *worth of the agent*."[2] He goes on to argue that morally right actions are independent of, and to be distinguished from, morally right motives. His point is that we need not know anything about the quality of motives or character in order to know whether actions are right or wrong.

Mill's point is well taken, but the exponent of virtue ethics will not think enough has been said. Mill maintains that "the object of virtue" is "the multiplication of happiness" and that a morality of actions is primary, but he does not provide sufficient reasons to show that a morality based on virtues and the evaluation of

---

[2]John Stuart Mill, *Utilitarianism* (1863), chap. 2, para. 19 (italics added).

character is less primary than a morality based on principles and the evaluation of actions. Mill, and many theorists who write from the perspective of a theory of obligation, seldom analyzes what is meant by "virtue," a task to which we now turn.

## The Definition of Virtue

A virtue should not be thought of as a moral *requirement,* because this confuses it with a principle or statement of what ought to be done. It is better to say that a virtue is, at minimum, a character trait that is socially valued. Patience, attentiveness, concern, humanity, graciousness, and the like, are examples. A *moral* virtue is a character trait that is morally valued—for example, truthfulness, honesty, gentleness, politeness, and the like. Virtues can be other than moral; they can be amoral and even immoral.[3] For example, the virtues of soldiers and intelligence operatives (their socially valued character traits) may systematically involve moral violations. Virtues such as conscientiousness and resourcefulness may be socially valued without being morally valued. Admirable traits such as calmness and competitiveness are virtues, but not moral virtues, and some traits akin to moral virtue, such as devotion and loyalty, are not specifically moral virtues. The virtue of personal integrity has something of a foot in all camps, because it is the trait of being faithful to one's values while standing up in their defense. Some of these values will be moral, others will not. (We tend to think of moral virtues as being the most important, but this claim needs defense.)

Some theorists have defined moral virtue as a disposition to act or a habit of acting in accordance with moral obligations and ideals,[4] but this approach seems flawed. On this definition, the moral virtue of justice, for example, is nothing but the trait a person has of acting fairly. The reason behind the person's actions is not considered; yet virtue clearly has something to do with the *motivational composition* that leads the agent to behave morally. Perhaps it is better to say that we are interested in the person's *characteristic* motivational structure, because we are dealing with character, not merely with the consistency of a person's performance. A just person—that is, a person with the virtue of fairness—not only has a disposition to act fairly but, when so acting, has a morally appropriate desire to do so. The person characteristically has a moral concern and reservation about acting in a way that would be unfair. Having only the motive to act in accordance with a rule of obligation—as Kant demands—is not morally sufficient for virtue in this sense.

---

[3]Aristotle required that virtue involve deliberate purpose to pursue virtuous ends (*Nichomachean Ethics,* bk. 2, chap. 6). Thomas Aquinas (relying on a formulation by Peter Lombard) additionally held that virtue is a good quality of mind by which we live rightly and cannot be put to bad use (*Summa Theologiae,* I–II, question 55, arts. 3–4). Neither condition is necessary in the analysis given here.

[4]This form of definition has been defended by Alan Gewirth, "Rights and Virtues," *Review of Metaphysics,* 38 (1985): 751, and earlier by William Frankena. See also Edmund Pincoffs, *Quandaries and Virtues: Against Reductivism in Ethics* (Lawrence: University Press of Kansas, 1986), pp. 9, 73–100. Alternatively, some utilitarian philosophers have defined virtues as character traits that tend to produce good consequences. See Julia Driver, "The Virtues and Human Nature," in Roger Crisp, ed., *How Should One Live?: Essays on the Virtues* (New York: Oxford University Press, 1996), pp. 111–29.

## Right Actions and Right Motives

Consider a person who always performs his or her obligation *because* it is an obligation, but intensely dislikes having to allow the interests of others to be of importance. Such a person, let us imagine, does not cherish, feel congenial toward, or think fondly of others, and respects others only because obligation requires it. This person can nonetheless, on a theory of moral obligation such as Kant's or Mill's, perform a morally right action, have an ingrained disposition to perform that action (because the person has a disposition to follow rules of obligation), and intend to act from obligation. But if the desire is not right, then a necessary condition of moral worth and virtue seems to be lacking.

Persons who exhibit traits of acting on morally inferior motives should be judged deficient in virtue, even if they consistently perform actions that are right actions from the moral point of view. Judgments of a person's merit, praiseworthiness, demerit, blameworthiness, and the like, are always tied to that person's motives, not merely to actions. The *reason why* the person acted is central. Our evaluation of a good and praiseworthy action is a way of expressing our evaluation of the motive underlying the action. That is, a praiseworthy or virtuous action is only a sign of a praiseworthy or virtuous motive, and the action derives its moral merit from that underlying motive.

This brief analysis of virtue raises important questions about the topics to be addressed in the remaining sections of this chapter: Aristotelian ethics, the relationship between an ethics of virtue and an ethics of obligation, and the role of moral ideals and moral excellence in a moral theory. Each of these topics will be explored in turn, beginning with Aristotle, whose philosophy is widely accepted as the most influential exposition of virtue ethics.

## ARISTOTELIAN ETHICS

Aristotle's *Nichomachean Ethics* is a piece of a much larger philosophical system held together by a functional (or goal-directed) view of nature and social organization: Things are to be understood in terms of their natural functions and their proper goals. Aristotle used the word *telos* to refer to the end toward which a thing moves; for example, an acorn has a *telos* to be an oak tree. The opening lines of the *Nichomachean Ethics* state that the good is "that at which all things aim." For human beings this state is *eudaimonia* or well-being, often translated as "happiness" (see the selection that follows) or even "fulfillment of function." We can begin our analysis of Aristotle's ethics with this concept.

One who achieves *eudaimonia* is one who flourishes and makes a success of life, in accordance with distinctive human faculties. Aristotle considers whether pleasure (as distinct from happiness) is the one intrinsic good, a view he finds generally accepted among the uncultivated masses, but in the end not compelling. Because there is a pleasure appropriate to each of our activities, the value of the pleasure depends upon the value of the activity. Some pleasures follow from acts of vice or vicious character traits, while other pleasures stunt growth or maturation. Moreover, whatever makes pleasure desirable seems to be supplemented or augmented by other goods, such as wisdom.

## The Social Context of Ethics

Aristotle proclaims ethics a "branch of politics." This has a strange sound to modern ears, but the word *politikos* in Greek encompasses what is meant in English by "the political" and "the social" jointly. Ethics is the study of how to live well as an individual; politics is the study of how to live well as a polis, or community. Second, Aristotle holds that both politics and ethics study the nature and promotion of human happiness or well-being (*eudaimonia*), and that these topics can be studied only within the context of society. This orientation led W. D. Ross to quip, appropriately, that Aristotle's ethics are social and his politics ethical.[5]

Perhaps the best way to view Aristotle's thesis is as follows: Ethics and politics alike are branches of practical knowledge. Ethics deals with how the individual lives best, politics with how the group lives best. Both seek the good, *eudaimonia*. Whereas Mill and Kant often emphasize human individuality and autonomy, Aristotle sees individuals as essentially members of a social unit. He believes that moral actions can be promoted only by the support of a social group and that laws and the threat of punishment are required to foster morality and to elevate ideals of virtuous conduct.

It might be said, then, that the design and implementation of institutions that make living well a possibility are the tasks of one who administers the state or some part of the state. Thus, because ethics is an essential dimension of political leadership, it should be studied by those who arrange and lead communities. Also important is the way Aristotle presents the methodology of ethics. Whereas an abstract discipline such as mathematics involves the intuitive apprehension of first principles, the first principles of ethics are deeply embedded in the nonabstract world of conduct in society. The philosopher's procedure must be the reverse of the mathematician: In ethics the philosopher finds first principles by pulling them out of the concrete mass of human actions. We start with the moral beliefs embedded in conduct and social practice—not with pure reason, as with Kant, or with abstract principles, as with Mill.

Nonetheless, Aristotle's ethics is reminiscent of Mill's, because it is a consequential (or teleological) ethics. Morality is essentially bound up with bringing about human good, and Aristotle proceeds, like Mill, to search for that which is intrinsically good. He reasons that all human objectives lead to further objectives until finally we reach some supreme objective or end, an ultimate good for the sake of which all other goods are pursued. Well-being or happiness (*eudaimonia*) is again reminiscent of Mill's happiness, and Aristotle also employs the means-to-ends thinking that characterizes Mill's ethics: He looks for proper ends and the best means to achieve those ends.

---

[5]W. D. Ross, *Aristotle,* 5th ed. (New York: Barnes and Noble, 1964), p. 183.

However, Aristotle does not have a principle that requires *maximizing* utility, and indeed has nothing like the principle of utility, which is Mill's central principle. Moreover, Aristotle regards human happiness as consisting in various forms of good activity, not in the satisfaction of desire, as Mill perceives it. In an extreme interpretation of the differences between Aristotle's ethical theory and more modern, obligation-based systems, such as those of Mill and Kant, some philosophers have held that the Greeks, because of their emphasis on rationality and individual and communal well-being, were not concerned with a moral way of life. This view is expressed by William Frankena:

> The Greeks were seeking the *rational* way to live, without making special mention of the *moral* way to live; their solutions do not center on our relations to other persons. However, the moderns conceive of a specifically *moral* way to live that is largely a matter of our relations to our fellow human beings. A prevailing egoism in Greek ethics runs counter to the altruism featured in modern ethics.[6]

This thesis is difficult to defend, as can be shown by a single quotation from Aristotle: "The excellent person labors for his friends and for his native country, and will die for them if he must; he will sacrifice money, honours, and contested goods in general, in achieving what is fine for himself. For he will choose . . . a single fine and great action over many small actions."[7]

## Excellence of Character

Aristotle uses the word *ethika* (from which we derive "ethics") to mean, roughly, "matters having to do with character." The best title for his work, then, might have been "On the Nature of Character." The right character is modeled on the person of virtue, which is understood in terms of a certain form of excellence.

Aristotle maintains that the good of anything in nature—its excellence or virtue—consists in its doing its work well, that is, in functioning successfully: A good heart is one that pumps blood well, a good sculptor is one who makes sculptures well, and so forth. From this framework, Aristotle constructs a theory of the moral life and the virtues that attend it. His word for virtue in Greek is *arete,* a word that encompasses much more than moral virtue and is close in meaning to "goodness," "virtue," and "excellence." We can speak of the arete of a knife, an oration, or the like, and virtually mean the goodness, virtue, or excellence of the knife or oration. Human excellence is human virtue, and Aristotle discusses not only the moral virtues but also the virtues of magnificence, cheerfulness, and excellence involved in activities requiring special skills.

The breadth of virtues subsumed by the term *arete* is illustrated by the range of excellence that Jane Addams possessed. Her oratorical skills, her devotion, and— above all for Aristotle—her intelligence and the way she applied it to practical

---

[6]William K. Frankena, *Thinking about Morality* (Ann Arbor: University of Michigan Press, 1980), p. 11.

[7]Aristotle, *Nichomachean Ethics,* Terence Irwin, trans. (Indianapolis: Hackett Publishing Co,. 1985), bk. 9, chap 8, 1169ª18–25.

affairs are all forms of excellence, developed through the careful nurturing of one's capacities for living the human life well. We are not born morally virtuous, but must be trained so that virtuous activity becomes habitual, just as we must be trained in other technical skills. Because everyone can be, and should strive to be, morally virtuous, Aristotle distinguishes moral virtues from virtues, or excellences, that occur for one particular type of function or work in which persons engage. For example, the virtues that make cobblers good cobblers depend upon the goals of the craft. Moral virtues, by contrast, are generally praiseworthy features of human character.

Virtue is neither a feeling nor an innate capacity. It is a disposition *bred from an innate capacity by proper training and exercise of that capacity.* We acquire virtues much as we do skills such as carpentry, playing an instrument, or cooking. We become just by performing just actions, temperate by doing temperate actions, and so forth. Aristotle reasons that there must be some proper function and state of well-being for all human beings *as human beings,* as distinct from human beings as carpenters, musicians, or cooks. He equates this proper function with what he sees as the distinctive attribute of the human species: reasoning or intelligence. Humans share many capacities and tendencies with other species in nature (for example, processes of nutrition and growth), and it is the exercise of rational capacities that is alone distinctive. The specifically *human* part of human excellence consists in the proper exercise of this faculty. Aristotle thus defines human well-being as an active life in accord with virtue (excellence), especially in accord with the best of the virtues—that is, reasoning or intelligence.

Although Aristotle links the performance of a unique human function with human well-being and holds that life controlled by reason is the highest form of well-being, he does not infer that *only* a life of reason can promote human well-being. Any correct performance of a proper function should result in human well-being, even if it is not a form of well-being distinctive to the human species. Aristotle describes the good for human beings in terms of activities that accord with a variety of virtues or excellences. He goes on to distinguish virtue of intellect from virtue of character, the latter constituting moral virtue.

## Practical Wisdom

Aristotle distinguishes between desire and reason, the latter being the rational part of the person that formulates plans and arguments. Two kinds of virtue correspond to these two parts of the person: "intellectual virtue," or the virtues of intellect, and "practical virtue," the virtues of character and practical life. Intellectual cleverness may lead to vicious actions, Aristotle declares, but a person of practical wisdom knows which ends should be chosen and knows how to achieve them in particular circumstances, at the same time keeping emotions within proper bounds and carefully selecting from among the range of possible actions that might be taken. The required factor is the practical judgment that skilled and admired group leaders exhibit when they combine experience and good judgment. Such persons know, for example, both when to be courageous and how to use money for good causes, in each case without excess or overreaction. Jane Addams's courageousness, efficiency, prudence, innovativeness, and financial skill make her a prime example of practical wisdom.

Although Aristotle leaves his account of practical judgment largely undeveloped, if this account of judgment could be worked out as a practical decision theory, it would acquire an advantage over rule-oriented theories such as Kant's. The latter theories falter on the problem of how to handle a conflict of rules or obligations, leaving unclear what should be done and what counts as good judgment. It appears that the theory of practical judgment in Aristotle could be designed to treat circumstances in which rules either conflict or provide insufficient guidance.

Fortunately, Aristotle does not leave us completely uninstructed in the details of practical moral judgment. In a famous discussion, he says that a training in virtuous conduct and good judgment involves learning to avoid two extremes: one is the vice of excess ("too much"), and the other is the vice of defect ("too little"). The virtuous person is one who aims at moderation between these extremes. Just as we must learn that eating too much or too little food is bad for our health, so we must learn that courage, for example, is a mean between rashness and cowardice. Courage is a virtue because it consists in appropriate decisions and consequent actions that avoid poor judgment and excessive fears that might arise from pain, risk of death, public disapproval, possible error, and the like. The courageous person has learned not to fear and thus act in a cowardly manner, but has also learned not to be foolhardy or rash by neglecting to fear that which is dangerous.

All virtues can be similarly analyzed, according to Aristotle. Every art and technique of skill involves making judgments about the right amount. Carpentry, for example, involves the proper cutting of wood and proper positioning after it has been cut. Too short or too long a cut, and too much or too little of the wood displayed, constitute poor carpentry. As with carpentry, so it is with other dimensions of life.

Aristotle does not claim that the mean is the same for all persons and circumstances. It is, he says, "relative to ourselves" and "determined by reason, or as a right-minded person would determine it." In morality, the proper mean between extremes is best judged by persons of practical wisdom who have experience and skill of judgment in facing situations that present new subtleties. They understand how to act with just the right intensity of feeling, in just the right way, at just the right time. These are virtuous persons in whom a right relation exists between reason, feeling, and desire.

The following selection from Aristotle concentrates on the virtuous person and the mean between extremes. One cautionary note deserves mention for those new to Aristotle. The *Nichomachean Ethics* was not composed as a book and was not intended to be published. It was originally little more than a set of outlines and lecture notes, and may have been compiled later from notes taken by students at Aristotle's lectures. Aristotle's works lay decaying in a cellar for decades, and they were subsequently mistranscribed and issued in editions that contained inaccuracies and gaps. Later scholarship has repaired many flaws, but the work unavoidably reads somewhat like well-prepared lecture notes and should be approached accordingly.

# *Moral Virtue**

### Aristotle

## The Good Is the End of Action

If there is some end of everything that is pursued in action, this will be the good pursued in action; and if there are more ends than one, these will be the goods pursued in action.

Our argument has progressed, then, to the same conclusion [as before, that the highest end is the good]; but we must try to clarify this still more.

## The Good Is Complete

Though apparently there are many ends, we choose some of them, e.g. wealth, flutes and, in general, instruments, because of something else; hence it is clear that not all ends are complete. But the best good is apparently something complete. Hence, if only one end is complete, this will be what we are looking for; and if more than one are complete, the most complete of these will be what we are looking for.

## Criteria for Completeness

An end pursued in itself, we say, is more complete than an end pursued because of something else; and an end that is never choiceworthy because of something else is more complete than ends that are choiceworthy both in themselves and because of this end; and hence an end that is always [choice-

*Aristotle, *Nichomachean Ethics*, T. Irwin, trans. (Indianapolis, Ind.: Hackett Publishing Company, 1987).

worthy, and also] choiceworthy in itself, never because of something else, is unconditionally complete.

## Happiness Meets the Criteria for Completeness, but Other Goods Do Not

Now happiness more than anything else seems unconditionally complete, since we always [choose it, and also] choose it because of itself, never because of something else.

Honour, pleasure, understanding and every virtue we certainly choose because of themselves, since we would choose each of them even if it had no further result, but we also choose them for the sake of happiness, supposing that through them we shall be happy. Happiness, by contrast, no one ever chooses for their sake, or for the sake of anything else at all.

## The Good Is Self-Sufficient; So Is Happiness

The same conclusion [that happiness is complete] also appears to follow from self-sufficiency, since the complete good seems to be self-sufficient.

Now what we count as self-sufficient is not what suffices for a solitary person by himself, living an isolated life, but what suffices also for parents, children, wife and in general for friends and fellow-citizens, since a human being is a naturally political [animal]. Here, however, we must impose some limit; for if we extend the good to parents' parents and children's children and to friends of friends, we shall go on without limit; but we must examine this another time.

Anyhow, we regard something as self-sufficient when all by itself it makes a life choiceworthy and lacking nothing; and that is what we think happiness does.

## What Is Self-Sufficient Is Most Choiceworthy; So Is Happiness

Moreover, we think happiness is most choiceworthy of all goods, since it is not counted as one good among many. . . .

Happiness, then, is apparently something complete and self-sufficient, since it is the end of the things pursued in action.

## A Clearer Account of the Good: The Human Soul's Activity Expressing Virtue

But presumably the remark that the best good is happiness is apparently something [generally] agreed, and what we miss is a clearer statement of what the best good is.

## If Something Has a Function, Its Good Depends on Its Function

Well, perhaps we shall find the best good if we first find the function of a human being. For just as the good, i.e. [doing] well, for a flautist, a sculptor, and every craftsman, and, in general, for whatever has a function and [characteristic] action, seems to depend on its function, the same seems to be true for a human being, if a human being has some function. . . .

## The Human Function

What, then, could this be? For living is apparently shared with plants, but what we are looking for is the special function of a human being; hence we should set aside the life of nutrition and growth. The life next in order is some sort of life of sense-perception; but this too is apparently shared, with horse, ox and every animal. The remaining possibility, then, is some sort of life of action of the [part of the soul] that has reason.

## Clarification of "Has Reason" and "Life"

Now this [part has two parts, which have reason in different ways], one as obeying the reason [in the other part], the other as itself having reason and thinking. [We intend both.] Moreover, life is also spoken of in two ways [as capacity and as activity], and we must take [a human being's special function to be] life as activity, since this seems to be called life to a fuller extent.

## The Human Good Is Activity Expressing Virtue

(a) We have found, then, that the human function is the soul's activity that expresses reason [as itself having reason] or requires reason [as obeying reason]. (b) Now the function of F, e.g. of a harpist, is the same in kind, so we say, as the function of an excellent F, e.g. an excellent harpist. (c) The same is true unconditionally in every case, when we add to the function the superior achievement that expresses the virtue; for a harpist's function, e.g. is to play the harp, and a good harpist's is to do it well. (d) Now we take the human function to be a certain kind of life, and take this life to be the soul's activity and actions that express reason. (e) [Hence by (c) and (d)] the excellent man's function is to do this finely and well. (f) Each function is completed well when its completion expresses the proper virtue. (g) Therefore [by (d), (e) and (f)] the human good turns out to be the soul's activity that expresses virtue.

## The Good Must Also Be Complete

And if there are more virtues than one, the good will express the best and most complete virtue. Moreover, it will be in a complete life. For one swallow does not make a spring, nor does one day; nor, similarly, does one day or a short time make us blessed and happy. . . .

## How a Virtue of Character Is Acquired

Virtue, then, is of two sorts, virtue of thought and virtue of character. Virtue of thought arises and grows mostly from teaching, and hence needs experience and time. Virtue of character [i.e. of ēthos] results from habit [ethos]; hence its name "ethical," slightly varied from "ethos."

## Virtue Comes About, Not by a Process of Nature, but by Habituation

Hence it is also clear that none of the virtues of character arises in us naturally.

## What Is Natural Cannot Be Changed by Habituation

For if something is by nature [in one condition], habituation cannot bring it into another condition. A stone, e.g., by nature moves downwards, and habituation could not make it move upwards, not even if you threw it up ten thousand times to habituate it; nor could habituation make fire move downwards, or bring anything that is by nature in one condition into another condition.

Thus the virtues arise in us neither by nature nor against nature, but we are by nature able to acquire them, and reach our complete perfection through habit.

## Natural Capacities Are Not Acquired by Habituation

Further, if something arises in us by nature, we first have the capacity for it, and later display the activity. This is clear in the case of the senses; for we did not acquire them by frequent seeing or hearing, but already had them when we exercised them, and did not get them by exercising them.

Virtues, by contrast, we acquire, just as we acquire crafts, by having previously activated them. Fore we learn a craft by producing the same product that we must produce when we have learned it, becoming builders, e.g., by building and harpists by playing the harp; so also, then, we become just by doing just actions, temperate by doing temperate actions, brave by doing brave actions.

## Legislators Concentrate on Habituation

What goes on in cities is evidence for this also. For the legislator makes the citizens good by habituating them, and this is the wish of every legislator; if he fails to do it well he misses his goal. [The right] habituation is what makes the difference between a good political system and a bad one.

## Virtue and Vice Are Formed by Good and Bad Actions

Further, just as in the case of a craft, the sources and means that develop each virtue also ruin it. For playing the harp makes both good and bad harpists, and it is analogous in the case of builders and all the rest; for building well makes good builders, building badly, bad ones. If it were not so, no teacher would be needed, but everyone would be born a good or a bad craftsman.

It is the same, then, with the virtues. For actions in dealings with [other] human beings make some people just, some unjust; actions in terrifying situations and the acquired habit of fear or confidence make some brave and others cowardly. The same is true of situations involving appetites and anger; for one or another sort of conduct in these situations makes some people temperate and gentle, others intemperate and irascible.

## Conclusion: The Importance of Habituation

To sum up, then, in a single account: A state [of character] arises from [the repetition of] similar activities. Hence we must display the right activities, since differences in these imply corresponding differences in the states. It is not unimportant, then, to acquire one sort of habit or another, right from our youth; rather, it is very important, indeed all-important. . . .

## The Right Sort of Habituation Must Avoid Excess and Deficiency

First, then, we should observe that these sorts of states naturally tend to be ruined by excess and deficiency. We see this happen with strength and health, which we mention because we must use what is evident as a witness to what is not. For both excessive and deficient exercises ruin strength; and likewise, too much or too little eating or drinking ruins health, while the proportionate amount produces, increases and preserves it.

The same is true, then, of temperance, bravery and the other virtues. For if, e.g., someone avoids and is afraid of everything, standing firm against nothing, he becomes cowardly, but if he is afraid of nothing at all and goes to face everything, he becomes rash. Similarly, if he gratifies himself with every pleasure and refrains from none, he becomes intemperate, but if he avoids them all, as boors do, he becomes some sort of insensible person. Temperance and bravery, then, are ruined by excess and deficiency but preserved by the mean. . . .

## . . . Crafts Versus Virtues

Moreover, in any case what is true of crafts is not true of virtues. For the products of a craft determine by their own character whether they have been produced well; and so it suffices that they are in the right state when they have been produced. But for actions expressing virtue to be done temperately justly [and hence well] it does not suffice that they are themselves in the right state. Rather, the agent must also be in the right state when he does them. First, he must know [that he is doing virtuous actions]; second, he must decide on them, and decide on them for themselves; and, third, he must also do them from a firm and unchanging state.

As conditions for having a craft these three do not count, except for the knowing itself. As a condition for having a virtue, however, the knowing counts for nothing, or [rather] for only a little, whereas the other two conditions are very important, indeed all-important. And these other two conditions are achieved by the frequent doing of just and temperate actions.

Hence actions are called just or temperate when they are the sort that a just or temperate person would do. But the just and temperate person is not the one who [merely] does these actions, but the one who also does them in the way in which just or temperate people do them.

It is right, then, to say that a person comes to be just from doing just actions and temperate from doing temperate actions; for no one has even a prospect of becoming good from failing to do them.

## Virtue Requires Habituation, and Therefore Requires Practice, Not Just Theory

The many, however, do not do these actions but take refuge in arguments, thinking that they are doing philosophy, and that this is the way to become excellent people. In this they are like a sick person who listens attentively to the doctor, but acts on none of his instructions. Such a course of treatment will not improve the state of his body; any more than will the many's way of doing philosophy improve the state of their souls.

## A Virtue of Character Is a State Intermediate between Two Extremes, and Involving Decision . . .

Next we must examine what virtue is. Since there are three conditions arising in the soul—feelings, capacities and states—virtue must be one of these.

By feelings I mean appetite, anger, fear, confidence, envy, joy, love, hate, longing, jealousy, pity, in general whatever implies pleasure or pain.

By capacities I mean what we have when we are said to be capable of these feelings—capable of, e.g., being angry or afraid or feeling pity.

By states I mean what we have when we are well or badly off in relation to feelings. If, e.g., our feeling is too intense or slack, we are badly off in relation to anger, but if it is intermediate, we are well off; and the same is true in the other cases.

## Virtue Is Not a Feeling . . .

First, then, neither virtues nor vices are feelings. (a) For we are called excellent or base in so far as we have virtues or vices, not in so far as we have feelings. (b) We are neither praised nor blamed in so far as we have feelings; for we do not praise the angry or the frightened person, and do not blame the person who is simply angry, but only the person who is angry in a particular way. But we are praised or blamed in so far as we have virtues or vices. (c) We are angry and afraid without decision; but the virtues are decisions of some kind, or [rather] require decision. (d) Besides, in so far as we have feelings, we are said to be moved; but in so far as we have virtues or vices, we are said to be in some condition rather than moved.

## Or a Capacity . . .

For these reasons the virtues are not capacities either; for we are neither called good nor called bad in so far as we are simply capable of feelings. Further, while we have capacities by nature, we do not become good or bad by nature; we have discussed this before.

## But a State

If, then, the virtues are neither feelings nor capacities, the remaining possibility is that they are states. And so we have said what the genus of virtue is. . . .

## Virtue and the Human Function

It should be said, then, that every virtue causes its possessors to be in a good state and to perform their functions well; the virtue of eyes, e.g., makes the eyes and their functioning excellent, because it makes us see well; and similarly, the virtue of a horse makes the horse excellent, and thereby good at galloping, at carrying its rider and at standing steady in the face of the enemy. If this is true in every case, then the virtue of a human being will likewise be the state that makes a human being good and makes him perform his function well. . . .

## Arguments from the Nature of Virtue of Character

By virtue I mean virtue of character; for this [pursues the mean because] it is concerned with feelings and actions, and these admit of excess, deficiency and an intermediate condition. We can be afraid, e.g., or be confident, or have appetites, or get angry, or feel pity, in general have pleasure or pain, both too much and too little, and in both ways not well; but [having these feelings] at the right times, about the right things, towards the right people, for the right end, and in the right way, is the intermediate and best condition, and this is proper to virtue. Similarly, actions also admit of excess, deficiency and the intermediate condition.

Now virtue is concerned with feelings and actions, in which excess and deficiency are in error and incur blame, while the intermediate condition is correct and wins praise, which are both proper features of virtue. Virtue, then, is a mean, in so far as it aims at what is intermediate.

Moreover, there are many ways to be in error, since badness is proper to what is unlimited, as the Pythagoreans pictured, and good to what is limited; but there is only one way to be correct. That is why error is easy and correctness hard, since it is easy to miss the target and hard to hit it. And so for this reason also excess and deficiency are proper to vice, the mean to virtue; "for we are noble in only one way, but bad in all sorts of ways."

## Definition of Virtue

Virtue, then, is (a) a state that decides, (b) [consisting] in a mean, (c) the mean relative to us, (d) which is defined by reference to reason, (e) i.e., to the reason by reference to which the intelligent person would define it. It is a mean between two vices, one of excess and one of deficiency.

## Proper Motive and Good Habits

Aristotle has made an important but much underdeveloped distinction between right action and proper motive. His point seems to be that we need to distinguish the *external performance* from the *internal motive*. An action can be the right action without being virtuous; but an action can be virtuous only if performed from the proper motive. Both right action and right motive must be present in a truly moral action. This distinction is reflected in the following passage, drawn from the preceding selection (italics added): "The *agent must . . . be in the right state when he does them* [the actions]. . . . The just and temperate person is not the one who [merely] does these actions, but the one who also does them *in the way in which just or temperate people do them.*"

This account suggests that if these conditions of knowledge and motivation are not present, the action performed cannot be of the same type of virtue that it otherwise would be. For example, an apparently courageous act would be viewed as something other than courageous—or a friendly act as other than friendly—if we find that the underlying motive was, say, lust for revenge. Such a person is not performing the act in the way in which courageous persons perform such acts.

Aristotle also discusses how we can create and nourish a virtuous or good character. His answer is that we are given by nature the raw materials for a good character, but we must learn the right habits of action and must practice them. Virtuous character is neither natural nor unnatural; it is cultivated and made a part of us, much as a language or musical performance is cultivated and made a part of us. Virtue can be improved through practice and wasted through lack of use. Whereas a stone by nature moves downward and cannot be habituated otherwise, virtue is always a matter of habit. We acquire virtues in the way we acquire skills—for example, by building furniture or playing a harp. Similarly, we become just by performing just actions, temperate by performing temperate actions, and so forth.

## THE SPECIAL PLACE OF THE VIRTUES

A few contemporary philosophers have bluntly defended the view that virtue ethics should be primary in ethical theory, not merely an appendix to, or the complement of, obligation-based ethics. They believe there are major differences in how people understand what it is to be morally good, and they find virtue theory to contain the deeper understanding. From this perspective, one can be a moral individual in every significant sense without being directed by obligations.

### The Claim of Primacy

Some writers in virtue theory seem to think that the moral life requires only right motives and desires, and that we can oust the categories of obligation, good, right, and the like. Other virtue theorists believe that we do need moral notions of obligation and rights for a complete account of the moral life, but they too believe that the person who is disposed by character to have the right motives and desires and to act on them is the proper model of the moral person.

Kant's view, by contrast, seems to be that the right motive or desire is to do the right thing *for the sake of the obligation* that requires it. This view has a difficult time dealing with moral worth. When a friend performs an act of friendship, we would hope it is not from a sense of the obligation to be our friend, but rather because the person has a desire to be friendly, feels friendly, and values our friendship. The friend who acts strictly from obligation seems to lack the virtue of friendliness, which is all important. Friendship, in a sense we would recognize as having moral worth, entails conscientious, benevolent, caring behavior, in which the friend values the friendship as a friendship, and not for what it will yield in the way of personal advancement or satisfaction. The more a person is concerned for a friend, the deeper is the moral worth of the person's attitudes and dispositions. Friendship, under this description, is a virtue; but if it fails to satisfy this description, then the cultivation of another may only be a self-serving project. Aristotle would say that having the trait of prizing friendship as such is essential for living human life well. This is a characteristic of the truly human life, and to the extent it is degraded by the wrong motives, something central has been lost.

The strength of this view is that a morally good person with the right kind of desires or motivations is more likely than a morally bad person to understand what should be done, more likely to be motivated to perform the acts that are required, and even more likely to form and act on moral ideals. A person we trust to do what is morally right is one who has an ingrained motivation and desire to perform right actions and who characteristically cares about a morally appropriate response. The person who simply follows rules of obligation, and otherwise exhibits no special moral character, may not be trustworthy in critical circumstances. Not the rule follower, then, but the person disposed by character to be generous, caring, compassionate, sympathetic, fair, and so on, is the one we will recommend, admire, praise, and hold up as a moral model.

This position is inviting in many respects. Persons of generous character and warm personality are not judged by the way they live up to the demands of rules. A person extremely conscientious in attending to the needs and desires of others lies close to our ideal of moral praiseworthiness, especially when that person sets aside his or her own desires in order to promote the welfare of others. The compassion guiding Jane Addams's life was no matter of moral obligation; and most figures celebrated for compassion have been moved by the plight of others, not by obligation to them. St. Francis of Assisi, for example, was known for the tenderness and compassion he exhibited toward the poor and the sick. St. Francis expressed reservations about both appeals to reason and appeals to obligation, because he found them irrelevant in the moral life.

Being moved from natural sympathy, rather than obligation, is undeniably virtuous; yet it has no clear moral place in Kant's philosophy. As Philippa Foot puts it, "The man who acts charitably out of a sense of obligation is not to be undervalued, but it is the other who most shows virtue and therefore to the other that most moral worth is attributed."[8] In this regard, Foot sees Aristotle's moral theory as more pre-scient and acceptable than an obligation-based theory, and she considers it superior, in particular, to Kant's account of moral worth. "Virtue par excellence," says Foot, is found in one who is prompt and resourceful in doing good, where this may be ac-complished as much by one's "innermost desires" as by a deliberate action.[9]

Another argument that speaks in favor of giving a special status to virtue ethics is the following: Even though we evaluate persons through our knowledge of their actions, we do not evaluate their moral worth or goodness simply by adding up all their actions. Rather, we take account of their total set of virtues. It will not matter that morally good persons act occasionally from blameworthy motives, or that evil persons act occasionally from good motives. None of us is unfailingly good, and even saints and heroes, such as Jane Addams, can and do act out of character. Only when we discover that telling a lie is "in character" do we appropriately label the lie teller a "liar" or conceive the person as having a vice rather than a virtue. An over-all assessment of the person thus depends fundamentally on whether we are confi-dent that any given act exhibits the person's *character.*

## MacIntyre's Aristotelian Program

Alasdair MacIntyre has been at the forefront of recent attempts to give primacy to a theory of virtue. He continues an Aristotelian program, although one including ele-ments not found in Aristotle. His work begins with the thesis we saw him advance in Chapter 2 (and see again in Chapter 9): Moral philosophy and morality are in dis-array in our time, and there is no way to grasp a moral philosophy without under-standing its historical content in a culture. In ancient Greece, medieval Europe, and the like, morality could be understood in terms of a whole cloth, but in our culture the cloth is interwoven with many different, rival, and incompatible fabrics.

MacIntyre maintains that escape from this cultural circumstance will be difficult, but the best chance for rescue lies with Aristotelian virtue theory. In ancient Greece and in the Middle Ages, he argues, we had a controlled sense of the nature of virtue, which we have now lost. MacIntyre approaches virtue theory by using a few tech-nical terms, the most important of which are "practice" and "internal good." A prac-tice is a cooperative arrangement in pursuit of goods that are internal to the arrangement. Our various social roles or ways of life, for example, involve prac-tices. These include being a parent, teacher, physician, architect, and the like. Thus, practices are found in disciplines, political institutions, and professions—for exam-ple, in music, government, and medicine. Each has a history that sustains a tradition, and each requires participants internal to the practice to cultivate and sustain certain virtues:

---

[8]Philippa Foot, *Virtues and Vices* (Oxford, England: Basil Blackwell, 1978), pp. 12–14.

[9]Ibid., p. 5, and "Morality as a System of Hypothetical Imperatives."

[A practice is] any coherent and complex form of socially established cooperative human activity through which goods internal to the form of activity are realized in the course of trying to achieve those standards of excellence which are appropriate to, and partially definitive of, that form of activity, with the result that human powers to achieve excellence, and human conceptions of the ends and goods involved, are systematically extended.[10]

"Goods internal to a practice" are achievable only by engaging in the practice and conforming to its standards of excellence. The virtues are character traits that dispose a person to act in accordance with the ends or objectives of the practices. These dispositions sustain practices and enable us to achieve the goods internal to practices. Consider, for example, the practice of medicine. Several goods are internal to the profession and are naturally associated with the idea of being a good physician. These include specific skills in the care of patients, the application of specific forms of knowledge, and teaching health behaviors. These goods are achievable if, and only if, one abides by the standards of the good physician, standards that have a history and that in part define the practice. Although these practices are not immune to revision, historical development of a body of standards is definitive of the idea of medicine as a practice.

In addition to these goods, which are all internal to a practice, there are external and contingently attached goods, including financial rewards, job security, status among friends, prestige among colleagues, and the like. These goods are external because they may be achieved by many paths of life other than medicine; and they are only contingently attached to the role of physician (thus any physician could consistently reject them as goods worthy of attention).

This distinction between internal and external goods also leads MacIntyre to an important distinction between practices and institutions. The latter are characteristically concerned with external goods and are structured in terms of power and status. Practices cannot survive without the institutions that sustain them, but they are not to be identified with institutions. A hospital is an institution, as is a medical school, but medicine is a practice that occurs in these institutions. Paradoxically, the institution that sustains a practice also threatens the practice because of the constant search for external goods. For example, a hospital's concern with costs and prestige, and a medical school's concern with status as a research center, may threaten various practices in medicine—such as developing more fulfilling patient-physician relationships. One essential function of the virtues is to resist the "corrupting power of institutions" that negatively affect practices.

MacIntyre further maintains that a practice is not merely a set of technical skills. Practices are to be understood in terms of the regard practitioners have for the goods internal to the practice(s). In the following essay MacIntyre explains why the historical dimension of practices is critical and how the virtues help us define our relationships to other persons in the context of our mutual purposes and practices.

---

[10]Alasdair MacIntyre, *After Virtue,* 2d ed. (Notre Dame, IN: University of Notre Dame Press, 1984), p. 17.

# *The Nature of the Virtues\**

## Alasdair MacIntyre

One response to the history might well be to suggest that even within the relatively coherent tradition of thought which I have sketched there are just too many different and incompatible conceptions of a virtue for there to be any real unity to the concept or indeed to the history. Homer, Sophocles, Aristotle, the New Testament and medieval thinkers differ from each other in too many ways. They offer us different and incompatible lists of the virtues; they give a different rank order of importance to different virtues; and they have different and incompatible theories of the virtues. If we were to consider later Western writers on the virtues, the list of differences and incompatibilities would be enlarged still further; and if we extended our enquiry to Japanese, say, or American Indian cultures, the differences would become greater still. It would be all too easy to conclude that there are a number of rival and alternative conceptions of the virtues, but, even within the tradition which I have been delineating, no single core conception.

The case for such a conclusion could not be better constructed than by beginning from a consideration of the very different lists of items which different authors in different times and places have included in their catalogues of virtues. Some of these catalogues—Homer's, Aristotle's and the New Testament's—I have already noticed at greater or lesser length. Let me at the risk of some repetition recall some of

their key features and then introduce for further comparison the catalogues of two later Western writers, Benjamin Franklin and Jane Austen.

The first example is that of Homer. At least some of the items in a Homeric list of the *aretai* would clearly not be counted by most of us nowadays as virtues at all, physical strength being the most obvious example. To this it might be replied that perhaps we ought not to translate the word *aretê* in Homer by our word "virtue," but instead by our word "excellence"; and perhaps, if we were so to translate it, the apparently surprising difference between Homer and ourselves would at first sight have been removed. For we could allow without any kind of oddity that the possession of physical strength is the possession of an excellence. . . .

The question can therefore now be posed directly: are we or are we not able to disentangle from these rival and various claims a unitary core concept of the virtues of which we can give a more compelling account than any of the other accounts so far? I am going to argue that we can in fact discover such a core concept and that it turns out to provide the tradition of which I have written the history with its conceptual unity. It will indeed enable us to distinguish in a clear way those beliefs about the virtues which genuinely belong to the tradition from those which do not. Unsurprisingly perhaps it is a complex concept, different parts of which derive from different stages in the development of the tradition. Thus the concept itself in some sense embodies the history of which it is the outcome.

*From Alasdair MacIntyre, *After Virtue,* 2d ed. (Notre Dame, Ind.: University of Notre Dame Press, 1984), pp. 181, 186–8, 190, 194, 201, 203.

One of the features of the concept of a virtue which has emerged with some clarity from the argument so far is that it always requires for its application the acceptance for some prior account of certain features of social and moral life in terms of which it has to be defined and explained. So in the Homeric account the concept of a virtue is secondary to that of *a social role,* in Aristotle's account it is secondary to that of *the good life for man* conceived as the *telos* of human action and in Franklin's much later account it is secondary to that of utility. What is it in the account which I am about to give which provides in a similar way the necessary background against which the concept of a virtue has to be made intelligible? It is in answering this question that the complex, historical, multi-layered character of the core concept of virtue becomes clear. For there are no less than three stages in the logical development of the concept which have to be identified in order, if the core conception of a virtue is to be understood, and each of these stages has its own conceptual background. The first stage requires a background account of what I shall call a practice, the second an account of what I have already characterized as the narrative order of a single human life and the third an account a good deal fuller than I have given up to now of what constitutes a moral tradition. Each later stage presupposes the earlier, but not *vice versa.* Each earlier stage is both modified by and reinterpreted in the light of, but also provides an essential constituent of each later stage. The progress in the development of the concept is closely related to, although it does not recapitulate in any straightforward way, the history of the tradition of which it forms the core. . . .

By a "practice" I am going to mean any coherent and complex form of socially established cooperative human activity through which goods internal to that form of activity are realized in the course of trying to achieve those standards of excellence which are appropriate to, and partially definitive of, that form of activity, with the result that human powers to achieve excellence, and human conceptions of the ends and goods involved, are systematically extended. Tic-tac-toe is not an example of a practice in this sense, nor is throwing a football with skill; but the game of football is, and so is chess. Bricklaying is not a practice; architecture is. Planting turnips is not a practice; farming is. So are the enquiries of physics, chemistry and biology, and so is the work of the historian, and so are painting and music. In the ancient and medieval worlds the creation and sustaining of human communities—of households, cities, nations—is generally taken to be a practice in the sense in which I have defined it. Thus the range of practices is wide: arts, sciences, games, politics in the Aristotelian sense, the making and sustaining of family life, all fall under the concept. . . .

A practice involves standards of excellence and obedience to rules as well as the achievement of goods. To enter into a practice is to accept the authority of those standards and the inadequacy of my own performance as judged by them. It is to subject my own attitudes, choices, preferences and tastes to the standards which currently and partially define the practice. Practices of course, as I have just noticed, have a history: games, sciences and arts all have histories. Thus the standards are not themselves immune from criticism, but nonetheless we cannot be initiated into a practice without accepting the authority of the best standards realized so far. . . .

We are now in a position to notice an important difference between what I have called internal and what I have called external goods. It is characteristic of what I have called external goods that when achieved they are always some individual's property and possession. Moreover characteristically they are such that the more someone has of them, the less there is for other people. This is sometimes necessarily the case, as with power and fame, and sometimes the case by reason of contingent circumstance as with money. External goods are therefore characteristically objects of competition in which there must be losers as well as winners. . . .

To enter into a practice is to enter into a relationship not only with its contemporary practitioners, but also with those who have preceded us in the practice, particularly those whose achievements extended the reach of the practice to its present point. It is thus the achievement, and *a fortiori* the authority, of a tradition which I then confront and from which I have to learn. And for this learning and the relationship to the past which it embodies the virtues of justice, courage and truthfulness are prerequisite in precisely the same way and for precisely the same reasons as they are in sustaining present relationships within practices. . . .

. . . The most notable difference so far between my account and any account that could be called Aristotelian is that although I have in no way restricted the exercise of the virtues to the context of practices, it is in terms of practices that I have located their point and function. Whereas Aristotle locates that point and function in terms of the notion of a type of whole human life which can be called

good. And it does seem that the question "What would a human being lack who lacked the virtues?" must be given a kind of answer which goes beyond anything which I have said so far.

For such an individual would not merely fail *in a variety of particular ways* in respect of the kind of excellence which can be achieved through participation in practices and in respect of the kind of human relationship required to sustain such excellence. His own life *viewed as a whole* would perhaps be defective; it would not be the kind of life which someone would describe in trying to answer the question "What is the best kind of life for this kind of man or woman to live?" And that question cannot be answered without at least raising Aristotle's own question, "What is the good life for man?" . . .

I have suggested so far that unless there is a *telos* which transcends the limited goods of practices by constituting the good of a whole human life, the good of a human life conceived as a unity, it will *both* be the case that a certain subversive arbitrariness will invade the moral life *and* that we shall be unable to specify the context of certain virtues adequately. These two considerations are reinforced by a third: that there is at least one virtue recognized by the tradition which cannot be specified at all except with reference to the wholeness of a human life—the virtue of integrity or constancy. Purity of heart," said Kierkegaard, "is to will one thing." This notion of singleness of purpose in a whole life can have no application unless that of a whole life does.

It is clear therefore that my preliminary account of the virtues in terms of practices captures much, but very far from all, of what the Aristotelian tradition taught about the virtues.

## CAN VIRTUES AND OBLIGATIONS COEXIST?

Despite the arguments by MacIntyre, Foot, and others, many prominent writers in philosophy have rejected the primacy of virtue and have defended systems composed primarily of principles of obligation. Perhaps the major reason for their reservations about an independent virtue theory is that traits of the person without principles of right action seem blind; we cannot know which traits to encourage or admire unless we already subscribe to some principles.[11] One cannot know how to be a virtuous person unless one makes judgments about what is the best way to manifest one's characteristic forms of sympathy, desire, and the like. Thus when Aristotelians discuss right actions as flowing from being the right type of person, there arises the worry that they have the wrong order. Must we, then, make a choice as to whether obligation or virtue is the more primary category in moral theory, or is it an issue we can circumvent?

The two kinds of theory—obligation-based and virtue-based—have different emphases, but they arguably are compatible, and perhaps even mutually reinforcing. Theories of ethics based on obligation presume that the central question in ethics concerns what is morally required and what is morally desirable in conduct. Statements of obligations entail that there are good moral reasons for performing actions and that society should exercise suitable forms of influence and control in order to ensure the maintenance of these standards. By contrast, theories of ethics grounded in virtue presume that the central question in ethics concerns what is morally desirable *in character rather than conduct.* Unless morality itself is inconsistent, there is no reason why the right type of person would do other than perform the right type of action in the right way for the right reasons. From this perspective, there is nothing incompatible about virtue ethics and obligation ethics.

A stronger thesis, and one more difficult to sustain, is that virtues *correspond to* moral obligations in the sense that every moral principle of obligation has a corresponding moral virtue. This correspondence can be depicted in schematic form ("exceptional standards" are moral ideals, a category we will examine later):

Action Guides (Correspond to) Virtue Standards

|                      | Fundamental obligations | Primary virtue standards   |
| -------------------- | ----------------------- | -------------------------- |
| Ordinary standards   | ↓                       | ↓                          |
|                      | Derivative obligations  | Derivative virtue standards |
| Exceptional standards | Ideals of action       | Ideals of virtue           |

[11]See William K. Frankena, *Ethics,* 2d ed. (Englewood Cliffs, NJ: Prentice-Hall, 1973), p. 65.

The point of this schema is not that virtue standards are equivalent in meaning to standards of obligation. There is no such equivalence. The point is that both types of standards are complementary in the moral life and can be shown to correspond in certain respects. The following list is not devised as a full inventory of the virtues or as a correct account of moral derivation, but it illustrates the correspondence between fundamental derivative action guides, virtues, and ideals.

| *Fundamental Obligations* | *Primary Virtues* |
|---|---|
| Respect for autonomy | Respectfulness |
| Beneficence | Benevolence |
| Justice | Justice (or fairness) |
| Veracity | Truthfulness |

| *Derivative Obligations* | *Secondary Virtues* |
|---|---|
| Due diligence | Conscientiousness |
| Confidentiality | Confidentialness |
| Respect for privacy | Respectfulness for privacy |
| Fidelity | Faithfulness |

| *Ideals of Action* | *Ideals of Virtue* |
|---|---|
| Forgiveness | Clemency |
| Generosity | Generosity |
| Compassion | Compassion |
| Kindness | Kindness |

Deontologists and utilitarians can point out that nothing in their theories disallows statements about the moral importance of the virtues in the right-hand column. Nonetheless, there are reasons to be cautious about this schema of correspondence. First, many virtue standards do not in any straightforward respect correspond to action guides. There is no one-to-one correspondence. Consider compassion, caring, sympathy, courage, modesty, and long-sufferingness. Which principle or principles of obligation correspond? This problem is broader than an absence of one-to-one relationships. Many virtues seem to have no connection whatever to principles of obligation, let alone a one-to-one connection. Typical examples are modesty, cautiousness, integrity (in the sense of upholding and standing firm in one's values), cheerfulness, sincerity, appreciativeness, cooperativeness, and commitment. The list could be greatly expanded. What corresponds to sobriety, friendship, courteousness, promptness, and prudence? Or compassion, conscientiousness, devotion, civility, and caring? Further, a virtue such as integrity may involve a commitment to uphold and stand fast in all our obligations and ideals; and an obligation or ideal such as beneficence may embody and camouflage many virtues.

A related point is that mainstream deontological and utilitarian ethics may not be able to support or otherwise account for a large area of the moral life that virtue ethics covers. If so, virtue ethics may be elevated in importance. For example, traits such as generosity, compassion, kindness, sincerity, patience, love, sympathy, and dozens of others are important moral notions that obligation-based ethics has generally ignored and seems to have no way to address.

The absence of a category of *obligation* in virtue ethics does not entail that the virtue theorists must dispense with the category of *right action.* This category seems basic for Aristotle, and it is difficult to understand why a philosopher would want to isolate virtues from right actions. Consider the virtue of compassion as a standard case: This virtue involves a disposition to attend to and attempt to soothe or ease the defeats, upsets, or mishaps of others. The compassionate person is one who acts to lend assistance; whether or not we understand the act as obligatory, we certainly frame the act as *right,* and even as what ought to be done.

On the one hand, an Aristotelian theory can accommodate categories such as right action, requisite action, and virtuous action without recourse to deontological or utilitarian conceptions of law, obligation, and the like. On the other hand, an ethics of obligation readily acknowledges a division into obligatory actions and right but not nonobligatory actions, such as philanthropy, good samaritan acts, and the like. An obligation-based theory requires that we be able to distinguish what is obligatory and what exceeds obligation, whereas a virtue-based theory has a less pressing need for this distinction, because the virtues do not inherently require actions. This difference does not show that obligation-based and virtue-based theories are incompatible; it merely indicates that one theory adds a perspective on the moral life that the other downplays.

This problem can be illuminated by a discussion of moral ideals, to which we now turn.


## MORAL IDEALS AND MORAL EXCELLENCE

We have previously distinguished between "ordinary moral standards" and "exceptional moral standards," noting that exceptional standards are moral ideals calling for moral excellence in the person who accepts them. We also discussed Aristotle's account of excellence in character. In the following selection we will treat these topics in detail.


### Aristotelian Excellence

Aristotelian ethical theory has long insisted that moral excellence is a supremely important topic and one closely connected to both virtues and moral ideals. Here is a passage from Aristotle that compactly summarizes this idea:

> A truly good and intelligent person . . . from his own resources at any time will do the finest actions he can, just as a good general will make the best use of his forces in war, and a good shoemaker will produce the finest shoe he can from the hides given him.[12]

This passage indicates how distant Aristotle's vision is from ethical theories that focus on the moral minimum of obligations. A theory of moral excellence structured in accordance with Aristotle's account shows what is worthy of our aspiration, and not as a matter of obligation. According to this model, if we reach only an ordinary

---

[12]*Nichomachean Ethics,* 1101ªff.

level of moral achievement, it is a matter of disappointment and regret, because each individual should aspire to a level as elevated as his or her ability permits.

Some persons are so advanced morally that what they aspire to do or achieve is different from what those who are less morally developed must do or can expect to achieve. The Aristotelian proposes that standards of moral excellence grow as we develop morally. The implication is that every person who has already achieved a certain level of virtue has the opportunity to strive for a higher level of virtue. What persons should strive to achieve when at a lower level of moral development is different from what should be attempted at a more advanced level. But wherever one is on the continuum of development, there will always be a goal of moral excellence that exceeds what has already been achieved. What we *ought* to do, then, in an Aristotelian framework, is set by a moving target of moral excellence.

This Aristotelian model does not expect moral perfection, but it does expect that one strive for perfection. Ideals are central in this model, not merely ornaments to an already commendable life. Being *our* ideals they motivate us in a way that obligations likely will not, and they also set out a path that can be climbed in stages, with a renewable sense of growth and achievement.

## Two Moralities

Ordinary moral standards are within the reach of everyone, but an elevated morality of high standards is within the reach only of a person of extraordinary talents, dedication, and drive. The general term "morality" includes both kinds of morality; but only the former involves moral obligations that we are all expected to accept. The life of Jane Addams, by contrast, illustrates a second morality, beyond the one practiced by most of us. This is a morality based on a set of moral ideals to which the rest of us are neither faithful nor bound.

There is a tendency in contemporary ethical theory to classify anything in the domain of morality either as a matter of obligation or as truly exceptional, thus omitting what might be situated in between. However, we often distinguish between strong and weak demands of the moral life—as well as between forms of principles that are strictly obligatory, others that are borderline, and still others that are not obligatory. These distinctions suggest that there is a continuum running from strong obligation through weaker forms and on to the domain of the morally nonrequired, including lower-level supererogation (e.g., assisting a person lost on the city streets) and ending with higher-level supererogation (e.g., heroic and saintly acts).

| Obligation | | Beyond obligation (Supererogation) | |
|---|---|---|---|
| Strict obligation | Weak obligation | Ideals beyond the obligatory | Saintly and heroic ideals |

This continuum moves from the strictest obligation to the most arduous personal ideal. An absence of charitableness and a failure of generosity—which we could construe as *vices*—are defects in the moral life even if they are not failures of obligation. The category of obligation (or obligations) does not exhaust what we ought to do, as various interpretations of the general form "*X ought* to do it" indicate. "Ought" might mean "is required by obligation," but it also can mean "should do it because it is the most honorable or decent thing to do" or "should do it because it is the best thing to do." Terms like "ought," then, operate within the boundary between obligation and that which exceeds obligation. Even if one believes that virtue exceeds obligation, there is still room for using the language of "ought" to explicate the demands of the moral life under the category of virtue.

In the following essay, Joel Feinberg addresses some of these issues about moral demands. He maintains that there is more to the moral life than an ethics of obligation and that what we *ought* to do often cannot be translated into a statement of obligations.

# Obligation and Supererogation*

## Joel Feinberg

The fundamental error committed by [philosophers who emphasize obligations] is the uncritical acceptance of jural laws and institutional "house rules" as models for the understanding of all counsels of wisdom and all forms of human worth. Many institutions have rules which allow persons to accumulate extra points of credit by oversubscribing their assigned quotas of cash or work. Merely acknowledging the existence of saintly and heroic actions which go beyond duty will not help if they are understood on the model of these institutional oversubscriptions. To so understand them is to commit the same sort of mistake as that committed by philosophers who take the prohibitory rules of jural law and other institutions as a model for understanding all so-called moral rules which contain the word "ought" and thus commit themselves to identifying all meritorious actions with the performance of "duties." . . .

First, consider how the word "ought" differs from the word "duty." Suppose a stranger approaches me on a street corner and politely asks me for a match. Ought I to give him one? I think most people would agree that I should, and that any reasonable man of good will would, offer the stranger a match. Perhaps a truly virtuous man would do more than that. He would be friendly, reply with a cheerful smile, and might even volunteer to light the stranger's cigarette.

Now suppose that Jones is on the street corner and another stranger politely requests a light from him. Jones is in a sour mood this morning, and even normally he does not enjoy encounters with strangers. He brusquely refuses to

*From Joel Feinberg, "Supererogation and Rules," *Ethics*, 71 (1961), as reprinted in Feinberg, *Doing and Deserving* (Princeton, N.J.: Princeton University Press, 1970), pp. 3–7, 16.

give the stranger a match. I think we
can agree that Jones's behavior on the
street corner does not constitute an ideal
for human conduct under such circumstances; that it is not what a perfectly
virtuous man would have done; that it
was not what Jones ought to have done.

If we reproach Jones, however, for
his uncivil treatment of the stranger, he
may present us with a vigorous self-
defense. "Perhaps I was not civil," he
might admit, "but surely I was under no
*obligation to* give a match to that man.
Who is he to me? He had no *claim* on
me; he has no authority to *command* any
performance from me: I don't *owe* him
anything. It may be nice to do favors for
people; but a favor, by definition, is
nothing that we are legally or morally
*required* to do. I am an honorable man.
In this instance I did not fail to honor
a commitment; neither did I fail to
discharge an obligation, moral or legal; nor did I break any rule, of man or
God. You have, therefore, no right to reproach me."

Jones's defense makes me think no
better of him. Still, from a certain legal-
like point of view, it appears perfectly
cogent. Everything Jones said in his
own defense was true. The moral I draw
from this tale is that there are some actions which it would be desirable for a
person to do and which, indeed, he
*ought* to do, even though they are actions he is under no *obligation* and has
no *duty* to do. It follows logically that to
say that someone has a duty or an obligation to do X is not simply another way
of saying that he ought to do X.

We speak of duties and obligations in
three different connections. First, there
are actions required by laws and by authoritative command. These can be
called "duties of obedience." Second,
there are the assigned tasks which "at-

tach" to stations, offices, jobs, and roles,
which for some reason seem better
named by the word "duty" than by the
word "obligation." Third, there are those
actions to which we voluntarily commit
ourselves by making promises, borrowing money, making appointments, and
so on. When we commit ourselves, we
put ourselves "under an obligation"
("duty" seems to fit less comfortably
here) to some assignable person or persons to behave in the agreed-upon way;
and we do this by utilizing certain social
contrivances or techniques designed for
just this purpose. When a person in-
vokes these procedures, he creates his
own "artificial chains," dons them, and
hands the key to the other. This act
"binds" or "ties" him to the agreed-upon
behavior and gives the other the authority to require it of him. The other can, if
he chooses, release him from his chains,
or he can, in Mill's much quoted words,
exact performance from him "as one ex-
acts a debt."[1]

All duties and obligations, whether
imposed by authoritative injunctions
and prohibitions, acquired through accepting or inheriting an office, job, or
role, or voluntarily incurred through
promises and other contractual agreements, share the common character of
being *required;* and this in turn, while it
may involve more than coercion or pressure, rarely involves less. In the legal
sense, to have a duty or an obligation is
to be subject to civil liability or criminal
punishment for nonperformance. In general, the law requires citizens to discharge their legal duties *or else* face up
to the unpleasant legal consequences.
Similarly, it follows from the rules of

[1]John Stuart Mill, *Utilitarianism* (Indianapolis:
Bobbs-Merrill Company, 1948), p. 60.

nonjural institutions (house rules) that a member who does not pay his dues can be dropped; an employee who fails to perform the duties of his job is liable to be fired; a negligent bureaucrat is liable to demotion, a wayward student to flunking, a disobedient soldier to court-martial.

That liability for failure to perform is an essential part of what we mean by "duty," when we talk of the duties of stations and positions, is suggested by our willingness to substitute in many contexts the word "responsibility" for the word "duty." To be assigned a task or a job in some organization is to be made responsible (answerable, accountable) for its performance. Without this associated accountability, I submit, we should be unwilling to speak of "the job" as involving any *duties* at all. . . .

We have seen that the word "ought" can be used to prescribe or give advice in particular cases. Singular pieces of advice, such as "You ought to keep your promise in this case," are often generalized into such principles as "you ought to keep your promises (generally)," "You ought to be kind," and "You ought to do favors." There is no harm in calling statements of generalized advice "rules"; indeed, it is consonant with us-age to do so. But it is important to notice that these rules do not enjoin, prohibit, or confer obligations and duties. They are rules in a quite different sense, better named "maxims" or "precepts" than "injunctions" or "commands." Perhaps "counsels of wisdom" or "rules of advice" would be the most appropriate designations, since these names suggest, quite correctly, that these are rules of thumb rather than "laws" on some jural or institutional model.

Counsels of wisdom guide the wise man's conduct and sometimes, also, that of the fool; for to have the right precepts without knowing how to apply them in puzzling circumstances or where they come into conflict is to be merely sententious, not wise. The better part of wisdom is a kind of knack or flair which cannot be bottled up in simple formulas. A man is on his own when he must decide whether to stick safely by his station or do the "meritorious, abnormally risky nonduty," or whether to honor his duty or an opposing commitment of a different order—whether to stay with Mother or join the Free French forces. There are, unfortunately, no strict super-rules for applying counsels of wisdom in such situations and no simple commands to obey.

---

The obligation-nonobligation distinction may have been overplayed in contemporary moral theory. The distinction is not as sharp as some theories suggest and does not exhaust the relevant alternatives. The distinction has also been mistakenly interpreted as a way of distinguishing between moral obligation and that which is not even advised, recommended, urged, or encouraged by morality. This approach may do more to obscure than to illuminate the richness and variety of the moral life.

Most theories that specify obligations can readily acknowledge a division into obligatory actions (those required by principles of obligation) and morally praiseworthy, nonrequired actions. Such a theory requires that a principle be formulated to specify both what is obligatory and what exceeds obligation. However, a virtue-based theory has no obvious need for this distinction, because the virtues do not inherently require, command, or compel actions.

Even so, this difference is not as telling as it at first appears. A moral virtue is a disposition to do what is morally good, not what is morally *supergood.* A virtue standard is not a high enough target for the person of saintly, heroic, or excellent character. Virtues like respectfulness, benevolence, and fairness, for example, establish our shared moral expectations for good and decent human relationships. Persons who violate those standards violate ordinary canons of morality.

## Models from Saints and Heroes

Recent literature on moral ideals has explored the exemplary character traits of saints and heroes. These traits provide developed models of supererogation. Normally, we do not expect or demand of anyone that they adopt the standards of a saint or hero; and most people do not and could not perform heroic or saintly acts. However, the saintly or heroic figure performs what he or she accepts as "obligation." The hero, for example, acts when others would generally succumb to fear, and the saint when others would generally yield to personal interest. Typically such persons do not regard their own actions as heroic or saintly. Rather, they tend to set higher standards for themselves than other people do. Saintliness, in particular, involves consistent fulfillment of, or transcendence of, obligation over time. Saintliness thus cannot be determined until a person's history is substantially complete. However, a person may become an instant hero through a single act, such as assuming a substantial risk in the attempt to save another's life.

The "ought" and "must" language of saints and heroes belongs in the realm of self-assumed moral ideals beyond the "ought" and "must" language of an obligation. If people fail to fulfill their obligations, we can blame or castigate them for nonperformance, but we cannot blame the saint or hero who fails to live up to his or her moral ideals. At most, we are disappointed that the person did not turn out as we had hoped.

Another aspect of saintliness that makes it particularly suited for study in virtue ethics is character and motive, which we discussed earlier. A person who acts in a manner normally deserving the accolade "saintly," but who does so purely for self-advancement or public recognition, is not a saint—and may not be a hero, depending on the exact motive involved. A saint *must* have a certain kind of character, with character traits that consistently dispose him or her to proper deeds over time. By contrast, a single act of courage can make someone a hero.

Finally, many actions exceed obligation without being either heroic or saintly. For example, a teacher may put in extra hours of work without being saintly or heroic. On many occasions, we are uncertain where to draw the line between the obligatory and the supererogatory, and thus we may be unclear about what kind of action exceeds obligation. What is the teacher's obligation to his or her students and to the entire school? Is it to grade tests and papers thoroughly? To serve as a friend or counselor? To assist all senior majors in the department in obtaining admission for advanced study? If the obligation is that of spending, say, forty hours a week in conscientious performance of tasks, then the teacher can go beyond that obligation by working forty-five hours. Many actions that exceed obligation are genuine instances of living up to moral ideals, but not ideals so high that we wish to apply the honorific titles "heroic" and "saintly" to them.

It would be a mistake to think that the only persons who serve as models of virtue are saints and heroes. One reason a person becomes a saint or hero is that he or she possesses many virtues, and thereby is admired and comes to influence us deeply. We can and often do learn about virtuous conduct from persons with a more limited repertoire of virtues. Jane Addams learned about the virtuous life from her father, and by her own account, his influence became the dominant influence in her life. Whereas we often learn conscientiousness from our parents and diligence from our teachers, neither our parents nor our teachers need, on the whole, lead exceptionally virtuous lives to exert such influence. We learn about virtue and how to practice it where we find it, and for most of us most of the time, our admired instructors are neither saints nor heroes. Nonetheless, it is worth remembering that many persons have a moral capacity, maturity, or authority that serves as a valid ideal of the moral life.

## CRITICISMS AND DEFENSES OF VIRTUE ETHICS

Virtue ethics has been challenged to prove its independence as a moral theory, or at least to show that it adds a dimension lacking in obligation-based theories. We can now investigate a criticism of virtue theories, together with some possible responses. These criticisms center on the indispensable role of obligations and rights in ethics.

If a climate of trust prevails, virtue and character are likely to be emphasized in many human relationships. Principles or rules of obligation may, in these contexts, be seen more as intrusions than essential elements. However, the categories in virtue theory do not always best capture some areas of moral experience. When strangers meet in many circumstances, character may play a less significant role than principles and rules. Here it does not seem that we can *dispense* with rules of obligation or the sanctions that back them as primary constituents in the moral life. For example, when a patient first encounters a physician, the physician's conformity to rules, principles, and even explicit contracts backed by sanctions may be essential to subsequent moral relationships involving disclosure, mutual decision-making, and legitimate authority. Many physicians may likewise believe that they cannot always trust their patients, especially if something goes wrong and litigation looms as a possibility. As a consequence, these physicians will welcome mutually agreed-upon rules and may demand signed consent forms to document mutual decisions.

Public rules of moral behavior are useful in situations such as doctor-patient relationships, where people need specific standards to determine the right course of action. Here virtue ethics does not seem to provide adequately specific guidance. Rules and principles can also serve to remind us of the moral minimum expected of everyone, and sanctions may deter morally good (but imperfect) persons from cutting moral corners. Such a reliance on principles and rules, accompanied by sanctions, need not entail a general presumption of distrust. A presumption of trust can be combined with a recognition that people who are generally trustworthy may sometimes fail to perceive what they ought to do or lack sufficient motivation to do it. Sometimes even the most virtuous person needs guidance by rules.

In the selection that follows Robert Louden develops these lines of criticism of virtue theory.

# On Some Vices of Virtue Ethics*

## Robert B. Louden

It is common knowledge by now that recent philosophical and theological writing about ethics reveals a marked revival of interest in the virtues. . . . Is there a price to be paid for its different perspective, and if so, is the price worth paying? . . .

While I am sympathetic to recent efforts to recover virtue from its long-standing neglect, my purpose in this essay is not to contribute further to the campaign for virtue. Instead, I wish to take a more critical look at the phenomenon, and to ask whether there are certain important features of morality which a virtue-based ethics either handles poorly or ignores entirely. In the remainder of this essay, I shall sketch some objections which (I believe) point to genuine shortcomings of the virtue approach to ethics. . . .

As noted earlier, it is a commonplace that virtue theorists focus on good and bad agents rather than on right and wrong acts. In focusing on good and bad agents, virtue theorists are thus forced to deemphasize discrete acts in favor of long-term, characteristic patterns of behavior. Several related problems arise

for virtue ethics as a result of this particular conceptual commitment.

## Applied Ethics

It has often been said that for virtue ethics the central question is not "What ought I to *do*?" but rather "What sort of person ought I to *be*?" However, people have always expected ethical theory to tell them something about what they ought to do, and it seems to me that virtue ethics is structurally unable to say much of anything about this issue. If I'm right, one consequence of this is that a virtue-based ethics will be particularly weak in the areas of applied ethics. . . . As virtue theorists from Aristotle onward have rightly emphasized, virtues are not simply dispositions to behave in specified ways, for which rules and principles can always be cited. In addition, they involve skills of perception and articulation, situation-specific "know-how," all of which are developed only through recognizing and acting on what is relevant in concrete moral contexts as they arise. These skills of moral perception and practical reason are not completely routinizable, and so cannot be transferred from agent to agent as any sort of decision procedure "package deal." Due to the very nature of the

*From *American Philosophical Quarterly,* 21 (no. 3, July 1984).

moral virtues, there is thus a very limited amount of advice on moral quandaries that one can reasonably expect from the virtue-oriented approach. We ought, of course, to do what the virtuous person would do, but it is not always easy to fathom what the hypothetical moral exemplar would do were he in our shoes, and sometimes even he will act out of character. Furthermore, if one asks him why he did what he did, or how he knew what to do, the answer—if one is offered—might not be very enlightening. One would not necessarily expect him to appeal to any rules or principles which might be of use to others. . . .

Virtue theory is not a problem-oriented or quandary approach to ethics: it speaks of rules and principles of action only in a derivative manner. And its derivative oughts are frequently too vague and unhelpful for persons who have not yet acquired the requisite moral insight and sensitivity. Consequently, we cannot expect it to be of great use in applied ethics. . . . The increasing importance of these two subfields of ethics in contemporary society is thus a strike against the move to revive virtue ethics.

## Tragic Humans

Another reason for making sure that our ethical theory allows us to talk about features of acts and their results in abstraction from the agent and his conception of what he is doing is that sometimes even the best person can make the wrong choices. There are cases in which a man's choice is grounded in the best possible information, his motives honorable and his action not at all out of character. And yet his best laid plans may go sour. . . .

Virtue ethics, however, since its conceptual scheme is rooted in the notion of the good person, is unable to assess correctly the occasional (inevitable) tragic outcomes of human action. . . .

## Intolerable Actions

A third reason for insisting that our moral theory enable us to assess acts in abstraction from agents is that we need to be able to identify certain types of action which produce harms of such magnitude that they destroy the bonds of community and render (at least temporarily) the achievement of moral goods impossible. In every traditional moral community one encounters prohibitions or "barriers to action" which mark off clear boundaries in such areas as the taking of innocent life, sexual relations, and the administration of justice according to local laws and customs. Such rules are needed to teach citizens what kinds of actions are to be regarded not simply as bad (a table of vices can handle this) but as intolerable. Theorists must resort to specific lists of offenses to emphasize the fact that there are some acts which are absolutely prohibited. We cannot articulate this sense of absolute prohibition by referring merely to characteristic patterns of behavior.

In rebuttal here, the virtue theorist may reply by saying: "Virtue ethics does not need to articulate these prohibitions—let the law do it, with its list of do's and don't's." But the sense of requirement and prohibition referred to above seems to me to be at bottom inescapably moral rather than legal. Morality can (and frequently does) invoke the aid of law in such cases, but when we ask *why* there is a law against e.g., rape or murder, the proper answer is that it is morally intolerable. To point merely to a legal convention when asked why an act is prohibited or intolerable raises more questions than it answers.

## Character Change

A fourth reason for insisting that a moral theory be able to assess acts in abstraction from agents and their conception of what they're doing is that peoples' moral characters may sometimes change. . . .

If skills can become rusty, it seems to me that virtues can too. Unless we stay in practice we run the risk of losing relative proficiency. We probably can't forget them completely (in part because the opportunities for exercising virtues are so pervasive in everyday life), but we can lose a certain sensitivity. People do become morally insensitive, relatively speaking—missing opportunities they once would have noticed, although perhaps when confronted with a failure they might recognize that they had failed, showing at least that they hadn't literally "forgotten the difference between right and wrong." If the moral virtues are acquired habits rather than innate gifts, it is always possible that one can lose relative proficiency in these habits. Also, just as one's interests and skills sometimes change over the course of a life as new perceptions and influences take hold, it seems too that aspects of our moral characters can likewise alter. (Consider religious conversion experiences.) Once we grant the possibility of such changes in moral character, the need for a more "character free" way of assessing action becomes evident. Character is not a permanent fixture, but rather plastic. A more reliable yardstick is sometimes needed. . . .

I have argued that there is a common source behind each of these vices. The virtue theorist is committed to the claim that the primary object of moral evaluation is not the act or its consequences but rather the agent—specifically, those character traits of the agent which are judged morally relevant. This is not to say that virtue ethics does not ever address the issue of right and wrong actions, but rather that it can only do so in a derivative manner. Sometimes, however, it is clearly acts rather than agents which ought to be the primary focus of moral evaluation. . . .

The last vice I shall mention has a more socio-historical character. It seems to me that there is a bit of utopianism behind the virtue theorist's complaints about the ethics of rules. Surely, one reason there is more emphasis on rules and regulations in modern society is that things have gotten more complex. Our moral community (insofar as it makes sense to speak of "community" in these narcissistic times) contains more ethnic, religious, and class groups than did the moral community which Aristotle theorized about. Unfortunately, each segment of society has not only its own interests but its own set of virtues as well. There is no general agreed upon and significant expression of desirable moral character in such a world. Indeed, our pluralist culture prides itself on and defines itself in terms of its alleged value neutrality and its lack of allegiance to any one moral tradition. This absence of agreement regarding human purposes and moral ideals seems to drive us (partly out of lack of alternatives) to a more legalistic form of morality. To suppose that academic theorists can alter the situation simply by re-emphasizing certain concepts is illusory. Our world lacks the sort of moral cohesiveness and value unity which traditional virtue theorists saw as prerequisites of a viable moral community.

The table of vices sketched above is not intended to be exhaustive, but even in its incomplete state I believe it spells trouble for virtue-based moral theories. For the shortcomings described are not esoteric—they concern mundane features of moral experience which any minimally adequate moral theory should be expected to account for. While I do think that contemporary virtue theorists are correct in asserting that any adequate moral theory must account for the fact of character, and that no ethics of rules, pure and unsupplemented, is up to this job, the above analysis also suggests that no ethics of virtue, pure and unsupplemented, can be satisfactory.

Louden does not deny that virtues are important or that virtue ethics is an important supplement to other ethical theories. He maintains only that virtue ethics cannot replace theories of obligation. According to Louden, virtue theory cannot itself supply the standards of right and wrong action needed to judge acts and hold agents responsible.

Especially unsettling would be a claim that if persons display a virtuous character, then their acts are therefore morally acceptable, or at least not prohibited. People of remarkably fine character who are acting virtuously sometimes perform wrong actions. Virtues such as loyalty, courage, and kindness can easily lead persons to act inappropriately and unacceptably. For example, the airline pilot who acts kindly and loyally by not reporting the incompetence of a fellow airline pilot acts improperly. Such human failures do not suggest that loyalty and kindness are not virtues, but only that virtuous motives require appropriate judgment in determining whether to act on the motives underlying these virtues. The virtues need to be accompanied by an understanding of what is right in the circumstance and deserving of kindness, generosity, and the like.[13]

Suppose an investigative journalist involved in examining a political scandal conscientiously collects information and with eminent fairness publishes a story. Although this journalist is virtuous (let us suppose), it does not follow that the action is right, or even that the actor is, on balance, acting virtuously. The story may involve violations of privacy rights and may fail to take into account limitations on the public's "right to know." The journalist also may not have considered whether it was proper or improper to manipulate a source in order to gather vital information. In such circumstances even the most ideal person of virtue may need to rely on rules of obligation.

How now might the defender of virtue ethics respond to this line of criticism? Neither Aristotle nor any other careful advocate of a virtue ethics would divorce it from an account of the *object* or *purpose* of morality. The end of morals and politics

---

[13]Rosalind Hursthouse and other philosophers have argued that virtue ethics does guide actions. While she thinks it unreasonable to expect virtue ethics to resolve moral dilemmas, Hursthouse claims that this is actually a strength of the theory and a more accurate representation of the moral life. See her "Normative Virtue Ethics," in Roger Crisp, ed., *How Should One Live?: Essays on the Virtues,* pp. 19–36; and "Applying Virtue Ethics," in Rosalind Hursthouse, Gavin Lawrence, and Warren Quinn, eds., *Virtues and Reasons* (New York: Oxford University Press, 1995), pp. 57–75.

is to produce well-being (*eudaimonia*); the person of practical wisdom must know both what constitutes proper ends and how to achieve them. Because acts may be wrong even though they exhibit a virtue, the morally virtuous person is one who makes judgments about appropriate actions by reference to moral goals. In conjunction with what he calls the "Aristotelian principle," John Rawls has expressed this view in the following terms:

> The excellences are a condition of human flourishing; they are goods from everyone's point of view.
>
>     The virtues are [moral] excellences. . . . The lack of them will tend to undermine both our self-esteem and the esteem that our associates have for us.[14]

Finally, we need to distinguish between having a moral virtue, having a morally virtuous character, and performing a virtuous action. One can exhibit a single virtue while performing unspeakably evil actions. History reveals thousands of misguided individuals whose loyalty to evil leaders was flawless. A thorough display of the virtue of loyalty does not make one a virtuous person, and one may even possess many moral virtues while at the same time acting in an evil manner.

## CONCLUSION

In the chapters constituting Part Two of this volume, three broad-ranging approaches to morality have now been discussed: utilitarian theories, deontological theories, and virtue theories. In this chapter we have seen that virtues and moral ideals enrich the framework of obligations developed in the previous chapters. Ideals transcend obligations, and some virtues dispose persons to act in accord with principles and rules as well as ideals. One important objective of the cultivation of virtue is to render fulfillment of obligation a routine matter, rather than a continuous struggle, and this is one reason why Aristotle's ethics has a stronger appeal to some than Kant's or Mill's.

Each of the conceptions of the moral life developed in these three chapters offers a worthy perspective from which to reflect on morality. We can extract valuable insights from each approach, while rejecting any excessive or overreaching emphases. Although the moral philosophies involved seem very different, the one sometimes neglecting what another takes to be of chief importance, we have found several common themes and even shared conclusions among them. Whatever their differences in approach and content, there is reason to believe that each type of theory has treated some important problems well and has provided insights not found in the others.

Now we will turn, in Chapter 7, to a theory that, like Aristotle's, has a concentrated commitment to the virtues. This theory will add a rich layer of moral psychology and an understanding of the nature and role of communal rules.

---

[14]John Rawls, *A Theory of Justice* (Cambridge, MA: Harvard University Press, 1971), pp. 443, 445.

## SUGGESTED SUPPLEMENTARY READINGS

### Aristotle's Works

Aristotle: *Eudemian Ethics.*
————: *Magna Moralia.*
————: *Nichomachean Ethics.*
————: *Politics.*

### Commentaries on Aristotle

Ackrill, J. L.: *Aristotle's Ethics* (New York: Humanities Press, 1980).
Barnes, Jonathan, ed.: *The Cambridge Companion to Aristotle* (New York: Cambridge University Press, 1995).
Broadie, Sarah: *Ethics with Aristotle* (New York: Oxford University Press, 1991).
Cooper, John M.: *Reason and the Human Good in Aristotle* (Cambridge, MA: Harvard University Press, 1975).
Engberg-Pedersen, Troels: *Aristotle's Theory of Moral Insight* (Oxford, England: Clarendon Press, 1983).
Hardie, W. F. R.: *Aristotle's Ethical Theory* (Oxford: Clarendon Press, 1968).
Rorty, Amelie, ed.: *Essays on Aristotle's Ethics* (Berkeley: University of California Press, 1980).
Ross, W. D.: *Aristotle,* 5th ed. (New York: Barnes & Noble, 1964), chap. 7.
Sherman, Nancy: *The Fabric of Character: Aristotle's Theory of Virtue* (Oxford: Clarendon Press, 1989).
————: *Making a Necessity of Virtue: Aristotle and Kant on Virtue* (New York: Cambridge University Press, 1997).
Urmson, J. O.: *Aristotle's Ethics* (Oxford: Clarendon Press, 1988).
Williams, B. A. O.: "Aristotle on the Good," *Philosophical Quarterly,* 12 (1962): 289–96.

### Virtue Ethics

Aquinas, St. Thomas: *Treatise on the Virtues,* John A. Oesterle, trans. (Notre Dame, IN: Notre Dame Press, 1984).
Baron, Marcia: "The Alleged Moral Repugnance of Acting from Duty," *The Journal of Philosophy,* 81 (1984): 197–220.
————: "Varieties of Ethics of Virtue," *American Philosophical Quarterly,* 22 (1985): 47–53.
Baron, Marcia W., Philip Pettit, and Michael Slote: *Three Methods of Ethics: A Debate* (Cambridge, England: Blackwell, 1997).
Becker, Lawrence C.: "The Neglect of Virtue," *Ethics,* 85 (1975): 110–22.
Blum, Lawrence: *Friendship, Altruism, and Morality* (London: Routledge and Kegan Paul, 1980).
Cordner, Christopher: "Aristotelian Virtue and Its Limitations," *Philosophy,* 69 (July 1994): 291–316.

Crisp, Roger, ed.: *How Should One Live?: Essays on the Virtues* (New York: Oxford University Press, 1996).

Crisp, Roger, and Michael Slote, eds.: *Virtue Ethics* (New York : Oxford University Press, 1997).

Dent, N. J. H.: *The Moral Psychology of the Virtues* (Cambridge, England: Cambridge University Press, 1984).

Driver, Julia: "Monkeying with Motives: Agent-Basing Virtue Ethics," *Utilitas,* 7 (1995): 281–8.

Foot, Philippa: *Virtues and Vices* (Oxford, England: Basil Blackwell, 1978), chap. 1.

Frankena, William K.: *Ethics,* 2d ed. (Englewood Cliffs, NJ: Prentice-Hall, 1973), chap. 4.

French, P., T. Uehling, and H. Wettstein, eds.: *Ethical Theory: Character and Virtue* (South Bend, IN: Notre Dame University Press, 1988). Originally published as *Midwest Studies in Philosophy,* 13 (1988). Special Issue. Includes an extensive bibliography.

Herman, Barbara: "Rules, Motives, and Helping Actions," *Philosophical Studies,* 45 (May 1984): 367–77.

Hursthouse, Rosalind: *On Virtue Ethics* (New York: Oxford University Press, 1999).

Hursthouse, Rosalind, Gavin Lawrence, and Warren Quinn, eds.: *Virtues and Reasons: Philippa Foot and Moral Theory* (Oxford, England: Clarendon Press, 1995).

Knight, Kevin M., ed.: *The MacIntyre Reader* (Notre Dame, IN: University of Notre Dame Press, 1988).

Kraut, Richard: *Aristotle on the Human Good* (Princeton, NJ: Princeton University Press, 1991).

Kruschwitz, Robert B., and Robert C. Roberts, eds.: *The Virtues: Contemporary Ethics and Moral Character* (Belmont, CA: Wadsworth Publishing Co., 1987).

MacIntyre, Alasdair: *After Virtue* (Notre Dame, IN: University of Notre Dame Press, 1981).

———: *Whose Justice? Which Rationality?* (Notre Dame: University of Notre Dame Press, 1988).

———: *Dependent Rational Animals: Why Human Beings Need the Virtues* (Chicago: Open Court, 1999).

Mayo, Bernard: *Ethics and the Moral Life* (London: Macmillan and Company, 1958).

Nussbaum, Martha: *The Fragility of Goodness* (Cambridge, England: Cambridge University Press, 1986).

———: "Non-Relative Virtues: An Aristotelian Approach," *Midwest Studies in Philosophy,* 13 (1988): 32–53.

*Philosophia,* 20 (1990). Double Issue on Virtue Theory.

Pincoffs, Edmund L.: *Quandaries and Virtues* (Lawrence: University Press of Kansas, 1986).

Schneewind, Jerome: "Moral Crisis and the History of Ethics," *Midwest Studies in Philosophy,* 8 (1983): 525–42.

Shelp, Earl, ed.: *Virtue and Medicine* (Dordrecht, Holland: D. Reidel, 1985).

Sherman, Nancy: "The Role of Emotions in Aristotelian Virtue," *Proceedings of the Boston Colloquium on Ancient Philosophy,* 9 (1993): 1–33.

Slote, Michael: *Goods and Virtues* (Oxford, England: Clarendon Press, 1983).

————: *From Morality to Virtue* (New York : Oxford University Press, 1992).

Statman, Daniel, ed.: *Virtue Ethics* (Washington, DC: Georgetown University Press: Edinburgh, Scotland: Edinburgh University Press, 1997).

Stocker, Michael: "The Schizophrenia of Modern Ethical Theories," *Journal of Philosophy,* 73 (1976): 453–66.

Walker, A. D. M.: "Virtue and Character," *Philosophy,* 64 (July 1989): 363–80.

Wallace, James D.: *Virtues and Vices* (Ithaca, NY: Cornell University Press, 1978).

## Saints, Heroes, and Moral Ideals

Feinberg, Joel, ed.: *Moral Concepts* (Oxford, England: Oxford University Press, 1969), selections 5–7, 9, and 11.

————: *Doing and Deserving* (Princeton, NJ: Princeton University Press, 1970), especially chap. 1.

Heyd, David: *Supererogation* (Cambridge, England: Cambridge University Press, 1982).

Jeske, Diane: "Friendship, Virtue, and Impartiality," *Philosophy and Phenomenological Research,* 57 (1997): 51–72.

Kamm, Frances M.: "Supererogation and Obligation," *Journal of Philosophy,* 82 (1985): 118–38.

Montague, Phillip: "Acts, Agents and Supererogation," *American Philosophical Quarterly,* 26 (1989): 101–11.

Pybus, Elizabeth: "Saints and Heroes," *Philosophy,* 57 (1982): 193–200.

Trianosky, Gregory: "Supererogation, Wrongdoing, and Vice: On the Autonomy of the Ethics of Virtue," *Journal of Philosophy,* 83 (1986): 26–40.

Urmson, J. O.: "Saints and Heroes," in A. I. Melden, ed., *Essays in Moral Philosophy* (Seattle: University of Washington Press, 1958).

Wolf, Susan: "Moral Saints," *Journal of Philosophy,* 79 (1982): 410–39.

————: "Above and Below the Line of Duty," *Philosophical Topics,* 14 (1986).

CHAPTER 7

# Hume and Humean Theories

## DRINKING DESSERT WINES

On the night of May 27, 1990, intoxicated Maryland teenager Donnell Petite hurled rocks at motorists passing by on the Washington, D.C. Beltway, causing permanent brain damage to a teenage passenger. Before the incident, Petite and his friends had purchased and consumed two 24-ounce bottles of Cisco, a wine strengthened with grape brandy and manufactured by the Canandaigua Wine Company in New York State.

The incident marked a new development in a preexisting controversy between Cisco's manufacturer, state and local governments, and public interest activists. Cisco's clear glass container and wraparound neck label made its appearance almost identical to standard wine coolers. However, it contained a higher level of alcohol. The wine industry divides its products into three categories, each roughly defined by average alcohol content. Most wine coolers contain 4 to 5 percent alcohol. In comparison, the industry defines "table wines" as products containing up to a 14 percent alcohol level. Finally, the "dessert wine" category includes all wines with alcohol content above 14 percent, usually an 18 to 20 percent level. Classified by Canandaigua as a "fortified dessert wine," Cisco has a 20 percent alcohol content, even though its packaging gave Cisco a "cooler style" appearance.

Consumer advocates like the National Council on Alcoholism and Drug Dependence (NCADD) allege that purchasers, particularly underage drinkers, do not realize the wine's potency. Cisco therefore represents a danger to ill-informed drinkers. When compounded by its stylish packaging, Cisco's potency prompted Surgeon General Antonia Novello to declare Cisco "a dangerous fortified wine, and the ultimate 'wine fooler.'" Consumer complaints about Cisco surfaced shortly after the company marketed the wine on a national level.

Canandaigua used the slogan "Cisco takes you by surprise" as a marketing technique. Canandaigua sells Cisco in 12-ounce (375 ml) and 24-ounce (750 ml) bottles. The two sizes supply purchasers with approximately four and eight (normal-sized) drinks, respectively. Research has shown that consumption of the 12-ounce bottle (equivalent to five shots of 80 proof vodka) within one hour by a person weighing

150 pounds or less will result in a 0.11 blood alcohol content level, which renders people legally unfit to drive in every state except Georgia. Consumption of two 12-ounce Cisco bottles within one hour by a 100-pound person may induce acute alcohol poisoning and death.

Disturbed by the results of the research, NCADD—in cooperation with CSPI, Mothers Against Drunk Driving (MADD), and Representative John Conyers (D-MI)—asked Canandaigua to voluntarily withdraw Cisco from sale and to alter its marketing techniques to better inform the public of Cisco's alcohol content. These interest groups feared that the wine's cooler style of packaging could cause people to mistake Cisco for a regular wine cooler with a low-alcohol content. Because it is inexpensively priced, like wine coolers, retail dealers often stock Cisco near or with the wine cooler displays.

Canandaigua's management has never shared these opinions or had similar concerns. Though the company has acknowledged that Cisco's 12-ounce bottle bears "some resemblance" to coolers produced by the Seagram's and Gallo companies, it has contended that the superficial likenesses did not warrant a packaging adjustment. Canandaigua highlighted Cisco's distinctive packaging: "Whereas wine coolers are almost universally sold in 4-packs of bottles, Cisco is sold in single bottles." The company also maintained that "Cisco's 'hot,' high-alcohol taste immediately tells the consumer it is not a low-alcohol cooler."

The public uproar over Cisco attracted the U.S. government's attention. Congress, the Treasury Department's Bureau of Alcohol, Tobacco and Firearms (BATF), the U.S. Surgeon General, and the Federal Trade Commission all became involved in the Cisco controversy. This involvement gave consumer advocates the opportunity to effect national regulatory action against Cisco.

Ultimately faced with a potential ban on all Cisco shipments outside New York State—unless it altered Cisco's bottle and label design—Canandaigua's management reached an agreement with federal authorities. Canandaigua officials presented their proposed modifications in Cisco's packaging to Surgeon General Novello. The plans changed Cisco's bottle color from clear to dark green and replaced the bottle's short neck with a longer, more slender neck. Canandaigua altered the 12-ounce bottle label so that it read "THIS CONTAINER SERVES 4 PEOPLE AND IS BEST SERVED OVER ICE." The company retained its warning label "This is not a wine cooler" on all Cisco bottles. The surgeon general and the Federal Trade Commission announced that the changes satisfactorily addressed their objections about the former package, and the government abandoned plans for regulatory action against Canandaigua.[1]

---

[1]This case was prepared by John Cuddihy, Jeff Greene, and Tom L. Beauchamp. The public statement of Antonia C. Novello, M.D., M.P.H., U.S. Surgeon General occurred at a press conference, January 9, 1991. Quotations pertaining to the views of the Canandaigua Wine Company come from interviews with legal counsel Robert Sands and from *Cisco: The Controversy, The Facts, Actions* (privately published by the Canandaigua Wine Company, 1990), p. 12.

## HUME'S MORAL PHILOSOPHY

In the previous three chapters, we surveyed three influential approaches to moral philosophy, all linked to a single philosopher of major historical significance. We come now to a fourth theory, which bases important aspects of ethics in moral sentiments and social agreements. David Hume is one of the great figures in the history of virtue theory, but he is equally notable for his views on the importance of historical traditions and social conventions.

Hume's philosophy is sufficiently diverse that various philosophers have regarded him as primarily an emotivist, a subjectivist, or an antirealist (to recall categories from Chapter 3), but such labels are quite misleading and fall far short of capturing the rich layers of his moral philosophy. In his later work (after 1750), three interconnected propositions were at the core of his theory:

1. *Reason and sentiment.* Reason plays a subordinate (although important) role in moral judgment, whereas desire, sentiment, or the passions determine human interests and goals.
2. *Virtue.* Moral virtues are qualities of the human mind that are universally approved by impartial observers.
3. *The conventions of communities.* Both social ethics and moral philosophy are rooted in historical traditions and community decisions.

Hume's moral philosophy is a unique blend of these three propositions, which we will examine in the order above.

### Reason and Moral Sentiment

The best-known statement Hume made in his writings on moral philosophy came early in his career, and he may have regretted it because it was dropped in his later work. He said in *A Treatise of Human Nature* that *reason is, and ought only to be, the slave of the passions.*[2] He called this view an "extraordinary opinion," and it has provoked criticism down to the present day. Hume's view is that sentiment, taste, desire, and the like, present our goals in life and that reason assists us in achieving those goals. By "taste" he means a properly cultivated capacity to reach good judgments and opinions regarding what is appropriate, excellent, beautiful, and the like. Hume uses "taste" and "sentiment" to refer to both judgment and opinion.

Reason and sentiment generally work together to reach moral conclusions. Sentiment sets practical goals, and reason determines how to reach those goals. Being incapable by itself of providing goals, reason discovers the means to achieve them. Hume insists that reason and passion, so understood, can never be in opposition or compete for the role of determining the will. For example, in the fortified wine case above, a person can have a passion for Cisco wine, and reason can tell the person that it is a dangerous product. Reason can tell a person how to obtain a product, that

---

[2] *A Treatise of Human Nature* 2.3.3.4. This work is cited by paragraph numbers. See the edition of the *Treatise* by David Fate Norton and Mary Norton (Oxford, England: Oxford University Press, 2000).

a product is dangerous, that there is a public controversy about the marketing of the product, and the like. But reason cannot, by itself, determine that you should or should not sell, purchase, or drink the product. In Hume's philosophy, only your passions or desires can give you such goals or lead you away from such goals.

**The Place of the Passions**   Hume's account of the human passions, which he often calls *sentiments,* is one of his distinctive contributions to philosophy. For him, passions are perceptions and can be studied like other perceptions. Passions are impressions caused in the mind by previous impressions or ideas. For example, we currently fear, hope, and desire based on some prior experience we have had, such as witnessing an event or meeting another person.

Many philosophers before Hume had disapproved of behavior driven by passion. Plato, the Stoics, St. Augustine, Spinoza, and others viewed the passions as irrational and sometimes overpowering influences needing the disciplined control of reason. These philosophers regarded the passions as alien forces, not parts of one's real self or one's intended actions; a person is acted upon by passions, rather than acting as an agent. Spinoza, for example, said that a "passion of the mind is a confused idea" and that persons are often in bondage to their passions, from which reason alone can free them.[3]

Hume, by contrast, thought that passions need not be confused, misleading, or censurable. They are vital and worthy dimensions of human nature, and Hume regarded it as incorrect to say that reason should always control the passions. Such advice will only distract persons from proper moral behavior and make them miserable. We should accept our nature rather than fight it. Reason cannot move us to action and cannot liberate us from the passions. Reason can only be the faithful servant of the passions. For example, the desire to promote a friend's happiness motivates us to acts of friendship, and reason helps us figure out the best means to achieve those goals. Passions of love and devotion drive family life and close personal relationships. Passions such as fellow-feeling have constructive roles in Hume's ethics, eclipsing the role attributed to reason in other philosophers' systems.

**The Place of Reason**   Kant and many other philosophers denounced Hume's depictions of sentiment and reason, on grounds that although we are often driven to act by sentiment or desire, the domain in which we must resist such motives is moral thinking and acting. For Kant, as we saw in Chapter 5, the word "reason" refers to something that can make us act; moral actions are precisely those undertaken for no motive or end other than that which is given by a principle of reason. For example, we should know by consulting reason that manipulative advertising of drinks with dangerous levels of alcohol is morally wrong, and we should act in accordance with moral rules that protect persons from such advertising. A rational principle, not a desire, determines the right action. Many critics of Hume likewise believe that desire and reason often conflict and that desire can be contrary to

---

[3]Spinoza, *Ethics,* 3, Conclusion. Compare the language of "bondage," "service," and "affect" at many points in Spinoza's *Ethics.* See the edition by Edwin Curley, in *The Collected Works of Spinoza* (Princeton, NJ: Princeton University Press, 1985).

reason. They maintain that reason has the power to determine how we should act, and they see moral actions as undertaken for ends that reason approves.[4]

Although Hume would not agree with these Kantian ideas about reason, he does acknowledge that reason can control our actions by giving us information that will redirect our desires and attitudes. For example, once we understand how dangerous it is to consume sweet, high-alcohol wines, our desires may change from a desire for the wine to a desire to avoid it. This new desire to avoid the wine will be based, for example, on our desire to avoid dangerous situations.

Hume also holds that there are cases in which personal desire conflicts with a *moral* faculty that many persons take to be a *rational* faculty. He recognizes that calm desire, for example, is similar in function to what other philosophers call reason. He thinks that other philosophers mistake the clash between calm and agitated desires for a clash between reason and desire. For example, if a desire to contact the police about a crime takes precedence over an intensely violent urge to take personal revenge for the crime, Hume would say that a calm desire, not reason, has gained ascendancy over a violent desire.

Moreover, Hume does not maintain that grossly immoral beliefs about the permissibility of torture, genocide, and slavery (even if accompanied by correct judgments of fact) are "reasonable" in the broad sense that we now often use the term "reasonable." He himself uses "reasonable" in this broader sense. For example, he speaks about "the conduct of any reasonable man" and "a reasonable frugality."[5] From this perspective, an excessive drinker who is ruining his health is unreasonable, whereas the temperate drinker is reasonable.

This problem of what is reasonable obviously depends on how broadly or narrowly one uses the terms "reason" and "passion." Hume generally uses them in stark opposition: Reason is nonpassionate; passion is nonrational. Hume is simply convinced that human motivation comes fundamentally from desires, aversions, and other passions, not from reason. If reason could inform us which desires and aversions are rational or otherwise acceptable, then reason alone could lead us to act. But reason is impotent in this regard.[6]

That Hume does not entirely repudiate a significant role for reason in morals is evident in the following selection.

[4]See, e.g., Terence Penelhum, "Hume's Moral Psychology," in David Norton, ed., *The Cambridge Companion to Hume* (Cambridge, England: Cambridge University Press, 1993), pp. 139–40; Kurt Baier, *The Moral Point of View* (Ithaca, NY: Cornell University Press, 1958), pp. 258–60.

[5]*An Enquiry concerning the Principles of Morals* 3.20; 6.11. This work is cited by section (or appendix) and paragraph numbers. See the edition edited by Tom L. Beauchamp (Oxford, England: Oxford University Press, 1998).

[6]Hume distinguishes two rival schools of thought about the general foundation (source or origin) of morals: (1) morals are derived from *reason;* (2) morals are derived from *sentiment* or an internal *sense*. Hume discusses this controversy and names the primary parties during a discussion of "The Foundations of Morality," in *A Letter from a Gentleman to his Friend in Edinburgh*. He identifies Samuel Clarke (English philosopher and theologian, 1675–1729) and William Wollaston (English moral philosopher and theologian, 1659–1724) as primary figures on the side of reason, and Scottish philosopher Francis Hutcheson (1696–1746) and Lord Shaftesbury (Anthony Ashley Cooper, third earl of Shaftesbury, English philosopher and politician, 1671–1713) as influential figures on the side of sentiment. Clarke and his followers hold that moral distinctions and knowledge are conveyed by reason. This is the main tradition to which Hume is opposed.

# The Principles of Morals*

David Hume

## Reason and Sentiment

There has been a controversy started of late, much better worth examination, concerning the general foundation of MORALS; whether they be derived from REASON, or from SENTIMENT; whether we attain the knowledge of them by a chain of argument and induction, or by an immediate feeling and finer internal sense; whether, like all sound judgment of truth and falsehood, they should be the same to every rational intelligent being; or whether, like the perception of beauty and deformity, they be founded entirely on the particular fabric and constitution of the human species. . . .

These arguments on each side . . . are so plausible, that I am apt to suspect, they may, the one as well as the other, be solid and satisfactory, and that *reason* and *sentiment* concur in almost all moral determinations and conclusions. The final sentence, it is probable, which pronounces characters and actions amiable or odious, praise-worthy or blameable; that which stamps on them the mark of honour or infamy, approbation or censure; that which renders morality an active principle, and constitutes virtue our happiness, and vice our misery: It is probable, I say, that this final sentence depends on some internal sense or feeling, which nature has made universal in

*From *An Enquiry concerning the Principles of Morals* (London, 1772, 9th edition), pp. 224, 227, 231–3, 237, 261, 264–7, 306–7, 335, 338–41, 353–56, 362–3, 367, 369, 371, 398 (with emendations based on corrections in the posthumous edition of 1777).

the whole species. For what else can have an influence of this nature? . . .

One principal foundation of moral praise being supposed to lie in the usefulness of any quality or action; it is evident, that *reason* must enter for a considerable share in all decisions of this kind; since nothing but that faculty can instruct us in the tendency of qualities and actions, and point out their beneficial consequences to society and to their possessor. . . .

The object of municipal laws is to fix all the questions with regard to justice: The debates of civilians; the reflections of politicians; the precedents of history and public records, are all directed to the same purpose. And a very accurate *reason* or *judgment* is often requisite, to give the true determination, amidst such intricate doubts arising from obscure or opposite utilities.

But though reason, when fully assisted and improved, be sufficient to instruct us in the pernicious or useful tendency of qualities and actions; it is not alone sufficient to produce any moral blame or approbation. Utility is only a tendency to a certain end; and were the end totally indifferent to us, we should feel the same indifference towards the means. It is requisite a *sentiment* should here display itself, in order to give a preference to the useful above the pernicious tendencies. This sentiment can be no other than a feeling for the happiness of mankind, and a resentment of their misery; since these are the different ends which virtue and vice have a tendency to promote. Here, therefore, *reason* instructs us in the several tendencies of actions, and *humanity* makes a distinction in favour of those which are useful and beneficial. . . .

Examine the crime of *ingratitude,* for instance; which has place, wherever we observe good-will, expressed and known, together with good offices performed, on the one side, and a return of ill-will or indifference, with ill-offices or neglect on the other: Anatomize all these circumstances, and examine, by your reason alone, in what consists the demerit or blame: You never will come to any issue or conclusion.

Reason judges either of *matter of fact* or of *relations.* Enquire then, *first,* where is that matter of fact, which we here call *crime;* point it out; determine the time of its existence; describe its essence or nature; explain the sense or faculty, to which it discovers itself. It resides in the mind of the person, who is ungrateful. He must, therefore, feel it, and be conscious of it. But nothing is there, except the passion of ill-will or absolute indifference. . . . The crime of ingratitude is not any particular individual *fact;* but arises from a complication of circumstances, which, being presented to the spectator, excites the *sentiment* of blame, by the particular structure and fabric of his mind? . . .

The hypothesis which we embrace is plain. It maintains, that morality is determined by sentiment. It defines virtue to be *whatever mental action or quality gives to a spectator the pleasing sentiment of approbation;* and vice the contrary. . . .

Thus the distinct boundaries and offices of *reason* and of *taste* are easily ascertained. The former conveys the knowledge of truth and falsehood: The latter gives the sentiment of beauty and deformity, vice and virtue. . . . Reason, being cool and disengaged, is no motive to action, and directs only the impulse received from appetite or inclination, by showing us the means of attaining happiness or avoiding misery: Taste, as it gives pleasure or pain, and thereby constitutes happiness or misery, becomes a motive to action, and is the first spring or impulse to desire and volition. . . .

## Benevolence and Self-Love

There is a principle, supposed to prevail among many, which is utterly incompatible with all virtue or moral sentiment. . . . This principle is, that all *benevolence* is mere hypocrisy, friendship a cheat, public spirit a farce, fidelity a snare to procure trust and confidence; and that, while all of us, at bottom, pursue only our private interest, we wear these fair disguises, in order to put others off their guard, and expose them the more to our wiles and machinations. . . .

There is another principle, somewhat resembling the former; which has been much insisted on by philosophers, and has been the foundation of many a system; that, whatever affection one may feel, or imagine he feels for others, no passion is, or can be disinterested; that the most generous friendship, however sincere, is a modification of self-love; and that, even unknown to ourselves, we seek only our own gratification, while we appear the most deeply engaged in schemes for the liberty and happiness of mankind. . . . But, at bottom, the most generous patriot and most niggardly miser, the bravest hero and most abject coward, have, in every action, an equal regard to their own happiness and welfare.

Whoever concludes, from the seeming tendency of this opinion, that those, who make profession of it, cannot possibly feel the true sentiments of benevolence, or have any regard for genuine virtue, will often find himself, in practice, very much mistaken. . . . Among the moderns, HOBBES and LOCKE, who maintained the selfish system of morals, lived irreproachable lives. . . .

The most obvious objection to the selfish hypothesis, is, that, as it is contrary to common feeling and our most unprejudiced notions, there is required the highest stretch of philosophy to establish so extraordinary a paradox. To the most careless observer, there appear to be such dispositions as benevolence and generosity; such affections as love, friendship, compassion, gratitude. These sentiments have their causes, effects, objects, and operations, marked by common language and observation, and plainly distinguished from those of the selfish passions. . . .

Tenderness to their offspring, in all sensible beings, is commonly able alone to counterbalance the strongest motives of self-love, and has no manner of dependence on that affection. What interest can a fond mother have in view, who loses her health by assiduous attendance on her sick child, and afterwards languishes and dies of grief, when freed, by its death, from the slavery of that attendance? . . .

These and a thousand other instances are marks of a general benevolence in human nature, where no *real* interest binds us to the object. And how an *imaginary* interest, known and avowed for such, can be the origin of any passion or emotion, seems difficult to explain. . . .

It is sufficient for our present purpose, if it be allowed, what surely, without the greatest absurdity, cannot be disputed, that there is some benevolence, however small, infused into our bosom; some spark of friendship for human kind; some particle of the dove, kneaded into our frame, along with the elements of the wolf and serpent. Let these generous sentiments be supposed ever so weak; let them be insufficient to move even a hand or finger of our body; they must still direct the determinations of our mind, and where every thing else is equal, produce a cool preference of what is useful and serviceable to mankind, above what is pernicious and dangerous. A *moral distinction,* therefore, immediately arises; a general sentiment of blame and approbation; a tendency, however faint, to the objects of the one, and a proportionable aversion to those of the other. . . .

## Justice, Convention, and Convenience

In general, we may observe, that all questions of property are subordinate to the authority of civil laws, which extend, restrain, modify, and alter the rules of natural justice, according to the particular *convenience* of each community. The laws have, or ought to have, a constant reference to the constitution of government, the manners, the climate, the religion, the commerce, the situation of each society. . . .

*What is a man's property?* Any thing, which it is lawful for him, and for him alone, to use. *But what rule have we, by which we can distinguish these objects?* Here we must have recourse to statutes, customs, precedents, analogies, and a hundred other circumstances; some of which are constant and inflexible, some variable and arbitrary. But the ultimate point, in which they all professedly terminate, is, the interest and happiness of human society. . . .

These reflections are far from weakening the obligations of justice, or diminishing any thing from the most sacred attention to property. On the contrary, such sentiments must acquire new force from the present reasoning. For what stronger foundation can be desired or conceived for any duty, than to observe, that human society, or even human nature could not subsist, without the establishment of it; and will still arrive at greater degrees of happiness and perfection, the more inviolable the regard is, which is paid to that duty? . . .

But farther, . . . when a definition of *property* is required, that relation is found to resolve itself into any possession acquired by occupation, by industry, by prescription, by inheritance, by contract, &c. Can we think, that nature, by an original instinct, instructs us in all these methods of acquisition? . . .

Does nature, whose instincts in men are all simple, embrace such complicated and artificial objects, and create a rational creature, without trusting any thing to the operation of his reason? . . .

Judges too, even though their sentence be erroneous and illegal, must be allowed, for the sake of peace and order, to have decisive authority, and ultimately to determine property. Have we original, innate ideas of praetors and chancellors and juries? Who sees not, that all these institutions arise merely from the necessities of human society? . . .

The convenience, or rather necessity, which leads to justice, is so universal, and every where points so much to the same rules, that the habit takes place in all societies; and it is not without some scrutiny, that we are able to ascertain its true origin. The matter, however, is not so obscure, but that, even in common life, we have, every moment, recourse to the principle of public utility, and ask, *What must become of the world, if such practices prevail? How could society subsist under such disorders? . . .*

It has been asserted by some, that justice arises from HUMAN CONVENTIONS, and proceeds from the voluntary choice, consent, or combination of mankind. If by *convention* be here meant a *promise* (which is the most usual sense of the word) nothing can be more absurd than this position. The observance of promises is itself one of the most considerable parts of justice; and we are not surely bound to keep our word, because we have given our word to keep it. But if by convention be meant a sense of common interest; which sense each man feels in his own breast, which he remarks in his fellows, and which carries him, in concurrence with others, into a general plan or system of actions, which tends to public utility; it must be owned, that, in this sense, justice arises from human conventions. . . .

Thus two men pull the oars of a boat by common convention, for common interest, without any promise or contract: Thus gold and silver are made the measures of exchange; thus speech and words and language are fixed, by human convention and agreement. Whatever is advantageous to two or more persons, if all perform their part; but what loses all advantage, if only one perform, can arise from no other principle. There would otherwise be no motive for any one of them to enter into that scheme of conduct. . . . The word, *natural,* is commonly taken in so many senses, and is of so loose a signification, that it seems vain to dispute, whether justice be natural or not. If self-love, if benevolence be natural to man; if reason and forethought be also natural; then may the same epithet be applied to justice, order, fidelity, property, society. . . .

We may just observe, before we conclude this subject, that, after the laws of justice are fixed by views of general utility, the injury, the hardship, the harm, which result to any individual from a violation of them, enter very much into consideration, and are a great source of that universal blame, which attends every wrong or iniquity. . . .

## A Common Point of View

The notion of morals implies some sentiment common to all mankind, which recommends the same object to general approbation, and makes every man, or most men, agree in the same opinion or decision concerning it. It also implies some sentiment, so universal and comprehensive as to extend to all mankind, and render the actions and conduct, even of the persons the most remote, an object of applause or censure, according as they agree or disagree with that rule of right which is established. These two requisite circumstances belong alone to the sentiment of humanity here insisted on. The other passions produce, in every breast, many strong sentiments of desire and aversion, affection and hatred; but these neither are felt so much in common, nor are so comprehensive, as to be the foundation of any general system and established theory of blame or approbation.

When a man denominates another his *enemy,* his *rival,* his *antagonist,* his *adversary,* he is understood to speak the language of self-love, and to express sentiments, peculiar to himself, and arising from his particular circumstances and situation. But when he bestows on any man the epithets of *vicious* or *odious* or *depraved,* he then speaks another language, and expresses sentiments, in which, he expects, all his audience are to concur with him. He must here, therefore, depart from his private and particular situation, and must choose a point of view, common to him with others: He must move some universal principle of the human frame, and touch a string, to which all mankind have an accord and symphony. If he mean, therefore, to express, that this man possesses qualities, whose tendency is pernicious to society, he has chosen this common point of view, and has touched the principle of humanity, in which every man, in some degree, concurs. While the human heart is compounded of the same elements as at present, it will never be wholly indifferent to public good, nor entirely unaffected with the tendency of characters and manners. And though this affection of humanity may not generally be esteemed so strong as vanity or ambition, yet, being common to all men, it can alone be the foundation of morals, or of any general system of blame or praise. One man's ambition is not another's ambition; nor will the same event or object satisfy both: But the humanity of one man is the humanity of every one; and the same object touches this passion in all human creatures. . . .

Whatever conduct gains my approbation, by touching my humanity, procures also the applause of all mankind, by affecting the same principle in them: But what serves my avarice or ambition pleases these passions in me alone, and affects not the avarice and ambition of the rest of mankind. There is no circumstance of conduct in any man, provided it have a beneficial tendency, that is not agreeable to my humanity, however remote the person. . . .

The principles upon which men reason in morals are always the same;

though the conclusions which they draw are often very different. That they all reason aright with regard to this subject, more than with regard to any other, it is not incumbent on any moralist to show. It is sufficient, that the original principles of censure or blame are uniform, and that erroneous conclusions can be corrected by sounder reasoning and larger experience. Though many ages have elapsed since the fall of GREECE and ROME; though many changes have arrived in religion, language, laws, and customs; none of these revolutions has ever produced any considerable innovation in the primary sentiments of morals. . . .

Particular customs and manners alter the usefulness of qualities: They also alter their merit. Particular situations and accidents have, in some degree, the same influence. He will always be more esteemed, who possesses those talents and accomplishments, which suit his station and profession, than he whom fortune has misplaced in the part which she has assigned him . . . Whatever conduct promotes the good of the community is loved, praised, and esteemed by the community, on account of that utility and interest, of which every one partakes. . . . This affection and regard be, in reality, gratitude, not self-love.

Although reason has no power to *fix* moral motivation in Hume's philosophy, reason does discover how to bring about the outcomes that we desire. These discoveries can make a decisive difference in the actions we take, because reason can have the effect of modifying desire, and thereby lead us to modify our action plans. If one discovers through reason that an outcome is not what one initially expected— for example, if one discovers that one's fiancé is a liar and a cheat—one's desire may turn to aversion. Similarly, a person who wants to be healthy and discovers through reason that aerobic exercise is very healthy can come to have a desire for aerobic exercise that did not previously exist. Reason may be the slave of passion, in that it requires the existence of a motivating desire to do something, but reason also informs and corrects the passions.

In the example that begins this chapter, much in the case turns on the acceptability of a government health policy. This is a reasoned activity of planning, but there must first be a desire to stop companies from manipulative marketing of products and to prevent injury or death from excessive alcoholic intake. Our motives may shift as we find out the empirical facts about marketing strategies, about teenage drinking patterns, and the like. Reason assists and redirects our desire to help in this circumstance, but reason does not by itself *motivate* us to formulate a health policy to govern such activities.

### Virtue beyond Egoism

**The Rejection of Egoism**   Hume maintains that his predecessors Thomas Hobbes and John Locke had maintained a "selfish system of morals"—the theory that human benevolence should be dismissed in favor of a theory that moral behavior is motivated entirely by self-interest. Hume maintains that psychological egoism is bad psychology. He thinks that any careful observer of human action will see that in addition to a principle of self-love (self-interest) there are "such dispositions as benevolence and generosity; such affections as love, friendship, compassion, gratitude." Hume's example of a devoted mother (in the above selection) is a favored example.[7]

Hume sees our benevolence as serving the public interest. He thinks our natural benevolence "accounts, in great part, for the origin of morality."[8] This principle, embedded in human nature, causes humans to act benevolently. However, Hume was aware of the mixture of motives in human nature. This is the point of his example of "some particle of the dove, kneaded into our frame, along with the elements of the wolf and serpent." Hume knew that we are far from selfless benefactors; but we are also not entirely self-interested. Human nature being what it is, we cannot reasonably expect to find persons so free of self-interest and jealousy that they exhibit perfect levels of trustworthiness and helpfulness in their dealings with others. This thesis that generous elements and self-interested elements are fused in human nature is an attempt to advance a balanced moral psychology. Whereas the egoist views human nature as limited to motives such as fear and self-love, Hume regards persons as motivated by a variety of passions, both generous and ungenerous.

Hume offers numerous arguments to support the idea of motives freed of self-interest. One argument starts with what Hume calls "qualities useful to ourselves," that is, qualities useful to the people who possess the qualities. Hume considers numerous examples of these qualities of people, including discretion, industry, frugality, and strength of mind. These qualities confer advantages on us without conferring any social benefits on those people who judge us favorably for having these qualities. Why, then, Hume asks, are these qualities ever approved by others? He answers that observers of these qualities do not approve of them because it is in their self-interest to do so, but rather from a principle of human nature that leads us to take an interest in the happiness of other persons. This principle also gives us pain and feelings of disapprobation when we see people who are incapacitated by their faults and imperfections. Hume argues that our capacity for fellow-feeling with others causes us to respond favorably to people with these qualities. He thinks we experience the same sentiments of favorable response to others when we encounter people who are far removed from our personal lives and who are not in a position to contribute to our welfare or interests.

**The Acceptance of Real Virtue**    Hume also believes that persons have real moral virtues; they do not merely pretend to have them, as the egoist suggests. He offers a definition of virtue as follows: "It is the nature, and, indeed, the definition of virtue, that it is a quality of the mind agreeable to or approved of by every one, who considers or contemplates it."[9] A virtue is whatever motive (quality of mind) gives observers a common sentiment of approval of that motive.

---

[7]*An Enquiry concerning the Principles of Morals* appx. 2.3, 6.
[8]*An Enquiry concerning the Principles of Morals* 5.17.
[9]*An Enquiry concerning the Principles of Morals*, 1st note in sect. 8 (n. 50).

This definition, and the surrounding analysis in Hume's text, indicates that a virtue is a fusion of two analytically distinct components: (1) a mental quality in the person contemplated and (2) a perception by those who contemplate the person. The latter perception is not merely a single individual's perception; all impartial individuals will have the requisite perception. Virtues exist only if the component parts are fused: neither (1) nor (2) is sufficient by itself to qualify as a virtue. Hume's thesis is that virtues are mental qualities that produce pleasure in impartial observers; the pleasure then produces esteem for those mental qualities. Conversely, vices are mental qualities that provoke displeasure in impartial observers, producing contempt for those qualities.

Hume maintains that only motives are virtuous; actions have no moral virtue even if they happen to conduce to public utility. For example, if a head of a charitable organization provides a program of public assistance to teenagers who might be victimized by the marketing of a product such as Cisco wine, the public official's motive must be one of assistance to victims—not one, say, of impressing city officials or potential donors—if the action of assistance is to be properly classified as moral. Similarly, when making a negative moral judgment on a person's harmful action we condemn malevolent motives, not merely acts that cause harm (these might be accidental). We can speak of virtuous actions, but only derivatively for Hume: Actions are virtuous if, and only if, there is an underlying motive that receives universal approval. Actions are our only *access* to motives, but the motives underlying the actions are the true objects of our appraisal.

Here is Hume's precise statement in his first work, *A Treatise of Human Nature:*

> 'Tis evident, that when we praise any actions, we regard only the motives that produced them, and consider the actions as signs or indications of certain principles in the mind and temper. The external performance has no merit. We must look within to find the moral quality. This we cannot do directly; and therefore fix our attention on actions, as on external signs. But these actions are still considered as signs; and the ultimate object of our praise and approbation is the motive, that produc'd them.[10]

For example, a person's act of benefiting someone merits moral praise only if the person's motive is to benefit the other person; it cannot be a moral motive if the action springs primarily from a desire to receive a reward for supplying the benefit.

Consider the following case: A lawyer discovers that she has a conflict of interest when a potential client discloses a legal problem. The lawyer would like to have the fee for doing the work for this client, but instead the lawyer arranges, free of charge, for the client to have legal representation with another firm. If the lawyer performs these actions only because the lawyer expects a kickback, there is no virtuous motive and therefore no virtuous action. The lawyer must have a desire to be of assistance or to maintain a sense of personal integrity. These motives are universally approved; the desire for kickbacks is not.

The postulate that virtues are approved of by all impartial inquirers leads Hume to say that qualities such as "friendship, sympathy, mutual attachment, and fidelity"

---

[10]*A Treatise of Human Nature* 3.2.1.2.

are "esteemed in all nations and all ages."[11] This thesis of *universality* in morals will be discussed in the next section.

## The Historical, the Conventional, and the Universal

Despite his downplaying of reason, Hume never denies that we can have "good reasons" for actions. Good reasons can be understood in terms of having the proper motives and also in terms of having "good evidence" in the sense of having the relevant empirical facts. But we can also have good reasons in that we are acting within the bounds of the operative moral rules, rather than against them or out of indifference to them.

One of Hume's assumed premises is that what we morally ought to do is what the institution of morality determines we ought to do, and that the rules in the institution of morality are a consensual, social matter. A community's determination of its moral interests is the only basis there is for morality—except, of course, a psychological grounding in human nature. The moral rules, then, are not merely the formulation of what an *individual* feels. They are fixed points in a *cultural matrix* of guidelines and controls, and they flow from our common human nature.

**Historicism and Conventionalism**    Hume is both a conventionalist and a historicist. His theory is historicist in the sense that morality rests on its historical development in cultures. It is conventionalist in the sense that moral rules derive their acceptability and correctness from human agreements, rather than from the way the world is independent of human agreements. A convention is simply a tradition or fixed pattern of doing things in a certain way. For example, Hume regards obligations to keep promises as resting on conventions. He refers to a convention as "a general sense of common interest; which sense all the members of the society express to one another, and which induces them to regulate their conduct by certain rules."[12] However, these views do not for him amount to a cultural relativism in which there is nothing but human choice and convention, as we shall now see.

**Universality in Morals**    Kant and many later philosophers have been concerned that Hume's apparently subjectivistic ethical theory lacks *universality* in its moral judgments. Hume, however, tries to make room for universality and to make it consistent with his idea that morality is rooted in the moral sentiment of individuals and the rules of the community. He argues that moral sentiment has a universal dimension: "The notion of morals implies some sentiment common to all mankind, which recommends the same object to general approbation, and makes every man, or most men, agree in the same opinion or decision concerning it. It also implies some sentiment, so universal and comprehensive as to extend to all mankind."[13]

Nonmoral beliefs and sentiments are often relative to the particular responses of individuals, but Hume thinks that persons universally have the same moral

---

[11]*An Enquiry concerning the Principles of Morals* 9.6 and "A Dialogue" 28.
[12]*A Treatise of Human Nature* 3.2.2.10.
[13]*An Enquiry concerning the Principles of Morals* 9.5.

sentiments and universally reach the same moral judgments when unbiased and placed in relevantly similar circumstances. For example, when we have the same information about another person and take an impartial view of the person, we all make the same judgments about that person's virtues and vices. In the case that begins this chapter, an impartial person will feel compassion for any young teenager who dies because he has been manipulated into a form of excessive drinking that he did not anticipate. Such manipulation is universally condemned. Sympathy for the youngster and his family is also a universal sentiment.

## Utility and Justice

Hume does not claim, however, that purely conventional rules such as the rules of justice are universal. In his account of the origin and nature of justice, public utility is "the sole origin of justice." Whereas we approve benevolent actions *primarily* because of their social utility, we approve systems of justice *exclusively* because of their social utility. Moreover, unlike benevolence (which is in human nature), justice requires a system of socially constructed rules. The rules of justice spring from human arguments and traditions that are observed and enforced because of the utility that particular communities find in those agreements and traditions, and these rules are relative to particular cultural circumstance.

Hume's point is that rules of justice are universally needed in complex societies, but particular rules of justice depend on particular conditions of need and utility and therefore differ from society to society. The rules of justice spring up, grow, and develop over time. "Justice" is, in effect, Hume's term for the virtue of following the rules and institutions that society creates to thwart the elements of the wolf and serpent in our nature, whereas "benevolence" is his term for the element of the dove. The more diversified a social arrangement becomes and the greater the extent to which persons are strangers rather than intimates, the more useful Hume considers the rules of justice (and the less useful is natural benevolence).

In a famous discussion, Hume lays out the circumstances in which rules of justice arise in human communities and how the rules function in those circumstances. He maintains that rules of justice emerge and become accepted in a community because they promote social utility. To persuade us, Hume reflects on situations in which rules of justice would be useless, unnecessary, or impossible—that is, without social utility. The circumstances that he considers are (1) an unlimited availability of the goods a person desires, (2) an unlimited benevolence in the members of society, (3) an extreme lack of necessary resources (because of famine or war), and (4) a situation in which we must interact with persons or creatures who are ignorant of the rules of justice.

Conventions of justice require both personal conflict and social cooperation; in the absence of either conflict or cooperation, rules of justice are useless and would never be formulated. Conflict is simply part of the human condition. We are by nature partial to ourselves and those close to us, and our beneficence is usually confined to this small group of intimates. Justice arises because almost all persons have this natural partiality and limited benevolence. (Compare the selection by Warnock in Chapter 1, which is indebted to Hume on just this point.) They want as many goods as possible, and they seek stability in the possession of their goods. Rules of justice are developed in order to ameliorate problems that arise from the competition for scarce resources, the limited benevolence in persons, and the vulnerability of personal property to damage or theft.

Hume maintains that justice "would never once have been dreamed of" if we lived in a society in which goods were freely available and our every desire satisfied.[14] However, many goods are scarce and competition for them is keen. To avoid destructive competition, we institute conventions of justice that establish rights for individuals and that protect the common interest. Conventions are rules that almost all members of society follow in almost all circumstances. For example, Hume regards basic rules of language, etiquette, promise-keeping, and contracting as conventions. Justice, in particular, requires a background framework of publicly accepted rules that are inlaid in the social mosaic of expected behaviors. Each person who follows the rules understands that the interests of everyone in society are advanced by conformity to these rules.

As stability, reciprocity, and trust grow, the conventions are strengthened and their social utility increases. If the utility of these institutions erodes or vanishes, causing a slippage in the trust and social cooperation that originally allowed the institutions to flourish, the mutual respect that supports the institutions will be impaired and they can then be expected to disintegrate. However, once the rules are in place and become respected, public-spiritedness—a motive to act in the common interest—motivates us to abide by the rules. Hume calls our personal identification with the rules of justice a "sense of common interest" and the "sentiment of justice."[15] This sense of justice is reinforced by parents, teachers, peers, and politicians in the community.

In discussing rules of justice, Hume points out that these rules are specified in different ways in different societies. Particular duties and rights vary from one society to the next, each of which gives a different specific content to the general rules found in all societies. Hume compares different houses to different rules of property: People in many different times and places construct houses, but construct them differently; similarly, persons in many different times and places fashion rules of property, but design them differently in accordance with the necessities of the particular society.

Conventions of property hold a special fascination for Hume. These conventions are specified in communities by social rules of justice, typically using enforceable laws. The rules specify legitimate forms of the possession and transfer of property and state the obligations, rights, and responsibilities of the various parties. These rules vary in accordance with historical precedent, new circumstance, and community orientation. For example, different countries establish different holdings in land and water, different lengths of time that property can be held, different rules about permissible gifts and inheritances, and different laws governing the transfer of rights.

---

[14]*An Enquiry concerning the Principles of Morals* 3.3.

[15]*An Enquiry concerning the Principles of Morals* appx. 3.7, 9.

Hume's interest in the specification of duties and rights in different cultures led him to consider the nature and role of social practices. He provides an account of "common life and practice" in which, despite the existence of many of "the same rules" in all cultures, the different practices in different cultures can be explained by the different utilities that the practices have in those communities.[16] He argues that many forms of human conduct in these cultures make no sense unless we grasp the underlying practices. For example, conventions surrounding the exchange of private property, such as selling it, make sense only to someone who already understands the institution of property and its accompanying practices.

Finally, Hume maintains that the purpose of moral rules and practices is to be *utility-promoting* and that these rules are universally approved by impartial persons. This perspective leads him to condemn merely customary rules and laws that fail to meet these conditions: "Where a civil law is so perverse as to cross all the interests of society, it loses all its authority. . . . Thus, the interests of society require, that contracts be fulfilled; and there is not a more material article either of natural or civil justice."[17] Customs, traditions, or standards that fail to be utility-promoting or to be approvable by impartial persons have no authority irrespective of plans or votes in a community.

However, beyond these general conditions of acceptable rules, Hume is reluctant to judge the acceptability or unacceptability of a community's particular moral rules. He indicates that any set of conventional rules that has been adopted in a particular moral or legal system is satisfactory if it satisfies these two general conditions. Thus, two communities can have very different, but perfectly legitimate, rules of justice and property.

## MORALS BY INVENTION

Appeals to historical traditions, morals by agreement, and the legitimacy of social conventions have increased in recent years in ethical theory. Some of the most prominent theories are not Humean or even influenced by Hume; but several are heavily indebted to him. Just as many Kantians and Aristotelians depart widely from Kant's and Aristotle's theories, so many Humean theories highlight certain themes and make connections to contemporary philosophy in ways that Hume could not have imagined. A variety of such theories will be considered in the remainder of this chapter (and some non-Humean theories in Chapter 8).

One way of extending Hume's theory is to defend the broad outlines of his theory of *sentiments* as a subjectivist account of morals and his theory of *convention* as an account of communal invention and agreement. In two previous chapters, we have already seen some indication that John Mackie follows precisely this approach in his ethical theory. Mackie's book, we saw, is subtitled "Inventing Right and Wrong," by which he does not mean that we are individual creators of personal

---

[16]*An Enquiry concerning the Principles of Morals* 3.47; 5.43.
[17]*An Enquiry concerning the Principles of Morals*, n. 12.

moralities, but that we invent and agree to moral rules as a collective social body, thereby bringing morality into existence by powers of authorization in a community.

Mackie's emphasis on invention is rooted in a skepticism about the objectivity of moral values that is indebted to his interpretation of Hume. Mackie regards Hume's views, as well as his own, as a "subjective" account of morals that is skeptical of any form of objective grounding for morality. His famous "error theory" of moral values (see Chapters 2 and 3) rests on the claim that there are no objective moral values, although ordinary moral judgments maintain a tacit commitment to objectivity—and in this respect our ordinary moral judgments are all mistaken.

Despite this thesis, Mackie is not a skeptic about the normative guidance given by morality, because he accepts that its principles often do constitute a valid social institution with a foundation in communal decision-making. Mackie thinks it is quite possible to shed the belief that there are objective moral properties, while continuing to use the same moral terms. Many substantive moral views can be retained, as well, but we should also appreciate that morality is a process of invention in which we put norms in place to limit human conflicts and make relations as smooth as possible. Morality can be given whatever content best helps us achieve this goal.

Mackie therefore opposes the view that morality is a matter of what we *discover* rather than what we *decide*. For example, we do not discover a morally correct set of rules for protecting teenagers from manipulative marketing or overdrinking; we decide what to do and create a body of rules and a public policy that is adequately protective. We do not discover whether Canandaigua Wine Company can with moral warrant make a wine or market a wine drink with a 20 percent alcoholic content. We invent the rules of licensing, acceptable marketing, and punishable offenses. Apart from our traditions, questions of right and wrong in such cases are not even meaningful.

Mackie expresses his views on justification in ethics by using the term "intersubjective standards," meaning that communitywide agreements form the basis of convenient and acceptable moral rules, although intersubjectivity cannot itself be further validated. Mackie understands morality in terms of social practices expressing what is demanded, enforced, and condemned.

# *The Contents of Ethics**

## J. L. Mackie

. . . When I speak of the requirements of an institution, I am referring not only to the normative content of the abstract rules and principles, but to various

*From J. L. Mackie, *Ethics: Inventing Right and Wrong* (London, England: Penguin Books Ltd, 1977).

things actually being demanded, condemned, enforced or encouraged. These requirements, then, are constituted by human thought, behavior, feelings, and attitudes. To speak within an institution is to use its characteristic concepts, to assert or appeal to or implicitly invoke its rules and principles, in fact to speak in those distinctive ways by speaking and thinking in which the participants help to constitute the institution.

An institution, as I am using the word, does not need to be instituted. It need not be such an artificial creation as the game of chess. Promising may well be a universal human practice, to be found in all societies; it is certainly one that could grow very naturally out of the ordinary conditions of human life. But that does not alter its logical status, or the logical status of conclusions that can be established only within and by invoking that institution.

A promise, and the apparent obligation to keep a promise, are created not merely by a speaker's statement of intention in conjunction with the desire of the person to whom the promise is made that it should be fulfilled, or even by these together with the hearer's reliance on the statement and the speaker's expectation that the hearer will, and intention that he should, so rely. What creates the institution of promising is all these being embedded in and reinforced by general social expectations, approvals, disapprovals, and demands: promising, in contrast with the stating of an intention, can be done only where there is such a complex of attitudes. . . .

. . . Morality is not to be discovered but to be made: we have to decide what moral views to adopt, what moral stands to take. No doubt the conclusions we reach will reflect and reveal our sense of justice, our moral consciousness—that is, our moral consciousness as it is at the end of the discussion, not necessarily as it was at the beginning. But that is not the object of the exercise; the object is rather to decide what to do, what to support and what to condemn, what principles of conduct to accept and foster as guiding or controlling our own

choices and perhaps those of other people as well.

However, even if we are looking at morality in this way, there is a distinction to be drawn. A morality in the broad sense would be a general, all-inclusive theory of conduct: the morality to which someone subscribed would be whatever body of principles he allowed ultimately to guide or determine his choices of action. In the narrow sense, a morality is a system of a particular sort of constraints on conduct—ones whose central task is to protect the interests of persons other than the agent and which present themselves to an agent as checks on his natural inclinations or spontaneous tendencies to act. In this narrow sense, moral considerations would be considerations from some limited range, and would not necessarily include everything that a man allowed to determine what he did. In this second sense, someone could say quite deliberately, "I admit that morality requires that I should do such-and-such, but I don't intend to: for me other considerations here overrule the moral ones." And he need not be putting "morality" here into either visible or invisible inverted commas. . . .

## A Device for Counteracting Limited Sympathies

It is of morality in the narrow sense that G.J. Warnock [see Chapter 1 in this text] is thinking when he argues that we shall understand it better if we ask what it is for, what is the object of morality. Morality is a species of evaluation, a kind of appraisal of human conduct; this must, he suggests, have some distinctive point, there must be something that it is supposed to bring about. Warnock explains this in terms of certain general and persistent features of the human predicament, which is "inherently such that things are liable to go very badly"—badly in the natural, non-moral sense that human wants, needs, and interests are likely to be frustrated in large measure. Among the factors which contribute to make things go badly in the natural course of events are various limitations—limited resources, limited information, limited intelligence, limited rationality, but above all limited sympathies. Men sometimes display active malevolence to one another, but even apart from that they are almost always concerned more with their selfish ends than with helping one another. The function of morality is primarily to counteract this limitation of men's sympathies. We can decide what the content of morality must be by inquiring how this can best be done. . . .

Hume is another in this tradition: "It is," he says, "only from the selfishness and confined generosity of man, along with the scanty provision nature has made for his wants, that justice derives its origin." Justice (by which he means particularly respect for property and for rules governing its possession and transfer, honesty, and the keeping of promises) is an artificial virtue; it is not something of which we would have any natural, instinctive, tendency to approve, but a device which is beneficial because of certain contingent features of the human condition. If men had been overwhelmingly benevolent, if each had aimed only at the happiness of all, if everyone had loved his neighbour as himself, there would have been no need for the rules that constitute justice. Nor would there have been any need for them if nature had supplied abundantly, and without any effort on our part, all

that we could want, if food and warmth had been as inexhaustibly available as, until recently, air and water seemed to be. The making and keeping of promises and bargains is a device that makes possible mutually beneficial cooperation between people whose motives are mainly selfish, where the contributions of the different parties need to be made at different times. . . .

. . . Hume points out that conventions can grow up gradually as men repeatedly experience the advantages of conforming to them and the disadvantages of violating them. And we can develop this hint. For the reasons given, moral sentiments which "annex the idea of virtue to justice" will enable social groups in which they take root to flourish. Consequently the ordinary evolutionary pressures, the differential survival of groups in which such sentiments are stronger, either as inherited psychological tendencies or as socially maintained traditions, will help to explain why such sentiments become strong and widespread. . . .

But is it so obvious that what is conventionally accepted as morality is exactly what is required? As all our writers have stressed, the device of morality is beneficial because of certain contingent features of the human condition. But if they are contingent they may also have changed. The contrast between Protagoras and Hobbes points at least to a change in the scale of the problem. Protagoras was looking for the ordering principles of a city, a *polis,* and in Greece a *polis* could be pretty small: his problem was how men could form social units large enough to compete with the wild beasts. But for Hobbes the problem was how to maintain a stable nation state. Today the scale has changed again: we can no longer share

Hobbes's assumption that it is only civil wars that are really a menace, that international wars do relatively little harm. . . .

Changes in the human situation which may well be relevant to morality have occurred in the last hundred and fifty and particularly in the last fifty years. Though they are obvious and well known, they should at least be summarized. One is the growth of worldwide mutual dependence. This is partly economic: an increased proportion of what people see as their needs is supplied directly or indirectly by goods from distant countries. It is partly a matter of possibilities of assistance: in 1700 the inhabitants of Europe would not have known, at least till much later, of an earthquake or a famine in India, and even if they had known they could have done nothing about it; but this is no longer so. It is partly, also, that there are worldwide political movements, and that local wars and changes of government can have repercussions far away. . . .

It does not follow, on the other hand, that an individual is free to invent a moral system at will. If a morality is to perform the sort of function described [above], it must be adopted socially by a group of people in their dealings with one another. Of course, there can be and are larger and smaller social circles. The rules and principles that govern relations within a relatively small group will in general be more detailed than those that govern relations between people who are less intimately involved with one another. The morality, or fragment of a morality, of a small group for its internal relations needs to be accepted, on the whole, by the members of that group: but they can change it as long as they manage to keep fairly well in step with one another. The fragment of a morality that regulates dealings between people who are more remote will be not only less detailed but also much less open to change. But in either case a fragment of a morality has to be a social reality, a going concern, and therefore something that some number of people jointly know of and understand, so that each can rely to some considerable extent on the others' observance of it. Privately imagined rules or principles of action are worthless. It is idle to point out how good (or how bad) would be the results of everyone's doing such-and-such if there is no likelihood that they will. What counts is rules that are actually recognized by the members of some social circle, large or small, and that thus set up expectations and claims. Innovations and reforms are not excluded, but they must be possibly actual, not purely utopian.

The prescription "Think of a set of rules and principles the general adoption of which would best promote what you value and see as worthwhile, and then follow them yourself, regardless of what you think others will do" may well be a recipe for disaster. The prescription "Think of such a set of rules, and try to secure their general acceptance" may be impractical. What the individual can do is to remember that there are, in the different circles of relationship with which he is concerned, various fragments of a moral system which already contributes very considerably to countering specifiable evils which he, like others, will see as evils; that he can at once take advantage of this system and contribute to its upkeep; but that he may be able, with others, to put pressure on some fragments of the system, so that they come gradually to be more favourable to what he sees as valuable or worthwhile.

For Mackie, "The moral codes . . . reflect ways of life."[18] Morality is needed to resolve the problem of limited resources and limited sympathies that create a social circumstance of potentially vicious competition and conflict. Morality is our tool to turn this situation into a scheme of beneficial cooperation. (For this idea Mackie acknowledges a debt both to Hume and to G. J. Warnock's views, found in this text in Chapter 1.) Mackie calls this conception "morality in the narrow sense," which for him is what morality *actually is,* in contrast to "morality" in some *extended sense* of the term. He means that morality is a set of constraints on conduct whose function is to check the behavior of persons who might otherwise be overly aggressive in advancing their personal interests. Rights, obligations, and social schemes of justice have all developed from these motives.[19]

Morality in the narrow sense deals with what is right and what can be validly claimed. It is the arena of principles of justice, fundamental rights, basic obligations, and the like. Mackie approvingly cites Hume's view (in *A Treatise of Human Nature*) that it is "only from the selfishness and confin'd generosity of men, along with the scanty provision nature has made for his wants, that justice derives its origin."[20] Mackie accepts Hume's view that if everyone were overwhelmingly benevolent, there would be no need for justice. For example, when we consider the devices used by corporations such as the Canandaigua Wine Company to make a profit, we realize the limits of natural benevolence in these companies and we see the need for government agencies and regulations, as well as the laws of justice. If such companies always acted in the public interest, or at least without danger to the public, there would be no need to impose laws and regulations on them.

In his analysis of what is correct or acceptable in the moral life, Mackie rejects accounts that incorporate forms of objective morality other than what is made objective by agreement. Persons have moral entitlements and moral obligations only if convention has so determined, and they have them because they are members of the community. A belief in natural rights, say, is simply one form of a truth theory that Mackie seeks to replace with an error theory.

Although Mackie maintains that certain beliefs about moral objectivity, justification, and truth are erroneous, it does not follow that the beliefs people have about *moral practices* are false or even that they need to be corrected. Here we move from the ontological to the normative, to use Mackie's language. Although a community of persons may have false ontological beliefs (presuppositions) about the foundations of ethics, its normative beliefs are definitive, indeed constitutive, of morality. This line of reasoning suggests that the *ethical theory* one holds may not make any difference in determining the acceptability of a *moral practice* (morality), however meaningful such differences may be to philosophers.

---

[18]Mackie, *Ethics*, pp. 30, 37.
[19]Mackie, *Ethics*, pp. 106–11.
[20]Hume, *Treatise* 3.2.2.18.

# MORALS BY AGREEMENT

Mackie emphasizes a side of Hume's thought that views morality as a set of social agreements that enable people to overcome limited resources and limited sympathy in order to protect their interests. This view of morality is similar to (though not identical to) the contractarian tradition that descends from Locke and Hobbes. In this tradition, morality arises as a result of a social contract between individuals for the purpose of mutual benefit.

In recent years an interpretation of the contraction view indebted to both Hobbes and Hume has been forcefully defended by David Gauthier, most prominently in his book *Morals by Agreement.*[21] As we saw in Chapter 2, Gauthier is a leading propo-nent of Hobbesian views of mutual advantage. Gauthier emphasizes the benefits that individuals gain from self-acceptance of the constraints of morality; it is ratio-nal to follow morality as long as others do so. Because they stand to gain from moral agreements, individuals have what both Gauthier and Hume term "interested obligations" to abide by and promote the terms of morality. (Hume speaks of an in-terested obligation *to virtue,* which means a reason from self-interest to act virtu-ously.) Morality is what rational individuals would agree to in order to maximize personal utility. That is, individuals accept moral obligations *because* the system of morality benefits them, and not for any other reason.

In the selection below, Gauthier develops an innovative account that both draws out the contractarian themes in Hume and develops the theories we encountered in Chapter 2 about social cooperation, mutual adherence to constraints, and utility maximization. Though Gauthier situates Hume in the contractarian and rational choice tradition to which Gauthier is himself committed, he does not attribute to Hume an entire moral theory rooted in self-interest. As we saw in Chapter 2 (see the discussion of the sensible knave) and earlier in the present chapter, Hume rejects egoism and insists that many of our moral sentiments are directed at love of and concern for family, friends, and community.

It does not follow, Gauthier would point out, that in Hume's theory we are moti-vated by reasons other than self-protection and mutual advantage to enter into moral and political contracts. Hume's theories of justice, political union, and allegiance to government are all built on such assumptions about contract. Just as rules of justice originate by contractual agreements under social circumstances of competition for scarce resources and limited benevolence in persons, so political society originates under circumstances in which some persons put their own pleasure and advantage ahead of the rules of justice. If we lived in a society in which "natural justice" were steadfastly maintained, without need for social mechanisms of enforcement, there would be no reason for political controls and law. Neither local government nor the laws of nations (international law) would exist. The sole foundation of allegiance to government, Hume argues, is advantage (usefulness) to society. Obligations to obey political authorities and social rules hold only in proportion to this usefulness. As in-dividuals, we would agree to a social contract only if the resulting government served this purpose.

---

[21]Gauthier, *Morals by Agreement* (Oxford, England: Clarendon Press, 1986).

For Hume, all social conventions are, like social contracts, mutually advantageous. Even in societies of robbers and pirates, common interest and utility generate standards of right and wrong that are mutually advantageous. This theme about advantage, contract, and political union is the one on which Gauthier is building in the following selection.

# David Hume, Contractarian*

## David Gauthier

David Hume's moral and political inquiries comprise three theories: a theory of moral sentiment, a theory of property and justice, and a theory of government and obedience. My concern is with the latter two, and my basic thesis is that, contrary to what may seem Hume's explicit avowals, these theories are both contractarian. . . .

Hume's account of justice in the *Enquiry* begins with the claim: "That public utility is the *sole* origin of justice, and that reflections on the beneficial consequences of this virtue are the *sole* foundation of its merit." . . .

Central to Hume's moral theory is the thesis that whatever has beneficial consequences receives moral approbation.[1] Whatever, then, is generally useful, or useful on the whole, receives overall moral approbation, and so may be denominated a virtue. Since justice has mutual expected utility, it must be generally useful, and so receives moral approbation. We may thus say, with Hume, that the beneficial consequences of justice establish its moral merit.

But to say that justice has public utility, or is mutually advantageous, is to say more than to say merely that justice is generally useful, or that justice has beneficial consequences. It is, of course, to say that each person may expect beneficial consequences *for himself* from justice. This additional factor does not enter into the moral approbation accorded to justice. That beneficial consequences extend to each person does not affect our moral sentiments, except insofar as overall, more beneficial consequences arise. However, it is this additional factor which is essential to *justice;* it is not the beneficial consequences themselves, but the expectation of benefit by each person, that is just-making. Thus we may again say, with Hume, that public utility, understood as mutual expected advantage, is the origin of justice.

Hence we distinguish public utility as the origin of justice, from general utility, or overall advantage, as the basis of our moral approbation of justice. Arrangements may be expected to be useful to each person; therefore they are just. These arrangements may also be expected to have beneficial consequences; therefore they receive moral approval, and justice is a virtue. In this way Hume's contractarian theory of justice may be clearly distinguished from his noncontractarian theory of morality. His initial claim should then read, with words added [thus]: "That public utility

*From *The Philosophical Review,* 88 (no. 1, January 1979).
[1]See, for example, Hume's discussion in *Enquiry,* Sec. V, Pt. I.

[i.e. mutually expected advantage] is the *sole* origin of justice, and that reflections on the generally beneficial consequences of this virtue are the *sole* foundation of its merit [i.e. moral approbation]." . . .

In examining Hume's text, we shall consider first whether mutual advantage is a necessary condition for the convention of property or whether overall advantage is sufficient. Hume develops his account of justice in the *Enquiry* by distinguishing six sets of circumstances in which justice would be useless, and no rules determining property would arise, or be maintained. Analysis of these situations will show how he is to be understood.

The first two sets of circumstances lend themselves equally to contractarian or utilitarian interpretation. Hume first supposes a situation of natural super-abundance, in which the objects of all of our desires are provided without need for our efforts. He next supposes a situation of universal fellow-feeling, in which each person has the same concern for the interests of all of his fellows as for his own. In both of these circumstances, Hume insists, there would be no rules of property. . . .

After considering circumstances in which abundance or benevolence makes justice superfluous, Hume turns to circumstances in which extreme scarcity or excessive rapaciousness leads each individual to a concern with his own self-preservation which must override all conventions. Hume's treatment of these situations strongly suggests that mutual advantage is the necessary condition of justice. . . .

In conditions of extreme scarcity, the institution of property ceases to be mutually advantageous, and the rules of

justice are then suspended. However morality does not lapse altogether, for even in these circumstances humanity may lead us to moderate our treatment of our fellows, so that we do not press small gains for ourselves at the expense of their lives. . . .

But Hume's argument proceeds from the standpoint of each individual; when the social order maintained by justice becomes useless to him, then he must seek his own survival by whatever means are prudent and humane. . . .

The fifth set of circumstances concerns the relation between human beings and inferior creatures. Hume's position here is decisively against total advantage, and for mutual advantage.

> Were there a species of creatures intermingled with men, which, though rational, were possessed of such inferior strength, both of body and mind, that they were incapable of all resistance, and could never . . . make us feel the effects of their resentment; the necessary consequence . . . is that we should be bound by the laws of humanity to give gentle usage to these creatures, but should not . . . lie under any restraint of justice with regard to them, nor could they possess any right or property, . . .

Hume insists that humanity requires us to use inferiors gently; "compassion and kindness [are] the only check, by which they curb our lawless will." Since moral approbation extends to whatever is generally beneficial, we approve what benefits them, but this is sharply distinguished from considerations of justice.

Finally, Hume considers the situation of persons who have neither the desire nor the need for society. Did

> each man . . . love himself alone, and . . . depend only on himself and his own activity for safety and happiness, he would, on every occasion, . . . challenge the prefer-

ence above every other being, to none of which he is bound by any ties, either of nature or of interest.

Property and justice could have no place among such men. . . .

A convention [is] a contract if and only if either it is selected from alternatives by a process of interested recognition or it commands adherence on the basis of interested obligation. . . . I shall [now] consider whether Hume's theory of property and justice satisfies either or both of these contractarian requirements. First, how are the conventions or rules which constitute a system of property selected?

Hume's basic supposition is that the need for rules determining rights in use and possession is sufficiently strong and evident that it effectively overrides opposed preferences among different rules, dictating the simplest form of agreement.

> Public utility is the general object of all courts of judicature; and this utility too requires a stable rule in all controversies; but where several rules, nearly equal and indifferent, present themselves, it is a very slight turn of thought which fixes the decision in favour of either party. [*Enquiry,* Appendix III] . . .

Hume's argument, then, is that the expected benefit, to each person, of a system of property, in comparison with no system, is very great, so that each has a strong interest in reaching and maintaining agreement with his fellows on some system. On the other hand, the expected differential benefit, to any person, between any two systems of property, is comparatively small, so that each is much more concerned with agreement on some system, than with the choice among possible systems. This concern then results in acceptance of

"the most obvious rule, which could be agreed on." . . .

Hume conceives the problem of selecting among rules as one of coordination, rather than bargaining. Bargaining, the typical contractarian device, is a relatively costly procedure for reaching agreement, suitable only when our differential preferences among possible conventions are strong in comparison with our interests in the selection of some convention rather than none. But the absence of bargaining does not affect the fundamentally contractual character of the procedure. For selection by salience, as Hume employs it, is based on interested recognition. Each person, given his own interests, recognizes that salience is relevant to the possibility of agreement on conventions of property. Each regards the appeal to present possession, to labor, to precedent, and so forth—the appeal, that is, to the various specific salient features which determine particular rules of possession and use—as in his own interest, insofar as it resolves opposed preferences among ways of affording "a separation and constancy in men's possessions" at less expected cost than any other form of appeal.

It will be noted that the use of salience to select among possible conventions and rules is highly conservative in its effects. This conservatism, of course, reflects Hume's insistence that, while a system of property is essential, the choice among systems is of much less importance. In a critical discussion of Hume's theory we might wish to question this insistence. We might question whether present possession, inheritance, precedent, would command the interested recognition of all concerned. But such questions would only express our doubt that Hume has chosen the appropriate contractarian device to select among systems of property and justice. The basis in interested recognition, essential to contractarian thought, would only be confirmed by this critique. . . .

Two species of obligation enter into the argument of the *Enquiry*—moral obligation and interested obligation.[2] Were Hume consistently to maintain the view that only extraordinary circumstances cause our real interests to diverge from the dictates of justice, then we might expect the latter to suffice. Given the real benefits of just behavior, one is obligated, against present temptation, to conform to the conventions determining property. But Hume's actual discussion of our interested obligation to be just reveals a rather different picture.

Treating vice with the greatest candour, and making it all possible concessions, we must acknowledge that there is not . . . the smallest pretext for giving it the preference above virtue, with a view of self-interest; except, perhaps, in the case of justice, where a man . . . may often seem to be a loser by his integrity. And though it is allowed that without a regard to property, no society could subsist; yet . . . a sensible knave [see Chapter 2 of this text. Ed.], in particular incidents, may think an act of iniquity or infidelity will make a considerable addition to his fortune, without causing any considerable breach in the social union . . . That *honesty is the best policy*, may be a good general rule, but is liable to many exceptions; and he, it may perhaps be thought, conducts himself with most wisdom, who observes the general rule, and takes advantage of all the exceptions. [*Enquiry*, Sec. IX, Pt. II]

[2]Interested obligation is discussed in the *Enquiry*, Sec. IX, Pt. II. The phrase "moral obligation" occurs, I believe, but once in the *Enquiry*, in Sec. IV, and is quoted later in this section of my paper.

Hume's sensible knave, like Hobbes' Foole, perceives the fundamental instability involved in justice. Each person prefers universal conformity to the conventions of property, to the expected outcome of general nonconformity. But each person also prefers, in many particular situations, not to conform, even if others do conform. Each expects to benefit from the just behavior of others, but to lose from his own; hence, whenever his own injustice will neither set an example to others, nor bring punishment on himself, his interests will dictate that injustice.

Recognizing the force of the sensible knave's argument, Hume continues the passage quoted above:

I must confess that, if a man think this reasoning much requires an answer, it would be a little difficult to find any which will to him appear satisfactory and convincing.

His further remarks constitute an appeal to our moral sentiments, tacitly admitting that there is no sufficient interested obligation to justice.

But before concluding that Hume's theory of property does not provide a contractarian ground for just behavior, we should consider whether the moral obligation to justice has a basis in interest. The *Enquiry* contains only brief references to this obligation, but these relate it clearly to public utility. . . .

What Hume must intend is the usefulness of the convention which gives rise to the obligation. Insofar as it is useful, so that general conformity to it is preferred to the expected outcome of general nonconformity, then there is a moral obligation to conform to it. . . .

Each person reflects, not on the consequences of his own failure to conform to the conventions of property, but on the consequences of general failure.

And this reflection gives rise to a judgment, representing conformity as obligatory, which checks the inclination not to be just. Both the obligation and the inclination, it should be noted, rest on interest. The inclination not to be just rests on the interest, expressed by the sensible knave, in taking advantage of "the exceptions"—in violating the rules of justice when violation would go uncopied and unpunished. The obligation to be just rests on the interest, which each man shares with his fellows, in maintaining the rules of justice rather than abandoning all conventions of property. Although in the absence of any checks the former interest will tend to dominate the latter, Hume supposes that reflection will lead us to weigh our interest in maintaining society more heavily than our interest in pursuing direct advantage. . . .

Since moral obligation combines an appeal to interest with an appeal to moral approbation, Hume, after admitting that there is no sufficient interested obligation to justice, reintroduces an appeal to moral sentiment. Recognizing that the maxim: Follow the general rule but take advantage of all the exceptions, can not strictly be refuted, he shifts his ground and considers the man of moral feeling, saying:

> If his heart rebel not against such pernicious maxims, if he feel no reluctance to the thoughts of villainy and baseness, he has indeed lost a considerable motive to virtue; and we may expect that his practice will be answerable to his speculation. [*Enquiry,* Sec. IX, Pt. II]

Hume's account of our obligation to be just, to conform to the conventions of property, is thus not purely contractarian, insofar as it reflects his theory of moral sentiment. But insofar as it also reflects his theory of property, it has a strong contractarian component. Although justice is not sufficiently upheld by a directly interested obligation, it is upheld by an obligation which, in a larger sense, conforms to the contractarian requirement, in being the effect of moral sentiment on what is acknowledged from the standpoint of individual interest.

Gauthier ends with some reflections on the role of sentiments in Hume's thought. However, neither Gauthier nor Mackie pursues this aspect of Hume's moral theory in any detail in the development of their own moral views. In the next section, however, we examine a theory by Annette Baier that is heavily indebted to Hume and his views on the moral sentiments.

## THE VOICE OF MORAL SENTIMENT

Baier has been at the forefront of some developments in ethics that are indebted to Hume's accounts of virtue, family, and community. She thinks that too much emphasis has been placed on justice in modern moral theory, to the exclusion of fundamental categories like care and trust. Baier's theory will be the focal point of this section, just as Mackie's and Gauthier's were in the previous two sections.

However, before we examine Baier's philosophy, we need some background in what has been called "the ethic of care" and its connection to virtue theory.

An eloquent group of philosophers have explored the theme that women exhibit an ethic of care, in contrast to men, who are dominated by the ethic of rights and obligations so evident in the utilitarian and deontological theories we examined in Chapters 4 and 5. Philosophers who have emphasized the ethic of care are indebted to feminist theory and to psychological studies of the differences between men and women. They defend the view, as psychologist Carol Gilligan put it, that there is a separate ethic for women such that "women speak in a different voice," a voice that traditional ethical theory, with its emphasis on universal principles and impartiality, has drowned out.

Internal to this discussion are some issues regarding whether the traditional ethic of rights and obligations—represented paradigmatically by Locke, Kant, and Mill—should be either replaced or reconstructed within a broader, more comprehensive view of ethics. To understand some of the foundations of this work as well as part of its motivation, we need first to look at Gilligan's conclusions.

In her book *In a Different Voice,* Gilligan maintains that women's moral development is distinct from men's and that this has generally been disregarded by influential psychological studies of moral development. She found through research on girls and women that they focus "not on the primacy and universality of individual rights, but rather on . . . a very strong sense of being responsible to the world." She found that women typically view morality primarily in terms of responsibilities of care deriving from attachments to others in their community, whereas men usually see morality in terms of rights and justice. A woman's problem is thus not "how to exercise one's rights without interfering with the rights of others," but instead how to lead a moral life of responsibilities in community with others.[22]

These conclusions are drawn from various studies conducted by Gilligan in which women and girls tended to see morality in terms of preserving bonds and connections with other persons. Men and boys tended, in her findings, to see morality more like a game of rules analogous to traffic regulations. The goal seemed to be to make the right moves without frustrating others' legitimate objectives.

Gilligan claims to have discovered gender differences over two "modes of relationship" and two modes of moral thinking, an ethic of care in contrast to an ethic of rights: The ethic of rights sees the world quasi-legally, as a conflicting arena of rights in which balancing is necessary and hierarchies are set up to resolve conflicts. Contract is often fundamental to this vision, and the contract account posits autonomous agents operating exclusively on impartial reason. The ethic of care, by contrast, centers on responsiveness and responsibility, as determined within an interconnected network of sentiments, relationships, and responsibilities created in community. Responsibility and responsiveness are understood in terms of sentimental attachment to others, caring for them, preventing harm from befalling them, and the like. Taking care of others in a network of personal relationships becomes the core notion.

---

[22]Carol Gilligan, *In a Different Voice* (Cambridge, MA: Harvard University Press, 1982), p. 21.

According to Gilligan, women typically see an ethic of care as an assumption or axiom of the moral world. Giving and helping are key categories, whereas resolution of dilemmas and principles of obligation are not high on the agenda. Again, equal consideration of persons is central; an overriding obligation or right is not. (Gilligan does not argue for the superiority of one ethic over another. She tends to see them as complementary, each supplying what the other lacks.)

### Feminism and the Concept of Trust

We can now turn to Baier's philosophical extension of Gilligan's psychological investigations, and her manner of combining Hume's moral theory with these contemporary feminist concerns.

Baier finds the reasoning and methods of women in ethical theory different from that in the traditional theories, all of which were written by men. She claims to hear in contemporary female philosophers, despite their diversity, the same "different" voice that Gilligan heard in her studies, but one made "reflective and philosophical." What women *want* in a ethical theory is just "what they are [beginning to] provide." What women theorists *need* is "to connect their ethics of love with what has been the men theorists' preoccupation, namely, obligation."[23]

Baier goes on to inquire into what would serve as a key concept, principle, or guiding motif in a broader theory, if it were to be developed as distinctively feminist. In casting about for a connecting bridge to span an ethic of love with an ethic of obligation, she proposes "appropriate trust" as the bridging concept. She does not propose that we drop categories of obligation, but rather that we make room for an ethic of love and trust, including an account of human bonding in family and community. Both relationships of care and relationships of obligation, she thinks, require trust as a necessary condition.

### Implications for Moral "Theory"

Although Baier is willing to build on the viable parts of traditional utilitarian and deontological ethical theory, she finds much of it defective for reasons other than mere incompleteness. She decries Kantian ethics for having too narrow of a conception of morality that left no room for virtues of caring, loving, trusting, gentleness, and the like. She sees a need to revalue caring as a fundamental moral relationship. Baier "deplores" the emphasis in modern moral philosophy on moral judgment as an instance of law or principle, and she also wonders whether there can be a moral "theory" in any meaningful sense.

> A theory, in its traditional and oldest sense, is an outcome of contemplation of some world or independently existing reality, a way of representing what it is, how it works, how its various different parts are [for example] a theory of God [or] a scientific system. . . . But normative moral "theory" does not describe an existent world, at best it guides the conduct

---

[23]"What Do Women Want in a Moral Theory?" *Nous,* 19 (1985): 53, 56.

of one species of living things within that world, a species a little prone to hubris and megalomania.[24]

Baier sees no way to effectuate a program of clear moral intuitions systematized to confirm theories and decide cases. A genuine communal morality may not be codifiable, let alone codifiable in the traditional, rationalistic language of what is universally *right* and what *ought* to be done. She sternly rejects contractarian models with their distinct emphasis on justice and rights, because they omit integral virtues of cooperation and trust, placing instead a premium on *autonomous choice* among free and equal agents. They also misrepresent persons as individual agents separated from others in their moral choices and determinations of responsibility, rather than as selves in a relational network of community. Baier is obviously not keen on autonomy, choice, or equality as central doctrines in ethical theory. The terms of social cooperation, especially in families and in communal decision-making, are, as she sees it, unchosen, intimate, and between unequals.

## Hume and the History of Ethics

We noted earlier that Baier credits Hume's ethics for some of her reflections on "the ethic of care." Although Baier finds traditional ethical theory disappointing, she credits Hume, Hegel, and Mill with noticing some forms of intimate relationship, unlike Hobbes, Butler, Bentham, and Kant, who tend to ignore them entirely. She thinks the great moral traditions have also generally been silent on questions of who should be trusted, in what ways, and why.

Hume and a few select others become "honorary women" for Baier, and she declares Hume the "best of the lot." She believes that philosophers can find resources in Hume that support feminist ideals, and she claims to have been inspired by those writings herself. Hume gave her insight into a morality that "gave authority to feeling, custom, and tradition" rather than giving authority to sovereign reason.[25] Like Hume, Baier insists that emotions guide one's moral responsiveness in relationships such as friendship and family.

Baier regards Hume's moral philosophy as highly relevant for today's concerns. What she prizes in Hume seems primarily to be (1) his total distance from Kant's paradigm of obedience to universal law (the quintessential theory predicated on equality and autonomy); (2) his emphasis on character and community; (3) the particular relational traits he emphasizes, such as capacity for sympathy; (4) the centrality of family life and related character traits of love in his work; and (5) the consistency of all the above with the morality that women commonly practice.[26] In the following selection, Baier joins her interpretation of Hume with her vision of the ethic of care ("the care perspective").

[24]Annette Baier, *Postures of the Mind* (Minneapolis: University of Minnesota Press, 1985), p. 210.
[25]*Postures of the Mind,* p. xii.
[26]Baier, "Hume, The Women's Moral Theorist?" in *Women and Moral Theory,* Eva Feder Kittay and Diana T. Meyers, eds. (Totowa, NJ: Rowman and Littlefield, 1987), pp. 38ff.

# *Hume, the Women's Moral Theorist?*\*

## Annette Baier

As every student of the history of philosophy knows, Hume was the philosopher Kant set out to "answer," and both Kant's theory of knowledge and his ethics stand in significant contrast to Hume's. And Kant's views, through their influence on Jean Piaget and John Rawls, are the views which are expressed in Kohlberg's version of moral maturity and the development leading to it, the version which Gilligan found not to apply to girls and women as well as it did to boys and men. So anyone at all familiar with the history of ethics will wonder whether other non-Kantian strands in Western ethics, as developed in the philosophical tradition, might prove less difficult to get into reflective equilibrium with women's (not specifically philosophical) moral wisdom than the Kantian strand. For there certainly is no agreement that Kant and his followers represent the culmination of all the moral wisdom of our philosophical tradition. Alasdair MacIntyre's recent attacks on the Kantian tradition, and all the controversy caused by attempts to implement in high schools the Kohlberg views about moral education shows that not all men, let alone all women, are in agreement with the Kantians. Since the philosopher Kant was most notoriously in disagreement with Hume, it is natural to ask, after Gilligan's work, whether Hume is more of a women's moral theorist than is Kant. We might do the same with Aristotle, Hegel, Marx, Mill, Mac-

Intyre, with all those theorists who have important disagreements with Kant, but a start can be made with Hume.

He is inviting, for this purpose, in part because he did try to attend, for better or worse, to male-female differences, and in his life, did, it seems, listen to women; and also because he is close enough in time, culture, and in some presuppositions to Kant, for the comparison between their moral theories to hold out the same hope of reconciliation that Gilligan wants or in her book wanted to get, between men's and women's moral insights. There are important areas of agreement, as well as of disagreement, or at least of difference of emphasis. . . . When I read Gilligan's findings that mature, apparently intelligent and reflective women appeared to "revert" to Kohlberg's stage three (lower stage of level two, the conventional level) my immediate thought was "perhaps we women tend to be Humeans rather than Kantians." That is the thought I want to explore here.

I shall list some striking differences between Kant's and Hume's moral theories, as I understand them, then relate these to the differences Gilligan found between men's and women's conceptions of morality.

Hume's ethics, unlike Kant's, make morality a matter not of obedience to universal law, but of cultivating the character traits which give a person "inward peace of mind, consciousness of integrity," (Hume 1975, p. 283) and at the same time make that person good company to other persons, in a variety of senses of "company," ranging from

\*From *Women and Moral Theory*, Eva Feder Kittay and Diana T. Meyers, eds. (Totowa, N.J.: Rowman & Littlefield Publishers, 1987).

the relatively impersonal and "remote" togetherness of fellow citizens, to the more selective but still fairly remote relations of parties to a contract, to the closer ties between friends, family, lovers. To become a good fellow-person one doesn't consult some book of rules, but cultivates one's capacity for sympathy, or fellow feeling, as well as for that judgment needed when conflicts arise between the different demands on us such sympathy may lead us to feel. Hume's ethics requires us to be able to be rule-followers, in some contexts, but do not reduce morality to rule-following. Corrected (sometimes rule-corrected) sympathy, not law-discerning reason, is the fundamental moral capacity.

Secondly, there is Hume's difference from Kant about the source of what general rules he does recognize as morally binding, namely the rules of justice. Where Kant sees human reason as the sole author of these moral rules, and sees them as universal, Hume sees them as authored by self-interest, instrumental reason, and rationally "frivolous" factors such as historical chance, human fancy and what it selects as salient, and by custom and tradition. He does not see these rules, such as property rules, as universal, but as varying from community to community and changeable by human will, as conditions or needs, wishes, or human fancy change. His theory of social "artifice," and his account of justice as obedience to the rules of these social artifices, formed by "convention," and subject to historical variation and change, stands in stark opposition to rationalist accounts, like Aquinas's and Kant's, of justice as obedience to laws of pure practical reason, valid for all people at all times and

places. Hume has a historicist and conventionalist account of the moral rules which we find ourselves expected to obey, and which, on reflection, we usually see it to be sensible for us to obey, despite their elements of arbitrariness and despite the inequalities their working usually produces. He believes it is sensible for us to conform to the rules of our group, those rules which specify obligations and rights, as long as these do redirect the dangerous destructive workings of self-interest into more mutually advantageous channels, thereby giving all the "infinite advantages" of increased force, ability, and security (compared with what we would have in the absence of any such rules). . . .

This difference from Kantian views about the role of general principles in grounding moral obligations goes along in Hume with a downplaying of the role of reason, and a playing up of the role of feeling in moral judgment. Agreeing with the rationalists that when we use our reason we all appeal to universal rules (the rules of arithmetic, or of logic, or of causal inference) and failing to find any such universal rules of morality, as well as failing to see how, even if we found them, they should be able, alone, to *motivate* us to act as they tell us to act, he claims that morality rests ultimately on sentiment, on a special motivating feeling we come to have once we have exercised our capacity for sympathy with others' feelings, and also learned to overcome the emotional conflicts which arise in a sympathetic person when the wants of different fellow-persons clash, or when one's own wants clash with those of one's fellows. Morality, on Hume's account, is the outcome of a search for ways of eliminating contradictions in the "passions" of sympathetic persons who are aware both of their own and their fellows' desires and needs, including emotional needs. Any moral progress or development a person undergoes will be, for Hume, a matter of "the correction of sentiment," where what corrects it will be contrary sentiments, plus the cognitive-cum-passionate drive to minimize conflict both between and within persons. Reason and logic are indispensable "slaves" to the passions in this achievement, since reason enables us to think clearly about consequences or likely consequences of alternative actions, to foresee outcomes and avoid self-defeating policies. But "the ultimate ends of human actions can never, in any case, be accounted for by *reason,* but recommend themselves entirely to the sentiments and affections of mankind, without any dependence upon intellectual faculties" (Hume 1975, p. 293). A lover of conflict will have no reason, since he will have no motive, to cultivate the moral sentiment, and nor will that man of "cold insensibility" who is "unaffected with the images of human happiness or misery" (Hume 1975, p. 225). A human heart, as well as human reason, is needed for the understanding of morality, and the heart's responses are to particular persons, not to universal principles of abstract justice. Such immediate responses may be corrected by general rules (as they will be when justice demands that the good poor man's debt to the less good miser be paid) and by more reflective feeling responses, such as dismay and foreboding at unwisely given love and trust, or disapproval of excessive parental indulgence, but what controls and regulates feeling will be a wider web of feelings, which reason helps us apprehend and

understand, not any reason holding authority over all feelings.

The next point to note is that Hume's version of what a typical human heart desires is significantly different from that both of egoists and of individualists. "The interested passion," or self-interest, plays an important role, but so does sympathy, and concern for others. Even where self-interest is of most importance in his theory, namely in his account of justice, it is the self-interest of those with fairly fluid ego boundaries, namely of family members, concerned with "acquiring goods and possessions for ourselves and our nearest friends" (Hume 1978, pp. 491–2). This is the troublesome passion that needs to be redirected by agreed rules, whereby it can control itself so as to avoid socially destructive conflict over scarce goods. Its self-control, in a society-wide cooperative scheme, which establishes property rights, is possible because the persons involved in it have already learned, in the family, the advantages that can come both from self-control and from cooperation (Hume 1978, p. 486). Had the rough corners of "untoward" and uncontrolled passions, selfish or unselfish, not been already rubbed off by growing up under some parental discipline, and were there no minimally sociable human passions such as love between man and woman, love of parents for their children, love of friends, sisters and brothers, the Humean artifice of justice could not be constructed. Its very possibility as an artificial virtue depends upon human nature containing the natural passions, which make family life natural for human beings, which make parental solicitude, grateful response to that, and the restricted cooperation thereby resulting, phenomena that do not need to be contrived by artifice. At the very heart of Hume's moral theory lies his celebration of family life and of parental love. Justice, the chief artificial virtue, is the offspring of family cooperativeness and inventive self-interested reason, which sees how such a mutually beneficial cooperative scheme might be extended. And when Hume lists the natural moral virtues, those not consisting in obedience to agreed rules, and having point even if not generally possessed, his favourite example is parental love and solicitude. The good person, the possessor of the natural virtues, is the one who is "a safe companion, an easy friend, a gentle master, an agreeable husband, an indulgent father" (Hume 1978, p. 606). We may deplore that patriarchal combination of roles—master, husband, father, but we should also note the virtues these men are to display—gentleness, agreeability, indulgence. These were more traditionally expected from mistresses, wives, and mothers than from masters, husbands, and fathers. Of course, they are not the only virtues Humean good characters show, there is also due pride, or self-esteem, and the proper ambition and courage that that may involve, as well as generosity, liberality, zeal, gratitude, compassion, patience, industry, perseverance, activity, vigilance, application, integrity, constancy, temperance, frugality, economy, resolution, good temper, charity, clemency, equity, honesty, truthfulness, fidelity, discretion, caution, presence of mind, "and a thousand more of the same kind" (Hume 1975, p. 243). . . .

The next point I want to stress in Hume's moral theory is that in his attention to various interpersonal relations, in which our Humean virtues or vices show, he does not give any special cen-trality to relationships between equals, let alone autonomous equals. Since his analysis of social cooperation starts from cooperation within the family, relations between those who are necessarily unequals, namely parents and children, is at the center of the picture. He starts from a bond which he considers "the strongest and most indissoluble bond in nature" (Hume 1975, p. 240), "the strongest tie the mind is capable of" (Hume 1978, p. 352), namely the love of parents for children, and in his moral theory he works out, as it were, from there. This relationship, and the obligations and virtues it involves, lack three central features of relations between moral agents as understood by Kantians and contractarians—it is intimate, it is unchosen, and is between unequals. Of course, the intimacy need not be "indissoluble," the inequality may be temporary, or later reversed, and the extent to which the initial relationship is unchosen will vary from that of unplanned or contrary-to-plan parenthood, to intentional parenthood (although not intentional parenting of a given particular child) to that highest degree of voluntariness present when, faced with an actual newborn child, a decision is taken not to let it be adopted by others, or, when a contrary decision is taken by the biological parent or parents, by the decision of adoptive parents to adopt such an already encountered child. Such fully chosen parenthood is rare, and the norm is for parents to *find themselves* with a given child, perhaps with any child at all, and for parental affection to attach itself fairly indiscriminately to its unselected objects. The contractarian model of morality as a matter of living up to self-chosen commitments gets into obvious trouble both with duties of young children to their unchosen parents, to whom no binding commitments have been made, and of initially involuntary parents to their children. Hume has no problem with such unchosen moral ties, since he takes them as the paradigm moral ties, one's giving rise to moral obligations more self-evident than any obligation to keep contracts.[1]

The last respect in which I wish to contrast Hume's moral philosophy with its more Kantian alternative is in his version of what problem morality is supposed to solve, what its point is. For Kantians and contractarians, the point is freedom, the main problem how to achieve it given that other freedom-aspirants exist and that conflict between them is likely. The Rousseau-Kant solution is obedience to collectively agreed-to general law, where each freedom-seeker can console himself with the thought that the legislative will he must obey is as much his own as it is anyone else's. For Hume, that problem, of the coexistence of would-be unrestrained self-assertors, is solved by the invention of social artifices and the recognition of the virtue of justice, namely of conformity to the rules of such mutually advantageous artifices. . . .

I have drawn attention to the limited place of conformity to general rules in Hume's version of morality, to the historicist conventionalist account he gives of such rules, to his thesis that morality depends upon self-corrected sentiments, or passions, as much or more than it depends upon the reason that concurs with

and serves those passions; to the non-individualist, nonegoistic version of human passions he advances, to the essentially interpersonal or social nature of those passions which are approved as virtues, the central role of the family, at least at its best, as an exemplar of the cooperation and interdependency morality preserves and extends, the fact that moral cooperation, for him, includes cooperation in unchosen schemes, with unchosen partners, with unequal partners, in close intimate relations as well as distanced and more formal ones. And finally, I emphasized that the need for morality arises for Hume from conflicts within each person, as well as from interpersonal conflict. It is a fairly straightforward matter to relate these points to at least some of the respects in which Gilligan found girls' and women's versions of morality to differ from men's. Hume turns out to be uncannily womanly in his moral wisdom. "Since the reality of interconnexion is experienced by women as given rather than freely contracted, they arrive at an understanding of life that reflects the limits of autonomy and control" (Gilligan 1982, p. 172). Hume lived before autonomy became an obsession with moral and social philosophers, or rather lived while Rousseau was making it their obsession, but his attack on contractarian doctrines of political obligation, and his clear perception of the given-ness of interconnection, in the family and beyond, his emphasis on our capacity to make others' joys and sorrows our own, on our need for a "seconding" of sentiments, and the inescapable mutual vulnerability and mutual enrichment that the human psychology and the human condition, when thus understood, entail, make autonomy not even an ideal, for Hume.

[1][In her article, "The Need for More than Justice," Baier writes that "women's traditional work, of caring . . . for the young, is obviously socially vital. One cannot regard any version of morality that does not ensure that caring for children gets well done as an adequate 'minimal morality.' . . . A moral theory . . . cannot regard concern for new and future persons as an optional charity left for those with a taste for it." Ed.]

Baier's article is an indication that writers in feminism need not abandon great historical figures in philosophy merely because their philosophies contain no distinctly feminist theory. Baier's bottom line seems to be that Hume is not everything one would wish to see in a feminist theory, but he is nonetheless a reflective source of ethics that forms a real resource available to this tradition.

## CRITICISMS OF HUMEAN ETHICS

### The Dangers of Skepticism

Hume was widely regarded as a skeptic by his contemporaries, and this reputation lives on today. In the eighteenth century, skeptics were regarded as philosophers who maintained that no absolute certainty exists and that a person should suspend judgment rather than cling to dogmatic beliefs. Skeptics of this description thought that methods of reasoning often leave us unable to choose between competing truth claims. Hume accepts the proposition that we do not know anything with absolute certainty and that truth is not achievable in many areas of inquiry, including ethics. As we saw in Chapter 3, many contemporary philosophers think the abandonment of moral truth is a dangerous mistake in a moral theory.

There are at least two reasons why Hume has been viewed as a skeptic about morals—and why many who are attracted to his theory, such as Mackie, have likewise been considered skeptics. First, by grounding morals in taste and passion, while denying all grounding in reason (other than instrumental reason), Hume places morals beyond demonstration, knowledge, and truth. Moral judgments cannot be supported exclusively by appeal to facts and cannot, therefore, be rationally demonstrated to be correct or incorrect. Second, Hume denies that moral values of goodness, obligation, and virtue exist independently of the human mind. That is, moral values require human nature and human communities for their existence. They do not exist in the form of objective facts. These philosophical theses may seem plausible in many matters of morals such as moral compassion, which clearly requires compassionate persons, but Hume's theses are less clearly correct in other areas of moral conduct. For example, is justice like compassion? Are there not objective moral standards of justice that are independent of human responses?

Hume's critics have regarded Hume's answers to such questions as so skeptical and dangerous that they threaten the very existence of morality. However, Hume himself did not think of his views either as skeptical of conventional moral standards or as a threat to those standards. His goal, like Mackie's, was to explain the nature and origin of those standards. Hume and Mackie are more skeptical of certain moral philosophies and moral theologies than skeptics about morality itself. Here they are both very skeptical indeed.

### The Limits of Subjectivism

Hume's theory and Mackie's have also been criticized for making the subjective self the sole source of moral approval and disapproval, virtue and vice, and right and wrong. The basis of this interpretation is rooted in statements such as the following from Hume's *Treatise of Human Nature:* "vice entirely escapes you, as long as you consider the object. You never can find it, till you turn your reflection into your own breast, and find a sentiment of disapprobation, which arises in you."[27] Such statements have led some commentators to maintain that Hume makes morality relative to each individual's particular feelings and tastes—elevating moral sentiment well beyond its true importance.

Whatever the merits of this interpretation, it needs to take account of the fact that moral sentiment has a *universal* dimension for Hume (though not for Mackie) and that by definition, virtue is *"a quality of the mind agreeable to or approved of by every one."* Hume tries to depict a moral agent as one who retreats from his or her "private and particular situation" to achieve an impartial perspective. By abstracting from particular situations and personal sentiments, the agent is affected only by sentiments of humanity. In the light of this theory, it seems inaccurate to say that Hume renders morality entirely dependent on the particular feelings of individual observers.

However, many critics find this claim of universality to be naive. Why, they say, should we believe that our subjective responses have something in common, when we see so much relativity of response and judgment? Why should we believe that recognition of virtue in a person requires some process of universal subjective response by impartial persons? From the perspective of these critics, once you start down Hume's road of the moral sentiments, you will inevitably wind up with Mackie's radical subjectivism.

## Problems about Justice and Utility

An anonymous reviewer of Hume's work published a monograph in 1753 under the title *Some Late Opinions Concerning the Foundation of Morality, Examined.* This review used the background of Hume's skepticism and subjectivism to state an objection to Hume's account of justice and utility that has troubled Humean theory to the present day:

> [T]he author is a very agreeable writer. . . . But . . . I am afraid, the love of simplicity has betrayed him. . . . Utility is his favourite and capital principle, to which he reduces all the several branches of morals. . . . [W]ith regard to justice, his notions are very singular.

Since Hume uses utility as the "capital principle" of morals, the reviewer argued that Hume's philosophy is "of dangerous tendency": Hume has degraded justice "in a dishonourable manner" to the point that it has no power to determine how social resources should be justly distributed. The reviewer maintained that "utility cannot possibly be any part of the foundation of morals" and that "justice has a deeper foundation . . . than . . . [Hume's basis in] utility." Even if Hume were to succeed in showing that "justice and public good coincide," his conclusion "will never prove, that we have no sentiment of justice but what arises from a reflection on public good."

[27]Hume, *Treatise* 3.1.1.26.

This critic interpreted Hume as holding that "whatever, in character or conduct, is approved as useful, is virtue," thereby "reducing morality into the same class in which we place some very trifling qualities," even including some purely intellectual qualities, such as industry and secrecy. The root of the problem is that *moral* approbation effectively means for Hume "whatever we take pleasure in; whatever we consider useful or agreeable," and that even "the greatest villain" and inanimate things can possess these traits. Moreover, this critic asserts that we are often more concerned with the motives of others than with the utility of their actions. Motives of gratitude, for example, are independent of considerations of utility. While it is true that we approve as virtuous that which is useful, it is moral motive, not utility, that is the source of the approbation.

These criticisms march to the conclusion that Hume has most fundamental matters of morals backwards. We will be in a good position to assess these criticisms of justice, in particular, when we have completed Chapter 9, where we will take up theories of justice and their proper grounding.

## CONCLUSION

In this chapter, we have considered several approaches to the role of moral sentiment, moral agreement, and social convention. Humean theories have perhaps forced us to think through the issue of moral pluralism more seriously than any other type of philosophy. The virtue of the diversity in these theories is that they cheerfully acknowledge a wide variety of moral conflicts, recognize the extraordinary range of disagreement in contemporary moral philosophy, and tolerate different traditions without attempting to force them into an artificial unity. Perhaps these theories are wrongheaded approaches to contemporary moral philosophy, but they deserve consideration as we shift now to the disputed territories of rights, justice, and liberty.

## SUGGESTED SUPPLEMENTARY READINGS

### Hume's Writings on Ethics

Hume, David: Knud Haakonssen, ed., *Political Essays* (Cambridge, England: Cambridge University Press, 1994).

———: Tom L. Beauchamp, ed., *An Enquiry concerning the Principles of Morals* (Oxford, England: Oxford University Press, 1998). Available in a student edition and in the Clarendon Hume edition for scholars.

———: David and Mary Norton, eds., *A Treatise of Human Nature* (Oxford, England: Oxford University Press, 2000).

Oxford University Press is currently publishing a critical edition of Hume's philosophical, political, and literary works.

## Commentaries on Hume

Baier, Annette: "Hume, the Women's Moral Theorist?" in E. Kittay and D. Meyers, eds., *Women and Moral Theory* (Totowa, NJ: Rowman & Littlefield, 1987), pp. 37–55.

————: *A Progress of Sentiments* (Cambridge, MA: Harvard University Press, 1991).

————: "Hume, David," in Lawrence Becker and Charlotte Becker, eds., *Encyclopedia of Ethics* (New York: Garland, 1992), vol. 1.

————: "David Hume, 1711–1776," in Edward Craig, ed., *Routledge Encyclopedia of Philosophy* (London: Routledge, 1997).

Buckle, Stephen: *Natural Law and the Theory of Property: Grotius to Hume* (Oxford, England: Clarendon Press, 1991).

Darwall, Stephen: "Motive and Obligation in Hume's Ethics," *Nous,* 27 (1993): 415–48.

Harrison, Jonathan: *Hume's Theory of Justice* (Oxford: Clarendon Press, 1981).

Hope, Vincent M.: *Virtue by Consensus* (Oxford: Clarendon Press, 1989).

Jones, Peter: "Hume," in N. F. Bunnin, ed., *The Blackwell Companion to Philosophy* (Oxford, England, and Cambridge, MA: Blackwell Reference, 1996).

MacIntyre, Alasdair: "Hume on 'Is' and 'Ought,'" in V. C. Chappell, ed., *Hume* (Garden City, NJ: Anchor Books, 1966), pp. 240–64.

Martin, Marie A.: "Hume on Human Excellence," *Hume Studies,* 18 (1992), 383–99.

Norton, David Fate: *David Hume: Common Sense Moralist, Sceptical Metaphysician* (Princeton, NJ: Princeton University Press, 1982).

————, ed.: *The Cambridge Companion to Hume* (Cambridge, England: Cambridge University Press, 1993).

Penelhum, Terence: *David Hume: An Introduction to His Philosophical System* (West Lafayette, IN: Purdue University Press, 1992).

Russell, Paul: *Freedom & Moral Sentiment: Hume's Way of Naturalizing Responsibility* (New York: Oxford University Press, 1995).

Snare, Francis: *Morals, Motivation, and Convention: Hume's Influential Doctrines* (Cambridge, England: Cambridge University Press, 1991).

Stewart, John B.: *Opinion and Reform in Hume's Political Philosophy* (Princeton, NJ: Princeton University Press, 1992).

Stewart, M. A., and John Wright, eds.: *Hume and Hume's Connexions* (Edinburgh, Scotland: Edinburgh University Press; University Park: Pennsylvania State University Press, 1995).

Tweyman, Stanley: *David Hume: Critical Assessments,* 6 vols. (London: Routledge, 1995).

## Morals by Invention and by Agreement

Baier, Annette: "Artificial Virtues and the Equally Sensible Non-Knaves: A Response to Gauthier," *Hume Studies,* 18 (1992): 429–39.

Gauthier, David: "David Hume, Contractarian," *Philosophical Review,* 88 (1979), 3–38.

————: *Morals by Agreement* (Oxford, England: Clarendon Press, 1986).

————: *Moral Dealing: Contract, Ethics, and Reason* (Ithaca, NY: Cornell University Press, 1990).

————: "Artificial Virtues and the Sensible Knave," *Hume Studies,* 18 (1992), 401–27.

Honderich, Ted, ed.: *Morality and Objectivity: A Tribute to J. L. Mackie* (Boston: Routledge & Kegan Paul, 1985).

Mackie, John: *Hume's Moral Theory* (London: Routledge & Kegan Paul, 1980).

————: *Ethics: Inventing Right and Wrong* (London: Penguin Books, 1990).

Narveson, Jan: "The Agreement to Keep Our Agreements: Hume, Prichard, and Searle," *Philosophical Papers,* 23 (1994): 75–87.

Vallentyne, Peter, ed.: *Contractarianism and Rational Choice: Essays on David Gauthier's Morals by Agreement* (New York: Cambridge University Press, 1991).

## The Voice of Moral Sentiment

Baier, Annette: "What Do Women Want in a Moral Theory?" *Nous,* 19 (1985): 53–63.

————: "Trust and Antitrust," *Ethics,* 96 (1986): 231–60.

————: *A Progress of Sentiments* (Cambridge, MA: Harvard University Press, 1991).

————: "Response to My Critics," *Hume Studies,* 20 (1994): 211–8.

————: *Moral Prejudices* (Cambridge, MA: Harvard University Press, 1994).

Carse, Alisa: "The Voice of Care: Implications for Bioethical Education," *Journal of Medicine and Philosophy,* 16 (1991): 5–28.

Gilligan, Carol: *In a Different Voice* (Cambridge, MA: Harvard University Press, 1982).

———— et al., eds.: *Mapping the Moral Domain* (Cambridge, MA: Harvard University Press, 1988).

Hanen, M., and Kai Nielsen, eds.: "Science, Morality and Feminist Theory," *Canadian Journal of Philosophy,* supp. vol. 13 (1987).

Jaggar, Alison: *Feminist Politics and Human Nature* (London: Rowman and Allenheld, 1983).

Johnson, Clarence Shole: "Annette Baier on Reason and Morals in Hume's Philosophy," *Dialogue,* 34 (1995): 367–80.

Kittay, Eva Feder, and Diana T. Meyers: *Women and Moral Theory* (Totowa, NJ: Rowman & Littlefield, 1987).

MacKinnon, C. A.: *Toward a Feminist Theory of the State* (Cambridge, MA: Harvard University Press, 1989).

Okin, Susan M.: *Justice, Gender, and the Family* (New York: Basic Books, 1989).

Ruddick, Sara: *Maternal Thinking* (Boston: Beacon Press, 1989).

# PART THREE

# Topics in Moral and Social Philosophy

# CHAPTER 8

# *Rights*

## THE TALIBAN IN CONTROL

Afghanistan is a mountainous, landlocked country in central Asia that is about the size of Texas. It is bordered by Iran, Pakistan, and several former Soviet republics. Afghanistan has been torn by civil war for the past twenty years. Recently the Taliban, a fundamentalist Muslim militia, has established moral, political, and economic control over most of the country.

In 1979 the Soviet Union invaded Afghanistan to support a communist government against Muslim insurgents. The United States responded by aiding the rebels, known as the mujahedin. After ten years of war Soviet forces withdrew in 1989, and the communist government fell in 1992. This did not result in peace, however, as the various rebel factions began to fight among themselves for control of the country. In September 1996 the Taliban took control of Kabul, the capital of Afghanistan, and thereby controlled almost all of the country.

The political changes brought by the Taliban have had a tragic impact on the lives of many people in Afghanistan. Torture, amputations, and stonings are common forms of punishment, and the courts lack due process and the right to legal counsel. Perhaps the most striking aspect of Afghanistan under the Taliban is the severe restrictions they have imposed on women, which have made the society almost unrecognizable compared to pre-Taliban years. For the past hundred years women in Afghanistan had been making significant progress, especially in urban areas. For example, they were guaranteed equal rights and the right to vote, and made up the majority of students in Kabul. These reforms were begun by turn-of-the-century ruler Amir Abdul Rahman, who banned child marriage and legalized divorce in order to bring Afghan practices in line with Islamic law. Under Taliban rule this process has been reversed and women face special discrimination.

Immediately after taking control of Kabul in September 1996, the Taliban issued the order that, except for those in the health care professions, no woman could work outside the home, attend school, or leave her home unless accompanied by a male relative. In addition, women must be covered from head to toe in a burqa (shroud) which has only a mesh opening to see and breathe through. Women are not allowed to wear white socks or shoes because white is the color of the Taliban flag, nor are they allowed to wear shoes that make noise as they walk.

Perhaps the most shocking Taliban policy is discrimination against women in health care. In January 1998, the Taliban declared a policy of segregating men and women in hospitals. They began to enforce this policy seriously in July when hospital directors were ordered to cease services to women and discharge female staff. The Taliban reversed this decision on November 6, 1998, but only limited hospital services and staff, with poor equipment, are available for women. All these restrictions are carried out in the name of an interpretation of Islamic law, but this interpretation has been rejected by most international Islamic authorities.

Although women have rarely experienced highly favorable conditions or the protection of human rights in Afghanistan, the Taliban has imposed a policy that appears to be an alien concept compared with previous conditions, particularly in the cities. Before the Taliban, universities in Kabul were coeducational. Women constituted 70 percent of the teaching force, about 50 percent of the civil servant corps, and 40 percent of physicians. Women were free to choose their dress, move about by themselves in public, and pursue their careers. Now they are commonly beaten and punished for "wrong" choices. In addition, for seventeen straight years (including the years of Taliban control), Afghans have been the largest single group of refugees according to the United Nations. Women and children compose three-quarters of this refugee population.

The Taliban has not been silent in the face of international criticism of its record on human rights. Its leaders justify their rule with the claim that greater peace requires restricted freedoms. Prior to their takeover, violence, including rape, was rampant and the nation was in a state of anarchy. By imposing severe criminal penalties and by banning TV, radio, music, and nonreligious books and magazines, the Taliban claim to have brought security as well as true Islamic law to the people of Afghanistan.

Some Taliban government officials have stated that the current condition is only temporary. The deputy minister of education has claimed that school for girls is only suspended, not ended. However, in the Taliban's view, any loosening of restrictions must wait until peace is secured throughout the country. Finally, many Taliban officials complain of what appears to them to be the world's hypocrisy. In the words of Al-Haj Maulavi Qalamuddin, the head of the General Department for Preservation of Virtue and Prevention of Vice, "Why is there such concern about women? Bread costs too much. There is no work. Even boys are not going to school. And yet all I hear about are women. Where was the world when men here were violating any women they wanted?"[1]

This case and all the sections in this chapter raise profound questions about the nature and foundation of rights.

---

[1]This case was developed from Zohra Rasekh et al., "Women's Health and Human Rights in Afghanistan," *Journal of the American Medical Association,* 280, no. 5 (August 5, 1998): 449–50; U.S. Department of State, "Afghanistan Country Report on Human Rights Practices for 1997" (Washington, D.C.), January 30, 1998, p. 11; Physicians for Human Rights, *The Taliban's War on Women: A Health and Human Rights Crisis in Afghanistan* (Boston: Physicians for Human Rights, 1998); Barry Barek, "Afghans Ruled by Taliban: Poor, Isolated, but Secure," *The New York Times* (October 10, 1998), A4–6; and the Taliban Website: http://www.ummah.net/taliban.

## RIGHTS AND HUMAN RIGHTS

In Chapters 4 through 7, terms from moral discourse such as "goal," "obligation," and "virtue" dominated the discussion. Principles of obligation and standards of virtue were invoked in various theories to determine appropriate actions and character traits. The language of rights has been in the background of these discussions, despite the fact that rights language underlies many current controversies in ethics—for example, the right to health care, the right to privacy, the right to life, and the rights of women. Moral protections for persons who are vulnerable to abuse, enslavement, neglect, and vendetta have often been stated in terms of rights—as is dramatically illustrated by the complaints of refugee agencies and women under the control of the Taliban.

### The Nature of Rights

Rights occupy a prominent place in political writing because they are powerful assertions of legitimate claims on others. Rights have been depicted by metaphors such as "stronghold" and "bulwark" to stress that they are justified *demands* that individuals and groups can make upon others or upon society. In this respect rights contrast with privileges, personal ideals, optional acts of charity, group ideals, and the like. Unlike rights, none of the latter can be demanded as one's due.

Rights to food or to health care are, as rights, no different than rights to receive an insurance benefit if required premiums have been paid: Anyone *eligible* under the fixed rules and requirements for a program may validly demand due services and goods provided by that program. Similarly, if students have a right to appeal a teacher's failing grade in a course, they are authorized by established procedures to a review. They are not dependent merely upon the good will and friendly cooperation of the teacher or others in the institutional setting. Thus, if women had political rights in Afghanistan, which they do not, then they would be protected against many of the rules made by the Taliban. H. J. McCloskey has defended an analysis of rights in terms of *entitlements:*

> A right is an entitlement to do, to demand, to enjoy, to be, to have done for us. Rights may be rights to act, to exist, to enjoy, to demand. We speak of rights as being *possessed, exercised,* and *enjoyed.* . . . We speak of our rights as being *rights to*—as in the rights to life, liberty and happiness—not as *rights against,* as has so often mistakenly been claimed.[2]

McCloskey maintains that entitlements are rights *to* something, whereas claims are *against* someone or some institution; therefore, he thinks entitlement rather than claim is the appropriate concept for analyzing rights. However, McCloskey seems to overstate his case. "Rights against" correctly indicates that rights are held against others, a use of language that has long prevailed in the law. Consider, for example, the right to privacy, which has been invoked in law to prevent governmental interference with personal decision-making on issues such as abortion and family decision-making about reproduction. An individual holds this right, like other

<hr>

[2]H. J. McCloskey, "Rights," *Philosophical Quarterly,* 15 (1965): 118.

constitutional rights, against the state and against parties acting on behalf of the state. Perhaps the best formulation of the language of rights is to say one holds a right *to* something (personal privacy, say) as a claim *against* another party. The following passage from a court opinion supports this analysis:

> As this constitutional guaranty [to privacy] reaches out to protect the freedom of a woman to terminate pregnancy under certain conditions, . . . so it encompasses the right of a patient to preserve his or her right to privacy *against* unwanted infringements of bodily integrity in appropriate circumstances.[3]

So understood, a right gives us a kind of claim, where claiming is the mode of action employed in appealing to a system of rules that permits us to demand, affirm, or insist upon that which is due. Valid "claiming" (or being able to claim) is a large part of what makes rights distinctive. If a person possesses a right, others are validly constrained from interfering with the exercise of that right, and the right holder is protected from failures to provide that which is owed. Thus rights can be analyzed as a combination of *entitlements to* perform or abstain from an action, together with *valid claims against* another party who interferes with the performance or abstention from that particular action.

Hereafter the language of both "valid claim" and "entitlement" will be used in discussing rights, and these notions can be understood as shorthand for discretionary holdings that express morally valid demands on others. Claiming will be understood as a form of rule-governed activity. The rules may be legal rules, moral rules, institutional rules, or rules of games; but all rights exist or fail to exist because the relevant rules either allow or disallow the appropriate claiming or conferral of entitlements. The rules distinguish between valid and invalid claims, and so between claims that amount to rights and those that do not.

## Human Rights

Many believe that fundamental human rights of the sort not recognized by the Taliban or by a great many oppressive governments transcend national boundaries and are not contingent on particular conferrals of rights. Yet, in the sweep of human history the language of rights is a distinctly modern phenomenon. Until the seventeenth century, problems of political ethics were rarely discussed in terms of rights. In the philosophy and political theory of that period, particularly in the works of major writers of the Enlightenment, crucial new ideas were introduced, including the notion of universal rights, international rights, and natural rights—now generally called human rights. These rights became instrumental in securing freedoms from authoritarian religions or governments—for example, freedom of the press, freedom of religious expression, and freedom of commerce. (The older vernacular was the "rights of man.")

---

[3]*Superintendent of Belchertown State School v. Saikewicz*, 370 N.E.2d 417, 424 (Mass. 1977), citing, inter alia, *In re Quinlan*, 70 N.J. 10, 355 A.2d 647 (1976). Italics added.

These rights are alleged to be universally valid and independent of particular, historical human arrangements, by contrast to rights that are conferred within human institutions and practices at specific historical moments. Human rights are possessed inherently by being a human person, whether or not the rights are legally recognized in a society such as modern Afghanistan. These rights are often touted as inalienable and possessed equally by all persons.

The idea of natural or human rights grew up in philosophy around the influential social contract theories of Hugo Grotius, Thomas Hobbes, John Locke, and Jean Jacques Rousseau. These theories viewed government as justified by the consent of the governed and served to delimit legitimate government authority and intervention, so that subjects were protected against illegitimate intervention. Major eighteenth-century revolutionaries such as Thomas Jefferson and the authors of the French Declaration of the Rights of Man and Citizen embraced these theories and declared the truth of the natural rights and natural justice doctrines to be self-evident. These ideas became the background for justifying revolutionary activity when a state had violated universal rights, and they spawned the added layer of protection by rights found in the American Bill of Rights and the French Declaration of the Rights of Man (both 1789), which safeguarded natural rights by law.

These and many other landmark historical documents hold that certain kinds of actions and policies violate fundamental rights and are therefore not to be tolerated. For example, rules legitimating slavery are unacceptable in any possible "moral" framework. Slavery is inconsistent with morality itself; rights against such treatment rest on a cross-cultural moral norm that no culture can legitimately reverse whatever its traditions, culture, or religion.

However, even the mainstays of this tradition have not always agreed on *which* rights are natural. Locke maintained that the rights to life, liberty, and property are natural rights, whereas the framers of the United States Declaration of Independence held that the rights to life, liberty, and the pursuit of happiness form the core of natural rights. Authors of the French Declaration added rights to security and resistance to oppression, whereas Thomas Hobbes had focused first and foremost on the right of self-preservation. These authors shared many political goals in common, but their lists of rights range over considerably different territories.

Many philosophers are skeptical of the validity of the natural-rights theories in these philosophical and political traditions. In the nineteenth century Jeremy Bentham derided the natural-rights tradition as "nonsense upon stilts" because of the claim that rights exist prior to an established political community that confers the rights. Bentham saw claims of natural rights as wishful thinking. In the same century, Karl Marx argued that the idea of natural rights was the product not of a philosophically justified body of arguments but rather of particular historical circumstances that cried out for protections against brutal economic systems and governments. Like Bentham, Marx found natural rights to be political weapons, rather than eternal truths.

These issues will be addressed in several sections of this chapter. However, we begin with the general moral and political theory that has been most closely associated with the tradition of firm individual rights. The term "liberalism" is the label now generally used to refer to this tradition.

## LIBERALISM AND ITS COMMUNITARIAN CRITICS

### The Protection of Rights in Liberal Theory

Liberalism places the individual at the center of moral and political life and views the state as limited in the event of a conflict with individual rights (such as freedom of association, expression, and religion). The state's role is to protect and enforce basic moral and political rights, often called *civil rights*. This liberal tradition can be introduced for present purposes through some cardinal premises we have already encountered in the types of theory discussed in other chapters in this book, especially some features of utilitarian, Kantian, and Humean ethics.

What makes these theories jointly "liberal" is their commitment to what Mill defended as "individuality," to what Kant called "autonomy," and to the freedom from state and religious authority championed by Hume. Liberalism embodies an attitude of distrust toward use of the coercive power of the state (and other powerful social institutions) against the less powerful individual. The liberal tradition presupposes separate individuals with at least some opposed interests that come into contingent conflict, both with one another and with the community. In cases of conflict, some guide to our thinking about the community's legitimate role in their adjudication is needed. Rights are intended to provide the necessary guidance.

Liberals are particularly concerned about the violation of rights by government authorities, such as the stern measures taken against women that we encountered in the Taliban case. A liberal is not deterred by the fact that we might be called upon to make a judgment about a violation of rights in another culture. Although multiculturalism (as we studied it in Chapter 2) requires a certain tolerance of different ways of life, liberals insist that certain rights must be protected irrespective of cultural differences. In particular, forms of oppression against the vulnerable are illicit rights violations wherever they occur. This liberal point of view is defended in the following article by Joel Feinberg.

# *Liberalism and Dogmatism**

## Joel Feinberg

Liberalism would be more obviously plausible and easier to defend if it were meant to apply only to pluralistic secular societies like the United States and most of the other "First World" countries. Even without such a restriction,

*From Joel Feinberg, *The Moral Limits of Criminal Law, Vol. 4: Harmless Wrongdoing* (New York: Oxford University Press, 1988).

counterexamples that are situated in such societies would be the most telling since they would strike against liberalism in its home terrain where it could be presumed to be least vulnerable. A liberalism restricted to such societies, however, would be too modest. A more ambitious and significant liberalism would also include within its scope traditional homogeneous societies, both small (like Amish villages, and ethnic neighborhoods), and large (ethnically and racially homogeneous nations like Sweden and Japan and religiously uniform ones like Ireland and Iran). To attempt to subject such societies to the requirements of liberalism is definitely to swim against the current, for most of these societies have used their criminal law (or would use it if they could), often with popular support, to protect their traditional ways of life against individual nonconformity. And yet we must attempt to justify the imposition of liberalism even in these cases if our arguments are to achieve coherence, and if we are to avoid ending up with a doctrine which is plausible within a shrunken domain, but which in its diminished form would become an anemic, parochial, and ultimately trivial ideology.

Those who would confine liberalism to the pluralist societies of modern industrial nations, however, often justify this restriction of liberalism on liberal or liberal-like grounds. Three types of arguments are characteristically used by these modest liberals: the argument from liberal tolerance, the closely related condemnation of "cultural imperialism," and an application to *societies* of Mill's famous celebration of individual diversity. Let us take these in order. Tolerance of cultural differences is of course characteristic of liberalism historically. . . . The liberal need not extend his tolerance to the point of skeptical relativism, the denial that there are any rational grounds for affirming some cultural practices' superiority to others, though in respect to some aspects of culture, such relativism might be justified. The liberal need only insist that while some transcultural comparative judgments are possible in principle they are

very difficult to make in fact, and so he puts forward "the useful warning that because our moral knowledge is tenuous we ought to be very careful about imposing our moral beliefs on others."[1] Just as we expect Third World zealots to acknowledge the rationality *for us* of permitting a wide variety of modes of dress for men and women, foods of all kinds, and religious observances in diverse churches as well as religious laxity and indifference, so in all consistency we should acknowledge the rationality of *their* enforcement of sartorial uniformity (especially for women), and religious dietary laws, and universal daily public prayer. We liberals liberate "our" women; they cover up and isolate theirs. Just as we have a right to our liberal indulgences so they have a right to their unmixed traditions. They don't presume to judge us; we should show a similar respect for them. So the liberal-appearing argument goes.

Often the modest liberal supplements his plea for mutual respect and tolerance with the charge that the dogmatic liberal's critique of the legal enforcement of tradition in some Third World countries is just another form of Western cultural imperialism, like exporting television programs, perfumed soaps and luxury cars, and rock and roll, or sending missionaries to "convert the natives" to Christianity. These impositions are an illicit use of our superior economic muscle and show no respect for local cultural forms.

Finally, some "tolerant liberals" might even invoke John Stuart Mill's impressive arguments for "experiments in living"—with a twist—to support a

[1]James W. Nickel, *Making Sense of Human Rights* (Berkeley: University of California Press, 1987), p. 70.

worldwide diversity not only of religion and culture, but of political and economic regimes. Mill's original arguments,[2] of course, supported the experiments of groups of nonconforming individuals within a nation-state, not the political nonconformity of political states themselves. He argued in three ways for the tolerance of such experiments as utopian socialist communes, Eastern mystic settlements, religious villages, nudist camps, and so on. First of all, by allowing each individual to experiment among a great variety of alternatives in his efforts to discover what kind of life is good for him, we increase the likelihood of each discovering the life that best fits his own aptitudes and ideals, that is, which best fulfills his nature. Second, by putting alternative forms of group organization to the test, the experiments show the rest of us how these systems succeed or fail—valuable lessons for us all. Third, these experiments create a rich and harmonious diversity which is good in itself and pleasant to behold, but also, from our social point of view, prudent in the manner of a balanced portfolio of investments, or a diverse gene pool in protecting the species from epidemics. If tolerance of many living styles and forms of social organization produces these advantages within a state, why should it not be equally valuable when applied to the worldwide collection of nation-states themselves? If liberalism works for individuals within one nation, why should it not work equally for nations within one world? Tolerant liberalism would allow each nation to seek its own collective good in its own way, thus putting the different ways to the test to the benefit of us all, maximizing the likelihood of national self-fulfillment, creating a pleasing diversity to counter

what would otherwise be a deadening uniformity, and ensuring that the world community—"the human race"—does not put all its eggs in one basket, thus risking universal disaster. John Stuart Mill, if he reasoned in this way, would prefer a world in which some nations were organized according to Mill's own liberal principles while others followed the teachings of Lenin, Mussolini, Mao Tse-tung, and Khomeini, to a world in which all nations followed the principles of Mill. In short, he would want even liberalism "put to the test" of competition.

How should we reply to these arguments from our fellow liberals? The doctrine of personal sovereignty . . . essential to liberalism would not permit liberalism to be "put to the test" at the expense of sovereign individuals who can no more properly be the objects of political experiments than they can properly be the objects of medical experiments without their consent. The more dogmatic liberalism endorsed in this book absolutely requires a doctrine of human rights to act as a moral restraint on what governments may do to individuals whether by law (our subject) or by arbitrary action. If all of us Americans are blessed (or cursed) with personal sovereignty—the natural right of self-determination—how could it be that individual Iranians are not similarly endowed? Are we Americans (and British, French, German, Japanese, etc.) God's chosen peoples? On the contrary, . . . all individual human beings have these basic rights, and any state that suppresses its minorities by means of illiberal criminal laws and refuses to permit nonconforming conduct even when it is directly victimless and

[2]John Stuart Mill, *On Liberty,* chap. III.

discreet, violates those rights, whatever its own political and legal traditions may be. One must be free to be an atheist even in Ireland, to eat pork even in Israel, and to go unveiled even in Iran. In a way, the smaller and more unprotected the minority, the greater the injustice of the legal repression of autonomy. The rare dissenter bucks overwhelming social pressures even without legal coercion. When the state adds its powers to an already unequal contest, it becomes mere bully.

To the claim that the Western human-rights activists are the true bullies in virtue of their transmission of the liberal message along with their rock and roll music and television soap operas, the liberal has a ready reply. Not one jot less respect is shown for a nation's cultural traditions, its folkways and music, its religious faith, its family organization, its wedding and burial customs, and its traditional festivals and holidays, when the liberal shows equal respect for its sovereign individuals and condemns its political repression. One cannot rejoice in a hundred blooming flowers in the nations of the world when some of the "flowers" are liberal governments, and other are tools for terrorizing and subduing individuals, even when those political instruments are ancient and traditional in the country in question. Quite apart from this point, the dogmatic liberal might find that it is his more tolerant cousin who has the patronizing "imperial" attitude toward (say) the Third World theocracies. He too readily assumes that human rights have a place in our political culture but not in theirs. Thomas Scanlon takes up the charge from there:

> . . . this argument rests on the attribution to "them" of a unanimity that does not in fact exist. "They" are said to be different from us and to live by different rules. Such stereotypes are seldom accurate, and the attribution of unanimity is particularly implausible in the case of human rights violations. These [governmental] actions have victims who generally resent what is done to them and who would rarely concede that, because such behavior is common in their country, their tormentors are acting quite properly.[3]

Cultural and political traditions may vary greatly among the peoples of the world, and that is a good thing, but it does not follow that anyone enjoys repression, or should tolerate being prevented forcibly by his government from doing what he wants to do.

The argument, purportedly derived from Mill, from the advantages of diversity misconstrues the sorts of diversity a liberal ideology must treasure. Some kinds of cultural diversity might well be unlimited in their variety, the liberal maintains, but the diversity of kinds of *political* institutions must be limited by the very reasons that count against limits of other kinds. Even if limits to acceptable forms of political authority are adopted, there will still remain different languages and literature, different religions, different economic and political structures, different characteristic cultural styles. James Nickel's way of making the point is just right:

> Cultural diversity is an important value, I think, but it is not absolute nor does it rule out many of the changes involved in complying with human rights. One may see the value of preserving, say, the cultural and

[3]Thomas M. Scanlon, "Human Rights as a Neutral Concern," in Peter G. Brown and Douglas MacLean, eds., *Human Rights and U.S. Foreign Policy* (Lexington, Mass.: D.C. Heath, 1979), p. 88. As quoted by James W. Nickel, *Making Sense of Human Rights, op. cit.* (see n. 4), p. 72.

religious traditions of India without concluding that the Indian caste system should have been preserved. Cultures and value systems typically have many parts, and it is sometimes possible to preserve the best and most distinctive features while jettisoning the most repugnant—particularly when making the changes required for compliance with human rights. These rights have the behavior of governments as their central focus, and government practices are seldom central to the identity and persistance of a culture.[4]

The most comprehensive liberal ideal envisions a world community that is not only diverse in the kinds of countries that make it up but also diverse within each of these parts. But the pleasing character of that double diversity (diversity within parts and diversity between parts) is not further enhanced by a certain diversity of prevailing political moralities. A world in which socialist and capitalist nations coexist is benignly diverse. Even a world in which there is a division between poor-simple (pastoral, elemental) peoples and rich-complicated (industrial, neurotic) peoples has something to be said for it. But a world in which some parts permit diversity and others forbid it does not achieve the kind of overall diversity that Mill had in mind. A world that is half slave and half free is not thereby "pleasingly diverse."

Even in the most homogeneous cultures there will be some natural diversity, some of it derived from differences in basic temperament. In our own large and multiform land, there are many other forms of diversity with many more origins. But it is a serious mistake to insist that human beings acquire human rights only by membership in a political community of the relatively mixed-up kind. If anything, human beings need the protection of human rights more in the smaller and simpler homogeneous kinds of community. Years ago Ruth Benedict, in a study of four relatively simple "primitive civilizations," pointed out that because of the malleability of their natures most human beings can and do assume the behavior dictated by the prevailing norms of their society. This is not because the institutions of that society "reflect an ultimate and universal sanity," but only because people are, for the most part, "plastic to the moulding force of the society into which they are born." "They do not all, however, find it equally congenial, and those are favored and fortunate whose potentialities most nearly coincide with the type of behavior selected by their society."[5] The unfortunate ones whose natural proclivities are not favored by the prevalent expectations are then labeled "misfits" (or worse), even though their characters conform to other cultural patterns that prevail in other cultural groups. In a large pluralistic country every type of person can find subcommunities in which his own kind of character can find respect and dignity. But where diverse subcommunities have been abolished and only one prevalent character type is permitted by the state, then the acknowledgment of the human rights of endangered minorities becomes most urgent. From Ayatollah Khomeini's point of view, the inevitable nonconformists are gangrenous appendages on the body politic that must be surgically removed.[6] But from the liberal's point of view each misfit is a

---

[4]Nickel, *op. cit.* (see n. 4), p. 79.

[5]Ruth Benedict, *Patterns of Culture* (New York: Mentor Books, 1946), p. 235.
[6]*Supra,* Chap. 29, note 2.

real flesh and blood human being, harmlessly seeking his or her own fulfillment; not a gangrenous infection or a cancerous growth, rather a beauty mark.

Anyway, diversity keeps breaking out, Benedict's point about natural differences aside. The economy generates classes; overall size produces regional differences; more efficient transport mixes things up. Foreign influences get harder and harder to keep out. Some come from trade, some from television, some from new communications media. People do tend to become different unless ruthlessly kept the same. Efforts to join them all into one mold are a constant struggle against the odds. There is no danger, as the confused "tolerant liberal" fears, that restrictions on the political power to accomplish this homogenization will somehow diminish the world's overall diversity.

My conclusion is that if there is personal sovereignty anywhere, then it exists everywhere, in traditional societies as well as in modern pluralistic ones. Liberalism has long been associated with tolerance and caution, but about this point it must be brave enough to be dogmatic.

## THE COMMUNITARIAN REJECTION OF LIBERALISM

Several approaches in contemporary philosophy and political theory have little sympathy with a rights theory like Feinberg's that confers strong rights to individuals. These theories see everything fundamental in ethics as deriving from communal values, the common good, social goals, traditional practices, and the promotion of the cooperative virtues. Conventions, traditions, loyalties, and the social nature of life and institutions play a more prominent role in communitarianism than in any theories we have encountered in previous chapters. We will now discuss these so-called communitarian theories that reject both liberalism and strong individual rights.

Unfortunately, there is no systematic account of communitarianism that rivals the systematic theories in Mill, Kant, and other liberal philosophers. Contemporary communitarianism is usually analyzed in terms of a few key themes to emerge from a few key philosophers. The most prominent themes are the influence of society on individuals (by contrast to the alleged emphasis in theories like Kant's and Mill's on free individual choice) and the roots of values in communal history and practices (by contrast to an emphasis on basic rights of the individual). Key philosophers in this tradition are Alasdair MacIntyre (whose views we have already encountered in Chapters 2, 6), Michael Sandel, Charles Taylor, and Michael Walzer.

Communitarian arguments usually contain both normative components and descriptive components. Descriptively, communitarians seem to believe that their conception of the individual as culturally developed ("socially embedded") is a true conception of the reality of the human world, which reflects the cultural, historical, and linguistic constitution of individuals—unlike the contrasting liberal account of atomic individuals with individual rights. Normatively, the communitarian claim is that human affairs will go better if public, community-controlled values guide communal interactions and control individual lives. In some communitarian theories, the claim seems to be the still stronger one that conceptions of society developed in terms of individual rights are nonviable; society will founder if erected on an overdose of freedom and rights.

Much of what one *ought* to do in communitarian theories is determined by prevailing social practices, including the social roles assigned to or acquired by a person as a member of a community. Understanding a particular system of moral rules, then, requires an understanding of the community's history, a sense of communal life, and a conception of social welfare built on some conception of the good adopted in that community. (See MacIntyre's theory in Chapter 6.)

Liberalism seems to some communitarians to be a *repudiation* of the historical landmarks in moral and political philosophy that preceded it. One of the critical assumptions in the liberal theory is that the individual is not a creature of the state, someone to be molded or sacrificed without limit for the state's own purposes, or for the purposes and interests of other institutions or authorities to which the state itself must answer. Liberalism tends to emphasize the importance of protecting political and civil liberties and rights against political threats to liberty, especially coercive interventions of the state achieved through the criminalization of conduct or thought. Each type of liberal theory offers a range of protections for the individual against state powers, and—so communitarians insist—each also asserts that the state should neither reward nor penalize different conceptions of the good life held by individuals. Persons are free in liberalism to hold whatever conception they wish to hold, because they have rights to precisely this liberty of choice.

The liberal principle that the rights of individuals cannot legitimately be sacrificed for the good of the community has been a particular target of communitarian censure. These communitarian criticisms of liberal theories seem to come to the following: Liberalism (1) fails to appreciate the constructive role of the cooperative virtues and the political state in promoting values and creating the conditions of the good life, (2) fails to acknowledge shared goals and obligations that come not from freely made contracts among individuals but from communal ideals and responsibilities, and (3) fails to understand the human person as historically constituted by and embedded in communal life and social roles.

Every major communitarian thinker has contested the thesis of the priority of individual rights over the common good. Charles Taylor's challenge is perhaps the most straightforward. He has argued that all conceptions of the rights of individuals already contain within their fabric some conception of the individual and social good, at least in the form of the good of moral agency and the good of human associations and friendship. The liberal's claim of the priority of right is itself, from this perspective, premised on a conception of the human good (the good of autonomous moral agency, in particular).

Taylor argues that the type of autonomy valued by liberals cannot be developed in the absence of family and other community structures. However, liberalism's emphasis on individual rights makes no provision for the development and maintenance of the necessary communities, and instead views individuals as isolated atoms existing independently of one another.

In the following selection, Charles Taylor provides a broad schematic argument in defense of communitarian ideals.

# *Atomism**

## Charles Taylor

The term "atomism" is used loosely to characterize the doctrines of social contract theory which arose in the seventeenth century and also successor doctrines which may not have made use of the notion of social contract but which inherited a vision of society as in some sense constituted by individuals for the fulfilment of ends which were primarily individual. Certain forms of utilitarianism are successor doctrines in this sense. The term is also applied to contemporary doctrines which hark back to social contract theory, or which try to defend in some sense the priority of the individual and his rights over society, or which present a purely instrumental view of society. . . .

Perhaps I am dealing with the wrong term. But there is a central issue in political theory which is eminently worth getting at under some description. And perhaps the best way of getting at it is this: what I am calling atomist doctrines underlie the seventeenth-century revolution in the terms of normative discourse, which we associate with the names of Hobbes and Locke.

These writers, and others who presented social contract views, have left us a legacy of political thinking in which the notion of rights plays a central part in the justification of political structures and action. The central doctrine of this tradition is an affirmation of what we could call the primacy of rights.

Theories which assert the primacy of rights are those which take as the fundamental, or at least a fundamental, principle of their political theory the ascription of certain rights to individuals and which deny the same status to a principle of belonging or obligation, i.e., a principle which states our obligation as men to belong to or sustain society, or a society of a certain type, or to obey authority or an authority of a certain type. Primacy-of-right theories in other words accept a principle ascribing rights to men as binding unconditionally, binding, that is, on men as such. But they do not accept as similarly unconditional a principle of belonging or obligation. Rather our obligation to belong to or sustain a society, or to obey its authorities, is seen as derivative, as laid on us conditionally, through our consent, or through its being to our advantage. The obligation to belong is derived in certain conditions from the more fundamental principle which ascribes rights.

The paradigm of primacy-of-right theories is plainly that of Locke. But there are contemporary theories of this kind, one of the best known in recent years being that of Robert Nozick. Nozick too makes the assertion of rights to individuals fundamental and then proceeds to discuss whether and in what conditions we can legitimately demand obedience to a state. . . .

Primacy-of-right theories have been one of the formative influences on modern political consciousness. Thus arguments like that of Nozick have at least a surface plausibility for our contemporaries and sometimes considerably

*From Charles Taylor, "Atomism," in Alkis Kontos, ed., *Powers, Possessions and Freedom* (Toronto: University of Toronto Press, 1979).

more. At the very least, opponents are brought up short, and have to ponder how to meet the claims of an argument, which reaches conclusions about political obedience which lie far outside the common sense of our society; and this because the starting point in individual rights has an undeniable *prima facie* force for us.

This is striking because it would not always have been so. In an earlier phase of Western civilization, of course, not to speak of other civilizations, these arguments would have seemed wildly eccentric and implausible. The very idea of starting an argument whose foundation was the rights of the individual would have been strange and puzzling—about as puzzling as if I were to start with the premise that the Queen rules by divine right. You might not dismiss what I said out of hand, but you would expect that I should at least have the sense to start with some less contenious premise and argue up to divine right, not take it as my starting point.

Why do we even begin to find it reasonable to start a political theory with an assertion of individual rights and to give these primacy? I want to argue that the answer to this question lies in the hold on us of what I have called atomism. Atomism represents a view about human nature and the human condition which (among other things) makes a doctrine of the primacy of rights plausible; or to put it negatively, it is a view in the absence of which this doctrine is suspect to the point of being virtually untenable.

How can we formulate this view? Perhaps the best way is to borrow the terms of the opposed thesis—the view that man is a social animal. One of the most influential formulations of this view is Aristotle's. He puts the point in terms of the notion of self-sufficiency (*autarkeia*). Man is a social animal, indeed a political animal, because he is not self-sufficient alone, and in an important sense is not self-sufficient outside a polis. Borrowing this term then we could say that atomism affirms the self-sufficiency of man alone or, if you prefer, of the individual. . . .

The kind of freedom valued by the protagonists of the primacy of rights, and indeed by many others of us as well, is a freedom by which men are capable of conceiving alternatives and arriving at a definition of what they really want, as well as discerning what commands their adherence or their allegiance. This kind of freedom is unavailable to one whose sympathies and horizons are so narrow that he can conceive only one way of life, for whom indeed the very notion of a way of life which is *his* as against everyone's has no sense. Nor is it available to one who is riveted by fear of the unknown to one familiar life-form, or who has been so formed in suspicion and hate of outsiders that he can never put himself in their place. Moreover, this capacity to conceive alternatives must not only be available for the less important choices of one's life. The greatest bigot or the narrowest xenophobe can ponder whether to have Dover sole or Wiener schnitzel for dinner. What is truly important is that one be able to exercise autonomy in the basic issues of life, in one's most important commitments.

Now, it is very dubious whether the developed capacity for this kind of autonomy can arise simply within the family. Of course, men may learn, and perhaps in part must learn, this from those close to them. But my question is whether this kind of capacity can develop within the compass of a single family. Surely it is something which only develops within an entire civilization. Think of the developments of art, philosophy, theology, science, of the evolving practices of politics and social organization, which have contributed to the historic birth of this aspiration to freedom, to making this ideal of autonomy a comprehensible goal men can aim at—something which is in their universe of potential aspiration (and it is not yet so for all men, and may never be).

But this civilization was not only necessary for the genesis of freedom. How could successive generations discover what it is to be an autonomous agent, to have one's own way of feeling, of acting, of expression, which cannot be simply derived from authoritative models? This is an identity, a way of understanding themselves, which men are not born with. They have to acquire it. And they do not in every society; nor do they all successfully come to terms with it in ours. But how can they acquire it unless it is implicit in at least some of their common practices, in the ways that they recognize and treat each other in their common life (for instance, in the acknowledgment of certain rights), or in the manner in which they deliberate with or address each other, or engage in economic exchange, or in some mode of public recognition of individuality and the worth of autonomy?

Thus we live in a world in which there is such a thing as public debate about moral and political questions and other basic issues. We constantly forget how remarkable that is, how it did not have to be so, and may one day no longer be so. What would happen to our capacity to be free agents if this debate should die away, or if the more specialized debate among intellectuals who attempt to define and clarify the alternatives facing us should also cease, or if the attempts to bring the culture of the past to life again as well as the drives to cultural innovation were to fall off? What would there be left to choose between? And if the atrophy went beyond a certain point, could we speak of choice at all? How long would we go on understanding what autonomous choice was? Again, what would happen if our legal culture were not constantly sustained by a contact with our traditions of the rule of law and a confrontation with our contemporary moral institutions? Would we have as sure a grasp of what the rule of law and the defence of rights required?

In other words, the free individual or autonomous moral agent can only achieve and maintain his identity in a certain type of culture, some of whose facets and activities I have briefly referred to. But these and others of the same significance don't come into existence spontaneously each successive instant. They are carried on in institutions and associations which require stability and continuity and frequently also support from society as a whole—almost always the moral support of being commonly recognized as important but frequently also considerable material support. These bearers of our culture include museums, symphony orchestras, universities, laboratories, political parties, law courts, representative assemblies, newspapers, publishing houses, television stations, and so on. And I have to mention also the mundane elements of infrastructure without which we couldn't carry on these higher activities: buildings, railroads, sewage plants, power grids, and so on. Thus the requirement of a living and varied culture is also the requirement of a complex and integrated society, which is willing and able to support all these institutions.

I am arguing that the free individual of the West is only what he is by virtue of the whole society and civilization which brought him to be and which nourishes him; that our families can only form us up to this capacity and these aspirations because they are set in this civilization; and that a family alone outside of this context—the real old patriarchal family—was a quite different animal which never tended to develop these horizons. And I want to claim finally that all this creates a significant obligation to belong for whoever would affirm the value of this freedom; this includes all those who want to assert rights either to this freedom or for its sake. . . .

The crucial point here is this: since the free individual can only maintain his identity within a society/culture of a certain kind, he has to be concerned about the shape of this society/culture as a whole. He cannot, following the libertarian anarchist model that Nozick sketched,[1] be concerned purely with his individual choices and the associations formed from such choices to the neglect of the matrix in which such choices can be open or closed, rich or meagre. It is important to him that certain activities and institutions flourish in society. It is even of importance to him what the moral tone of the whole society is—shocking as it may be to libertarians to raise this issue—because freedom and individual diversity can only flourish in

a society where there is a general recognition of their worth. . . .

Thus the thesis just sketched about the social conditions of freedom is based on the notion, first, that developed freedom requires a certain understanding of self, one in which the aspirations to autonomy and self-direction become conceivable; and second, that this self-understanding is not something we can sustain on our own, but that our identity is always partly defined in conversation with others or through the common understanding which underlies the practices of our society. The thesis is that the identity of the autonomous, self-determining individual requires a social matrix, one for instance which through a series of practices recognizes the right to autonomous decision and which calls for the individual having a voice in deliberation about public action.

The issue between the atomists and their opponents therefore goes deep; it touches the nature of freedom, and beyond this what it is to be a human subject; what is human identity, and how it is defined and sustained. It is not surprising therefore that the two sides talk past each other. For atomists the talk about identity and its conditions in social practice seems impossibly abstruse and speculative. They would rather found themselves on the clear and distinct intuition which we all share (all of us in this society, that is) about human rights.

For non-atomists, however, this very confidence in their starting point is a kind of blindness, a delusion of self-sufficiency which prevents them from seeing that the free individual, the bearer of rights, can only assume this identity thanks to his relationship to a developed liberal civilization; that there is an absurdity in placing this subject in

[1][See Chapters 4 and 10 in the present text.]

a state of nature where he could never attain this identity and hence never create by contract a society which respects it. Rather, the free individual who affirms himself as such *already* has an obligation to complete, restore, or sustain the society within which this identity is possible. . . .

Many liberals recognize that Taylor has reasonable concerns about the legitimacy of community control, but they do not agree that Taylor has understood the true commitments of liberalism. They think that communitarians such as Taylor present us with two false dichotomies: (1) either liberal accounts of rights and justice have priority or the communal good has priority, and (2) either radical autonomy in decision-making is protected or communal determination of social goals is protected against the individual. Liberals think that a more accurate picture is that we inherit various social roles and goals from traditions. We then critique, adjust, and attempt to improve our beliefs over time through free discussion and collective arrangements. Individuals and groups alike progressively interpret, revise, and sometimes even replace traditions with new conceptions that adjust and foster community values.

Feinberg has argued that this liberal outlook is entirely compatible with communal interests: "It is impossible to think of human beings except as part of ongoing communities, defined by reciprocal bonds of obligation, common traditions, and institutions. . . . The ideal [in liberals' accounts] of the autonomous person is that of an authentic individual whose self-determination is as complete as is consistent with the requirement that he is, of course, a member of a community."[4] Liberals such as Feinberg have found several other shortcomings in communitarianism, especially the paucity of space left in these theories for individual rights. In the following selection, Jeremy Waldron suggests that communitarians fail to appreciate the absolutely central role that rights play in protecting both individual and social interests:

# *When Justice Replaces Affection: The Need for Rights**

Jeremy Waldron

Why do individuals need rights? In a world crying out for a greater emphasis on fraternity and communal responsibility in social life, what is the point of an institution that legitimates the making of querulous and adversarial claims by individuals against their fellows? . . .

*From Jeremy Waldron, "When Justice Replaces Affection: The Need for Rights," *Harvard Journal of Law & Public Policy*, **11** (Summer 1988): 625–41.

[4]Joel Feinberg, *Harm to Self,* in *The Moral Limits of the Criminal Law* (New York: Oxford University Press, 1986), vol. 3, p. 47.

[Consider the example of marriage:] Claims of right should have little part to play in the context of a normal loving marriage. If we hear one partner complaining to the other about a denial or withdrawal of conjugal *rights,* we know that something has already gone wrong with the interplay of desire and affection between the partners. The same would be true if people started talking about their *right* to a partner's fidelity, their *right* to be freed from child-care or domestic chores once in a while, their equal *right* to pursue a career, their *right* to draw equally on the family income, and so on. In each case, the substance of the claim may be indispensable for a happy and loving marriage in the modern world. But it is its presentation *as a claim*—that is, as an entitlement that one party presses peremptorily, querulously, and adversarially against the other—that would lead to our misgivings. We would certainly look for all these things in a marriage, but we would hope to see them upheld and conceded, not as matters of right, but as the natural outcome of the most intimate mutual concern and respect brought to bear by the partners on the common problems that they face. Even if rights like these were acknowledged as the ground-rules of the relationship in some sort of formal agreement drawn up by the partners, there would still be something unpleasant about their *asserting* them as rights or, as the phrase goes, *"standing on their rights"* in the normal functioning of the relationship. Such behavior would be seen as a way of blocking and preventing warmth and intimacy, replacing relatively unbounded and immediate care and sensitivity with rigid and abstract formulas of justice.

The point can be generalized: To stand on one's rights is to distance oneself from those to whom the claim is made; it is to announce, so to speak, an opening of hostilities; and it is to acknowledge that other warmer bonds of kinship, affection, and intimacy can no longer hold. . . .

Though marriage is certainly more than a matter of rights and correlative duties, and though one will not expect to hear claims of right in a happily functioning marriage, nevertheless the strength and security of the marriage commitment in the modern world depends in part on there being an array of legalistic rights and duties that the partners know they can fall back on, if ever their mutual affection fades. . . .

I want to explore this idea against the background of some criticisms that have been made of rights-based liberalism. In recent years, liberal theories have come under attack from socialists and communitarians for their implausible suggestion that the bonds of social life should be thought of as constituted primarily by the rights and rights-based relations of initially atomistic individuals. I will consider how much of that attack would be mitigated or refuted if liberals were to concede that the structure of rights is not constitutive of social life, but instead to be understood as a position of fall-back and security in case other constituent elements of social relations ever come apart. To go back to the marriage example, I will suggest that there is a need for an array of formal and legalistic rights and duties, not to constitute the affective bond, but to provide each person with secure knowledge of what she can count on in the unhappy event that there turns out to be no other basis for her dealings with her erstwhile partner in the relationship. The importance of rights ought to be much easier to defend from this somewhat less inflated position.

But the argument is not merely a strategic retreat for liberals. Liberals are entitled to ask their communitarian critics how this important function of security is to be performed in a community that repudiates rights and legalism, and under the auspices of a theory that gives individual rights no part to play at all. Is it to be supposed that the intimate and affective relations that characterize various forms of community will never come apart, that affections will never change, and that people will never feel the urge to exit from some relationships and initiate others? If so, communitarianism in the modern world presents itself as naive or desperately dangerous, and probably both. . . .

I chose marriage as my starting point because I wanted to illustrate two things. The first is the claim I have already outlined. The function of matrimonial law, with its contractual rules and formulas and rigid rights and duties, is not necessarily to constitute the marriage bond; its function is to provide a basis on which affective ties can be converted into legal responsibilities in the unhappy situation where affection can no longer be guaranteed.

But I also want to develop a second point. The structure of impersonal rules and rights not only provides a background guarantee; it also furnishes a basis on which people can act to initiate *new* relations with other people even from a position of alienation from the affective bonds of existing attachments and community. Impersonal rules and rights provide a basis for new beginnings and for moral initiatives which challenge existing affections, driving them in new directions or along lines that might seem uncomfortable or challenging to well-worn traditional folkways. Such initiatives may be valued on social as well as individual grounds: Not only do they make life bearable for alienated individuals by allowing them to start out in new directions, but they also provide a dynamic for social progress by challenging the existing types of relationships with new ones. . . .

I want to illustrate this with an example. At a superficial level, Shakespeare's *Romeo and Juliet* is a noble and lamentable tragedy of star-crossed "death-marked" love: The fates bring the lovers together and, at the end, it is the fates who cruelly divide them. But *Romeo and Juliet* can also be read as a deeper text about the dangers that beset a new and unforeseen social initiative—in this case a romantic initiative—in circumstances where the only available structures for social action are those embedded in the affections and disaffections of the existing community. The bonds which tie together the members of the respective clans of Capulet and Montague, and which divide the clans from one another, are such as to rule out of the question the union that the young lovers seek. Driven by their need for each other, Juliet and Romeo seek to create a marriage for themselves outside those inhibiting bonds.

The tragedy is that this cannot reliably be done in that social world, for there is no framework of public or impersonal law, standing apart from communal attachments, of which people can avail themselves in circumstances like these. Even the apparent voice of order in the play—Prince Escalus—is presented as head of a third clan and himself deeply implicated in the disaffection between Capulet and Montague. So the lovers have to take their chances in a world outside the public realm. The arrangements they make are of necessity covert and clandestine. There is no public and hence no visible and reliable way of coordinating actions and expectations. There is no way of counting on any but their own resources in a world where formally and publicly their relationship does not exist. Secret letters go astray. Another marriage is contracted for Juliet because it is thought this one did not exist. Communications break down, actions are misread, and timing fails as the lovers try to act in concert in a world that provides no structure or landmarks for co-ordination. Their only hope of success is for Juliet to assume "the form of death" to the social world in which she was brought up, and to resurrect herself in the giddy space of a world beyond the city walls. . . .

There is nothing outside the structures of their warring clans that these two can rely on—no points of salience, no common framework of expectations, and no public knowledge—just their own meagre resources and those of their understandably pusillanimous allies. Man is a social animal; only a god can live outside a state. . . .

What this implies is that it is important for there to be a structure of rights that people can count on for organizing their lives, a structure which stands somewhat apart from communal or affective attachments and which can be relied on to survive as a basis for action no matter what happens to those attachments. . . .

I have used the marriage example to illustrate these points, but I do not want to give the impression that marriage is my sole concern. There are other areas of law and politics that can be used to make related points about the indispensability of individual rights.

One is the area of welfare rights. It is common to hear laments about the loss of face-to-face charity and caring, whether by individuals or in family groups, and its replacement in modern society by more impersonal systems of welfare agencies and formalized welfare entitlements. Certainly, there is a very important debate to be had about the nature and extent of our provision for need in society—one that I cannot go into here. But it may be worth pointing out why the replacement of face-to-face caring by more impersonal structures is not altogether the disaster that some people make it out to be.

Consider care for the elderly. Age brings with it a certain amount of dependence: As one gets older, one's capacity to secure an income diminishes while one's needs increase. There have been societies, perhaps ours in an earlier age, or China, both now and in the past, where the old have been able to count on the support of their adult children as their needs increase and their capacities diminish. That mode of caring strikes us as an attractive one, for it is based on ties of kinship, affection, and love, and it reciprocates in an almost symmetrical way the care that the parent once lavished on her children.

Moreover, it has the advantage of being personal: The care is between this particular old person and her children (who can be sensitive to the detail of her needs), rather than between old people and young people in general. Still, there are good reasons in the modern world why many old people feel less than confident about relying on their children's support. One problem is demographic:

Even in kin-oriented societies such as China, there are proportionately fewer working adults to support an increasing population of the aged. But other problems go deeper into modern life. People's lives and careers are complex, shifting, and often risky and demanding. They cannot always guarantee a secure base for themselves, let alone provide an assurance of security for their parents. And people are torn by other motives in modern life which, though not intrinsically hostile to the provision of this care, make it somewhat less certain that this will be something they necessarily want to do. . . .

Instead, we have opted for less personal, less affective modes of care. People are encouraged to purchase an income for their old age in the marketplace, so they can rely on a pension check from a finance house even if they cannot rely on the warm support of their children. And, as a fall-back position, the impersonal agencies of the state guarantee an income, either to all the elderly, or to those who have not made or have not been able to make impersonal provision for themselves. Thus, although we may not care for them on a face-to-face basis, we both provide impersonal structures to enable them to care for themselves, and respond collectively and impersonally as a society to the rights that they have to our support. . . .

A similar analysis is possible in the area of market relations—the area that liberals and their critics see as the domain *par excellence* of individual rights. . . . At first sight, it is tempting, to say about markets, not what we have said so far about rights—that they involve fallback positions for social relations constituted by affection or community—but rather that markets involve an area of social relations that *is* actually constituted by structures of contract and individual right, an area in which there is no prominent component of affection or community at all. We know, of course, that this is sociologically naive: A market cannot exist without an ethic of fidelity and without some underpinning for its property entitlements. But still, the ethics, the ideology, and the force that make markets possible are not much more than what is presupposed by the idea of rights anyway, and the point is that they do not necessarily include any of the more robust and substantial ideas and affections associated in the modern mind with the idea of community.

Certainly the higher levels of the capitalist market—secondary capital markets, commodity markets, international trade and so on—have this character of being mainly rights-constituted (though even there the network of individual rights is supplemented by more or less rigid codes of professional honor among those who trade in them). Similarly, in more mundane markets, we buy and sell in department stores with little more to bond us to our market partners than reciprocal self-interest and the laws of contract.

Waldron's point is not to contest the importance of communities. Rather, he argues that rights are necessary in communities both to enable individuals to safely live in liberal communities and to protect individuals from oppressive communities. Liberals like Waldron remind their communitarian critics that not all communities are morally decent. For example, liberals maintain that the type of community imposed on the women of Afghanistan by the Taliban is an abomination. To claim that this community helps women lead virtuous lives is to misunderstand what is morally virtuous. Communities are necessary for healthy human development, but not all communities contribute to this goal. When communities themselves become oppressive, rights become all the more important (see the essay by Susan Moller Okin below).

## RIGHTS AGAINST OPPRESSION

Among the group of rights now generally mentioned by liberals are rights against oppression. Many vulnerable groups such as political dissidents and ethnic minorities have been the subject of treatises that defend a range of rights against oppression. In recent decades, several writers have carefully investigated the oppression of women and the importance of rights in contexts of sexual discrimination. In this section we will look especially closely at this problem and how feminists and liberal defenders of rights view these problems.

As the Taliban case dramatically illustrates, women continue to be denied even basic human rights in many parts of the world. In various societies women may be subjected to surgery without consent, beaten by their husbands or fathers, sold as wives or sold into slavery, and generally denied the economic, political, and social opportunities open to men. These rights-violations may be ignored or neglected even in liberal societies committed to universal human rights. Many nations that are signatories to the Universal Declaration of Human Rights do not vigorously protect women's basic human rights, or at least have a narrow vision of what those rights entail. When complaints are raised, as by the women affected in the Taliban case, governments often claim that they are treating women in accord with their cultural and religious traditions. They also maintain that attempts by strangers to press for rights of women are nothing less than "cultural imperialism." Because they reject such imperialism, they defend standards that are "culturally relevant" or "culturally sensitive," thereby rejecting the transcultural applicability of competing rights standards.

The charge of "cultural imperialism" stems from hundreds of years of western political and economic domination over many parts of the world. During this period western nations forcibly imposed their cultures, languages, and political systems on other peoples. Westerners were often quite blunt about the superiority of their culture, and often about their "duty" to impose it on the rest of the world. This duty has been sarcastically referred to as "the white man's burden." Not only did the colonial powers of this ilk show little respect for local culture and traditions, but the systems they imposed often worked to benefit the colonial power while harming the people in the colonies.

Many people in nonwestern nations worry that current talk of universal human rights is a guise for more of the same. They see western efforts to safeguard such rights as a strategy designed to destroy other cultures and force them to adopt western political and economic policies that will enrich the west at their expense. They maintain that the west talks of human rights when it has other goals at stake, but ignores such issues when dealing with rights-impoverished, pro-western governments such as Saudi Arabia.

Many people opposed to the concept of universal rights also point out that the western experiment with extreme individualism has lead to social problems such as high rates of murder, divorce, and drug abuse—a point made by several communitarians. Even if universal rights make sense in multiethnic, pluralistic western societies, such solutions will not necessarily work well in other cultural contexts.

Despite these objections, many people in both western and nonwestern nations insist that universal human rights are important and must be protected. They hold that cultural difference should not be allowed to obscure the injustice of oppression. In the following selection, Susan Okin argues that we need to recognize that women are being denied human rights and that when this fact is recognized, the inadequacy of cultural and religious defenses becomes apparent.[5]

# Feminism, Women's Human Rights, and Cultural Differences*

## Susan Moller Okin

The recognition of women's rights as human rights has been taking place on the global stage—from the grassroots to the international conference levels—in the last two decades. This has required considerable rethinking of human rights.

Because some of women's most basic rights—to freedom of movement and to work outside of the home, and to bodily integrity and freedom from violence—have been very much in the international news lately, I shall refer to these examples fairly often. But by doing this I do not mean to downplay the importance of other crucial rights, such as rights to health care, to an adequate standard of living, and so on.

*Hypatia*, vol. 13, no. 2 (Spring 1998) © by Susan Moller Okin

From the beginning of the post-World War II human rights movement, women have been formally included as holders of human rights. The Universal Declaration of Human Rights (1948) and many subsequent declarations, including the two United Nations International Covenants, that on Economic, Social and Cultural Rights (UNICESCR) and that on Civil and Political Rights (UNICCPR) proclaim the equal rights of human beings without regard to their sex. In practice, though, women are discriminated against in all of the world's countries, both in differing and in similar ways, and to a widely varying extent. Moreover, the grounds for this distinction have often been, and still are in many parts of the world (in some cultural or religious groups in all

[5]For more information about the living conditions of women in various parts of the world, as discussed by Okin, see Martha Nussbaum and Jonathan Glover, eds., *Women, Culture, and Development* (Oxford, England: Oxford University Press, 1995).

countries), seen as far more natural, inevitable, and benign than other grounds for distinction that human rights declarations prohibit—such as race, religion, or political opinion. Indeed, discrimination on the grounds of sex is frequently justified as being in accordance with many of the cultures—including religious aspects of these cultures—practiced in the world today.

It now seems quite startling that the Universal Declaration of Human Rights of 1948 should have so clearly repudiated distinctions of sex, given that there was not a country in the world at that time whose laws did not routinely make distinctions of sex, often on matters of basic rights. France and Italy had only just enfranchised women, and the Swiss did not do so (in national elections) until 1973. In most countries, sex discrimination in employment, family law, and many other areas of life remained routine for many years to come, and in many countries, violations of women's basic human rights are still commonplace. . . . Nevertheless, the vast gap between declarations of rights and actual practice turns out to be a common pattern. This could make one quite cynical; for, as a few examples cited later will show, even declarations explicitly aimed at women's rights—such as the Universal Declaration of Women's Rights (1967) and the Convention on the Elimination of All Forms of Discrimination Against Women, or CEDAW (1979)—have been signed and even ratified by governments of countries whose laws or accepted practices are far from fulfilling the provisions of these conventions. . . .

Why was it necessary to rethink human rights—as it was—in order to address many important women's rights?

Basically, because both the early conception of "the rights of man" in the seventeenth century and the original conception of international "human rights" in the mid-twentieth century were formulated with male household heads in mind. They were conceived as rights of such individuals against each other and, especially, against the governments under which they lived. It was generally recognized that there existed a sphere of privacy, protected by rights from outside intrusion, but not necessarily governed internally in accordance with the rights of its members. There can be little doubt that both Locke and his contemporaries and the framers of the Universal Declaration had male household heads foremost in mind when thinking about those who were to hold the "natural" and the "human" rights they respectively argued for and proclaimed. . . .

[E]xisting theories, compilations, and prioritizations of human rights have been constructed after a male model. When women's life experiences are taken equally into account, these theories, compilations, and prioritizations change significantly. Examples of issues that come to the fore, instead of being virtually ignored, include rape (including marital rape and rape during war), domestic violence, reproductive freedom, the valuation of childcare and other domestic labor as work, and unequal opportunity for women and girls in education, employment, housing, credit, and health care. The aim has been—and it has largely been achieved, by the Vienna Human Rights Conference and then further by the Fourth World Conference on Women in Beijing—to incorporate into the center of the discourse of human rights issues that are often matters of life and death for women (and for children). . . .

Some generally recognized human rights abuses have specifically gender-related forms that were not typically recognized as human rights abuses. Frequently, these abuses are perpetrated by more powerful family members against less powerful ones. For example, slavery is generally recognized as a fundamental violation of human rights. But parents' giving their daughter in marriage in exchange for money or even selling her to a pimp has not typically been seen as an instance of slavery. If a husband pays a bride price for his wife or marries her without her adult consent; if he confines her to their home, forbids her to work for pay, or appropriates her wages; if he beats her for disobedience or mishap; these manifestations of slavery would not be recognized as violations of human rights in many parts of the world. In some parts, indeed, most of these acts would be regarded as quite within the limits of normal, culturally appropriate behavior in parents or husbands. Also, there was little acknowledgement until recently of women's particular vulnerability to poverty and need for basic social services, such as health care, because of both their biological reproductive capacity and their assumption, in virtually all societies, of greater responsibility for children.

Even most human rights activists, until very recently, have been unwilling to recognize many culturally sanctioned abuses and instances of neglect of women as serious violations of human rights. Recently, though, especially over the last decade, this perception has been very strongly challenged. For example,

it took until 1995 in Beijing for the international community to recognize women's right to say no to sexual intercourse. . . .

Those seeking to establish women's rights as human rights also point out that much earlier human rights thinking focuses on *governments* as violators of human rights. . . .

But whereas governments can often affect, and act to reduce or try to eliminate, many violations of women's human rights, the violations themselves are much more likely to be carried out by individual men (and sometimes women, too). Part of the reason for the "invisibility" of gender-based violations has been the neglect in human rights talk of the private or domestic sphere. For it is in this sphere that great numbers of the world's women live most (in some cases, virtually all) of their lives, and in which vast numbers of violations of women's human rights take place. . . .

This situation of private rights violations is exacerbated by the fact that "respecting cultural differences" has increasingly become a euphemism for restricting or denying women's human rights. As feminist activist-scholars have been making clear, the relevance and even the sanctity of "cultural practices" is most often claimed when issues of sexuality, marriage, reproduction, inheritance, and power over children are concerned (issues that play a larger part in most women's lives than they do in most men's). And this often happens in contexts where traditions or rules of that same culture or religion are *not* called on in other areas of life, such as commerce or crime. . . . In India, for example, partly because of the history of violent religious intolerance, this distinction is built into the formal frame-work of the state; the different religious communities enforce their own "per-sonal laws," and there is no uniform civil code of family law. This can have grave consequences for women, who are differently (albeit usually unfairly) treated in divorce, and in custody and inheritance issues, depending on which religious group they belong to.

It is important to note, in this context, that the rise and the growth in political power of religious fundamentalism in many parts of the world are closely re-lated to rejection of the imposition of "Western" or "white" culture and ideas. Women's freedom and equality are often understood as clear symbols of Western values, in contrast to which and in reac-tion against which religious, conserva-tive, or nationalist movements define themselves. . . .

The continuing and rising influence of cultural or religious justifications for women's inequality is one impor-tant reason why it is so significant for women's rights to be recognized as hu-man rights. Many people fail to perceive what or how big the problems are, and many serious inequalities between the sexes are still regarded by many people as invisible, insignificant, natural, or culturally appropriate. This is true of some people in positions of power both inside and outside the cultures in which some of the most obvious and egregious violations of women's basic rights are taking place. For example, in Afghan-istan in the fall of 1996, when the Tali-ban regime closed girls' schools, denied all women the right to go to work or to leave their homes without being com-pletely covered up (rules enforced partly by beatings of those who broke them, by Taliban adolescent thugs), the (male) medical director of a hospital in Kabul

said (and was regarded by *New York Times* reporter John F. Burns, as "typi-cal" in saying) that the restrictions placed on women were "a small price to pay for the peace" that the Taliban vic-tory had secured. Burns himself asked whether Amnesty Internationals's de-scription of the situation as "a reign of terror" might not be "exaggerated" (*New York Times* 1996a).

Also in the fall of 1996, government officials in the Ivory Coast, when asked about the practice of clitoridectomy, were reported as conceding the "evils of genital cutting," or female genital muti-lation, adding that, although they had a plan to educate people about the con-sequences of that practice, they had no budget or staff. The U.S. Embassy spokesman in Abidjan said, "it's a mat-ter for local society to determine the extent to which these practices are to be tolerated." He was outdone in his cava-lierness toward the girls and women harmed by the practice only by the French embassy spokesman, who said, "this is a marginal problem." Then, per-haps thinking again, this person added, "it's important, but to feed people is probably more important" (*New York Times* 1996b).

Such reactions shed some light on why it is important to fight the struggle for women's rights as a human rights struggle. It makes it *more difficult* for the old double standard, which obvi-ously is still alive and well, to continue to convince people. It is difficult to imagine reactions similar to those just mentioned, to a situation in which all the men living under a given regime were kept under virtual house arrest. It is even more difficult to imagine such mild re-actions to a sexual custom in which a man, in order to become marriageable and therefore able to survive economically, were allowed to ejaculate some sperm to be saved so that he could still reproduce, and then were pinned down by four or five people in order for his penis to be cut off with a knife. But this *would be* the closest male equivalent to female genital mutilation which, in its least invasive commonly practiced form, involves the removal of the clitoris, removing with it the possibility of female sexual satisfaction. These are the kinds of parallels that become entirety plausible, once one draws attention to wrongs done to women as violations of human rights. . . .

One reaction to this might be to say: So what difference does it make to recognize abuses of women as human rights violations? My answer is that . . . it enables the international community to put these issues unambiguously on the table. Most governments do not like to be international pariahs, to have the eyes of the world focus on them only for their worst practices or their failure to prevent practices harmful to women and children. It has been clear from some of the recent news reports that ethnic and

religious groups, too, can develop the same distaste for being seen as condoning serious harms done to women. Not surprisingly, Muslims in many countries—and even the governments of countries with strict Islamic laws—have distanced themselves from the particularly brutal fundamentalist types of behavior that the Taliban regime in Afghanistan has tried to justify as being in accordance with "Muslim principles."

## References

*New York Times.* 1995. Women's meeting agrees on a right to say no to sex. 11 September.
———. 1996a. Walled in, shrouded and angry in Afghanistan. 4 October.
———. 1996b. African ritual pain: Genital cutting. 5 October.
———. 1996c. New law bans genital cutting in United States. 10 October.
United Nations. 1948. *Universal Declaration of Human Rights.* G.A. Res. 217A(III), U.N. Doc. A/810. Adopted December 10, 1948.

Okin has forcefully maintained that more attention needs to be paid to violations of women's human rights committed under the guise of tradition, culture, or religion. Practices such as the Taliban's exclusion of girls from school or the denial of adequate health care to women are not merely different cultural lifestyles; they are violations of human rights. Once this fact is recognized, Okin seems to say, the importance of issues that might have previously been categorized as relatively minor cultural variations becomes urgent. Viewing women's rights as *human rights* allows us to separate mere cultural diversity from oppression and domination. (As we will see in Chapter 9, Okin has related concerns about the role that gender plays in societies committed to a liberal view of rights.)

These problems of rights and cultural differences point beyond the oppression of women. They direct us to inquire into the oppression of other vulnerable groups, some of which were mentioned at the beginning of this section. Some groups consist of persons who are vulnerable in a *categorical* sense, so that all individuals who fall into that category are vulnerable. Infants and small children, patients in a persistent vegetative state, and persons with severe mental illness or cognitive disability might be said to be vulnerable in this way. However, many other parties, such as the homeless and economically disadvantaged people, are vulnerable situationally rather than categorically. Their vulnerability stems from sources such as a lack of coping skills, mental illness, or a lack of economic and social power. Such parties need economic resources and social standing to be brought to bear on their behalf, and this will likely happen only if they have carefully protected rights.

By focusing on individual rights, it often becomes easier to see forms of oppression and domination that are otherwise obscured by cultural assumptions and practices. For example, an approach rooted in rights has helped to expose negative cultural stereotypes and insensitivity toward racial minorities, aboriginal peoples, and handicapped persons. The claims of cultural sovereignty and religious authority that are sometimes used to justify the oppression of women are often strikingly similar to arguments from a "distinct way of life" that justify the oppression of other populations, including the arguments that were once used to justify slavery.

## TYPES OF RIGHTS

In her arguments about the rights of women, Okin drew attention to several different rights—for example, the rights not to be beaten, subjected to unwanted surgery, or sold into slavery. These rights are often referred to as negative or liberty rights. Okin also emphasized the right to receive an education, which is generally categorized as a positive or welfare right. In his article, Jeremy Waldron used examples of rights as diverse as rights against oppressive social relations (see his *Romeo and Juliet* example) and also what he called "welfare rights," such as the provisions we make for the care of the elderly. These are very different kinds of rights, and the distinctions between them have played a prominent and critical role in recent discussions of rights.

At another point in his analysis, Waldron noted that "marriage is certainly more than rights and correlative duties." The correlativity of rights and duties (or obligations) is another important thesis in the rights literature that we need to analyze and one that liberals such as Feinberg have explicitly endorsed as basic in moral theory. We begin this section with an analysis of the correlativity thesis and then turn to the distinction between negative (liberty) and positive (welfare) rights. These distinctions will then lead us to a final distinction between legal, moral, and institutional rights.

### The Correlativity of Rights and Obligations

What is the relationship between one person's rights and another's obligations? Consider the meaning of the general expression "$X$ has a right to do or have $Y$." $X$'s right entails someone else having an obligation not to interfere (if $X$ does $Y$) or to provide something (to provide $X$ with $Y$). If a state promises or otherwise incurs an obligation to provide goods such as food or therapeutic care to needy citizens, then citizens can claim an entitlement to food or therapy if they meet the relevant criteria of need. The right to die, the right to privacy, and the right to a healthy environment, as well as all rights not to be interfered with are analyzable in parallel fashion: Each entails the obligation to abstain from interfering with another person's intended course in life.

If this analysis is correct, there is a correlativity between obligations and rights. "*X* has a right to do or to have *Y*" means that the moral system of rules (or the legal system, if appropriate) imposes an obligation on someone to act or to refrain from acting so that *X* is enabled to do or have *Y*. The language of rights is, therefore, always translatable into the language of obligations: A right entails a prima facie obligation, and all prima facie obligations similarly entail rights.[6]

The thesis that rights language is the flip side of obligation language is very attractive. Nonetheless, the correlativity thesis has been challenged on grounds that many obligations do not entail rights, and that certain rights do not entail obligations. Obligations of charity, obligations to be kind to animals, obligations of love, and obligations of conscience, for example, do not seem to confer correlative rights. The problem with these alleged counterexamples to the correlativity thesis is that some of these apparent "obligations" are actually expressions of what we believe we *ought* to do because we hold personal *ideals*. They are self-imposed rules that are not obligations required by morality. We voluntarily pledge to be charitable, but this "obligation" need not be discharged toward any particular person or at any particular time; persons and times are left to individual discretion. If this view is correct, then only real moral obligations that must be discharged are correlative to rights; and the main problem for a theory of rights is how to express which rights are based on general moral obligations.

This task has proved difficult, because, in a surprisingly large number of cases, it is not clear whether an obligation is a genuine moral obligation or rather is subject to discretion. Consider, for example, obligations of beneficence. Obligations of beneficence such as obligations to rescue those in serious distress where the rescuer is at no significant risk seem very different from self-imposed "obligations" of beneficence such as our sense that an entirely optional contribution should be made to a charity. "Obligations" of this second type are only "requirements" in an extended sense, because they are purely elective. However, if an obligation of the first type is required by moral principles or rules of ordinary morality, then the correlativity thesis does seem to always hold and to generate rights to be benefited.

Also worth considering is the problem of rights without apparent correlative obligations. Consider rights to goods such as adequate housing, clothing, food, health care, education, and a clean environment, all of which are on the United Nations list of "human rights." Do these rights have correlative obligations? Not obviously. In a situation of scarce resources, it may be impossible to provide the goods and services to which one would, under ordinary circumstances, be entitled. The "right" often cannot be *exercised* because no one can provide the needed goods and services. It seems to follow that in contexts in which there can be no obligations, the

---

[6]A weaker version of the correlativity thesis holds that rights entail obligations, although not all obligations entail rights.

term "rights" has no appropriate usage. For example, in a famine in which food *cannot* be supplied no one has a right to be supplied with food or a right to be saved from starvation. People may at some later point come to have such a right, but they have none if there is no possibility of fulfilling the correlative obligation.

## Positive and Negative Rights

Throughout their early history, the human rights or natural rights discussed earlier in this chapter were regarded as rights not to be interfered with, or liberty rights. Only much later did proclamations of rights such as those to health care, housing, and welfare appear in political and legal documents. Then in 1948, the Universal Declaration of Human Rights of the United Nations General Assembly extended rights claims into new territory. This document contains an extensive list of rights, moving beyond those of liberty to include rights to benefits and to services and forms of welfare, such as rights to clothing and food. As the list of rights expands, controversies increase over the precise scope of legitimate rights.

Philosophers often distinguish positive and negative rights in order to clarify which range of rights is at stake. A positive right is a valid claim on goods or services. A negative right is a valid claim to liberty, that is, a right not to be interfered with. Presumably, all that must be done to honor negative rights is to leave people alone, but the same is not true with respect to positive rights. To honor positive rights, someone must provide something. Because of the correlativity between rights and obligations, everything true of positive rights is true of positive obligations, and everything true of negative rights is true of negative obligations. If a person has a positive right to food, medical care, and insurance, then others have a positive obligation to provide them. If a person has a negative right against interference, then another person has an obligation to abstain from interfering.

Negative rights have sometimes been explicated as involving only forbearance on the part of others, hence not requiring active intervention. Yet, many liberty rights normally classified as negative rights do suggest a need for an active intervention. For example, to assert a right to health (not health *care*) is to claim more than mere freedom from interferences that might cause others to be unhealthy. It asserts that the state is obligated to enforce the rights of citizens by protecting them against dangerous chemicals, emissions, pollution, contagion, and the like. Some rights may be best treated as rights both to freedom *and* to state protection—a dual claim to a negative right and a positive right. In this way, some rights can be treated as complex and as analyzable into both negative and positive components.

The political documents mentioned earlier as landmarks in the history of rights have generally been interpreted as affirming negative rights, because these documents were intended to be primarily protective of liberty. However, in the United States, the Bill of Rights also enforces some positive rights, such as the right to an appointed counsel, the right to a speedy and public trial, the right to a jury trial, and the right to compensation for government confiscations of property. Far broader declarations of positive rights have emerged only in the twentieth century. Contemporary concern about positive rights to goods such as food, shelter, and employment is often traced to the aforementioned 1948 Universal Declaration of Human Rights of the United Nations General Assembly, which specifies rights to a standard of living adequate to provide for one's health and well-being.

Nevertheless, the United Nations document and many other such assertions of positive rights do not always declare *entitlements* or introduce a mechanism to ensure the rights they declare. Rights can also be viewed as *guiding ideals,* rather than existing entitlements, as has been given explicit recognition in some documents. This use of the term "rights" may even be the prevailing political use today. The word "right" in this usage functions to establish a commendable or perhaps obligatory target, without claiming a specific obligation on the state's part to enforce its citizens' right or to provide the funding at present that would make those rights anything other than a future goal.

## Legal, Moral, and Conventional Rights

Another important distinction is between moral rights and other types of rights, especially legal rights. We all are familiar with legal rights and their enforcement by the state through a network of penalties. Moral rights have no comparable penalties, but if people believe moral rights have been violated, they will sanction the violators through contempt, social ostracism, disregard, criticism, and the like.

The nature and status of moral rights and other nonlegal rights is a controversial topic. There is neither a system of rights nor a network of codified punishments in morality. Moreover, the proliferation of claims about rights has generated skepticism about their existence and importance.[7] For example, some people claim that there is a right to have an abortion, whereas others argue that the right to life precludes a right to have an abortion. Such controversy has extended to rights to privacy, rights to health care, the rights of children, the rights of animals, the rights of the elderly, smokers' rights, and so forth. In some quarters there has been a persistent suspicion that there are no moral rights, only legal rights.

This reduction of rights to legal rights is implausible. Virtually everyone reacts vigorously if cherished legal rights are withdrawn by legislators or overturned in courts. "Those rights are fundamental!" we say. This complaint cannot mean that rights are "legally fundamental," because the rights (once legally withdrawn) are no longer legal rights. These outcries seem to presuppose independent, nonlegal rights that support claims to legal rights. How, then, can we disentangle legal, moral, and other forms of rights?

Whereas legal rights are supported by existing law, moral rights are supported by moral principles and rules. Legal systems do not require reference to moral systems for their understanding, just as moral systems require no reference to legal systems. One may have a legal right to do something immoral—for example, to treat one's spouse rudely—or have a moral right in the absence of a corresponding legal guarantee. Legal rights are derived from codified bodies of law, legislative enactments, common law, and the executive orders of the highest government official. Moral

---

[7]See Carl Wellman, *The Proliferation of Rights: Moral Progress or Empty Rhetoric?* (Boulder, CO: Westview Press, 1999).

rights, by contrast, exist independently of and form a basis for criticizing or justifying legal rights. Finally, legal rights can be eliminated by existing bodies of law (or by revolution), but moral rights cannot be eroded or banished through any legal or political process. For example, critics of the Taliban maintain that women have moral rights to freedom of movement and to an education—yet, women in Afghanistan do not have legal rights to either because the Taliban has eliminated them. Women's moral rights form the basis for criticizing the legal system instituted by the Taliban.

Other rights, often referred to as conventional, are conferred by special groups on their members. Examples include trade associations, professional societies, labor unions, private clubs, and fraternal organizations. These rights are neither moral nor legal. They contrast with moral rights in that they usually do not exist independently of conventions and practices. They differ from legal rights in that they are generally not recognized as rights within the law.

## THE CONTINGENCY OF RIGHTS

Some liberals and rights theorists have claimed that rights are inalienable and even that they trump all other social considerations. They believe that certain rights must absolutely be respected, irrespective of the effect of doing so on the community and irrespective of the individual's own wishes in the matter. What are we to make of such claims?

### Prima Facie and Absolute Rights

Owing perhaps to political documents that assert fundamental or inalienable human rights, many persons assume that rights are absolute. Yet there are numerous counterexamples to this thesis: Parents have the right to rear their children as they see fit *unless* they abuse them; corporations have a right to increase productivity *unless* they become monopolies, and so forth. Moreover, if the correlativity thesis is correct, absolute rights would entail absolute obligations. However, we saw in Chapter 5 that this is an extremely dubious moral category. Prima facie obligations were analyzed as strong moral demands that may be validly overridden by more stringent, competing demands. This same form of competition presumably could arise if rights conflict, a possibility suggesting that rights no less than obligations may be overridden by competing rights (or some other moral claims). One person's pursuit of happiness will bump up against another's, and one of their rights will be overridden (or perhaps both will be compromised). But is *every* right, even a fundamental right, prima facie, and so capable of being validly overridden?

Consider the right to life. Some assume that this right is absolute, irrespective of competing claims or social conditions. This thesis is contradicted by common moral judgments about capital punishment, international agreements about killing in war, and beliefs about the justifiability of self-defense. Writers on ethics generally agree that we have only a right not to have our lives taken *without sufficient justification.* Though some disagree concerning all the conditions under which it is justifiable to take lives, many agree on at least two conditions: self-defense and defense of one's country against aggression. Even the right to life, then, is not absolute: It can be legitimately exercised and can impose obligations on others only if it has an overriding status.

In times of national emergency such rights as freedom of movement and freedom of the press are often restricted. The government may also impose rationing and require businesses to produce war-related materials instead of consumer goods. As we saw earlier, Taliban officials claim that some of the restrictions they have imposed on women are justified by the need to bring peace and security to Afghanistan after twenty years of war. However, although emergencies do justify the infringement of some rights, it is unlikely that the Taliban's actions against women can be justified on this basis. Even if rights are not absolute, the burden of proof is on the government to justify an infringement.

All rights appear, like all obligations, to be prima facie—that is, presumptively valid—claims that sometimes must yield to other claims. However, Ronald Dworkin has argued the well-known thesis that *some* rights are so basic that ordinary justifications for interference by the state, such as lessening inconvenience or promoting utility, are insufficient. The stakes must be far more significant to justify such invasions, he argues, because rights are "trumps" held by an individual against general plans and background justifications in a political state.[8] Governments typically frame their policies to promote the general welfare and to conform to the decisions of the majority. Rights function to guarantee that individuals cannot be sacrificed to government or majority interests. Rights are above the state's utilitarian goals for Dworkin, much in the way deontologists have maintained that rights secured by justice cannot be traded off by political bargaining or a utilitarian calculus of social interests. Rights to freedom of religion, speech, travel, and association have all been formed with this objective in mind—to place limits on what can be done to an individual. Here it makes good sense to say that the individual's right trumps even the admirable objective of the good of society as an aggregate unit.

The model of rights as trumps has a strong appeal, but the metaphor needs careful assessment. Utilitarians, for example, are very suspicious of the trumping thesis. Consider a typical utilitarian example: A large segment of the population might be made better off by evicting a small group of persons from land they own in order to build a road, park, or university (while compensating persons for the value of the land that they would not voluntarily sell). Utilitarianism sanctions such action and therefore rejects the notion of individual rights to property that trump the state's constructive use of land. The utilitarian reasons that the idea of something that is a trumping "right" in and of itself, without reference to some human good or objective, is unintelligible and disconnected from all human endeavors.

This is a debate in ethical theory that we have previously encountered (see pp. 130–32), but its reincarnation in the context of rights is instructive. The utilitarian, like virtually all other ethical theorists, wants to construct exactly the right *account* of rights in a theory, not to reject rights altogether. The importance of rights and their role in protecting the individual against the desires of others is not seriously questioned in contemporary ethical theory, but the *basis* for the belief in rights and

---

[8]Ronald Dworkin, *Taking Rights Seriously* (Cambridge, MA: Harvard University Press, 1977), p. xi; and *Law's Empire* (Cambridge, MA: Harvard University Press, 1986), p. 223.

the *strength* of rights—for example, whether they have the status of trump cards—continue to stir controversy.

Dworkin himself does not say that rights are so absolute that they may never be overridden. Rather, he has argued that if the rights of others need to be protected—for example, the state faces the need to prevent the spread of a catastrophic disease—then rights can legitimately be overridden. What cannot be done, Dworkin insists, is to act as if the right did not exist and so make decisions based entirely on net social utility. Mere benefit to the community is not of itself sufficient to override rights, and this is the whole point of rights guarantees. Dworkin's qualifications make "trumps" rather more tame than they first appear to be, and it is not clear that utilitarians need to protest his milder formulation.

## Fundamental and Derivative Rights

Another illuminating distinction—one that recalls the distinction between human rights and other types of rights—is the distinction between fundamental rights and derivative rights. For example, the rights to self-determination at issue in Afghanistan have been presented by some philosophers as the basis for derivative rights such as the right to die, the right to commit suicide, and the right to have an abortion. Similarly, some have argued that the right to food is derived from the more general right to be protected from starvation, which in turn is derived from the right to life. Underlying these claims about "more general" or "more fundamental" rights is the conviction that some rights *ground* other rights.

Rights can be fundamental in at least four senses. First, they may be primary and may form the basis for other rights. For example, the right to an adequate standard of living might be regarded as fundamental because it is *not* derived from another right (such as the right to life). By contrast, the right to have a nutritionally sound diet may turn out to be derived from the right to an adequate standard of living. Second, there are some fundamental rights that are rights to create other rights. This form of fundamental right is sometimes said to be composed of powers. If a state legislature, for example, has a basic right to create welfare benefits, and legislators exercise the right properly, other secondary rights such as rights to food and housing derive from their legislative powers.

The remaining two categories bear a certain resemblance. The third category refers to rights that are fundamental because they are causally necessary conditions of other rights. Life, liberty, and equality have some claim to status as fundamental in this sense, because having them is causally necessary for having or doing other things. Samuel Gorovitz has argued that the right to food is fundamental in this third sense, because it is causally necessary for the exercise of other rights, and "no right has meaning or value once starvation strikes."[9] The fourth category includes fundamental rights to the goods or liberties that are essential for a decent standard of

---

[9]Samuel Gorovitz, "Bigotry, Loyalty, and Malnutrition," in Peter G. Brown and Henry Shue, eds., *Food Policy: The Responsibility of the United States in the Life and Death Choices* (New York: Free Press, 1977), pp. 131ff; see also James W. Nickel, *Making Sense of Human Rights: Philosophical Reflections on the Universal Declaration of Human Rights* (Berkeley, CA: University of California Press, 1987), pp. 84–90.

living. Just as we often draw a line between a level of income that puts persons below or above the poverty line, we could draw a line and say that those conditions without which our existence would be impoverished are conditions to which we have fundamental rights. These needs generate rights to a minimally decent level of liberty, political access, security, subsistence, and the like.

The fourth category can be drawn close to the third category by specifying that all rights in the fourth category are those whose exercise is a necessary condition of all other rights. One way of stating this thesis is to say that fundamental rights are those such that persons must possess them for other rights to be capable of being exercised. For example, a right to health in the sense of a protection against environmental polluters who cause fatal diseases seems to be a right such that, unless it is in place, no other right can be enjoyed.

## Waivers and Releases of Rights

If one person holds a right against another, the first person is *entitled to* but *not required to* press the claim against the second party. The first party can *release* the second of the obligation owed, if he or she wishes, because the claimant of a right has discretion over its exercise. With legal rights, for example, one maintains the option to sue over the failure of another to discharge a legal obligation. Any rights holder may, under any circumstances, *waive* his or her right. In doing so, the party who waives the right releases the party having the obligation; the second party is off the hook. For example, if I have a right to a yearly contract from my university, the university is obligated to supply me with the appropriate signed agreement. However, if I waive my right to the contract, the university is no longer obligated to provide it.

A controversial and instructive example of the use of waiver is found in situations involving medical treatment. A patient may relinquish his or her right to give an informed consent to a physician, for example, in the case of an exploratory operation. The patient thereby delegates decision-making authority to the physician, freeing the physician from what the law views as a strict disclosure obligation. In effect, the patient is making an informed decision not to make another informed decision. According to well-established law, a person can waive a legal right only if the waiver is informed, reasoned, and voluntary. Thus the medical circumstances under which a waiver can legally occur are not clear, and there are problems about legitimate waivers. An attached moral problem concerns how much the physician must disclose about the possible consequences of a waiver. Should waivers be discouraged, on grounds that they are difficult to bring in line with the basic purpose of informed consent requirements, which is to allow for autonomous decision-making?

Another issue of similar complexity involves the validity of a suspect's waiver of so-called *Miranda* rights to silence and to the presence of counsel during a custodial interrogation. The U.S. Supreme Court has recognized that certain procedures are necessary to ensure that the "inherent coerciveness" of such an interrogation does not force a voluntary confession from the suspect that could later be used against him or her, thereby violating the constitutional right against self-incrimination.

Because police read and explain *Miranda* rights to suspects, many argue that any waiver is the product of the interrogation's inherent coerciveness, and therefore is invalid. Courts tend to view waivers of *Miranda* rights with skepticism and have contrived tests to determine a waiver's validity.[10]

Philosophers have occasionally suggested that some rights cannot be waived because they are inalienable, and therefore not something that can be either voluntarily given up or taken away. Many rights in criminal law have been said to be inalienable, and therefore not waivable. In some cases one can waive the exercise of these rights but cannot waive the rights in the sense that those rights will be *lost.* In other cases, as a matter of social policy, we do not permit people to *enact* certain waivers at all. For example, we deny someone the right to waive his or her right not to be enslaved. As a general principle rights can always be waived, but when we have valid reasons of social policy to disallow the waivers, an exception to the general principle should be recognized.

## Losing and Forfeiting Rights

Waivers and releases are different from circumstances in which a person forfeits a right as a result of unacceptable conduct. "Forfeit" means the loss of a valid claim (a right) as a result of one's neglect or misdeed. Even if inalienable rights cannot be lost, revoked, or forfeited, many rights can be. Criminals forfeit rights of freedom by their activities, and, as a result, correlative obligations to them cease. For example, courts have held that while a person's home is protected against unreasonable governmental searches, a prison cell has no similar protection, though it is in effect a prisoner's home.

Questions of forfeiture have emerged about various forms of societal coverage or possible societal coverage for injuries, diseases, or catastrophic losses as a result of the person's lifestyle or individual actions. Many forms of insurance or other programs of entitlement now incorporate conditions of forfeiture. Recent debates about the forfeiture of insurance or public assistance have occurred in regard to patients with AIDS as a result of sexual activities or intravenous drug use, patients with lung cancer as a result of smoking cigarettes, and patients with liver disease as a result of heavy consumption of alcohol. Those who engage in these actions are regarded by many as *causing* their ill health, injury, and medical needs, thereby forfeiting their right to insured care, coverage, or a place on a waiting list for organ transplants. It is unfair, critics of these behaviors say, for other individuals to pay higher premiums or taxes to support those who voluntarily engage in risky actions; and it is fair, from this perspective, to withhold public funds from certain entitlement programs. This is a way of declaring that citizens have forfeited their rights by engaging in certain forms of voluntary risk-taking.

The general idea behind forfeiture is reasonable and defensible. However, in practice it has proved difficult to implement in public policy. In dealing with the issue of risky lifestyle, for example, it is necessary to distinguish the many possible causes of a problem—such as heredity, social conditions, and environmental

---

[10]*Miranda* v. *Arizona,* 384 U.S. 436 (1966).

exposures—in order to confirm that an illness or injury is the result of personal activities. It is also essential to show that the activities were voluntarily undertaken, in that actors were aware of the risks and voluntarily accepted them.

It has proved to be extremely difficult to isolate the relevant causal factors of ill health because of the complexity of causal links and the limitations of our knowledge. Medical needs, for example, can result from the conjunction of genetic predispositions, personal actions, and environmental and social conditions. The causal roles of these different factors are often impossible to establish with sufficient evidence. It may be possible to determine responsibility for an injury incurred while mountain climbing or skiing, but it is rarely possible to determine with any precision whether a particular individual's lung cancer resulted from cigarette smoking, environmental pollution, work conditions, or heredity (or some combination of these causal factors)—despite the clear evidence linking cigarette smoking with lung cancer.

Forfeiture is a defensible moral concept, but it can also be a dangerous precedent for social policy and law.

## RIGHT-BASED ETHICAL THEORIES

The correlativity thesis about rights and obligations suggests that obligation-oriented theories are committed to rights, and vice versa. However, this conclusion does not determine whether rights or obligations, if either, is the more fundamental or primary category in ethical theory. Nor does it determine whether rights can be reduced in content or in meaning to obligations. In previous chapters, we have encountered goal-based theories (for example, utilitarianism), duty-based theories (for example, Kantian ethics), virtue-based theories (for example, Aristotelian ethics), and conventionalist theories (for example, one side of Hume's ethics). The first two types of theory share a concentration on obligations, and both are commonly said to be obligation-based. Now we come to the question of whether this typology needs to be expanded to include right-based theories as another type.

Some philosophers maintain that ethical theory or some part of it *must be* "right-based."[11] They seek to ground ethical theory in an account of rights that (1) is not reducible to a theory of obligations or virtues, and (2) is prior in the order of justification to obligations. Consider, for example, a theory we encounter in Chapter 9, as a theory of justice. The "libertarian" theory of justice (one type of liberalism) is often developed through a principle that specifies rights to social and economic liberty as the basis for determining just distributions. What makes such theory libertarian is its insistence that liberty rights are basic and not reducible to anything further. Persons have fundamental rights to freedom of choice and to own and dispense with the fruits of their labor as they choose. One representative of this theory, Robert Nozick, refers to his social philosophy (see pp. 133–36, 315–19 in Chapters

---

[11]Ronald Dworkin argues that *political* morality is right-based in *Taking Rights Seriously* (London: Duckworth, 1977), p. 171. John Mackie has applied this thesis to *morality generally* in "Can There Be a Right-Based Moral Theory?" *Midwest Studies in Philosophy,* 3 (1978).

4 and 9) as an "entitlement theory" of justice. The appropriateness of that description is apparent from the provocative line with which his book begins: "Individuals have rights, and there are things no person or group may do to them (without violating their rights)." Starting from this assumption, Nozick defends a political state in which government action is justified only if it protects the fundamental rights of its citizens. Such a conception is the very antithesis of the current state of affairs in Afghanistan.

Nozick's theory might be viewed as a political and legal theory, not a right-based *moral* theory. But his claim can be recast as a purely moral one. Nozick takes the following rule to be basic in the moral life: All persons must be (have a right to be) left free to do as they choose. This rule expresses a right. The duty not to interfere with this right follows from the right. That it *follows* is an indication of the *priority of a rule of right over a rule of obligation.* That is, a duty seems to be derived from a right, in this case a *liberty* right.

A related right-based argument uses *benefit* rights, as Alan Gewirth has proposed:

> Rights are to duties as benefits are to burdens. For rights are justified claims to certain benefits, the support of certain interests of the subject or right-holder. Duties, on the other hand, are justified burdens on the part of the respondent or duty-bearer; they restrict his freedom by requiring that he conduct himself in ways that directly benefit not himself but rather the right-holder. But burdens are for the sake of benefits, and not vice versa. Hence duties, which are burdens, are for the sake of rights, whose objects are benefits.
>
> Rights, then, are prior to duties in the order of justifying purpose . . . in that respondents have correlative duties *because* subjects have certain rights.[12]

These right-based conceptions accept the correctness of the correlativity thesis, but contend that obligations follow from rights, rather than the converse. Rights form the justifying basis of duties because they best express the purpose of morality, which is the securing of liberties or other benefits or goods for a right-holder. Some might object that obligations are not necessarily burdens and may be welcomed as expressions of our rationality or as a basic form of human activity. But Gewirth and other rights theorists insist that obligations are essentially what Mill and Kant said they were, namely, *constraints* on autonomy and, hence, burdens placed on autonomous action. Duties restrict in a way rights do not, and the purpose of morality is to benefit, not to burden.

Despite the arguments by Gewirth and Nozick, critics of rights theories believe that rights are not the fundamental or primary category in ethical theory. Rights are nonprimitive, they maintain, because the defense of rights requires appeal to justifying reasons that are themselves rooted in an ethical theory in which the language of rights emerges from some other structure of rules. Rights, on this account, tend to be recognized and asserted if we have achieved a sufficiently heightened sensitivity to the needs of individuals, a sensitivity rooted in some more basic account of

---

[12]"Why Rights Are Indispensable," *Mind,* 95 (1986): 333. A similar thesis was defended in the article cited above by John Mackie.

moral obligation, value, or procedure. The rights we possess follow from a more general account of ethics that stakes out what *makes* a claim *valid*. If a moral theory is the activity of justifying the rules within which claiming occurs, then the moral theory cannot be right-based.

## CONCLUSION

The issues about rights raised in this chapter leave us with several unresolved questions. Many of these questions lead to a consideration of theories of justice, the subject of Chapter 9. Claims of justice yield particularly strong rights, and it is likely that there is a conceptual link between rights claims and justice claims. Many believe that justice is the deeper and more significant moral notion. This thesis will now be tested.

## SUGGESTED SUPPLEMENTARY READINGS

### Rights and Liberalism

Benditt, Theodore M.: *Rights* (Totowa, NJ: Rowman and Littlefield, 1982).

Buchanan, Allen E.: "What's So Special about Rights?" *Social Philosophy and Policy,* 2 (1984): 61–83.

Burnyeat, Myles: "Did the Ancient Greeks Have the Concept of Human Rights?" *Polis,* 13 (1994): 1–11.

Coleman, Jules L., ed.: *Rights and Their Foundations* (New York: Garland, 1994).

Dworkin, Ronald: *Taking Rights Seriously* (Cambridge, MA: Harvard University Press, 1977).

Feinberg, Joel: "Duties, Rights, and Claims," *American Philosophical Quarterly,* 3 (1966): 137–44.

———: *Social Philosophy* (Englewood Cliffs, NJ: Prentice-Hall, 1973), chaps. 4–6.

———: *Rights, Justice, and the Bounds of Liberty* (Princeton, NJ: Princeton University Press, 1980).

Finnis, John: *Natural Law and Natural Rights* (Oxford, England: Clarendon Press, 1980).

Flathman, Richard E.: *The Practice of Rights* (Cambridge, England: Cambridge University Press, 1977).

Frey, R. G., ed.: *Utility and Rights* (Minneapolis: University of Minnesota Press, 1984).

Gewirth, Alan: *Human Rights* (Chicago: University of Chicago Press, 1982).

———: "Why Rights Are Indispensable," *Mind,* 95 (1986): 329–44.

———: *The Community of Rights* (Chicago: University of Chicago Press, 1996).

Hart, H. L. A.: "Are There Any Natural Rights?" *Philosophical Review,* 64 (1955): 175–91.

————: "Between Utility and Rights," in Alan Ryan, ed., *The Idea of Freedom: Essays in Honour of Isaiah Berlin* (Oxford, England: Oxford University Press, 1979), pp. 77–98.

Hohfeld, Wesley Newcomb: *Fundamental Legal Conceptions as Applied in Judicial Reasoning* (London and New Haven, CT: Greenwood Press, 1964 [1919]).

Korsgaard, Christine: "The Right to Lie: Kant on Dealing with Evil," *Philosophy and Public Affairs,* 15 (1986): 325–49.

Lomasky, Loren E.: *Persons, Rights, and the Moral Community* (New York: Oxford University Press, 1987).

Lyons, David: "Rights, Claimants, and Beneficiaries," *American Philosophical Quarterly,* 6 (1969): 173–85.

————: "The Correlativity of Rights and Duties," *Nous,* 4 (1970): 45–55.

————, ed.: *Rights* (Belmont, CA: Wadsworth Publishing Company, 1979).

Mackie, John L.: "Can There Be a Right-Based Moral Theory?" *Midwest Studies in Philosophy,* 3 (1978).

Martin, Rex A.: *A System of Rights* (Oxford, England: Clarendon Press, 1993).

Martin, Rex, and James W. Nickel: "Recent Work on the Concept of Rights," *American Philosophical Quarterly,* 17 (1980): 165–80.

Melden, Abraham I.: *Human Rights* (Belmont, CA: Wadsworth Publishing Company, 1970).

————: *Rights and Persons* (Berkeley, CA: University of California Press, 1977).

Meyers, Diana: *Inalienable Rights: A Defense* (New York: Columbia University Press, 1985).

Pettit, Philip: "Rights, Constraints, and Trumps," *Analysis,* 47 (1987): 8–14.

Pollock, Lansing: "Moral Rights and Moral Equality," *Public Affairs Quarterly,* 9 (April 1995): 139–54.

Shue, Henry: *Basic Rights* (Princeton, NJ: Princeton University Press, 1980).

Simmons, A. John: *The Lockean Theory of Rights* (Princeton, NJ: Princeton University Press, 1994).

Spector, Horacio: *Autonomy and Rights: The Moral Foundations of Liberalism* (Oxford, England: Clarendon Press, 1992).

Sumner, L. W.: *The Moral Foundation of Rights* (Oxford: Clarendon Press, 1987).

Sunstein, Cass R.: *After the Rights Revolution: Reconceiving the Regulatory State* (Cambridge, MA: Harvard University Press, 1993).

Thomson, Judith J.: *The Realm of Rights* (Cambridge, MA: Harvard University Press, 1990).

Tuck, Richard: *Natural Rights Theories* (Cambridge, England: Cambridge University Press, 1979).

Waldron, Jeremy, ed.: *Theories of Rights* (Oxford, England. Oxford University Press, 1984).

————, ed.: *Nonsense upon Stilts: Bentham, Burke, and Marx on the Rights of Man* (New York: Methuen, 1987).

Wellman, Carl P.: *A Theory of Rights* (Totowa, NJ: Rowman & Allanheld, 1985).

————: *Real Rights* (New York: Oxford University Press, 1995).

————: *The Proliferation of Rights: Moral Progress or Empty Rhetoric?* (Boulder, CO: Westview Press, 1999).

White, Alan R.: *Rights* (Oxford, England: Clarendon Press, 1984).

Winston, Morton E., ed.: *The Philosophy of Human Rights* (Belmont, CA: Wadsworth Publishing Co., 1989).

Wolf, Clark: "Contemporary Property Rights, Lockean Provisos, and the Interests of Future Generations," *Ethics,* 105 (1995): 791–818.

Wolgast, Elizabeth: *Equality and the Rights of Women* (Ithaca, NY: Cornell University Press, 1980).

## Communitarian Ethics

Arneson, Richard J.: "Liberalism, Freedom, and Community," *Ethics,* 100 (1990): 368–85.

Avineri, Shlomo, and Avner de-Shalit, eds.: *Communitarianism and Individualism* (Oxford, England: Oxford University Press, 1992).

Bell, Daniel A.: *Communitarianism and Its Critics* (Oxford: Clarendon Press, 1993).

Buchanan, Allen: "Assessing the Communitarian Critique of Liberalism," *Ethics,* 99 (1989): 852–82.

Care, Norman S.: *On Sharing Fate* (Philadelphia: Temple University Press, 1987).

Ewin, R. W.: *Liberty, Community, and Justice* (Totowa, NJ: Rowman & Littlefield, 1987).

Freeden, Michael: "Human Rights and Welfare: A Communitarian View," *Ethics,* 100 (1990): 489–502.

Gauthier, David: *Morals by Agreement* (Oxford, England: Clarendon Press, 1986).

————: *Moral Dealing: Contract, Ethics, and Reason* (Ithaca, NY: Cornell University Press, 1990).

Gutmann, Amy: "Communitarian Critics of Liberalism," *Philosophy and Public Affairs,* 14 (1985): 308–22.

Kymlicka, Will: *Liberalism, Community, and Culture* (Oxford: Clarendon Press, 1989).

MacIntyre, Alasdair: *Whose Justice? Which Rationality?* (Notre Dame, IN: University of Notre Dame, 1988).

Rasmussen, David, ed.: *Universalism vs. Communitarianism: Contemporary Debates in Ethics* (Cambridge, MA: MIT Press, 1990).

Rosenblum, Nancy L., ed.: *Liberalism and the Moral Life* (Cambridge, MA: Harvard University Press, 1989).

Sandel, Michael J.: *Liberalism and the Limits of Justice* (Cambridge, England: Cambridge University Press, 1982).

————: *Democracy's Discontent: America in Search of a Public Philosophy* (Cambridge, MA: Harvard University Press, 1996).

Taylor, Charles: *Philosophical Papers*, 2 vols. (Cambridge, England: Cambridge University Press, 1985).

Walzer, Michael: *Spheres of Justice: A Defense of Pluralism and Equality* (New York: Basic Books, 1983).

————: *Politics: A Work in Constructive Social Theory*, 3 vols. (Cambridge: Cambridge University Press, 1987).

————: "The Communitarian Critique of Liberalism," *Political Theory,* 18 (1990).

## CHAPTER 9

# *Justice*

## NUCLEAR FALLOUT IN THE MARSHALL ISLANDS

At the end of the Second World War the United States government chose the Marshall Islands—a scattered cluster of atolls just north of the equator above New Zealand—as a site for its newly developed nuclear weapons testing program. The United Nations designated these islands a trust territory of the United States in 1947. According to the agreement at the time, the United States, as trustee, "shall . . . protect the health of the inhabitants." The Marshall Islands first came under foreign control in 1885, when Germany made them a protectorate. During World War I they were seized by the Japanese, who received a League of Nations mandate under the treaty of Versailles. The United States seized the islands from Japan during World War II, a development welcomed by the inhabitants. After the war, independence for the islands was never considered a serious option in the United States; debate centered on whether they should be annexed or made into a United Nations protectorate under U.S. control. The people of the Marshall Islands were given no role in making this decision, which ultimately turned on U.S. political and strategic interests. From 1944 until the establishment of a United Nations mandate in 1947, the islands continued to be occupied by U.S. forces.

The United States officially obtained permission from Chief Juda of the Bikinians to use their island as a test site for nuclear bombs and to temporarily relocate the population. In return, the United States promised to take care of the Bikinians. However, President Truman had already approved the choice of Bikini as test site before this permission was granted, and an American ship was already blasting in the lagoon in preparation.

Called "Operation Crossroads," two tests were conducted at Bikini Atoll. To avoid possible radiation contamination from fallout, the Bikinians had been evacuated. Despite the promises made to the Bikinians, during the second shot in the series—a 21-kiloton underwater blast—the surviving test ships and the atoll itself were seriously contaminated. The Bikinians were unable to return to their atoll for over twenty years. At that time (1969), it was thought that the island had been decontaminated, but after the Bikinians were resettled and lived there for a decade (until 1978), it was discovered that the radiological cleanup had been inadequate and that unacceptable levels of nuclear materials had been consumed with native foods, as well as absorbed in the skin. The Bikinians were again evacuated. Over a half century later, the Bikinians remain spread out in the Marshall Islands awaiting adequate radiological cleanup of their atoll, which is still in progress.

In 1954, the Bravo shot was detonated at the Bikini Atoll; it tested a thermonuclear (hydrogen) bomb roughly a thousand times the power of the Hiroshima bomb. An unanticipated wind shift carried fallout toward Rongelap and other inhabited atolls. The Rongelap and Utirik Atolls were evacuated, but only after persons on those islands had received serious radiation exposure. No formal investigation has ever been conducted of this affair by the U.S. government, but it is known that an evacuation capability was not standing by at the time of the blast.

After these radiation exposures, the U.S. government set in motion a program to provide medical care for those exposed, as well as a research program to better understand the long-term effects of radiation exposure. The Marshallese came to feel that they were pawns in a careless U.S. nuclear testing program. Surviving historical evidence indicates that U.S. officials had ignored weather forecasts about wind patterns at the time of the Bravo shot and had proceeded without taking adequate precautions to protect the population.

The Rongelapese were, after three years, resettled onto their atoll. It was recognized at the time that contamination problems were serious and required careful controls—for example, dietary restrictions. As it turned out, these measures underestimated the seriousness of the conditions. Unlike the Bikini case, the medical follow-up program has continued to the present day, indicating both the seriousness of the radiation exposure and a persisting belief that it can be controlled and the population successfully resettled.

Five years after the Bravo shot, Dr. Robert A. Conard, the director of the medical team from the Brookhaven National Laboratory of the U.S. Atomic Energy Commission, wrote that:

> The people of Rongelap received a high sub-lethal dose of gamma radiation, extensive beta burns of the skin, and significant internal absorption of fission products. . . . Very little is known of the late effects of radiation in human beings. . . . The seriousness of their exposure cannot be minimized.
>
> From these considerations it is apparent that we are obligated to carry out future examinations on the exposed people to the extent that they are deemed necessary as time goes on so that any untoward effects that may develop may be diagnosed as soon as possible and the best medical therapy instituted. Any action short of this would compromise our responsibility and lay us open to criticism.

Brookhaven researchers agreed with the Marshallese that the medical care provided by the Trust Territory government was inadequate. They faced this situation: The Marshallese had been exposed to highly penetrating gamma radiation (whole-body exposure), radiation from deposition of fission products on the skin, radiation from consumption of contaminated food and water, and some inhalation of fallout particles. These problems were, for the most part, handled in on-island medical facilities by visiting U.S. physicians. When medical problems were noticed that required treatment in the United States, such as thyroid nodules requiring surgery, patients were flown to Metropolitan General Hospital in Cleveland or other U.S. treatment facilities.

Primary care, however, was seriously inadequate on the island. Epidemics of poliomyelitis, influenza, chicken pox, and pertussis developed. All of these diseases had been imported to the islands by the treating U.S. medical teams. The epidemics proved to be severe, with very high mortality rates. These rates could have been significantly lowered by the use of available vaccines, but they were not made available on the islands by U.S. officials. The Atomic Energy Commission insisted that all primary care was the responsibility of the Trust Territory, but it had no personnel or equipment for these services. Even as late as 1978, when administrative responsibilities were realigned on the islands, the needed supplies had not been made available.

In 1985, the people of Rongelap expressed grave concerns about the levels of radioactivity still in their food chain. They rejected the U.S. Department of Energy's advice to remain on their island. They moved themselves, using the Greenpeace ship *Rainbow Warrior,* to Majetto Island in Kwajelein Atoll, where they remain today. In 1994–95 an Advisory Committee to the U.S. President confirmed the above facts in this case and reported them publicly.[1]

This case illustrates several problems of justice that are central to this chapter. Moral arguments turn on whether the Marshallese were unjustly treated and whether the compensation package and medical care efforts offered by the U.S. government were fair or unfair. There has been, and continues to be, strong disagreement about what, if anything, constitutes a claim of *justice* in these devastating and tragic circumstances.

## THE NATURE OF JUSTICE

Philosophical work on justice usually begins with how the terms "justice" and "distributive justice" have been used in classical and contemporary moral philosophy— and also how they *should* be used.

### The Meaning of "Justice"

Justice has been explicated in terms of *fairness,* in terms of *desert* (what is deserved), and in terms of *entitlement* (that to which one is entitled). These notions, though different, all have something to do with what is due or owed. Justice, in the general sense, arises if a person is accorded those benefits or burdens due or owed to the person because of the person's particular properties or situation. What persons are due or owed is based on morally relevant properties or situations, such as their being productive or their having been harmed by the acts of another party in the way the Marshallese were harmed by U.S. testing.

[1]This case was developed primarily from Advisory Committee on Human Radiation Experiments (ACHRE), *Final Report of the Advisory Committee on Human Radiation Experiments* (New York: Oxford University Press, 1996), chap. 12. See also Jonathan M. Weisgall, *Operation Crossroads: The Atomic Tests at Bikini Atoll* (Annapolis, MD: Naval Institute Press, 1994); Robert Conard, *Fallout: The Experiences of a Medical Team in the Care of a Marshallese Population Accidentally Exposed to Fallout Radiation* (Upton, NY: Associated Universities, Inc., September 1992).

We often express what a person deserves or is entitled to through specific rules and laws, such as those governing state lotteries, food stamp allocation, health care coverage, admission procedures for universities, and the like. However, these specific rules may be evaluated, criticized, and revised by reference to abstract moral principles such as equality of persons, property ownership, and compensatory justice.

## Distributive Justice

Theories of justice deal with either *distributive* or *criminal* matters. Issues of criminal justice concern the corrective actions or punishments meted out to redress criminal wrongs. Distributive justice, the sole concern of this chapter, refers to the just distribution of benefits and burdens in society. Distributive justice covers the distribution of benefits and burdens through society's major and pervasive institutions, governing and judicial bodies, lending institutions, and health-care systems. Paying taxes, being drafted into the armed services to fight a war, and serving jury duty are distributed burdens, whereas welfare checks, grants to perform research, and newly paved neighborhood streets are distributed benefits.

A theory of distributive justice attempts to establish a connection between the properties or characteristics of persons and the morally correct distribution of benefits and burdens in society. The connection may be found, for example, in the effort a person expends or in the misfortune a person suffers. For example, the misfortune and neglect suffered by injured persons in the Marshall Islands bear a connection to the financial compensation and the distribution of health resources that followed these tragic events. We can assess the fairness of how the Marshallese were treated by a general and comprehensive perspective on justice. One function of a general theory of distributive justice is to justify basic principles of justice and the design of institutions that control the distribution of goods, services, and burdens.

Recent literature on distributive justice has tended to focus on economic considerations, especially inequalities in income distribution among different groups and unfair tax burdens. But there are many problems of distributive justice besides strictly economic ones, including the issues raised in prominent contemporary debates over preferential hiring and reverse discrimination, the distribution of health care, and public environmental policies that regulate uses of private property.

## Comparative Justice

Issues of distributive justice often involve a comparison of individuals. Justice is said to be *comparative* if what one person deserves is determined by balancing his or her claims against the competing claims of others. Here the condition of others affects how much an individual is due; what a person is owed is relative to how much others are owed. For example, it is common for an employer to use a merit system for annual salary increases, while making a flat percentage increase (3 percent over the previous year, say) available to each department to distribute among its members. Each individual's claim to a salary increase is relative to how much others are owed in the scheme of distribution. In this system one does not have a claim to a particular increase (3 percent, say) that is independent of what others are owed.

Not all problems of justice, however, involve such a comparison. Issues of criminal justice are essentially *noncomparative:* What is owed is judged by a standard independent of others' claims and has nothing to do with others' circumstances. For example, when a crime has been committed, certain rules must be followed: Legal dictates of justice such as the right to a fair trial or to due process must never be affected by the condition of other people in a society.

Distributive justice, by contrast, applies to the distribution of scarce benefits under the condition of competition for those benefits, and this context is often comparative. If there were plenty of fresh water for industries to use when dumping their waste materials, with no subsequent problems of contamination, rules to restrict dumping would not be needed. Only because we are worried that the supply of drinking water will be contaminated, or that public health will be affected by the pollutants, or that certain forms of marine life will disappear, do we limit the amount of permissible discharge. Many schemes for distributing jobs, determining salaries, or setting limits on waste-water effluents will involve a balancing of competing claims and interests.

David Hume pointed out that rules of justice function to handle problems of conflicting claims or interests (see Chapter 7, pp. 227–29, 234–36). Rules of justice, he maintained, would have no point unless society consisted of persons with limited sympathy for others in the competition for scarce resources. The rules of justice serve to strike a balance between conflicting interests. Because law and morality are our tools for balancing conflicting claims, there is a close link between the lawful society and the just society. Nonetheless, the law may be unjust, and not all rules of justice are connected to the law or to legal enforcement.

## PRINCIPLES OF JUSTICE

### The Formal Principle of Justice

Justice has been analyzed in many different ways in what we will later call rival theories. But common to all theories of justice is a minimal principle traditionally attributed to Aristotle: Equals must be treated equally, and unequals may legitimately be treated unequally (in proportion to their relevant similarities and differences). This elementary principle is referred to as the principle of formal justice, or sometimes as the principle of formal equality. It is formal because it provides no particular respects in which equals ought to be treated the same and provides no criteria for determining whether two or more individuals are equals. It asserts that no matter which relevant respects are under consideration, persons equal in those respects should be treated equally. Put in a negative form, this principle says that no person should be treated unequally, despite all his or her differences from another person, until it has been shown that there is a difference between them relevant to the treatment at stake. This principle does not reject inequality of treatment, only inequality of treatment for irrelevant reasons.

Because the formal principle of justice does not tell us how to determine equality or proportion, it lacks substance as a specific guide to conduct. In any group of persons, there will be many respects in which they are both similar and different, and we will have to establish equality in relevant respects. Not *all* respects, however, are relevant to justice—race and sex being prominent examples. In circumstances of hiring and promoting employees, for instance, the formal principle stipulates that an employer ought to treat equally those among its employees who are equal; but it does not indicate whether differences in sex or race make employees unequal for purposes of distributing jobs and salaries. Our normal presumption is that sex-based or race-based hiring is unjust, but nothing in the skeletal formal principle recommends this conclusion.

Consider an example of how little is excluded by the formal principle. A longstanding principle on many stock exchanges is the so-called one-share–one-vote, or equal-voting-rights, principle, which states that any company traded on the stock exchange must allow persons holding common stock to cast one vote for each share held. Each company traded is required to adopt this rule, which is considered a matter of justice by stock exchange officials. Several years back, Gordon Macklin, president of the National Association of Securities Dealers, argued that the over-the-counter (OTC) market should not follow the one-share–one-vote principle, but instead should allow companies to have two classes of common stock with unequal voting rights, a practice already followed by several corporations, including Hershey Foods and Dow Jones, publisher of the *Wall Street Journal.* A year later the New York Stock Exchange ended a sixty-year-old one-share–one-vote rule and followed Macklin's suggestion. Nothing in the formal principle of justice rules out unequal voting rights or declares them unjust; even classes of stock that would have *no* voting rights could be created under this rule. The formal principle says only that whatever *class* of stock you own, you must be treated equally as an owner under that classification. Thus, if you hold a class of stock with no voting rights, you must be treated like all other persons in that class: You may not vote!

Philosophers generally maintain that the formal principle gives no egalitarian recommendations for action; it cannot be presumed on this principle that all should be treated equally. The formal principle of justice is not, then, identical with a substantive principle of equality. The formal principle does not have the power to rule out many forms of unequal treatment. The principle does not even make a *presumption* in favor of treating persons equally rather than unequally. Many immoral "principles of distributive justice" could, under the formal principle, be applied equally to all—for example, rules of taxation constructed to favor those who are already wealthy while penalizing the poor.

Theories of justice attempt to avoid these problems of substantive injustice by systematically elaborating the notions of equality in distribution and by specifying the differences that count as relevant for personal comparisons. This function is served by material principles of justice, to which we now turn.

## Material Principles of Justice

The formal principle requires equal treatment for equals, but it is not to be presumed that all people are equal for purposes of distributing every social burden and benefit.

Indeed, the contrary assumption is generally appropriate. Different people possess different properties on the basis of which they deserve different distributions. Any plausible theory of justice, then, must specify relevant properties; and not just any proposed properties are morally acceptable. If the fact that the inhabitants of the Marshall Islands are not *citizens of the United States* is judged a good reason for not compensating them for the harm done by U.S. nuclear testing, this fact introduces a *proposed* relevant property for purposes of compensation, but this property is morally irrelevant under the circumstances of the case. The proposed property of citizenship allows a distribution of benefits based on the morally irrelevant property (in this case though not in all cases) of not being a citizen of a particular country.

Material principles of justice identify a relevant property on the basis of which burdens and benefits should be distributed. The following is a somewhat short, but representative, list of some major candidates for the position of valid material principles of distributive justice: (1) to each person an equal share; (2) to each person according to individual need; (3) to each person according to that person's rights; (4) to each person according to individual effort; (5) to each person according to societal contribution; (6) to each person according to merit; and (7) to each person according to free market exchanges.

Nothing bars accepting more than one of these principles, and some theories of justice accept all seven. Many societies use several in the belief that different rules are appropriate to different situations. In many countries, for example, prevailing principles demand that welfare payments be distributed according to *need,* that jobs and promotions be distributed on the basis of *achievement* and *merit,* and that compensation for injury be distributed in accordance with the inconvenience or disability suffered. *Equality* is often invoked as a principle that entitles everyone to a free basic education and to vote in public elections.

A plausible moral thesis is that each of these material principles specifies an obligation that—like other obligations such as respecting another's autonomy, maintaining confidentiality, and avoiding harm—is prima facie and may be overridden by one of the other principles. It is attractive, on this presumption, to try to protect each of the above-listed principles in a theory of justice. But conflicts between them will still create a serious weighting or priority problem.

Conflicts between the different material principles of justice, as well as their prima facie status, are illustrated by the following example: A university professor hires three male students to help move the furniture in her house to a new location, promising each the standard hourly wage for professional movers in the city. One student turns out to be capable of lifting large items by himself and is both more efficient and more careful than either of the other students. The second student, the professor learns, desperately needs money, owing to a severe financial crisis that threatens his enrollment for the next semester. The third student carelessly breaks two vases and scars a table, but otherwise fulfills the conditions of the agreement, although in an undistinguished manner. The first mover deserves greater compensation on the basis of performance, the second has a greater need for money than the others do, and the third deserves less on the basis of performance, but deserves an equal share on the basis of the agreement.

Although the professor knows she must abide by her agreement and pay each student equally, she is distressed by the "unfairness" of the situation. Suppose she resorts to *justice in general* to tell her what ought to be done. Such an appeal to a general notion of justice would likely prove worthless, because the material principles of justice are in conflict and justice itself does not give priority to one of these principles. She would perhaps wish for a general account of justice that would order this fragmented array of considerations, but no material principle clearly outweighs any other.

In the face of this untidy circumstance of conflicting appeals, theories of justice have been devised to systemize, simplify, and order our diverse rules and judgments. Several well-reasoned and systematic theories have been advanced to determine how goods and services should be distributed or, as some insist, redistributed. The theories largely differ according to the particular material criteria they emphasize. The following are the most prominent theories: (1) egalitarian theories, which emphasize equal access to the goods in life that every rational person desires (often invoking the material criteria of need and equality); (2) libertarian theories, which emphasize rights to social and economic liberty (invoking fair procedures and systems rather than substantive outcomes); and (3) utilitarian theories that emphasize a mixture of criteria so that public utility is maximized (an example is public health policy, as it has generally been formulated). The acceptability of any theory of justice is determined by the quality of its moral argument that one or more selected material criteria or principles ought to be given priority, or perhaps exclusive consideration, over others.

Consideration will now be given to the libertarian and the egalitarian theories. The utilitarian theory was explained in Chapter 4, where we saw utilitarians argue that justice is the name for the most paramount and stringent forms of obligation created by the principle of utility.

## THE LIBERTARIAN THEORY

The libertarian theory is based on a material principle that specifies rights to social and economic liberty. Justice consists not in some distributed *result,* such as increasing public utility, but in the unhindered working of fair *procedures.* Events in a true free market should not be a matter of social planning, but rather of individual choosing. Social intervention in the free market perverts justice by constraining individual liberty. What makes these theories libertarian is their advocacy of distinctive processes, procedures, or mechanisms for ensuring that liberty rights are preeminent. Typical of all libertarian theories is the premise that coercion—that is, the restriction of liberty by threat—is justified only to prevent or punish criminal activity, the infliction of harm, the violation of contracts, and other violations of liberty rights.

In the libertarian theory, the central social mechanisms are typically the rules and procedures governing economic acquisition and exchange in free market systems. Adam Smith classically described well-functioning capitalistic economic systems as people acting in an individually self-interested fashion yet thereby exhibiting behavior patterns that collectively further the interests of everyone in the larger society. He called the market forces that operate to produce this outcome the "invisible hand."

People are seen as freely entering and withdrawing from economic arrangements in accordance with a controlling perception of their interest. Choices are considered the morally relevant bases on which to discriminate between individuals in distributing economic burdens and benefits, because the choices are free. This feature supports Robert Nozick's characterization of the underlying material principle informing libertarian theory: "From each as they choose, to each as they are chosen."

In seeing free choice as central to an account of justice in economic distribution, libertarian writers often commit themselves to a particular conception of economic production and value that is individualist. Libertarians maintain that people should receive economic benefits in proportion to how much they freely contribute to production in an open marketplace, a theory which assumes that it is possible to recognize meaningful distinctions between individual contributions to production of such benefits. The industrious and imaginative business executive, for instance, is contributing far more to his or her company's success than the similarly exemplary assembly-line worker or secretary, and the executive therefore deserves a proportionately greater share of the profits than the assembly-line worker or secretary.

The underlying assumption in this theory corresponds to certain economic presuppositions in Anglo-American society, but many philosophers challenge it. They maintain that, however great the differences between particular people's contributions, many individual contributions shrink to insignificance once the broader context of production is appreciated. On this account, economic value is generated through an essentially communal process that renders differences between individual contributions morally spurious.

These critics might admit that it was possible to identify more precisely the importance of an individual contribution to something of economic value when, for example, frontier settlers turned virgin forests into productive farmland. But they would argue that this possibility has long since been eliminated by the complexity and interdependence of modern economic systems. The initiative and ideas of the business executive, for example, would be only one among the many factors at work in a corporation's success, each factor itself reflecting a diversity of formative influences including family background, education, and interaction with professional colleagues. If this view of economic production and value were accepted, a material principle of contribution would result in broadly egalitarian or perhaps utilitarian distributions, because no single individual would be able to make a contribution to economic wealth truly distinguishable from the contributions of other members of the relevant social group.

Libertarians reject the conclusion that egalitarian patterns of distribution somehow represent a normative ideal after which we should pattern society. People may be equal in a host of morally significant respects (for example, entitled to equal treatment under the law), but for the libertarian, it is a basic misconception of "justice" to regard people as a priori deserving of equal economic returns. In particular, people are seen as having a fundamental right to own and dispense freely with the products of their labor. This right must be respected even if its unrestricted exercise leads to vast inequalities of wealth within a single society.

However, a libertarian is not opposed to utilitarian or egalitarian distribution schemes if they are freely chosen by a group. Free choice by members of the group makes a rule right. Justice has nothing to do with the collection and redistribution of social resources, unless the redistribution is contractually accepted by those whose goods are redistributed. For the libertarian, justice is fundamentally about respecting individual choice.

## Nozick's Theory

The role of individual rights in a libertarian theory of justice is emphasized by contemporary philosopher Robert Nozick in his book *Anarchy, State, and Utopia*.[2] He elaborates and defends many classic notions of property ownership found in the seventeenth-century philosopher John Locke, who held that we make natural resources into our personal property by "mixing our labour" with the resources. Nozick presents social justice in terms of fundamental rights that derive from three principles: justice in acquisition, justice in transfer, and justice in rectification. There is no pattern of just distribution independent of free-market procedures for acquiring unowned property without violating the rights of others (though we must provide rectification for those who had property wrongfully extracted or otherwise were illegitimately obstructed in the free market). Justice consists in the unhindered operation of just *procedures* (such as fair play), not in the production of just *outcomes* (such as an equal distribution of resources).

Nozick refers to the social philosophy presented in his book as an "entitlement theory" of justice. The appropriateness of this description is apparent from the provocative line with which the book begins: "Individuals have rights, and there are things no person or group may do to them (without violating their rights)." Under this assumption, Nozick defends the minimal or "night-watchman" state, a conception according to which government action is justified only if it protects the fundamental rights or entitlements of its citizens.

Nozick's theory of legitimate state power presents a challenge to many assumptions underlying political realities in contemporary industrial societies. In both socialist and capitalist countries, government activity beyond protection of individual rights is allowed on grounds of social justice. Governments take pronounced steps to *redistribute* the wealth that has been acquired by individuals exercising their economic rights in accordance with free market laws. For example, the wealthy are taxed at a progressively higher rate than those who are less wealthy, with the proceeds underwriting state support of the indigent through welfare payments and unemployment compensation. Both Nozick's conception of the role of the state and his principles of justice are developed in the following selection.

---

[2]Robert Nozick, *Anarchy, State, and Utopia* (New York: Basic Books, 1974), especially pp. 149–82.

# The Entitlement Theory*

### Robert Nozick

The term "distributive justice" is not a neutral one. Hearing the term "distribution," most people presume that some thing or mechanism uses some principle or criterion to give out a supply of things. Into this process of distributing shares some error may have crept. So it is an open question, at least, whether re-distribution should take place; whether we should do again what has already been done once, though poorly. However, we are not in the position of children who have been given portions of pie by someone who now makes last minute adjustments to rectify careless cutting. There is no *central* distribution, no person or group entitled to control all the resources, jointly deciding how they are to be doled out. What each person gets, he gets from others who give to him in exchange for something, or as a gift. In a free society, diverse persons control different resources, and new holdings arise out of the voluntary exchanges and actions of persons. . . .

The subject of justice in holdings consists of three major topics. The first is the *original acquisition of holdings,* the appropriation of unheld things. This includes the issues of how unheld things may come to be held, the process, or processes, by which unheld things may come to be held, the things that may come to be held by these processes, the extent of what comes to be held by a

particular process, and so on. We shall refer to the complicated truth about this topic, which we shall not formulate here, as the principle of justice in acquisition. The second topic concerns the *transfer of holdings* from one person to another. By what processes may a person transfer holdings to another? How may a person acquire a holding from another who holds it? Under this topic come general descriptions of voluntary exchange, and gift and (on the other hand) fraud, as well as reference to particular conventional details fixed upon in a given society. The complicated truth about this subject (with placeholders for conventional details) we shall call the principle of justice in transfer. (And we shall suppose it also includes principles governing how a person may divest himself of a holding, passing it into an unheld state.)

If the world were wholly just, the following inductive definition would exhaustively cover the subject of justice in holdings.

1. A person who acquires a holding in accordance with the principle of justice in acquisition is entitled to that holding.

2. A person who acquires a holding in accordance with the principle of justice in transfer, from someone else entitled to the holding, is entitled to the holding.

3. No one is entitled to a holding except by (repeated) applications of 1 and 2. The complete principle of distributive justice would say simply that a distribution is just if everyone is entitled to the

*From Robert Nozick, *Anarchy, State, and Utopia* (New York: Basic Books, Inc., Publishers, 1974), pp. 149–54, 156–7, 159–63, 168, 174–5, 178–9, 182. Copyright 1974 by Basic Books, Inc., Publishers, New York. Reprinted by permission of Basic Books, Inc., and Basil Blackwell Publisher.

holdings they possess under the distribution. . . .

Not all actual situations are generated in accordance with the two principles of justice in holdings: the principle of justice in acquisition and the principle of justice in transfer. Some people steal from others, or defraud them, or enslave them, seizing their product and preventing them from living as they choose, or forcibly exclude others from competing in exchanges. None of these are permissible modes of transition from one situation to another. And some persons acquire holdings by means not sanctioned by the principle of justice in acquisition. The existence of past injustice (previous violations of the first two principles of justice in holdings) raises the third major topic under justice in holdings: the rectification of injustice in holdings. If past injustice has shaped present holdings in various ways, some identifiable and some not, what now, if anything, ought to be done to rectify these injustices? . . .

## Historical Principles and End-Result Principles

The general outlines of the entitlement theory illuminate the nature and defects of other conceptions of distributive justice. The entitlement theory of justice in distribution is *historical;* whether a distribution is just depends upon how it came about. In contrast, *current time-slice principles* of justice hold that the justice of a distribution is determined by how things are distributed (who has what) as judged by some *structural* principle(s) of just distribution. A utilitarian who judges between any two distributions by seeing which has the greater sum of utility and, if the sums

tie, applies some fixed equality criterion to choose the more equal distribution, would hold a current time-slice principle of justice. As would someone who had a fixed schedule of trade-offs between the sum of happiness and equality. According to a current time-slice principle, all that needs to be looked at, in judging the justice of a distribution, is who ends up with what; in comparing any two distributions one need look only at the matrix presenting the distributions. No further information need be fed into a principle of justice. It is a consequence of such principles of justice that any two structurally identical distributions are equally just. . . .

Most persons do not accept current time-slice principles as constituting the whole story about distributive shares. They think it relevant in assessing the justice of a situation to consider not only the distribution it embodies, but also how that distribution came about. If some persons are in prison for murder or war crimes, we do not say that to assess the justice of the distribution in the society we must look only at what this person has, and that person has, and that person has, . . . at the current time. We think it relevant to ask whether someone did something so that he *deserved* to be punished, deserved to have a lower share. . . .

## Patterning

Almost every suggested principle of distributive justice is patterned: to each according to his moral merit, or needs, or marginal product, or how hard he tries, or the weighted sum of the foregoing, and so on. The principle of entitlement we have sketched is *not* patterned. There is no one natural dimension or weighted sum or combination of a small number of natural dimensions that yields the distributions generated in accordance with the principle of entitlement. The set of holdings that results when some persons receive their marginal products, others win at gambling, others receive a share of their mate's income, others receive gifts from foundations, others receive interest on loans, others receive gifts from admirers, others receive returns on investment, others make for themselves much of what they have, others find things, and so on, will not be patterned. . . .

To think that the task of a theory of distributive justice is to fill in the blank in "to each according to his _____" is to be predisposed to search for a pattern; and the separate treatment of "from each according to his _____" treats production and distribution as two separate and independent issues. On an entitlement view these are *not* two separate questions. Whoever makes something, having bought or contracted for all other held resources used in the process (transferring some of his holdings for these cooperating factors), is entitled to it. . . .

So entrenched are maxims of the usual form that perhaps we should present the entitlement conception as a competitor. Ignoring acquisition and rectification, we might say:

> From each according to what he chooses to do, to each according to what he makes for himself (perhaps with the contracted aid of others) and what others choose to do for him and choose to give him of what they've been given previously (under this maxim) and haven't yet expended or transferred.

This, the discerning reader will have noticed, has its defects as a slogan. So as a summary and great simplification (and not as a maxim with any independent meaning) we have:

*From each as they choose, to each as they are chosen.*

## How Liberty Upsets Patterns

It is not clear how those holding alternative conceptions of distributive justice can reject the entitlement conception of justice in holdings. For suppose a distribution favored by one of these non-entitlement conceptions is realized. Let us suppose it is your favorite one and let us call this distribution $D_1$; perhaps everyone has an equal share, perhaps shares vary in accordance with some dimension you treasure. Now suppose that Wilt Chamberlain is greatly in demand by basketball teams, being a great gate attraction. (Also suppose contracts run only for a year, with players being free agents.) He signs the following sort of contract with a team: In each home game, twenty-five cents from the price of each ticket of admission goes to him. (We ignore the question of whether he is "gouging" the owners, letting them look out for themselves.) The season starts, and people cheerfully attend his team's games; they buy their tickets, each time dropping a separate twenty-five cents of their admission price into a special box with Chamberlain's name on it. They are excited about seeing him play; it is worth the total admission price to them. Let us suppose that in one season one million persons attend his home games, and Wilt Chamberlain winds up with $250,000, a much larger sum than the average income and larger even than anyone else has. Is he entitled to this income? Is this new distribution $D_2$, unjust? If so, why? There is *no* question about whether each of the people was entitled to the control over the resources they held in $D_1$; because that was the distribution (your favorite) that (for the purposes of argument) we assumed was acceptable. Each of these persons *chose* to give twenty-five cents of their money to Chamberlain. They could have spent it on going to the movies, or on candy bars, or on copies of *Dissent* magazine, or of *Monthly Review*. But they all, at least one million of them, converged on giving it to Wilt Chamberlain in exchange for watching him play basketball. If $D_1$ was a just distribution, and people voluntarily moved from it to $D_2$, transferring parts of their shares they were given under $D_1$ (what was it for if not to do something with?), isn't $D_2$ also just? If the people were entitled to dispose of the resources to which they were entitled (under $D_1$), didn't this include their being entitled to give it to, or exchange it with, Wilt Chamberlain? Can anyone else complain on grounds of justice? Each other person already has his legitimate share under $D_1$. Under $D_1$, there is nothing that anyone has that anyone else has a claim of justice against. After someone transfers something to Wilt Chamberlain, third parties *still* have their legitimate shares; *their* shares are not changed. By what process could such a transfer among two persons give a rise to a legitimate claim of distributive justice on a portion of what was transferred, by a third party who had no claim of justice on any holding of the others *before* the transfer? To cut off objections irrelevant here, we might imagine the exchanges occurring in a socialist society, after hours. After playing whatever basketball he does in his daily work, or doing whatever other daily work he does, Wilt Chamberlain decides to put in *overtime* to earn additional money. (First his work quota is set; he works time over that.) Or imag-

ine it is a skilled juggler people like to see, who puts on shows after hours. . . .

The general point illustrated by the Wilt Chamberlain example is that no end-state principle or distributional patterned principle of justice can be continuously realized without continuous interference with people's lives. Any favored pattern would be transformed into one unfavored by the principle, by people choosing to act in various ways; for example, by people exchanging goods and services with other people, or giving things to other people, things the transferrers are entitled to under the favored distributional pattern. To maintain a pattern one must either continually interfere to stop people from transferring resources as they wish to, or continually (or periodically) interfere to take from some persons resources that others for some reason chose to transfer to them. . . .

Patterned principles of distributive justice necessitate *re*distributive activities. The likelihood is small that any actual freely-arrived-at set of holdings fits a given pattern; and the likelihood is nil that it will continue to fit the pattern as people exchange and give. From the point of view of an entitlement theory, redistribution is a serious matter indeed, involving, as it does, the violation of people's rights. (An exception is those taking that fall under the principle of the rectification of injustices.) . . .

## Locke's Theory of Acquisition

Before we turn to consider other theories of justice in detail, we must introduce an additional bit of complexity into the structure of the entitlement theory. This is best approached by considering

Locke's attempt to specify a principle of justice in acquisition. Locke views property rights in an unowned object as originating through someone's mixing his labor with it. This gives rise to many questions. What are the boundaries of what labor is mixed with? If a private astronaut clears a place on Mars, has he mixed his labor with (so that he comes to own) the whole planet, the whole uninhabited universe, or just a particular plot? Which plot does an act bring under ownership? . . .

Locke's proviso that there be "enough and as good left in common for others" is meant to ensure that the situation of others is not worsened. . . .

. . . I assume that any adequate theory of justice in acquisition will contain a proviso similar to [Locke's]. . . .

I believe that the free operation of a market system will not actually run afoul of the Lockean proviso. . . . If this is correct, the proviso will not . . . provide a significant opportunity for future state action.

Nozick's emphatic opposition to redistributive accounts of justice is apparent in the opening three sentences of the above selection. Justice, in his theory, does not extend beyond free and fair exchanges in the marketplace. It has nothing to do with redistribution, which necessarily involves the coercive extraction of legitimate holdings, which is a form of theft through taxation. A libertarian insists on a system in which, for example, health-care insurance is privately and voluntarily purchased by individuals. This entirely voluntary system is preferable because no one has had his or her property coercively extracted by the state in order to benefit someone else. In this theory, use of the tax code to effect social goals such as alleviating poverty, saving lives through advanced medical technology, and supporting the arts are forms of social engineering based on what a majority prefers rather than on what justice demands. All such state actions are illegitimate.

Many libertarians would object to the type of actions taken by the U.S. government in the Marshall Islands. There are two major libertarian arguments against the morality of what the United States did, both based on the violation of rights. First, since the Marshall Islands were legally occupied territory at the time of the first nuclear tests, the U.S. seems to have violated international conventions regarding the property rights of those in an occupied territory. Even after the establishment of the U.S. trusteeship, the U.S. actions were unjustified from a libertarian perspective, because they were undertaken with U.S., not Marshallese, interests in mind. As trustee, this was not the role assigned to the United States by the United Nations.

Second, it is not clear that the Bikinians acted freely in agreeing to turn over their land. To the extent that they felt they had no choice in the matter, the agreement they reached with the United States could be construed as more akin to theft. If the Bikinians had only a forced choice, then the seizure of their land was akin to an act of eminent domain, which many libertarians consider to be illegitimate because it violates individual rights for the sake of utilitarian social goals. This is a major and fundamental difference between utilitarians and libertarians on questions of social justice.

## Critiques of the Libertarian Theory

**Types of Procedural Justice**   Nozick's theory of legitimate acquisition and transfer, together with his thesis that justice consists not in any particular distributional outcome but in the unhindered operation of just procedures, suggests that he is committed to a form of "procedural" justice. This term, however, has a variety of meanings that need to be specified. John Rawls, whose theory of justice is discussed in the following section, has identified three distinct forms of procedural justice.[3] The first is "perfect" procedural justice, a type illustrated by considering the problem of how justly to divide a pizza. One solution to this problem would be to require that the person who cuts the pizza take the last piece. There would then be both an independent criterion or pattern of justice (i.e., each person should receive an equal share) and a procedure guaranteeing that a just distribution was achieved. The person who cuts the pizza would be certain to receive the largest possible share only if he or she made every slice the same size.

"Imperfect" procedural justice also has an independent criterion of just distribution, but it is not possible to design procedures that can guarantee outcomes in conformity with the criterion. An example is criminal trials. The independent criterion specifies that those who have committed crimes, and only those who have committed crimes, are to be found guilty. The procedures of the criminal trial have been established as the most reliable means of achieving this outcome; but no matter how strictly those procedures are followed, just outcomes will not *always* result.

"Pure" procedural justice differs from both the perfect and imperfect forms in that any criterion or pattern of justice independent of the demands of the procedure itself is absent. With this type of justice, any outcome is just as long as it results from the consistent operation of the specified procedures. Gambling is an example. We consider the result of a lottery or a game of chance unjust only if the rules and procedures of those practices are violated (for example, if a lottery is fixed or weighted). If a wealthy person wins money, we do not declare it unjust that he or she should win when poor people lost in the same game. We may think it unjust that the rich winner is not taxed more heavily, but this consideration of justice is distinct.

Nozick's entitlement theory advocates procedural justice of the pure procedural type. There is no pattern of just distribution independent of the procedures of acquisition, transfer, and rectification, and justice is served whenever individual rights are respected in the protected operation of these procedures. This claim has been at the center of philosophical controversy over the libertarian account, and many influential theories of justice are, in part, reactions against the libertarian commitment to pure procedural justice. Philosophers who have these reservations often maintain that some independent substantive criterion or pattern is essential to an adequate account of justice, even if there are no procedures that always produce outcomes in conformity with the independent standard. Consideration will now be given briefly to some of the alternative theories.

---

[3]John Rawls, *A Theory of Justice* (Cambridge, MA: Harvard University Press, 1971), pp. 84–86.

**Rights-Based Objections to Libertarianism**   Many objections to the libertarian theory take as their starting point assumptions that at least formally resemble the libertarian's assumptions. It is possible, for instance, to reach conclusions radically different from Nozick's without abandoning his commitment to fundamental individual rights. The mistake in the libertarian theory, claim these writers, is the overriding importance ascribed to a limited set of *economic* rights. Many philosophers would argue that a more inclusive conception of fundamental individual rights must be recognized. They challenge the proponent of libertarianism to answer the following questions: Why should we assume that people's economic rights extend only to the acquisition and dispensation of private property according to the free market rules? Is it not equally plausible to posit more substantive moral rights in the economic sphere—say, the right to a decent level of education, to health care, and to a decent living standard?

Moreover, Nozick's ideal is most plausible for free transactions among informed and consenting parties who start as equals in the bargaining process. In the real world, however, this is rarely the case. Contracts, voting privileges, ventures in the stock market, and family relationships may involve bluffing, differentials of power and wealth, manipulation, and the like, that work systematically to disadvantage individuals. Imagine, for example, that over the course of time one group in society gains immense wealth and thereby political influence and power over another group. Although each of the transactions leading to this immense imbalance was legitimate, it does not follow that the outcome is a morally acceptable or just state of affairs. For example, the centuries of transactions leading up to control of resources and the distribution of goods in the Marshall Islands might be understandable—and many of them legitimate—but the outcome may be an unjust arrangement requiring redistribution of resources or power. Here, as elsewhere, it seems that an individual or group whose bargaining position has been deeply eroded has a right to be protected against social inequalities that are seriously harmful and disadvantaging. These inequalities seem especially unjust if they are the result of actions taken before the individual was born or could have exerted influence over the state of affairs.

If additional, more substantive rights are recognized, a different picture of the requirements of justice emerges. The broader and more substantive conception of economic and noneconomic rights introduces a criterion of just distribution by which the outcomes of economic processes can be evaluated. Moreover, if people have a right to a minimal level of material means, their rights are violated whenever economic distributions leave some persons with less than the minimal level. A commitment to individual rights may result in a theory of justice that requires a more activist role for government than Nozick's rights-based theory condones.

**The Material Principle of Need**   These considerations lead many philosophers to reject the pure procedural commitments of the libertarian theory. In their place, some philosophers propose a material principle specifying need as the relevant respect in which people are to be compared for purposes of determining the justice of economic distributions.

Much in these theories turns on how the notion of a need is delineated. Generally, to say that someone has a need for something is to say that the person will be harmed or detrimentally affected if that thing is not obtained. For purposes of justice, a material principle of need would be less controversial if it were restricted to *fundamental* needs. If malnutrition, serious bodily injury, and the withholding of information involve fundamental harms, then we have a fundamental need for nutrition, health-care facilities, and education. According to theories based on this material principle, justice requires that the satisfaction of fundamental human needs is a higher social priority than the protection of rights to economic opportunity. Such a principle seems especially important in the circumstance of limited resources in the Marshall Islands, where the failure to gain access to certain medical supplies and uncontaminated foods will cause avoidable deaths.

This construal of the material principle of need has provided historically important alternatives to libertarian justice, but there may be room for reconciling libertarianism with theories that emphasize need. Many advanced industrial countries have the capacity to produce far more than is strictly necessary to meet their citizens' fundamental needs. One might argue that once everyone's fundamental needs have been satisfied, justice requires no particular pattern of distribution and will allow the operation of the free market mechanisms that libertarians support. For example, some current discussions of the right to free health care and national health insurance are rooted in the idea of everyone's receiving basic medical needs, but no more than basic needs. In this way, a single unified theory of justice might require the maintenance of certain patterns in the distribution of basic goods (for example, a decent minimum level of income, education, and health care), while allowing the market to determine distributions of goods beyond those which satisfy fundamental needs.

This approach accepts a two-tiered system of access to goods and services—(1) social coverage for basic and catastrophic needs and (2) private purchase of other goods and services. On the first tier, distribution is based on need, and everyone's basic needs are met by the government. Better services may be made available for purchase at personal expense on the second tier. This proposal offers an attractive point of negotiation between libertarians, utilitarians, and egalitarians. It provides a modicum of welfare for all on a premise of equal access, while also allowing unequal additional purchase through individual initiative and contract. Theories such as utilitarianism may find the compromise attractive because it serves to minimize public dissatisfaction and to maximize social utility. The egalitarian finds an opportunity to use an equal access principle, and the libertarian retains free-market production and distribution.

However, some contemporary moral philosophers consider need-based theories of justice to be nothing more than one form of egalitarian theory of justice. We now turn to this theory.

## THE EGALITARIAN THEORY

Some notion of equality has a pivotal place in many ethical theories. For example, deontologists and utilitarians alike express a commitment to the idea of equality of persons. In utilitarianism, people are equal in the value accorded their preferences and goals, whereas the Kantian considers persons to deserve equal respect. Also, as Ronald Dworkin has suggested in his theory of rights, the notion that everyone possesses fundamental and inviolable moral rights is one way of giving expression to the idea of equality. In each of these theories, it is a requirement of morality that people be treated equally, regardless of individual differences.

Nonetheless, a commitment to some form of basic equality is compatible with a belief that justice allows people to be *unequal* in many other respects. People may be considered equal or treated equally for purposes such as distributing basic political rights and moral obligations, and yet be considered unequal or treated unequally for other purposes, such as salaries and taxes.

The justification of both equality and inequality is central to egalitarian theories of justice. In its most extreme form, egalitarianism holds that individual differences are no more significant in an account of social justice than elsewhere in morality. An inequality is an inequity; and distributions of burdens and benefits in a society are just to the extent that they are equal. Deviations from absolute equality in distribution can be determined to be unjust without consideration of the respects in which members of the society may differ.

Consider how a radical egalitarian might interpret studies conducted by the Survey Research Center at the University of Michigan and other survey research centers. Their surveys showed that in the United States wealth had become more concentrated in the three decades between 1963 and 1995. Only 1 percent of all U.S. citizens owned 39 percent of the total household wealth (up from 25 percent in 1963); the top 20 percent owned 84 percent. Although the share of wealth owned by this small top group was rising rapidly throughout this period, the share of every other group below it was declining. By 1997 a single person, Bill Gates, was worth as much as the forty million American households at the lowest level of wealth distribution. These three decades reversed a long-standing trend in the United States toward less concentration of wealth. The radical egalitarian would view these figures as evidence that American society is now seriously unjust.

Stated in this form, egalitarianism seems implausible, because it leaves no room for individual differences to be permissible by justice. Less rigid egalitarian accounts, by contrast, permit certain inequalities to be just. Often these theories recommend only the equal distribution of goods necessary to satisfy fundamental human needs, and some egalitarian accounts of justice move still further away from radical egalitarian commitments. Some maintain that equality of distribution meeting fundamental needs is not the crucial matter, because egalitarianism requires nothing more than a basic equality of *opportunity,* namely, that individuals be given the opportunity to satisfy their fundamental needs.

The most powerful and influential egalitarian theory has been developed by John Rawls. His is not a radical theory, but it does have distinctive ingredients of egalitarianism.

## Rawls's Theory

Rawls presents his theory as a direct challenge to utilitarianism. His objections to utilitarianism help explain his principles of justice.

Rawls's basic objection is that the distributions produced by maximizing utility could entail violations of basic individual liberties and rights that ought to be guaranteed by social justice. "Each person possesses an inviolability founded on justice that even the welfare of society as a whole cannot override."[4] Utilitarianism, being indifferent to the *distribution* of satisfactions among individuals but not to the total satisfaction in society, would presumably permit the infringement of some people's rights and liberties if this infringement promised to produce a proportionately greater utility for others. For example, during a war or an incident of civil violence, it might be possible to justify restricting freedom of the press, confiscating weapons, searching private homes, denying the right to vote to certain groups, torturing prisoners, and experimenting on nuclear weapons if there were sufficient utility for others. Rawls argues that there is something fundamentally awry in an ethical theory that makes individual rights depend on changeable (perhaps temporary) social facts such as individual happiness and majority interests. This utilitarian approach, according to Rawls, fundamentally affronts our conception of social justice.

Utilitarians have not been persuaded by this idea. They maintain that the principle of utility is alone sufficient to ground an adequate account of justice. They argue that Rawls's objections seem plausible only because they are abstracted from the conditions in which considerations of justice arise and because he uses excessively exaggerated examples. For these philosophers, a complete assessment of the social consequences reveals that allegedly justified violations of common notions of justice in truth do not satisfy the principle of utility.

Rawls is as unmoved by these arguments as utilitarians are by egalitarian considerations. To him, it seems enough that violations of justice could *in principle* be allowed on utilitarian grounds. Here he might point to the Marshall Islands case, where it was very tempting at the end of the Second World War to use a remote island population to test what was considered the single most important national security device in the world, namely, nuclear bombs. Under a utilitarian theory it would appear that the justification of such testing was not problematic: Few persons stand to suffer, and all free nations stand to benefit. Rawls regards such thinking as undercut by the principle that the Marshallese are due the same equal respect and rights as anyone else.

The task of moral philosophy, as Rawls sees it, is to advocate an ethical theory capable of grounding principles of justice in conditions other than utility. Here begins the constructive side of his theory. Rawls turns for this purpose to a hypothetical social-contract procedure indebted to what he calls the "Kantian conception of equality." In this account, valid principles of justice are those to which we would agree if we could freely and impartially consider the social situation from a standpoint (the "original position") outside any actual society. Impartiality is guaranteed in this situation by a conceptual device Rawls calls the "veil of ignorance." This notion stipulates that, in the original position, each person is ignorant of all his or her particular fortuitous advantages or disadvantages. For example, the person's sex, race, intelligence, family background, and special talents or handicaps are not re-

---

[4]John Rawls, *A Theory of Justice*, p. 3.

vealed in this hypothetical circumstance; nor does the person know whether he or she is a government official in Washington or a farmer in the Marshall Islands. The veil of ignorance prevents people from promoting principles of justice that are biased toward personal combinations of fortuitous talents and characteristics, for example, various combinations of need, merit, experience, and sexual advantage that lead different parties to promote competing material principles.

Rawls argues that under these conditions of impartiality, people would unanimously agree on two fundamental principles of justice. The first requires that each person be permitted the maximum amount of basic liberty compatible with a similar liberty for others. The second stipulates that once this equal basic liberty is assured, inequalities in social primary goods (including, for example, income, rights, and opportunities) are to be allowed only if they benefit everyone. Rawls considers social institutions just if, and only if, they conform to these two basic principles.

By contrast to an individual-centered theory, such as Nozick's, a social arrangement, in Rawls's view, is a communal effort to advance the good of all in the society. Because inequalities of birth, natural endowment, and historical circumstance are undeserved, persons in a cooperative society should make more equal the unequal situation of naturally disadvantaged members. Those naturally endowed with more advantageous properties or more fortunate in their social position do not *deserve* those advantaging properties, and a just society seeks to nullify the advantages stemming from accidents of birth and history. As Rawls puts it, these fortuitous advantaging properties seem arbitrary from the moral point of view. (See pp. 332–34 below on "fair opportunity" for amplification of this thesis.)

# An Egalitarian Theory of Justice*

## John Rawls

### The Role of Justice

Justice is the first virtue of social institutions, as truth is of systems of thought. A theory however elegant and economical must be rejected or revised if it is untrue; likewise laws and institutions no matter how efficient and well-arranged must be reformed or abolished if they

*Reprinted by permission of the publishers from *A Theory of Justice* by John Rawls, Cambridge, Mass.: The Belknap Press of Harvard University Press, Copyright ©1971 by the President and Fellows of Harvard College.

are unjust. Each person possesses an inviolability founded on justice that even the welfare of society as a whole cannot override. For this reason justice denies that the loss of freedom for some is made right by a greater good shared by others. It does not allow that the sacrifices imposed on a few are outweighed by the larger sum of advantages enjoyed by many. Therefore in a just society the liberties of equal citizenship are taken as settled; the rights secured by justice are not subject to political bargaining or to the calculus of social interests. The only thing that permits us to acquiesce in an erroneous theory is the lack of a better one; analogously, an injustice is tolerable only when it is necessary to avoid an even greater injustice. Being first virtues of human activities, truth and justice are uncompromising.

These propositions seem to express our intuitive conviction of the primacy of justice. No doubt they are expressed too strongly. In any event I wish to inquire whether these contentions or others similar to them are sound, and if so how they can be accounted for. To this end it is necessary to work out a theory of justice in the light of which these assertions can be interpreted and assessed. I shall begin by considering the role of the principles of justice. Let us assume, to fix ideas, that a society is a more or less self-sufficient association of persons who in their relations to one another recognize certain rules of conduct as binding and who for the most part act in accordance with them. Suppose further that these rules specify a system of cooperation designed to advance the good of those taking part in it. Then, although a society is a cooperative venture for mutual advantage, it is typically marked by a conflict as well as by an identity of interests. There is an identity of interests since social cooperation makes possible a better life for all than any would have if each were to live solely by his own efforts. There is a conflict of interests since persons are not indifferent as to how the greater benefits produced by their collaboration are distributed, for in order to pursue their ends they each prefer a larger to a lesser share. A set of principles is required for choosing among the various social arrangements which determine this division of advantages and for underwriting an agreement on the proper distributive shares. These principles are the princi-

ples of social justice: they provide a way of assigning rights and duties in the basic institutions of society and they define the appropriate distribution of the benefits and burdens of social cooperation. . . .

## The Original Position and Justification

. . . The idea here is simply to make vivid to ourselves the restrictions that it seems reasonable to impose on arguments for principles of justice, and therefore on these principles themselves. Thus it seems reasonable and generally acceptable that no one should be advantaged or disadvantaged by natural fortune or social circumstances in the choice of principles. It also seems widely agreed that it should be impossible to tailor principles to the circumstances of one's own case. We should insure further that particular inclinations and aspirations, and persons' conceptions of their good, do not affect the principles adopted. The aim is to rule out those principles that it would be rational to propose for acceptance, however little the chance of success, only if one knew certain things that are irrelevant from the standpoint of justice. For example, if a man knew that he was wealthy, he might find it rational to advance the principle that various taxes for welfare measures be counted unjust; if he knew that he was poor, he would most likely propose the contrary principle. To represent the desired restrictions one imagines a situation in which everyone is deprived of this sort of information. One excludes the knowledge of those contingencies which sets men at odds and allows them to be guided by their prejudices. In this manner the veil of ignorance is arrived at in a natural way. . . .

## Two Principles of Justice

I shall now state in a provisional form the two principles of justice that I believe would be chosen in the original position. . . .

The first statement of the two principles reads as follows.

First: each person is to have an equal right to the most extensive basic liberty compatible with a similar liberty for others.

Second: social and economic inequalities are to be arranged so that they are both (a) reasonably expected to be to everyone's advantage, and (b) attached to positions and offices open to all. . . . [The Difference Principle].

By way of general comment, these principles primarily apply, as I have said, to the basic structure of society. They are to govern the assignment of rights and duties and to regulate the distribution of social and economic advantages. As their formulation suggests, these principles presuppose that the social structure can be divided into two more or less distinct parts, the first principle applying to the one, the second to the other. They distinguish between those aspects of the social system that define and secure the equal liberties of citizenship and those that specify and establish social and economic inequalities. The basic liberties of citizens are, roughly speaking, political liberty (the right to vote and to be eligible for public office) together with freedom of speech and assembly; liberty of conscience and freedom of thought; freedom of the person along with the right to hold (personal) property; and freedom from arbitrary arrest and seizure as defined by

the concept of the rule of law. These liberties are all required to be equal by the first principle, since citizens of a just society are to have the same basic rights.

The second principle applies, in the first approximation, to the distribution of income and wealth and to the design of organizations that make use of differences in authority and responsibility, or chains of command. While the distribution of wealth and income need not be equal, it must be to everyone's advantage, and at the same time, positions of authority and offices of command must be accessible to all. One applies the second principle by holding positions open, and then, subject to this constraint, arranges social and economic inequalities so that everyone benefits.

These principles are to be arranged in a serial order with the first principle prior to the second. This ordering means that a departure from the institutions of equal liberty required by the first principle cannot be justified, or compensated for, by greater social and economic advantages. The distribution of wealth and income, and the hierarchies of authority, must be consistent with both the liberties of equal citizenship and equality of opportunity.

It is clear that these principles are rather specific in their content, and their acceptance rests on certain assumptions that I must eventually try to explain and justify. A theory of justice depends upon a theory of society in ways that will become evident as we proceed. For the present, it should be observed that the two principles (and this holds for all formulations) are a special case of a more general conception of justice that can be expressed as follows.

> All social values—liberty and opportunity, income and wealth, and the bases of self-respect—are to be distributed equally

unless an unequal distribution of any, or all, of these values is to everyone's advantage.

Injustice, then, is simply inequalities that are not to the benefit of all. Of course, this conception is extremely vague and requires interpretation.

As a first step, suppose that the basic structure of society distributes certain primary goods, that is, things that every rational man is presumed to want. These goods normally have a use whatever a person's rational plan of life. For simplicity, assume that the chief primary goods at the disposition of society are rights and liberties, powers and opportunities, income and wealth. These are the social primary goods. Other primary goods such as health and vigor, intelligence and imagination, are natural goods; although their possession is influenced by the basic structure, they are not so directly under its control. Imagine, then, a hypothetical initial arrangement in which all the social primary goods are equally distributed: everyone has similar rights and duties, and income and wealth are evenly shared. This state of affairs provides a benchmark for judging improvements. If certain inequalities of wealth and organizational powers would make everyone better off than in this hypothetical starting situation, then they accord with the general conception.

Now it is possible, at least theoretically, that by giving up some of their fundamental liberties men are sufficiently compensated by the resulting social and economic gains. The general conception of justice imposes no restrictions on what sort of inequalities are permissible; it only requires that everyone's position be improved. . . .

Now the second principle insists that each person benefit from permissible inequalities in the basic structure. This means that it must be reasonable for each relevant representative man defined by this structure, when he views it as a going concern, to prefer his prospects with the inequality to his prospects without it. One is not allowed to justify differences in income or organizational powers on the ground that the disadvantages of those in one position are outweighed by the greater advantages of those in another. Much less can infringements of liberty be counterbalanced in this way. Applied to the basic structure, the principle of utility would have us maximize the sum of expectations of representative men (weighted by the number of persons they represent, on the classical view), and this would permit us to compensate for the losses of some by the gains of others. Instead, the two principles require that everyone benefit from economic inequalities. . . .

## The Tendency to Equality

I wish to conclude this discussion of the two principles by explaining the sense in which they express an egalitarian conception of justice. Also I should like to forestall the objection to the principle of fair opportunity that it leads to a callous meritocratic society. In order to prepare the way for doing this, I note several aspects of the conception of justice that I have set out.

First we may observe that the difference principle gives some weight to the considerations singled out by the principle of redress. This is the principle that undeserved inequalities call for redress; and since inequalities of birth and natural endowment are undeserved, these inequalities are to be somehow compensated for. Thus the principle holds that in order to treat all persons equally, to provide genuine equality of opportunity, society must give more attention to those with fewer native assets and to those born into the less favorable social positions. The idea is to redress the bias of contingencies in the direction of equality. In pursuit of this principle greater resources might be spent on the education of the less rather than the more intelligent, at least over a certain time of life, say the earlier years of school.

Now the principle of redress has not to my knowledge been proposed as the sole criterion of justice, as the single aim of the social order. It is plausible as most such principles are only as a prima facie principle, one that is to be weighed in the balance with others. For example, we are to weigh it against the principle to improve the average standard of life, or to advance the common good. But whatever other principles we hold, the claims of redress are to be taken into account. It is thought to represent one of the elements in our conception of justice. Now the difference principle is not of course the principle of redress. It does not require society to try to even out handicaps as if all were expected to compete on a fair basis in the same race. But the difference principle would allocate resources in education, say, so as to improve the long-term expectation of the least favored. If this end is attained by giving more attention to the better endowed, it is permissible; otherwise not. And in making this decision, the value of education should not be assessed only in terms of economic efficiency and social welfare. Equally if not more important is the role of education in enabling a person to enjoy the culture of his society and to take part in its affairs, and in this way to provide for each individual a secure sense of his own worth.

Thus although the difference principle is not the same as that of redress, it does achieve some of the intent of the latter principle. It transforms the aims of the basic structure so that the total scheme of institutions no longer emphasizes social efficiency and technocratic values. . . .

The natural distribution is neither just nor unjust; nor is it unjust that men are born into society at some particular position. These are simply natural facts. What is just and unjust is the way that institutions deal with these facts. Aristocratic and caste societies are unjust because they make these contingencies the ascriptive basis for belonging to more or less enclosed and privileged social classes. The basic structure of these societies incorporates the arbitrariness found in nature. But there is no necessity for men to resign themselves to these contingencies. The social system is not an unchangeable order beyond human control but a pattern of human action. In justice as fairness men agree to share one another's fate. In designing institutions they undertake to avail themselves of the accidents of nature and social circumstance only when doing so is for the common benefit. The two principles are a fair way of meeting the arbitrariness of fortune; and while no doubt imperfect in other ways, the institutions which satisfy these principles are just. . . .

There is a natural inclination to object that those better situated deserve their greater advantages whether or not they are to the benefit of others. At this point it is necessary to be clear about the notion of desert. It is perfectly true that given a just system of cooperation as a scheme of public rules and the expectations set up by it, those who, with the prospect of improving their condition, have done what the system announces that it will reward are entitled to their advantages. In this sense the more fortunate have a claim to their better situation; their claims are legitimate expectations established by social institutions, and the community is obligated to meet them. But this sense of desert presupposes the existence of the cooperative scheme; it is irrelevant to the question whether in the first place the scheme is to be designed in accordance with the difference principle or some other criterion.

Perhaps some will think that the person with greater natural endowments deserves those assets and the superior character that made their development possible. Because he is more worthy in this sense, he deserves the greater advantages that he could achieve with them. This view, however, is surely incorrect. It seems to be one of the fixed points of our considered judgments that no one deserves his place in the distribution of native endowments, any more than one deserves one's initial starting place in society. The assertion that a man deserves the superior character that enables him to make the effort to cultivate his abilities is equally problematic; for his character depends in large part upon fortunate family and social circumstances for which he can claim no credit. The notion of desert seems not to apply to these cases. Thus the more advantaged representative man cannot say that he deserves and therefore has a right to a scheme of cooperation in which he is permitted to acquire benefits in ways that do not contribute to the welfare of others. There is no basis for his making this claim. From the standpoint of common sense, then, the difference principle appears to be acceptable both to the more advantaged and to the less advantaged individual.

Rawls's theory is not concerned with the burdens and benefits to be distributed to identifiable individuals, but rather with the cooperative institutional arrangements that produce the benefits and create the burdens that are to be distributed. His principles of justice do not, for example, mention properties possessed by an individual on the basis of which that person's share of social resources is determined. Nor do the principles determine how wealth or other primary goods are to be distributed directly to individuals.

Rawls sets as his theory's exclusive objective "the basic structure of society." The basic structure is "the primary subject of justice" and encompasses the "all-inclusive social system that determines background justice." Rawls argues that other philosophers have superficially presupposed the basic institutions as a mere background against which moral judgments are to be reached, while failing to theorize regarding the justice of the institutions themselves. His concern in a theory of justice is with the all-inclusive system of political, legal, economic, and familial institutions whose "effects are so profound and present from the start," and not with superficial tinkering with allocational principles.[5]

To consider an example, suppose the structure of the market system is not fair because only those born wealthy are able to make investments, and investments alone

---

[5]In his later work Rawls has continued to emphasize the importance of the basic structure of society as the subject matter for theories of justice. See "The Basic Structure as Subject," in *Political Liberalism* (New York: Columbia University Press, 1996), pp. 256–88.

permit an ample standard of living. Those not born into wealth are systematically excluded from the possibility of living well. This situation of advantage and disadvantage could be adjusted by taxing and redistributing wealth according to a principle of need. Wealth theoretically could even be distributed to equalize individual income. Yet the social system would remain unjust because the background conditions generating the problem had not been adjusted. To the extent that these background conditions are themselves the cause of unjust outcomes requiring compensatory actions, they are unjust no matter which compensatory measures are introduced.

Rawls's theory is *egalitarian* in several respects. First, it makes equality a basic characteristic of the original position from which the social contract is forged. Equality is built into that hypothetical position in the form of a free and equal bargain between all parties, under the condition that there is equal ignorance of all individual characteristics and advantages that persons have or will have in their daily lives. Furthermore, people in this position would choose a scheme of equal possession of basic liberties as the first commitment of their social institutions. Given the "serial order" (also called "lexical ordering") of the two principles, this commitment to equal liberty assumes a rigid priority in the Rawlsian account of justice. Rawls also thinks it expresses the inviolability of persons that utilitarian theories fail to express.

Because parties in the original position are free and *equal,* one might suppose that the overriding principle of distributive justice should be strictly equal distribution. No perfectly free and equal person, after all, would expect either more or less than an equal share of primary social goods. Rawls notes that "the obvious starting point is to suppose that . . . social primary goods . . . should be equal: everyone should have an equal share."[6] Nevertheless, Rawls rejects radical egalitarianism, arguing that equal distribution cannot be justified as the sole primary principle. If there were inequalities rendering everyone better off in comparison to initial equality, these inequalities would be desirable, as long as they were consistent with equal liberty and fair opportunity. More particularly, if these inequalities worked to enhance the position of the most disadvantaged persons, as measured by a higher level of primary goods for them, then it would be self-defeating for the least advantaged or anyone else to seek to prohibit them. Rawls thus rejects radical egalitarianism in favor of his second principle of justice.

The first part of his second principle is called the "difference principle." This principle permits inequalities of distribution as long as they are consistent with equal liberty and fair opportunity. Rawls formulates this principle so that inequalities are justifiable only if social and economic institutions are arranged to maximally benefit the position of the "*representative* least advantaged" person—that is, a hypothetical individual particularly unfortunate in the distribution of fortuitous characteristics or social advantages. Rawls is unclear about the range of types of individuals who might qualify under this category, but we can imagine that, for example, an uninsured worker at the poverty level who has been incapacitated from exposure to asbestos would qualify.

[6]John Rawls, "A Kantian Conception of Equality," *Cambridge Review* (February 1975): 97.

The difference principle could in theory allow extraordinary economic rewards to entrepreneurs if the resulting economic stimulation were to produce improved job opportunities and working conditions for the least advantaged members of society. Despite this measure of justified inequality, a strong egalitarian quality is retained, in that inequalities are permissible only if they maximally enhance the position of those worst off. Rawls points out that the "first problem of justice" is to delineate principles that can regulate inequalities while rearranging the long-lasting effects of social, natural, and historical contingencies. "The idea," says Rawls, "is to redress the bias of contingencies in the direction of equality."[7]

## Fair Opportunity

The difference principle expresses Rawls's conviction that the justice of social institutions is to be gauged by their tendency to counteract the inequalities caused purely by luck of birth, natural endowment, and historical circumstances and events. This approach accommodates many common beliefs about justice, which agree that it is unjust to distribute social burdens and benefits on the basis of purely fortuitous characteristics. But *why* are fortuitous characteristics such as race, religion, intelligence, national origin, sex, and social status inappropriate as material principles of distributive justice? The most plausible reason is that to use principles based on the merely fortuitous would be to treat people differently, sometimes with devastating consequences, because of circumstances over which they have no control. This fairness-based reason holds that differences between persons are relevant only if those persons are responsible for the differences.

The "fair-opportunity principle," as it may be called, says that no person should be granted social benefits on the basis of undeserved advantaging properties (because no person is responsible for having these properties) and that no person should be denied social benefits on the basis of undeserved disadvantaging properties (because he or she also is not responsible for these properties). Such advantaging or disadvantaging properties are not grounds for morally acceptable discrimination between persons, because they are not the sorts of properties that one has a fair chance to acquire or overcome. Although religion and social status are not acquired in many societies and can be changed, race, sex, and intelligence—those natural properties that plague justice more than any others—are not alterable and are the kinds of properties we must consider in addressing issues of fair opportunity.

Consider the familiar example of the distribution of resources needed to obtain a basic education. This benefit is conventionally conferred on all citizens equally, and a person would be deprived or harmed if denied the benefit. Imagine a community in which an efficient school system provides a uniform opportunity for a quality education to all students with basic skills, regardless of sex, race, or religion. However, this system does not have special facilities for students with reading difficulties or mental handicaps, and therefore does not offer them an equal educational opportunity. These students require special training in order to overcome their

---

[7]John Rawls, *A Theory of Justice*, pp. 100 ff.

problems and to receive what for them would be a minimally adequate education. If they were responsible for their slowness, we might say that they deserved no special training and must expend greater effort. But if we discover that they are not responsible, owing to learning deficiencies or handicaps produced through injury, we sometimes say that they deserve special consideration. Distinctive levels of education are introduced for different kinds of students, disregarding the differential in cost (within reasonable financial limits).

At stake is not an *equal* distribution of economic resources to each individual. We do not say that slow learners with special reading problems or mental handicaps should be offered amounts of money or training or resources equal to what other pupils receive. Rather, we say they should receive a quality education because the principle of fair opportunity morally requires it. Any alternative distribution would lead to an undue burden for this group of persons. The burden would be undue because placed in violation of justice—or, at least, this is the claim of those who support a principle of fair opportunity.

If one accepts the fair opportunity rule in an account of distributive justice, it provides a revisionary perspective on many common forms of social distribution. A commitment to this principle suggests that whenever persons are set back in the advancing of their interests by "disadvantageous" properties for which they are not responsible, they should not be denied benefits because of those properties. In the case of the Marshall Islands, for example, it might be argued that the U.S. intervention set back the Marshallese and handicapped them. If so, justice seems to require that the United States provide the resources to give them at least the level of opportunity they enjoyed prior to the intervention—for example, adequate health-care resources to restore health, decontamination of the land, and so on.

But suppose that almost all our chief abilities and disabilities are a function of what Rawls refers to as the "natural lottery." That is, suppose that almost all our talents and deficiencies are a causal function of heredity and environment and that we consequently are not responsible for them. This could mean that among one's advantaging properties are one's ability to work long hours, one's competitive drive, and one's sense of dedication. Suppose also that disadvantaging properties such as a raspy voice, an ugly scar, or a thick accent were also undeserved. How far should we extend the range of *undeserved properties* that create a right in justice to some form of assistance?

If this theory of the causal origins of advantageous and disadvantageous properties were accepted, along with the justification based on fair opportunity previously outlined, one would be led to views about distributive justice radically different from the ones we now generally acknowledge. It is uncertain what the full implications of this approach would be, but several conclusions are anticipated in Rawls's own work. He argues as follows (against views such as Nozick's):

> [A free market society] permits the distribution of wealth and income to be determined by the natural distribution of abilities and talents. Within the limits allowed by the background arrangements, distributive shares are decided by the outcome of the natural lottery; and this outcome is *arbitrary from a moral perspective.* There is no more reason to permit the distribution of income and wealth to be settled by the distribution of natural assets than by historical and social fortune. . . . The extent to which natural capacities develop and reach

fruition is affected by *all kinds of social conditions and class attitudes.* Even the willingness to make an effort, to try, and so to be deserving in the ordinary sense is itself dependent upon happy family and social circumstances.[8]

Social rewards and punishments would be conceived in a strikingly revisionary manner if Rawls's approach were extended to many social contexts. Rather than allowing radical inequalities based on effort, contribution, and merit, one would see justice as done if radical inequalities were diminished (so long as disadvantaged persons were advantaged by such a system of conferring benefits). On the other hand, as Bernard Williams has correctly pointed out, this ideal procedure of reducing inequalities will have to stop somewhere, especially if it is assumed that everything about a person is environmentally controlled.[9] Some disadvantages may properly be viewed as *unfortunate,* whereas others will be viewed as *unfair* (and therefore obligatory in justice to correct). If needs are unfortunate, they may still be ameliorated by benevolence or compassion; but only if they are unfair does the obligation of justice require intervention by the state to redistribute resources.

It remains uncertain what the broader implications of a use of the fair opportunity principle approximating Rawls's would be. This problem also provides a reason why some have argued (Nozick, for example) that the principle of fair opportunity is not a valid principle at all.

### Critiques of Rawls's Egalitarianism

Rawls contends that people situated behind a veil of ignorance would adopt the difference principle as a way of protecting themselves against the unknown contingencies that could conceivably befall them. This contention has been among the most controversial in his theory. Some philosophers have argued that Rawls unjustifiably assumes that any rational person would agree to the difference principle. This assumption implies a particular conception of the process of human deliberation in situations involving choice, but is Rawls's thesis accurate? Specifically, does he ignore the possibility that people would agree to a riskier system of basic rules that permits more dramatic wins (as well as losses) in the distribution of social benefits? Other philosophers, including some utilitarians, suggest that the difference principle represents a departure from Rawls's commitment to the equal inviolability of all people, because it means that the wants, preferences, and happiness of the most advantaged individuals do not count for as much as the wants, preferences, and happiness of those who are less advantaged.

A second line of criticism springs from Nozick's libertarianism, perhaps the single most visible alternative account of justice in contemporary philosophy. His theory guarantees equal liberties without any attempt to compensate for advantages resulting from natural and social contingencies. He argues, specifically against Rawls, that a theory of justice should be structured to protect individual rights

---

[8]John Rawls, *A Theory of Justice,* pp. 73ff.
[9]Bernard Williams, "The Idea of Equality," in Hugo Bedau, ed., *Justice and Equality* (Englewood Cliffs, NJ: Prentice-Hall, 1971), p. 135.

against state interference and should not promote patterning arrangements that in effect *redistribute* economic benefits and burdens. In *Anarchy, State, and Utopia,* Nozick argues against Rawls's views as follows:

> If things fell from heaven like manna, and no one had any special entitlement to any portion of it, and no manna would fall unless all agreed to a particular distribution, and somehow the quantity varied depending on the distribution, then it is plausible to claim that persons placed so that they couldn't make threats, or hold out for specially large shares, would agree to the difference principle of distribution. But is *this* the appropriate model for thinking about how the things people produce are to be distributed?[10]

However, Rawls reasons that Nozick fails to consider how the justice of acquisitions, holdings, transfers, and rectification is to be monitored by social institutions, thus ignoring problems of regulation and basic institutional structures in society. In response, Nozick accuses Rawls of neglecting the underlying reason for someone's having an entitlement to something in the first place, including the significant reason that the person *produced* it. Rawls stands accused of incorrectly regarding social goods as given, like manna, independently of a background history of individual enterprise and desert.

Rawls went on to defend his egalitarian theory and views on fair opportunity in his second major work, *Political Liberalism.* There he responds to Nozick's charge that he incorrectly views social goods as a given, by arguing that Nozick incorrectly views the talents that allow individuals to create wealth as a given. "[W]e cannot view the talents and abilities of individuals as fixed natural gifts." Rawls argues that talents and abilities require favorable social conditions, and that our potential abilities reflect "our personal history, opportunities, and social position."[11]

For this reason, Rawls maintains that the structure of systems in which people compete must be fair. If, through fair market transactions, people come to have radically different opportunities in life, then the agreements that they make are no longer fair. Since just decisions may lead to unjust situations, society has an obligation to intervene and restore justice.

## CRITICISMS OF THEORIES OF JUSTICE

### Rival Theories and Competing Principles

Mill and Rawls both believe that our commonsense treatments of justice address issues too obliquely because they operate with what Rawls calls mere "precepts of justice," which are the material principles of distribution preferred by commonsense.[12] Rawls relies on Mill's perceptive treatment of the subject in *Utilitarianism* (chap. V), in which Mill argues that commonsense precepts or principles such as "to each according to effort" or "to each according to need" lead to perplexing conflicts

---

[10]Robert Nozick, *Anarchy, State, and Utopia,* p. 198.
[11]John Rawls, *Political Liberalism,* p. 269.
[12]Section 47 of *A Theory of Justice* is devoted exclusively to "The Precepts of Justice."

between principles and to contrary moral injunctions. The principles themselves assign no relative weight to their demands when they stand in conflict with other principles. Consequently, they are of no help if a decision must be made as to which principle will be overriding. These precepts fall short of providing a theory of justice because they result in an unhelpful pluralism in which a higher principle is needed to arbitrate their conflicts.

Rawls declares that "in order to find suitable first principles one must step behind them" and develop a philosophical theory.[13] We have seen, however, that several theories of justice can claim a strong measure of coherence and consistency with commonsense ideas, while also stepping beyond common sense. The particular principles that are declared "first principles," in Rawls's sense, differ from one theory to the next, without any definitive reason for choosing one first principle over another. Rawls, Nozick, and their utilitarian opponents seem to capture some but not all of our intuitive convictions about justice with their first principles. Rawls's difference principle and fair-opportunity principle, for example, capture a common belief about the role of fortuitous human characteristics (i.e., those determined by natural or historical contingency); but Nozick's theory also makes a strong appeal in the domains of taxation, property ownership, and liberty rights, whereas utilitarianism seems appealing in many areas of public policy.

Accordingly, some have argued that there are several equally valid, or at least equally viable, theories of justice. A less generous view is that there are several rival and incommensurable theories of justice, with no clear path for choosing among them. These kinds of questions about the work of philosophers in delineating theories of justice are addressed in the following essay by Alasdair MacIntyre. His essay picks up and develops the treatment found in the selection by MacIntyre in Chapter 2, as well as the communitarian theories presented in Chapter 8.

# *Rival Justices, Competing Rationalities**

## Alasdair MacIntyre

Begin by considering the intimidating range of questions about what justice requires and permits, to which alternative and incompatible answers are offered by contending individuals and groups within contemporary societies. Does justice permit gross inequality of income and ownership? Does justice require compensatory action to remedy inequalities which are the result of past injustice, even if those who pay the costs of such compensation had no part in that injustice? Does justice permit or require the imposition of the death penalty and, if so, for what offences? Is it just to permit legalized abortion?

*From Alasdair MacIntyre *Whose Justice? Which Rationality?* (South Bend, Ind.: University of Notre Dame Press, 1988), pp. 1–5.

[13]*A Theory of Justice,* pp. 307f.

When is it just to go to war? The list of such questions is a long one.

Attention to the reasons which are adduced for offering different and rival answers to such questions makes it clear that underlying this wide diversity of judgments upon particular types of issue are a set of conflicting conceptions of justice, conceptions which are strikingly at odds with one another in a number of ways. Some conceptions of justice make the concept of desert central, while others deny it any relevance at all. Some conceptions appeal to inalienable human rights, others to some notion of social contract, and others again to a standard of utility. Moreover, the rival theories of justice which embody these rival conceptions also give expression to disagreements about the relationship of justice to other human goods, about the kind of equality which justice requires, about the range of transactions and persons to which considerations of justice are relevant, and about whether or not a knowledge of justice is possible without a knowledge of God's law.

So those who had hoped to discover good reasons for making this rather than that judgment on some particular type of issue—by moving from the arenas in which in everyday social life groups and individuals quarrel about what it is just to do in particular cases over to the realm of theoretical enquiry, where systematic conceptions of justice are elaborated and debated—will find that once again they have entered upon a scene of radical conflict. What this may disclose to them is not only that our society is one not of consensus, but of division and conflict, at least so far as the nature of justice is concerned, but also that to some degree that division and conflict is within themselves. For what many of us are educated into is, not a coherent way of thinking and judging, but one constructed out of an amalgam of social and cultural fragments inherited both from different traditions from which our culture was originally derived (Puritan, Catholic, Jewish) and from different stages in and aspects of the development of modernity (the French Enlightenment, the Scottish Enlightenment, nineteenth-century economic liberalism, twentieth-century political liberalism). So often enough in the disagreements which emerge within ourselves, as well as in those which are matters of conflict between ourselves and others, we are forced to confront the question: How ought we to decide among the claims of rival and incompatible accounts of justice competing for our moral, social, and political allegiance?

It would be natural enough to attempt to reply to this question by asking which systematic account of justice we would accept if the standards by which our actions were guided were the standards of rationality. To know what justice is, so it may seem, we must first learn what rationality in practice requires of us. Yet someone who tries to learn this at once encounters the fact that disputes about the nature of rationality in general and about practical rationality in particular are apparently as manifold and as intractable as disputes about justice. To be practically rational, so one contending party holds, is to act on the basis of calculations of the costs and benefits to oneself of each possible alternative course of action and its consequences. To be practically rational, affirms a rival party, is to act under those constraints which any rational person, capable of an impartiality which accords no particular privileges to one's own interests, would agree should be imposed. To be practically rational, so a third party contends, is to act in such a way as to achieve the ultimate and true good of human beings. So a third level of difference and conflict appears. . . .

Modern academic philosophy turns out by and large to provide means for a more accurate and informed definition of disagreement rather than for progress toward its resolution. Professors of philosophy who concern themselves with questions of justice and of practical rationality turn out to disagree with each other as sharply, as variously, and, so it seems, as irremediably upon how such questions are to be answered as anyone else. They do indeed succeed in articulating the rival standpoints with greater clarity, greater fluency, and a wider range of arguments than do most others, but apparently little more than this. And, upon reflection, we should perhaps not be surprised.

Consider, for example, one at first sight very plausible philosophical thesis about how we ought to proceed in these matters if we are to be rational. Rationality requires, so it has been argued by a number of academic philosophers, that we first divest ourselves of allegiance to any one of the contending theories and also abstract ourselves from all those particularities of social relationship in terms of which we have been accustomed to understand our responsibilities and our interests. Only by so doing, it has been suggested, shall we arrive at a genuinely neutral, impartial, and, in this way, universal point of view, freed from the partisanship and the partiality and onesidedness that otherwise affect us. And only by so doing shall we be able to evaluate the contending accounts of justice rationally.

One problem is that those who agree about this procedure then proceed to disagree about what precise conception of justice it is which is as a result to be accounted rationally acceptable. But even before *that* problem arises, the question has to be asked whether, by adopting this procedure, key questions have not been begged. For it can be argued and it has been argued that this account of rationality is itself contentious in two related ways: its requirement of disinterestedness in fact covertly presupposes one particular partisan type of account of justice, that of liberal individualism, which it is later to be used to justify, so that its apparent neutrality is no more than an appearance, while its conception of ideal rationality as consisting in the principles which a socially disembodied being would arrive at illegitimately ignores the inescapably historically and socially context-bound character which any substantive set of principles of rationality, whether theoretical or practical, is bound to have.

Fundamental disagreements about the character of rationality are bound to be peculiarly difficult to resolve. For already in initially proceeding in one way rather than another to approach the disputed questions, those who so proceed will have had to assume that these particular procedures are the ones which it is rational to follow. A certain degree of circularity is ineliminable. . . .

. . . How is it rational to respond [to the claims of different traditions]? The initial answer is: that will depend upon who you are and how you understand yourself. This is not the kind of answer which we have been educated to expect in philosophy, but that is because our education in and about philosophy has by and large presupposed what is in fact not true, that there are standards of rationality, adequate for the evaluation of rival answers to such questions, equally available, at least in principle, to all persons, whatever tradition they may happen to find themselves in and whether or not they inhabit any tradition. When this false belief is rejected, it becomes clear that the problems of justice and practical rationality and of how to confront the rival systematic claims of traditions contending with each other in the *agōn* of ideological encounter are not one and the same set of problems for all persons. What those problems are, how they are to be formulated and addressed, and how, if at all, they may be resolved will vary not only with the historical, social, and cultural situation of the persons whose problems these are but also with the history of belief and attitude of each particular person up to the point at which he or she finds these problems inescapable.

What each person is confronted with is at once a set of rival intellectual positions, a set of rival traditions embodied more or less imperfectly in contemporary forms of social relationship and a set of rival communities of discourse, each with its own specific modes of speech, argument, and debate, each making a claim upon the individual's allegiance. It is by the relationship between what is specific to each such standpoint, embodied at these three levels of doctrine, history, and discourse, and what is specific to the beliefs and history of each individual who confronts these problems, that what the problems are for that person is determined.

MacIntyre suggests that the theories we have examined in this chapter are rivals without possible mediation. A more charitable view is that we should expect only partial success from these philosophical efforts in their attempts to develop theories that bring full consistency and comprehensiveness to our fragmented visions of social justice. It does not follow that these theories can never agree about right principles or about correct social practices. For example, if the libertarian holds that it is *virtuous* and *ideal* from the moral point of view to provide social plans for health care, child care, and job assistance, but not strictly a matter of *justice,* there may in the end be little or no dispute over which health policies, child-care policies, and programs of job assistance we should adopt. The bigger dispute may be over how to defend those policies adequately.

## A Feminist Critique

Several feminist writers have criticized theories of justice such as those offered by Nozick and Rawls for failing to consider the implications their theories have for gender relations and the need for more than justice in moral relationships. These critics contend that the traditional theories of justice, all developed by males, implicitly assume that women will continue to do almost the bulk of the domestic work necessary in society, and that justice is only applicable to the relations between heads of households or their functional equivalents.

In the following selection Susan Okin develops such a line of criticism against both Nozick and Rawls by discussing the importance of family life. Picking up some strands of her argument in Chapter 8, she argues that Nozick's theory leads to unacceptable consequences and that Rawls's theory reflects the need for a radical rethinking of family structure.

# The Family: Beyond Justice?*

## Susan Moller Okin

The substantial inequalities that continue to exist between the sexes in our society have serious effects on the lives of almost all women and an increasingly large number of children. Underlying all these inequalities is the unequal distribution of the unpaid labor of the family. . . .

In fact, many social "goods," such as time for paid work or for leisure, physical security, and access to financial resources, typically are unevenly distributed within families. Though many may be "better than just," at least most of the time, contemporary gender-structured families are *not* just. But they *need* to be just. They cannot rely upon the spirit of generosity—though they can still aspire to it—because the life chances of millions of women and children are at stake. They need to be just, too, if they are to be the first schools of moral development, the places where we first learn to develop a sense of justice. And they need to be just if we are even to begin to approach the equality of opportunity that our country claims as one of its basic ideals. . . .

Thus, it is only when the family is idealized and sentimentalized that it can be perceived as an institution that undermines the primacy of justice. When we recognize, as we must, that however

much the members of families care about one another and share common ends, they are still discrete persons with their own particular aims and hopes, which may sometimes conflict, we must see the family as an institution to which justice is a crucial virtue. When we recognize, as we surely must, that many of the resources that are enjoyed within the sphere of family life—leisure, nurturance, money, time, and attention, to mention only a few—are by no means always abundant, we see that justice has a highly significant role to play. When we realize that women, especially, are likely to change the whole course of their lives because of their family commitments, it becomes clear that we cannot regard families as analogous to other intimate relations like friendship, however strong the affective bonding of the latter may be. . . .

## Libertarianism

What becomes of libertarian arguments when we apply them to all the adult members of society, women as well as men? Focusing mainly on the work of the most influential of contemporary academic libertarians, Robert Nozick, I conclude that his theory is reduced to absurdity when women are taken into account. Instead of the minimal state that he argues for in *Anarchy, State and*

*From Susan Moller Okin, *Justice, Gender, and the Family* (New York: Basic Books, 1989).

*Utopia,*[1] what results is a bizarre combination of matriarchy and slavery. . . . Libertarianism in any form tacitly assumes, beyond the reach of its principles, a realm of private life in which the reproductive and nurturant needs of human beings are taken care of. It also assumes that work performed in this realm is not work in the same sense, or deserving of the same rewards, as that done outside this sphere. Behind the individualist facade of libertarianism, the family is assumed but ignored.

The rebirth of feminism has raised fundamental and sometimes difficult issues concerning the basic rights of individuals. Arguments for women's rights to control their own bodies have raised the dilemma, previously obscured or ignored by both liberal and libertarian theories of rights, that results from the fact that the potential lives of some are radically dependent upon (because contained within) the bodies of others. Abortion is not the only moral issue raised by this fact. It is also relevant to the claim of paternity rights concerning fetuses (including those of so-called surrogate mothers), the right of a pregnant woman to take drugs, and the issue of whether a dying woman who is pregnant should be subjected to a Caesarean section against her will. All of these and other related issues have reached the courts in recent years. In addition, reformers' arguments about just allocations of property and income after divorce have raised the fundamental question of what is and what is not to be regarded as productive labor, deserving of monetary reward. . . .

Nozick's entitlement theory is clearly predicated on the belief, though he

never *argues* for it, that each person owns himself. Without this initial assumption, his Lockean theory of acquisition would make no sense. He states that people have the right to control their own bodies, and he writes as a paradigm case of entitlement people's rights to the parts of their own bodies. Objecting to redistributive principles, which he regards as justifying forced labor, he says that they "involve a shift from the classical liberals' notion of self-ownership to a notion of (partial) property rights in *other* people."[2]

The assumption that each person owns himself, however, can work only so long as one neglects two facts. First, persons are not only producers but also the *products* of human labor and human capacities. Anyone who subscribes to Nozick's principle of acquisition must explain how and why it is that persons come to own themselves, rather than being owned, as other things are, by whoever made them. Second, the natural ability to produce people is extremely unequally distributed among human beings. Only women have the natural ability. . . .

I will suggest . . . why Nozick's theory, in spite of its apparent dedication to self-ownership, cannot avoid the conclusion that women's entitlement rights to those they produce must take priority over persons' rights to themselves at birth.

The first reason is Nozick's consistent preference for legitimately acquired property rights over all other claims, including basic need and the right to life. It is difficult to see how a theorist who claims that a starving person has no right to food that is owned by another person, even if that other person has

---

[1]Robert Nozick, *Anarchy, State, and Utopia* (New York: Basic Books, 1974).

[2]Nozick, *Anarchy, State, and Utopia*, p. 172.

food to throw away, could relax his stringent adherence to property rights in order to give an infant, who is after all the product of someone else's body and labor, the right of self-ownership, in contravention of the principle of acquisition. As Nozick writes: "No one has a right to something whose realization requires certain uses of things and activities that other people have rights and entitlements over."[3] If I am (already) my mother's property, I cannot claim a conflicting right to own myself. . . .

It is equally difficult to see how one might successfully employ Nozick's second potential escape route from the dilemma that persons seem to be the property of those who produce them. Much more obviously (and literally) than most other produced things, they "come into the world already attached to people." If, as Nozick claims, it is such attachment that entails entitlement, here is a clear case of it! . . .

The immediate problem of this analysis for Nozick, however, is that it leaves the core of his theory—the principle of acquisition—mired in self-contradiction. If persons do not even "own" themselves, in the sense of being entitled to their own persons, bodies, natural talents, abilities, and so on, then there would appear to be no basis for anyone's owning anything else. Nozick's theory of entitlement is clearly premised on the notion that each person owns himself. But as I have shown, when we consider women's reproductive capacities and labor, the notion of self-ownership that is so central to the principle of acquisition turns out to be completely undermined by that very principle. . . .

Like a number of other contemporary theorists, Nozick is able to reach the

conclusions he does without confronting the absurdities we have examined only because of his neglect of women and his implicit assumption that the gender-structured family exists—crucial to, but outside of, the scope of his theory. His argument occasionally mentions wives (in order to illustrate points having nothing in particular to do with women or wifehood) and children. In his final discussion of the utopian framework of voluntaristic communities that he endorses, he mentions family obligations as an obstacle to the individual's ability to shift from one community to another. He also admits that children "present yet more difficult problems. In some way it must be ensured that they are *informed* of the range of alternatives in the world." But of course in any real world, children need a lot more than this if they are to become those moral agents, capable of living meaningful lives, that Nozick requires as subjects of his theory. They need years and years of attentive care, at least some of which needs to be provided by persons who love them and know them very well—in most cases, their parents. Nozick's theory is able to ignore this fact of life, and childhood in general, only by assuming that women, in families, continue to do their work of nurturing and socializing the young and of providing a sphere of intimate relations. As we are finding to be so often the case, the family and a large part of the lives of most women, especially, are assumed by the theory but are not part of it in the important sense of having its conclusions applied to them. . . .

## Justice as Fairness: For Whom?

John Rawls's *A Theory of Justice* has had the most powerful influence of any

[3]Ibid., p. 238.

work of contemporary moral and political theory.[4] . . . Now, I turn to Rawls's theory of justice as fairness, to examine not only what it explicitly says and does not say, but also what it *implies,* on the subjects of gender, women, and the family. . . .

The significance of Rawls's central, brilliant idea, the original position, is that it forces one to question and consider traditions, customs, and institutions from all points of view, and ensures that the principles of justice will be acceptable to everyone, regardless of what position "he" ends up in. The critical force of the original position becomes evident when one considers that some of the most creative critiques of Rawls's theory have resulted from more radical or broad interpretations of the original position than his own. The theory, in principle, avoids both the problem of domination that is inherent in theories of justice based on traditions or shared understandings and the partiality of libertarian theory to those who are talented or fortunate. For feminist readers, however, the problem of the theory as stated by Rawls himself is encapsulated in that ambiguous "he." . . . While Rawls briefly rules out formal, legal discrimination on the grounds of sex (as on other grounds that he regards as "morally irrelevant"), he fails entirely to address the justice of the gender system, which, with its roots in the sex roles of the family and its branches extending into virtually ever corner of our lives, is one of the fundamental structures of our society. If, however, we read Rawls in such a way as to take seriously both the notion that those behind the veil of ignorance do not know what sex they are and

the requirement that the family and the gender system, as basic social institutions, are to be subject to scrutiny, constructive feminist criticism of these contemporary institutions follows. So, also, do hidden difficulties for the application of a Rawlsian theory of justice in a gendered society.

I shall explain each of these points in turn. But first, both the critical perspective and the incipient problems of a feminist reading of Rawls can perhaps be illuminated by a description of a cartoon I saw a few years ago. Three elderly, robed male justices are depicted, looking down with astonishment at their very pregnant bellies. One says to the others, without further elaboration: "Perhaps we'd better reconsider that decision." This illustration graphically demonstrates the importance, in thinking about justice, of a concept like Rawls's original position, which makes us adopt the positions of others—especially positions that we ourselves could never be in. It also suggests that those thinking in such a way might well conclude that more than formal legal equality of the sexes is required if justice is to be done. As we have seen in recent years, it is quite possible to enact and uphold "gender-neutral" laws concerning pregnancy, abortion, childbirth leave, and so on, that in effect discriminate against women. The United States Supreme Court decided in 1976, for example, that "an exclusion of pregnancy from a disability-benefits plan providing general coverage is not a gender-based discrimination at all."[5] One of the virtues of the cartoon is its suggestion that one's thinking on such matters is likely to be affected by the knowledge that one

---

[4]John Rawls, *A Theory of Justice* (Cambridge: Harvard University Press, 1971).

[5]*General Electric v. Gilbert,* 429 U.S. 125 (1976), 136.

might become "a pregnant person." The illustration also points out the limits of what is possible, in terms of thinking ourselves into the original position, as long as we live in a gender-structured society. While the elderly male justices can, in a sense, imagine themselves as pregnant, what is a much more difficult question is whether, in order to construct principles of justice, they can imagine themselves as women. This raises the question of whether, in fact, sex *is* a morally irrelevant and contingent characteristic in a society structured by gender.

Let us first assume that sex is contingent in this way, though I shall later question this assumption. Let us suppose that it is possible, as Rawls clearly considers it to be, to hypothesize the moral thinking of representative human beings, as ignorant of their sex as of all the other things hidden by the veil of ignorance. It seems clear that, while Rawls does not do this, we must consistently take the relevant positions of both sexes into account in formulating and applying principles of justice. In particular, those in the original position must take special account of the perspective of women, since their knowledge of "the general facts about human society" must include the knowledge that women have been and continue to be the less advantaged sex in a great number of respects. In considering the basic institutions of society, they are more likely to pay special attention to the family than virtually to ignore it. Not only is it potentially the first school of social justice, but its customary unequal assignment of responsibilities and privileges to the two sexes and its socialization of children into sex roles make it, in its current form, an institution of crucial importance for the perpetuation of sex inequality.

In innumerable ways, the principles of justice that Rawls arrives at are inconsistent with a gender-structured society and with traditional family roles. The critical impact of a feminist application of Rawls's theory comes chiefly from his second principle, which requires that inequalities be both "to the greatest benefit of the least advantaged" and "attached to offices and positions open to all."[6] This means that if any roles or positions analogous to our current sex roles—including those of husband and wife, mother and father—were to survive the demands of the first requirement, the second requirement would prohibit any linkage between these roles and sex. Gender, with its ascriptive designation of positions and expectations of behavior in accordance with the inborn characteristic of sex, could no longer form a legitimate part of the social structure, whether inside or outside the family. . . .

After the basic political liberties, one of the most essential liberties is "the important liberty of free choice of occupation."[7] It is not difficult to see that this liberty is compromised by the assumption and customary expectation, central to our gender system, that women take far greater responsibility for housework and child care, whether or not they also work for wages outside the home. In fact, both the assignment of these responsibilities to women—resulting in their asymmetric economic dependence on men—and the related responsibility of husbands to support their wives compromise the liberty of choice of occupation of both sexes. . . .

Finally, Rawls argues that the rational moral persons in the original position

[6]Rawls, *Theory,* p. 302.
[7]Ibid., p. 274.

would place a great deal of emphasis on the securing of self-respect or self-esteem. They "would wish to avoid at almost any cost the social conditions that undermine self-respect," which is "perhaps the most important" of all the primary goods.[8] In the interests of this

[8]Rawls, *Theory,* pp. 440, 396; see also pp. 178–9.

primary value, if those in the original position did not know whether they were to be men or women, they would surely be concerned to establish a thoroughgoing social and economic equality between the sexes that would protect either sex from the need to pander to or servilely provide for the pleasures of the other.

## CONCLUSION

We should not underestimate the theoretical differences between utilitarianism, libertarianism, egalitarianism, and their critics, but we also should not underestimate potential agreements that might be reached in their judgments of what constitutes a good and decent society. Because there is presently neither social consensus about problems of justice nor a paramount theory of justice, we should expect our public policies governing economic distribution, racial and sexual discrimination, access to health care, corporate responsibility, and the like, to oscillate, sometimes latching onto the premises of one theory, then emphasizing another theory. Such fluctuation is common in public policy and does not necessarily entail that policies are unjust. Each influential theory of justice has developed from a distinct perspective on the moral life that only partially captures the diversity of that life. The richness of our moral traditions, practices, and theories helps explain why egalitarian theories, libertarian theories, and utilitarian theories of justice have all been skillfully defended throughout the history of modern philosophy.

## SUGGESTED SUPPLEMENTARY READINGS

### Concepts and Principles of Justice

Baier, Annette C.: *Moral Prejudices: Essays on Ethics* (Cambridge, MA: Harvard University Press, 1995).

Campbell, Tom: *Justice* (London: Macmillan, 1988).

Copp, David. "The Right to an Adequate Standard of Living: Justice, Autonomy, and the Basic Needs," *Social Philosophy and Policy,* 9 (1992): 231–61.

Galston, William A.: *Justice and the Human Good* (Chicago: University of Chicago Press, 1980).

Johnston, David: "Is the Idea of Social Justice Meaningful?" *Critical Revue,* 11 (1997): 607–14.

Kymlicka, Will, ed.: *Justice in Political Philosophy: Schools of Thought in Politics,* 2 vols. (Brookfield, VT.: Ashgate, 1992).

Miller, Richard: *Moral Differences: Truth, Justice, and Conscience in a World of Conflict* (Princeton, NJ: Princeton University Press, 1992).

Nagel, Thomas: *Equality and Partiality* (New York: Oxford University Press, 1991).

Pinkard, Terry: *Democratic Liberalism and Social Union* (Philadelphia: Temple University Press, 1987).

Solomon, Robert C., ed.: *What Is Justice? Classic and Contemporary Readings* (New York Oxford University Press, 1990).

Sterba, James P.: *Justice for Here and Now* (New York: Cambridge University Press, 1998).

Stewart, Robert M., ed.: *Readings in Social and Political Philosophy* (New York: Oxford University Press, 1996).

## Libertarian Theories

Boaz, David: *The Libertarian Reader: Classic and Contemporary Readings, from Lao-tzu to Milton Friedman* (New York: The Free Press, 1997).

Engelhardt, H. Tristram, Jr.: *The Foundations of Bioethics*, 2d ed. (New York: Oxford University Press, 1996).

Fried, Barbara: "Wilt Chamberlain Revisited: Nozick's 'Justice in Transfer' and the Problem of Market-Based Distribution," *Philosophy and Public Affairs,* 24 (1995): 226–45.

Friedman, Milton: *Capitalism and Freedom* (Chicago: University of Chicago Press, 1962).

Hayek, Friedrich A.: *The Mirage of Justice* (London: Routledge & Kegan Paul, 1976).

Machan, Tibor R., and Douglas B. Rasmussen, eds.: *Liberty for the Twenty-First Century: Contemporary Libertarian Thought* (Lanham, MD: Rowman and Littlefield, 1995).

Paul, Jeffrey, ed.: *Reading Nozick* (Totowa, NJ: Rowman and Littlefield, 1981).

Perry, Stephen R.: "Libertarianism, Entitlement, and Responsibility," *Philosophy and Public Affairs,* 26 (1997): 351–96.

Scanlon, Thomas M.: "Nozick on Rights, Liberty, and Property," *Philosophy and Public Affairs,* 6 (1976): 3–25.

Wolff, Jonathan: *Robert Nozick: Property, Justice, and the Minimal State* (Stanford, CA: Stanford University Press, 1991).

## Egalitarian Theories

Barry, Brian: *The Liberal Theory of Justice, a Critical Examination of the Principal Doctrines in a Theory of Justice by John Rawls* (Oxford, England: Clarendon Press, 1973).

Blocker, H. Gene, and Elizabeth H. Smith, eds.: *John Rawls' Theory of Social Justice: An Introduction* (Athens: Ohio University Press, 1980).

Christman, John P.: *The Myth of Property: Toward an Egalitarian Theory of Ownership* (New York: Oxford University Press, 1994).

Cohen, G. A.: "Where the Action Is: On the Site of Distributive Justice,"
    *Philosophy and Public Affairs,* 26 (1997): 3–30.
Daniels, Norman, ed.: *Reading Rawls: Critical Studies of a Theory of Justice*
    (New York: Basic Books, 1975).
Kane, John: "Justice, Impartiality, and Equality: Why the Concept of Justice Does
    Not Presume Equality," *Political Theory,* 24 (1996): 375–93.
Nagel, Thomas: "Equality," in *Mortal Questions* (Cambridge, England:
    Cambridge University Press, 1979).
Okin, Susan: *Justice, Gender, and the Family* (New York: Basic Books, 1989).
Pogge, Thomas W.: *Realizing Rawls* (Ithaca, NY: Cornell University Press, 1991).
Pojman, Louis, and Robert Westmoreland, eds.: *Equality: Selected Readings* (New
    York: Oxford University Press, 1997).
Rawls, John: "Kantian Constructivism in Moral Theory: The Dewey Lectures
    1980," *Journal of Philosophy,* 77 (1980): 515–72.
————: *Political Liberalism* (New York: Columbia University Press, 1996).
Roemer, John E.: *Theories of Distributive Justice* (Cambridge, MA: Harvard
    University Press, 1996).
Vallentyne, Peter: "Self-Ownership and Equality: Brute Luck, Gifts, Universal
    Dominance, and Leximin," *Ethics,* 107 (1997): 321–43.
Williams, Bernard: "The Idea of Equality," in Peter Laslett and W. G. Runciman,
    eds., *Philosophy, Politics and Society*, 2d series (New York: Barnes and
    Noble, 1962).

## Utilitarian Theories

Allison, Lincoln, ed.: *The Utilitarian Response: Essays on the Contemporary
    Viability of Utilitarian Political Philosophy* (London: Sage, 1990).
Arneson, Richard J.: "Liberalism, Distributive Subjectivism, and Equal
    Opportunity for Welfare," *Philosophy and Public Affairs,* 19 (1990): 158–94.
————: "Primary Goods Reconsidered," *Nous,* 24 (1990): 429–54.
Berger, Fred R.: "Mill's Substantive Principles of Justice: A Comparison with
    Nozick," *American Philosophical Quarterly,* 19 (1982): 373–80.
Braybrooke, David: *Meeting Needs* (Princeton, NJ: Princeton University Press,
    1987).
Feldman, Fred: "Justice, Desert, and the Repugnant Conclusion," *Utilitas,* 7
    (1995): 189–206.
Frey, Raymond G., ed.: *Utility and Rights* (Oxford, England: Blackwell, 1985).
Hardin, Russell: *Morality within the Limits of Reason* (Chicago: University of
    Chicago Press, 1988).
Harsanyi, John C.: "Rule Utilitarianism, Equality, and Justice," *Social Philosophy
    and Policy,* 2 (1985): 115–27.
————: "Equality, Responsibility, and Justice as Seen from a Utilitarian
    Perspective," *Theory and Decision,* 31 (1991): 141–58.
Lyons, David: "Rawls versus Utilitarianism," *Journal of Philosophy,* 69 (1972):
    535–45.
Quinton, Anthony: *Utilitarian Ethics*, 2d ed. (La Salle, IL: Open Court, 1989).
Sidgwick, Henry: *The Methods of Ethics* (New York: Dover Publications, 1966).

## CHAPTER 10

# Liberty

In Chapters 8 and 9, the topics of "rights" and "justice" were explored. Now we turn to the subject of liberty and its connection to personal autonomy. This topic concludes our treatment of the intersection between moral philosophy and social and political philosophy.

## RESTRICTING ACCESS TO THE INTERNET

In recent years the Internet has grown rapidly, and so have disputes over whether and to what extent its content should be regulated by the government, Internet providers, schools, parents, and the like. Legislative efforts to regulate the Internet have focused primarily on protecting minors from online pornography. The first such attempt, the Communications Decency Act (CDA), sought to criminalize the "knowing" transmission of "obscene or indecent" messages and pictures to anyone under the age of eighteen, and to prohibit knowingly sending or displaying to a minor any message "that, in context, depicts or describes, in terms patently offensive as measured by contemporary community standards, sexual or excretory activities or organs." However, the U.S. Supreme Court ruled on June 26, 1997, that the CDA was unconstitutional (by a vote of 9 to 0).

In 1998 Congress passed the Child Online Protection Act (COPA), which attempted to require webmasters to verify the age of a surfer before allowing him or her into a site with material that may be injurious to minors. Representatives of the media argued vigorously that this regulation was an attack on legally guaranteed rights of free speech. In 1999, enforcement of the COPA was blocked by a federal judge, a decision that was then appealed by the Justice Department.

Since the Supreme Court's 1997 decision, software companies have developed a number of more sophisticated Internet filtering programs to protect minors from potentially harmful materials. However, these programs are not perfect and often block sites that discuss issues such as breast cancer and homosexuality, but that contain no pornographic content. These programs also often fail to block brand new pornographic sites, which are created daily. Recently some public libraries have begun to install filtering programs on their computers in order to protect children from accessing pornographic material and to prevent offense to other library patrons. But one such use of filtering programs in Louden County, Virginia, was blocked by a federal judge in November 1998 on grounds that it had the side effect of violating the rights of adults to free speech.

Free speech advocates like the American Civil Liberties Union (ACLU), which brought the case leading to the overturning of CDA, argue that the government does not have the right to restrict access to pornography on the Internet. They maintain that doing so results in restricting minors' access to important information, and that any attempt to prohibit children from accessing pornography will inevitably result in restricting adult access.

Many people disagree, arguing that pornography should not be considered protected free speech. According to Focus on the Family, "Behind the shelter of anonymity, millions of young boys, as well as older men, have viewed pornographic images. Not only can these stolen glances affect a male's ability to relate intimately with other women in the 'real world,' but in some cases obscene online images such as bestiality, bondage, and child pornography can create in males a desire to 'act out' in dangerous ways."

Pornographic sites are not the only Internet sites under dispute. In early 1999, a jury awarded $107 million in damages to a group of doctors who sued antiabortion activists over a site called The Nuremberg Files. This site featured—in the form of wanted posters—a list of physicians who perform abortions. These physicians were characterized as "baby butchers." One person listed on the site was Barnett Slepian, a physician who worked at an abortion clinic in Amherst, New York. He was killed by a sniper, and the next day his name was crossed off the list of "baby butchers." At the trial physicians testified that they have feared for their lives since they were targeted on the Nuremberg Files site. The physicians won their case against the creators of the web site on grounds that the list was tantamount to a death threat.[1]

The question of whether, and under what conditions, states, corporations, or other groups may legitimately control the Internet, or leave it free of controls, remains highly controversial.

## THE CONCEPTS OF AUTONOMY AND LIBERTY

Concerns about respecting autonomy and protecting liberty have been hallmarks of some of the most famous political developments in modern history. For example,

[1]Sources for this case include Leslie Miller, "Peacefire.org at War with Cyber-Censors," *USA Today*, April 7, 1999, p. 6D; Tunku Varadarajan, "U.S. Courts Confuse Issue," *The Times* (London), February 10, 1999; Jerry Zremski, "Internet 'Hit List' Case Reflects Free Speech Dilemma Facing Courts," *The Buffalo News*, February 4, 1999, p. 1A; Rita Ciolli, "U.S. Court Blocks Internet Porno Law," *The Gazette* (Montreal), February 2 1999, p. D11; Patrick McGreevy, "6 City Libraries to Test Internet Porn Blocking," *Los Angeles Times*, January 28, 1999, Metro B1; Eric Schoch, "Freedom from Filtering," *The Indianapolis Star*, December 21, 1998, p. C12; David Nakamura, "Libraries Restore Internet, Ease Access Curbs," *The Washington Post*, December 3, 1998, Loudon Extra, p. V1; Rene Sanchez, "Doctors Win Suit against Anti-Abortion Site," *The Washington Post*, February 3, 1999, p. A1; *Janet Reno, Attorney General of the United States et al., Appellants v. American Civil Liberties Union et al.*, 521 U.S. 844, 117 S. Ct. 2329 (1997); as well as the Internet web site for *Focus on the Family* at http://www.family.org; and the web site for the *American Civil Liberties Union* at http://www.aclu.org.

the French and American revolutions advertised the fundamental importance of "liberty and equality," where equality is a principle of justice and both notions are used in defense of rights. Major documents in the history of moral philosophy have been no less oriented toward justice and liberty. Bentham's *Principles of Morals and Legislation,* which was published in Great Britain in the year of the French Revolution, had many of the same objectives of social reform, justice, and liberty found in French and American political documents.

Many moral and social problems of liberty emerge where law clashes with liberty, as it does dramatically in the proposed Internet regulations mentioned above. By protecting rights or liberties for one group, such as children, the law may impose obligations on, or restrict the liberty of, others. Even laws that protect the rights of individuals are restrictive, because they place a limit on what otherwise would be an option. Nonetheless, it is generally accepted that some liberties should be traded off in favor of state protections. If a right to liberty or autonomous action entailed a zone of absolute freedom of action, there could be no control of pornography or anything else. Former U.S. Chief Justice Warren Burger once noted the impracticality of this view in the case of *Paris Adult Theatre I v. Slaton.*[2] Burger wrote that "totally unlimited play for free will is not allowed in our or any other society." Even ardent advocates of liberty may seek restrictions if they see others using their freedom to engage in repulsive, degrading, or harmful actions. Questions thus arise about the conditions under which limiting individual liberty is justified.

The terms "liberty" and "autonomy" might be analyzed as referring only to *acceptable* autonomy and *acceptable* liberty, and so to a zone of actions in which people ought to be free to engage. But it is a conceptual mistake to identify the term "autonomy" with acceptable autonomy and "liberty" with acceptable liberty. Persons can perform unacceptable but autonomous actions. This suggests a need to analyze "autonomy" and "liberty," as well as "autonomy right" and "liberty right."

## Autonomous Actions

First, what is autonomy and what is its connection to liberty? "Autonomy" has evolved from the Greek terms *autos* ("self") and *nomos* ("governance" or "law"), used to refer to self-governance in Greek city-states. Autonomy has since come to refer to personal self-governance: personal rule of the self by adequate understanding while remaining free from controlling interferences by others and from personal limitations that prevent choice. Autonomy, so understood, has been analyzed in terms of freedom from external constraint and the presence of critical internal capacities integral to self-governance. However, autonomy has also been used to refer to individual choice, being one's own person, authenticity, and several other quite different notions. It is necessary, then, to sharpen the meaning of the term "autonomy" in light of the objectives of this chapter.

[2]413 U.S. 49, 93 S.Ct. 2628 (1973).

A satisfactory account of autonomy requires at least three conditions: (1) acting intentionally, (2) acting with understanding, and (3) acting free of influences that control behavior. First, intentional actions require plans, in the form of representations of the series of events proposed for the execution of the action, and an attempt to execute the plan so that there is intention-in-action. Although an outcome might not materialize as projected, an intentional act must correspond to the actor's conception to qualify as intentional. Second, the actor needs an *understanding* of his or her action, which involves apprehending the nature of the action and all its foreseeable consequences or outcomes. Consider Mill's example of a man who wants to cross what he believes to be an *intact* bridge. Unfortunately, the bridge is out. The man's understanding of the facts pertinent to walking across the bridge fails to include at least one relevant act description, namely, that if he attempts to cross the bridge, he will fall into the river. The third of the three conditions constituting autonomy is that a person, like an autonomous political state, must be free of—that is, independent of, not governed by—controls, especially controls exerted by others that rob the person of self-directedness. This may be called the "liberty condition." It must be treated separately and in greater detail than the other two conditions of autonomy, because liberty is central to autonomy and to every topic under discussion in this chapter.

## Liberty as Free Action

Free action entails not being under external control. This does not mean there can be no *influences* on the action. There are many kinds and degrees of constraining influences, not all of which *control* human behavior. Many influences are resistible, and some are trivial in their impact on a person's autonomy. Influence is a broad category, and influences come from many sources and take many forms. For example, threats of physical harm, promises of love and affection, economic incentives, reasoned argument, lies, and appeals to emotional weaknesses are all influences.

Completely controlled acts, the ones we primarily worry about in discussing liberty, are *entirely dominated* by the will of another person. The thief who forces you to hand over a wallet at gunpoint subjects your will to his. These influences cause one person to serve as the means to another's ends; in no respect do they serve the actor's ends. Coercion is the most frequently mentioned form of *controlling* influence; and some believe it is the only kind of influence that truly controls. Coercion occurs if one person intentionally uses a credible and severe threat of harm or force to control another. The threat of state force underlying legal rules of limited Internet access is an example. For a threat to be credible, either both parties must know that the person making the threat—the police, say—can effect it, or the one making the threat must successfully deceive the person threatened into believing it is credible. Some threats will coerce virtually all persons, whereas others will coerce only a few persons. Whether coercion occurs, therefore, depends ultimately on the subjective responses of those at whom coercion is directed.

Coercion entirely compromises autonomy and should be placed at one end of a continuum of the types of influence that affect us. At the other end of the continuum are weak forms of influence such as rational persuasion. In *persuasion,* a person must be convinced to believe something through the merit of reasons advanced by another person. By contrast, *manipulation* refers to a class of influences whose common feature is that they are neither instances of persuasion nor instances of co-ercion. The essence of manipulation is getting people to do what the manipulator wants, without recourse to coercion. For example, if a salesperson manages to suc-cessfully influence a customer to purchase a product by filling the customer with unfounded fears about a competitive product, the person does what the agent of in-fluence intends and has thereby been manipulated. Various forms of informational manipulation involve lying, withholding information, and exaggerating so as to mislead. Each of these strategies limits another's liberty.

In modern moral and political theory, we have been concerned primarily with so-cial restrictions on autonomy in the form of limitations that specifically affect lib-erty (rather than understanding or intention). This subject of liberty and its limitation is the one to which the remainder of this chapter is devoted.

## THE VALID RESTRICTION OF LIBERTY

No right is encompassing enough to entail unrestricted exercise of autonomy in public life. Some valid restrictions on our liberty are entirely appropriate. But which ones? We generally agree that laws prohibiting immoral actions, such as murder and theft, not only are justified but are justified by moral reasons. Because persons are significantly *harmed,* we legally prohibit these actions, even at the "expense" of a loss of liberty to murderers and thieves. But what are we to say if no harm is caused? Should laws or moral restrictions ever prohibit conduct involving consent-ing parties, such as purchasing pornography, showing X-rated movies, running gambling casinos, climbing mountains during dangerous seasons, and the like?

### Autonomy-Limiting Principles

The basic moral problem is that the value of liberty sometimes conflicts with other values that we treasure, such as the health and welfare of parties who are affected by another person's free action. For example, in a welfare state people are legiti-mately taxed against their will—a deprivation of their liberty to spend their money voluntarily—in order to benefit those in the state who need assistance in the form of health care, job insurance, food, child care, and the like. In the case of the Internet, we would like to have full access to available data, but we also want to protect chil-dren against harmful influences. Such conflicts between liberty and other goods present a need to establish the proper limits on liberty for individuals, groups, and institutions. We need to be able to specify what limits, if any, will be placed on In-ternet access, public nudity, the use of controversial reading material in public schools, the dissemination of pornography, high-risk behaviors, and the like.

Various principles, generally assumed to be *moral* principles, have been ad-vanced in order to justify the limitation of individual human liberties. Joel Feinberg

has called them both "liberty-limiting principles" and "coercion-legitimizing principles."[3] Expressed either way, the generic issue is that of the proper moral justification for coercion, usually by law. For Feinberg these principles specify morally
relevant reasons supporting penal legislation and constitute the moral underpinnings
and limits of criminal law. In this chapter, Feinberg's interest in penal legislation,
criminal prohibition, legal limits, and the like, will be expanded to include moral
uses of these principles that have no clear legal implications (as, for example, in
"medical paternalism").

These principles will here be referred to as "autonomy-limiting" principles.
Through these principles, allegedly valid restrictions of an autonomous agent's liberty (whether recognized in law as valid or not) occur by balancing the principle of
respect for autonomy against other principles such as protection against harm and
protection against offensive behavior. These principles are said by their defenders to
provide a good *reason* for interference with autonomy and for any corresponding
use of coercion necessary for the interference.

The following four autonomy-limiting principles have been defended by a number of philosophers and will be defended in the selections in this chapter. These
principles have played a significant role in recent philosophical controversies.

1. *The harm principle.* A person's autonomy is justifiably restricted to prevent
   harm to others caused by that person.
2. *The principle of paternalism.* A person's autonomy is justifiably restricted to
   prevent harm to the person caused by that person, irrespective of whether
   harm is caused to others.
3. *The principle of legal moralism.* A person's autonomy is justifiably restricted
   to prevent that person's immoral behavior, irrespective of whether that
   person's conduct is harmful or offensive.
4. *The offense principle.* A person's autonomy is justifiably restricted to prevent
   hurt or offense (as contrasted to harm or injury) to others caused by that
   person.

A person who supports any one of these principles need not support the others.
The offense principle, for example, directly relates to the issue of Internet regulation
of offensive materials, but close examination of all features of the Internet case
shows all four of these principles at work in the arguments by proponents of regulation (that is, limited access). The harm principle (or harm to others principle) is repeatedly invoked in discussing clear and present dangers to minors involved in
pornography and costly institutional harms involved in controlling it.

The harm principle is almost universally accepted as a valid autonomy-limiting
principle. However, certain ambiguities surround the concept of a harm and how far
the harm principle stretches. Feinberg rightly notes that "$X$ harmed $Y$" means, in its
*normative* sense, that $X$ wronged $Y$ or treated $Y$ unjustly; but in a *nonnormative*
sense, it means only that $X$ invaded and thereby thwarted, defeated, or set back $Y$'s

---

[3]See Feinberg's four-volume work on *The Moral Limits of the Criminal Law,* in particular, the final volume,
*Harmless Wrongdoing* (New York: Oxford University Press, 1988), p. ix. The schema of principles in the present chapter is heavily indebted to Feinberg's work.

interests.[4] The many problems that surround analysis of the notion of harm cannot be treated here, but we can stipulate the minimal sense that will be employed, which is that of a thwarting, defeating, or setting back of the interests of one party by the invasive actions of another. In this sense, not every harmful invasion of another's interests is wrong, or even wrong on balance. Some harmful actions are justifiable and excusable ways of thwarting, frustrating, or restricting another's interests. For example, justified criminal punishments satisfy this description.

Some definitions of harm are broad enough to include setbacks to reputation, property, privacy, or liberty—all of which involve interests of persons. Within this broad definition, trivial harms can be distinguished from serious harms by the order and magnitude of the interests affected. Other definitions have a narrower focus and view harms exclusively as setbacks to physical and perhaps mental interests (for example, health and survival), disallowing setbacks to interests such as property and liberty. Whether the broad or the narrow account of harm is preferable is not vital for present purposes. We can concentrate on physical and psychological harms, including pain, disability, and death, without denying the importance of other kinds of harm and setbacks to other interests.

Little debate now surrounds the justifiability of the harm principle, but substantial debate surrounds the other principles considered in this chapter, for reasons we will now consider.

### Mill's *On Liberty*

John Stuart Mill's classic monograph *On Liberty* (1859) has occupied a prominent position in these discussions. Mill inquired after the nature and limits of justifiable social control over the individual. Although he does not use the term "autonomy," he defends a personal and community ideal of "the *free development* of *individuality*"—the functional equivalent for him of autonomy.[5] One central line of argument, in modified vocabulary, is as follows: The individual autonomous agent is independent, that is, free of dependent relationships. Such a person does not act from decisions reached by others and is neither subtly constrained by environmental influences in forming beliefs nor unreflectively submissive to control by social customs. The measure of a person's autonomy is the measure of the person's independence from such overpowering influences.

Among Mill's favorite examples are imposed sanctions, coercive force, and censorship. Such causal factors must be absent for a person's intentionally and actively formed attitudes, values, beliefs, and the like, to be autonomous. Whereas freedom from constraint is a condition making "individual spontaneity" *possible,* Mill says there would be no point to this freedom unless one could exercise a positive *capacity of spontaneity.*[6] A controlled effort to be autonomous by developing oneself and

---

[4]See Joel Feinberg, *The Moral Limits of the Criminal Law:* vol. I, pp. 32–36; and vol. IV, p. x.

[5]John Stuart Mill, *On Liberty,* 4th ed., in *Collected Works of John Stuart Mill,* vol. XVIII (Toronto: University of Toronto Press, 1977), p. 261.

[6]*On Liberty,* pp. 261–77

distinguishing one's thoughts and character from others is judged by Mill to be one of the treasured features of human existence. He considers positive freedom—the ideal of using distinctive human faculties in the process of self-development—to be as essential as negative freedom, or freedom from constraint. These distinctive endowments center on what Mill calls "choice." They include judgment, reasoning, decision, discriminative feeling, and moral preference. Sheep and cattle, Mill argues, can be (negatively) free but cannot exercise these faculties of choice, because they lack the capacities.[7]

Mill extends his theses beyond what we commonly think of as understanding and rational choice, into the realm of desires and impulses. "There is not the same willingness that our desires and impulses should be our own," he writes, insisting that it is no less crucial to individuality that one place one's impulses "under the government of a strong will" and thereby establish one's character *as one's own.* Strong impulses, he argues, are but another name for an energetic nature, which can be cultivated for good purposes as well as bad. Autonomy requires more than negative freedom, because negative freedom does not make values and beliefs *one's own by choice.* Mill holds that positive freedom results *only if* negative freedom prevails; nonetheless, negative freedom, though necessary, is not a sufficient condition of positive freedom.[8]

**One's Life Plan**   Mill believes, largely on the basis of anecdotal empirical observations, that most members of society have never been trained to develop their mental and moral imaginations. Yet he holds that these faculties, being vital components of individuality, must be exercised regularly, just as the physical body must be exercised, and they can be exercised only by making choices that exhibit "firmness and self-control."[9] Public opinion and social controls that restrict or abridge personal development retard the growth of individual autonomy. Mill displays particular irritation with those who promote conformity by using as their guideline, "Is it suitable to my position to do so-and-so?" One ought always to ask instead, "Is it something that it would be valuable for me to do?" One must "choose a plan of life," or else suffer the fate of having it chosen by others. "The plan of our life," he says, must be framed "to suit our own character," and the person who "chooses his plan for himself" is the one who uses distinctive human faculties to maximize positive freedom.[10]

**Character and Culture**   Mill argues that a person with "true character" makes discriminating choices and appropriates from the culture only what he or she *judges* to be valuable. A person "without character," by contrast, is profoundly, even if passively, governed by entities such as church, state, parents, or family. Mill's rejection of cultural influence as "ape-like imitation" is grounded in his theory of the autonomous person. The person without character does not choose, does not develop his

[7]*On Liberty,* pp. 262–3, 267, 270.
[8]*On Liberty,* pp. 263–4.
[9]*On Liberty,* pp. 262–3.
[10]*On Liberty,* p. 264.

or her beliefs and values, and does not exercise his or her precious and distinctive mental faculties: "Character is formed *for* him, and not by him." Like Calvinism, which demands surrender to the will of God, like the "paternal despotism of China," or like submission to Russian bureaucrats, modern society for Mill crushes human spontaneity by demanding conformity to custom and, in the end, "gets the better of individuality."[11]

Mill, then, decisively rejects all *constraining* traditions, customs, and social influences—unless one, upon reflection, freely accepts them. He argues that society generally overlooks the paramount importance of individuality, that the social majority has little appreciation for the importance of individual expressiveness, and that spontaneity of character forms no part of prevailing social goals. His ideal individual is capable of making new discoveries, developing new practices, self-prescribing rules of behavior, and enjoying individual tastes, without rejecting what is best in cultural and family life.

Mill has been accused by some critics of confusing individuality with idiosyncrasy, singularity, and eccentricity.[12] However, this criticism fails to appreciate much of the argument in *On Liberty*. Mill castigates those who criticize eccentricity, but he does not insist on a *rejection* of culture or tradition. He resists only an *enslaving* influence, which he seeks to surmount through his account of human choice. The individual is urged to choose that which is valuable in culture, while discarding that which has no value.[13]

The following selection presents a summary and outline of Mill's central theses regarding liberty and the harm principle.

# *On Liberty**

## John Stuart Mill

There is, in fact, no recognised principle by which the propriety or impropriety of government interference is customarily tested. People decide according to their personal preferences. Some, whenever they see any good to be done, or evil to be remedied, would willingly instigate the government to undertake the business; while others prefer to bear almost any amount of social evil, rather than add one to the departments of human interests amenable to governmental control. And men range themselves on one or the other side in any particular case, according to this general direction of their sentiments; or according to the degree of interest which they feel in the particular thing which it is proposed that the government should do, or according to the belief they entertain that the government would, or would not, do it in the manner they prefer; but very rarely

*From John Stuart Mill, *On Liberty* (1863).

[11]*On Liberty,* pp. 262–65, 271–4, 286, 302.
[12]See R. P. Anschutz, *The Philosophy of J. S. Mill* (London: Oxford University Press, 1963), pp. 25ff.
[13]*On Liberty,* pp. 262–3, 265, 268–9, 291.

on account of any opinion to which they consistently adhere, as to what things are fit to be done by a government. And it seems to me that in consequence of this absence of rule or principle, one side is at present as often wrong as the other; the interference of government is, with about equal frequency improperly invoked and improperly condemned.

The object of this Essay is to assert one very simple principle, as entitled to govern absolutely the dealings of society with the individual in the way of compulsion and control, whether the means used be physical force in the form of legal penalties, or the moral coercion of public opinion. That principle is, that the sole end for which mankind are warranted, individually or collectively, in interfering with the liberty of action of any of their number, is self-protection. That the only purpose for which power can be rightfully exercised over any member of a civilized community, against his will, is to prevent harm to others. His own good, either physical or moral, is not a sufficient warrant. He cannot rightfully be compelled to do or forbear because it will be better for him to do so, because it will make him happier, because, in the opinions of others, to do so would be wise, or even right. These are good reasons for remonstrating with him, or reasoning with him, or persuading him, or entreating him, but not for compelling him, or visiting him with any evil in case he do otherwise. To justify that, the conduct from which it is desired to deter him, must be calculated to produce evil to some one else. The only part of the conduct of any one, for which he is amenable to society, is that which concerns others. In the part which merely concerns himself, his independence is, of right, absolute. Over himself, over his own body and mind, the individual is sovereign.

It is, perhaps, hardly necessary to say that this doctrine is meant to apply only to human beings in the maturity of their faculties. We are not speaking of children, or of young persons below the age which the law may fix as that of manhood or womanhood. Those who are still in a state to require being taken care of by others, must be protected against their own actions as well as against external injury. . . .

This, then, is the appropriate region of human liberty. It comprises, first, the inward domain of consciousness; demanding liberty of conscience, in the most comprehensive sense; liberty of thought and feeling; absolute freedom of opinion and sentiment on all subjects, practical or speculative, scientific, moral, or theological. The liberty of expressing and publishing opinions may be seen to fall under a different principle, since it belongs to that part of the conduct of an individual which concerns other people; but, being almost of as much importance as the liberty of thought itself, and resting in great part on the same reasons, is practically inseparable from it. Secondly, the principle requires liberty of tastes and pursuits; of framing the plan of our life to suit our own character; of doing as we like, subject to such consequences as may follow: without impediment from our fellow-creatures, so long as what we do does not harm them, even though they should think our conduct foolish, perverse, or wrong. Thirdly, from this liberty of each individual, follows the liberty, within the same limits, of combination among individuals; freedom to unite, for any purpose not involving harm to others: the persons combining being supposed to be of full age, and not forced or deceived.

No society in which these liberties are not, on the whole, respected, is free, whatever may be its form of government; and none is completely free in which they do not exist absolute and unqualified. The only freedom which deserves the name, is that of pursuing our own good in our own way, so long as we do not attempt to deprive others of theirs, or impede their efforts to obtain it. Each is the proper guardian of his own health, whether bodily, or mental and spiritual. Mankind are greater gainers by suffering each other to live as seems good to themselves, than by compelling each to live as seems good to the rest. . . .

Again, there are many acts which, being directly injurious only to the agents themselves, ought not to be legally interdicted, but which, if done publicly, are a violation of good manners, and coming thus within the category of offences against others, may rightfully be prohibited. Of this kind are offences against decency; on which it is unnecessary to dwell, the rather as they are only connected indirectly with our subject, the objection to publicity being equally strong in the case of many actions not in themselves condemnable, nor supposed to be so. . . .

If all mankind minus one, were of one opinion, and only one person were of the contrary opinion, mankind would be no more justified in silencing that one person, than he, if he had the power, would be justified in silencing mankind. Were an opinion a personal possession of no value except to the owner; if to be obstructed in the enjoyment of it were simply a private injury, it would make some difference whether the injury was inflicted only on a few persons or on many. But the peculiar evil of silencing the expression of an opinion is, that it is robbing the human race; posterity as well as the existing generation; those who dissent from the opinion, still more than those who hold it. If the opinion is right, they are deprived of the opportunity of exchanging error for truth: if wrong, they lose, what is almost as great a benefit, the clearer perception and livelier impression of truth, produced by its collision with error. . . .

The strongest of all the arguments against the interference of the public with purely personal conduct, is that when it does interfere, the odds are that it interferes wrongly, and in the wrong place. On questions of social morality, of duty to others, the opinion of the public, that is, of an overruling majority, though often wrong, is likely to be still oftener right; because on such questions they are only required to judge of their own interests; of the manner in which some mode of conduct, if allowed to be practised, would affect themselves. But the opinion of a similar majority, imposed as a law on the minority, on questions of self-regarding conduct, is quite as likely to be wrong as right; for in these cases public opinion means, at the best, some people's opinion of what is good or bad for other people; while very often it does not even mean that; the public, with the most perfect indifference, passing over the pleasure or convenience of those whose conduct they censure, and considering only their own preference.

Mill defends his views by appeal to the utilitarian framework discussed in Chapter 4. In particular, he argues that his general principle of freedom from social control, however dangerous to prevailing social beliefs, will produce the best possible conditions for social progress and for the development of individual talents. Although he never carefully analyzes the concept of harm, presumably he allows more than physical and psychological pain and damages to count, and does not accept mere inconvenience as harmful. Harm often seems to mean "serious injury to another's interests," because he speaks of certain important interests that should be protected by specific legal rights.

**Mill's Critics**    Some have attacked Mill's theory as useless, because he is too vague in drawing the line between harm and nonharm and between proper and improper government intervention, with the result that individuals and governments are free to draw the line wherever they wish. His principles seem to some critics so broad that they are capable of supporting virtually any form of criminal legislation. "Harm," they say, covers damaging the public welfare, not promoting the public interest, breaking contracts, unilaterally declaring a marriage ended, invading privacy, treating another as unequal, forgery, damaging reputation, and so forth. So broad is the term "harm" for Mill that it seems to expand indefinitely to embrace almost every kind of reason for restricting autonomous action. If his notion of harm is construed narrowly (for example, as bodily harm), it is argued, then many serious nonbodily invasions of a person's freedom will not be restricted. But if his notion of harm is construed broadly, virtually no freedom will be permitted and government regulation will extend to every phase of our lives.

We will be in a better position to assess this criticism of Mill's framework after an examination of the other autonomy-limiting principles that have been proposed by some philosophers as valid ways to augment the harm principle.

## LEGAL MORALISM

Most of us tend to be skeptical that the legal enforcement of controversial moral claims can be justified. Nevertheless, the justification of many commendable laws is based on some structure of moral beliefs, which indicates that we are not reluctant to see our laws underwritten by moral premises. For example, the Supreme Court's various decisions concerning pornography rest on moral appraisals of the nature of "obscene conduct" and matters of "redeeming social value." It is reasonable, then, to ask whether moral views are legitimately enforceable if they are perceived to be of overwhelming social importance.

"Legal moralism" is the philosophical principle that it is morally legitimate to use criminal or other severe social sanctions to prohibit actions that constitute moral evils, but that cause neither harm nor offense. This principle is independent of the harm principle and thereby raises questions regarding the *kinds* and *degree* of moral content, if any, that may properly be described as "evil," including whether socially deviant conduct can justifiably be outlawed in a pluralistic society. This issue has proved troublesome. Certain private sexual acts or pictorial representations involving consenting adults may turn out to be widely regarded in society as perverse, as we have seen in the issue of Internet regulation. Community standards were translated into laws in the COPA and CDA laws and through the use of filtration programs in public libraries. The following additional categories have been candidates in many countries for legislation as criminal offenses: homosexual and bisexual relations, prostitution, private use of pornographic films, gambling, private use of drugs and stimulants, voluntary active euthanasia, and suicide.

## Morally Wrong Behavior without Victims

In considering these problems it is useful to distinguish between (1) morally wrong behavior in which there is no damaged party and all parties involved voluntarily consent, and (2) morally wrong behavior in which there is a damaged party or victim. In the first range of cases, an act is wrong for some reason other than a harm caused. Feinberg calls such actions "harmless wrongdoing" because an (allegedly) illicit act occurs that does not harm anyone's interests. Criminal sanctions against prostitution, homosexuality, gambling, the use of marijuana, enticement through the Internet, and sexual stimulation in "massage parlors" are now-familiar examples of laws designed to prohibit what is considered to be morally wrongful behavior, though it is not directly harmful to those involved. By contrast, rape is a crime that always has a victim and, as such, falls under the harm principle.

The ethical issue is whether morally wrongful behavior without victims should be considered criminal or otherwise be socially constrained. Perhaps legal restrictions on gambling, for example, constitute unwarranted restrictions of liberty. Even if certain forms of sexual conduct are considered perverse, perhaps society should nonetheless allow individuals the personal freedom to engage in such conduct, if only consenting adults are involved. What gives these questions much of their punch is not the issue of whether the allegedly degrading, evil, or perverse wrongdoing is truly that, but rather whether the state has the right to criminalize the behavior.

Sometimes harm plays a related role in these arguments and controversies. For example, it has been argued that child pornography and street solicitation by prostitutes may legitimately be penalized under criminal law, because the sexual development of young children is perverted and street prostitutes are harmed by degradation, exploitation, and physical violence. These particular arguments are based on the harm principle, not on the principle of legal moralism. Only legislation against such acts for reasons of moral wrongdoing, *rather than harm,* are straightforwardly involved in the use of the principle of legal moralism—that is, in using sanctions to protect and maintain a community's moral standards.

Since the publication of Mill's *On Liberty,* there have been many sympathetic attempts to oppose the imposition of moral views on society and to eliminate existing restrictive legislation. The so-called Wolfenden Committee Report, issued in England in the 1950s, emerged as a landmark document on the issues of sexual practices and the law. The committee was established in 1954 to study existing laws regarding homosexuality and prostitution. It recommended that the current law be softened so that homosexuality was no longer a crime between consenting adults, but that there be no change in existing laws governing prostitution.

The recommendations of this committee often seemed to follow directly from Mill's arguments in *On Liberty.* The committee argued, for example, that firm distinctions should be drawn between crime and sin, and between public decency and private morality. Its members maintained that whereas the law must govern matters of public decency, private morality is not a matter to be legislated: "The function of the criminal law is to preserve public order and decency, to protect the citizen from what is offensive or injurious, and to provide sufficient safeguards against exploitation and corruption of others." They further maintained that the law should not function "to intervene in the private lives of citizens, or to seek to enforce any pattern of behavior" unless matters of public decency or harm are involved.

The clear message of the Wolfenden Committee was that unless it could be shown that public indecency or personal harm was involved, the law should not prohibit activities such as homosexuality and prostitution. This position is less relevant in cases involving pornography, where a criterion of "decency" is involved, as we have seen in the Internet controversies of today. The Wolfenden Committee maintained that the state should not have the right to restrict any private actions affecting only consenting adults. The state should not have this right, because of the supreme importance placed in social ethics and law on "individual freedom of choice and action in matters of private morality . . . which is, in brief and crude terms, not the law's business."

## Arguments in Support of Legal Moralism

The conclusions reached by Mill and embraced by the Wolfenden Committee have not stood unchallenged. Several reasons have been advanced to show that society has a right to preserve its traditional morality, that virtue and good character are legitimate goals of the law, and that personal advancement by immoral means is intolerable under law. Perhaps the two main arguments in support of legal moralism are arguments based on (1) rights to community control in a democracy and (2) the social importance of morality.

The first is an argument founded on the idea of legitimate exercise of authority under democratic rule. There is no tradition in western democracies, ethical or legal, that disallows the legislation of morality where no technical harm occurs. If some practice is regarded as immoral by the vast majority of citizens in a community, their reaction has been considered *in itself* sufficient to justify the claim that the behavior should be illegal. Both democratic rule and the institution of morality must be protected at all costs, according to this argument, at the expense of risk to individual liberties. Community sentiment makes the law in democracies, and laws set forth the prevailing standards of justice. Any majority-sanctioned law is valid and appropriate unless it is unconstitutional. In the instance of Internet access one could argue that states have a right to maintain a "decent society" and that in democracies a majority standard is appropriate. Supporters of legal moralism conclude that a society is partially constituted by a set of moral ideas, and that if some practice is widely detested, society cannot be denied the right to restrict it.

A second argument for legal moralism is based on the social necessity and importance of morality. In the nineteenth century, it was argued against Mill that one of the law's primary functions is to promote virtue while discouraging vice—two notions that cannot be reduced to benefit and harm. More recently, it has been argued that legal moralism is justified whenever threats to moral rules challenge the social order. Just as law and order through government are necessary for a stable society, according to this view, a moral environment conclusive to virtue is essential to a society's continuity. Individual liberties deserve protection only if they do not erode standards essential to the promotion of virtue and development of good character in society.

All supporters of this second argument agree that we ought to be cautious in declaring a practice intolerably immoral. But the point remains, they insist, that society has the *right* to pass criminal laws legislating morality in extenuating circumstances. This is just as true, they think, of messages and images on the Internet as of any other form of activity.

In the following selection Robert P. George argues that society has the right to outlaw immoral behavior such as the use of pornography when that behavior threatens what he calls the society's "moral environment." According to George, the widespread presence of vices such as pornography and the use of illegal drugs makes it more difficult for people to develop into virtuous, upstanding citizens. Even if they want to resist engaging in such transparently unacceptable behavior themselves, the influences and temptation may in some circumstances prove overwhelming. In a society allowing such vice, people may not be able to become the sort of persons they seek to become. Parents who are themselves virtuous may also have a difficult time raising their children in a vicious environment. George's point is not that such behavior should always be illegal; rather, he argues, there is nothing wrong in principle with using legislation based on morals to preserve a society's moral environment.

# *Making Men Moral**

## Robert P. George

[G]overnments have conclusive reasons not to attempt to enforce certain obligations which are essential to valuable social practices whose meaningfulness depends on the parties fulfilling their obligations freely. For example, compelling the expressing of gratitude, or the giving of gifts, or the acknowledging of achievements, where people ought to express gratitude, give gifts, or ac-

knowledge achievements, would have the effect of robbing these important practices of their meaning and value in social life. The reasons for not bringing coercion to bear with respect to such practices do not depend on the circumstances; they are not merely prudential. And they place significant ranges of morality beyond the reach of legislation as a matter of principle.

Nevertheless, the existence of justice- or rights-based grounds, as well as prudential reasons, for "not repressing every vice," does not entail that there

*From Robert P. George, *Making Men Moral: Civil Liberties and Public Morality* (Oxford, England: Clarendon Press, 1993).

are never valid reasons to legally prohibit *any* vice on the ground of its immorality. The legal prohibition of a vice may be warranted precisely to protect people from the *moral* harm it does to them and their communities. I have already observed that people do not become morally good by merely conforming their outward behavior to moral rules. Someone who refrains from a vice merely to avoid being caught and punished under a law prohibiting the vice realizes no moral good (though he may avoid further moral harm). Laws can compel outward behavior, not internal acts of the will; therefore, they cannot compel people to realize moral goods. They cannot, in any direct sense, "make men moral." Their contribution to making men moral must be indirect.

People become morally bad by yielding to vice; and they can be protected from the corrupting influence of powerfully seductive vices by laws that prohibit them (in so far as they are manifest in outward behavior) and prevent them from flourishing in the community. By suppressing industries and institutions that cater to moral weakness, and whose presence in the moral environment makes it difficult for people to choose uprightly, such laws can protect people from strong temptations and inducements to vice. To the extent that morals laws help to preserve the quality of the moral environment, they protect people from moral harm.

Any social environment will be constituted, in part, by a framework of understandings and expectations which will tend, sometimes profoundly, to influence the choices people actually make. People's choices, in turn, shape that framework. The significance of common understandings and expectations with respect to sex, marriage, and family life is obvious. The point extends well beyond these matters, however: the moral environment as constituted, in part, by the framework of understandings and expectations which exists in a particular society will affect everything from people's tendency to abuse drugs, to their driving habits on the highways, to their honesty or dishonesty in filling out their tax returns. If people's moral understandings are more or less sound, and if these understandings inform their expectations of one another, the moral environment thus constituted will be conducive to virtue. In contrast, if human relations are constituted according to morally defective understandings and expectations, the moral environment will seduce people into vice. In neither case will the moral environment eliminate the possibility of moral goodness and badness, for people can be good in bad moral environments and bad in good moral environments. The point remains, however, that a good moral ecology benefits people by encouraging and supporting their efforts to be good; a bad moral ecology harms people by offering them opportunities and inducements to do things that are wicked.

A physical environment marred by pollution jeopardizes people's physical health; a social environment abounding in vice threatens their moral well-being and integrity. A social environment in which vice abounds (and vice might, of course, abound in subtle ways) tends to damage people's moral understandings and weaken their characters as it bombards them with temptations to immorality. People who sincerely desire to avoid acts and dispositions which they know to be wrong may nevertheless find themselves giving in to prevalent vices and more or less gradually being corrupted by them. Even people who themselves stand fast in the face of powerful temptations may find their best efforts to instill in their children a sense of decency and moral integrity thwarted by a moral environment filled with activities and images or representations which, in the unfashionable but accurate phrase of the common law, "tend to corrupt and deprave."

Moreover, even people who wish to perform immoral acts but fear doing so lest they be caught and punished, or who would wish to perform them if their opportunities to do so had not been eliminated by the effective enforcement of a morals law, can be protected by effective laws from the (further) moral harm that they would do to themselves. A morals law may prevent moral harm, thus benefiting a potential wrongdoer, simply by protecting him from the (further) corrupting impact of acting out the vice. It is not that the person deterred solely by the law from wrongdoing realizes a moral good by not engaging in the vice. Moral goods cannot be realized by direct paternalism. Rather, it is that he avoids, albeit unwillingly, the bad impact of (further) involvement in the vice on his character.

Of course, it is a mistake to suppose that laws by themselves are sufficient to establish and maintain a healthy moral ecology. It is equally a mistake to suppose, however, that laws have nothing to contribute to that goal. Even apart from their more direct effects in discouraging particular vices or eliminating occasions for people to commit them, morals laws can help to shape the framework of understandings and expectations that helps to constitute the moral environment of any community. As Aristotle and Augustine rightly held, a community's laws will inevitably play an important educative role in the life of the community.

They can powerfully reinforce, or fail to reinforce, the teachings of parents and families, teachers and schools, religious leaders and communities, and other persons and institutions who have the leading roles in the moral formation of each new generation. . . .

I now want to focus . . . on the specific question of a right to pornography, . . . demonstrating that anti-pornography legislation need neither violate anyone's rights, nor sacrifice anyone's welfare, for the sake of advancing collective interests.

The human interest in dignity and beauty in sexual relationships, and in the creation and maintenance of a "cultural structure" which supports these goods, is a "collective" interest (just) in the sense that (1) these goods are genuine interests of each and every individual member of the collectivity, and (2) such a cultural structure cannot exist without collaboration, common endeavor, and common restraints. It is a "common" interest, and a matter of the common good, (just) in the sense that it is shared by all and may be preserved and advanced by common action. It is worth noticing that among those people whose interests anti-pornography legislation may preserve and advance are those very individuals who would be inclined to use pornography were it freely available. Dignity and beauty in sexual relationships (and a supporting cultural structure) are no less goods for them than for anyone else. To the extent that it serves these (truly common) goods, anti-pornography legislation preserves and advances, rather than harms, *their* interests as well as the interests of everybody else.

Such would not be the case, of course, if human interests were ultimately matters of desire-satisfaction. . . .

**365**

Individual rights, if they existed, would constrain the collective pursuit of desire-satisfaction. They would specify immunities which would, in effect, entitle the individual to certain types of desire-satisfaction of his own—even at a cost to the overall desire-satisfaction of the collectivity.

But once we understand interests as having to do with human goods not reducible to desire-satisfaction, individual rights need not be viewed as fundamentally in conflict with collective interests. Anti-pornography legislation, to the extent it is effective, frustrates the desires (or potential desires) of persons inclined to use pornography, but it does so precisely in the interests of, among others, those very individuals. In so far as it does not treat their interests as in any sense inferior to those of anyone else, it does not fail to treat them with equal concern and respect.

## Arguments Opposed to Legal Moralism

The central objection to legal moralism is that it is intolerant and repressive of individual rights, failing to respect privacy and the differing views inevitably present in a pluralistic society that constitutionally protects autonomy. For example, rights of "privacy," "constitutional rights," "protected speech," and freedom of "private thoughts" are often appealed to in defense of rights to Internet access.

There are several forms of this argument against legal moralism; the central claim, however, is that any attempt to make immoral conduct criminal, when the conduct is not harmful to others, is unacceptable because it directly violates principles of respect for autonomy. If one is to be justifiably punished under law, it must be because one's action harms someone else. Accordingly, the law should never be based on views that a certain *moral* perspective is intolerable, but rather on the view that *harmful* treatment is intolerable.

H. L. A. Hart has been perhaps the leading critic of legal moralism, as well as a selective defender of both Mill and the Wolfenden Report. For many years he has argued that proof of moral wrongness is an insufficient justification for legislation against acts such as homosexuality, because laws create undue frustration and misery of a special degree for those legislated against. Hart sees legal moralism as a disguised conservative defense of the conventional moral order, one that attempts to sweep all valid legal restrictions against immoral practices (for example, bigamy and dishonesty) under the same rug.

It must not be thought that Hart and Mill are attacking antiquated views that are now outmoded in liberal societies (as defined in Chapter 8). Prohibitions based on legal moralism are permitted and in some cases prevalent in both English common law and American constitutional law. Moreover, it is not clear from the arguments presented by these philosophers that legal moralism is *in principle* unacceptable. If, as we noted at the beginning of this section, laws are commonly justified by appeal to moral reasons, and if Mill and Hart accept the premise that whatever on balance maximizes utility is justified, then it would seem to follow that any criminal sanctions that maximized social utility by preventing moral evils would be justified. If sound, this argument indicates that legal moralism may find adequate justification even on the moral theories that have most famously opposed it.

## THE OFFENSE PRINCIPLE

Consider the following hypothetical newscast: "Publisher $X$ was jailed last evening for the publication and distribution of pornographic materials on the Internet. The decision to jail $X$ followed an extensive police investigation into his traffic in pornography and other obscene materials." Such a newscast might be followed by reports on the local reaction: Favorable reaction to the news of $X$'s jailing indicates that some people in the community believe $X$ deserved everything he got. Unfavorable reaction indicates that some people in the community feel the low quality of $X$'s material is irrelevant, and that one probably ought to be free to publish whatever one wishes on the Internet without restriction, as long as it does not harm other persons.

Here we encounter the problem of whether a public perception of inherent *offensiveness* is a proper ground for restricting liberty when there is no direct harm to individual persons. When offensive displays and the dissemination of offensive materials are public, they may be neither consented to nor avoidable. These public displays should be contrasted with private displays such as the showing of films and the like in homes or theaters, with only consenting adults present. Theaters can be interpreted as places of public accommodation, but this characterization is not sufficient to qualify them as "public" in the relevant sense, which is that of freely open to all. The Internet, by contrast, seems clearly to be public in the relevant sense. Magazines displayed on racks, pamphlets handed out on the street, and advertisements over the radio are also public in the relevant sense. These public spots are the more common sources of concern when it comes to pornography and obscenity.

### The Meanings of "Offense" and "Obscene"

"Offense" is not reducible either to harm (as in the harm principle) or to moral wrong (as in legal moralism). If pornographic plays, novels, photographs, and the like, are condemned as "offensive," the word does not have the *descriptive* meaning of "psychologically painful" or "causing displeasure." The appropriate sense of "offense" is "a wrongful but not harmful action causing dissatisfaction in others."

The word "obscenity," by contrast, refers in ordinary English to something foul, repulsive, and disgusting, particularly when compared to that which is modest and decent. The term has come to have definite associations with lewdness, nudity, sexual display, and excretion. Both law and ethical theory use the terms similarly, but with a more direct ethical import attached: To say that something is "obscene" is to say that *because of its offensiveness, it does not deserve to be protected from legal interference.*

This judgment leaves open precisely which criteria should be used to delineate offensiveness. A common strategy, as with legal moralism, is to appeal to community standards or community sentiment. Any acceptable standard must be publicly testable and socially well entrenched in order to qualify as stipulating what is "offensive" for the purpose of law and ethics. To avoid the accusation that a judgment of offensiveness is purely subjective, one strategy is to gauge the level of community sentiment objectively by reference to social facts—in particular, facts about whether the norms that underlie the judgment are the prevailing social norms of proper conduct.

## Offensiveness and Public Policy

An instructive instance of a government struggling with these issues occurred when the U.S. Congress, citing traffic in obscene and pornographic materials as "a matter of national concern," created the National Commission on Obscenity and Pornography. This commission, whose members were appointed by the President, was charged with studying social and moral issues of obscenity and pornography. Its eventual report reads like a document prepared by Mill, and it contrasts sharply with the judicial findings of the Supreme Court. The commission recommended that all legal restrictions on the public sale, exhibition, and distribution of sexual materials to *consenting adults* be repealed, but that nonconsenting adults be protected from sexually explicit materials encountered through public displays and unsolicited mailings. The commission based its final recommendations more on factual than ethical premises: There was no evidence to connect exposure to explicit sexual materials with antisocial behavior. Both the factual and the ethical theses of the commission are in general agreement with Mill's claims.

The report of the National Commission on Obscenity and Pornography was not well received in several quarters. Six of the commission's eighteen members did not support its final recommendations. Some members filed a minority report that challenged the factual findings, as well as the recommendations. Then President Richard Nixon was angered by the report, and members of Congress and their constituents were also less than enthusiastic. As a result, the commission's recommendations were never implemented. Still, this and other studies, and judicial discussions such as the current controversies about Internet access, challenge us to consider what conditions, if any, would justify a government's limitation of access to pornographic and other obscene materials.

## Arguments against Social Controls

An argument commonly employed to resist the offense principle (and, indeed, the argument used by the National Commission on Obscenity and Pornography) is a consequentialist one based on the insufficiency of relevant evidence: There is no factual evidence to indicate that unrestricted dissemination of pornography and controversial displays will bring about a substantial social evil. For this reason, restricting access to printed materials or Internet materials of any sort, including public displays that may be offensive by prevailing standards, is regarded as unjustified.

Justice William Brennan used this argument and related ones several times in a dissenting opinion in the previously mentioned *Paris Adult Theatre* case. Brennan argued that state efforts to suppress obscene material inevitably lead to the erosion of protected speech, thereby violating both the First Amendment and the Fourteenth Amendment of the Constitution. He noted that in the past the Supreme Court had agreed that there was no compelling evidence of a causal connection between exposure to obscene materials and unacceptable behavior. As he put it, the Court's traditional view has been that there is "little empirical basis for" the claim that "exposure to obscene materials may lead to deviant sexual behavior or crimes of sexual violence."

One striking argument on behalf of sexually explicit materials takes the optimistic view that they are actually beneficial to those exposed to them and to society as a whole. It is claimed, for example, that exposure to sexual materials can promote normal rather than deviant sexual development, that sexual relationships can be enhanced by it, and that for some people it provides a socially harmless release from sexual tension. Supporters of this point of view favor easy access to sexually explicit publications, including in readily available places such as the Internet. Their arguments, if correct, provide maximally strong reasons in favor of free access, because they claim *benefits* for allegedly offensive materials, as well as *harms* from the loss of the liberty to acquire them.

## Mixed Arguments for Social Controls

Only rarely is a case for the social control of offensive materials (through criminal sanctions, for example) based purely on the offense principle. Usually the appeal is to a mixture of the autonomy-limiting principles under examination in this chapter. Several appeals are found in the literature on pornography and other obscene materials or actions. For example, the harm principle is a common basis for the claim that exposure to pornography is a direct cause of the crime of rape. Proponents of this position often cite studies or examples of persons exposed to pornographic material who subsequently commit sex-related crimes. They cite studies purporting to show that an arguable correlation exists between obscene material and crimes. The acknowledged problem with such examples is that they fail to establish that the crime, which follows exposure to pornography, is a direct *causal result* of the exposure itself. Sociological data indicating a causal relation are weak. The National Commission on Obscenity and Pornography claimed that, on the basis of the available data, there was virtually no evidence to support causal claims.

*If* a causal connection between the use of pornography and antisocial behavior could be demonstrated, the argument would have found a solid basis in the harm principle; but then there would be no need for a supplementary offense principle. The principle of paternalism is also sometimes invoked on grounds that those exposed to pornography will harm *themselves* by such exposure—for example, pornography might reinforce their emotional problems or render them incapable of love and other distinctively human relationships.

It is difficult to balance questions of liberty against problems of mere offense, but in the following selection, Joel Feinberg attempts to convince us by the use of examples and argument that there is at least some offensive conduct that we should not tolerate and may legitimately prohibit by law.

# "Harmless Immoralities" and Offensive Nuisances*

## Joel Feinberg

The American Civil Liberties Union, adopting an approach characteristic of both the friends and the foes of censorship in an earlier period, insists that the offensiveness of obscenity is much too trivial a ground to warrant prior restraint or censorship.[1] The A.C.L.U. argument for this position treats literature, drama, and painting as forms of expression subject to the same rules as expressions of opinion. The power to censor and punish, it maintains, involves risks of great magnitude that socially valuable material will be repressed along with the "filth"; and the overall effect of suppression, it insists, can only be to discourage nonconformist and eccentric expression generally. In order to override these serious risks, the A.C.L.U. concludes, there must be in a given case an even more clear and present danger that the obscene material, if not squelched, will cause even greater harm; and evidence of this countervailing kind is never forthcoming (especially when "mere offense" is not counted as a kind of harm).

The A.C.L.U. stand on obscenity seems clearly to be the position dictated by the [harm principle and its] corollary, the clear and present danger test. Is there any reason at this point to introduce the offense principle into the discussion? Unhappily, we may be forced to do just that if we are to do justice to all of our particular intuitions in the most harmonious way. Consider an example suggested by Louis B. Schwartz. By the provisions of the new Model Penal Code, he writes, "a rich homosexual may not use a billboard on Times Square to promulgate to the general populace the techniques and pleasures of sodomy."[2] If the notion of "harm" is restricted to its narrow sense that is contrasted with "offense," it will be hard to reconstruct a rationale for this prohibition that is based on a harm principle. It is unlikely that there would be evidence that a lurid and obscene public poster in Times Square would create a clear and present danger of injury to those unfortunate persons who fail to avert their eyes in time as they come blinking out of the subway stations. And yet it will be surpassingly difficult even for the most dedicated liberal to advocate freedom of expression in a case of this kind. Hence, if we are to justify coercion in this case, we will likely be driven, however reluctantly, to the offense principle.

There is good reason to be "reluctant" to embrace the offense principle

---

*From Joel Feinberg, "'Harmless Immoralities' and Offensive Nuisances," in *Issues in Law and Morality* (Cleveland: Case Western Reserve University Press, 1973), pp. 99–104, 133–34.

[1]"Obscenity and Censorship" (New York: American Civil Liberties Union, March 1963). The approach that was characteristic of the late fifties and early sixties was to assimilate the obscenity question to developed free speech doctrine requiring a showing of a "clear and present danger" of substantive harm to justify government suppression. Obscene materials pertaining to sex (but not excretion!) were taken to be dangerous, if at all, because they are alluring and thus capable of tempting persons into antisocial (harmful) conduct. As Herbert Packer points out (Limits of Criminal Sanctions, p. 319), the clear and present danger test is virtually certain to be passed by even the most offensive materials.

[2]Schwartz, "Morals Offenses," p. 681.

until driven to it by an example of the above kind. People take offense—perfectly genuine offense—at many socially useful or harmless activities, from commercial advertisements to inane chatter. Moreover, as we have seen, irrational prejudices of a very widespread kind can lead people to be disgusted, shocked, even morally repelled by perfectly innocent activities, and we should be loath to permit their groundless repugnance to override the innocence. The offense principle, therefore, must be formulated in a very precise way so as not to open the door to wholesale and intuitively unwarranted repression.

It is instructive to note that a strictly drawn offense principle would not only justify prohibition of public conduct and publicly pictured conduct that is in its inherent character repellent (e.g., buggery, bestiality, sexual sadomasochism), but also conduct and pictured conduct that is inoffensive in itself but offensive only when it occurs in inappropriate circumstances. I have in mind so-called indecencies such as public nudity. . . .

If we are to accept the offense principle as a supplement to the harm principle, we must accept two mediating norms of interpretation which stand to it in a way similar to that in which the clear and present danger test stands to the harm principle. The first is the *standard of universality* which has already been touched upon. The interracial couple strolling hand in hand down the streets of Jackson, Mississippi, without question cause shock and mortification, even shame and disgust, to the overwhelming majority of white pedestrians who happen to observe them; but we surely don't want our offense principle applied to justify preventive coercion on that ground. To avoid that consequence

let us stipulate that in order for "offense" (repugnance, embarrassment, shame, etc.) to be sufficient to warrant coercion, it should be the reaction that could reasonably be expected from almost any person chosen at random, taking the nation as a whole, and not because the individual selected belongs to some faction, clique, or party.

That qualification should be more than sufficient to protect the interracial couple, but, alas, it may yield undesirable consequences in another class of cases. I have in mind abusive, mocking, insulting behavior or speech attacking specific subgroups of the population—especially ethnic, racial, or religious groups. Public cross-burnings, displays of swastikas, "jokes" that ridicule Americans of Polish descent told on public media, public displays of banners with large and abusive caricatures of the Pope[3] are extremely offensive to the groups so insulted, and no doubt also offensive to large numbers of sympathetic outsiders. But still, there will be many millions of people who will not respond emotionally at all, and many millions more who may secretly approve. Thus, our amended offense principle will not justify the criminal proscription of such speech or conduct. I am inclined, therefore, simply to patch up that principle in an *ad hoc* fashion once more. For that special class of offensive behavior that consists in the flaunting of abusive, mocking, insulting behavior of a sort bound to upset, alarm, anger, or irritate those it insults, I would allow the offense principle to apply, even though the behavior would *not* offend the entire

[3]For a penetrating discussion of an actual case of this description, see Zechariah Chafee, *Free Speech in the United States* (Cambridge, MA: Harvard University Press, 1964), p. 161.

population. Those who are taunted by such conduct will understandably suffer intense and complicated emotions. They might be frightened or wounded; and their blood might boil in wrath. Yet the law cannot permit them to accept the challenge and vent their anger in retaliatory aggression. But again, having to cope with one's rage is as burdensome a bore as having to suffer shame, or disgust, or noisome stenches, and the law might well undertake to protect those who are vulnerable, even if they are—indeed, precisely because they are—a minority.

The second mediating principle for the application of the offense principle is the standard of reasonable avoidability. No one has a right to protection from the state against offensive experiences if he can easily and effectively avoid those experiences with no unreasonable effort or inconvenience. If a nude person enters a public bus and takes a seat near the front, there may be no effective way whatever for the other patrons to avoid intensely shameful embarrassment (or other insupportable feelings) short of leaving the bus themselves, which would be an unreasonable inconvenience. Similarly, obscene remarks over a loudspeaker, homosexual billboards in Times Square, pornographic handbills thrust into the hands of passing pedestrians all fail to be reasonably avoidable.

On the other hand, the offense principle, properly qualified, can give no warrant to the suppression of *books* on the grounds of obscenity. When printed words hide decorously behind covers of books sitting passively on the shelves of a bookstore, their offensiveness is easily avoided. The contrary view is no doubt encouraged by the common comparison of obscenity with "smut," "filth," or "dirt." This in turn suggests an analogy

to nuisance law, which governs cases where certain activities create loud noises or terrible odors offensive to neighbors, and "the courts must weigh the gravity of the nuisance [substitute "offense"] to the neighbors against the social utility [substitute "redeeming social value"] of the defendant's conduct."[4] There is, however, one vitiating disanalogy in this comparison. In the case of "dirty books," the offense is easily avoidable. There is nothing like the evil smell of rancid garbage oozing right out through the covers of a book whether one looks at it or not. When an "obscene" book sits on a shelf, who is there to be offended? Those who want to read it for the sake of erotic stimulation presumably will not be offended (else they wouldn't read it), and those who choose not to read it will have no experience of it to be offended by. . . .

I should like to take this opportunity to try one final example and to rest my case on it. It is an example that illustrates not just one but virtually all the categories of offensiveness mentioned in my article; and if the reader fails to concede that it provides a legitimate occasion for legal interference with a citizen's conduct on grounds other than harmfulness, then I must abandon my effort to convince him at all, at least by the use of examples. Consider then the man who walks down the main street of a town at midday. In the middle of a block in the central part of town, he stops, opens his briefcase, and pulls out a portable folding camp-toilet. In the prescribed manner, he attaches a plastic bag to its under side, sets it on the sidewalk, and proceeds to defecate in it, to the utter amazement and disgust of the

[4]William L. Prosser, *Handbook of the Law of Torts* (St. Paul, MN: West Publishing Company, 1955).

passers-by. While he is thus relieving himself, he unfolds a large banner which reads "This is what I think of the Ruritanians" (substitute "niggers," "Kikes," "Spics," "Dagos," "Polacks," or "Hunkies"). Another placard placed prominently next to him invites ladies to join him in some of the more bizarre sexual-excretory perversions mentioned in Krafft-Ebbing and includes a large-scale graphic painting of the conduct he solicits. For those who avert their eyes too quickly, he plays an obscene phonograph record on a small portable machine, and accompanies its raunchier parts with grotesquely lewd bodily motions. He concludes his public performance by tasting some of his own excrement, and after savoring it slowly and thoroughly in the manner of a true epicure, he consumes it. He then dresses, ties the plastic bag containing the rest of the excrement, places it carefully in his briefcase, and continues on his way.

Now I would not have the man in the example executed, or severely punished. I'm not sure I would want him punished at all, unless he defied authoritative orders to "move along" or to cease and desist in the future. But I would surely want the coercive arm of the state to protect passers-by (by the most economical and humane means) from being unwilling audiences for such performances. I assume in the example (I hope with some plausibility) that the offensive conduct causes no harm or injury either of a public or a private kind. After all, if the numerous tons of dog dung dropped every day on the streets of New York are no health hazard, then surely the fastidious use of a sanitary plastic bag cannot be seriously unhygienic.

Feinberg has attempted to show why the prevention of harmless offenses is a legitimate purpose of the criminal law and how we can apply the offense principle by using balancing tests, at the same time minimizing the possibility that this principle will be abused. He proposes in other writings that balancing tests must be devised for weighing the seriousness of the offense and inconvenience caused to an offended party against the purposes and reasonableness of the party causing the offense. He argues that the seriousness of the offense must be gauged by the level of repugnance produced by the action, as well as the extent to which this outcome might have reasonably been predicted in the circumstances. He would also have us consider whether the offended person might possibly have avoided the offense and whether those offended might perhaps avoid contact with the action. Factors such as these must be weighed against the importance of the conduct to the actor, the social importance of permitting such conduct generally, alternatives that might be substituted for the conduct, and the extent to which the motives behind the conduct are malevolent, vengeful, or spiteful. Feinberg argues that there is no fixed recipe for balancing these considerations in order to determine whether conduct should be prohibited, and in hard cases there may be no clearly correct decision in light of the above criteria.[14] Those who are struggling today with limiting Internet access seem to be weighing precisely these factors.

[14]See Feinberg, *Offense to Others,* in *The Moral Limits of the Criminal Law* (New York: Oxford University Press, 1985), vol. II, chap. 8.

Feinberg's standard of reasonable avoidability proposes a minimum requirement for judging offensive displays or actions. But how is the boundary to be drawn between the avoidable and the unavoidable? Can adequately precise *conditions* be established under which restrictions of liberty are justified on grounds of offensiveness? These are important questions, and they apply not only to pornography in the forms usually brought to public attention but potentially to many forms of poetry, dance, drama, pictorial representations, language, and music. It seems likely that wherever one draws the line as to what is permissible and impermissible in conduct, there will be difficult cases that fall on each side of the line.

## PATERNALISM

Kant once denounced paternalistic government as "the worst conceivable despotism." He was referring to a government that "cancels the freedom of subjects." He never seriously contemplated a parental model that likens the state to a protective parent caring for a heavily dependent minor. Nor did Mill in *On Liberty* contemplate the possibility that paternalism might include intervention involving those who have limited or no autonomy.[15] Yet the very model that these two philosophers never contemplated has become the most widely accepted model of paternalism. The root idea is government of another as by a loving father: The father acts beneficently (that is, in accord with his conception of the interests of his children) and makes decisions relating to his children's welfare, rather than letting them make their own decisions.

### The Nature of Paternalism

This model of paternalism is, however, insufficient to capture the appropriate sense of that which is central to the issues we will examine in this section, which turn on the intentional limitation of the autonomy of one person by another. Paternalists maintain that restricting the autonomy of persons is justified if these persons would otherwise produce serious harm to themselves or would fail to secure an important benefit for themselves. The main ethical issue is whether—and, if so, under which conditions—these paternalistic interventions are morally justified.

The word "paternalism" refers loosely to acts of treating adults as a benevolent father treats his children, but the term has been given both a narrow and a broad meaning in ethical theory. In the narrow sense, "paternalism" refers to acts or practices that restrict the autonomy or liberty of individuals without their explicit consent; the justification for such actions is either the prevention of some harm they stand to do to themselves or the production of some benefit for them that they would not otherwise secure. This *narrow conception* of paternalism suggests the following definition: *Paternalism* is the intentional limitation of the autonomy of one person

---

[15]Immanuel Kant, *On the Old Saw: That May Be Right in Theory but It Won't Work in Practice,* E. B. Ashton, trans. (Philadelphia: University of Pennsylvania Press, 1974), pp. 290–91; John Stuart Mill, *On Liberty, passim.*

by another, where the person who limits autonomy justifies the action exclusively by the goal of helping the person whose autonomy is limited. (Gerald Dworkin, in the selection below, relies on a similar definition.) An act of paternalism, then, overrides the value of autonomous choice on grounds of beneficence.

Some writers object to this analysis of paternalism, because it does not capture an established traditional meaning of the term, especially as it has descended from legal precedent. They view the notion as linked to guardianship, surrogate decision making, and government intervention to protect the vulnerable. The root sense of "paternalism" here is "government as by a benevolent father." This meaning incorporates interventions with both autonomous actions and nonautonomous actions. Those who follow this *broad conception* recommend the following definition: *Paternalism* is the intentional overriding of one person's known preferences by another person, where the person who overrides justifies the action by the goal of benefiting the person whose will is overridden. Under this second definition, if a person's stated preferences do not derive from a substantially autonomous choice, the act of overriding their preferences is still paternalistic.[16]

Defenders of the first definition argue that there are compelling reasons for rejecting this second definition. First, paternalism originates in ethical theory, as we have seen throughout this chapter, as an issue about the valid limitation of liberty and autonomy. To include cases involving persons who lack substantial autonomy, such as drug addicts or the severely mentally handicapped, broadens the term in a way that obscures the central issue, which is how, whether, and when liberty or autonomy can be justifiably limited. Second, the legal concept of paternalism (often expressed in terms of *parens patriae* powers) has its own subtleties and complexities. Courts do not apply this notion across the same range of thought and conduct treated in ethical theory.

These two definitions are both established in current literature, but the first will be emphasized here because of its consistency with problems of the limitation of liberty or autonomy. Many believe that paternalism in this sense is pervasively present in modern society. Numerous actions, rules, and laws are commonly justified by appeal to a paternalistic principle. Examples include court orders for blood transfusions when patients have refused them, involuntary commitments to medical institutions for treatment, intervention to stop rational suicides, withholding information that persons have requested, and some government efforts to restrict risky recreational activities of citizens (for example, in national parks). The CDA and COPA laws proposed for the Internet were clearly paternalistic because their stated objectives were limiting the liberty of mature minors to prevent harm that these young persons might bring upon themselves by exploring web sites.

Two classic cases in American law involving requirements that helmets be worn when riding motorcycles illustrate the dilemma presented by paternalistic legislation. In one case, a judge relied extensively on Mill's views about liberty. He argued that requiring motorcyclists and their passengers to wear crash helmets for paternalistic reasons was an instance of reasoning that could lead to unlimited state

---

[16]See Donald VanDeVeer, *Paternalistic Interventions: The Moral Bounds on Benevolence* (Princeton, NJ: Princeton University Press, 1986); John Kleinig, *Paternalism* (Totowa, NJ: Rowman and Allenheld, 1983).

paternalism. He acknowledged that highway safety is a relevant reason for legal restrictions in cases in which *other* persons are involved, but not where the *cyclist alone* is at risk. The opinion quoted Justice Brandeis to the effect that we ought to be especially careful to protect human liberty if government becomes overprotective through its beneficence. Like the Wolfenden Report, this legal opinion reads almost as if it were an immediate application of Mill's moral and social philosophy.[17]

By contrast, a different judge in a different case argued that "we ought to admit frankly that the purpose of the helmet [requirement] is to preserve the life and health of the cyclist"—and not to promote public health or highway safety. The judge saw the issue as a case of justifiable paternalism. He found at least some paternalistic laws to be acceptable and pointed out that suicide, for example, has been "a common-law crime for centuries." The judge also appealed to Mill for support, quoting him to the effect that "no person is an entirely isolated being" and that one cannot perform actions free of responsibilities to other persons.[18]

These two opinions, and many like them, indicate that the issue of paternalism is as unsettled in contemporary American law as it is in philosophy.

### Weak (Soft) Paternalism and Strong (Hard) Paternalism

Joel Feinberg's distinction between weak and strong paternalism has profoundly affected the literature on paternalism. Although he switched to the language of "soft" and "hard" paternalism in his later work, the terms "weak" and "strong" seem to have more deeply influenced the literature and will be used here.

In *weak paternalism,* one "has the right to prevent self-regarding conduct only when it is substantially nonvoluntary or when temporary intervention is necessary to establish whether it is voluntary or not."[19] This type of paternalism confines permissible limitations of autonomy to substantially nonautonomous (or nonvoluntary) behaviors. For example, it is permissible to pick up injured, partially incoherent victims of automobile accidents who refuse ambulance service and to involuntarily admit mentally ill persons who are dangerous to themselves. In *strong paternalism,* however, it is proper to protect or benefit a person by autonomy-limiting measures even if the person's contrary choices are autonomous. This paternalism supports interventions that protect competent adults against their will; that is, it controls or restricts substantially autonomous behaviors. For example, it is an act of strong paternalism to refuse to release a competent hospital patient who will die outside the hospital but requests the release knowing the consequences.

Weak paternalism is built on conditions of compromised ability or dysfunctional incompetence. When conduct that affects only the actor is restricted, *some* degree of autonomy may be present in the restricted actor, but the action must be *substantially* nonautonomous. Conditions that can significantly compromise the ability to act

---

[17]*American Motorcycle Association v. Department of State Police,* 158 N.W. 2d 72 (Mich. App. 1968). The quote from Brandeis is found in *Olmstead v. U.S.,* 277 U.S. 438, 478 (1928), in a dissenting opinion.
[18]*Florida v. Eitel,* 227 So. 2d 489 (Fla. 1969).
[19]Feinberg, "Legal Paternalism," *Canadian Journal of Philosophy,* 1 (1971): 113; see vol. III of *The Moral Limits of the Criminal Law* (1986) for detailed argument.

autonomously include the influence of psychotropic drugs, painful labor while delivering a child, a blow to the head that affects memory and judgment, and the immaturity of childhood. In medical situations, a patient's illness can be so devastating that it affects decision-making capacity. Every increase in illness, ignorance, or quantity of medication can increase the patient's dependence on his or her physician. A member of the medical profession who overturns the preferences of a substantially nonautonomous patient in the interests of the person's medical welfare acts paternalistically and justifiably by the standards of weak paternalism. For this reason, weak paternalism has been widely accepted in law, medicine, and moral philosophy as an appropriate basis for intervention.

Strong paternalism, by contrast, supports some interventions intended to benefit a person whose choices and actions are informed and autonomous. Strong paternalism *usurps* autonomy by either restricting the information available to a person or overriding the person's informed and voluntary choices. These choices may not be *fully* autonomous or voluntary, but in order to qualify as strong paternalism the choices of the beneficiary of paternalistic intervention must be substantially autonomous. For example, a strong paternalist would prevent a patient capable of autonomous choice from receiving diagnostic information that might lead to suicide. Unlike weak paternalism, strong paternalism does not require any conditions of compromised ability, dysfunctional incompetence, or encumbrance as the basis of intervention.

### The Justification of Weak Paternalism

Any careful proponent of a principle of paternalism will specify which goods and needs deserve paternalistic protection and the conditions under which intervention is warranted. In recent formulations, it has been argued that one is justified in interfering with a person's autonomy only if the interference protects the person against his or her actions where those actions are extremely and unreasonably risky (for example, waterfall rafting, hang gliding, refusing to wear a seat belt, or refusing a lifesaving therapy) or have potentially dangerous or irreversible effects (such as taking some drugs or choosing some forms of surgery). In this conception, paternalism can be justified only if (1) the harms prevented or the benefits provided to the person outweigh the loss of independence and the sense of invasion caused by the interference, (2) the person's condition seriously limits his or her ability to choose autonomously, and (3) the interference is universally justified under relevantly similar circumstances.

Roughly this position has been defended by a number of recent writers, some of whom regard paternalism as a form of "social insurance policy" that fully rational persons would take out in order to protect themselves.[20] Such persons would know, for example, that they might be tempted at times to make decisions that were far-reaching, potentially dangerous, or irreversible. In still other cases, persons might not sufficiently understand or appreciate such dangers as the effects of smoking or

[20]See Gerald Dworkin, "Paternalism," *The Monist* (January 1972): 64–84; John Rawls, *A Theory of Justice* (Cambridge, MA: Harvard University Press, 1971): 248–49.

of too much drinking. Thus, these paternalists conclude, it is rational to consent to a limited authorization for others to control our actions by paternalistic policies and interventions.

Many supporters of paternalism accept that a heavy burden of justification is needed to limit free actions by competent persons, especially if there is never direct consent (even if there might be proxy consent) to be placed under a paternalistic power. Gerald Dworkin espouses one form of this justified paternalism in which the justification of the position rests on the argument that completely rational agents fully aware of their circumstances *would consent* to paternalism and *would consent* to a scheme of penalties that would deter them from any motive to undertake a foolish action. Those whose autonomy is reduced would consent were it not for their compromised condition.

# *Paternalism**

## Gerald Dworkin

I suggest that since we are all aware of our irrational propensities, deficiencies in cognitive and emotional capacities and avoidable and unavoidable ignorance it is rational and prudent for us to in effect take out "social insurance policies." We may argue for and against proposed paternalistic measures in terms of what fully rational individuals would accept as forms of protection. Now, clearly since the initial agreement is not about specific measures we are dealing with a more-or-less blank check and therefore there have to be carefully defined limits. What I am looking for are certain kinds of conditions which make it plausible to suppose that rational men could reach agreement to limit their liberty even when other men's interests are not affected.

Of course as in any kind of agreement schema there are great difficulties in deciding what rational individuals

would or would not accept. Particularly in sensitive areas of personal liberty, there is always a danger of the dispute over agreement and rationality being a disguised version of evaluative and normative disagreement.

Let me suggest types of situations in which it seems plausible to suppose that fully rational individuals would agree to having paternalistic restrictions imposed upon them. It is reasonable to suppose that there are "goods" such as health which any person would want to have in order to pursue his own good—no matter how that good is conceived. This is an argument that is used in connection with compulsory education for children but it seems to me that it can be extended to other goods which have this character. Then one could agree that the attainment of such goods should be promoted even when not recognized to be such, at the moment, by the individuals concerned.

An immediate difficulty that arises stems from the fact that men are always faced with competing goods and that

*From Gerald Dworkin, "Paternalism," *Monist* 56 (1): 78–84, with permission of the author and publisher.

there may be reasons why even a value such as health—or indeed life—may be overridden by competing values. Thus the problem with the Christian Scientist and blood transfusions. It may be more important for him to reject "impure substances" than to go on living. The difficult problem that must be faced is whether one can give sense to the notion of a person irrationally attaching weights to competing values.

Consider a person who knows the statistical data on the probability of being injured when not wearing seat belts in an automobile and knows the types and gravity of the various injuries. He also insists that the inconvenience attached to fastening the belt every time he gets in and out of the car outweighs for him the possible risks to himself. I am inclined in this case to think that such a weighing is irrational. Given his life-plans which we are assuming are those of the average person, his interests and commitments already undertaken, I think it is safe to predict that we can find inconsistencies in his calculations at some point. I am assuming that this is not a man who for some conscious or unconscious reasons is trying to injure himself nor is he a man who just likes to "live dangerously." I am assuming that he is like us in all the relevant respects but just puts an enormously high negative value on inconvenience—one which does not seem comprehensible or reasonable. . . .

Some of the decisions we make are of such a character that they produce changes which are in one or another way irreversible. Situations are created in which it is difficult or impossible to return to anything like the initial stage at which the decision was made. In particular some of these changes will make it impossible to continue to make rea-soned choices in the future. I am thinking specifically of decisions which involve taking drugs that are physically or psychologically addictive and those which are destructive of one's mental and physical capacities.

I suggest we think of the imposition of paternalistic interferences in situations of this kind as being a kind of insurance policy which we take out against making decisions which are far-reaching, potentially dangerous and irreversible. Each of these factors is important. Clearly there are many decisions we make that are relatively irreversible. In deciding to learn to play chess I could predict in view of my general interest in games that some portion of my free time was going to be preempted and that it would not be easy to give up the game once I acquired a certain competence. But my whole life-style was not going to be jeopardized in an extreme manner. Further it might be argued that even with addictive drugs such as heroin one's normal life plans would not be seriously interfered with if an inexpensive and adequate supply were readily available. So this type of argument might have a much narrower scope than appears to be the case at first.

A second class of cases concerns decisions which are made under extreme psychological and sociological pressures. I am not thinking here of the making of the decision as being something one is pressured into—e.g., a good reason for making duelling illegal is that unless this is done many people might have to manifest their courage and integrity in ways in which they would rather not do so—but rather of decisions such as that to commit suicide which are usually made at a point where the individual is not thinking clearly and calmly about the nature of his decision. . . .

Using my argument schema the question is whether rational individuals would consent to such limitations. I see no reason for them to consent to an absolute prohibition but I do think it is reasonable for them to agree to some kind of enforced waiting period. . . .

A third class of decisions—these classes are not supposed to be disjoint—involves dangers which are either not sufficiently understood or appreciated correctly by the persons involved. Let me illustrate, using the example of cigarette smoking, a number of possible cases.

1. A man may not know the facts—e.g., smoking between one and two packs a day shortens life expectancy 6.2 years, the costs and pain of the illness caused by smoking, etc.
2. A man may know the facts, wish to stop smoking, but not have the requisite will-power.
3. A man may know the facts but not have them play the correct role in his calculation because, say, he discounts the danger psychologically because it is remote in time and/or inflates the attractiveness of other consequences of his decision which he regards as beneficial.

In case 1 what is called for is education, the posting of warnings, etc. In case 2 there is no theoretical problem. We are not imposing a good on someone who rejects it. We are simply using coercion to enable people to carry out their own goals. (Note: There obviously is a difficulty in that only a subclass of the individuals affected wish to be prevented from doing what they are doing.) In case 3 there is a sense in which we are imposing a good on someone since

given his current appraisal of the facts he doesn't wish to be restricted. But in another sense we are not imposing a good since what is being claimed—and what must be shown or at least argued for—is that an accurate accounting on his part would lead him to reject his current course of action. Now we all know that such cases exist, that we are prone to disregard dangers that are only possibilities, that immediate pleasures are often magnified and distorted.

If, in addition, the dangers are severe and far-reaching, we could agree to allowing the state a certain degree of power to intervene in such situations. The difficulty is in specifying in advance, even vaguely, the class of cases in which intervention will be legitimate.

A related difficulty is that of drawing a line so that it is not the case that all ultra-hazardous activities are ruled out, e.g., mountain-climbing, bull-fighting, sports-car racing, etc. There are some risks—even very great ones—which a person is entitled to take with his life.

A good deal depends on the nature of the deprivation . . . e.g., does it prevent the person from engaging in the activity completely or merely limit his participation—and how important to the nature of the activity is the absence of restriction when this is weighed against the role that the activity plays in the life of the person? In the case of automobile seat belts, for example, the restriction is trivial in nature, interferes not at all with the use or enjoyment of the activity, and does, I am assuming, considerably reduce a high risk of serious injury. Whereas, for example, making mountain-climbing illegal prevents completely a person engaging in an activity which may play an important role in his life and his conception of the person he is.

In general, the easiest cases to handle are those which can be argued about in terms which Mill thought to be so important—a concern not just for the happiness or welfare, in some broad sense, of the individual, but rather, a concern for the autonomy and freedom of the person. I suggest that we would be most likely to consent to paternalism in those instances in which it preserves and enhances for the individual his ability to rationally consider and carry out his own decisions.

I have suggested in this essay a number of types of situations in which it seems plausible that rational men would agree to granting the legislative powers of a society the right to impose restrictions on what Mill calls "self-regarding" conduct. However, rational men knowing something about the resources of ignorance, ill-will, and stupidity available to the law-makers of a society—a good case in point is the history of drug legislation in the United States—will be concerned to limit such intervention to a minimum. I suggest in closing two principles designed to achieve this end.

In all cases of paternalistic legislation there must be a heavy and clear burden of proof placed on the authorities to demonstrate the exact nature of the harmful effects (or beneficial consequences) to be avoided (or achieved) and the probability of their occurrence. The burden of proof here is twofold—what lawyers distinguish as the burden of going forward and the burden of persuasion. That the authorities have the burden of going forward means that it is up to them to raise the question and bring forward evidence of the evils to be avoided. Unlike the case of new drugs where the manufacturer must produce some evidence that the drug has been tested and found not harmful, no citizen has to show with respect to self-regarding conduct that it is not harmful or promotes his best interests. In addition the nature and cogency of the evidence for the harmfulness of the course of action must be set at a high level. To paraphrase a formulation of the burden of proof for criminal proceedings—better ten men ruin themselves than one man be unjustly deprived of liberty.

Finally I suggest a principle of the least restrictive alternative. If there is an alternative way of accomplishing the desired end without restricting liberty then although it may involve great expense, inconvenience, etc. the society must adopt it.

An appeal to some kind of consent—be it rational, subsequent, or some other type—is central to the strategy of this and other prominent theories of justified paternalism. As Dworkin puts it, "the basic notion of consent is important and seems to me the only acceptable way to try to delimit an area of justified paternalism." However, one major source of the distance between the supporters and the opponents of paternalism rests on the emphasis each places on capabilities for autonomous action by persons making "choices." Supporters of paternalism tend to cite examples of persons of diminished or compromised capacity, for example, persons lingering on kidney dialysis, chronic alcoholics, compulsive smokers, and seriously depressed, suicidal individuals. Opponents of paternalism, by contrast, cite examples of persons who are capable of autonomous choice but have been socially restricted in exercising their capacities—for example, those involuntarily committed to institutions because of eccentric behavior, prisoners not permitted to volunteer for risky research, and those who might rationally elect to refuse treatment in life-threatening circumstances. One element of this controversy, then, concerns the quality of consent or refusal by the persons whose autonomy might be restricted by such policies.

Another and alternative form of argument in support of weak paternalism is that the justifying ground is not consent but beneficence. If the paternalist's basic objective is to protect or improve the welfare of another, then intervention can be justified by harm-avoidance or benefit-production, as is the case in the justification of parental actions that override the wishes of their children. Children are treated paternalistically not because they will subsequently consent or would have consented were they rational, but because they will have better lives.

However, a general problem is generated by the restriction of paternalistic intervention to cases in which persons are of diminished or compromised ability. Virtually everyone acknowledges that some forms of weak paternalism are justified (for example, preventing persons under the influence of cocaine from harming or killing themselves). If "paternalistic interventions" do not necessarily override autonomy (because little autonomy is present), it is easier to justify paternalistic interferences with a person's actions than it would otherwise be. The difficulty is that weak paternalism may not be paternalism in any interesting sense, because it is not an autonomy-limiting principle that is *independent* of the harm principle. This is one reason why the meaning of the word "paternalism" probably should be restricted to a definition that recognizes only *strong* paternalism as real paternalism.

## The Justification of Strong Paternalism

Although autonomy is overridden in strong paternalism, conditions can be specified by a strong paternalist that will severely restrict the range of justifiable interventions. For example, the strong paternalist might maintain that interventions are justified only if no acceptable alternative to the paternalistic action exists, if a person is at risk of serious harm, if risks to the person that are introduced by the paternalistic action itself are not substantial, if projected benefits to the person outweigh risks to the person, and if any infringement of the principle of respect for autonomy is minimal.

Strong paternalism, so interpreted, will stand or fall on the strength of the argument that major welfare interests legitimately override relatively minor autonomy interests (under some specifiable conditions). Many plausible cases of strong paternalism can be found that fit this model; for instance, several healthy persons with no heart disease once volunteered as subjects in a research protocol to have an artificial heart implanted at the University of Utah. A research review committee declared that the risk relative to benefit for a *healthy* subject (unlike a cardiology patient in need of a new heart) is morally unacceptable and that they should not be allowed to undergo the procedure despite their desire to do so.

Not all supporters of strong paternalism would accept the broad restrictions often placed on it. As we saw in the Internet case, some people argue that very substantial autonomy interests may be overridden if important human values are at stake. If persons are using their autonomy in a way that will diminish their ability to engage in important human goods in the future, then restrictions on autonomy are justified in order to preserve the person's future choices. For example, if the use of pornography destroys a man's ability to form meaningful sexual relationships, then some supporters of paternalism argue that society is justified in preventing him from accessing such material in the interests of his future well-being.

## Antipaternalistic Individualism

Some believe that paternalistic intervention cannot be justified under any circumstances because it violates individual rights and unduly restricts free choice. The serious adverse consequences of giving paternalistic powers to the state, or to any class of individuals in positions of authority, motivate antipaternalists to reject the view that the completely rational person would accept paternalism. However, the dominant reason why paternalism is thought to be unacceptable is that the right to make a decision resides in the individual whose life would be controlled, not in the controller. The right to make a decision about what to view or subscribe to on the Internet, for example, is rightly the choice of every autonomous person, not of some alleged authority on the subject.

Despite his intense opposition to paternalism, Mill considered temporary beneficent interventions in a person's intentional actions to be justified on some occasions. He argued in *On Liberty* that a person who is ignorant of a potential risk or is otherwise temporarily encumbered may justifiably be restrained in order to ensure that he or she is acting intentionally with adequate knowledge of the consequences of the action. Once warned, however, the autonomous person should be free to choose whatever course he or she desires. Because Mill did not regard this temporary intervention as a "real infringement" of liberty, he did not view it as paternalistic. Liberty, he says, consists in doing what one desires, and—in his example mentioned on p. 351 above—a person about to cross a river over a bridge he does not know has been destroyed does not desire to fall into the river.

In this account, it is not a question of protecting men and women *against themselves* or of interfering with their *liberty of action*. The man attempting to cross a washed-out bridge is not acting at all in regard to the danger of the bridge. He needs protection from something which is not himself, not his intended action, not in any sense of his making.

A fairly common theme found among those who follow Mill's general approach is the following: We may (assuming objectivity and knowledge on our part) justifiably protect a person from harm that might result directly from partially nonvoluntary acts—for example, those due to drunkenness or other mental impairment. One justifiably intervenes to protect a person from causes beyond his or her knowledge and control. If a person has "cloudy judgment" or is deceived by ignorance, his or her choices are not entirely voluntary.

In the end, much of the disagreement between paternalists and antipaternalists seems to turn on whether acceptance of the principle of paternalism would create a situation in which, as Dworkin puts it, the "ignorance, ill-will and stupidity" of those in power might be used to override legitimate, although risky, exercises of freedom. Dworkin believes the risk of such unwarranted interference is worth taking in order to gain a personal insurance policy. By contrast, the followers of Mill maintain both that the stakes are too high to justify the risk and that the harm principle alone will suffice.

## CONCLUSION

The sometimes narrow focus on law in this chapter may lead some readers to the conclusion that whatever ought to be legally permissible is also morally permissible, a clearly questionable assumption. There are many immoral acts, such as violating another's friendship or trust, that are not legally proscribed. Furthermore—as Aristotle, Hume, Kant, and Mill all recognized—the coercive arm of the law should not be allowed to reach into every dimension of the moral life. A conclusion that an act is morally wrong, offensive, or self-harming does not necessarily lead to a judgment that it should be legally prohibited. Nevertheless, as we have repeatedly seen in this chapter, if the problems are serious enough, legal prohibition may be a justifiable remedy.

## SUGGESTED SUPPLEMENTARY READINGS

### The Nature of Autonomy and Liberty

Benn, Stanley I.: *A Theory of Freedom* (Cambridge, England: Cambridge University Press, 1988).

Berofsky, Bernard: *Liberation from Self: A Theory of Personal Autonomy* (Cambridge: Cambridge University Press, 1995).

Christman, John, ed.: *The Inner Citadel: Essays on Individual Autonomy* (New York: Oxford University Press, 1989).

Dworkin, Gerald: *The Theory and Practice of Autonomy* (Cambridge: Cambridge University Press, 1988).

Faden, Ruth R., and Tom L. Beauchamp: *A History and Theory of Informed Consent* (New York: Oxford University Press, 1986), chap. 7.

Young, Robert: *Personal Autonomy: Beyond Negative and Positive Liberty* (New York: St. Martin's Press, 1986).

### Mill, Harm, and Autonomy-Limiting Principles

Coleman, Jules L., and Allen Buchanan, eds.: *In Harm's Way: Essays in Honor of Joel Feinberg* (Cambridge, England: Cambridge University Press, 1994).

Donchin, Anne: "Reworking Autonomy: Toward a Feminist Perspective," *Cambridge Quarterly of Health Care Ethics,* 4 (1995): 44–55.

Doppelt, Gerald: "The Moral Limits of Feinberg's Liberalism," *Inquiry,* 36 (1993): 255–86.

Dworkin, Gerald, ed.: *Morality, Harm, and the Law* (Boulder, CO: Westview Press, 1994).

————, ed.: *Mill's On Liberty* (Lanham, MD: Rowman & Littlefield, 1997).

Epstein, Richard: *Principles for a Free Society: Reconciling Individual Liberty with the Common Good* (Reading, MA: Perseus Books, 1998).

Feinberg, Joel: *Harm to Others*, in *The Moral Limits of the Criminal Law* (New York: Oxford University Press, 1984), vol. I.

————: *Rights, Justice, and the Bounds of Liberty* (Princeton, NJ: Princeton University Press, 1984).

————: "Harm and Offense," in L. C. and C. B. Becker, eds., *Encyclopedia of Ethics* (New York: Garland, 1992), pp. 437–40.

Gray, John: *Mill on Liberty: A Defense*, 2d ed. (London: Routledge & Kegan Paul, 1996).

Hart, Herbert L. A.: *Law, Liberty, and Morality* (Stanford, CA: Stanford University Press, 1963).

Hodson, John D.: *The Ethics of Legal Coercion* (Dordrecht, Holland: D. Reidel Publishing Co., 1983).

Kernohan, Andrew: "Accumulative Harms and the Interpretation of the Harm Principle," *Social Theory and Practice,* 19 (1993): 51–72.

McCloskey, H. J.: "Mill's Liberalism," *Philosophical Quarterly,* 13 (1963): 143–54.

Narveson, Jan: *The Libertarian Idea* (Philadelphia: Temple University Press, 1988).

Pyle, Andrew, ed.: *Liberty: Contemporary Responses to John Stuart Mill* (Bristol, England: Thoemmes, 1994).

Radcliff, Peter, ed.: *Limits of Liberty: Studies of Mill's "On Liberty"* (Belmont, CA: Wadsworth Publishing Company, 1966).

————: *Routledge Philosophy Guidebook to Mill* On Liberty (London: Routledge & Kegan Paul, 1998).

Ten, C. L.: *Mill on Liberty* (Oxford, England: Clarendon Press, 1980).

## Paternalism

Arneson, Richard: "Paternalism," in Edward Craig, ed., *Routledge Encyclopedia of Philosophy,* vol. 7, 1998, pp. 250–2.

Beauchamp, Tom L., and Laurence McCullough: *Medical Ethics* (Englewood Cliffs, NJ: Prentice-Hall, 1984), chap. 4.

Childress, James: *Who Should Decide?: Paternalism in Health Care* (New York: Oxford University Press, 1982).

Dworkin, Gerald: "Paternalism," *The Monist,* 56 (1972): 64–84.

————: "Paternalism," in L. C. and C. B. Becker, eds., *Encyclopedia of Ethics* (New York: Garland, 1992), pp. 939–42.

Feinberg, Joel: *Harm to Self,* in *The Moral Limits of the Criminal Law* (New York: Oxford University Press, 1986), vol. III.

————: "Paternalism," in Donald M. Borchert, ed., *Encyclopedia of Philosophy,* Supplement (New York: Macmillan, 1996), pp. 390–2.

Gert, Bernard, and Charles M. Culver: "Paternalistic Behavior," *Philosophy and Public Affairs*, 6 (1976): 45–57.

Gutmann, Amy: "Children, Paternalism, and Education," *Philosophy and Public Affairs*, 9 (1980): 338–58.

Hunt, Ian: "Risking One's Life: 'Soft Paternalism' and Feinberg's Account of Legal Liberalism," *Canadian Journal of Law and Jurisprudence*, 8 (1995): 311–24.

Husak, Douglas: "Paternalism and Autonomy," *Philosophy and Public Affairs*, 10 (1981): 27–46.

Kultgen, John H.: *Autonomy and Intervention: Parentalism in the Caring Life* (Oxford, England: Oxford University Press, 1995).

Parker, Lisa S.: "Social Justice, Federal Paternalism, and Feminism: Breast Implantation in the Cultural Context of Female Beauty," *Kennedy Institute of Ethics Journal*, 3 (1993): 57–76.

Purdy, Laura M.: *In Their Best Interest: The Case against Equal Rights for Children* (Ithaca, NY: Cornell University Press, 1992).

Sartorius, Rolf, ed.: *Paternalism* (Minneapolis: University of Minnesota Press, 1983).

VanDeVeer, Donald: *Paternalistic Interventions: The Moral Bounds on Benevolence* (Princeton, NJ: Princeton University Press, 1986).

## Legal Moralism

Carroll, Noel: "Moderate Moralism versus Moderate Autonomism," *British Journal of Aesthetics*, 38 (1998): 419–24.

Cicchino, Peter M.: "Reason as the Rule of Law: Should Bare Assertions of 'Public Morality' Qualify as Legitimate Government Interferences for the Purposes of Equal Protection Review?" *Georgetown Law Journal*, 87 (1998): 139–93.

Dworkin, Ronald: "Lord Devlin and the Enforcement of Morals," *Yale Law Journal*, 75 (1966): 986–1005. Reprinted in his *Taking Rights Seriously*.

Feinberg, Joel: *Rights, Justice, and the Bounds of Liberty* (Princeton, NJ: Princeton University Press, 1980).

———: *Harmless Wrongdoing*, in *The Moral Limits of the Criminal Law* (New York: Oxford University Press, 1988), vol. IV.

George, Robert, ed.: *Natural Law, Liberalism, and Morality* (New York: Oxford University Press, 1996).

Greenawalt, Kent: "Legal Enforcement of Morality," *Journal of Crime and Criminology*, 85 (1995): 710–24.

Hart, H. L. A.: *The Morality of the Criminal Law* (Jerusalem: Magner Press, 1964), lecture 2.

Hayry, Heta: "Liberalism and Legal Moralism," *Ratio Juris*, 4 (1991): 202–18.

Simmonds, N. E.: "Law and Morality," in Edward Craig, ed., *Routledge Encyclopedia of Philosophy*, vol. 5, 1998, pp. 438–42.

Wasserstrom, Richard, ed.: *Morality and the Law* (Belmont, CA: Wadsworth Publishing Company, 1970).

Wertheimer, Alan: "Victimless Crimes," *Ethics,* 87 (1977).

*The Wolfenden Report:* Report of the Committee on Homosexual Offences and Prostitution, 1957, cmd. 247 (New York: Stein and Day, 1963).

## Offensiveness

Baier, Kurt: "The Liberal Approach to Pornography," *University of Pittsburgh Law Review,* 40 (1979).

Berger, Fred R., ed.: *Freedom of Expression* (Belmont, CA: Wadsworth Publishing Company, 1980).

Carse, Alisa: "Pornography: An Uncivil Liberty?" *Hypatia,* 10 (1995): 155–82.

————: "Pornography's Many Meanings: A Reply to C. M. Concepcion," *Hypatia,* 14 (1999): 101–11.

Ellis, Anthony: "Offense and the Liberal Conception of the Law," *Philosophy and Public Affairs,* 13 (1984): 3–23.

Feinberg, Joel: *Offense to Others,* in *The Moral Limits of the Criminal Law* (New York: Oxford University Press, 1985), vol. II.

————: "Harm and Offense," in L. C. and C. B. Becker, eds., *Encyclopedia of Ethics* (New York: Garland, 1992), pp. 437–40.

MacKinnon, Catharine A., and Andrea Dworkin, eds.: *In Harm's Way: The Pornography Civil Rights Hearings* (Cambridge, MA: Harvard University Press, 1997).

Mellema, Gregory: "Offense and Virtue Ethics," *Canadian Journal of Philosophy,* 21 (1991): 323–9.

Orser, Mari E.: "Pornography and the Justifiability of Restricting Freedom of Expression," *Journal of Social Philosophy,* 25 (1994): 40–64.

*The Report of the Commission on Obscenity and Pornography* (Washington, DC: Government Printing Office, 1970).

Scanlon, Thomas: "A Theory of Freedom of Expression," *Philosophy and Public Affairs,* 1 (1972): 204–26.

Scoccia, Danny: "Can Liberals Support a Ban on Violent Pornography?" *Ethics,* 106 (1996): 776–99.

Stark, Cynthia A.: "Pornography, Verbal Acts, and Viewpoint Discrimination," *Public Affairs Quarterly,* 12 (1998): 429–45.

Thomson, Judith Jarvis: "Feinberg on Harm, Offense, and the Criminal Law," *Philosophy and Public Affairs,* 15 (1986): 381–95.

Vernon, Richard: "John Stuart Mill and Pornography: Beyond the Harm Principle," *Ethics,* 106 (1996): 621–32.

West, Robin: "The Feminist-Conservative Anti-pornography Alliance and the 1986 Attorney General's Commission on Pornography Report," *American Bar Foundation Research Journal* (1987): 681–711.

# Index

**387**

Please remember that this is a library book, and that it belongs only temporarily to each person who uses it. Be considerate. Do not write in this, or any, library book.